THE WORLD OF COLONIAL AMERICA

The World of Colonial America: An Atlantic Handbook offers a comprehensive and in-depth survey of cutting-edge research into the communities, cultures, and colonies that comprised colonial America, with a focus on the processes through which communities were created, destroyed, and recreated that were at the heart of the Atlantic experience. With contributions written by leading scholars from a variety of viewpoints, the book explores key topics such as

- The Spanish, French, and Dutch Atlantic empires
- The role of the indigenous people, as imperial allies, trade partners, and opponents of expansion
- Puritanism, Protestantism, Catholicism, and the role of religion in colonization
- The importance of slavery in the development of the colonial economies
- The evolution of core areas, and their relationship to frontier zones
- The emergence of the English imperial state as a hegemonic world power after 1688
- Regional developments in colonial North America.

Bringing together leading scholars in the field to explain the latest research on Colonial America and its place in the Atlantic World, this is an important reference for all advanced students, researchers, and professionals working in the field of early American history or the age of empires.

Ignacio Gallup-Diaz is Associate Professor of History at Bryn Mawr College.

THE WORLD OF COLONIAL AMERICA

An Atlantic Handbook

Edited by Ignacio Gallup-Diaz

NEW YORK AND LONDON

First published 2017
by Routledge
711 Third Avenue, New York, NY 10017

and by Routledge
2 Park Square, Milton Park, Abingdon, Oxon OX14 4RN

Routledge is an imprint of the Taylor & Francis Group, an informa business

© 2017 Taylor & Francis

The right of Ignacio Gallup-Diaz to be identified as the author of the editorial material, and of the authors for their individual chapters, has been asserted in accordance with sections 77 and 78 of the Copyright, Designs and Patents Act 1988.

All rights reserved. No part of this book may be reprinted or reproduced or utilised in any form or by any electronic, mechanical, or other means, now known or hereafter invented, including photocopying and recording, or in any information storage or retrieval system, without permission in writing from the publishers.

Trademark notice: Product or corporate names may be trademarks or registered trademarks, and are used only for identification and explanation without intent to infringe.

Library of Congress Cataloging in Publication Data
Names: Gallup-Diaz, Ignacio, 1963- editor.Title:The world of colonial America : an Atlantic handbook/edited by Ignacio Gallup-Diaz.Description: New York: Routledge, 2017. | Includes bibliographical references and index.
Identifiers: LCCN 2016047498 (print) | LCCN 2016058650 (ebook) | ISBN 9781138786905 (alk. paper) | ISBN 9781315767000 (ebook)Subjects: LCSH: United States–History–Colonial period, ca. 1600-1775.Classification: LCC E188.W66 2017 (print) | LCC E188 (ebook) | DDC 973.2–dc23LC record available at https://lccn.loc.gov/2016047498

ISBN: 978-1-138-78690-5
ISBN: 978-1-315-76700-0

Typeset in Bembo
by Deanta Global Publishing Services, Chennai, India

Printed in the United Kingdom
by Henry Ling Limited

For Anjali

CONTENTS

Acknowledgments   x

Introduction: Atlantic Perspectives   5

PART I
Spanish Empire; Spanish Influences   15

1   From Monarchy to Empire: Ideologies, Institutions, and the Limits of Spanish Imperial Sovereignty, 1492–1700   17
Alexander Ponsen

2   "The Oversight of King Henry VII": Imperial Envy and the Making of British America   39
Jorge Cañizares-Esguerra and Bradley J. Dixon

3   Indo-Hispano Borderlands in the Americas: Entanglements, North and South   59
Bianca Brigidi and James F. Brooks

PART II
Unfree Labor   83

4   Labor, Empire, and the State: The English Imperial Experience in the Seventeenth Century   85
Abigail L. Swingen

5   The Early English Caribbean: Conflict, the Census,
    and Control   105
    Jenny Shaw

6   The Development of Slavery in the British Americas   123
    Justin Roberts

PART III
British Colonial Developments and the Fates of Indigenous Polities   151

7   Spiritual Giants, Worldly Empires: Indigenous Peoples
    and New England to the 1680s   153
    Neal Salisbury

8   "Vast and Furious": Understanding an Atlantic New England   171
    Wendy Warren

9   The Middle Colonies: Region, Restoration, and Imperial Integration   189
    Ned C. Landsman

10 His Own, Their Own: Settler Colonialism, Native Peoples, and
    Imperial Balances of Power in Eastern North America, 1660–1715   209
    Daniel K. Richter

11 The Chesapeake: Putting Maryland on the Map   235
    Kathleen M. Brown

12 Protestantism as Ideology in the British Atlantic World   263
    Carla Gardina Pestana

13 Was Knowledge Power? Science in the British Atlantic   281
    Joyce E. Chaplin

PART IV
Competition and Imperial Frontiers   301

14 Defying Mercantilism: Dutch Interimperial Trade
    in the Atlantic World   303
    Willem Klooster

15 Atlantic, Western, and Continental Early America   321
    Paul W. Mapp

16 Native–European Interactions in North America and the Trade in Furs   339
    Ann M. Carlos and Frank D. Lewis

17 Dismantling the Dream of "France's Peru": Indian and
    African Influence on the Development of Early
    Colonial Louisiana   355
    Elizabeth Ellis

PART V
Revolutions   **373**

18 How to Lose an Empire: British Misperceptions of the Sinews
    of the Transatlantic System   375
    Andrew Shankman and Ignacio Gallup-Diaz

19 The Revolutionary Black Atlantic: From Royalists
    to Revolutionaries   393
    Jane Landers

Index   409

ACKNOWLEDGMENTS

It is a genuine pleasure to express my deep and abiding sense of gratitude to John M. Murrin, advisor and friend, from whom I learned to understand early American history. I am also heartily pleased to thank Andrew Shankman, fast friend and longtime colleague, at whose suggestion I took up this project in the first place. Peter Magee's true friendship buoyed me throughout both the good and less good times. I thank the authors for their enthusiasm, earnest cooperation, and trust in the value of the endeavor.

I am fortunate in working alongside inspiring colleagues in Bryn Mawr College's history department: Sharon Ullman, Madhavi Kale, Elly Truitt, Anita Kurimay, Brigid Gurtler, and Kalala Ngalamulume. (Elly's engagement with this work was especially sustained and welcome.) I gained moral support from Bryn Mawr colleagues Rosi Song and Jamie Taylor. The intellectual stimulation of my companions at the McNeil Center for Early American Studies and the Forum on European Expansion and Global Interaction remains vital to all my scholarly endeavors. I have benefited from my interactions with Christian A. Crouch, Steve Pincus, Ada Ferrer, Sinclair Thomson, and Elena Schneider.

My wife, Anjali, has provided me with unremitting love and support, and it is not hyperbole to say that this project is possible only because of her.

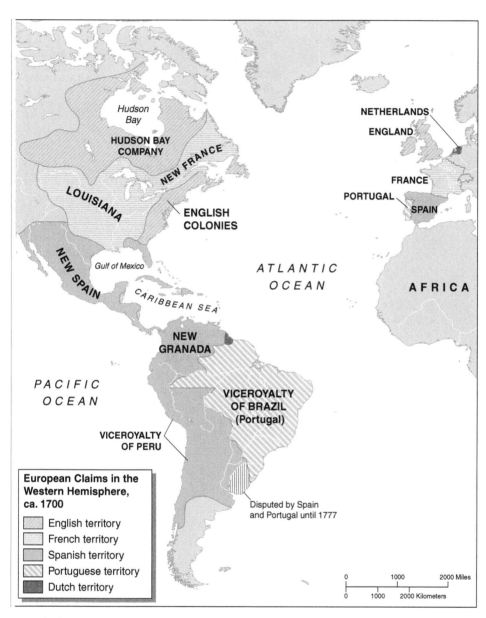

Map 1   European Claims in Western Hemisphere, ca. 1700.
Source: Courtesy of Carto-graphics.

Map 2 European Claims in Western Hemisphere, ca. 1760.
Source: Courtesy of Carto-graphics.

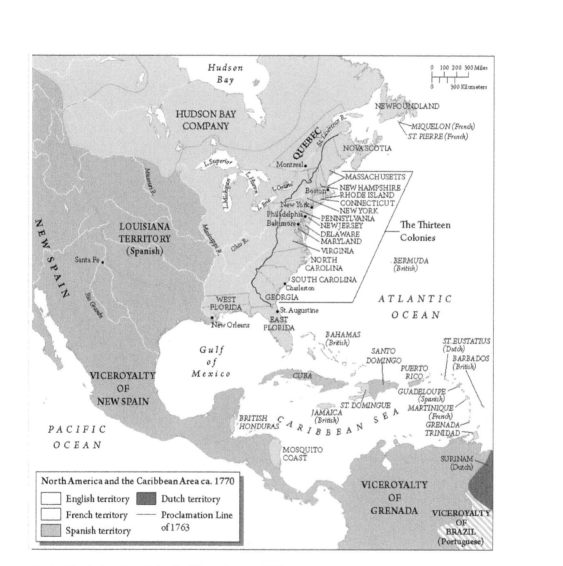

Map 3　North American & the Caribbean Area, ca. 1770.
Source: Courtesy of Carto-graphics.

INTRODUCTION
Atlantic Perspectives

Ignacio Gallup-Diaz

What is an Atlantic Approach?

Colonial America: An Atlantic Handbook provides the reader with an understanding of important developments across the broad chronological and geographic scope of colonial American history. The authors of the chapters have been selected based on the strength of their contributions to their areas of expertise and the innovative nature of their published scholarship. Taking an Atlantic perspective, the *Handbook* is attentive to the interconnections between empires and states, allowing the authors to explore how colonies, communities, and individuals interact with and influence one another.

The *Handbook* joins several recent publications that strive to present colonial American history using an Atlantic framework. In an essay titled 'Atlantic History: A Circumnavigation',[1] J. H. Elliott provides an insightful capsule description of what an Atlantic perspective is, and what it allows historians to bring into our frameworks of analysis.

> The new Atlantic history might be defined as the history, in the broadest sense, of the creation, destruction and re-creation of communities as the result of the movement, across and around the Atlantic basin, of people, commodities, cultural practices, and ideas. It is not the history of the advent—or non-advent—of modernity, a concept that has bedeviled the history of the Americas, but rather of change and continuity in the face of new experiences, new circumstances, new contacts, and new environments. Both the change and the continuity only become understandable if set into the context of an Atlantic that is seen as at once a unifying element, connecting peoples and events across the great expanses of the ocean, and a divisive element, fragmenting and distancing communities through space and time, and promoting, in a multiplicity of different environments, a whole spectrum of responses.[2]

Rather than an arbitrary or simply scholastic exercise, the adoption of an Atlantic perspective allows researchers to access a view of the world that approximates that held by the subjects of their studies. Historians can produce narratives and analytical frameworks that place previously ignored or misunderstood historical actors—especially indigenous and African actors—at the center of the frame.

On larger scales, an Atlantic perspective allows for the experiences of colonial regions and communities to be properly contextualized over long periods of time. Colonies that were adjacent to each other could have held and nurtured ties to competing European states, and communities within individual colonies could have had ties, if not allegiances, to other imperial powers.

On a more intimate level, the Atlantic approach is the only viable method through which to explore the history of indigenous peoples who engaged in a series of complex interactions with a wide range of Europeans. Since many successful indigenous leaders were multilingual and did not need to tie themselves to a single European state, primary sources describing them are embedded in the archives produced by several different empires.

What an Atlantic Perspective Allows Historians to Do

The *Handbook's* chapters bring into focus salient points about the morphology and chronology of empire in North America. A morphological approach allows us to categorize what we know along the lines of central processes that were shared by the various empires, although they were not happening at the same point in time, or in the same space. Morphology allows us to think, for example, in terms of "early," "middle," and "late" kinds of processes in the colonial experience, while allowing us to understand that the English empire might have experienced its "early" processes two hundred years after Spain had done so. Events in individual colonies can be similarly analyzed, with the understanding that a neighboring colony in the same empire might have been experiencing a different range of processes.

Processes common to imperial experiences are

- extended interactions with indigenous polities and the acquisition of alliances (and, by extension, enmities)
- the transferal of administrative and legal institutions, and the (attempts to effect the) subjugation of indigenous peoples to those forms
- the establishment of labor regimes
- the establishment of core regions, with associated hinterlands, and less-than-secure frontier peripheries
- frontier areas in which indigenous polities or, in some cases, escaped slaves held sway
- anchoring processes—such as the acquisition of reliable staple activities such as mining, and tobacco and sugar production
- demographic security in the form of a self-reproducing population
- shifting administrative and political relationships with an increasingly more attentive imperial center
- the intertwining of warfare driven by local concerns with broader concerns related to imperial competition

Competing Powers and British Hegemony

Drawing attention to morphological and chronological anchor points—parts of the deep structure of the big picture that shaped the Atlantic experience—allows for a richer contextualization by way of the localized elements of that history. The trajectories of individual colonies, polities, communities, and peoples are more fully illuminated by an understanding of morphology and chronology. The big picture elements—monarchies establishing boundaries to fix their realms and contending with other states through warfare—are illuminated through careful attention to the actions of local proxies, indigenous allies, legislatures, militias, and naval forces.

Introduction

And while boundary making and marking were of critical importance to imperial planners, boundary crossing was a frequent experience for individuals and groups, one that could be especially embedded in the experiences of indigenous and African communities inhabiting frontier zones. The cross-boundary connections made by peoples living and operating in border zones formed dense, overlapping networks that crisscrossed the continent and straddled the lines on imperial maps. They formed a nexus of economic, military, cultural, and, in some cases, familial ties. Actors on the margins—escaped slaves, "unconquered" Indians, and smugglers—thrived due to their nurturing of and negotiation through these networks, and these connections, as well as the actions taken by those maintaining them, could influence and change the course of empire.

An Atlantic perspective makes it possible to keep the macro and micro levels of the system in the same frame of analysis. For this reason, many of the *Handbook's* chapters are concerned with illuminating for the reader the experiences of individuals within their communities. What daily life was like for an individual—a planter, merchant, woman, indigenous person, or slave—depended greatly upon the manner in which local laws, regulations, ideologies, social norms, and mores were made real and embodied in the actions of elites and people with power, as well as those who were subject to the power of others. The complex interplay of forces that came together to produce a community's range of local practices was just as important, if not more important, than the statutes rendered by the Parliament in London. Colonialism could be experienced differently in separate locations—even locations within the same colony—and, over time, how people lived and were guided by these complex forces formed and framed what we might term *local colonial cultures*.

As the Atlantic system evolved, a succession of states emerged as world powers, which fed a cycle of international relations characterized by competition between aggressive nation-states. The study of developments in the Americas serves as a prism through which to track Spanish, Dutch, French, and English periods of economic and political hegemony. After the Spanish attained a world empire, that nation's foes oriented and ordered themselves through a complex set of alliances in order to challenge Hapsburg supremacy. One of the results of these rearrangements was the emergence of the United Provinces of the Netherlands as an imperial power, and the weakening of Spain through the Thirty Years' War (1618–48), which ultimately saw England, the Netherlands, and France joining their forces in order to defeat the Hapsburgs.

Extended periods of disorder in the politics of France and England after 1648 allowed Dutch merchants and ship captains to integrate themselves into the colonial staple trades of the American colonies. The English republican regime established after the overthrow of King Charles I took a pugilistic stance toward the former Dutch ally; Cromwell guided a Navigation Act through parliament whose aim was to exclude Dutch ships from carrying staple goods from English colonies to European markets. (That Act sparked the first Anglo-Dutch War.)

England attained hegemonic world power status through a systematic undermining of the Dutch and through fighting off the challenge made by a resurgent and belligerent Louis XIV of France. The restoration of the English monarchy in 1660 played a key role in this process. The crown's actions—aimed at bringing a more centralized administration to the "reality on the ground"—were an attempt to reign in the English subjects in the colonies settled through a series of fairly disconnected expansionist ventures. The colonies chartered after 1660 were licensed by a crown interested in deriving a regular income from staple goods that could allow it some substantial breathing room in the form of allowing the crown to rule without parliamentary intervention.

The later Stuarts were innovators in the development and exploitation of a bureaucracy of empire, using the Privy Council, Board of Trade, and Royal Philosophical Society as mechanisms through which to gather information, frame, and implement policy. In a continuance of the aggressive policies of the Cromwellian regime, Restoration-era Navigation Acts were ushered through Parliament, sparking additional wars against the Dutch in 1664 and 1672. These Acts were aimed at completing the process of excluding the Dutch from colonial carrying trades so that the crown could derive the maximum customs revenue from the staple crops grown in the colonies. (Notably, customs rates were neither set by Parliament nor subject to its review.)

The Glorious Revolution that upset the Restoration Settlement was a violent reaction to the concentration of power in the hands of Charles II and James II, Catholic kings who pursued pro-French foreign policies. However, *the revolution was by no means a rejection of empire.* The revolution was a rejection of a system that allowed Catholic monarchs to garner the fruits of empire so that they might rule without parliaments. This concentration of power in the colonial sphere was reflected by an equivalent process in the metropole.

The accession of William and Mary that anchored the revolution settlement entirely reoriented these processes. Members of parliament were quite willing to support a centralizing, taxing, standing army–wielding monarchy, so long as that monarchy was Protestant and constrained to act within a system of parliamentary supremacy. The crown's tolerance and respect for the legitimacy of colonial legislatures—something James II had placed under threat—removed an irritant, allowing the colonies to reflect in their royal governor, governor's council, and elected legislature the king-in-parliament that Britons believed brought perfection to their polity.

Warfare was central to the experiences of the colonies, and the importance of the War of Spanish Succession (1700–15) cannot be overstated. In this struggle an alliance led by England confronted Louis XIV, who threatened to integrate the Spanish world into the French system, and placed the survival of the United Netherlands at risk as an independent Protestant nation. On the domestic front, the burdens of the war fueled the financial revolution in England, and were the impetus for several other important events. First, the Union of Scotland and England in 1707, driven by William's desire to remove any possibility that a restive kingdom might distract his attention while he battled France on the continent; and, second, an enhanced reliance upon experts to manage colonial affairs through the Board of Trade.

As the Treaty of Munster that ended the Thirty Years' War in 1648 enshrined in the Netherlands as an independent nation and an imperial power. The Treaty of Utrecht that ended the War of Spanish Succession in 1715 recognized France's eclipse and Great Britain's emergence as a hegemonic world power. Each treaty made provision for the important *asiento* contract—the license to bring African slaves into the Spanish empire for sale. The *asiento* was granted to a Dutch firm in 1648 and then, in 1715, to a British one.

The emergence of Great Britain as a powerful, fiscal-military state held great importance for eighteenth-century domestic politics. The implications for colonial integration with the home country were immense, as a fiscal-military state had the ability to integrate the empire and conceive of it as a single unit. In addition, the eighteenth-century state also provided the benefits of protection and guaranteed domestic markets to colonial merchants and elites—benefits unavailable to the Tudor crown that had initiated English expansion. The years 1689–1720 were crucial decades for the colonies, with changes in the home country providing the necessary conditions for the period of imperial integration that occurred between 1720 and 1740.

In order to encompass the wider field of vision required by the Atlantic perspective, the geographic scope of the *Handbook* takes the reader far beyond the thirteen North American and British colonies. In order to cover the various elements of the multimodal world of competing European empires, authors have contributed chapters on the Caribbean, the Lower Mississippi Valley, Hudson's Bay, Central and South America, and the North American continent as a whole.

The chapters written by the *Handbook's* authors can be grouped into the following categories, which reflect the predominant themes of the collection as a whole. The first, "Spanish Empire; Spanish Influences," includes chapters that deal with the importance of a nexus of ideological and administrative structures that Europeans transferred from Europe to the Americas, adapting and transforming them under the force of the new environments. In the second section, authors write about the nature of "Unfree Labor" systems imposed by Europeans throughout the Americas. The third grouping sees authors examining "Colonial Developments and the Fate of Indigenous Polities." In the fourth group, authors examine "Competitors, Frontiers, and Peoples on the Borders," doing so from fresh perspectives and through innovative approaches, and, in the last section, the "Revolutions" that sundered the British Atlantic empire are examined.

Spanish Empire; Spanish Influences

In "From Monarchy to Empire: Ideologies, Institutions, and the Limits of Spanish Imperial Sovereignty, 1492–1700," Alexander Ponsen examines the manner in which the Spanish crown deployed institutions and administrative forms (some derived from the peninsular *reconquista*) as it struggled to centralize and bring under its control processes of overseas conquest that had been set in motion by individuals. Historians, Ponsen argues, should conceive of the Spanish as having engaged in a series of conquests, rather than a single decisive one. They should be seen "as processes, rather than as discrete events, which often played out over decades if not centuries and in many cases never reached completion." Even after indigenous state systems were replaced by Spanish institutions, the monarchy's effective sovereignty remained, Ponsen writes, "surprisingly diffuse." As was the case with the conquests themselves, indigenous polities and leaders were crucial in making the empire an entity that controlled, guided, and profited from the lives and labor of the peoples of the Americas.

In "'The Oversight of Henry VII': Imperial Envy and the Making of British America," Jorge Cañizares-Esguerra and Bradley Dixon explore the importance of a process of imperial mimesis to English expansionists, as they wished to emulate Spain's successes in bringing the lands and peoples of the Americas under its administrative and financial control. Going beyond the desire to replicate what their enemies had done, Englishmen expressed admiration for Spanish deeds, and the authors make clear that the planners of the Virginia venture saw themselves through the lens of what the Spanish had done. However, English admiration was diminished by the structural changes that were introduced to the European balance of power by the Spanish imposition of dominion over the Americas and its peoples. Protestant Englishmen came to fear and decry the development of what they saw as a universal Catholic monarchy, one poised and eager to wield the material riches of the Americas in order to oppress Protestants and extinguish Protestantism.

In "Indo-Hispano Borderlands in the Americas: Entanglements, North and South," Bianca Brigidi and James Brooks explore interactions between Spaniards and indigenous peoples in the borderlands, areas far removed from the core regions that emerged in the Spanish Indies after the dismantling of the Aztec and Inca state systems. On the borderlands, indigenous peoples experienced the loss of power associated with colonialism through their forced engagement with a set of religious institutions managed by missionaries who were members of religious orders. The authors' discussion of daily life within the missions shows the contestation between representatives of colonial power and the peoples being ruled, and challenges previously argued notions that the Guarini people living in the Jesuit missions experienced a different kind of colonialism than did other indigenous peoples outside of that system.

Unfree Labor

Abigail Swingen's "Labor, Empire, and the State: The English Imperial Experience in the Seventeenth Century" examines the actions taken by the later Stuart monarchs to foster the slave trade and promote the development of their Caribbean colonies after the Restoration. The Royal African Company became the means through which the Stuart monarchs acted to foster commerce in commodities such as sugar and tobacco which were of special benefit to them, as well as to exercise their authority by making clear that colonial development—and the profits from that development—was to happen solely under their authority, directed through entities such as the Company whose charters were reliant upon crown approval. Like the Spanish monarchy before it, the English crown attempted to centralize colonial activity. However, after the overthrow of James II in 1688, the company's monopoly over the slave trade was destroyed—having been painted by its enemies as a relic of Stuart tyranny. By the 1690s the state shared the Stuart's interest in fostering the slave trade; eliminating the Company's monopoly was its means to do so.

Jenny Shaw, in "The Early English Caribbean: Conflict, the Census, and Control," examines the importance of numerical information to the state after the Glorious Revolution, as it worked to control the economic, political, and demographic developments taking place across the Atlantic. For Shaw, censuses chart several things: the state's attentiveness to a colonial population and its economic changes; the colonials' willingness to provide the information the state needs; and, most importantly, the racial attitudes expressed through the categories describing enslaved and free populations. With populations filled with rebellious Irish transportees, the islands' early censuses reflected an interest in counting Catholic subjects. However, the nature of the counts changed as England (and, after 1707, Great Britain) attained greater power, political stability, and firmer control of the colonies. Reflecting these changes, "categories that connoted ethnicity or religious status disappeared [...] as their importance waned. [...] In Jamaica and Barbados, the primary categories were those of freedom and slavery conflated with skin color: 'white' and 'negro' featured prominently." The censuses became carefully recorded enumerations of who owned land, how many men were available for militia service, and the supply of enslaved, servant, and free labor.

Justin Roberts, in "The Development of Slavery in the British Americas" explores the exploitation of slaves as laborers as a constant reality in the history of the British Americas. Having emerged as an institution in the absence of any specific legal framework to legitimate or define it or of any legal mechanisms of coercion, local elites took the lead in formalization through statutes without input from the imperial center. Roberts notes the distinctions between the manner in which the Caribbean and Chesapeake regions developed as slave societies within the same empire; the regions achieved a rough parity in the 1720s, with the slave population of Chesapeake becoming naturally reproductive, and Jamaica overtaking the smaller islands in sugar production.

British Colonial Developments and the Fates of Indigenous Polities

Neal Salisbury, in "Spiritual Giants, Worldly Empires: Indigenous Peoples and New England to the 1680s," shows the benefits to be derived from a scholarly perspective that centers indigenous communities, illuminates their cultural understandings of their relationships to the land and their environment, in addition to elucidating long-standing networks of diplomacy and trade that predated European encroachment by millennia. Salisbury describes the complex process through which Europeans established their hegemony over "New England," first by inserting themselves into pre-existing trade and diplomatic networks, and then entering into treaties with groups that led them to exercise enmity toward others. During the Pequot War (1637) and King Philip's War (1676) settlers massacred large communities of indigenous peoples, depriving them of the means to resist (and in some cases, persist). Ultimately, the Great Migration delivered the population and the Restoration the administrative attention that enabled settlers to overpower indigenous nations and subordinate them to English authority. Salisbury's analytical approach explores the strategies used by indigenous leaders as they confronted the Europeans who had invaded their worlds.

In "'Vast and Furious': Understanding an Atlantic New England," Wendy Warren delineates the nature of the development of New England with a local economy that included small farmers, the provision of raw materials to the state, and merchants engaged in a trade relationship with the Caribbean islands, providing food for islands in which all the land had been placed under the cultivation of cash crops. While New England was not a plantation slave society, it was nevertheless *a society with slaves* and its social and legal system fostered settler colonialism, the effacement of indigenous sovereignty over land by European treaty, law, and settlement. While the Atlantic Ocean is often described as a highway across which people travelled back and forth, Warren elucidates the concept of an *Atlantic chasm*—with the ocean acting as a difficult-to-surmount barrier that locked slaves and settlers in place in the Americas and opened northern Europeans to captivity by Barbary pirates in the North Atlantic closer to their original home. Warren's New England is *in and of* the Atlantic—farmers in the interior were implicated in Caribbean slavery; slaves were an integral part of New England life. Rather than being unique, *New England is representative of the exploitative Atlantic*.

Ned C. Landsman, in "The Middle Colonies: Region, Restoration, and Imperial Integration," provides a useful framework for contextualizing the Middle Colonies of New York, New Jersey, Pennsylvania, and Delaware: rather than representing the archetype of a diverse society, Landsman argues that "the region mattered because of its place within early American development." The Middle Colonies "would function as critical centralizing forces within eastern North America at a time of intense imperial rivalry affecting Europeans and Indians." Emerging after the restoration, these colonies reflected the monarchy's attempt to use its charters, trade regulations, and officials in order to exercise greater control in North America. The heightened competition between European states after 1660 was played out in the Middle Colonies, with New York City changing hands several times, and European conflicts being connected to local indigenous warfare. Due to their geographic positioning as the meeting-points of opposing empires, New York and Pennsylvania were scarred by war and competition. Landsman argues that the regional focus on trade and commerce, coupled with the presence of the Dutch, Quakers, and Germans did come together to produce a *particular commercial culture*.

Daniel Richter, in "His Own, Their Own: Settler Colonialism, Native Peoples, and Imperial Balances of Power in Eastern North America, 1660–1715," examines settler colonialism as a complex process, with the chapter exploring the preconditions that made it possible and settler success inevitable. In North America, he writes, "multiple metropolitan sovereignties contested with multiple Native sovereignties and multiple incipient settler colonial projects." (7) As do Neal Salisbury, and Ned Landsman, Richter describes the process of indigenous polity shattering that needed to occur—through processes of enslavement and relentless warfare under the rubric of imperial competition—*before* settlers could exert their dominance over what had been indigenous lands. The decisions taken by Haudensaunee leaders—to ally with Europeans in order to further their own strategic and economic goals—had ripple effects throughout the Northeast, effects that would be felt amongst indigenous communities for decades. These ripples were not solely North American, either, "[a]s European settlers increasingly set their minds on lands west of the Appalachians, in 1754 the Indian war […] broke out with a vengeance in the Ohio country, and then spread throughout the globe in the great conflict known as the Seven Years War."

Kathleen Brown, in "The Chesapeake: Putting Maryland on the Map," explores the reasons why Maryland and Virginia—places so similar to one another—occupy such markedly different places in the historiography of colonial North America. The new social history, whose practitioners were interested in the lives of people poorly represented in that historiography, pursued an interest in small tobacco producers, and applied quantitative methods to Maryland's well-kept records relating to small and middling planters. These scholars produced studies establishing the processes through which white settlers and African slaves overcame high mortality rates and family rupture to attain demographic stability in the eighteenth century. There was no cause for celebration in this fact with regard to the slave community, since it did not produce a creole population until 1750, *decades* after the white community had done so. Brown explores the tension presented by a plethora of county records available in Maryland, and their relative paucity in Virginia, a situation in which the question of whether research results from either Virginia or Maryland can represent 'the Chesapeake' endures.

Carla Pestana, in "Protestantism as Ideology in the British Atlantic World," explores the manner in which "Protestantism serves as a placeholder for certain understandings of liberty and aversion to Roman Catholic superstition and authoritarianism [that] proved an enduring legacy that worked to smooth over differences and to obscure disparities between reality and idealism." Pestana argues that the binding together of liberty and Protestantism formed a powerful cultural ideology for people in England, one well suited to overseas expansion. While Spaniards exploited indigenous people and persecuted them in the name of a false religion, Englishmen acted in order to build an empire that would not only enhance the liberty of European Protestants, but also improve the lives of the indigenous peoples with whom they came into contact with and engaged in commerce. Pestana argues that such an ideology would be crucial for an empire that experienced great in-migration and incorporated many different kinds of Protestants under its aegis as the eighteenth century progressed.

In "Was Knowledge Power?: Science in the British Atlantic," Joyce E. Chaplin writes that "the Americas were parts of a global unfolding of information about places unknown or little known to Europeans before 1492." The chapter traces the integration of this storehouse of knowledge and information as Europeans investigated questions "of weather and climate on the one hand, and blood and soil on the other," and a consensus emerged that "the greatest source of colonial wealth lay in the British Atlantic's population. In a shift that underscores the development of colonial societies in the Americas, by the eighteenth century colonial elites considered themselves members of a transatlantic community of thinkers, and vied to be recognized as equals by the Royal Philosophical Society. Britons in the Americas could study their own environments, peoples, and effectively produce knowledge. "The possibility of being informants to the Society set up for colonists three aspirational goals [...]: publishing in the society's Philosophical Transactions, becoming a Fellow of the Royal Society, and winning the Copely Medal for a particularly distinguished contribution to natural knowledge."

Competition, Frontiers, and Peoples on the Borders

Willem Klooster, in "Defying Mercantilism: Dutch Interimperial Trade in the Atlantic World" describes the multiple foreign ties that were the distinguishing marks of the Dutch Atlantic, exposing how limited our understanding would be through studying Atlantic history within purely national frameworks. Dutch investors and merchants were not solely involved in colonial trades; they fostered developments throughout the Americas, assisting in the takeoff of French Guadalupe as a sugar island. Having established themselves as the carriers of colonial staple goods to Europe in the period before the Restoration, the English promulgated a series of Navigation Acts aimed at undercutting the Dutch carrying trade—these acts led to warfare between the normally allied nations. The Dutch experience brought together settlement, imperial competition, indigenous trade, investment and knowledge transferal, and the establishment of Statia and Curacao as regional entrepôts, serving roles similar to the one Amsterdam played in Europe.

Paul W. Mapp, "Atlantic, Western, and Continental Early America," integrates the history of the far west of the North American continent into the Atlantic history paradigm. While England did not expand west until late in its imperial experience, France was deeply involved in the North American West, and Spain established an even earlier western presence (although their settlements did not penetrate into North America). Integrating the West into Atlantic history is essential, because the temporal depth, geographic connections, and cultural interactions at the continent's western reaches expose so much more of the kinds of material investigators are currently and rightly interested in. Mapp argues that attention to the continent as a whole highlights global connections, brings the human contacts that were creating hybrid American populations and cultures into sharper relief, and brings many Indian peoples into the frame of view for a much longer time. Understanding the ways in which the Spanish empire was a kind of hybrid entity—composed of many different peoples—also sheds light on the British and French imperial experiences.

Ann M. Carlos and Frank D. Lewis, in "Native–European Interactions in North America and the Trade in Furs," provide a study of the North American fur trade, with their focus being the activities of the Hudson's Bay Company. The Company carried out trade through factories established throughout the bay, each with a salaried manager running the post, assisted by accountants, tradesmen, and laborers. Indigenous agents were the key to the trade, and this was reflected in the use of Cree as the language of the trade (used by both the English and the French), and the incorporation of practices derived from ceremonial gift giving into the trade at the factories. Through a study of the Company's records, the authors conclude that the tools and goods acquired by indigenous peoples who traded furs afforded them an increased standard of living, one even higher than that of eighteenth-century Europeans.

In "Dismantling the Dream of 'France's Peru': Indian and African Influence on the Development of Early Colonial Louisiana," Elizabeth Ellis examines how mutual need led to working partnerships between indigenous peoples of the *petite nations* and French settlers and soldiers. As she writes, "when Iberville and his men landed in 1699, they entered a geopolitical world that had been thrown into chaos by the expansion of the Southeastern Indian slave trade." The colony's lifeline came through two factors: its alliance with the Choctaws and its improved relations with the Upper Creeks, which halted their attacks on French settlements. Ellis makes clear that the failure of Louisiana to develop as a profitable plantation society was neither accidental nor the result of poor planning. Rather, it was the direct result of the resistance of African peoples and the hostility and noncompliance of local indigenous polities.

Revolutions

In "How to Lose an Empire: British Misperceptions of the Sinews of the Transatlantic System," Andrew Shankman and I examine the dissolution of the first British empire, a late eighteenth-century occurrence that was countercyclical to the previous half century of colonial development, which was typified by increasing integration between London and its dependencies. Officials dealing with a massive public debt after the Seven Years' War misperceived the workings of the imperial system, legislating a series of measures aimed at forcing the colonies to support the British troops residing in North America. These measures failed and ultimately fostered an irreparable rupture. Discussing the nature of prior successful efforts illuminates how badly the politicians at the imperial center misperceived the key to success, the importance of engaging the voluntarism of English subjects residing in the colonies.

In "The Revolutionary Black Atlantic: From Royalists to Revolutionaries," Jane Landers provides a comparative study of the free black experience in the age of revolutions, exploring the motivations of the free peoples of African descent who chose military service in the Spanish empire. By the mid-seventeenth century, the Spanish crown accepted that free men of color could serve with valor in the defense of the American realms. In return for their service, black men won grants of land, and, in some cases, free black towns were chartered with blacks in positions of civic authority. During the war that followed the French Revolution, and the slave uprising that developed into the Haitian Revolution, Spain offered an alliance to Georges Biassou, Jean-Francois Papillon and Toussaint Louverture, the leaders of the rebellion. They accepted, and in 1793 became officers in the army of Black Auxiliaries of Charles IV. While Toussaint later switched his allegiance to the French, the other two generals remained loyal to the Spanish crown. The history of the Americas would never be the same.

Notes

1 Joseph C. Miller, ed., *The Princeton Companion to Atlantic History* (Princeton University Press, 2015); D'Maris Coffman, Adrian Leonard, and William O'Reilly, *The Atlantic World* (Routledge, 2014); Jack D. Greene and Philip D. Morgan, *Atlantic History: A Critical Appraisal* (OUP USA, 2009); Bernard Bailyn, *Atlantic History: Concept and Contours* (Harvard University Press, 2005); Bernard Bailyn, *Soundings in Atlantic History* (Harvard University Press, 2009); Thomas Benjamin, *The Atlantic World: Europeans, Africans, Indians and Their Shared History, 1400–1900* (Cambridge University Press, 2009); T. H. H. Breen, *Colonial America in an Atlantic World* (Longman, 2003); Nicholas Canny, *Colonial Identity in the Atlantic World, 1500–1800* (Princeton University Press, 1989); Jorge Cañizares-Esguerra, *The Atlantic in Global History: 1500–2000* (Prentice Hall, 2006).
2 David Armitage and Michael J. Braddick, *The British Atlantic World, 1500–1800* (Palgrave Macmillan, 2002), 239–40.

PART I

Spanish Empire; Spanish Influences

1
FROM MONARCHY TO EMPIRE
Ideologies, Institutions, and the Limits of Spanish Imperial Sovereignty, 1492–1700

Alexander Ponsen

The completion of the peninsular Reconquest in 1492, the expansion of Habsburg possessions across Europe, and the series of conquests in the Americas and Philippines gave rise to an increasingly messianic discourse lauding the exploits of the Spanish monarchy over the course of the sixteenth century. The enthusiastic fervor for Spanish imperium reached crescendo around 1581, when Philip II of Spain ascended the Portuguese throne, achieving the long sought reunification of the entire Iberian Peninsula for the first time since antiquity and bringing the two hemispheres of Iberian expansion together under his singular sovereignty. By adding Portuguese territories in Africa, Asia, and Brazil to his already sprawling possessions, Philip now looked out from his new Lisbon palace over what contemporary observers and modern historians alike have viewed as the world's first global empire.

The Americas, unknown to Europe prior to the late fifteenth century, soon became a major center of gravity within Spain's empire, providing enormous wealth, and endowing the metropolis with increased prestige. An array of authors, many under crown commission, sought to amplify Spain's exploits and bestow them with providential meaning in an effort to galvanize support among Spaniards across the empire and impress upon rivals its unprecedented power. If the total population of the monarchy with its Castilian and Aragonese subjects stood at some 6 million in 1491, within half a century it seemed to have multiplied by almost ten times, adding roughly 50 million more with the incorporation of the former Aztec and Inca empires and several other Native American polities.[1]

As we recognize the vast dimensions of Spain's early modern imperium, however, it is also worth asking to what extent the crown actually exercised sovereignty over the territories and peoples it purported to rule. What are we to make of vague claims stressing the unprecedented power of the empire and its globality? Despite the formidable efforts of conquerors, missionaries, humanists, jurists, and theologians in giving physical and ideological meaning to the Spanish empire as it expanded, the process of extending imperial rule was constantly contested. A gaping divide existed between theory and practice, between the monarchs' capacious claims and their ability to impose effective sovereignty over those claims. Distinct from the traditional portrayal of the empire as a domineering, centralized political unit exercising supreme control over vast swathes of uninterrupted territory and millions of colonial subjects, Spanish imperial rule was, in reality, highly fragmented and often indirect, especially beyond fortified enclaves.

In this chapter I examine the discourse developed to glorify and legitimize Spanish expansion, and the debates that expansion provoked. Exploring tensions between political theory, legal frameworks, and the practice of government, I analyze how large parts of the "New World" were integrated within Spain's composite monarchy, and the enormous institutional and intellectual challenges this process presented. Finally, I assess how the monarchy attempted to rule the vast and varied territories over which it laid claim, the persistence of indigenous forms of social, cultural, and political organization, and the generally diffuse nature of imperial power, including at the apex of Spain's global hegemony in the sixteenth and early seventeenth centuries.

Over two decades ago Jack Greene's study, *Negotiated Authorities: Essays in Colonial Political and Constitutional History*, subverted the idea of an absolutist, centralized structure of early modern European imperial rule.[2] Although his work focused on British America and the crown's relationship to its European colonial subjects, the fundamental argument that imperial authority was decentralized and constantly renegotiated can also be applied fittingly to the territories over which Spain laid claim. In many ways, Greene's work echoed that of European historians like António Manuel Hespanha and Pablo Fernández Albaladejo, who advanced related arguments for early modern Iberia and have, along with others like Víctor Tau Anzoátegui and Tamar Herzog, applied similar approaches in the Spanish American context as well.[3] Fusing the fields of geography, law, and cultural history, Lauren Benton's work has in its own way displayed how European and non-European empires alike sought to maintain order over diverse dominions through constant compromises between the imposition of top-down centralized forms of rule and the ceding of legal and political autonomy to local settler and indigenous groups within the larger structure of empire.[4] In addition, the largely ethnohistorical scholarship of the "New Conquest History," so termed and in part shaped by Matthew Restall, has emphasized the dynamism of Native peoples and the persistence of Indigenous social, cultural, and political forms during the long, complex process of encounter between Europeans and Native Americans.[5] These contributions, among others, have added significant depth to our understanding of the porosity, fluctuation, and imprecision of imperial boundaries, of the limits of European domination, and of the diffusion of power inherent to early modern empires, including that of Spain.

It is worth clarifying at the outset my use of the terms "empire" and "sovereignty." The Spanish Monarchy never officially defined itself as an "empire." In Castilian dictionaries of the sixteenth and seventeenth centuries, "empire," as a political unit, referred to the Roman Empire or its successor, the Holy Roman Empire. In strict semantic terms, the "Spanish Empire" never existed in its own day. Instead, contemporaries called that political unit, "the Spanish Monarchy," or "the Catholic Monarchy."[6] In its general sense, the concept of "empire"—*imperio* in Castilian and *imperium* in Latin—meant simply "lordship" and "power," "to reign," and "to command," and could be used with a geographical connotation to denote the territorial limits of a given realm. So although "empire" was not the official designation used to describe the multicontinental polity of early modern Spain, contemporaries did often use the term to convey the general vastness of Spanish monarchical power. And if we accept the capacious definition of empires proposed by Jane Burbank and Frederick Cooper as "large political units, expansionist or with a memory of power extended over space, polities that maintain distinction and hierarchy as they incorporate new peoples," then the Spanish monarchy was without doubt "imperial."[7]

The term "sovereign," on the other hand, had long been used by Europeans among alternatives to "majesty," "king," "monarch," and "lord," to refer to rulers, including non-European ones, to denote the supreme power they held within their respective realms. In a report compiled shortly after the conquest of Mexico, a Spanish scribe wrote of Montezuma, for example, as having been "sovereign of that land."[8] But "sovereignty," as a political concept, entered the European lexicon slowly, despite being first theorized by French jurist Jean Bodin in 1576.[9] While sovereign power then as now was absolute in theory, it has rarely been absolute in practice.[10] Including during the supposed height of European royal absolutism in the seventeenth century, crown power was often circumscribed and dependent on constant negotiations with elites and local interests over financial and military support to the crown, jurisdictional autonomy, and royal recognition of local custom and privilege.[11] As on the peninsula, the Spanish monarchs' sovereignty was also diffuse in America, especially beyond the confines of colonial strongholds like Mexico City and Lima, and to some degree within them, as we will see.[12] And in many places crown rule was only partial or indirect, extended through alliances or fluid relations of vassalage with local Indigenous polities, or through missionaries acting as intermediaries at the vanguard in the expansion of the faith and Spanish civilization.[13] Thus I use the term "sovereignty" primarily as an interpretive concept, which, importantly, reflects less an achieved reality than an ambition on the part of the monarchy to exercise full and indivisible rule in the territories it claimed to possess.

Peninsular Monarchy to Global Empire

As historians have long recognized, a combination of commercial and religious motives drove early Spanish expansion under Isabel and Ferdinand. In 1492, having completed the final phase of *reconquista*, the monarchs looked to new horizons and agreed to sponsor Columbus' voyage west in the hope of forging new frontiers of trade and evangelization. In less than a century, as a result of the expeditions of Hernán Cortés in Mexico, Francisco Pizarro in Peru, and others elsewhere, the most populous parts of America had been invaded and claimed for the Spanish monarchy and many of its colonial centers had been founded, including Santo Domingo, Havana, Mexico City, and Lima.

Even before any Spaniard had knowledge of the "New World," let alone set foot there, and before the *Inter cætera* bull of donation, Isabel and Ferdinand began laying the basic institutional and ideological foundations of their imperium over those distant lands and peoples. In the Capitulations of Santa Fe agreed upon with Columbus on April 30, 1492 the monarchs made explicit their intention to settle, govern, and exploit new lands to the west economically, and they provided a clear articulation of the religious political philosophy underpinning their claim as legitimate lords in the possessions they already ruled. They derived their sovereignty from God who, as "King over all Kings," "governs and maintains them."[14] Kings serve as God's "vice-regents" "set upon earth in the place of God to fulfill justice. So great is the authority of the power of kings, that all laws and rights are subject to their power, for they do not derive it from men, but from God, whose place they occupy in matters temporal."[15]

Once news of Columbus' "discovery" of Caribbean islands reached Europe, official legitimation followed swiftly. In May 1493 the Valencia-born Pope Alexander VI issued the *Inter cætera* bull, which claimed to legitimize Spain's conquest of the Americas in the name of Christianization. The bull granted the "kings of Castile and León" and their "heirs and successors," "forever, ... full and free power, authority, and jurisdiction of every kind."[16] It linked Spain's overseas expansion to "the honor of God himself and the spread of Christian rule," and thereby endowed it with a sacred mission "to instruct the [native] inhabitants and residents in the Catholic faith and train them in good morals."[17] The Papal donation provided the first foundation of Spain's claim to legitimate sovereignty in the New World, and imbued the enterprise with divine ideological meaning.

Celebration

By the second decade of the sixteenth century, authors across the monarchy were already developing a triumphalist discourse that hailed the exploits of the crown and conquistadors.[18] Michel

Foucault's concept of a "discourse" serves well in assessing the wide range of texts on Spain's early modern empire that furnished its ideological power.[19] A discourse, in the Foucauldian sense, is a reflection of power relations, which when enacted by and through speaking and writing subjects comes to form a unified system of thought, language, and action that in turn legitimates power. This is not to say there was always a singular, self-conscious, official "Spanish ideology of empire," however. Debates over the legitimacy of Spanish imperium were always polyphonic and contentious.[20] But even critics like Bartolomé de las Casas, who censured settlers' abuse of Native Americans, and Francisco de Vitoria, who criticized the Pope's secular authority and by extension the Spanish monarchs' initial claims to sovereign title over New World territory, did not advocate the total illegitimacy or abandonment of overseas empire. On the contrary, in critiquing specific features of Spanish imperialism they sought to reshape and improve the nature of the empire in order to justify it in the eyes of God and according to natural law.

On the other hand, writers like Juan Ginés de Sepulveda and Juan de Solórzano Pereira offered a more explicit, unfettered support for empire. They did so not only to bolster the monarchy's claims to moral and legal authority against those of competing empires, but also to justify the imperial mission to the crown's own subjects, including Spaniards and the masses of non-European subject populations overseas. Although not constituting an official Spanish imperial ideology, critics as well as unabashed champions of Spanish imperium did nonetheless draw on a shared vocabulary, grammar, and set of beliefs, which coalesced into a discourse rooted in the religious, juridical, and cultural traditions of early modern Christian Iberia.[21]

Between 1516 and 1530, the Milanese historian Pietro Martire d'Anghiera birthed the genre of the Spanish imperial chronicle, publishing his *On the New World*, which recounted Spaniards' early explorations and conquests throughout the circum-Caribbean and Pacific coasts of America.[22] Gonzalo Fernández de Oviedo y Valdés later wrote his own comprehensive *General and Natural History of the Indies*, which presents a providential vision of Spain's mission in the New World.[23] Several decades on, Bernal Díaz de Castillo, who had participated in several early expeditions to Mexico, composed his own account, the *True History of the Conquest of New Spain*, in which he emphasized the valor and sacrifice of common soldiers like himself to complement accounts extolling leaders like Cortés.[24]

More than simply praising the chivalry and heroism of conquistadors, many authors advanced specific justifications of Spanish sovereignty in the so-called Indies. Oviedo, for instance, cited the papal donation and, in an effort to provide a longer term historical basis for Spain's claim as first discoverer of America, claimed that mythical sailors had reached the Caribbean Antilles from ancient pre-Roman Hispania.[25] Francisco López de Gómara, commissioned by Cortés to write his own history of the Indies, cited the more recent past in glorifying Spain's religious imperial mission and portrayed Spaniards' efforts in the New World as a continuation of those in the Old.[26] They "began the conquest of the Indies having completed that of the Moors," he writes, "because the Spaniards always warred against infidels."[27] López de Gómara, like Oviedo, also invoked papal donation as a basis of legitimacy, and in his recounting of the invasion of Mexico tells of miraculous interventions by Spain's patron saint Santiago in the battles of Cintla and Tabasco to convey the sense of the "conquest" as preordained by God.[28] The idea of a willful *translatio imperii* from indigenous empires to Spanish rule, although discredited by Vitoria as legal and historical fiction, was another motif mobilized with increasing regularity to complement claims based on papal donation and divine providence.[29] López de Gómara, for instance, echoed Cortés himself in describing the voluntary relinquishing of the Aztec throne by Montezuma in favor of Charles V.[30]

After the Spanish invasions of Mexico and Peru and the discovery of massive silver mines nearby, the monarchy expanded its military activities throughout Europe, the Mediterranean,

East Asia, and the Americas in the second half of the sixteenth century. Excited by these events, many in Europe thought Spain would soon realize universal monarchy and unite the entire world under its singular sovereignty.[31] This view seemed all but assured when Philip II ascended the Portuguese throne in 1581 after the sudden death of his childless nephew, Sebastian I of Portugal. Philip's succession to the Portuguese throne initiated a further profusion of verbal and visual discourse celebrating Spanish imperium. The famous 1583 coin emblazoned with the phrase "The World is not Enough" was one of many examples.[32] Another was the *General History of the Deeds of the Castilians on the Islands and Mainland of the Ocean Sea Known As the West Indies*, published between 1601 and 1615, by Antonio de Herrera y Tordesillas, the crown's official "chronicler of the Indies."[33] Despite the many limits on its ability to impose imperial rule, the monarchy now claimed authority over large parts of Africa, Asia, and America, where, in the words of the chronicler and jurist Gregorio López Madera, "Roman power never reached, and which not even Alexander attempted to subject."[34]

Controversy

The celebratory discourse, however, was soon accompanied by intense debates about the treatment of native peoples and the titles by which the monarchy justified its claims to dominion in America.[35] In the effort to sustain the early colony of Hispaniola, officials there began allocating Native Americans as forced labor to Spanish settlers who in turn were entrusted with defending the land and instructing their charges in Catholicism and Spanish civilization. This institution, known as *encomienda*, became central to Spanish imperial rule in America, especially when transferred to the mainland. But it also became the focus of intense scrutiny as abuse grew rife and as native populations declined precipitously.

In 1511 Antonio de Montesinos, a Dominican priest in Hispaniola, was the first to publicly denounce the natives' harsh treatment at the hands of rapacious settlers. "Tell me, what right have you to enslave them?" he decried in a fiery sermon. "What authority did you use to make war against them who lived at peace on their territories? … And why don't you look after their spiritual health, so that they should come to know God? … Aren't they human beings? Have they no rational soul?"[36] In these brief lines, Montesinos defined the basic terms of a debate that would rattle Spain's imperial conscience for the next four decades. Bartolomé de las Casas, also a Dominican, a former *encomendero* himself who had been converted by Montesinos, soon catalogued the numerous crimes committed against Native Americans. His *Short Account of the Destruction of the Indies*, written in the 1540s, provided the first systematic account of the horrors of the conquest, and of the exploitative colonial regime that arose in its wake.

Several authors did rise to support the *encomenderos*, however. The most prominent was the humanist theologian Juan Ginés de Sepúlveda. Drawing primarily on Aristotelian philosophy, Sepúlveda argued that Spaniards were "natural masters," whereas the natives, as subhuman "barbarians," were "natural slaves." His treatises, in particular the 1547 *Demócrates Alter*, written in eloquent Latin, serve as an erudite albeit protoracist complement to the more popular celebratory works in support of empire by humanists like Gómara, Balbuena, and others.[37]

Tensions escalated to such an extent that in 1550 Charles V convened a public debate on the issue between Las Casas and Sepúlveda, and decreed that all conquests would cease until a ruling was made on the justness of Spanish conduct in America. Neither of the two interlocuters were declared the clear winner, but the fact that the 1573 *Ordinances for the Discovery, Settlement, and Pacification of the Indies* upheld the crown's long-professed intention to protect Native Americans shows that Las Casas and his camp had effectively prevailed. The 1573 *Ordinances*, like the 1513 *Laws of Burgos* and the 1542 *New Laws*, while aiming to shield Native Americans from mistreatment and thereby bolster the monarchy's claim to moral authority, also sought to curb the rise of an autonomous settler elite, which threatened the primacy of crown power in the New World. Settler abuse of Native Americans persisted across space and time, however. Intense, often violent opposition from settlers in Peru and Mexico compelled royal officials to rescind, delay, or soften several of these laws' key provisions. The series of laws and decrees failed to effectively eliminate such abuse, but did represent a systematic effort by the crown to consolidate its position as a benevolent moral authority among both its own subjects and imperial competitors.[38]

Alongside the debate over the treatment of the Indigenous peoples was the so-called Controversy of the Indies, which centered on the monarchy's lawful title to the territories it claimed in America. One of early modern Spain's most influential theologians and leading experts on natural law, Francisco de Vitoria, was deeply interested in the moral aspects of authority and of the exercise of power. He rejected the legality of the Pope, the Emperor, and of any other authority that claimed to possess universal power; and in 1534 he denied the Pope's authority in secular affairs. Although possessing authority in the spiritual world, Vitoria argued, "the Pope is not civil or temporal lord of the whole world, in the proper sense of civil lordship and power," so the rights he awarded Castile in the *Inter cætera* bull were null and void.[39] He argued further that the Native Americans, as rational beings, had held their territory as legitimate owners, and that Spanish occupation of it was thereby unlawful. Yet Vitoria did not categorically reject Spain's title to sovereignty in the New World. Drawing on theories from natural law he argued that Spanish war against Native Americans and the seizure of their territory could be considered just and legitimate if the natives' had impeded Spaniards' natural right to travel, trade, or preach the gospel in their lands. He also recognized that "Indian aborigines could have come under the sway of the Spaniards through true and voluntary choice," or "by a title of alliance or friendship."[40]

Debates over the monarchy's titles to the New World dissipated over the late sixteenth and early seventeenth centuries. This was in part because, as the Jesuit ethnographer José de Acosta argued in the 1580s, despite valid critiques of the conquest's initial legitimacy, Spanish claims in the Indies had become legally prescribed through their long and continuous occupation of the land.[41] By then the monarchy and its advocates drew upon a diversified range of arguments including the papal bulls, the voluntary vassalage of native peoples, the right of just conquest, and the right to occupy unclaimed or uncultivated lands.[42] The controversy culminated in 1629 with the publication of the first volume of *De Indiarum Jure*, by the jurist-bureaucrat Juan de Solórzano Pereira.[43] Synthesizing over a century of theological and juridical debate he recognized all the above titles as legitimate, arguing for Native Americans' true humanity and reaffirming the Pope's supreme authority in the spiritual world, including over non-Christians.[44] Solórzano's work provided the foundation for the first comprehensive corpus of Spanish American law, the *Compilation of Laws of the Indies*, published in 1681, and thereby concluded the legal debate within Spain over the monarchy's claim to sovereignty in the New World.[45]

Integrating a New World

The growing presence of Spaniards throughout "the Indies" also provoked intense discussions about the political status of those territories within the monarchy. From the beginning all the American territories over which Spain claimed sovereignty were in theory incorporated within the kingdom of Castile, as Granada and the Canaries had been. Isabel confirmed this in her will, declaring explicitly that the Indies "must remain incorporated within these realms of Castile and León, according to the Apostolic Bull."[46] In 1571 Philip II reiterated this, decreeing that the

"States [of the Indies] be governed according to the style and regime prevailing in the Kingdoms of Castile and León." He continued:

> Because the kingdoms of Castile and the Indies belong to one Crown, their laws and government system ought therefore to be as alike as possible. The members of the Council [of Indies] shall try, in the laws and institutions which they may establish for those States, to reduce the form and manner of their government to the style and order by which the kingdoms of Castile and León are ruled to the extent allowed by the diversity and difference of lands and peoples.[47]

The final line is significant. Although the intention was to reproduce Castilian legal and governmental frameworks, the king recognized that the Americas' distinctive social and geographical characteristics could result in adaptations to those frameworks when transferred across the ocean.

One such adaptation regarded social hierarchy. In American territories controlled by Spain the so-called *indios* were considered vassals of the king but part of the *República de indios*, a separate juridicopolitical body within the monarchy that maintained certain indigenous laws and institutions. Whereas the *República de españoles* was composed of Spaniards, Africans, mulattoes, and those mestizos recognized by their Spanish fathers, the *República de indios* included the entire Native American population. The reality was far more complex. There were, as we will see, several key exceptions. But in general legal terms the institution blurred the distinctions between the thousands of Indigenous groups and polities, creating a single overarching category of *indios*, which in theory encompassed all the diverse native peoples from northern California to Patagonia—as well as the Philippines.[48] According to Castilian law, *indios* were viewed as minors, as *gente sin razon* (people without reason), subjugated therefore to a relationship of legal and political dependence on the Castilian crown, and forced to provide tribute, often in the form of labor.

In the attempt to consolidate control over the rapidly expanding colonial world, the monarchy created a complex structure of institutions and officials charged with extending and maintaining relations of vassalage over both indigenous groups and colonists of European origin.[49] In the monarchy's political hierarchy, directly below the king was a polysynodial system of councils, including one for each constituent kingdom. The establishment of an independent Council of Indies in 1524 had great symbolic and practical significance as it acknowledged the prominence of those territories in relation to the monarchy's various kingdoms in Europe.

The Council of Indies advised the monarch on everything related to the administration of his American possessions and became the highest authority on all legislative, executive, and judicial matters concerning those territories, subject only to the orders of the king. It gained jurisdiction over the House of Trade (*Casa de Contratación*), the first institution of colonial government founded in 1503, which set and collected taxes and duties, licensed voyages, protected cartographic and commercial intelligence, and served as a court of maritime law. A century on, in 1629, Solórzano continued, in grandiose terms, to justify the existence of a separate council for the Indies with such broad powers. It was charged not only with "the government of a County or Kingdom," he proclaimed, "but that of an Empire which embraces so many Kingdoms and such rich and powerful Provinces, or, in better words, the broadest and most extended Monarchy the world has ever known, as it actually comprises another world."[50]

As Spaniards spread across the Americas they founded new towns and cities with municipal councils (*cabildos*), which provided them limited self-government at the local level. In Spanish America, towns served the same symbolic and administrative functions they had in Castile. They were centers of commerce, culture, and power.[51] Even seigniorial lords with vast rural landholdings resided in towns, their prestige reflected in the proximity of their residences to the central plaza with its church and municipal buildings, including the *cabildo*. Built on grid systems, Spanish American towns held great significance as symbols of European civilization and rational order. And, as during *reconquista*, newly founded towns in America served as bases for further invasions as Spaniards pushed deeper into native-controlled territory. Cortés, in the most famous example, founded Veracruz in Mexico, along with a *cabildo*, as a means to free himself from the authority of his rival, the governor of Cuba, to place himself under direct royal order, and to create the legal basis for a new, independent mandate to conquer the Aztec empire. According to Cortés,

> [I]t seemed best to all of us in the name of your Royal Highnesses to populate and found there a town in which there were justice, so that there were lordship in that land, as in your kingdoms and lordships [in Europe]; because being this land populated with Spaniards, in addition to increasing the kingdoms and lordships of your majesties and your revenues, you might bestow Graces and favors upon us and to the settlers that come from here forward.[52]

The founding of Veracruz provided a bastion of Castilian law and jurisdiction and an early symbol of Spanish permanence on the American mainland.

In its effort to centralize power, the monarchy itself also created several institutions in the Americas, the most important of which were the viceroyalties, *audiencias* (high courts of appeal), and royal treasuries.[53] Alongside these secular institutions, the monarchy encouraged the establishment of bishoprics and religious orders throughout the Indies as well. Their most important function, apart from caring for the spiritual needs of Spaniards in the New World, was to convert the Native Americans, and the hundreds of thousands of Africans brought there by force.[54]

The creation of viceroyalties, one with its seat in Mexico City in 1535, the other in Lima in 1543, signaled the first territorialization of Spanish imperial sovereignty in the New World by defining precise areas over which the crown claimed jurisdiction. Appointed to serve "in the king's living image," viceroys, according to the *Compilation of Laws of the Indies*, "had and exercise the same power, mandate and jurisdiction as the King."[55] They were the chief political, military, and treasury authority within their territory, and they confirmed ecclesiastical posts.[56]

Audiencias represented the second major institution of colonial government. The first American *audiencia* was founded in Santo Domingo in 1511, followed by one in New Spain in 1527, one in Lima in 1543, and several others throughout the rest of the sixteenth and seventeenth centuries. *Audiencia* judges maintained direct correspondence with the king through the Council of Indies and thus provided an independent check on viceregal power. In addition to being high courts of appeal for all legal disputes within their jurisdiction, hearing cases presented by both Spaniards and Native Americans, *audiencias* also served a legislative role in issuing laws and local ordinances, as well as a consultative one in advising viceroys and governors.

The royal treasury was another key institution. Colonial centers and every important port and mining town had one staffed by crown-appointed officials responsible for managing all royal payments and income, including tribute and spoils from conquest. The fact that their appointments came directly from Spain gave them a degree of autonomy from the viceroys, provincial governors, and *audiencia* judges, and further diffused power among the various colonial institutions, each of which reported directly to the Council of Indies.

Within the political, judicial, fiscal, and ecclesiastical institutions, including the bishoprics and missionary orders, there existed more or less clear orders of hierarchy, and all, with the exception of the regular clergy, were subject to the ultimate authority of the monarch and his Council of Indies. But between them, relations of hierarchy were not always clear. Jurisdictional disputes erupted frequently between the viceroy and *audiencia*, for instance, since both reported directly to Spain. Even town councils could appeal directly to the king through his Council of Indies if they felt the viceroy or another authority had violated their local rights or jurisdictions. Rather than provoking anarchy, however, this complex political structure actually produced a degree of cohesion while at the same time affording local colonial institutions substantial autonomy.[57] Factors like physical distance and communication lag, jurisdictional layering, and respect for local custom and privilege all converged to diffuse the monarch's effective power and ability to influence everyday decision making. But the checking of certain colonial institutions by the power of others also aimed to ensure that ultimate sovereignty remained in the hands of the king.

Conquest?

Despite the impressive advance of Spaniards throughout the New World after Columbus, and despite the vast institutional apparatus that arose in their wake, the so-called conquest was not as rapid, linear, or comprehensive in its domination of American territories and peoples as once thought. Classical historiography on the conquests of the Aztec and Inca empires, for instance, even if recognizing the violence of events, continued to emphasize the heroism of missionaries, or of vastly outnumbered conquistadors who by their faith and grit managed to defeat and subject America's two preeminent native polities with miraculous speed.[58] Interestingly, many of these nineteenth- and early twentieth-century histories were based on less-than-critical readings of Oviedo, Díaz del Castillo, and others, demonstrating the enduring ideological power of early modern Spain's celebratory discourse of empire. In recent decades, however, scholars have increasingly demonstrated the effective resistance, adaptation, and even collaboration of native peoples. In addition, this "New Conquest History" has underlined the need to conceive of the "conquests" as processes, rather than discrete events, which often played out over decades if not centuries and in many cases never reached completion.[59]

We now know in more concrete terms the fundamental role of Native allies in virtually every major "Spanish" victory over indigenous polities in mainland America. In Mexico, for instance, hundreds of thousands of Tlaxcalans, longtime enemies of the Aztecs, seized the opportunity to ally with the Spanish and were instrumental in the series of battles that led to the fall of Tenochtitlan in 1521. From there, many more thousands of Indigenous allies, including but not limited to Tlaxcalans, Cholulans, and even defeated Nahua groups from central Mexico joined the Spanish in their expeditions south and east into Yucatán, Guatemala and Honduras, northwest against the Cazcanes and Zacatecas, and later against a diverse confederation of Chichimeca peoples in the region of Bajío, in which Cazcanes fought alongside Spaniards.[60] Likewise, in their various campaigns in South America the Spanish relied on support from Nahuas, Mayas, Nicaraguans of various groups, as well as Cañaris and other local South American societies who had long resented and resisted Inca domination.[61]

Despite the Spaniards' technological superiority, the support of so many thousands of Native American allies, and the rapidity with which they deposed the titular heads of the Inca and Aztecs, for instance, it took many decades to consolidate rule over those pre-Hispanic empires. Soon after the indigenous ruler Atahualpa was captured in 1532, for instance, a large Inca force rebelled, harassed Spanish positions, and eventually established a neo-Inca state based in the mountains in Vilcabamba, which successfully resisted Spanish domination for nearly four decades. The effort to subjugate the Maya peoples of Yucatán was an even more complicated affair. Beginning in 1517 the Spanish began sending expeditions into the peninsula, faced pitched resistance, and after a series of violent clashes in the 1520s and 1530s only managed their first permanent settlements there in 1542. Still, Spanish control remained restricted to the northwest part of the peninsula, and was dependant on an unstable alliance with local Maya groups and other indigenous allies from central Mexico.[62] Mexico City too, the ostensible heart of Spanish imperial sovereignty in the New World, remained unstable well into the seventeenth century when two major Native American rebellions rocked the city, one as late as 1692, threatening Spanish colonial rule at its core.[63]

Spanish hegemony remained far from complete in other ways as well. Even in central Mexico the Nahua *altepetl* (city-state), the basis of indigenous sociopolitical organization, survived well into the postconquest period, as did traditional kinship and inheritance patterns.[64] Indigenous peoples across much of Spanish America continued residing in their traditional towns and villages where they maintained local leaders, customs, and legal norms. Although in reality the forms of these units derived from pre-Hispanic forms of sociopolitical organization like the *altepetl*, the semiautonomy they maintained was reminiscent of the *fueros* (local laws and privileges) granted to cities and lordships back in Spain, and were thus intelligible within Castilian legal frameworks as well.

In addition, despite being regarded in legal terms as a single homogenous population comprising the *República de indios*, Native Americans maintained many of their diverse customs, languages, and beliefs, sometimes covertly, and often in the face of brutal attempts to eradicate such traditions. Although in theory claiming the authority to abolish all indigenous law and custom, the monarchy acquiesced to preserve certain aspects of pre-Hispanic political and social organization. The intention was to provide continuity to facilitate the transition from indigenous to Spanish rule, making the latter more intelligible and legitimate in the eyes of Native Americans. But it was also a response to the reality, of which the monarchy was well aware, that it simply did not possess sufficient power to fully impose its cultural and institutional rule over such vast, varied, and complex indigenous societies.

To the extent that Nahuas, for instance, incorporated Spanish social and cultural forms, they did so through a gradual process of selective acculturation throughout the sixteenth and seventeenth centuries at least.[65] Like the Nahua, the Maya also retained many of their traditions, especially in religion, despite systematic Spanish efforts to impose Christianity.[66] They adopted certain Christian religious practices but imbued them with Maya meaning, and they maintained their traditional vision of the universe and concept of cyclical time. Similar processes played out across the empire, where indigenous peoples incorporated varying degrees of Spanish influence, but always maintained certain elements from the pre-Hispanic past.[67]

As part of the *República de indios*, indigenous peoples throughout the Americas and Philippines, in addition to maintaining certain forms of traditional legal culture at the local level, also had access to Castilian law. Native Americans often utilized this access to protest abusive *encomenderos* or protect their communities' local autonomy and customs. The General Indian Court, for instance, founded in Mexico City in 1592 served as a forum for complaints against abusive Spanish settlers, priests, and even royal officials, and, if only in its early phase, dealt with a combination of both Castilian and Native American law.[68]

In practice, there were key exceptions to the legal theory that subsumed Native Americans into the single juridico-political category of the *República de indios*. Particular Indigenous nations, like the Tlaxcala, for instance, secured special status in recognition of their collaboration in military campaigns against other native groups. That status exempted Tlaxcalans from certain tribute payments and enabled them to maintain their traditional culture relatively unmolested. Some members of the former indigenous elite also retained their elevated status under the new Spanish political regime. This was a prudent if necessary concession from the monarchy, designed to legitimate its transition to power among native peoples by preserving some of the traditional indigenous hierarchy. These individuals, although in theory prohibited from performing traditional religious functions, maintained their status, property, and power in the native community, and the hereditary nature of their titles, offices, and wealth.

Limits of Imperial Sovereignty

Long after Spain had proclaimed victory in conquering several of America's great indigenous polities and had created its central institutions of imperial administration, the monarchy's effective sovereignty in the New World remained surprisingly diffuse including among the colonial European population. The monarchs' power to determine basic decision making, for instance, was not absolute, nor was it expected to be. Even the highest crown officials, including viceroys and *audiencia* judges in the colonial centers, had wide power to interpret royal decrees as they saw fit and were not always required to execute them to the letter. The famous legal device captured in the phrase, *obedezco pero no cumplo* ("I obey but do not comply"), permitted officials to refuse to implement certain decrees while simultaneously affirming their obedience to the monarch's supreme authority.[69] According to the 1681 *Compilation of Laws of the Indies*, "Ministers and judges should obey, but not comply with our decrees and orders" if given local circumstances they seemed imprudent.[70] Such legal devices combined with jurisdictional overlapping between various institutions and the myriad customary privileges and exemptions of indigenous and local settler communities limited the king's sovereign power in the New World.[71] Practical, tangible forces like physical distance and limited and overstretched resources further diffused that control.[72]

Spanish American municipalities and their *cabildos* also enjoyed substantial legal, political, and economic autonomy from the crown and from its high institutions of colonial government. *Cabildos* held jurisdiction over both the municipality itself and the surrounding countryside, and served as bastions for the protection of local customary law, as in Europe. Describing the wide-ranging authority of the institution, the minutes of the municipal council of Buenos Aires explained in 1674 that

> *Cabildos* …, under their royal laws and *ius commune*, are vested with the power to rule the city and hear matters pertaining to it, by governing each and every part of it, paying attention to the protection of its fruits and crop fields, its sustenance and that of its people, peacefulness, price, amounts, and better distribution, in such a way as they may agree at any time, and deciding whatever they may deem convenient.[73]

Beyond the *cabildo* existed a range of other small yet no less important institutions. Convents, monasteries, unions, schools, universities, and even families—the base unit of Spanish colonial society—all had their own rules, customs, and leaders. Collectively, this integrated constellation of local and regional powers was fundamental in determining the legal and normative frameworks governing everyday life across Spain's American colonies.[74]

Moving outward from the cities and towns that served as islands of Castilian law and government, the monarchy's sovereignty grew increasingly diffuse. If throughout the sixteenth and seventeenth centuries Spanish imperial sovereignty was fragile and circumscribed within the core regions of central Mexico and Peru, it was even more so in remote places like the Río de la Plata, the Philippines, and Chile, to name just three examples, all territories the monarchy claimed within its extended imperium. In such remote regions isolated settlers, missionaries, or itinerant soldier-adventurers often represented the sole Spanish presence beyond fortified enclaves. All these individuals maintained their own unique relationships to the monarchy, and often served as intermediaries in the extension of Spanish cultural and political influence.[75]

The lush upper reaches of the Río de la Plata watershed, for instance, lay on the contested boundary line separating the Spanish- and Portuguese-claimed hemispheres of imperial jurisdiction in America and thus became a key site of conflict not only between Iberian and indigenous groups but also between the two Iberian empires themselves. In the late sixteenth century mixed-race *paulistas*, from São Paulo, in Brazil, began entering the region on expeditions to enslave the local Guaraní peoples.[76] To curb that process and provide a buffer against Portuguese movements into the territory claimed by Spain, the monarchy sanctioned Jesuit efforts to settle local indigenous groups into missions and thereby establish an indirect claim to occupation in the region by proxy.[77] Jesuit-run settlements steadily expanded over the period, despite several devastating *paulista* attacks, but even then the crown had no direct, permanent presence in the territory.[78] And although in perpetual conflict with each other, the Spanish Jesuits and Luso-Brazilian *paulistas* remained the prime representatives of their respective empires in the region until well into the mid-eighteenth century and beyond.

The Philippines became another key focus of strategic interest given its proximity to various Asian emporia, including China, and to the antimeridian separating the two hemispheres of Iberian jurisdiction.[79] Initially claimed for Spain in the 1560s, the monarchy's frustrations in consolidating sovereignty there were compounded by the archipelago's mountainous topography and the difficulty of conquering peoples dispersed across thousands of islands. Although the Spanish managed rather quickly to subjugate the indigenous peoples around Manila, they became embroiled in violent, cyclical conflict with the city's massive Chinese merchant community, making the seat of Spanish power in the Philippines too perpetually unstable.[80] Highlighting the fragility of Spanish sovereignty beyond its enclaves, Philip II instructed his new governor in Manila in 1589 that he "should live with the much vigilance and continuous caution that is required for the conservation of land so new, discontented and encircled by enemies."[81] The king went on to enumerate those enemies in detail: "First, the natives of the land, who are many and little subjected and firm in the faith. Second, the four or five thousand Chinese *indios* who reside there and come and go in trade. Third, the Japanese …. Fourth, the natives of Maluco and Brunei, who are irritated. … Fifth and most important, the English and Lutheran corsairs who come to those shores."[82] On the southern island of Mindanao the native Muslim inhabitants successfully repelled Spanish attempts to establish any lasting presence whatsoever. And although by the 1590s Spain claimed sovereignty over the entire northern island of Luzon, where Manila was located, the mountain peoples of the central cordillera always remained beyond the reach of Spanish power.

As in the New World, a sharp polyphonic debate erupted between missionaries and settlers, theologians and royal officials, over the Spanish abuse of natives through conquest and *encomienda*, viewed together as the prime cause of Filipino unrest.[83] The debates revived questions over the viability of *encomienda* as a central institution of Spanish colonialism, this time in Asia.[84] Yet despite the multipronged efforts to alleviate native suffering, abuses persisted, rebellions continued, and most of the archipelago remained beyond the reach of crown power and even missionary influence until well into the nineteenth century.[85]

Finally, the case of Chile is perhaps even more revealing given its proximity to Peru, one of the centers of Spanish colonial power in America. Hoping to find precious metals and establish a stronghold to protect Peru's southwestern flank, Pedro de Valdivia led the first significant expedition to the region in 1540–41, founding Santiago.[86] Over the following decade subsequent expeditions pushed south into the lands of the Mapuche, establishing a string of isolated settlements along the southern coast and initiating a fierce, persistent conflict with those native peoples.[87] During an escalation from 1599 to 1604 Mapuche forces permanently expelled the Spanish from all seven of their southernmost outposts.[88] Despite the fact that in Chile the monarchy maintained one of its largest standing armies in all the Americas, the Spanish presence there remained hemmed in along the narrow stretch of coast between the Atacama Desert to the north and the Bío-Bío River to the south. Missionary efforts in the south were largely fruitless as well, and the Mapuche repelled virtually every Spanish attempt to conquer, or "pacify," their territories throughout the entire remainder of the colonial era.[89]

Conclusion

In less than a century after Columbus' initial landing in Hispaniola in 1492, Spain had been transformed from an internally divided, relatively isolated group of kingdoms on the edge of Europe into one of the most extended empires the world had ever known. Contemporary observers were well aware of this fact, and the monarchy's most zealous supporters waxed lyrical about the seemingly unbridled potential of Spanish expansion. In his, *De Monarchia Hispanica*, published in 1600, the Calabrian theologian and political philosopher Tomasso Campanella proclaimed that given events of the past century the world now marveled at the "the Spanish Monarchy for its audacity and power because it conquered so many seas and girdled the entire globe."[90] Campanella's portrayal of the monarchy's global reach was accurate in a sense. By then, the monarchy possessed colonies in Europe, Africa, Asia, and America—all "four parts of the world."[91]

Yet despite the mellifluous discourse of Campanella, Oviedo and so many other champions of Spanish imperium, the monarchy's sovereignty over and within its imperial possessions was far from absolute, even at the height of Spanish global hegemony in the sixteenth and early seventeenth centuries. More than simply highlighting the dissonant tension between theory and practice, between ambition and effective rule, a focus on the limits of imperial sovereignty places in sharper relief the true reach of Spanish power and jurisdiction. It illuminates the relative efficacy (or inefficacy) of strategies of imperial domination, including both institutional and discursive ideological ones. It helps reveal the power of indigenous peoples in shaping colonial legal and political frameworks, patterns of conquest, and relations of vassalage and alliance. And it exposes the extension and maintenance of imperial rule as a continuous process of negotiation and adaptation, not only between Europeans and Indigenous peoples but also between Europeans themselves, including settlers, missionaries, and crown officials. These continuous negotiations balanced tendencies toward autonomy with the more centripetal forces of inclusion and subjugation within the larger structure of empire.

Notes

I would like to thank Ignacio Gallup-Díaz, Antonio Feros, Matthew Restall, Gabriel de Avilez Rocha and Roberto Saba for their helpful comments and suggestions.

1 This before the demographic crisis took its toll: J. H. Elliott, "The Spanish Colonization and Settlement of America," *The Cambridge History of Latin America*, ed. Leslie Bethell (Cambridge: Cambridge University Press, 1984), 171.
2 Jack Greene, *Negotiated Authorities: Essays in Colonial Political and Constitutional History* (Charlottesville: University Press of Virginia, 1994).
3 António Manuel Hespanha, *As Vésperas do Leviathan: Instituições e Poder Político em Portugal, século XVI* (Coimbra: Almedina, 1994); Pablo Fernández Albaladejo, *Fragmentos de monarquía: Trabajos de historia política* (Madrid: Alianza Editorial, 1992); Víctor Tau Anzoátegui, *Nuevos horizontes en el estudio histórico del Derecho indiano* (Buenos Aires: Instituto de Investigaciones de Historia del Derecho, 1997), and *El poder de la costumbre: Estudios sobre el Derecho consuetudinario en América hispana hasta la Emancipación* (Buenos Aires: Instituto de Investigaciones de Historia del Derecho, 2001); Thomas Duve and Heikki Pihlajamäki, ed., *New Horizons in Spanish Colonial Law: Contributions to Transnational Early Modern Legal History* (Frankfurt: Max Planck Institute for European Legal History, 2015); Tamar Herzog, *Frontiers of*

Possession: Spain and Portugal in Europe and the Americas (Cambridge: Harvard University Press, 2015); and Pedro Cardim, Tamar Herzog, José Javier Ruiz Ibáñez, and Gaetano Sabatini, eds., *Polycentric Monarchies: How did Early Modern Spain and Portugal Achieve and Maintain a Global Hegemony?* (Eastbourne: Sussex Academic Press, 2012).

4 See, among Lauren Benton's works, *Law and Colonial Cultures: Legal Regimes in World History, 1400–1900* (Cambridge: Cambridge University Press, 2001); and *A Search for Sovereignty: Law and Geography in European Empires, 1400–1900* (Cambridge: Cambridge University Press, 2009).

5 Matthew Restall, "The New Conquest History," *History Compass* 10, 2 (2012): 151–60; and Restall's, *Seven Myths of the Spanish Conquest* (Oxford: Oxford University Press, 2003).

6 Pedro Cardim, "La aspiración imperial de la monarquía portuguesa, siglos XVI y XVII," *Comprendere le monarchie iberiche: Risorse materiali e rappresentazioni del potere*, ed. Gaetano Sabatini (Roma: Viella, 2010), 37–72.

7 Jane Burbank and Frederick Cooper, *Empires in World History: Power and the Politics of Difference* (Princeton: Princeton University Press, 2010), 8.

8 "Información hecha ante las justicias de Tepeaca (México) de los descubrimientos, conquistas y pacificaciones de Hernán Cortés en Nueva España," c. 1521, AGI (Archivo General de Indias), *Patronato*, 15, R.17, my translation.

9 Jean Bodin, *Les Six Livres de la République* (Paris: Chez Iacques du Puys, 1576).

10 On the role of clientelism in mediating the relationship between central monarchical authority and elites and other local and regional powers, see Antonio Feros, "Clientelismo y poder monárquico en la España de los siglos XVI y XVII," *Relaciones* 73[19] (1998): 17–49.

11 Historians have long recognized this to be especially true in Aragon, and a substantial body of scholarship has shown it to be true in Castile as well, where royal power had conventionally been seen as having dominated local seigniorial and urban corporate interests. For scholarship interrogating the concept of absolutism, and of the state, in early modern Spain and Europe, see James Amelang, "The Peculiarities of the Spaniards: Historical Approaches to the Early Modern State", *Public Power in Europe: Studies in Historical Transformations*, eds. James Amelang and Siegfried Beer (Pisa: Pisa University Press, 2006), 31–56; Bartolomé Clavero, "Tejido de sueños: La historiografía jurídica española y el problema del estado," *Historia contemporánea* 12 (1996): 25–47; Charles Jago, "Habsburg Absolutism and the Cortes of Castile," *American Historical Review* 86[2] (April 1981): 307–26; I. A. A. Thompson, *Crown and Cortes: Government, Institutions and Representation in Early-Modern Castile* (Aldershot: Variorum, 1993); and Giorgio Chittolini, "The 'Private,' the 'Public,' the State," *Journal of Modern History* 67 (Dec. 1995): 34–61.

12 For an analysis of these dynamics from an economic perspective, see Alejandra Irigoin and Regina Grafe, "Bargaining for Absolutism: A Spanish Path to Nation-State and Empire Building," *Hispanic American Historical Review* 88,[2] (2008): 173–209.

13 The monarchy made clear its intention to use missionaries in such a capacity. See the *Recopilación de leyes de los reynos de las Indias (Compilation of Laws of the Indies)*, Book 4, Title 4, Laws 2–6 (Madrid: Boix, 1841 [1681]).

14 Ferdinand and Isabella, "Capitulations with Columbus: Agreement of April 30, 1492," *The Spanish Tradition in America*, ed. Charles Gibson (New York: Harper & Row, 1968), 29.

15 "Capitulations with Columbus," 30.

16 Pope Alexander VI, "Papal Bull *Inter cætera* of May 4, 1493," *The Philippine Islands, 1493–1803*, Vol. I, 1493–1529, eds. Emma Helen Blair and James Alexander Robertson (Cleveland, OH: The Arthur H. Clark Company, 1903), 100–01.

17 "Papal Bull *Inter cætera* of May 4, 1493," 101.

18 Carlos José Hernando Sánchez, *Las indias en la monarquía católica: Imágenes e ideas políticas* (Valladolid: Universidad de Valladolid, 1996).

19 Michel Foucault, *The Archaeology of Knowledge and the Discourse on Language* (New York: Pantheon Books, 1972); and *Discipline and Punish: The Birth of the Prison* (New York: Vintage Books, 1995).

20 Lewis Hanke, *The Spanish Struggle for Justice in the Conquest of America* (Dallas, TX: Southern Methodist University Press, 2002 [1949]); for a more recent appraisal of sixteenth century historiography on Spain's invasion of and early colonial presence in America, see Rolena Adorno, "The Discursive Encounter of Spain and America: The Authority of Eyewitness Testimony in the Writing of History," *The William and Mary Quarterly* 49[2] (April 1992): 210–28.

21 For a study on the narrative, literary aspect of this discourse, see Rolena Adorno, *The Polemics of Possession in Spanish American Narrative* (New Haven: Yale University Press, 2008).

22 Petri Martyris ab Anglería, *Decadas de Orbe Novo* (Alcalá de Henares: Michaele[m] d[e] Eguia, 1530).
23 Published in parts in the sixteenth century, the complete work was not published until the nineteenth century: Gonzalo Fernández de Oviedo y Valdés, *Historia general y natural de las Indias*, ed. José Amador de los Rios (Madrid: Real Academia de la Historia, 1851–55).
24 Bernal Díaz de Castillo, *Historia verdadera de la conquista de la Nueva España*, ed. Genaro García, 2 vols. (México: Oficina Tipográfica de la Secretaría de Fomento, 1904–05). Díaz de Castillo completed the original manuscript in 1568. Although a version of the work was first published in Madrid in 1632, the 1904 version is the first published edition based on the original manuscript.
25 *Las indias en la monarquía católica*, 57.
26 Francisco López de Gómara, *Historia general de las Indias* (Medina del Campo: Guillermo de Millis, 1553).
27 Francisco López de Gómara, *Hispania Victrix: Primera y segunda parte de la historia general de las Indias co[n] todo el descubrimiento, y cosas notables que han acaescido dende que se ganaron hasta el año de 1551, con la conquista de Mexico, y de la nueua España* (Medina del Campo: Guillermo de Millis, 1553), f.3r.
28 Alberto Pérez-Amador Adam, *De legitimatione imperii Indiae Occidentalis: La vindicación de la empresa Americana* (Madrid: Iberoamericana, 2011), 260.
29 Alongside that of Mexico, the conquest of Peru elicited a similar outpouring of laudatory discourse celebrating that event. The *Verdadera relación de la conquista del Perú*, (Seville: Bartolomé Pérez, 1534), by Pizarro's personal secretary Francisco de Jerez, was one example. In 1553 Pedro Cieza de León's *Parte primera de la chronica del Perú* (Seville) portrayed the Monarchy as a civilizing force. Two years later, in the *Historia del descubrimiento y conquista del Perú* (Amberes, 1555), Agustín de Zárate provided his own laudatory interpretation of the event.
30 *Hispania Victrix*, fs.53v–54r.
31 Franz Bosbach, "The European Debate on Universal Monarchy," *Theories of Empire, 1450–1800*, ed. David Armitage (Aldershot: Ashgate, 1998), 87; and Xavier Gil Pujol, *Imperio, Monarquía Universal, Equilibrio: Europea y la Política Exterior en el Pensamiento Político Español de los siglos XVI y XVII* (Perugia: Università di Perugia, 1995–96).
32 The phrase, "The World is not Enough" ("*Non Sufficit Orbis*" in Latin) was reincarnated by supporters of Philip II to invoke Alexander the Great's quest for universal empire under a single sovereign. Geoffrey Parker, *The World is not Enough: The Imperial Vision of Philip II of Spain* (Waco, TX: Markham Press Fund, 2001).
33 Antonio de Herrera y Tordesillas, *Historia general de los hechos de los castellanos en las Islas y Tierra Firme del mar Océano que llaman Indias Occidentales* (Madrid, 1601–15); on these "official histories," see Richard Kagan, *Clio and the Crown: The Politics of History in Medieval and Early Modern Spain* (Baltimore: Johns Hopkins University Press, 2009).
34 Gregorio López de Madera, *Excellencias de la Monarchia y Reyno de España* (Valladolid: Diego Fernández de Córdoba, 1597), 63v.
35 Anthony Pagden, *The Fall of Natural Man: The American Indian and the Origins of Comparative Ethnology* (Cambridge: Cambridge University Press, 1982); Tzvetan Todorov, *The Conquest of America*, trans. Richard Howard (New York: Harper and Row, 1984); and *The Spanish Struggle for Justice in the Conquest of America*.
36 Recorded in Bartolomé de las Casas, *Historia de las Indias*, ed. André Saint-Lu, Book 3, Ch. 4 (Caracas: Biblioteca Ayacucho, 1986) 13–14.
37 Juan Ginés de Sepúlveda, *Demócrates Alter sive de justis belli causis apud Indos*; for a bilingual Latin–Spanish version see *Democrates segundo, o, De las justas causas de la guerra contra los indios*, ed. Angel Losada (Madrid: CSIC, 1951).
38 Anthony Pagden, "Heeding Heraclides: Empire and its Discontents, 1619–1812," *Spain, Europe and the Atlantic World: Essays in Honor of John H. Elliott*, eds. Richard Kagan and Geoffrey Parker (Cambridge: Cambridge University Press, 1995), 316–33.
39 Francisco de Vitoria, *Relecciones teológicas del P. Fray Francisco de Vitoria*, ed. and trans. Jaime Torrubiano Ripoll (Madrid: Librería Religiosa Hernández, 1917), 41, my translation.
40 Ibid., 67–87.
41 Xavier Gil Pujol, "Spain and Portugal," *European Political Thought, 1450–1700: Religion, Law and Philosophy*, eds. H. A. Lloyd, G. Burgess, and S. Hodson (New Haven: Yale University Press, 2007), 431.
42 Juan de Solórzano Pereira, *Política Indiana*, Book 1, Ch. 9–12 (Madrid: Diego Díaz de la Carrera, 1647); Pérez-Amador Adam, *De legitimatione imperii Indiae Occidentalis*; Tamar Herzog, "Did European Law Turn American? Territory, Property and Rights in an Atlantic World," *New Horizons in Spanish Colonial Law*, 75; and Anthony Pagden, *Lords of All the World: Ideologies of Empire in Spain, Britain and France, c. 1500–c. 1800* (New Haven: Yale University Press, 1995).

43 Juan de Solórzano Pereira, *De Indiarum Jure sive de justa Indiarum Occidentalium Inquisitione, Acquisitione, & Retentione*, 2 vols. (Madrid: Ex Typographia Francisci Martínez, 1629–39). A Spanish version was subsequently published as *Política Indiana* in 1647.
44 James Muldoon, *The Americas in the Spanish World Order: The Justification for Conquest in the Seventeenth Century* (Philadelphia: University of Pennsylvania Press, 1994).
45 *Recopilación de leyes de los reynos de las Indias*.
46 *Las indias en la monarquía católica*, 32.
47 *Ordenanzas del Consejo de Indias*, Book 2, Title 2, Law 13, Ordinance 14, 1571, quoted in Rafael D. García Perez, "Revisiting the Americas' Colonial Status under the Spanish Monarchy," *New Horizons in Spanish Colonial Law*, 47.
48 In reality this distinction meant little to most Spaniards with firsthand experience in the New World, who recognized that understanding the complexity of indigenous politics and society was integral to any hope of successful settlement in the Americas.
49 On the need to reemphasize the importance of political culture and institutions in the history of Spanish colonial America, see, Alejandro Cañeque, "The Political and Institutional History of Colonial Spanish America," *History Compass* 11[4] (2013): 280–91.
50 Juan de Solórzano Pereira, "Memorial y discurso de las razones que se ofrecen para que el real y supremo Consejo de las Indias deba preceder en todos los actos públicos al que llaman de Flandes [1629]," *Obras varias posthumas del doctor Juan de Solórzano Pereyra* (Madrid: Imprenta Real de la Gaceta, 1776), 178, my translation. Not all observers shared this view. The Count-Duke of Olivares, for instance, argued that the conquest and occupation of the Americas had been a mistake, that it had weakened the monarchy and diminished its overall prestige.
51 Ángel Rama, *La ciudad letrada* (Hanover, NH: Ediciones del Norte, 1984).
52 Hernán Cortés, "Carta de la Justicia y Regimiento de la Rica Villa de la Veracruz, á la reina doña Juana y al Emperador Carlos V, su hijo, á 10 de julio 1519," *Cartas y relaciones de Hernán Cortés*, ed. Don Pascual de Gayangos (Paris: Imprenta Central de los Ferro-Carriles, 1866) 19, my translation.
53 John Leddy Phelan, "Authority and Flexibility in the Spanish Imperial Bureaucracy," *Administrative Science Quarterly* 5 (1960): 47–65.
54 Solórzano Pereira, *Política Indiana* (1647).
55 *Recopilación de leyes de los reynos de las Indias*, Book 3, Title 3, Law 2.
56 Alejandro Cañeque, *The King's Living Image: The Culture and Politics of Viceregal Power in Colonial Mexico* (New York: Routledge, 2004); and Pedro Cardim and J. L. Palos, "El gobierno de los imperios de España y Portugal en la Edad Moderna: Problemas y soluciones compartidas," *El mundo de los virreyes en las monarquías de España y Portugal*, eds. Pedro Cardim and J. L. Palos (Madrid: Iberoamericana-Vervuert, 2012), 11–32.
57 "Authority and Flexibility in the Spanish Imperial Bureaucracy."
58 Among the most representative of these works are Robert Ricard, *La "Conquête spirituelle" du Mexique: Essai sur l'apostolat et les méthodes missionnaires des Ordres mendiants en Nouvelle-Espagne de 1523–24 à 1572* (Paris: Institut d'Ethnologie, 1933); and those by William H. Prescott, including, *History of the conquest of Mexico: with a preliminary view of the ancient Mexican civilization, and the life of the conqueror, Hernando Cortés* (New York: Harper, 1843), and *History of the Conquest of Peru: with a Preliminary View of the Civilization of the Incas* (New York: Harper, 1847).
59 For elaboration of this argument, see Matthew Restall, "Under the Lordship of the King: The Myth of Completion," Ch. 4, *Seven Myths of the Spanish Conquest*, 64–76; and "The Incomplete Conquest," Ch. 7, *Latin American in Colonial Times*, ed. Matthew Restall and Kris Lane (Cambridge: Cambridge University Press, 2011), 109–28; for another author's argument for the need to reexamine conquests as processes rather than discrete events, see Barbara Mundy's *The Mapping of New Spain: Indigenous Cartography and the Maps of the Relaciones Geográficas* (Chicago: University of Chicago Press, 1996), and more recently her *The Death of Aztec Tenochtitlan: The Life of Mexico City* (Austin: University of Texas Press, 2015).
60 Laura E. Matthew and Michel R. Oudijk, eds., *Indian Conquistadors: Indigenous Allies in the Conquest of Mesoamerica* (Norman, OK: University of Oklahoma Press, 2007); Ida Altman, *The War for Mexico's West: Indians and Spaniards in New Galicia, 1524–1550* (Albuquerque, NM: University of New Mexico Press, 2010); and Matthew Restall, *Maya Conquistador* (Boston: Beacon Press, 1998).
61 *Indian Conquistadors*.
62 *Maya Conquistador*.
63 Douglas Cope, *The Limits of Racial Domination: Plebeian Society in Colonial Mexico City, 1660–1720* (Madison, WI: University of Wisconsin Press, 1994).

64 James Lockhart, *The Nahuas after the Conquest: A Social and Cultural History of the Indians of Central Mexico, Sixteenth through Eighteenth Centuries* (Stanford: Stanford University Press, 1992).

65 *The Nahuas after the Conquest*. See also Rebecca Horn, *Postconquest Coyoacan: Nahua-Spanish Relations in Central Mexico, 1519–1650* (Stanford: Stanford University Press, 1997); and Serge Gruzinski, *La colonisation de l'imaginaire: Sociétés indigènes et occidentalisation dans le Mexique espagnol, XVIe–XVIIIe siècle* (Paris: Gallimard, 1988).

66 Inga Clendinnen, *Ambivalent Conquests: Maya and Spaniard in Yucatan, 1517–1570* (Cambridge: Cambridge University Press, 1987).

67 For how this played out in Guatemala, see George W. Lovell, *Conquest and Survival in Colonial Guatemala: A Historical Geography of the Cuchumatán Highlands, 1500–1821* (Buffalo: McGill-Queen's University Press, 1985).

68 Woodrow Borah *Justice by Insurance: The General Indian Court of Colonial Mexico and the Legal Aides of the Half-Real* (Berkeley: University of California Press, 1983) and Brian Owensby, *Empire of Law and Indian Justice in Colonial Mexico* (Stanford: Stanford University Press, 2008). By the seventeenth century, however, Spanish judges decreasingly respected pre-Hispanic traditions or legal norms in forming their decisions. See, Susan Kellogg, *Law and the Transformation of Aztec Culture, 1500–1700* (Norman, OK: University of Oklahoma Press, 1995).

69 Colin MacLachlan, *Spain's Empire in the New World: The Role of Ideas in Institutional and Social Change* (Berkeley: University of California Press, 1988).

70 *Recopilación de leyes de los reynos de las Indias*, Book 2, Title 2, Law 22.

71 On the importance of local customary law in Spanish America see Víctor Tau Anzoátegui, *El poder de la costumbre: Estudios sobre el derecho consuetudinario en América hispana hasta la emancipación* (Buenos Aires: Instituto de Investigaciones de Historia del Derecho, 2001).

72 For discussion of the impact of physical distance on imperial governance see Christine Daniels and Michael V. Kennedy, eds. *Negotiated Empires: Center and Peripheries in the Americas, 1500–1820* (New York: Routledge, 2002).

73 Víctor Tau Anzoátegui, "Provincial and Local Law in the Indies," *New Horizons in Spanish Colonial Law*, 240–41.

74 "Provincial and Local Law in the Indies."

75 For the particular role of indigenous intermediaries in colonial Oaxaca, see Yanna Yannakakis, *The Art of Being In-Between: Native Intermediaries, Indian Identity, and Local Rule in Colonial Oaxaca* (Durham, NC: Duke University Press, 2008).

76 John Monteiro, *Negros da terra: Índios e bandeirantes nas origens de São Paulo* (São Paulo: Companhia das Letras, 1998).

77 Bartolomeu Meliá, *El Guarani conquistado y reducido* (Asunción: Litocolor, 1986).

78 Carlos Ernesto Romero Jensen, *El Guairá, caída y éxodo* (Asunción: Academia Paraguaya de História, 2009).

79 Alonso Álvarez, "La inviabilidad de la hacienda asiática: Coacción y mercado en la formación del modelo colonial en las islas Filipinas, 1565–1595," *Imperios y naciones en el Pacífico*, Vol. 1, eds. María Dolores Elizalde Pérez-Grueso, José María Fradera, and Luis Alonso (Madrid: CSIC, 2001), 181–206.

80 Alfonso Felix, ed., *The Chinese in the Philippines: 1570–1770* (Manila: Historical Conservation Society, 1966).

81 "Real Cédula a Gómez Pérez das Mariñas," 9 August 1589, AGI, *Filipinas*, Legajo 339, L.1, f.365v–389r, my translation.

82 "Real Cédula a Gómez Pérez das Mariñas."

83 John Leddy Phelan, "Some Ideological Aspects of the Conquest of the Philippines," *The Americas* 13[3] (January 1957): 221–39.

84 J. Gayo Aragón, "The Controversy Over Justification of Spanish Rule in the Philippines," *Studies in Philippine Church History*, ed. Gerald H. Anderson, 3–21 (Ithaca, NY: Cornell University Press, 1969).

85 Fernando Palanco, "Resistencia y rebelión indígena en Filipinas durante los primeros cien años de soberanía española, 1565–1665," *España y el Pacífico*, Vol. 2, ed. Leoncio Cabrero (Madrid: SECC, 2004), 71–98; and Patricio Hidalgo Nuchera, *La Recta Administración. Primeros tiempos de la colonización hispana en Filipinas: La situación de la población nativa* (Madrid: Ediciones Polifemo, 2001).

86 For a late seventeenth century account of these events, see Diego de Rosales, *Historia general de Chile: Flandes indiano*, ed. Mario Góngora (Santiago: Editorial Andrés Bello, 1989 [1674]).

87 Alonso de Ercilla famously immortalized these events in his epic poem, *The Araucaniad*, published between 1569 and 1589, in which he also lauded Mapuche (Araucanian) valor in resisting Spanish

encroachment. For an edition containing all three of the poem's parts, see Alonso de Ercilla, *La Araucana* (Madrid: Francisco Martínez Abad, 1733).
88 Guillaume Boccara, *Los vencedores: Historia del pueblo mapuche en la época colonial* (San Pedro de Atacama: Línea Editorial IIAM, 2007).
89 In the 1573 *Ordinances for the discovery, settlement, and pacification of the Indies* the monarchy ordered its subjects to "forego the word conquest, using instead pacification and settlement" in a clear effort to portray Spain's presence there as more benign and benevolent. See *Recopilación de leyes de los reynos de las Indias*, Book 4, Title 1, Law 6.
90 Tomasso Campanella, *La Monarquía Hispanica* (Madrid: Centro de Estudios Constitucionales, 1982 [c. 1601]), 255.
91 Serge Gruzinski, *Les quatre parties du monde: Histoire d'une mondialisation* (Paris: Martinière, 2004).

References

Adorno, Rolena. "The Discursive Encounter of Spain and America: The Authority of Eyewitness Testimony in the Writing of History," *The William and Mary Quarterly* 49[2] (April 1992): 210–28.
Adorno, Rolena. *The Polemics of Possession in Spanish American Narrative* (New Haven, CT: Yale University Press, 2008).
Altman, Ida. *The War for Mexico's West: Indians and Spaniards in New Galicia, 1524–1550* (Albuquerque, NM: University of New Mexico Press, 2010).
Álvarez, Alonso. "La inviabilidad de la hacienda asiática: Coacción y mercado en la formación del modelo colonial en las islas Filipinas, 1565–1595," *Imperios y naciones en el Pacífico*, vol. 1, eds. María Dolores Elizalde Pérez-Grueso, José María Fradera, and Luis Alonso (Madrid: CSIC, 2001), 181–206.
Amelang, James. "The Peculiarities of the Spaniards: Historical Approaches to the Early Modern State," *Public Power in Europe: Studies in Historical Transformations*, eds. James Amelang and Siegfried Beer (Pisa: Pisa University Press, 2006), 31–56.
Benton, Lauren. *A Search for Sovereignty: Law and Geography in European Empires, 1400–1900* (Cambridge: Cambridge University Press, 2009).
Benton, Lauren. *Law and Colonial Cultures: Legal Regimes in World History, 1400–1900* (Cambridge: Cambridge University Press, 2001).
Boccara, Guillaume. *Los vencedores: Historia del pueblo mapuche en la época colonial* (San Pedro de Atacama: Línea Editorial IIAM, 2007).
Borah, Woodrow. *Justice by Insurance: The General Indian Court of Colonial Mexico and the Legal Aides of the Half-Real* (Berkeley, CA: University of California Press, 1983).
Bosbach, Franz. "The European Debate on Universal Monarchy," *Theories of Empire, 1450–1800*, ed. David Armitage (Aldershot: Ashgate, 1998).
Burbank, Jane and Frederick Cooper. *Empires in World History: Power and the Politics of Difference* (Princeton: Princeton University Press, 2010).
Campanella, Tomasso. *La Monarquía Hispanica* (Madrid: Centro de Estudios Constitucionales, 1982 [c. 1601]).
Cañeque, Alejandro. *The King's Living Image: The Culture and Politics of Viceregal Power in Colonial Mexico* (New York: Routledge, 2004).
Cañeque, Alejandro. "The Political and Institutional History of Colonial Spanish America," *History Compass* 11, 4 (2013): 280–91.
Cardim, Pedro and J. L. Palos. "El gobierno de los imperios de España y Portugal en la Edad Moderna: Problemas y soluciones compartidas," *El mundo de los virreyes en las monarquías de España y Portugal*, eds. Pedro Cardim and J. L. Palos (Madrid: Iberoamericana-Vervuert, 2012), 11–32.
Cardim, Pedro. "La aspiración imperial de la monarquía portuguesa, siglos XVI y XVII," *Comprendere le monarchie iberiche: Risorse materiali e rappresentazioni del potere*, ed. Gaetano Sabatini (Roma: Viella, 2010), 37–72.
Cardim, Pedro, Tamar Herzog, José Javier Ruiz Ibáñez, and Gaetano Sabatini, eds. *Polycentric Monarchies: How did Early Modern Spain and Portugal Achieve and Maintain a Global Hegemony?* (Eastbourne: Sussex Academic Press, 2012).
Chittolini, Giorgio. "The 'Private,' the 'Public,' the State," *Journal of Modern History* 67 (Dec. 1995): S34–S61.
Clavero, Bartolomé. "Tejido de sueños: La historiografía jurídica española y el problema del estado," *Historia contemporânea* 12 (1996): 25–47.

Clendinnen, Inga. *Ambivalent Conquests: Maya and Spaniard in Yucatan, 1517–1570* (Cambridge: Cambridge University Press, 1987).
Cope, Douglas. *The Limits of Racial Domination: Plebeian Society in Colonial Mexico City, 1660–1720* (Madison, WI: University of Wisconsin Press, 1994).
Cortés, Hernán. "Carta de la Justicia y Regimiento de la Rica Villa de la Veracruz, á la reina doña Juana y al Emperador Carlos V, su hijo, á 10 de julio 1519," *Cartas y relaciones de Hernán Cortés*, ed. Don Pascual de Gayangos (Paris: Imprenta Central de los Ferro-Carriles, 1866).
Daniels, Christine and Michael V. Kennedy, eds. *Negotiated Empires: Center and Peripheries in the Americas, 1500–1820* (New York: Routledge, 2002).
Díaz de Castillo, Bernal. *Historia verdadera de la conquista de la Nueva España*, ed. Genaro García, 2 vols. (México: Oficina Tipográfica de la Secretaría de Fomento, 1904–05).
Duve, Thomas and Heikki Pihlajamäki, eds. *New Horizons in Spanish Colonial Law: Contributions to Transnational Early Modern Legal History* (Frankfurt: Max Planck Institute for European Legal History, 2015).
Elliott, J. H. "The Spanish Colonization and Settlement of America," *The Cambridge History of Latin America*, ed. Leslie Bethell (Cambridge: Cambridge University Press, 1984).
Felix, Alfonso, ed. *The Chinese in the Philippines: 1570–1770* (Manila: Historical Conservation Society, 1966).
Fernández Albaladejo, Pablo. *Fragmentos de monarquía: Trabajos de historia política* (Madrid: Alianza Editorial, 1992).
Fernández de Oviedo y Valdés, Gonzalo. *Historia general y natural de las Indias*, ed. José Amador de los Rios (Madrid: Real Academia de la Historia, 1851–55).
Feros, Antonio. "Clientelismo y poder monárquico en la España de los siglos XVI y XVII," *Relaciones* 73[19](1998): 17–49.
Foucault, Michel. *Discipline and Punish: The Birth of the Prison*. 2nd ed. (New York: Vintage Books, 1995).
Foucault, Michel. *The Archaeology of Knowledge and the Discourse on Language* (New York: Pantheon Books, 1972).
García Perez, Rafael D. "Revisiting the Americas' Colonial Status under the Spanish Monarchy," *New Horizons in Spanish Colonial Law*, eds. Duve and Pihlajamäki.
Gayo Aragón, J. "The Controversy Over Justification of Spanish Rule in the Philippines," *Studies in Philippine Church History*, ed. Gerald H. Anderson (Ithaca, NY: Cornell University Press, 1969), 3–21.
Gil Pujol, Xavier. *Imperio, Monarquía Universal, Equilibrio: Europea y la Política Exterior en el Pensamiento Político Español de los siglos XVI y XVII* (Perugia: Università di Perugia, 1995–96).
Gil Pujol, Xavier. "Spain and Portugal," *European Political Thought, 1450–1700: Religion, Law and Philosophy*, eds. H. A. Lloyd, G. Burgess, and S. Hodson (New Haven, CT: Yale University Press, 2007).
Greene, Jack P. *Negotiated Authorities: Essays in Colonial Political and Constitutional History* (Charlottesville, VA: University Press of Virginia, 1994).
Gruzinski, Serge. *La colonisation de l'imaginaire: Sociétés indigènes et occidentalisation dans le Mexique espagnol, XVIe–XVIIIe siècle* (Paris: Gallimard, 1988).
Gruzinski, Serge. *Les quatre parties du monde: Histoire d'une mondialisation* (Paris: Martinière, 2004).
Hanke, Lewis. *The Spanish Struggle for Justice in the Conquest of America* (Dallas, TX: Southern Methodist University Press, 2002 [1949]).
Hernando Sánchez, Carlos José. *Las indias en la monarquía católica: Imágenes e ideas políticas* (Valladolid: Universidad de Valladolid, 1996).
Herrera y Tordesillas, Antonio de. *Historia general de los hechos de los castellanos en las Islas y Tierra Firme del mar Océano que llaman Indias Occidentales* (Madrid, 1601–15).
Herzog, Tamar. "Did European Law Turn American? Territory, Property and Rights in an Atlantic World," *New Horizons in Spanish Colonial Law*, eds. Duve and Pihlajamäki.
Herzog, Tamar. *Frontiers of Possession: Spain and Portugal in Europe and the Americas* (Cambridge: Harvard University Press, 2015).
Hespanha, António Manuel. *As Vésperas do Leviathan: Instituições e Poder Político em Portugal, século XVI* (Coimbra: Almedina, 1994).
Hidalgo Nuchera, Patricio. *La Recta Administración. Primeros tiempos de la colonización hispana en Filipinas: La situación de la población nativa* (Madrid: Ediciones Polifemo, 2001).
Horn, Rebecca. *Postconquest Coyoacan: Nahua-Spanish Relations in Central Mexico, 1519–1650* (Stanford, CA: Stanford University Press, 1997).
Irigoin, Alejandra and Regina Grafe. "Bargaining for Absolutism: A Spanish Path to Nation-State and Empire Building," *Hispanic American Historical Review* 88[2] (2008): 173–209.

Jago, Charles. "Habsburg Absolutism and the Cortes of Castile," *American Historical Review* 86[2] (April 1981): 307–26.

Kagan, Richard. *Clio and the Crown: The Politics of History in Medieval and Early Modern Spain* (Baltimore, MD: Johns Hopkins University Press, 2009).

Kellogg, Susan. *Law and the Transformation of Aztec Culture, 1500–1700* (Norman, OK: University of Oklahoma Press, 1995).

las Casas, Bartolomé de. *Historia de las Indias*, ed. André Saint-Lu, Book 3, Ch. 4 (Caracas: Biblioteca Ayacucho, 1986).

Lockhart, James. *The Nahuas after the Conquest: A Social and Cultural History of the Indians of Central Mexico, Sixteenth through Eighteenth Centuries* (Stanford, CA: Stanford University Press, 1992).

López de Gómara, Francisco. *Hispania Victrix: Primera y segunda parte de la historia general de las Indias co[n] todo el descubrimiento, y cosas notables que han acaescido dende que se ganaron hasta el año de 1551, con la conquista de Mexico, y de la nueua España* (Medina del Campo: Guillermo de Millis, 1553).

López de Gómara, Francisco. *Historia general de las Ind*ias (Medina del Campo: Guillermo de Millis, 1553).

López de Madera, Gregorio. *Excellencias de la Monarchia y Reyno de España* (Valladolid: Diego Fernández de Córdoba, 1597).

Lovell, George W. *Conquest and Survival in Colonial Guatemala: A Historical Geography of the Cuchumatán Highlands, 1500–1821* (Buffalo, NY: McGill-Queen's University Press, 1985).

MacLachlan, Colin. *Spain's Empire in the New World: The Role of Ideas in Institutional and Social Change* (Berkeley, CA: University of California Press, 1988).

Matthew, Laura E. and Michel R. Oudijk, eds. *Indian Conquistadors: Indigenous Allies in the Conquest of Mesoamerica* (Norman, OK: University of Oklahoma Press, 2007).

Meliá, Bartolomeu. *El Guarani conquistado y reducido* (Asunción: Litocolor, 1986).

Monteiro, John. *Negros da terra: Índios e bandeirantes nas origens de São Paulo* (São Paulo: Companhia das Letras, 1998).

Muldoon, James. *The Americas in the Spanish World Order: The Justification for Conquest in the Seventeenth Century* (Philadelphia, PA: University of Pennsylvania Press, 1994).

Mundy, Barbara. *The Death of Aztec Tenochtitlan: The Life of Mexico City* (Austin: University of Texas Press, 2015).

Mundy, Barbara. *The Mapping of New Spain: Indigenous Cartography and the Maps of the Relaciones Geográficas* (Chicago, IL: University of Chicago Press, 1996).

Owensby, Brian. *Empire of Law and Indian Justice in Colonial Mexico* (Stanford, CA: Stanford University Press, 2008).

Pagden, Anthony. "Heeding Heraclides: Empire and its Discontents, 1619–1812," *Spain, Europe and the Atlantic World: Essays in Honor of John H. Elliott*, eds. Richard Kagan and Geoffrey Parker (Cambridge: Cambridge University Press, 1995), 316–33.

Pagden, Anthony. *Lords of All the World: Ideologies of Empire in Spain, Britain* and *France, c. 1500–c. 1800* (New Haven, CT: Yale University Press, 1995).

Pagden, Anthony. *The Fall of Natural Man: The American Indian and the Origins of Comparative Ethnology* (Cambridge: Cambridge University Press, 1982).

Palanco, Fernando. "Resistencia y rebelión indígena en Filipinas durante los primeros cien anos de soberanía española, 1565–1665," *España y el Pacífico*, vol. 2, ed. Leoncio Cabrero (Madrid: SECC, 2004), 71–98.

Parker, Geoffrey. *The World is not Enough: The Imperial Vision of Philip II of Spain* (Waco, TX: Markham Press Fund, 2001).

Pérez-Amador Adam, Alberto. *De legitimatione imperii Indiae Occidentalis: La vindicación de la empresa Americana* (Madrid: Iberoamericana, 2011).

Petri Martyris ab Anglería, *Decadas de Orbe Novo* (Alcalá de Henares: Michaele[m] d[e] Eguia, 1530).

Phelan, John Leddy. "Authority and Flexibility in the Spanish Imperial Bureaucracy," *Administrative Science Quarterly* 5 (1960): 47–65.

Phelan, John Leddy. "Some Ideological Aspects of the Conquest of the Philippines," *The Americas* 13[3] (January 1957): 221–39.

Prescott, William H. *History of the conquest of Mexico: with a preliminary view of the ancient Mexican civilization, and the life of the conqueror, Hernando Cortés* (New York: Harper, 1843); and *History of the Conquest of Peru: with a Preliminary View of the Civilization of the Incas* (New York: Harper, 1847).

Rama, Ángel. *La ciudad letrada* (Hanover, NH: Ediciones del Norte, 1984).

Restall, Matthew. *Maya Conquistador* (Boston, MA: Beacon Press, 1998).

Restall, Matthew. *Seven Myths of the Spanish Conquest* (Oxford: Oxford University Press, 2003).
Restall, Matthew. "The New Conquest History," *History Compass* 10[2] (2012): 151–60.
Restall, Matthew and Kris Lane. *Latin American in Colonial Times*, eds. (Cambridge: Cambridge University Press, 2011).
Ricard, Robert. *La "Conquête spirituelle" du Mexique: Essai sur l'apostolat et les méthodes missionnaires des Ordres mendiants en Nouvelle-Espagne de 1523–24 à 1572* (Paris: Institut d'Ethnologie, 1933).
Romero Jensen, Carlos Ernesto. *El Guairá, caída y éxodo* (Asunción: Academia Paraguaya de História, 2009).
Rosales, Diego de. *Historia general de Chile: Flandes indiano*, ed. Mario Góngora (Santiago: Editorial Andrés Bello, 1989 [1674]).
Solórzano Pereira, Juan de. *De Indiarum Jure sive de justa Indiarum Occidentalium Inquisitione, Acquisitione, & Retentione*, 2 vols. (Madrid: Ex Typographia Francisci Martínez, 1629–39).
Solórzano Pereira, Juan de. "Memorial y discurso de las razones que se ofrecen para que el real y supremo Consejo de las Indias deba preceder en todos los actos públicos al que llaman de Flandes [1629]," *Obras varias posthumas del doctor Juan de Solórzano Pereyra* (Madrid: Imprenta Real de la Gaceta, 1776).
Solórzano Pereira, Juan de. *Política Indiana*, Book 1, Ch. 9–12 (Madrid: Diego Díaz de la Carrera, 1647).
Tau Anzoátegui, Víctor. *El poder de la costumbre: Estudios sobre el Derecho consuetudinario en América hispana hasta la Emancipación* (Buenos Aires: Instituto de Investigaciones de Historia del Derecho, 2001).
Tau Anzoátegui, Víctor. *Nuevos horizontes en el estudio histórico del Derecho indiano* (Buenos Aires: Instituto de Investigaciones de Historia del Derecho, 1997).
Thompson, I. A. A. *Crown and Cortes: Government, Institutions and Representation in Early-Modern Castile* (Aldershot: Variorum, 1993).
Todorov, Tzvetan. *The Conquest of America*, trans. Richard Howard (New York: Harper and Row, 1984).
Vitoria, Francisco de. *Relecciones teológicas del P. Fray Francisco de Vitoria*, ed. and trans. Jaime Torrubiano Ripoll (Madrid: Librería Religiosa Hernández, 1917).
Yannakakis, Yanna. *The Art of Being In-Between: Native Intermediaries, Indian Identity, and Local Rule in Colonial Oaxaca* (Durham, NC: Duke University Press, 2008).

Figure 2.1 A reproduction of Theodore de Bry's illustration for Bartolome de Las Casas' 1598 book. It illustrates Las Casas' extravagant depiction of the Spanish abuses inflicted on the American Indians.

Source: 1598, Theodori de Bry illustration for Bartolomé de las Casas' Narratio regionum Indicarum per Hispanos quosdam deuastatarum verissima. Wikimedia Commons.

2

"THE OVERSIGHT OF KING HENRY VII"

Imperial Envy and the Making of British America

Jorge Cañizares-Esguerra and Bradley J. Dixon

In 1648 the former Dominican, Thomas Gage, tempted English readers with his description of the West Indies. Relating his travels across Spanish America, Gage hoped to rouse his fellow Englishmen to claim the inheritance that should have been theirs—if only Christopher Columbus had sailed under the Cross of St. George. "To my Country-men therefore I offer a New World," Gage declared, "to be the subject of their future Pains, Valour and Piety." In his book, the "English Nation may see what wealth and honour they have lost by the oversight of King Henry VII."[1] The Tudor monarch had cost England the greatest prize of all—a vast American empire, with millions of civil, indigenous vassals, and rivers of gold and silver flowing back to Bristol instead of Seville.

Gage was neither the first nor the last to lament England's late start in the New World. The English knew very well what empire their forefathers had forfeited. They spent much of the seventeenth century trying belatedly, as the Carolina Quaker John Archdale put it, "to get some Share in this American Continent."[2] Spain's success in America enflamed England's passion for overseas expansion—just as its physical presence in North America defined and at times hindered it.

Imperial envy took many forms. Englishmen coveted Spain's riches not only in precious metals but also in the valuable commodities and medicines the "Treasure House of the Indies" afforded. And they were desirous of emulating Spain's missionary success among the Indians while decrying the loss of so many souls to "popery." But Spain's presence also directly impacted the English colonial venture in more concrete ways. The geographic reach of Spain's empire contributed to the location of England's first colonies on what the Spanish considered to be their colonial hinterlands. Englishmen established outposts they hoped would be out of the effective reach of the Spanish, enacting—especially in early Virginia—colonial fantasies of replicating the successes of Cortes and Pizarro, and building an Anglo-Indian polity but this time for Protestantism.

To the Spanish, Virginia, England's first permanent American colony, surely looked small, howsoever dangerous. Spanish America defined the original geographical limits of English America. The first English colonies clung to the northernmost edges of the vast Spanish periphery and officials in Madrid were determined to keep it that way. Since 1513, Spanish *entradas* had penetrated the interior of North America. Indeed, a semipermanent Spanish presence had not left even that remote place untouched. Jesuits had formed a mission near the Chesapeake in the 1560s, taking with them an Indian man whom they christened Don Luis after the viceroy of New Spain the Indian met on his travels to Mexico.³ A decade later, the missionaries returned with Don Luis in tow, but he soon fled to his people and helped destroy the mission. Although the English colonists seem to have little knowledge of the Jesuit mission, they were well aware of the looming presence of the Spaniards—at once threatening and alluring. Virginia, then, was fundamentally an Indian space but it was also a Spanish zone where, at the outset, the English would follow Spanish rules.

Cosmography and Spanish Claims to British America

Spain had already laid claim over the lands the English would later settle. Regardless of whether the Spaniards actually trekked those lands and enacted ceremonies of transference of vassalage with local populations, Spaniards also claimed lands through cosmography. The *padrón real*—Spain's secret, all-encompassing chart of the world—was the means used by the crown to incorporate vast amounts of new lands into the patrimony of the monarchy. The *padrón* was constantly updated by trained cosmographers at the Casa de Contratación who used reports, questionnaires, and queries to pilots, officials, and conquistadors or who simply traveled themselves to the New World to gather empirical materials.⁴ Thus by the 1530s the contour of an entire hemisphere, that had previously been considered islands off the coast of Asia, was sketched and transformed into *mappae mundi* for the crown to give as presents to the Pope, financiers, and other monarchs. These *mappae mundi* sought to establish claims of sovereignty over lands barely explored.⁵ These were the lands the English would eventually demand as their own. The *planisférío* of Diego Ribero of 1529 for example carefully delineated the lands that would eventually become the Carolinas, Virginia, Pennsylvania, and New England. Diego Ribero, to be sure, gave these lands other names: Tierra de Garay, Tierra de Ayllón, Tierra de Estevan Gómez, and Tierra Nova de Corte Real.

Mapping, cartography, and cosmography allowed Spain and Portugal to lay claim to enormous swaths of land in the Americas, Africa, and Asia before any other European polity could begin to claim them as their own. Possession through mapping involved technologies and institutions that went well beyond voyages and expeditions. Iberians created the Casa do Guinea (Portugal) and the Casa de Contratación (Spain) to bring cosmographers and pilots

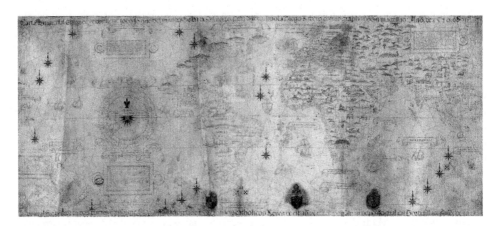

Figure 2.2 Spanish "map of the world," ca. 1533.

Source: Biblioteca Apostolica Vaticana, Vatican City, Carte Nautiche Borgiano III/Wikimedia Commons

together, so the learned could adjust maps to the tangled and conflicting empirical evidence offered by those who had come back from the Indies. The Iberians were also at the forefront of other technologies that complemented mapping through the collation of geographical and ethnographic information—travel compilations. By the 1530s there were already dozens of accounts of expeditions circulating as manuscripts. Soldiers of fortune, pilots, settlers, and adventurers described their journeys while requesting *mercedes* (rewards) from the king. The learned both in Spain and in the Indies would query conquistadors, pilots, and the curious to assemble chronicles, accounts, and compilations, yielding both manuscript and printed accounts of new lands and new conquests. By the early 1550s there were already printed compilations of these exploits written by the likes of Pedro Martir de Anglería, Hernán Cortes, Gonzalo Fernández de Oviedo, Giovanni Ramusio, Pedro Cieza de León, and many others. Maps and travel compilations offered Iberians virtual, narrative, and spatial possession of territories.

The English envied the printed records, compilations, and mapping institutions the Iberians established. Those Tudor and Stuart circles who pushed harder for the creation of an English empire in the Indies were the very ones who most contributed to the creation of a written record of travel narratives to ascertain and document possession. Richard Hakluyt and Samuel Purchas are a case in point. Hakluyt and Purchas sought to present the English as a nation prone to travel and expansion, going back in time to the Noachian monarchies.[6] The argument of possession through archived narratives of national peregrination was also accompanied by explicit calls to emulate Spanish institutions of cosmography and mapping. Hakluyt longed for the English to emulate the Spaniards and have their own Casa, namely, a clearing house for pilots' reports to be transformed by learned cosmographers into maps to ascertain possession.[7] It was the serendipitous outcome of the battle of Alcazarquivir in Morocco that would allow the English to gain access to more accurate cartographic knowledge of the Americas. When the king of Portugal, Sebastian, died in battle in 1578 it triggered a contest over the succession that was ultimately won by Philip II, who struck deals with the Portuguese nobles to respect the autonomy of the kingdom. Philip I of Portugal also militarily defeated his main rival Dom Antonio, Prior of Crato, in battles in Lisbon and the Azores. In 1581, Dom Antonio and his entourage that included cosmographers wound up in Paris from where he would later move to London.[8] If the English lacked the institutions that allowed the Iberians to cartographically possess the Americas, the geopolitical battles of the day made it possible nevertheless for the English to smuggle some of that precious knowledge to their domain.

Since the English arrived late to the game of mapping and colonization they sought to make their territorial aspirations explicit and unambiguous by branding maps of the Caribbean, Virginia, and New England with royal coats of arms.[9]

Like the Iberians, the English learned that possession came through mapping and naming. Early English maps did what the Spanish and Portuguese had long been doing, namely, treating America like a palimpsest giving the land new names at will. Like the Iberians, the English misinterpreted native names and plastered them on maps for islands, rivers, capes, and many other geographical features. The English also christened new villages with the names of the places from where they originally hailed. Thus Plymouth and Boston became the English later equivalents of the earlier Iberian-American Cuenca, Cartagena, and Guadalajara. Finally, the English also sought to honor their monarchs and thus christened Jamestown and Henrico after the first Stuart king and his (soon-to-be-deceased) heir. And yet the English often surrendered to the nomenclature the Iberians had first established. During the 1580s in Roanoke, the painter John White found himself reproducing Spanish and Portuguese names of the fauna and flora that he encountered.[10] The relationship of the English to Iberian mapping and naming was tortuous and

Figure 2.3 Captain John Smith's 1606 *Map of Virginia*.
Source: Courtesy of Library of Congress Prints and Photographs Division. LC-USZ62-116706.

ironic. Raleigh's "Virginia" was meant to be a place cleared from all Spanish impurity, a "Virgin Soile not yet polluted with Spaniards lust."[11] The English managed to turn geopolitical weakness into a virtue: possession of the northern periphery was in itself good because the Spaniards had considered these territories so marginal as not to be worth settling.

On the Limits of La Florida

In September 1608, Don Pedro de Zúñiga, the Spanish ambassador in England, dispatched a secret map of Virginia to King Philip III. Amidst the maze of broad, navigable rivers and the scores of populous Indian towns, only one of the map's features really mattered—the tiny, triangular fort *Jamestown*. The fort made clear England's intentions to settle a colony on the limits of La Florida. Little did Zúñiga or anyone in Spain know to what lengths the English in "Virginia" were going to parallel the Spanish achievements of the last century. At the town of Werowocomoco, the English crowned the Powhatans' mamanatowick or, "paramount chief," Wahunsonacock, in a farcical attempt to make him a vassal of King James I. With a smuggled map, depicting a fledgling settlement whose inhabitants were in truth not far from ruin, the centuries-long contest between Spain and England in North America at last began in earnest. But Spanish claims in North America were hardly settled.

In that same fateful year, 1608, far to the south, in that part of La Florida proper that would become the province of Apalachee, a barefoot Franciscan, Fray Martín Prieto, ministered to the people there and brokered a peace between them and their neighbors in the province of

Timucua.[12] In a missive to the governor at Saint Augustine, Spain's fortified presidio since 1565, Prieto guessed that half of Apalachee's population wished to receive Catholic baptism.[13]

When Fray Prieto entered Apalachee and forged the peace with Timucua, he did so with the permission of the *caciques* of both. For these early missions, the friars went without soldiers and only with the blessings of indigenous leaders. The wariness of the Apalachee *caciques* or their inability to protect the friars from others hostile to the mission obliged the Franciscans to leave the new province periodically between 1608 and 1612.[14] They declined martyrdom—a fate for the blessed—not out of fear but from respect for what had become the established doctrine of Spanish colonial possession. The friars had to be patient as they needed to win the consent of the region's *señores naturales* or, natural lords. As the legitimate rulers of the country, the *caciques'* assent was necessary for the Spanish to enter and eventually possess it in the king's name.

English ceremonies of possession seem mundane by comparison. Split-rail fences declared possession, not crosses; the strike of a hoe into the dirt was the English fashion, not the scratching of a notary's pen or the approving shout of a local *cacique*.[15] But the dictates of Roman law mattered for English colonizers as well.

When Christopher Newport led a party up the James River to the Falls in 1607, the high point of the adventure was the captain's order to "sett up a Crosse with this incriptyon Jacobus Rex. 1607. and his owne name belowe."[16] Gathering around the cross, Newport's men prayed for King James and with lusty shouts "proclaimed him kyng" over Virginia. The import of this ceremony of possession was great enough that Newport waited until all the Indians were gone lest they wonder at its intention. Only a single Indian, Navirans, was there to "admire" the spectacle. And to him the English leader spun a crafty lie, saying that "the two Armes of the Crosse signified kyng Powatah and himselfe, the fastening of it in the myddest was their united Leaug, and the shoute the reverence he dyd to Pawatah."[17] Erecting a cross, praying before it, and under its shadow proclaiming a distant king's sovereignty was the way that the Virginia Company's representatives claimed possession. No "ordinary house-building activity" had preceded the raising of the cross, either.[18] In fact, the very first act of the Virginia colonists, according to John Smith, was to build a fort for their planned "great cittie" and to do so "with as much speede as might bee."[19]

Fears of hostile Indians and of Spanish invaders prompted the dispatch with which the English built their fort. But the stockade possessed legal significance as well. The fort at Jamestown soon appeared on maps like Zúñiga's circulating back in Europe and signaled that the English claimed possession of the land and were ready to defend their rights under Roman law. English lawyers resorted to the Roman law of nations or, *jus commune*, when they wished to make arguments for New World possession that would satisfy other European princes.[20] In Roman law terms, valid possession required a combination of *animus* and *corpus*—a claim backed by knowledge of the territory and physical occupation that was defended by force if necessary. Forts were thus essential to making a respectable assertion of both *imperium* and *dominium* in the New World.

Making treaties with local indigenous rulers was another important way that English colonizers asserted their claims to North America.[21] Treaties did more than transfer land or establish rules for interactions between Indian nations and English colonies. In Roman law, treaties were the result of "*consensus ad idem*, a 'meeting of the minds' or voluntary agreement between parties, [that] served as proof that a claim was pacified, or under control."[22] The consent of local rulers was one sign of possession that other European powers would recognize under the law of nations. And both Las Casas and Francisco de Vitoria asserted that treaties offered a legitimate way to claim possession lawfully.

The Virginia "company-state" had before it a diverse array of precedents, policies, and proposals from which to choose when deciding how best to colonize the lands of America's natural lords. As the preeminent transatlantic empire for more than a century, Spain's example towered in the English imagination as it did in the French and the Dutch. And Spanish works provided the best information on the New World, short of what they were able to collect themselves first hand. The development of England's overseas colonies was dramatically influenced by Iberian ideas and the turns of Anglo-Iberian geopolitics.

Anglo-Iberian Geopolitics and the Making of Colonies

Up until the mid-seventeenth century English imperial projects (or lack thereof) were tethered to Iberians' actions and experiences. The Elizabethan expansion was wholly subordinated to the geopolitical rivalry with Spain. The colonization of Munster in Ireland, and of the Caribbean and Virginia in the Americas, was part of a global strategy that also included commercial and military alliances with the Ottomans in the Mediterranean and with the Dutch in the Low Countries, America, Africa, and Asia.[23] The colonization of Munster became a priority after rebellions in Ireland exposed the Spanish Habsburgs' deep support for Roman Catholic Irish rebels like Shane O'Neil (1560s) and Gerald Fitzgerald, earl of Desmond (1570s). Many of the Elizabethans involved in the English colonization of the Americas were deeply involved in the colonization of Munster, a project that for many English observers resembled that of the Spanish Reconquista: the expulsion of heretical local communities and their replacement by land-hungry coreligionists. After the Tudor failure to turn Irish peasants and their Scottish and English replacements in Munster into civilized Anglicans, the Stuarts initiated the century with a new colonial project in Ulster with the same blueprint: relocation of rebel Irish Catholics and their substitution with Scottish and English settlers. In 1606, Sir John Davies found the English colonial project in Ireland to have a clear precedent in the Spanish removal "of the Moor out of Grenada into Barbary."[24]

The Elizabethan colonization of America was wholly reactive and part of larger strategy of cutting Spanish supply lines. Colonies in Roanoke, Florida, and the Antilles were meant to be outposts for privateers like Hawkins or Drake, busy plundering Spanish vassals and ports in the Atlantic and the South Sea. The location of colonies was wholly subordinated to piracy, yet on occasion Tudor colonization sought to go beyond offering logistical support for filibustering. Raleigh's obsession with Guiana had little to do with cutting Spanish transoceanic routes. And yet Raleigh's Guiana could not escape Spain's shadow. Like many Elizabethans, Raleigh was obsessed with finding a society of great Incas who had buried their own in gilded treasure, available to plunder, and ruled over large pools of docile labor, available to work the mines. In short, Raleigh gave up his life and that of his son in the pursuit of the equivalent of Spanish Peru somewhere in the Orinoco and the Amazon.[25]

The transition from Tudor to Stuart rule came with big geopolitical changes. James I put an end to the Elizabethan strategy of global piracy aimed at weakening the behemoth that was Spain-Portugal. Colonies like Roanoke therefore no longer made sense. The types of colonial outposts that James I encouraged resembled Portuguese *feitorias*, from the Eastern Mediterranean to Africa to South Asia to America.[26] The very weakness of the English monarchy explains the turn to the sixteenth-century Portuguese model of colonization via royal charters of private merchant monopolies aimed at establishing vast commercial networks. Jamestown was originally designed to be a fortified trading post, not a settler colony. The Virginia and East India Companies were set up right after James I signed a peace treaties with Spain; these companies did not seek to incorporate indigenous lands and rulers into the composite monarchy that had become Scotland and England. The history of Jamestown from 1607 to 1614 is no more than the repeated frustrated efforts by a chartered company to extract a profitable local product through trade while holding onto a set of fortified enclaves. And since 1611 it was ruled as a military-commercial outpost through martial law. Upon arrival, the new military governor Sir Thomas Dale envisioned Jamestown as a Portuguese penal colony of *degradados*, those condemned to death would be sent to Virginia "thus doth the Spaniard people his indies."[27] The Company sent artisans to develop trades like iron- and glassworks to supply the Powhatan with hatchets and *wampum* in exchange for pelts or any other valuable potential commodity. Jamestown was also envisioned as an intermediary outpost on the way to Asia. The English launched cartographic expeditions into the riverine interior, convinced that a passage into the South Sea was within reach. Like any successful Portuguese *feitoria*, the model included the incorporation of indigenous allies through marriage alliances and the exchange of *criados*, namely, children who would grow up acculturated and fully familiar with each other's ways.[28] One of the initiators of the English *feitoria* model in the Americas, Martin Frobisher, was left behind by an English crew in Portuguese West Africa where he became a fluent translator.[29]

Since neither the *feitoria* nor the shortcuts to Asia materialized, the Company inaugurated in 1614 a new approach. The new approach aimed at agricultural diversification through local plantations. It originally sought to bring Asia to America by developing silk plantations (mulberry trees). It also encouraged the growth of agricultural staples, like Bermudan tobacco, for exports.[30] The new strategy was a deliberate attempt to imitate the successes of Spanish settler colonialism in the Americas: self-replicating European-like cities with their dependent indigenous hinterlands of Amerindian converts, both producing revenues for monarchs and financiers. The silver of England was cod from New England and Nova Scotia and tobacco from Virginia. For Captain John Smith the fisheries of New England "might beene as profitable as the best Mine the King of Spaine hath in the West Indies."[31]

The Company also deliberately imported Spanish models of urban settlement, including urban planning around grids and plazas.[32] The new model involved the creation of autonomous, self-ruling creole, settler colonies as well and by 1619 the Virginia Assembly met for the first time. The new model also actively sought the incorporation of the Powhatan as Christian vassals, who were to be converted and educated in colleges for Indians, like in Mexico and Peru. The Company invested both ideologically and financially in seeking to convert the natives to Christianity, deploying millennial Spanish-like eschatological discourses.[33]

At long last, Jamestown began to show signs of prosperity. Success with tobacco led to the expansion of settler colonialism into indigenous lands, which in turn led to a Native uprising in 1622. The Powhatans sought to issue a decisive check on the English in Virginia, killing one-third of the settler population. In the wake of the 1622 assault, the Spaniard of the Black Legend became a model to embrace. The Company continued to advocate conversion and missionary work but also the use of propaedeutic violence against Amerindians during the decade that followed. The rebellion also led to a reevaluation by the crown of its policies of ruling by commercial proxies. The Virginia Company was eliminated in 1624 and the Stuarts resorted to Spanish-like governing bodies to rule the colony directly; these included institutions that resembled the Council of the Indies, *audiencias*, and viceroys, among them the Virginia Council and a royal governor. More importantly, the Stuarts would begin seriously to consider the natives as vassals to be protected from predator settlers and Indian polities as bona fide members of the composite monarchy.[34]

Historians like Karen Kupperman have argued that the history of the colonization of Virginia was one of serendipity and discovery through trial and error. For decades the English tried and failed to get Roanoke and later Jamestown off the ground, until they finally discovered that colonies made up of young males and ruled through martial law were bound to end up in failure. It was only after the Company allowed for colonial self-rule, generous access to land for agricultural production for new arrivals, and the development of "normal" institutions (including the migration of women and families) that Virginia finally began to prosper and yield profits for shareholders. But the history of Virginia could also be read through the prism of an English "envy" of Spain. Roanoke was first meant as a privateering outpost against Spain. Jamestown was then designed as a Portuguese *feitoria* that included even the potential use of *degradados*. Finally, Jamestown only began to look viable to Englishmen after 1614 when the Company used Spanish models of settler colonialism and the full-fledged incorporation of Amerindians as converted vassals.

The process perhaps has the appearance of trial and error because of the many different uses to which Englishmen put Spanish experience and thinking. The lessons that Englishmen drew from Spain varied widely. Some Englishmen had hopes of freeing the Indians groaning under the Spanish yoke, while still others strove to follow the conquistadors to subdue a new Peru. For others, Spain was anti-Christian, its treatment of the Indians barbarous, and its record should stand only to inspire dread in the hearts of decent Protestants. Spain was a model to be avoided. And there were other Englishmen who furthered the "Black Legend," but who honored the Spanish reformers like Las Casas who had in fact created it, all the while drawing lessons from their writings about the best and most just means of proceeding with the Indians in the New World. There were "dreams of liberation" and dreams of emulation. Both had a lasting impact.

Dreams of Liberation and Dreams of Emulation

At his coronation at Werowocomoco in 1608, Powhatan had refused to kneel. Wahunsonacock's English attendants that day leaned hard on his shoulders as if to physically subject him to the Crown of England. The English were already grumbling that the ceremony was taking place at Powhatan's seat and not at Jamestown. To this proposal from Christopher Newport, the mamanatowick balked. John Smith reported that Wahunsonacock declared "If your king have sent me presents, I also am a king, and this my land."[35] The mamanatowick had stood on his rights as natural lord of the country, refusing the consent that the English sought. After Powhatan's astute response, was it any coincidence that Richard Hakluyt the younger brought out a translation of the Gentleman of Elvas's account of Hernando de Soto's brutal *entrada* in 1609, the following year?

The story of the Soto expedition in *Virginia Richly Valued*, writes Hakluyt in his dedicatory epistle to the Virginia Company, "doth yeeld much light to our enterprise now on foot," including "the qualities and conditions of the Inhabitants, or what course is best to be taken with them."[36] To the leaders of the Virginia colony, chagrined after the fiasco of the coronation and Powhatan's kingly response, Hakluyt notes that in Elvas's story they would find many "very eloquent and well spoken" Indians. "But for all their faire and cunning speeches, they are not ouermuch to be trusted: for they be the greatest traitors of the world, as their manifold most craftie contriued and bloody treasons, here set down at large, doe euidently proue." The caciques in the pages that followed were "vnconstant as the weathercock... great liars and dissemblers." Should fair means fail with them, then English soldiers, "trained vp in the Netherlands," would serve to hammer the rebellious Indians into submission. Richard Hakluyt, whose collections of voyages and travels came to form the intellectual foundation of a maritime commercial British empire, closed with a flourish worthy of a conquistador's chaplain. Hakluyt prayed "that the painfull Preachers shall be reuerenced and cherished, the valiant and forward soldiour respected, the diligent rewarded, the coward emboldened, the weake and sicke relieued, the mutinous suppressed, the reputation of the Christians among the Saluages preserued, our most holy faith exalted, all Paganisme and Idolatrie by little and little vtterly extinguished."[37] This was hardly his usual encomium to trade. The novelty of the circumstances in Virginia, a place on the edges of La Florida, meant that Englishmen turned to other precedents for guidance in what was for them an unprecedented situation.

Spanish America provided a major source of those precedents in the early years. But the relationship was ambivalent. As Eric Griffin has put it, "we can see Hispanophilia and Hispanophobia walking hand in hand" in much of the "corpus of England's colonial writing."[38] But what Englishmen made of Spain's record in the New World varied depending on the author, the time, the place, and the demands of the situation. From all these competing uses of the lore of Spain, scholars have identified two broader tributaries of thought.

In his classic account of colonial Virginia, Edmund S. Morgan characterized English aspirations in the New World as "dreams of liberation."[39] The English envisioned freeing the Indians from what Richard Hakluyt had called in 1585 the "more then Turkishe cruelties" of the Spaniards. The "poor Indians" whom they imagined groaning under the Spanish yoke offered the English a path both to riches and to redemption. The reports of reconnaissance missions and the voluminous works of anti-Spanish propaganda convinced many Englishmen that the Indians in places like Mexico and Peru were ripe for rebellion, that they would willingly overthrow their Spanish masters in favor of the "mild government" of the English. With Indian aid, the English could topple the Spanish and take their empire out from under them. The wealth gained would be as nothing in comparison with the spiritual fruits of such a victory. The saving of American souls would redeem England and propel her to the front rank of the Protestant nations in their crusade against popery. Spain as the antitype, as the antimodel, undoubtedly contributed much to the genesis of an English expansion.

Freeing the New World from Spanish domination was a persistent theme in English thinking and had a very long life, in spite of the atrocities that Indians would suffer at their hands beginning in the seventeenth century. Visions of oppressed Indians and friendly black maroon communities who had escaped slavery inspired Englishmen like Sir Francis Drake and the younger Hakluyt, to believe that Spanish America would easily yield itself to them. Even in Virginia, they imagined their work as liberating poor Indians from idolatry, ignorance, and the threat of Spanish rule. If the paradox of how liberty arose in the midst of slavery is at the heart of Edmund Morgan's classic work, then the other paradox is how, after professing such good intentions, the English managed to suppress the Indians as brutally as they imagined the Spanish had. The early ideal perceptions of innocent Indians—which the hard-headed materialist Morgan admittedly takes with a grain of salt—in Virginia led Englishmen to very different conclusions. As Morgan notes, over the course of the seventeenth century Indians *lost* their humanity in the eyes of the English colonists. "There was something different about the Indians," Morgan explains. "Whatever the particular nation or tribe or group they belonged to, they were not civil, not Christian, perhaps not quite human in the way that white Christian Europeans were. It was no good trying to give them a stake in society—they stood outside society."[40] Society by then meant the world that wealthy tobacco planters were forging in the Chesapeake with Indian land and African labor—not exactly the one that either liberators or emulators had in mind.

But just as powerful as these "dreams of liberation" were the "dreams of emulation." Even Henry VII himself tried to make up for his famed mistake, employing John Cabot in the 1490s to sail to North America under the flag of England. A vogue for imitating the Spanish reached a new height by the mid-sixteenth century when England's Queen Mary wed Prince Philip of Spain. A host of translators "Englished" Spanish works during this period, stoking renewed enthusiasm for the New World. These works—and countless others that went to press through 1600—provided the fodder for would-be conquistadors from Sir Walter Raleigh to Captain John Smith. They hoped to find a new Peru with Indian polities just as sophisticated and as wealthy as those they read about from the Andes. The works of Spanish thinkers heavily influenced the early policies of the Virginia Company as it set out to establish England's first permanent colony in North America.

The "dreams of emulation" took many forms and rode the currents of thought that flowed from Spain to England often in the form of books. English adventurers steeped in a heady brew of Spanish conquest narratives, New World pharmacopeias, legal and philosophical tracts. Spanish New World heroics encouraged English humanists and would-be conquistadors alike.[41] In the 1550s, following the nuptials of Mary Tudor to Philip II, Richard Eden penned verses like "stoope, England stoope, and learne to knowe thy lorde and master," urging his countrymen to learn from the Spanish. Eden hoped to stoke the fires of ambition for New World glory in English hearts. The Spanish in America he likened to "goddes made of men."[42] Sir Walter Raleigh in his *History of the World* paused to "commend the patient virtue of the Spaniard."

"We seldom or never find any nation hath endured so many misadventures and miseries as the Spaniards have done in their Indian discoveries," Raleigh wrote. "Yet persisting in their enterprises, with invincible constancy, they have annexed to their kingdom so many goodly provinces, as bury the remembrance of all dangers past."[43] Spanish tenacity, he must have hoped, would buoy the spirits of English colonizers who had by then tasted their share of disappointment and failure. Eventually great kingdoms and treasures would be theirs. Captain John Smith also praised the men who had sailed or fought under the banners of the Spanish for the vast domains they had won. The likes of "Columbus, Cortez, Pitzara, Soto, Magellanes" had "advanced themselves from poore Souldiers to great Captaines, their posterity to great Lords, their King to be one of the greatest Potentates on earth, and the fruites of their labours, his greatest glory, power and renowne."[44]

Books also offered glimpses of the wealth and felicity that Englishmen could hope to win. The Spaniards had proven that the Indies were a "treasure house." Emulation sprang from imperial envy—covetousness for Spanish riches. Recent scholars like Peter Mancall have reminded us that to the likes of Richard Hakluyt, England was a dreary isle of plagues and idleness and earthquakes, which various interpreters attempted to explain, usually in reference to the nation's sin. For Hakluyt, the Indies were at once a medicine cabinet to salve England's sick and also a place where the English population could grow free from European disease.[45] Mancall also pointed out that Hakluyt's perception of the roots of Spanish power were more sophisticated than scholars previously imagined. While gold had been the cry of the conquistador, English observers like Hakluyt noted that perhaps the real wealth of Spain was in agriculture, especially the herds of cattle and sheep that ranged on American *haciendas*. And once English settlement had begun, the sight of Spanish plantations during stopovers in the Caribbean provided their first impressions of American colonization.[46] Silver and gold of course merited English admiration. The English sought mines just about every place they went—even Tangier.[47] But in these early imaginings, the dreams of wealth depended upon English success in converting and ruling the Indians. Spain's example encouraged the aspirations of the English.

English travelers had also been reporting on the nature of Spain's government of the Indies since the mid-sixteenth century. Some of these "legal ethnographies" became part of the great compilations of the younger Richard Hakluyt and Samuel Purchas. Hakluyt's *Principall Navigations* in 1600 included the account of Mexico by an Anglo-Sevillan merchant called Henry Hawkes. "And if any Spaniard," Hawks reports, "should happen to do any of them harme, or to wrong him in taking anything from him, as many times they do, or to strike any of them, being in any towne, whereas justice is, they are aswell punished for the same as if they had done it one Spaniard to the other." However high the station of the Spaniard, however lowly the Indian whom he abused, however far from the city of Mexico the offense took place, Hawks saw justice done. In Mexico, "the Indians are much favoured by the Justices of the Countrey and they call them their orphanes."[48]

Protestant Peru

When the plan to make a pliant vassal out of Powhatan collapsed in 1608, the Virginia Company pursued another strategy of drawing in his people as tributaries who in turn could expect the protection of the English Crown. Spanish precedent in Mexico and Peru had as much to do with the decision as the fact that the Powhatan chiefdom was organized on a tributary basis. Indeed, Spanish colonization literature encouraged the early Virginia adventurers to conceive of the land they were invading in indigenous terms. The English carefully noted the political workings and boundaries of Tsenacommacah and hoped to superimpose their own authority on this Indian kingdom as they imagined the Spaniards had done in their great conquests.[49] The cumulative effect of such policies led Eliga Gould to claim without any irony that "the English spent their first 15 years in Virginia trying to turn the colony into a sort of Protestant Mexico."[50]

Perhaps "Protestant Peru" is just as apt. Typical of the Spanish-inspired visions that dazzled the imaginations of Virginia's early boosters was William Strachey's 1612 *Historie of Travell into Virginia Britania*. Finding Powhatan unwilling to submit as a vassal, Strachey and the Virginia Company branded him a tyrant whose people would live better under English rule. They would "hold their lands as free burgers and Cittizens with the English and Subjectes to king James, who will give them Justice and defend them against all their enemyes."[51] And the duties of tribute would encourage the "Naturalls" to further develop the agricultural capacity of the country. Having read John Ellis's 1590 descriptions of the Indian nobles living roundabout Potosí, Strachey argued that like them, the Powhatans would benefit from the rule of a European monarch. Much as the Andeans had under the King of Spain, the Powhatans, Strachey claimed, would "fynd themselves in far better estate, then now they are: the Cassiques or Comaunders of Indian Townes in Peru, whome the Virginians call Weroances, although they paie unto the king of Spayne great Tribute, yet because they make exchaunge with the Spaniards for what remaynes, they doe not only keep great Hospitality and are rich in their furniture horses and cattell, but as Capt Ellis vowes, who lived amongst them some few yeares, their diet is served to them in silver vessels and many of them have naturall Spaniardes, that attend them in their howses."[52] No doubt the first British Empire by the eighteenth century was indeed, in David Armitage's classic summation, "Protestant, commercial, maritime, and free."[53] But for a time, many Englishmen imagined an empire that was evangelizing, territorial, tributary, and just.

Yet justice was not a simple matter. William Strachey's Tidewater Tawantinsuyu with Powhatan "Cassiques" paying a light tribute as "free burgers and Cittizens" of King James, was one standard of justice—of just rule—to which the English aspired. And conquest might make it possible. After all, Peru's subjugation was a long, violent affair as Strachey well knew. The present happiness and riches of Andean nobles had come through law but not after arms had reduced them to obedience. The liberators had turned up their noses at the Spanish conquest as a bloody mess that had depopulated continents. What was their alternative and from what sources did they draw to shape it? Was there no soul-searching or trepidation among the English as they themselves sought to dispossess the country's natural lords?

The Lascasian Moral Dimensions of Planting

When Samuel Purchas introduced excerpts from the writings of Bartolomé de Las Casas to his English readers, he praised the Dominican friar for his courage and his devotion to the honor of his monarch. "For my part," Purchas averred, "I honour virtue in a Spaniard, in a frier, in a Jesuite."[54] The topic at "[i]ssue was the Alteration of government in the Indies by the gentlenesse of the kings of Spaine," Purchas explains, "which freed them [the Indians] from slaverie, and took better order both for their bodily and spiritual estate as before we have read in Herera."[55] To honor a virtuous Spaniard was perhaps the hardest part. But what might an Englishman actually have learned from him? Why publish the account at all if not to present the crimes of Spain to the world? Las Casas's writings had circulated in England long before Purchas published his compilation. In 1583, Las Casas's *Brevísima relación de la destrucción de las Indias* appeared in English translation as *The Spanish Colonie*. Along with Las Casas's denunciations of the conquistadors, the translator included excerpts from the Dominican's debate at Valladolid with Juan Ginés de Sepulveda. Admittedly, the interest of the person who "Englished" the compilation was on Las Casas's rejection of the papal bulls that had served as the original foundation of Spanish claims in the New World. There were also the friar's opinions on the capacity of the natives that entitled them to Christian regard and rights as vassals.

Lascasian and Salamanca School thought on the capacity and rights of the natives was susceptible to different interpretations. English colonizers of the seventeenth century—especially in Virginia—started where the most advanced Spanish thinkers like Las Casas had left off in their debate about indigenous rights. Early English colonizers started with the Indians' basic humanity and social nature as ideological premises. The Powhatans met several key criteria for civility. "These tests included having a complex language, government by a hereditary hierarchy, organization of society in towns, and agriculture that implied care to provide for the morrow. Religion was also required for true societies." To the English, like the Spanish, "town life was superior to any kind of scattered life."[56] To put this in the terms of the theologians and philosophers who debated the question in Spain, the Indians lived *políticamente*. They had their own religions, laws, and rulers. They were not, in the formulation of Jose de Acosta, *behetrías* or, men without lords—although some Englishmen at other times chose to brand them as such.[57]

In New England, the Lascasian influence was perhaps the strongest. The deeds of Cortes and Pizarro found few to envy them openly in Plymouth or Boston—though they shared structural similarities with Spanish colonialism, including the belief that colonization involved a holy mission to drive out the Devil.[58] The Separatist Pilgrims and the Massachusetts Bay Colony Puritans in the 1620s and '30s both abhorred collecting tribute from the Indians as it was a practice of the Spaniards throughout the New World.[59] Settler colonialism in New England valued Indian land—shorn of Indians—above all other commodities. But Roger Williams's famous lament from 1664 that "God Land will be as great a God with us English as God Gold was with the Spaniard" has a distinctly Lascasian ring.[60] English colonial thinkers drew from the history of the Spanish in the New World to craft their own "benevolent" mode of colonization, "planting." In Spanish, *poblar* denotes a similar action, but does not quite convey the same moral connotations that "to plant" assumes in English.[61] Planting worked by improving "unused" land. Indians were thus to be unaffected—only theoretically. Francis Bacon, for one, preferred "a *Plantation* in a Pure Soile; that is, where People are not *Displanted*, to the end, to *Plant* in Others. For else, it is rather an Extirpation, then a Plantation."[62] Whether English "planters" knew it or not, this was similar to what Las Casas proposed in the 1510s for settling Tierra Firme in modern-day Venezuela with Castilian farmers who would live peacefully alongside the Indians.[63] The Protestant powers read Lascasian literature not only for the Black Legend propaganda but also for a guide to colonizing justly.

Concern for justice did not prevent the English from enslaving Indians, eventually on a grand scale. Early colonists justified slavery as redemptive, converting and civilizing the enslaved.[64] But the English colony of Carolina, founded in 1670, soon made Indian slaves its top export just as the Spanish monarchy renewed the campaign to abolish Indian slavery throughout its empire.[65] Of the estimated 30,000 to 51,000 victims of Carolina's Indian slave trade, most came from Spanish Florida.[66] Some "Spanish Indians" came to Carolina as "free" people. Their predicament prompted the trader, Thomas Nairne, to urge Carolinians to imitate the Spanish. "Now if we take not leave equal of their Salvation as the Spaniards have always done," Nairne declared, "what a good fight have we been fighting to bring so many people from something of Christianity to downright Barbarity and Heathenism."[67] Even then, Spain was a spur to emulation and a reproach to inaction. But as the eighteenth century wore on, Anglo-Americans were less likely to imagine Spain as a model to emulate. Spanish thought informed English attitudes toward Indians. But the road to slavery also ran through Iberian terrain.

The Iberian Road to African Slavery

The early-modern English were fond of imagining themselves as a uniquely free people in a menacing world, creating narratives that have made it difficult for historians to see the pervasiveness of slavery from the beginning of their encounter with Africa and the Americas. The historiography has it that African slaves first arrived in Virginia in 1619. But African slaves were in English ships as cargo since the very origins of the Atlantic slave trade in the mid-fifteenth century.[68] Many of the so-called "Iberian" traders moving slaves from West African *feitorias* into the Canaries, Lisbon, and Seville were in fact English merchants; expatriates who felt at home both in the Peninsula and the British Isles and whose names in archives appear therefore Hispanicized. As the confessional divide between Catholic Spain and Protestant England hardened in the sixteenth century in the wake of the Reformation, these merchants were forced to take sides. Many returned permanently to England where they supplied the likes of Hakluyt with arresting amounts of oral and printed information on how the Portuguese and Spanish colonies actually worked, including many translations of Iberian texts into English as well as detailed knowledge of the Atlantic slave trade.[69] This was the knowledge that allowed the likes of John Hawkins (himself a chameleonic Anglo-Iberian figure)[70] get a foothold in the Spanish colonies as early as 1562 smuggling African slaves.[71]

The way Hawkins operated is emblematic of how the early English slave trade in the Americas worked for at least one century, namely, through interloping and smuggling, until the Company of Royal Adventurers in Africa gained its charter in 1660 and established a trading monopoly in Africa. The English would capture Iberian slavers off the coast of Africa to then smuggle hundreds of captured slaves into the Spanish Caribbean and Tierra Firme.[72] Both piracy and smuggling familiarized the English with African and Iberian ways of understanding slavery. These included the right of slaves to buy their freedom and own property, religious conversion as a way to secure some protections for the integrity of families through the institution of marriage, the hiring-out system (slaves for hire who would live independently from masters), and racial miscegenation.[73] The slavery that the English first introduced in Virginia until the third quarter of the seventeenth century was not different from the slave regimes that flourished in the Iberian world, both in the Peninsula and the Americas. It included sizeable populations of 'mixed bloods,' slaves-for-hire living on their own and with the right to own property, and growing communities of free colored.[74] What Ira Berlin has called the "Charter Generation" of "Creole" slaves is just a roundabout way of describing early Iberian forms of slavery first established in West Central Africa by the Portuguese. These forms arrived in the Chesapeake via Dutch and English smuggling of captives seized from the Portuguese through raids. Berlin himself has described these slaves as individuals with Hispanic names, familiar with Catholicism and other forms of European culture.[75]

Paradoxically, the English privateers smuggling slaves into the Americas and capturing Portuguese slavers off the coast of Africa saw themselves as liberators. Central to English ideas of how to limit the growing power of Spain-Portugal was the notion that slaves and communities of runaway slaves in the Americas would join them in their raids to topple the idolatrous Catholic empire, the sprawling monarchy of the Antichrist.[76]

From Envy to Enmity

Spain's influence was immense on English thinking about overseas expansion during the sixteenth and seventeenth centuries. But by the eighteenth century the Spanish increasingly looked to the English for a model of colonial development. At midcentury, just as imperial officials in Whitehall took pains to centralize American affairs after the Seven Years' War, officials in Spain loosened their grip in order to promote English-style policies, including managing Indian affairs through a commercial model.[77] The Spanish monarchy also sought to imitate the extractive models of the British and the French in the Caribbean, and thus it afforded Cuban planters greater commercial freedom to import slaves.[78] This historical twist reveals that Europe's oldest American empire was neither monolithic nor unchanging—that the Spanish had been the vanguard of the "modern" in the sixteenth century and were still adapting to changes in the eighteenth. The relationship between the two empires was entangled and thus far more dynamic than scholars have previously assumed.

The Spanish part in the founding of British America gradually receded from view. Spain's historical example continued to figure in the Anglo-American imaginary but chiefly as a cautionary tale. At the century's end Henry Knox, Washington's secretary of war and architect of federal Indian policy, held up Spain as a measuring stick of cruelty, saying that the United States had actually been "more destructive."[79] Given the opinion most people then had of Spain's conquest, Knox's was a harsh indictment. By the 1820s, as the country contemplated removing Indian tribes from the South, the Spanish still retained the associations of cruelty that were supposed to distinguish its record from that of the English-speaking world. When the Philadelphia traveler, James Pierce, visited Florida and met a Seminole chief, he made sure to record a tidbit that must have amused—and mortified—his readers and summarized the change in attitudes toward Spain's legacy. "The chief had heard of our Saviour, and his sufferings," reported Pierce on the response to his questions about Seminole knowledge of Christianity, "but supposed he had been put to death by the Spaniards."[80]

Notes

1 Thomas Gage, *The English-American his Travaill by Sea and Land*... (London: 1648).
2 John Archdale, "A New Description of that Pleasant and Fertile Province of Carolina, 1707," *Narratives of Early Carolina, 1650–1708*, ed. Alexander S. Salley, Jr. (New York: Charles Scribner's Sons, 1911), 287.
3 See Anna Brickhouse, *The Unsettlement of America: Translation, Interpretation, and the Story of Don Luis de Velasco, 1560–1945* (New York: Oxford University Press, 2015).
4 For more, see Maria Portuondo, *Secret Science: Spanish Cosmography and the New World* (Chicago: University of Chicago Press, 2009).
5 On early Spanish *mappae mundi* as instruments of possession, see Antonio Sánchez, *La Espada, la Cruz y el Padrón: soberanía, fe y representación cartográfica en el mundo ibérico bajo la Monarquía Hispánica, 1503–1598* (Madrid: CSIC, 2013).
6 Peter C. Mancall, *Hakluyt's Promise: An Elizabethan's Obsession for an English America* (New Haven, CT: Yale University Press, 2010).
7 Richard Hakluyt, *Principal Navigations of the English Nation*, 2 vols (London: 1599, original first edition 1589), 1:3r and 4v.

8 On the process of Portuguese succession triggered by the death of Sebastian, see Fernando Bouza, *Felipe II y el Portugal "dos povos." Imagenes de esperanza y revuelta* (Universidad de Valladolid, 2001); Pedro Cardim, *Portugal unido y separado: Felipe II, la unión de territorios y el debate sobre condición política del reino de Portugal* (Valladolid: Universidad de Valladolid, 2014); On the arrival of Portuguese cosmographic knowledge to England via the exile of Dom Antonio, see Karen Ordahl Kupperman, *The Jamestown Project* (Cambridge, MA: Harvard University Press, 2007), 31.
9 On the early English use of coats of arms to ascertain possession in New Word maps, see Ken MacMillan, "Centre and Periphery in English Maps of America, 1590–1685," *Early American Cartographies*, ed. Martin Bruckner (Chapel Hill, NC: University of North Carolina Press, 2011), 67–92.
10 Jorge Cañizares-Esguerra and Ben Breen, "Hybrid Atlantics: Future Directions for the History of the Atlantic World," *History Compass* 11[8] (2013): 597–609.
11 Samuel Purchas in 1614, quoted in *The Jamestown Project*, 150.
12 John Hann, *Apalachee: The Land Between the Rivers* (Gainesville, FL: University of Florida Press, 1988), 10.
13 *Apalachee*, 11.
14 *Apalachee*, 100–101.
15 Patricia Seed, *Ceremonies of Possession in Europe's Conquest of the New World, 1492–1640* (Cambridge, UK: Cambridge University Press, 1995).
16 Gabriel Archer, "A Relatyon of the Discovery of Our River," *Captain John Smith: Writings with Other Narratives of Roanoke, Jamestown, and the First English Settlement of America* (New York: Literary Classics of the United States, Inc., 2007), 940.
17 "Relatyon," *Captain Smith*, 941.
18 *Ceremonies*, 17.
19 John Smith, "A True Relation," *Captain Smith*, 5.
20 Ken MacMillan, *Sovereignty and Possession in the English New World: The Legal Foundations of Empire, 1576–1640* (Cambridge, UK: Cambridge University Press, 2006).
21 Jeffrey Glover, *Paper Sovereigns: Anglo-Native Treaties and the Law of Nations, 1604–1664* (Philadelphia, PA: University of Pennsylvania Press, 2014).
22 *Paper Sovereigns*, 3.
23 *Jamestown Project*, Ch. 1–2.
24 Davies quoted in *Jamestown Project*, 208–207. On the English colonization of Munster and Ulster, see Nicholas Canny, *Making Ireland British, 1580–1650* (New York: Oxford University Press, 2001). On the English colonial project in Ireland in relationship to Spanish geopolitics, see John J. Silke, *Kinsale: The Spanish Intervention in Ireland and the End of the Elizabethan Wars* (New York: Fordham University Press, 1970).
25 Christopher Heaney, "The Ingas of Inglatierra: English Grave-Opening in the Peruvian Atlantic and the Extirpation of Indigenous History, 1554–1622," under submission at the *American Historical Review*.
26 *Jamestown Project*, Ch. 6.
27 Dale quoted in *Jamestown Project*, 258.
28 *Jamestown Project*, Ch. 7.
29 James McDermott, *Martin Frobisher: Elizabethan Privateer* (New Haven, CT: Yale University Press, 2001).
30 *Jamestown Project*, Ch. 8–9.
31 John Smith, *Advertisements for the unexperienced Planters of New England, or any-where* (London: 1631), Ch. 8, p. 36.
32 On instructions on the creation of a Spanish-like urban grid in Virginia, see Virginia Company, "Instructions to Gates," *New American World: A Documentary History of North America to 1612*, ed. David B. Quinn, 5 vols. (New York: Arno Press, 1979), 5: 214–215 and "Virginia Company to Governor and Council of Virginia, August 1, 1622," *Records of the Virginia Company of London*, Susan Myra Kingsbury, 4 vols. (Washington DC, 1906–1935), 3: 666–673.
33 On Indian missions in Virginia and the college for Native Americans, see Kupperman, *Jamestown Project*, 244–245, 295–299.
34 On the success of settler colonialism as the cause of the 1622 Powhatan rebellion and the reforms it unleashed, see Kupperman, *Jamestown Project*, Ch. 9.
35 John Smith, "The Proceedings of the English Colonie in Virginia," *Captain Smith*, 73.
36 Richard Hakluyt, *Virginia richly valued, by the description of… Florida* (London: 1609), i.
37 *Virginia*, v–vi.

38 Eric Griffin, "The Specter of Spain in John Smith's Colonial Writing," *Envisioning an English Empire: Jamestown and the Making of a North Atlantic World*, eds. Robert Appelbaum and John Sweet (Philadelphia, PA: University of Pennsylvania Press, 2005), 132.
39 Edmund S. Morgan, *American Slavery, American Freedom: The Ordeal of Colonial Virginia* (1975; reprinted New York: History Book Club, 2005), Ch. 1.
40 *American Slavery, American Freedom*, 233.
41 Andrew Fitzmaurice, *Humanism and America: An Intellectual History of English Colonisation, 1500–1625* (Cambridge, UK: Cambridge University Press, 2003).
42 Discussed and quoted in Fitzmaurice, *Humanism and America*, 34–35.
43 Quoted in Irving Albert Leonard, *Books of the Brave: Being an Account of Books and of Men in the Spanish Conquest and Settlement of the Sixteenth-Century New World* (1949; reprinted Berkeley, CA: University of California Press, 1992), 10.
44 John Smith, "A Description of New England," *Captain Smith*, 136–137.
45 *Hakluyt's Promise*, 46–47.
46 April Lee Hatfield, *Atlantic Virginia: Intercolonial Relations in the Seventeenth Century* (Philadelphia, PA: University of Pennsylvania Press, 2004), 7.
47 Alison Games, *The Web of Empire: English Cosmopolitans in an Age of Expansion, 1560–1660* (New York: Oxford University Press, 2008), 11.
48 Henry Hawks, "A relation of the commodities of Nova Hispania, and the maners of the inhabitants, written by Henry Hawks merchant, which lived five yeeres in the sayd country, and drew the same at the request of M. Richard Hakluyt Esquire of Eiton in the county of Hereford, 1572," *The Principal Navigations, Voyages, Traffiques & Discoveries of the English Nation Made by Sea or Over-land to the Remote and Farthest Distant Quarters of the Earth at any time within the compasse of these 1600 Yeeres*, Richard Hakluyt, vol. IX (Glasgow: James MacLehose and Sons, 1903), 394.
49 See April Lee Hatfield, "Spanish Colonization Literature, Powhatan Geographies, and English Perceptions of Tsenacommacah/Virginia," *The Journal of Southern History* 69, 2 (May 2003): 245–282.
50 Eliga H. Gould, "Entangled Histories, Entangled Worlds: The English-Speaking Atlantic as a Spanish Periphery," *American Historical Review* 112[3] (June 2007): 769.
51 William Strachey, "The Historie of Travell into Virginia Britania," *Captain Smith*, 1074.
52 "Historie," *Captain Smith*, 1074.
53 David Armitage, *The Ideological Origins of the British Empire* (New York: Cambridge University Press, 2000), 173.
54 Samuel Purchas, *Hakluytus Posthumus or Purchas His Pilgrimes: Contayning a History of the World in Sea Voyages and Lande Travells by Englishmen and others by Samuel Purchas, B. D.*, Vol. XVII (Glasgow: James MacLehose and Sons, 1906), 81.
55 *Purchas His Pilgrimes XVII*, 81.
56 Karen Ordahl Kupperman, *Indians and English: Facing Off in Early America* (Ithaca, NY: Cornell University Press, 2000), 78.
57 Andrew Fitzmaurice, "Moral Uncertainty in the Dispossession of Native Americans," *The Atlantic World and Virginia, 1500–1624*, ed. Peter C. Mancall (Chapel Hill: University of North Carolina Press, 2007), 403.
58 See Jorge Cañizares-Esguerra, *Puritan Conquistadors: Iberianizing the Atlantic, 1550–1700* (Stanford, CA: Stanford University Press, 2006).
59 Jenny Hale Pulsipher, *Subjects unto the Same King: Indians, English, and the Contest for Authority in Colonial New England* (Philadelphia, PA: University of Pennsylvania Press, 2005), 17.
60 Quoted in Wesley Frank Craven, *The Colonies in Transition, 1660–1713* (New York: Harper & Row, 1968), 21.
61 John Elliott mentions that "poblador" in Spanish shares a meaning similar to "planter" in English but does not explore the different moral dimensions. J. H. Elliott, *Empires of the Atlantic World: Britain and Spain in America, 1492–1830* (New Haven, CT: Yale University Press, 2006), 9.
62 Quoted in *Humanism and America*, 166.
63 See Lewis Hanke, *The Spanish Struggle for Justice in the Conquest of America* (1949; reprinted Boston: Little, Brown and Company, 1965), 54–71.
64 Michael Guasco, *Slaves and Englishmen: Human Bondage in the Early Modern Atlantic World* (Philadelphia, PA: University of Pennsylvania Press, 2014), 180–192.
65 Tatiana Seijas, *Asian Slaves in Colonial Mexico: From Chinos to Indians* (New York: Cambridge University Press, 2014), 248.

66 Alan Gallay, *The Indian Slave Trade: The Rise of the English Empire in the South, 1670–1717* (New Haven, CT: Yale University Press, 2002), 295–296 and 299.
67 Frank J. Klingberg, "Early Attempts at Indian Education in South Carolina, a Documentary," *The South Carolina Historical Magazine* 61[1] (January 1960): 2.
68 *Slaves and Englishmen*.
69 Mark Sheaves, "The Anglo-Iberian Atlantic as a hemispheric system? English merchants navigating the Iberian Atlantic, 1550–1588" *Entangled Histories of the Early Modern British and Iberian Empires and their Successor Republics*, ed. Jorge Cañizares-Esguerra (Philadelphia, PA: University of Pennsylvania Press, forthcoming); Heather Dalton, "'Into Speyne to selle for Slavys': Slave trading in English and Genoese merchant networks prior to 1530," *Brokers Of Change: Atlantic Commerce And Cultures In Pre-Colonial Western Africa*, eds. Toby Green and José Lingna Nafafé (Oxford: Oxford University Press, 2012), 91–123.
70 On Hawkins as Spanish-English double agent, including his promises to help a Catholic uprising against Elizabeth by volunteering a fleet to set Mary of Scots free, see Geoffrey Parker, "The Place of Tudor England in the Messianic Vision of Philip II of Spain," *Transactions of the Royal Historical Society*, 12 (2002): 198–206.
71 Nick Hazlewood. *The Queen's Slave Trader: John Hawkyns, Elizabeth I, and the Trafficking in Human Souls* (New York: William Morrow, 2004); and Harry Kelsey, *Sir John Hawkins: Queen Elizabeth's Slave Trader* (New Haven, CT: Yale University Press, 2003).
72 Gregory E. O'Malley, *Final Passages: The Intercolonial Slave Trade of British America, 1619–1807* (Chapel Hill, NC: University of North Carolina Press, 2015), Ch. 2.
73 Christopher Schmidt-Nowara, *Slavery, Freedom, and Abolition in Latin America and the Atlantic World*. (Albuquerque: University of New Mexico Press, 2011).
74 *Slaves and Englishmen*, 8.
75 Ira Berlin. *Many Thousands Gone: The History of the First Two Centuries of Slavery in North America* (Cambridge, MA: Harvard University Press, 1998), part I; See also Linda M. Heywood and John K. Thornton. *Central Africans, Atlantic Creoles, and the Foundation of the Americas, 1585–1660* (New York: Cambridge University Press, 2007).
76 *Puritan Conquistadors: Iberianizing the Atlantic*.
77 David J. Weber, *Barbaros: Spaniards and Their Savages in the Age of Enlightenment* (New Haven, CT: Yale University Press, 2005), 1.
78 Jeremy Adelman *Sovereignty and Revolution in the Iberian Atlantic* (Princeton: Princeton University Press, 2007); and Elena Schneider, "African Slavery and Spanish Empire: Imperial Imaginings and Bourbon Reform in Eighteenth-century Cuba and Beyond," *Journal of Early American History* 5[1] (2015): 3–29; and Gabriel Paquette, *Enlightenment, Governance, and Reform in Spain and Its Empire, 1759–1808* (New York: Palgrave Macmillan, 2008).
79 *Barbaros*, Ch. 5.
80 James Pierce, "Notices of the Floridas, &c.," *The American Journal of Science and Arts* IX (June 1825), ed. Benjamin Silliman, 135.

References

Adelman, Jeremy. *Sovereignty and Revolution in the Iberian Atlantic* (Princeton: Princeton University Press, 2007).
Archdale, John. "A New Description of that Pleasant and Fertile Province of Carolina, 1707," *Narratives of Early Carolina, 1650–1708*, ed. Alexander S. Salley, Jr. (New York: Charles Scribner's Sons, 1911).
Armitage, David. *The Ideological Origins of the British Empire* (New York: Cambridge University Press, 2000).
Berlin, Ira. *Many Thousands Gone: The History of the First Two Centuries of Slavery in North America* (Cambridge, MA: Harvard University Press, 1998).
Bouza, Fernando. *Felipe II y el Portugal "dos povos." Imagenes de esperanza y revuelta* (Valladolid: Universidad de Valladolid, 2001).
Brickhouse, Anna. *The Unsettlement of America: Translation, Interpretation, and the Story of Don Luis de Velasco, 1560–1945* (New York: Oxford University Press, 2015).
Cañizares-Esguerra, Jorge. *Puritan Conquistadors: Iberianizing the Atlantic, 1550–1700* (Stanford, CA: Stanford University Press, 2006).
Cañizares-Esguerra, Jorge and Ben Breen. "Hybrid Atlantics: Future Directions for the History of the Atlantic World," *History Compass* 11[8] (2013): 597–609.

Canny, Nicholas. *Making Ireland British, 1580–1650* (New York: Oxford University Press, 2001).
Cardim, Pedro. *Portugal unido y separado: Felipe II, la unión de territorios y el debate sobre condición política del reino de Portugal* (Universidad de Valladolid, 2014).
Company, Virginia. "Instructions to Gates," *New American World: A Documentary History of North America to 1612*, ed. David B. Quinn, 5 vols. (New York: Arno Press, 1979), 5: 214–215.
Company, Virginia. "Virginia Company to Governor and Council of Virginia, August 1, 1622," *Records of the Virginia Company of London*, ed. Susan Myra Kingsbury, 4 vols. (Washington DC, 1906–1935), 3: 666–673.
Craven, Wesley Frank. *The Colonies in Transition, 1660–1713* (New York: Harper & Row, 1968).
Dalton, Heather. "Into Speyne to selle for Slavys: Slave trading in English and Genoese merchant networks prior to 1530," *Brokers Of Change: Atlantic Commerce And Cultures In Pre-Colonial Western Africa*, eds. Toby Green and José Lingna Nafafé (Oxford: Oxford University Press, 2012), 91–123.
Elliott, J. H. *Empires of the Atlantic World: Britain and Spain in America, 1492–1830* (New Haven, CT: Yale University Press, 2006).
Fitzmaurice, Andrew. *Humanism and America: An Intellectual History of English Colonisation, 1500–1625* (Cambridge, UK: Cambridge University Press, 2003).
Fitzmaurice, Andrew. "Moral Uncertainty in the Dispossession of Native Americans," *The Atlantic World and Virginia, 1500–1624*, ed. Peter C. Mancall (Chapel Hill: University of North Carolina Press, 2007).
Gage, Thomas. *The English-American his Travaill by Sea and Land...* (London: 1648).
Gallay, Alan. *The Indian Slave Trade: The Rise of the English Empire in the South, 1670–1717* (New Haven, CT: Yale University Press, 2002).
Games, Alison. *The Web of Empire: English Cosmopolitans in an Age of Expansion, 1560–1660* (New York: Oxford University Press, 2008).
Glover, Jeffrey. *Paper Sovereigns: Anglo-Native Treaties and the Law of Nations, 1604–1664* (Philadelphia, PA: University of Pennsylvania Press, 2014).
Gould, Eliga H. "Entangled Histories, Entangled Worlds: The English-Speaking Atlantic as a Spanish Periphery," *American Historical Review* 112[3] (June 2007), 764–786.
Griffin, Eric. "The Specter of Spain in John Smith's Colonial Writing," *Envisioning an English Empire: Jamestown and the Making of a North Atlantic World*, eds. Robert Appelbaum and John Sweet (Philadelphia, PA: University of Pennsylvania Press, 2005), 111–134.
Guasco, Michael. *Slaves and Englishmen: Human Bondage in the Early Modern Atlantic World* (Philadelphia, PA: University of Pennsylvania Press, 2014).
Hakluyt, Richard. *Principal Navigations of the English Nation*, 2 vols (London: 1599, original first edition 1589).
Hakluyt, Richard. *The Principal Navigations, Voyages, Traffiques & Discoveries of the English Nation Made by Sea or Over-land to the Remote and Farthest Distant Quarters of the Earth at any time within the compasse of these 1600 Yeeres*, vol. IX (Glasgow: James MacLehose and Sons, 1903).
Hakluyt, Richard. *Virginia richly valued, by the description of... Florida* (London: 1609).
Hanke, Lewis. *The Spanish Struggle for Justice in the Conquest of America* (1949; reprinted Boston: Little, Brown and Company, 1965).
Hann, John. *Apalachee: The Land Between the Rivers* (Gainesville, FL: University of Florida Press, 1988).
Hatfield, April Lee. *Atlantic Virginia: Intercolonial Relations in the Seventeenth Century* (Philadelphia, PA: University of Pennsylvania Press, 2004).
Hatfield, April Lee. "Spanish Colonization Literature, Powhatan Geographies, and English Perceptions of Tsenacommacah/Virginia," *The Journal of Southern History* 69[2] (May 2003), 245–282.
Hazlewood, Nick. *The Queen's Slave Trader: John Hawkyns, Elizabeth I, and the Trafficking in Human Souls* (New York: William Morrow, 2004).
Heaney, Christopher. "The Ingas of Inglatierra: English Grave-Opening in the Peruvian Atlantic and the Extirpation of Indigenous History, 1554–1622," under submission at the *American Historical Review*.
Heywood, Linda M., and John K. Thornton. *Central Africans, Atlantic Creoles, and the Foundation of the Americas, 1585–1660* (New York: Cambridge University Press, 2007).
Kelsey, Harry. *Sir John Hawkins: Queen Elizabeth's Slave Trader* (New Haven, CT: Yale University Press, 2003).
Klingberg, Frank J. "Early Attempts at Indian Education in South Carolina, a Documentary," *The South Carolina Historical Magazine* 61[1] (January 1960), 1–10.
Kupperman, Karen Ordahl. *Indians and English: Facing Off in Early America* (Ithaca, NY: Cornell University Press, 2000).
Kupperman, Karen Ordahl. *The Jamestown Project* (Cambridge, MA: Harvard University Press, 2007).

Leonard, Irving Albert. *Books of the Brave: Being an Account of Books and of Men in the Spanish Conquest and Settlement of the Sixteenth-Century New World* (1949; reprinted Berkeley, CA: University of California Press, 1992).

McDermott, James. *Martin Frobisher: Elizabethan Privateer* (New Haven, CT: Yale University Press, 2001).

MacMillan, Ken. "Centre and Periphery in English Maps of America, 1590–1685," *Early American Cartographies*, ed. Martin Bruckner (Chapel Hill, NC: University of North Carolina Press, 2011), 67–92.

MacMillan, Ken. *Sovereignty and Possession in the English New World: The Legal Foundations of Empire, 1576–1640* (Cambridge, UK: Cambridge University Press, 2006).

Mancall, Peter C. *Hakluyt's Promise: An Elizabethan's Obsession for an English America* (New Haven, CT: Yale University Press, 2010).

Morgan, Edmund S. *American Slavery, American Freedom: The Ordeal of Colonial Virginia* (1975; reprinted New York: History Book Club, 2005).

O'Malley, Gregory E. *Final Passages: The Intercolonial Slave Trade of British America, 1619–1807* (Chapel Hill, NC: University of North Carolina Press, 2015).

Paquette, Gabriel. *Enlightenment, Governance, and Reform in Spain and Its Empire, 1759–1808* (New York: Palgrave Macmillan, 2008).

Parker, Geoffrey. "The Place of Tudor England in the Messianic Vision of Philip II of Spain," *Transactions of the Royal Historical Society*, 12 (2002), 198–206.

Pierce, James. "Notices of the Floridas, &c.," *The American Journal of Science and Arts* IX (June 1825), Benjamin Silliman, ed., 135.

Portuondo, Maria. *Secret Science: Spanish Cosmography and the New World* (Chicago, IL: University of Chicago Press, 2009).

Pulsipher, Jenny Hale. *Subjects unto the Same King: Indians, English, and the Contest for Authority in Colonial New England* (Philadelphia, PA: University of Pennsylvania Press, 2005).

Purchas, Samuel. *Hakluytus Posthumus or Purchas His Pilgrimes: Contayning a History of the World in Sea Voyages and Lande Travells by Englishmen and others by Samuel Purchas, B. D.*, Vol. XVII (Glasgow: James MacLehose and Sons, 1906).

Sánchez, Antonio. *La Espada, la Cruz y el Padrón: soberanía, fe y representación cartográfica en el mundo ibérico bajo la Monarquía Hispánica, 1503–1598* (Madrid: CSIC, 2013).

Schmidt-Nowara, Christopher. *Slavery, Freedom, and Abolition in Latin America and the Atlantic World*. (Albuquerque, NM: University of New Mexico Press, 2011).

Schneider, Elena. "African Slavery and Spanish Empire: Imperial Imaginings and Bourbon Reform in Eighteenth-century Cuba and Beyond," *Journal of Early American History* 5[1] (2015): 3–29.

Seed, Patricia. *Ceremonies of Possession in Europe's Conquest of the New World, 1492–1640* (Cambridge, UK: Cambridge University Press, 1995).

Seijas, Tatiana. *Asian Slaves in Colonial Mexico: From Chinos to Indians* (New York: Cambridge University Press, 2014).

Sheaves, Mark. "The Anglo-Iberian Atlantic as a hemispheric system? English merchants navigating the Iberian Atlantic, 1550–1588," *Entangled Histories of the Early Modern British and Iberian Empires and their Successor Republics*, ed. Jorge Cañizares-Esguerra (Philadelphia, PA: University of Pennsylvania Press, forthcoming).

Silke, John J. *Kinsale: The Spanish Intervention in Ireland and the End of the Elizabethan Wars* (New York: Fordham University Press, 1970).

Smith, John. *Advertisements for the unexperienced Planters of New England, or any-where* (London: 1631), Ch. 8, p. 36.

Smith, John. *Captain John Smith: Writings with Other Narratives of Roanoke, Jamestown, and the First English Settlement of America*, ed. James Horn (New York: Literary Classics of the United States, Inc., 2007).

Weber, David J. *Barbaros: Spaniards and Their Savages in the Age of Enlightenment* (New Haven, CT: Yale University Press, 2005).

Figure 3.1 Castillo de San Marcos, located near present-day St. Augustine, Florida, and the oldest masonry fort in the continental United States.

Source: National Park Service/Wikimedia Commons.

3
INDO-HISPANO BORDERLANDS IN THE AMERICAS
Entanglements, North and South

Bianca Brigidi and James F. Brooks

Early in the autumn of 1540, the newly appointed *adelantado* of the Río de la Plata—a province that comprised portions of what are today Argentina, Paraguay, and Uruguay—gathered an expeditionary force of indigenous allies and some 200 Spanish settlers and set out on a 1,200-mile journey from the coast of present-day Brazil toward the provincial seat of government, Asunción. He had been charged to forge a royal road from that distant and fragile center of royal power across the Andean Cordillera into Peru. The arduous journey nearly broke the spirits of his colonial contingent, whom he inspired to forge on only by refusing to ride one of the 26 horses on the journey, walking barefoot instead to demonstrate both his toughness and humility. Once he arrived in Asunción he took charge of the province and assigned the path-forging duties to his predecessor, Domingo Martínez de Irala, then turned his attention to Indian affairs, especially as they pertained to the local Guarani peoples. Local *encomenderos*, he felt, had turned what the Spanish crown had intended as a relationship of mutual aid and trust—Indians would provide labor tribute in return for Catholic instruction and protection against enemies—into a one-sided exploitation of natural resources and people alike.

Irala's efforts proved inconclusive, however, so the *adelantado* shouldered trailblazing duties himself, an expedition that also proved a failure. In his absence, however, Irala fomented resistance to the new governor among the *encomenderos*, who frantically concocted trumped-up charges of malfeasance and dispatched couriers to the royal court in Spain. Convicted of 32 specific cases of the maltreatment of his Indian charges (none of which proved true), the fallen administrator found himself sentenced to five years of confinement in the penal colony of Oran in North Africa. Although he would ultimately have his sentence commuted after a series of appeals, he remained in Spain, reputation in tatters, until he died in 1559.

Such is not the story by which we generally recall the life of Álvar Núñez Cabeza de Vaca. Far better known is an earlier story, thousands of miles to the north, first published in Spain in 1542, even while his travails in Rio de la Plata were being enacted. Cabeza de Vaca's *Relación*, or account of his adventures between 1528 and 1536 as one of a handful of the survivors of the disastrous Pánfilo de Narváez expedition, would become the foundational work of ethnology and colonial travel literature in North America. Crossing the continent from Florida to northern Mexico with a dwindling group of survivors, finally just "four ragged castaways," Cabeza de Vaca would undergo transformation from slave to trader to healer. Cabeza de Vaca's narrative revealed the man's gradual transformation from a Spaniard contemptuous of *los indios salvages* into one

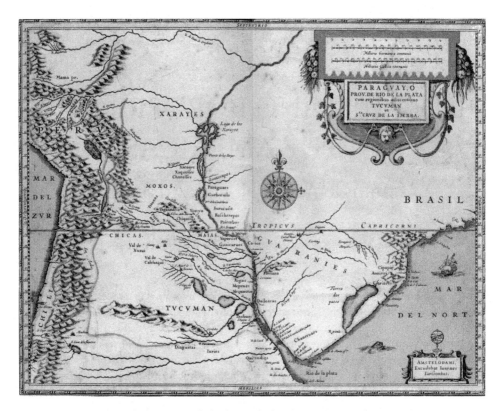

Figure 3.2 Map *c.* 1600 depicting Rio de la Plata and adjacent areas.

who came to appreciate, at least within his capacity, indigenous humanity. Carrying those sentiments into his new posting as *adelantado* of the Rio de la Plata would ultimately result in his imprisonment, as well as cost him his career and social standing. His is also the first, and remains one of the richest, chronicles of indigenous cultures in North America, one that continues to yield insights to scholars of the Gulf Coast societies and northern Mexico. He is among those few Spanish chroniclers whose experience traverses the northern and southern borderland of the Spanish Americas, and as such provides a crucial bridge in crafting the histories of each.[1]

The indigenous peoples of the Rio de la Plata that Cabeza de Vaca sought to protect from exploitation included the Guarani, whose history with Jesuit missionization and Spanish colonization forms the following illustrative example of borderland processes. Like those indigenous languages that continue to be spoken in the lands across which he traveled in North America, the survival of the Guarani language even today may speak to some distant echo of his attention to their fate—although more attributable to the complex interplay of Jesuit evangelical pedagogy (and Franciscan, in the far north) and the cultural determination of the Guarani (and the Puebloan) themselves. Our focus henceforth lies in the long century that unfolded after de Vaca's efforts to bring reform to the Platin borderlands, to suggest some processes and themes that precede David Weber's magisterial treatment of Spanish imperial Indian policy during the Bourbon era in *Bárbaros: Spaniards and their Savages in the Age of Enlightenment* (2005). That period signaled a transition in tactics from relying on missionaries to serve as the agents of pacification and civilization to an era of political and military engagement with powerfully transformed equestrian nations—an implicit acknowledgement that many indigenous peoples had increased, rather than exhausted, their sense of power and autonomy in the earlier centuries. Thus, Spanish

Map 3.1 A 1795 map of South America.
Source: Kitchin, Thomas, *Kitchin's General Atlas*, Laurie & Whittle, London, 1797/Wikimedia Commons.

interactions in the early colonial Platin borderlands, and those among the Puebloans, Comanches, and Apaches in el Norte, were both a sign of the strength and the weakness of the regime.

Colonial expansionism brought opportunities for the Society of Jesus and Friars Minor Capuchin (Franciscans) to establish settlements in so-called peripheral areas such as the Rio de La Plata and the northern reaches of New Mexico. Yet it was down in the Rio de La Plata—not in other viceroyalties like New Spain and Peru, where intense political struggles between the religious and secular arms of the Empire limited missionary autonomy—that the Jesuits found opportunities to expand their political influence and missionary experiments, which might help to explain the uniqueness of the Guarani missions.[2] On this "haunted frontier," in Gastón Gordillo's formulation, we observe early colonial Spanish-indigenous entanglements in their most intimate expression, as well as unexpected resonances. Jesuits would continue De Vaca's anti-*encomienda* agenda and thereby cordon the Guarani off from some of the worst colonial abuses observed elsewhere. And yet, by doing so, the indigenous group would also become segregated and simplified as a "pure ethnicity" dependent for their very survival on Jesuit paternalism and ethnolinguistic fetishization. As such, the case that follows hints toward some of the most provocative rethinking of the anthropological enterprise itself, like that of Lucas Besire's *Behold the Black Caiman: A Chronicle of Ayoreo Life*, whose subjects' precarious lives are likewise conditioned by "soul collecting missionaries, humanitarian NGOs, neoliberal economic policies, and the highest deforestation rate in the world." All too often, what's past is prologue.[3]

Entangled Worlds in Colonial Paraguay

For years, the survival of the Guarani language in Paraguay has attracted scholarly attention from scholars in a variety of disciplines. Even researchers who are not Latin Americanists, such as Benedict Anderson, have analyzed the pioneerism and practices of nationalism among Creoles in the Spanish Americas that relate to the Guarani language.[4] We complicate these studies by demonstrating ways in which the Guarani and other indigenous groups from Paraguay managed to establish relations that focused missionary work on language. By analyzing the missionary context of colonial Paraguay, we see the results of a complex transcultural process experienced on the South American indigenous border. Indigenous communities therefore played a much more active role in the survival of their language than previously thought.[5] Moreover, the Guarani language is just the "tip of the iceberg" through which we can access complex historical experiences captured by authors interested in languages.

While there are significant works showing the unmatched Guarani-missionary relations in Paraguay in terms of their benevolence,[6] a closer look at these relations' sociocultural context shifts our understanding of a borderland that was anything but peaceful. Instead, the borderland was characterized by nuanced complexities, especially in the early seventeenth century when ethnic and political identities were reaffirmed by institutionalized powers like the Spanish and Jesuit colonialists. Therefore the Indigenous-missionary relations in the Rio de La Plata borderlands should be characterized less by Jesuitic benevolence, and more by the everyday forms of resistance with which the indigenous community faced the missionaries in seventeenth-century Paraguay.[7]

Due to the uniqueness of the survival of the Guarani language, as well as to classic studies such as Anderson's, there is a common misconception that the communities now occupying what was the colonial Province of Paraguay are all descendants of Guarani-speaking groups. But recent studies have taken a more critical view of the information available about the early years, and have identified various ethnic and linguistic groups located in what would be the Río de La Plata.[8] This body of work reflects on variations within the ethnic identity formation of the so-called Guarani groups.[9] For instance, Baptista complicates the issue of ethnic identity among the indigenous communities in colonial Paraguay by asking questions about the "guaranization" of other ethnicities, understood as the process by which these other groups might have been absorbed by both the Guarani cultures as well as the primary sources written about them.[10]

Our essay relies on the interdisciplinary academic efforts of a lively community of scholars, whose questions complicated and generated advanced debates on indigenous studies and profoundly impacted generations of scholars on the Americas.[11] To that end, we analyze Father Antonio Ruiz de Montoya's writings, whose authorship was greatly immersed in the indigenous linguistic and colonial context of the Río de La Plata region. Ruiz de Montoya was a Jesuit who in seventeenth-century Paraguay translated the indigenous world into the Christian framework for the purpose of converting it. Montoya published the first chronicle—and the only one of its kind—about the first stages of colonial history in the Province of Paraguay.

Montoya was also the author of the *Tesoro de La Lengua Guarani* (1639), the *Catecismo de la Lengua Guarani* (1639), and the *Arte y Bocabulario de la Lengua Guarani* (1640). Additionally, Montoya wrote annual letters concerning the world he was attempting to translate from Guarani to Spanish, a translation that was aimed at modifying its core values and traditions through missionary work. In that process was born a rich body of literature that, once read closely and critically, allows for "thick" scholarship on indigenous ethnographies in late-sixteenth and early-seventeenth century Paraguay.[12] While other scholars have analyzed seemingly incontestable sources such as Montoya's writings, studies about them have been surprisingly few in number, and even less of them have done so for an English-speaking audience. Accordingly, we hope to shed light on new perspectives and approaches to the Indo-Hispano borderlands through the descriptions authored by missionaries, whose praxis deeply intersected with the language and cultures of these communities.

Indigenous Ethnographies in Antonio Ruiz De Montoya's Writings

The records left by the Jesuits about indigenous communities in colonial Paraguay are highly regarded for their ethnographic value.[13] All kinds of materials—from reports to annual letters, ranging in date from 1594 to 1639—have become main sources for Paraguayan and Guarani studies, due to the overwhelming cultural-informative data offered by this first stage of missionary-indigenous relations.[14] Of special interest are Ruiz de Montoya's writings, especially due to the breadth provided by his missionary lens, which sought primarily to know and to communicate with the communities in order to convert them to Christianity. Montoya's annual letters are not only very relevant to the cultural studies of indigenous groups in colonial Paraguay, but also crucial to understanding the historical process that retained aspects of the ethnic identities of the groups, as well as particular characteristics of the "Guarani way of being."

Although Paraguay's history is often linked to the Jesuits, its first missionaries were Franciscans who started their work in 1580. Indeed, the Franciscans' work was decisive for the appreciation and understanding of the importance of missionizing the indigenous communities by valuing their native language. Works by linguists suggest the influential impact of Fray Luis Bolaños, who was the first to preach catechism in an indigenous language among the local communities living in the surrounding areas of Asunción.[15] Almost 30 years after the Franciscans' first missions, the Spanish crown brought the Jesuits into the Province of Paraguay to "reduce" the indigenous groups to live in villages in order to closely learn how to work and live by the word of God.[16]

Around the late sixteenth century and early seventeenth century, Jesuits and Franciscans in the South American borderlands published works on indigenous languages to facilitate missionary work in the Americas. In 1610, Jesuits of Paraguay received the *Arte de Grammatica da Língua mais visada na costa Brasil* (1595), written by the Portuguese Jesuit José de Anchieta and published by Antonio de Mariz in 1595 in Coimbra, Portugal.[17] Padre Anchieta's grammar on the "universal tupí" was used as an instrument of conversion in the Brazilian coast of Bahia in Portuguese America. When Anchieta's book reached Paraguay, the missionaries had already been oriented and were working toward the same approach through the unpublished body of work on grammatical notes initiated by Fray Luis Bolaños in the 1580s.[18]

Scholarship on the missions of Paraguay often attributes their successes to the alignment of Guarani culture as amenable to the values of Christianity, or even to the peoples' natural inclination to docility.[19] Yet, Antonio Ruiz de Montoya's role in the missionizing project reveals rhetoric that, in addition to advocating for the protection of the indigenous communities in the missions from the Portuguese *bandeirantes* and the labor abuses of the Spanish crown,[20] also petitioned to arm the Indians with firearms.[21] In 1639, Montoya traveled to Spain to request arms from the crown that might be used for liberation. While there, he was able to publish some of his most important works on the indigenous language and his chronicles. Montoya's petition is dated a year later, in 1640, in which he argued for arming the mission Indians against the Portuguese invaders who sought to capture them in order to take them to São Paulo and sell them as labor for Brazil's sugar mills.[22] In 1644, Montoya was granted the right to use firearms among the indigenous communities.

Montoya played a key role in the missionary politics of the colonial borderlands of Paraguay, Brazil, and Argentina. He denounced abuses toward the mission groups of indigenous people, published major linguistic works to assist in the progress of missionary work in South America, served as an intermediary in political conversations and debates with the Portuguese *bandeirantes* and Spaniards, and left a rich body of work of key relevance for the study of indigenous groups. Ruiz de Montoya acted as the superior of the Missions of Guairá and, as such, led the difficult and necessary task of transferring the missions from the Guairá to the south of Paraguay with around 12,000 Guarani. He also had an important role as a translator of the Guaraní and Spanish languages, as well as of catechisms, publishing remarkable works on these topics.[23] Because his intellectual work transcends disciplinary boundaries, Montoya's writings are of major importance to the field of indigenous studies.

Anthropology, Polygamy, and Cacique Politics in Ruiz De Montoya's Cartas

Montoya's writings are a rich source of information that makes important distinctions between different indigenous groups in colonial Paraguay, thus providing more complex understandings of their ethnic diversity. For instance, when Ruiz de Montoya referred to the Gualachos Indians in San Xavier in 1628, he revealed aspects about anthropophagy while explaining other features about the traditional customs of this group: "The wildness of this people in killing and eating each other is incredible. At first they do it to avenge their enemies, but after enjoying the taste of human flesh," concludes Montoya, "they do it for pleasure." Montoya went on to explain the circumstances grounding his concerns. The padres were dealing with 40 congregated Indians, one of whom apparently had eaten 20 people, including the two sons of an Indian who accompanied the priest.

As the narrative continued to explain how the priests learned of the story, more interesting aspects of mission life came to light, demonstrating the balancing of power and how priests tried to come to terms with leadership. Montoya explained that the padres learned about the case due to the noteworthy frequency with which the Amerindians used to stand in front of the priests' house. Curious about the cause of this, the priest asked what the Indians were doing there, to which he obtained no response. One day a couple of women arrived in emotional torment, one of them explaining that she was mourning the death of her husband.[24] The indigenous woman said she had been accompanying her husband, who was hunting to sustain their children, and when he climbed a tree to wait for his prey, some Amerindians from that land passed by and struck him with arrows. Although the hunter had begged for his life to sustain his children, the "wild" group overpowered him, and "they roasted his body to eat him." Following this woman's declaration, the mission Amerindians who were guarding the priests' house declared they would leave. The padre then learned that the Amerindians were trying to protect the priests' house because the cannibal indigenous men wanted to kill and eat the padre. The mission Amerindians asked permission to engage in war in order to destroy the cannibals, but the priest persuaded them to give up on this idea, and, instead, sent out some Amerindians on a peaceful mission. They were to bring the cannibals to the mission with intents of "reducing" them at the village, believing that this would make them renounce such old habits of eating human flesh.[25]

The priests understood the powerful role of these leadership figures in spiritual life, and the role they played in the political structure of these communities. These understandings led the priests to persuade such leaders to ally with the missionary project in order to further gather candidates for conversion. At these borderlands, missionaries negotiated in political, religious, and cultural realms in the name of the missionary precepts knowing that,[26] for instance, some of the Amerindians continued to engage in warfare amongst themselves, sometimes conspiring against the priests as well—such as when they entered the land for the first time and the Amerindians wanted to eat them.[27]

The priests' understandings of the *caciques*' roles led to missionary intervention in political matters, so that they might become central to these social relations. Montoya describes the first Indian they saw in the bushes surrounding the San Xavier reduction at the time of the Jesuits' first entry, a *cacique* who was highly esteemed among the group for his "bravery and even for having a sorcerer's name." The cacique was the leader of around nine squares on this site. On that occasion, the cacique convened his Indians to kill the Jesuits, assuring he himself would be the first one to surrender to the missionaries. Although the cacique's plan did not succeed, Montoya suspected that the chief was only observing what the priests were doing, and learning from it while secretly planning another attack.[28]

Indeed, the cacique punished some of his vassals for having been baptized by the missionaries by stealing their belongings from their houses. Padre Francisco Diaz made the cacique return all the stolen items to the Indians, at which point the cacique invited the leading figures from the village to share his disgust for the priests. He claimed that he would never become a Christian, nor would he go to church. Montoya writes that, "when the church bell plays, he would hunt and kill deer, and that he would eat meat on Fridays," in order to contradict what the padres demanded of the baptized. Montoya added that for every Sunday mass, there was a line of Indians behind him to hunt, and the deer hunted were actually divided amongst the entire village on Fridays. Typically, it would be expected that the hunters and the chief would divide the hunt among the people.

When Padre Francisco Diaz rebuked the caciques, the leader threatened the priest by showing his bow and arc and targeting the small livestock in front of the entire village. Right after that, the cacique suffered an injury from a tree branch that fell on his head. Yet, even worse than that, "at that same day, four of his concubines fell ill." Three died that day, and the fourth died on the following day. Montoya explains that these deaths were God's punishment, and adds that the diseases and the great number of deaths recorded among the Indians in Guairá were in fact a divine response to the rebels' bad conduct. According to Montoya, after witnessing these deaths, the cacique asked the priest to ask for God's forgiveness, especially after having awakened even sicker one morning. He began proclaiming the goodness of the padres, showing regret for his past, and encouraging his people to listen to the priests. Indeed, the cacique even proposed building his own house at the reduction, which he ended up doing while living with his son in the village. Montoya concludes by affirming the importance of these people's devotion and proceeds with the healers' case, referring to these men as witchdoctors.[29]

The medical emergencies and diseases that plagued the Paraguayan missions were numerous, and were accompanied by elaborate explanations for their causes and effects, such as the polygamous practices among the Christianized Indians. Montoya devoted much of his 1628 annual letter presenting polygamy as a sin, and the plague as its divine punishment. Montoya mentioned the case of a Christian cacique whose involvement with indigenous infidel women was the cause of an illness that proved fatal, even after the man's confessions.[30] The caciques managed to maintain their sexual encounters with female partners outside of the physical and conceptual boundaries imagined by the Jesuits as a divide between the Christianized/mission Indians and infidels.[31]

In 1630, the climate of tension and the encroachment by the Portuguese on the border with Spanish America generated numerous changes that directly affected the Jesuit missions of Guairá led by Padre Montoya. Repercussions were felt in the province of Guairá, and responses to the strained relations were addressed by different individuals and in different languages. The letter of August 27, 1630, contained arguments made by both the Jesuits and the indigenous groups, in Spanish and Guarani. The Real Audiencia in the city of La Plata had made royal provision in order to allow the Indians in the Guairá to remain there for two months, and to move to the town of Maracayu, located in the east of Asunción, in times of disease.[32] Around that time, the town of Maracayu had become an important center that attracted harvesters due to the yerba-maté production that the Jesuits and mission Indians had already mastered. Yerba-maté had grown into an important commodity for the colonial economy of Paraguay, and, with it, the town of Maracayu represented a site of Indian labor and exploitation. Of course, the Guarani responses dated 1630 show no interest in a transition to the town at any point. The entire mission of Ignacio de Ypaumbucu Rio del Parana gathered to discuss the royal provisions, and padres Cataldino and Mendiola decided to include the Guarani's own words to "display the strength" of the indigenous arguments.[33] Their statement showed that the Indians from Guairá felt threatened by the Spaniards who consistently visited the reduction and violently took Indians to the *encomiendas* in Maracayu. The statement claimed that the colonialists assured that the Spanish king would never know what actually took place with these Indians, who were fighting to not be forgotten by the crown. Additionally, the Indians exposed the fatal conditions met by many indigenous people who went to Maracayu to die without the sacraments, thus using Christian rhetoric to condemn the transferal of the Guairá population and validate their request to stay.[34] Montoya started by confirming the quality of the translation of the Guarani words, and concluded his paragraph not only in agreement with the Indians, but also completely reinforcing their reasoning, advising the Majesty of Spain to refrain from sending the Guairá Indians to their graves in Maracayu.[35]

Indigenous Ways of Being in *Conquista Espiritual*

Montoya's chronicle reflected the historical context of the Paraguayan borderland communities: colonialists representing the Iberian Peninsula, missionaries from different religious orders, and a multitude of indigenous communities who fled *encomenderos* and exploitive labor systems taking place in their lands. Montoya spoke explicitly about the impact of colonization on the division of indigenous groups that the European presence provoked. Indeed, there were previous disagreements and misunderstandings between some communities, but the intensity of these had worsened due to the Iberian colonization that began in the sixteenth century. According to Montoya's chronicle *Conquista espiritual*, the indigenous communities in colonial Paraguay would have learned to negotiate the stealing and selling of each other's community members to trade with the *encomenderos*.[36]

Missionaries in the Paraguayan borderlands also recorded data about what they called the "old rituals" of indigenous communities. In order to replace these habits, the missionaries sought to disseminate descriptions of them amongst themselves, and at times, interpretations of these cultural categories, hoping to replace them with Christian ones. In the *Spiritual Conquest*, Montoya dedicates one chapter to the old beliefs and rituals[37] that are especially relevant because they are related to indigenous ways of being, and to the social identity of being Guarani.

According to Meliá, the way of being Guarani is closely linked to how "the Indians lived their geographical space."[38] Thus, the so-called *tekoha* Guarani relates to its geography, it means "where we live according to our customs."[39] Therefore, the cultural category *tekoha* means the "place of the way of life, culture, teko means and produce at the same time the economic relations, social relations and political-religious organization both essential for the Guarani life."[40] Meliá further explains that the very category of spatiality is "crucial to the Guarani culture," because "it ensures the freedom and the possibility of maintaining ethnic identity."[41] Once "reduced" to Jesuit space, the Guarani lived in a new form of spatial (and therefore social) organization.

This identity management could manifest itself in several ways, including in the mobility of this group. Such mobility is often related and referred to by scholars through the theme of the

Land without Evil,[42] although this obscured the fact that the Guarani were walkers rather than nomadic peoples. Either to visit friends and relatives, or to indeed search for this land, the Guarani's constant mobility was part of a way of living, thus the reductions led by the Jesuits would indeed represent simply *another* place for the communities.[43] The Guarani walked in search of a land that would offer an abundance of natural resources both physically and metaphysically, such as in dreams.[44]

While for the missionaries the reductions were spaces for the Guarani to live under "the priests diligence to larger villages, and to the political and human life," wearing "cotton to dress them since the Indians generally lived naked," and being in constant vigil,[45] it was also a place where their search could be carried on, and their way of being might continue to be lived. Although there are other aspects of this way of being, we will focus on the themes of shamanism; land, fields, and hills; agriculture; hunting, fishing, and recollection; polygamous relations; and leadership.

The missionaries learned a great deal about American nature, fauna, and geography through their attention to indigenous perspectives.[46] More importantly, the Jesuits also learned about the relations of those communities with their natural, animal, and, ultimately religious world.[47] A close analysis of the sources supports the notion of indigenous perspectives immersed within the Jesuits' words, especially when descriptions of animals and plots are cross-referenced with ethnographic data about the myths of these groups.[48] While the records vary on aspects of nature, such as animals, depending on the dialogical experiences between the individual authors and the indigenous groups, we will focus on Montoya's narratives involving animals like snakes, jaguars, and tapirs. These animals appear constantly in the records of other missionaries as well, and are often at the center of religious and mythic texts.[49]

The natural world appears to intersect with religion through practices of medicine, rites of healing, and hunting. Montoya's descriptions showed more complex understandings of these practices in colonial Paraguay, and allow us to see how nature was understood both in terms of scientific as well as magical terms, inside and outside of the limits of the reductions.[50] Missionaries made numerous references to vipers and the indigenous ways of treating their poisoned bite, including Montoya. Indigenous groups tended to use a range of natural ingredients and medicinal herbs (such as the São Paulo rock), and prepared a drink from smashed garlic. But of special interest was fire, which was regarded as the most important of medicines. It was used by the Amerindians to burn the bitten part of a wound, which would then be sprayed with sulfur. If done in time, this rite would likely save the victims' lives.[51]

While missionaries might have encouraged hunting in order to sustain the indigenous population, it was actually condemned for its ambiguous religious relation to indigenous cultures.[52] Indeed, the many references to hunting in the Jesuits' manuscripts and writings were made to condemn these practices, given their cultural relevance among the indigenous communities in the Rio de La Plata basin. After all, similar to the indigenous world, the animal world had a hierarchic representation in which equivalent social actors form the "socialization of the nature," with its "leaders, sorcerers, warriors, hunters, etc."[53] Thus, hunting among the colonial Paraguayan Indians had a socioreligious structure that permeated the relationships between humans and animals. Those narratives captured religious components related to hunting as a sacred activity, while simultaneously recording the indigenous people's knowledge about their environment and strategies formed in response to it. Thus, empirical and magical knowledge were present, and Montoya witnessed and chose to record the cultural institution of hunting.

Montoya described a water snake that was trying to kill an indigenous man, who, in turn, ended up hunting the snake. The story unfolds as the snake prepares to attack the man, who immediately "raises his arms." The snake, in turn, curls up his body. Using a knife hidden behind his back, he attacked the animal. After killing the snake, Montoya reports that the man fed himself from it for days.[54] The anecdote referred to the Indians' skillful ways of responding to these circumstances, but also addressed indigenous understandings of how to relate to the natural world.[55]

Jaguars were often the main characters in episodes involving spiritual and political leadership.[56] The priests seem particularly interested in knowing more about these creatures and their connections to indigenous communities due to their constant appearances in the everyday lives of these peoples.[57] Montoya recalled what the priests learned about them from the indigenous groups, as well as how they referred to jaguars.[58] In the *Vocabulario*, he clarified meanings for the Guarani word *jaguarete*: the once divided *jagua* and *ete* together refer to "really hideous creature," stressing the idea that any encounter with this animal is dramatic and evil. In his chronicle, he narrated a case that indicates that from a Guarani perspective, although the jaguars were endowed with force, they do not have the wisdom of the human, and therefore can be outwitted. One case demonstrated that human urine may be used to scare jaguars away. Montoya mentioned another time that an indigenous man, stalked by a jaguar, was able to get up in a tree. The man tried many strategies to scare the jaguar away, including throwing rocks and sticks, yet the only thing that kept the jaguar away was his urine.[59]

Jaguars also appeared in indigenous beliefs and explanations of natural phenomena such as eclipses. These animals apparently caused mixed feelings because their attitudes were unpredictable—they can be both bad and good. According to Montoya, the Amerindians explained that eclipses were caused by "a giant tiger or dog [who] lives in the sky, and in certain instances of rage, such animal devours the moon and the sun." The Indians' reactions to these phenomena showed both "apprehension and admiration." Jaguars clearly occupied a prominent place in indigenous culture—in the natural, spiritual, and religious realms.[60]

In ways similar to the jaguars, tapirs often populated narratives about indigenous peoples, revealing some of the strategies involved in hunting them and the cultural relation with these animals.[61] Montoya narrated how Amerindian hunters would approach a corral of tapirs during the evening, use fire to outshine them at night, and hunt them easily when the morning came. In terms of meat, Montoya drew a comparison between tapirs' meat and cows' meat, which led to the understanding that the Jesuits also enjoyed the hunted animals captured by the Indians—an especially interesting fact considering that missionaries tended to discourage hunting. Another note made by Montoya refers to the tapirs' nails, which were believed to hold poison.[62]

Of course, many of these references were categorized by Jesuit logic as mere superstitions. However, these narratives revealed deep cultural aspects of indigenous cultures, since the animal world reflected the social structure of Guarani society. For instance, with a description of the presence of a deer in a village, Montoya remarked that this animal "not being killed, someone from the village where the animal passed by, shall die." While retelling this case from "experimental observation" Montoya attested that the devil supports such false beliefs, since he witnessed the same occurring while a wedding celebration was taking place in a Spanish town, where, sure enough, the groom died after a deer's visit and unsuccessful attempts to kill it.[63] Such cases, when taken together, offered an explanation about the order of the supernatural world among indigenous groups, which dictated certain rules and expectations for relations between animals and humans.[64]

Indigenous resistance in the Rio de La Plata basin manifested itself in various ways and demonstrated distinct levels of engagement, regardless of community, region, or the scope of these responses. In the first decades of the missionary presence in colonial Paraguay, there are records of at least 25 spiritual leaders who challenged the missionaries. These leaders were often referred to by the priests as wizards, sorcerers, magicians, and by some scholars as shamans because of their roles as healers. Many references to sorcery were linked to animals, with sorcerers being the interpreters of birds' singing. As for the descriptions of medicine men, Montoya alluded to the "sucking of the wounds," followed by the removal of objects—these could be fish spine and coal—from the sorcerer's' mouth, suggesting that these were the reasons for the illness. Among the categories of sorcerers, there were those referred to as "gravediggers," because they bury "food, fruit peels, and coal," and sometimes "frogs crossed with fishbones" in the house of those whom they are targeting to kill, causing the victim to weaken to death. The sorcerers also handled the local plants and already were aware of the *yerba* before most Indians and the colonialists were. Montoya (1639, 45) investigated the origin of the *yerba* "among 80 to 100 Indians" to find out that "when these old Indians were young, this *yerba* wasn't to drink. The Indians knew of it only through the sorcerer or magician, who had a deal with the devil." Montoya concluded by affirming that the yerba was widely used to "do spells."[65]

When trying to identify the meanings of the terms held by the spiritual leaders for the members of the indigenous groups, Montoya also found meanings for the Jesuits in their linguistic terms. For instance, the Indians in the Tayati called the priests "Pay Abaré," which according to Montoya (98) meant they were different from others, because they were "chaste men." Montoya explains that "Pay" was used to refer to the spiritual leaders often categorized by the missionaries as sorcerers and wizards, as already discussed. Montoya offered a definition of a Guarini term that suggests that the indigenous people thought of priests in the same way as they thought of their own leaders. Even the sorcerers themselves referred to the priest as Abaré due to the priests' celibacy.[66]

Many names and stories about the spiritual leaders were told, while the cultural categories of war, revenge, and the constant displacement from and return to villages were invoked. Although names such as Taubici, Araguaye, Tayubay, Yeguaporú, Ñesú, and Guirabera were often associated with several religious aspects pertaining to the missionary project, they also revealed relevant data for the understanding of these indigenous communities within these cultural categories. When Montoya referenced his visit to the reduction of San Loreto with Padre Simon Masseta and Padre José Cataldino, he mentioned the "great cacique, besides magician, wizard, and a devil's relative" named "Taubici." According to Montoya, Taubici was a very well respected member of his community, "for fearing his cruelty," the priest was nonetheless very well regarded. He even prevented the priests from being killed when they were visiting the village for the first time. With time, Taubici and his village members came to live in the San Ignácio reduction under the direction of Padre Masseta, and to celebrate "Corpus Christi" day with a party, the cacique decided to leave the reduction with his vassals to return to his village. On the way, enemy Indians attacked them to "avenge an Indian killed by Taubici."[67] Taubici's case informs us of the groups' mobility inside and outside of the mission, the importance of the leadership in deciding where the group should go, and revenge and war among indigenous nations.

Frequently, indigenous ways of being were recorded as referring to a hidden *old* way of living, which was discovered by the missionaries while the Indians lived within the reduction. On occasions, this *old* way of living was revealed by the priest through the actions of some of the leaders. A ringleader unnamed by Montoya was among these cases, and his words defined the old way of living as "the ancestors' way." According to Montoya's chronicle, this rebel was disguised as a candidate for Christian conversion, living in a house built by mission Indians but at a distance from the center where the priests themselves were located. It was in this house where the rebel sorcerer performed the old ritual practices, and preached the old ways of living: "Let us live the way of our ancestors! What is the reason for the priests to think is evil for us to have women in abundance?! It's absurd that we shall abandon our customs and our good way of living of our ancestors, and instead, we subject ourselves to the news that these priests are introducing! The best remedy for this evil is to take this priest's life." Through this active threat to the priest's life, this unnamed rebel's case informs us of resistance in the borderlands, which is the very opposite of the commonly held notion of peaceful coexistence. Furthermore, the rebel's motives trace back to his ancestors' way of living in the time prior to the Europeans' arrival. It comes as no surprise that the Jesuits condemned this rebel's preachings, for not only did he threaten the priest's life, but he also articulated the revival of the custom of polygamy, a major sin combated by the religious orders.[68]

Although the Indians of the São Francisco Xavier mission present in these accounts responded with "joys and dances," one young Indian reported the fact to Padre Francisco de Cespedes, who had to escape during the night since sorcerers were hunting him. While many Indians accompanied the priest, others followed the sorcerer. Yet with pressure from armed Christians, the rebels were displaced and set out to different reductions in Paraná. The movement was initiated by an unnamed ringleader, who ended up being sent to the reduction in Loreto.

Other cases provide evidence of hidden ways of being serving to perpetuate indigenous identities at the missions. When Montoya referred to the indigenous groups *charruas* and *yaros* living in the same reduction, he mentioned that both were warrior groups, but also that they had no fixed homes and moved constantly. Another problem was faced in the reduction of Concepción de Nuestra Señora, defined by Montoya as a "wizard nest." In particular, one wizard, explained Montoya, pretended to become a Christian while he in fact remained a "devil's minister" for years before the priest found out about his disguised acts of defiance. Not too far from that reduction, another similarly disguised wizard lived among the priests in the reduction of Corpus Christi, and was equally rebellious.[69] The persistence of these famous sorcerers and their influence was an ongoing problem for the priests in colonial Paraguay. Missionaries put a lot of effort into combating the impact of these actions, as is shown in records and in Montoya's chronicle.[70]

Countless life-threatening movements are present in the Jesuits' writings, representing the complex relationships between the missionaries and Paraguayan indigenous groups. For instance, in the first reduction founded in the Province of Paraguay, called "Santo Ignácio del Parana," Montoya reported the existence of a group of Indians who were intent on killing priests as well as their supporters.[71] This threat demonstrated that the Indians who were allied with priests were in danger, since the rebels saw them as betrayers. Thus, when the missionaries argued that the colonialists divided these groups, they failed to observe their own share of guilt in this dynamic.

Yet, if on the one hand the groups were threatening each other because of the priests, on the other they also allied *against* the priests. On some occasions, ultimatums resulted in fatalities for the priests, as was the case of Padre Pedro Espinosa. At the same reduction of Santo Ignácio, a group of rebels allied with another group located in Loreto, and together they killed Padre Espinosa. They claimed to disapprove of Espinosa's preaching, and accused him of lying and adoring "fake gods," such as Maria, Jesus, and God. After disclosing all of this to the priest, the group attacked him and let him be "devoured by the tigers," which, as already has been discussed, were seen as being truly evil creatures.[72]

Indigenous identities were interpreted by and represented through the focused lenses of the missionary's intent on religious conversion. Nonetheless, it was precisely the urge to know these communities that triggered the Jesuits' interest in capturing as much information as possible to identify the markers of indigenous belief in order to target them. In Montoya's chronicle it is possible to learn about the Guarani rites and sociopolitical organization in small villages governed by their caciques.[73] Missionaries in Paraguay understood the caciques as the nobility among the Guarani, and Montoya even elaborated on this social structure as an inherent status passed through the caciques' ancestors.[74] Montoya also noted the main characteristics of successful leadership, including their nobility, as shown through their eloquence in speech—part of the importance of their language.[75] As Montoya was the author of the vocabulary and grammar of the Guarani language, he demonstrated a skill useful for political and religious purposes in colonial Paraguay.[76]

Although the benefits and privileges enjoyed by caciques varied, Montoya traced a pattern that helped in understanding the structure of these groups in order to reach their desired Christianity through the actions of the Jesuits.[77] The caciques had their houses built by their vassals, but they also planted and harvested the land along with the community. Their vassals would offer their daughters to the caciques should they want additional wives, as polygamy was permitted. As a matter of fact, Montoya revealed that he had news of some caciques who had 15, 20, and even 30 wives. While Montoya refered to polygamy among the caciques, he also concluded that the group as a whole was very respectful of women, especially mothers and sisters, and that they never broke the taboos of fornication with them. Once they became Christians, ensured Montoya, they left their various women, choosing only one to be their principal wife. Of special interest is that they were able to convince the caciques to have only one wife after becoming Christians, which represented a rupture with the old way of life as recalled by the aforementioned rebel chief of Santo Ignácio.

Indigenous women's worlds were often related to the social and family episodes described and interpreted by Montoya, who focused on the circumstances in which the Jesuits could possibly garner more candidates to the mission. Thus, Montoya also reported that when a woman was about to give birth, the husband and father would abstain from eating for 15 days: "no meat, and no hunting even with the prey right in front of them." This was believed to protect the child's health. Once the child was born, Montoya revealed that the Indians had a form of baptism or "special way to name the child."

Rituals of anthropophagy were recurrent even among natives considered already converted, suggesting the continuing relevance of these cultural practices to the groups. On one occasion, two Indians were killed by infidels who Montoya himself was trying to initiate through conversion rites. Often the missionaries entered for the first time into a "Gentile" village accompanied by converted Indians, seeking to make first contacts. In one case, as soon as the two Indians approached the infidels, they were offered women to "celebrate their baptism ceremonies." While one Indian engaged in taking wives, the other rejected them and was killed and eaten without ceremony. The Indian who chose his wives and accepted his fate, was "killed with solemnity, and eaten," showing that the ritual was carried out.[78] Montoya provided more details on such practices, informing the reader that the captive had freedom in terms of "food and women, all of his choosing." When the captive was ready, he was "killed with a lot of solemnity." Every member of the community touched the dead body, and added that name to their own, which explains the aforementioned "baptism" ritual. In a huge party involving different ceremonies, the Guarani prepared and cooked some sort of cereal with the body, and every member tastes it, including small children, and a new name was added to theirs.[79]

Priests often recorded rituals of death and the afterlife in colonial Paraguay. Montoya described that generally the widows would wail and hurl themselves from high places, often injuring themselves or even dying. The burial rituals involved the belief that the soul and the body went separately to the grave; once they brought their dead to the urns, they would also bring along small plates in their mouths to assure the soul would be "better fit." Even after the Indians were living in the missions as Christians, the persistence of these habits was noted when the priests would bury the dead. There was always a "sly old woman who" would use a small pot and in a "disguised manner would agitate that pot as if she was taking something from the grave." The Indians would say that that something was the soul.[80]

Although priests also put a lot of effort into preaching against the sin of adultery, and for the maintenance of chastity, the habit of keeping more than one wife and/or having sexual encounters with different partners persisted.[81] In order to minimize losses of potential Christians, priests had to be flexible on this matter, and ended up making exceptions—especially to caciques—since so many Indians were losing interest in conversion. Montoya's chronicle reveals that the priests avoided for two years any mention of the sixth commandment while they preached twice a day and at Sunday masses. Montoya even revealed that the caciques had offered the priests some women, since it was believed to be "against the nature if men to do the domestic work," like the missionaries did.

This was also true of caciques Roque Macaranan and Miguel Artiguaye, who lived in one of the colonies near Santo Ignácio. Maracanan was widely respected by his community and well known by the surrounding groups due to his "great eloquence," another relevant characteristic necessary to be a leader among the Guarani, reveals Montoya.[82] With respect to his marital status, Montoya recorded that Maracanan replaced his legitimate noble wife with another woman. Maracanan also performed the functions of a missionary priest: dressing up with "a feather cape," and preaching mass with "towels on a table, and … a cassava pie, a vase decorated, and corn wine." Maracanan would then perform as the priests he saw did by speaking to his vassals, performing ceremonies, eating and drinking that food, and being revered by faithful followers. Having observed the priests, Maracanan recreated his role within his community based on the detailed understanding he had of the priests' world.

Maracanan reinvented both the sacred host and wine by replacing it with cassava pie and corn wine, respectively. Maracanan maintained concubines—encouraging others to do the same—and was against the consecrated water used by priests to heal the ill. According to Montoya, Maracanan used to preach that the priests were actually brought by the "demons" since they were introducing "their new beliefs, [to] deprive us of the old and good way of living of our ancestors." Maracanan reminded his fellow Indians of their history and their ancestors who not only "had many women," but also "many domestic helpers," as well as the "freedom to choose whomever they wanted," whereas with the coming of the priests the Indians had "to be with only one woman." The cacique found this to be "unfair," and thus threatened directly the priests: "we either send them away from our lands, or you take their lives away." Cacique Maracanan was fighting to maintain this very specific habit of polygamy.[83]

Miguel Artiguaye's conclusions regarding the priests and their teachings were similar; when he first met the priests he engaged in a calm dialogue. But the importance of polygamy for indigenous communities was so great that it seemed non-negotiable. Artiguaye first accused the priests of being "hell demons, sent by your prince to our doom," then proceed to make remarks about the old way of being of the Indians and their ancestors: "Our greatest lived freely, and having the women they wanted, without anyone bothering them, with whom they lived and spent their days with joy. You, however, want to destroy their traditions and impose on us such a heavy load, that is of tie-in with one woman." On his way out, Artiguaye remarked that although the priests were freely living in the indigenous lands, he would not endure to live under the missionaries' "bad way of being." Through these interactions recorded by Montoya, we learn that polygamy was a fundamental and nonnegotiable aspect of the Guarani way of being.[84]

One day the mission was awakened by the sound of "drums, flutes, and other instruments," and about 300 well adorned Indians armed with arrows and bows led by Artiguaye gathered in the central plaza. Montoya, Padre Simon, and Padre José already suspected that the group was on its way to ask permission from Roque Maracanan to kill the missionaries, and as soon as Artiguaye arrived in San Loreto he clarified once again his intention to no longer suffer at the priests' hands: "they put us in a house – that they call church – and in there they talk and do the opposite of what our ancestors did. They had many women, and these priests take them away from us, and they want us to keep just one."

Cacique Maracanan came out to see Artiguaye, who once more emphasized "it is time to honor our ancestors and put an end to these priests, to enjoy our women and our freedom." Although Macaranan had threatened the priests before, he aggressively rejected Artiguaye's suggestion, pushing him down to the ground, and threatening him with punishment.[85] Perhaps because he had known that another cacique, Araráa, had offered help and to protect the priests should Artiguaye try to kill them, Maracanan canceled the plan altogether. Miguel Artiguaye returned to the mission of Loreto, and asked for the priests' forgiveness, despite, as later described, never having left his mistress. The priests ended up relocating the mistress to a faraway town, but Miguel was able to trace her, and left his wife and village members behind to pursue a life with his mistress. He moved with her small child to a distant wood, where he worked for years and died, leaving her without any option but to go back to the missions to be supported by the priests.[86]

Cacique Maracanan was one of many examples of indigenous chiefs who would manage their alliances flexibly. Although Cacique Maracanan at first threatened the Jesuits, he then allied with the missionaries, and prevented them from being attacked. Yet, not too long after that, the same cacique would be reported as uniting forces with another cacique and a spiritual leader in order to expel the missionaries from indigenous lands.[87] Although this plan was also unsuccessful and the three conspirators ended up dying in the attempt, Maracanan's case pointed to the strategic relationships within and between communities that the chiefs acted upon, sometimes in favor of and sometimes against the Jesuits.

It is important to point out that Artiguaye's call for a return to the traditions of their ancestors, including polygamy, was quoted three times in Montoya's chronicle, suggesting its relevance and charged meaning for the Guarani. In both cases, Artiguaye and Maracanan articulated a discourse that denied the imposition of the new way of life brought by the missionaries in favor of maintaining the old traditions, particularly the habit of polygamy.[88] More cases of caciques who openly or secretly maintained their polygamous family lives populate Montoya's chronicle and missionaries letters, some accepting Christian teaching only to seek out their concubines right after, while others would turn in some of their wives, while in fact having "left thirty concubines hidden."[89]

Antonio Ruiz de Montoya's reasoning supports the notion that all the difficulties the missionaries experienced among the indigenous communities were direct consequences of bad role models and the attitudes of the Spanish colonialists, to whom the Indians only mattered in terms of the labor system.[90] Montoya explicitly blamed the Spaniards' mistreatment of the Indians as the main cause for the remaining existence of the old practices among the converted Indians.[91] He affirmed that the colonialists were bad role models, and that this is the main reason for a lack of interest in the evangelical teachings brought by the Jesuits. Montoya definitively denounced the atrocities caused by the labor systems taking place in Paraguay, targeting the disclosure of the Indians' mistreatment at the *encomiendas*, and providing a full description of what was done with the *yerba*, and how the *encomenderos* abused this Indian labor system in colonial Paraguay.[92] Indeed as the chronicle was to be published in Madrid, Montoya was petitioning to arm the indigenous against the Spanish *encomenderos* and Portuguese *Bandeirantes*.[93]

★ ★ ★

As the colonial Spanish American world drew to its end, another key figure emerged to reach across the northern and southern borderlands and provide a sense of historical change and some closure to the complex entanglements of these regions of Indo-Hispano negotiation. Teodoro de Croix, a Frenchman who, by virtue of diplomatic alliances between the Catholic royalty of France and Spain, came to be appointed the first commandant general of the newly designed *Provincias Internas del Norte* in 1776. His charge reflected the changing nature of frontier relations that had unfolded between the 1540s and the later years of the eighteenth century. Where once administrators like Cabeza de Vaca were expected to protect vulnerable Indian peoples from exploitation by *encomenderos,* borderlands north *and* south had evolved toward striking military parity. The relatively defenseless hunters and gatherers or swidden farmers of the sixteenth century had, in some cases, become themselves transformed from the Spanish notion of *salvages* (simple savages) to that of *bárbaros,* peoples with real military power who might threaten Spanish control of the borderlands.[94]

Among the most threatening of *indios bárbaros* in the northern provinces were the various divisions of the Comanches, numic-speaking peoples who had emerged from their mobile hunter-gathering lives in the Great Basin of North America in the early eighteenth century to adopt an equestrian hunting and raiding economy, fully formed and fiercely effective by the 1770s. From the 1740s onwards, Comanche raiding plagued Spanish colonial missions and settlements in New Mexico and the province of Tejas, severely limiting provincial exchange and communications with Mexico. Among Croix's instructions from King Carlos V was to reorganize the presidial defenses of the frontier, but also, more importantly, to employ a combination of military action and diplomacy to bring the Comanches into treaty relationships with Spain. By February 1786, he and his lieutenant Juan Bautista de Anza had achieved that objective with a treaty executed in Santa Fe, New Mexico, complete with the exchange of hostages to ensure mutual compliance.[95]

But de Croix was not in Mexico City to enjoy the success in diplomacy. In 1781, a revolt among the Quechans of the lower Colorado River region in the province of Sonora pulled his attention westward from Comanche affairs. De Croix held himself responsible, for in addition to the Franciscan missions of La Purisima Concepcion and San Pedro y San Pablo in Quechan country, he encouraged the establishment of two secular *pueblos* among those whom the padres sought to evangelize. Hosting missionaries whom they supported with their own produce, in exchange for military defense against Halchidhoma raiders, was one thing; but seeing their fields trampled by grazing sheep, cattle, and horses proved to be quite another. By July 1781, tensions erupted, and within one week 105 Spanish *pobladores* died, including 21 women and children. Seventy-six settlers were taken war captive. So too did the two Franciscan priests, who had been warmly welcomed, only to find their mission hopelessly compromised by the addition of the *pobladores.* Punishments ensued, but de Croix was no longer calling the orders. He had been abruptly summoned to take up the duties of the Viceroy of Peru, charged to restore order in the aftermath of the uprising of the second Tupac Amaru.[96]

★ ★ ★

In the summer of 1770, eight-year-old Francisco Xavier Chaves drove his family's sheep to graze on the expanse of dry grasslands running up toward the Manzano Mountains from the Chaves' family home village of Tomé, in New Spain's northernmost province of New Mexico. Tomé was a frontier settlement, established in 1739 to provide rest, sustenance, and protection from Indian raids to travelers on El Camino Real, the royal road that linked the distant provincial capital of Santa Fe to cities far to the south—El Paso del Norte, cuidad Chihuahua, Durango, and finally Mexico City itself. Its settlers included some 172 *indios genízaros* (a unique caste of converted and hispanicized Indian slaves, the males among whom were raised and trained to act as frontier soldiers), as well as *vecinos* (Spanish colonial citizens) who sought new irrigable and grazable lands a day's ride south of Albuquerque. By 1760 it contained some 400 residents who carried forward the mixed ethnic character of the original *pobladores* (settlers).[97]

As young Francisco drove his sheep toward the forested mountains, a raiding band of Comanches swept both the boy and his livestock up and carried them across the steep passes to their vast homelands on the southern plains. He would grow to adulthood among his captors, but when his adoptive Comanche mother died, depriving him of the protections of captive kinship, he was sold to Taovayas, village farmers along the Red River who were often allies of the Comanches. In 1784, at the age of 22, he slipped away from his captors and presented himself to Governor Domingo Cabello at San Antonio de Bexar. Eyelids tattooed in the Taovayas' fashion, he then began a long career as cultural emissary in the service of Spain.

Along with a compatriot, the Frenchman-turned-Indian Pedro Vial, Francisco would participate in the earliest Euro-American trailblazing expeditions between Tejas and New Mexico in the 1780s and 1790s. Chaves also managed to reclaim kin and cultural ties with the Comanches, for as late as 1792 Vial encountered him on the Plains east of Pecos, traveling with seven Comanches and their wives. He had spent the last three years among his Comanche kinspeople, and now, Chaves told Vial, they were heading for New Mexico in order to visit his parents. In a final example of Indo-Hispano entanglement, Chaves had found ways to connect the violence of the borderlands to the flexible filaments of kinship among his captors and kinsmen with those of the blood relatives he had left behind more than 20 years before. His life, and those of the many enmeshed in borderlands north and south, illustrate the myriad social worlds that developed in these regions, their fluidity, and their fragility once the era of independence and state building would commence in the nineteenth century.[98]

Notes

1 The literature on Cabeza de Vaca's journey and life is extensive; the most recent and comprehensive from Andrés Reséndez, *A Land So Strange: The Epic Journey of Cabeza de Vaca* (New York: Basic Books, 2007; for a recent translation of his own account, see Álvar Núñez Cabeza de Vaca, *The Narrative of Cabeza De Vaca*, Translation of *La Relación*, eds. Rolena Adorno and Patrick Charles Pautz, (Lincoln, NE: University of Nebraska Press, 2003).
2 David J. Weber, *Bárbaros: Spaniards and Their Savages in the Age of Enlightenment* (New Haven: Yale University Press 2005).
3 Gaston Gordillo, *Rubble: The Afterlife of Destruction* (Durham and London: Duke University Press 2014); Lucas Besire, *Behold the Black Caiman: A Chronicle of Ayoreo Life* (Chicago, IL: University of Chicago Press, 2014).
4 Anderson argued that Paraguay was an exceptional case, where the Guarani language "achieved a status of print-language," because the Jesuits "established a benevolent dictatorship ... in early seventeenth century," and because the "indigenes were better treated than elsewhere in Spanish America," as argued by Anderson (*Imagined Communities: Reflections on the Origin and Spread of Nationalism* [New York: Verso, 2006], 64). A notion first discussed in the 18th century by the Jesuit missionary José Manuel Peramás in "The Republic of Plato and the Guarani," *The Paraguay Reader: History, Culture, Politics*, ed. Peter Lambert Durham (London: Duke University Press, 2013).
5 Julia Sarreal (*The Guarani and Their Missions*, 2014, 9) affirms that even in the post-Jesuit years Guarani leaders acting as *cabildos* kept exchanging letters and correspondence in Guarani, avoiding performing their work in Spanish.
6 Such as the works of the French scholar Maxime Haubert, *La Vie Quotidienne Des Indiens Et Des Jésuites Du Paraguay Au Temps Des Missions* (Paris: Hachette, 1986). (1967, 1986) And for an Anglophone audience, see Barbara Anne Ganson, *The Guaraní under Spanish Rule in the Río De La Plata* (Stanford, CA: Stanford University Press, 2003).
7 Missionary–indigenous relations in colonial Paraguay were, therefore a result of the interplay of these heterogeneous groups. As Mary Louise Pratt argues, it is also engendered by an asymmetry in its nature due to variables such as the imperial administration as well as the agendas placed in the hands of the missionaries, who authored the sources (Mary Louise Pratt, *Imperial Eyes: Travel Writing and Transculturation* [London: Routledge, 1992]).
8 Bartomeu Melià (*El Guaraní Conquistado Y Reducido: Ensayos De Etnohistoria* [Asunción: Centro De Estudios Antropológicos, Universidad Católica, 1986]) already called attention to this phenomenon in his early groundbreaking essays published in Paraguay. Influenced by Melià's work of linguistic anthro-

pology, a young group of scholars dedicated years of work to compiling data from primary sources derived in the first century of missions, and collectively published it in 2003 as a database in CD form entitled *Xamanismo e Cura na Coleção De Angelis*, with easy access and querying. This project was funded by the Coordenação de Aperfeiçoamento de Pessoal de Nivel Superior (CAPES) Foundation, and the research group was composed by Dr. Maria Cristina dos Santos (Pontifícia Universidade Católica do Rio Grande do Sul [PUCRS]), and research associates Dr. Jean Baptista (Universidade Federal de Goiás), Dr. Bianca Brigidi (Quest University Canada), Dr. Fabiana Pires, and Dr. Carla Berto.

9 In addition to the well-known works by Meliá (1997) and Alvarez Kern (2009), which point to the ethnic diversity of the La Plata region, there are the works authored by Santos and Baptista, and Wilde: Santos, Maria Cristina dos and Jean Baptista, "Reduções Jesuíticas e Povoados de Índios: Controvérsias Sobre a População Indígena (séc XVII–XVIII)," *Historia* Vol. 11, No. 2 (2007); and Guillermo Wilde, "Territorio y Etnogénesis Misional en el Paraguay del siglo XVIII," *Revista Fronteiras, Dourados*, Vol. 11, No. 19 (2009).

10 Jean Baptista. "A visibilidade étnica nos registros coloniais: missões Guaranis ou Missões Indígenas?" *Povos Indígenas: coleção História Geral do Rio Grande do Sul.*, 1 ed., (Passo Fundo: Meritos, 2009), Vol. 5, 207. Additionally, cases such as in the reduction of Nuestra Señora de los Reyes is described by Montoya (1639, 211, conquista) as composed by a diversity of indigenous groups and languages, in which everyone could "understand the common language, that is Guarani." Since the early years of the Spanish and Portuguese conquest, missionaries demonstrated interest in indigenous languages. These works can be found in Matthew Restall, Lisa Sousa, and Kevin Terraciano, *Mesoamerican Voices: Native Language From Colonial Mexico, Oaxaca, Yucatan, and Guatemala* (Cambridge: Cambridge University Press, 2005). Indeed, the dialogical records echo the nuances of these borderlands, where Spanish was definitely not the only language used to express historical borderlands' experiences (Mary Louise Pratt, "Arts of the Contact Zone," *Profession*, 1991, 33–40. Available online at www.jstor.org/stable/25595469). Further research on indigenous languages in the South American region are discussed in Lyle Campbell, ed. *The World of Linguistics: Volume 2: The Indigenous Languages of South America A Comprehensive Guide* (Berlin: De Gruyter, 2012). Foundational works on the early borderlands in the Spanish Americas provides insightful and well-known discussions on the linguistic approach, such as Robert Ricard, "Ethnographic and the Linguistic Training of the Missionaries" *The Spiritual Conquest of Mexico; an Essay on the Apostolate and the Evangelizing Methods of the Mendicant Orders in New Spain, 1523–1572* (Berkeley, CA: University of California Press, 1966).

11 Recent indigenous studies are numerous, and they help to illuminate more inclusive approaches to history and cultural studies about indigenous communities. Frameworks such as "reversed colonialism" (Pekka Hämäläinen, *The Comanche Empire.* [New Haven, CT: Yale University Press, 2008]), "contact zones" (Mary Louise Pratt), gender dynamics and the role of women within the Spanish Missions (Juliana Barr, *Peace Came in the Form of a Woman: Indians and Spaniards in the Texas Borderlands* [Chapel Hill, NC: University of North Carolina Press, 2007]), and the "middle ground" (Richard White, *The Middle Ground: Indians, Empires, and Republics in the Great Lakes Region, 1650–1815* [Cambridge: Cambridge University Press, 1991]), are just a few examples of critical works on the indigenous communities in the colonial Americas. More provocative frameworks on indigenous studies, such as Linda Tuhiwai-Smith's *Decolonizing Methodologies: Research and Indigenous Peoples* (London: Zed Books, 1999), invite us to rethink and reconsider the whole approach to research and its narrow views on non-Western cultures. On the same line of thinking, works by the Mohawk scholar Gerald Taiaiake Alfred (*Wasáse: Indigenous Pathways of Action and Freedom* [Peterborough, ON: University of Toronto Press, 2005]) shifted the paradigm by centralizing the analysis on indigenous identities in a contemporary context as transcendental of the negative asymmetrical relations engendered by current states (to coin the important framework brought by Hector Diaz Polanco in *Indigenous Peoples in Latin America: The Quest for Self-determination*. Translated by Lucía Rayas [Boulder, CO: Westview Press, 1997]).

12 Scholarship on the ethnographic state often considers the Jesuits' writings solely for their goal of serving the imperial administration, therefore, classifying the indigenous communities while conditioned by the need to produce a binary discourse opposing "Christian Indians" and "infidel Indians" (Guillermo Wilde, "De las crónicas jesuíticas a las 'etnografías estatales': realidades y ficciones del orden misional en las fronteras ibéricas," *Nuevo Mundo Mundos Nuevos* [En ligne], Débats, mis en ligne le 30 novembre 2011, consulté le 27 septembre 2015. Available online at http://nuevomundo.revues.org/62238; DOI : 10.4000/nuevomundo.62238).

13 Although the list of works is immensely long, note the works authored by Bartomeu Meliá and Graciela Chamorro (*Decir el Cuerpo: Historia y Etnografía del Cuerpo de los Pueblos Guarani*. [Asunción: Tiempo de Historia, 2009]).

14 Melià (El modo de ser, conquistado y reducido) established these dates to reflect the letter by Father Alonso Barzana a Juan Sebastián of 1594 published in Guillermo Furlong (1968), and the *Spiritual Conquest* by Father Antonio Ruiz de Montoya, published in 1639.
15 Bartomeu Melià, *La Lengua Guarani en el Paraguay Colonial* (Asunción: CEADUC, 2003).
16 According to Melià, the *reducción* "conducted by the Jesuits among the Guarani was a religious enterprise as well as a sociocultural achievement that played fully into the structure of the Guarani nation." Bartomeu Melià. *El Guaraní-conquistado Y Reducido: Ensayos De Etnohistoria* (Asunción: Centro De Estudios Antropológicos, Universidad Católica, 1986), 5.
17 Available at www.brasiliana.usp.br/bbd/handle/1918/00059200#page/1/mode/1up.
18 According to Melià (*La Lengua Guarani*, 42), from 1582–1585, Fray Bolaños had assistance from two "criollos" missionaries born in Paraguay and raised with the Guarani language as their mother tongue. Melià (2012, 2) also mentions the encounter between Ruiz de Montoya and Father Diego González Holguín, who authored the *Gramática y arte nueva de la lengva general de todo el Perú, llamada lengua Qquicua, o lengva del Inca* (1607) and *Vocabulario de la lengva general de todo el Perv, llamada lengua Qquichua o del Inca* (1608).
19 These ideas can be found in a variety of sources, such as in the works cited by Sarreal (*The Guarani and Their Missions*).
20 For more on the *bandeirantes*, see John M. Monteiro, *Negros Da Terra: Índios E Bandeirantes Nas Origens De São Paulo* (São Paulo: Companhia Das Letras, 1994).
21 Graciela Chamorro compares this revolutionary aspect of Montoya's request to "arming present peasantry" communities in Latin America in "Antonio Ruiz de Montoya: promotor y defensor de las lenguas indígenas," *História*,Vol. 11, No. 2 (2007), 252–260.
22 "Copia de la Petición del Pe. Antonio Ruiz de Montoya hecha a S.M, suplicando por el remedio de las Prov." s y *Reducciones de Indios en las hostilidades que padece (sic) de los Portugueses*, (MCA, Cortesão, Guairá), 433–4.
23 Dietrich W., "La importancia de los diccionarios guaranies de Montoya." *Amerindia: Revue d'Ethnolinguistique Amerindienne* 19–20 (1995): 287–299.
24 *1628. Carta Annua dei Guayra por el Pe. Antonio Ruiz, del año de 628.* (MCA, Cortesão, Guairá), 263.
25 *1628. Carta Annua dei Guayra por el Pe*. 264.
26 Sarreal 2014, 37.
27 Reduction of San Xavier, *1628. Carta Annua del Guayra por el Pe. Antonio Ruiz, del año de 628* (MCA, Cortesão, Guairá), 264.
28 Reduction of San Xavier, 264.
29 Reduction of San Xavier, 264–6. Jesuits often represented diseases as divine opportunities to convert more Amerindians. There are innumerable references to the health of mothers giving birth and to newborns, since the Jesuits would have a particular interest in baptizing the infants, such as in San Xavier's account from 1628 in which Montoya refers to a woman's labor in which the father searched for the priest's help in "saying the gospel." Two hours later, the padre assured, a young healthy infant was nursing (Reduction of San Xavier, 266).
30 *1628. Carta Annua del Guayra por el Pe. Antonio Ruiz, del año de 628* (MCA, Cortesão, Guairá), 267.
31 Wilde discusses the autonomy of movement that indigenous communities had. Guillermo Wilde, *Territorios y Etnogénesis Misional en el Paraguay Del Siglo XVIII*, *Revista de História*,Vol. 11, No. 19 (2009).
32 *1628. Carta Annua del Guayra por el Pe*, 352–6.
33 *1628. Carta Annua del Guayra por el Pe*, 352.
34 *1628. Carta Annua del Guayra por el Pe*, 355.
35 *1628. Carta Annua del Guayra por el Pe*, 357.
36 Antonio Ruiz de Montoya, *Conquista espiritual hecha por los religiosos de la Compañía de Jesús en las provincias del Paraguay, Paraná, Uruguay y Tape* (Madrid, 1639) (Bilbao: Corazón de Jesús, 1892), 40.
37 Montoya, *Conquista espiritual*, 221.
38 Bartomeu Melià, *El Paraguay Inventado* (Asunción: CEPAG, 1997), 105.
39 Melià, *El Paraguay Inventado*, 105.
40 Melià, *El Paraguay Inventado*, 105.
41 Melià, *El Paraguay Inventado*, 106.
42 Although this notion is widely known, it does not apply to all Guarani groups. In fact it is denied by the Mbyá, for instance (Interview with Melià, "A história de um guarani é a história de suas palavras").
43 Ivory Garlet, *Mobilidade Mbyá: História e Significação*, Dissertation (Porto Alegre: PUCRS, 1997).
44 A notion coined by Heléne Clastres, *The Land-without-Evil: Tupí-Guaraní Prophetism*. (Urbana, IL: University of Illinois Press, 1995).

45 Montoya, *Conquista espiritual*, 35.
46 Jean Baptista (2004, 70) demonstrated that among the Paraguayan populations, the natural world is conceived of as the very "means to exist, from where the myths are collected, the rules, and institutions are formed, and the pathways of life are walked."
47 AlthoughViveiros de Castro analyzes the Amazonian groups, there are plenty of references in his article to other works of ethnohistories—EduardoViveiros de Castro, "Cosmological Deities and Amerindian Perspectivism." *The Journal of the Royal Anthropological Institute* 4, 3 (September 1998), 469–488.
48 Let's not forget the value of cross-referencing sources to look at indigenous history since Harris' groundbreaking work on indigenous perspectives about the theme of the "discovery/arrival" of Spaniards in the Americas ("The Coming of the White People." Reflections on the Mythologisation of History in Latin America").
49 Besides the Nimuendajú's texts published in English in volumes 1 and 3 of the *Handbook of South American Indians* (1946–1959), more references can be found in Curt Nimuendajú, *As lendas da criação e distruição do mundo como fundamentos da religião dos Apapocúva-Guaraní* (São Paulo: Editora HUCITEC: Editora da Universidade de São Paulo, 1987).
50 Susnik B., "El hombre y lo sobrenatural," *Las Culturas Condenadas*, Augusto Roa Bastos (ed.) (Siglo XXI, Colección América Nuestra, México,1980), 136.
51 Montoya, *Conquista espiritual*, 24. Another interesting note refers to the ingestion of the vipers' liver mixed well with food, and apparently capable of saving the lives of those poisoned by vipers' bites.
52 "El hombre y lo sobrenatural," 136.
53 Jean Baptista, 2004, 73.
54 Montoya, *Conquista espiritual*, 25.
55 Western narratives would often purposefully portray Indigenous people as lacking any skills, making this source even greater in relevance.
56 Cadogan (*Ayvu Rapyta: Textos míticos de los Mbyá-Guaraní del Guairá*, São Paulo: Universidade de São Paulo, 1992, 119–136) had collected myths among the Mbyá-Guarani. Of special interest is one that refers to the twin brothers Kuaray and Jasy, who were raised by jaguars that had killed their mother. Upon discovering that fact, they avenge her death by killing all the jaguars in the world, except for one female jaguar pregnant with a male with whom she eventually breeds—hence the existence of other jaguars in the world. Kuaray curses the surviving jaguars making them all lose their "human appearance," reappearing in the known animal form. Humans learn how to survive in the forest with the jaguars, but as enemies, due to this traditional rupture between these cultures. Baptista (2004, 64) analyzes the myths and explains that the remaining jaguars end up becoming rival tribes with whom the Guarani engage in war, which partially explains why hunting and or killing a jaguar is so often recorded by both colonial sources as well as contemporary ethnographies.
57 An annual letter dated 1627 from the reduction of Iguaçú (MCA,Vianna, 67), retells how the Jesuits built a trap to hunt down a jaguar who had attacked a child at the mission. The trap worked, and the missionaries boast of acquiring the "fame of being killers of tigers," recognizing the importance of such a feat for effective group leadership. Jean Baptista (2004, 66) suggests that the missionaries were immersed in the Guarani world since they avenged the original history of the cultural heroes—the twin brothers.
58 Besides the aforementioned annual letter, there is another interesting reference dated 1633 that was authored by padre Pedro Romero (MCA, Cortesão, 42–3) who narrates a similar plot of trapping a jaguar by orchestrating with relatives of the jaguar's victims.
59 It is important to note that among the Kaingang people, the same animal reflects the group's being (Niumuendajú 1993, 72), while the Guarani see the jaguar as a horrible being, their historical enemy. The Kaingang are the jaguars, essentially.
60 Montoya, *Conquista espiritual*, 55.
61 Many traps are similar to hunt different animals such as pigs and deer (MCA, Cortesão,Tape, 81), and the tapirs' case described here.
62 Montoya, *Conquista espiritual*, 26–7.
63 Montoya, *Conquista espiritual*, 56. Another similar case of the presence of an animal and a resulting death was mentioned concerning frogs. To talk about this other superstition, Montoya recounts a time when they were aboard a vessel that carried frogs that could be heard for two days, making the Indians search for the animals due to their fear of their death. Although reported by Montoya as an unrelated matter, four Indians aboard these vessels died after the fact.
64 Montoya, *Conquista espiritual*, 57.
65 Montoya (*Conquista espiritual*, 45) compared the yerba with the tea from China since both are stimulating drinks that awake the one who drinks it, as well as with the coca leaves in Peru.

66 Montoya, *Conquista espiritual*, 99.
67 Montoya, *Conquista espiritual*, 51–2.
68 Montoya, *Conquista espiritual*, 216–7.
69 Montoya, *Conquista espiritual*, 208–11.
70 In many cases, the Jesuits would have to deal with wizards even before they died, due to the worship of the remains of famous wizards, which were sometimes worshiped within the church itself. Such was the case of four bodies and bones that had "been revered in the church," recorded by Montoya (*Conquista espiritual*, 117–122). Additionally, Sarreal (2015, 37) tells us that the Jesuits worked hard to "suppress the shaman" figures.
71 Montoya, *Conquista espiritual*, 200–1.
72 Montoya, *Conquista espiritual*, 187–8.
73 As Sarreal (2014, 56) reminds us that the "Guarani generally joined a mission as a part of a cacicazgo led by a cacique."
74 Jesuits gave the caciques the titles of "Don" (Sarreal 2014, 56).
75 Sarreal, 54.
76 Montoya acknowledges that each cacique converted represents a great possibility to convert more Indians, for instance, the great cacique Tayaoba, governor of the province with the same name, was leading several indigenous groups (Montoya, *Conquista espiritual*, 123–7 and 128–31).
77 These obligations and privileges were distinct in the Guarani mission and elsewhere in Latin America (Sarreal 2014, 56).
78 Montoya, *Conquista espiritual*, 94–5.
79 Montoya, *Conquista espiritual*, 55–6.
80 Montoya, *Conquista spiritual*, 55–6.
81 This was especially true of caciques and sorcerers, and if not observed was considered a "misfortune" (*Conquista espiritual*, 99).
82 There are several references in contemporary ethnographic works that suggest eloquence as one necessary trait of caciques (Schaden, *Aspectos Fundamentais*, and Melià, *Conquistado y Reducido*), especially in colonial sources such as Montoya's writings. For instance, there is a reference about a cacique who makes a "rather eloquent speech" and thus saves the missionaries from dying in the hands of the Indians during their arrival to the village that would later become San Francisco Xavier (*Conquista espiritual*, 96).
83 Montoya, *Conquista espiritual*, 59–61.
84 Montoya, *Conquista espiritual*, 62.
85 Montoya, *Conquista espiritual*, 65.
86 Montoya, *Conquista espiritual*, 92–3.
87 Montoya, *Conquista espiritual*, 77.
88 Both polygamy and adultery continued up to the 18th century (Wilde, *Religión y Poder*, 133).
89 Montoya, *Conquista espiritual*, 74–5.
90 Montoya, *Conquista espiritual*, 46.
91 Notion coined by many other missionaries, including classics works like Bartolomé De Las Casas, *The Destruction of the Indies* (New York: Penguin Classics, 1992).
92 *The Destruction of the Indies*, 41–45.
93 There are records of armed Guarani populations defending the missions dated 1639, yet only the Jesuits received firearms in 1647, and the Guarani militias became the king's militias in 1649 (Sarreal 2014, 33).
94 David J. Weber, *Bárbaros: Spaniards and their Savages in the Age of Enlightenment* (New Haven, CT: Yale University Press, 2005).
95 Brooks, *Captives & Cousins*, 72–79; Pekka Hämäläinen, *Comanche Empire* (New Haven, CT: Yale University Press, 2008).
96 Alfred Barnaby Thomas, trans., *Teodoro de Croix and the Northern Frontier of New Spain, 1776–1783* (Norman, OK: University of Oklahoma Press, 1941).
97 Brooks, *Captives & Cousins*, 67–69.
98 Brooks, *Captives & Cousins*, 68.

References

Alfred, Gerald Taiaiake. *Wasáse: Indigenous Pathways of Action and Freedom* (Peterborough, ON: University of Toronto Press, 2005).
Anderson, Benedict. *Imagined Communities: Reflections on the Origin and Spread of Nationalism* (New York: Verso, 2006).

Baptista, Jean. "A visibilidade étnica nos registros coloniais: missões Guaranis ou Missões Indígenas?" *Povos Indígenas: coleção História Geral do Rio Grande do Sul.*, 1 ed., (Passo Fundo: Meritos, 2009),Vol. 5, 207.
Barr, Juliana. *Peace Came in the Form of a Woman: Indians and Spaniards in the Texas Borderlands* (Chapel Hill, NC: University of North Carolina Press, 2007).
Besire, Lucas. *Behold the Black Caiman: A Chronicle of Ayoreo Life* (Chicago, IL: University of Chicago Press, 2014).
Brooks, James F. *Captives and Cousins*, (Chapel Hill, NC: University of North Carolina Press, 2002).
Cabeza de Vaca, Álvar Núñez. *The Narrative of Cabeza De Vaca*, Translation of *La Relación*, eds. Rolena Adorno and Patrick Charles Pautz. (Lincoln, NE: University of Nebraska Press, 2003).
Cadogan, L. "Ayvu Rapyta: Textos míticos de los Mbyá-Guaraní del Guairá," (*Revista de Antropoligia* Vol. 1, no. 2: 123–132.
Campbell, Lyle, ed., *The World of Linguistics: Volume 2: The Indigenous Languages of South America A Comprehensive Guide* (Berlin: De Gruyter, 2012).
Chamorro, Graciela. *Decir el Cuerpo: Historia y Etnografía del Cuerpo de los Pueblos Guarani* (Asunción: Tiempo de Historia, 2009).
Chamorro, Graciela. "Antonio Ruiz de Montoya: promotor y defensor de las lenguas indígenas," *História* 11, 2 (2007): 252–260.
Clastres, Helené. *The Land-Without-Evil: Tupí-Guaraní Prophetism* (Urbana, IL: University of Illinois Press, 1995).
de Anchieta, José. *Arte de Grammatica da Língua mais visada na costa Brasil* (Coimbra, Portugal: Antonio de Mariz, 1595).
de Montoya, Antonio Ruiz. *Tesoro de la Lengua Guarani* (Madrid: Juan Sanchez, 1639).
de Montoya, Antonio Ruiz. *Catecismo de la Lengua Guarani* (Madrid: Diego Diaz de Carrera, 1639).
de Montoya, Antonio Ruiz. *Arte y Bocabulario de la Lengua Guarani* (Madrid: Juan Sanchez).
Diaz Polanco, Hector. *Indigenous Peoples in Latin America: The Quest for Self-determination.* Translated by Lucía Rayas (Boulder, CO: Westview Press, 1997).
Ganson, Barbara Anne. *The Guaraní under Spanish Rule in the Río De La Plata* (Stanford, CA: Stanford University Press, 2003).
Garlet, Ivory. *Mobilidade Mbyá: História e Significação*, (Dissertation, PUCRS, 1997).
Gordillo, Gaston. *Rubble: The Afterlife of Destruction* (Durham and London: Duke University Press, 2014).
Hämäläinen, Pekka. *Comanche Empire*, (New Haven, CT: Yale University Press 2008).
Harris, Olivia. "'The Coming of the White People': Reflections on the Mythologisation of History in Latin America," *Bulletin of Latin American Research* 14 (1995): 9–24.
Haubert, Maxime. *La Vie Quotidienne Des Indiens Et Des Jésuites Du Paraguay Au Temps Des Missions* (Paris: Hachette, 1986).
Lambert, Peter, and José Manuel Peramás. *The Paraguay Reader: History, Culture, Politics* (Durham and London: Duke University Press, 2013).
Melià, Bartomeu. *El Guaraní Conquistado Y Reducido: Ensayos De Etnohistoria.* (Asunción: Centro De Estudios Antropológicos, Universidad Católica, 1986).
Melià, Bartomeu and Graciela Chamorro. *Decir el Cuerpo: Historia y Etnografía del Cuerpo de los Pueblos Guarani* (Asunción: Tiempo de Historia, 2009).
Melià, Bartomeu. *El Paraguay Inventado* (Asunción: CEPAG, 1997).
de Montoya, Antonio Ruiz. *Conquista espiritual hecha por los religiosos de la Compañía de Jesús en las provincias del Paraguay, Paraná, Uruguay y Tape* (Madrid, 1639) (Bilbao: Corazón de Jesús, 1892).
Melià, Bartomeu. *La Lengua Guarani en el Paraguay Colonial* (Asunción: CEADUC, 2003).
Nimuendajú, Curt. *As lendas da criação e distruição do mundo como fundamentos da religião dos Apapocúva-Guaraní* (São Paulo: Editora HUCITEC: Editora da Universidade de São Paulo, 1987).
Pratt, Mary Louise. "Arts of the Contact Zone," *Profession*, 1991, 33–40. Available online at www.jstor.org/stable/25595469
Pratt, Mary Louise. *Imperial Eyes: Travel Writing and Transculturation* (London: Routledge, 1992).
Reséndez, Andrés. *A Land So Strange: The Epic Journey of Cabeza de Vaca* (New York: Basic Books, 2007).
Restall, Matthew, Lisa Sousa, and Kevin Terraciano. *Mesoamerican Voices: Native Language From Colonial Mexico, Oaxaca, Yucatan, and Guatemala* (Cambridge: Cambridge University Press, 2005).
Ricard, Robert. "Ethnographic and the Linguistic Training of the Missionaries," *The Spiritual Conquest of Mexico; an Essay on the Apostolate and the Evangelizing Methods of the Mendicant Orders in* New Spain, *1523–1572* (Berkeley, CA: University of California Press, 1966).

Santos, Maria Cristina dos and Baptista, Jean. "Reduções Jesuíticas e Povoados de Índios: Controvérsias Sobre a População Indígena (séc XVII–XVIII)," *Historia* 11[2] (2007).

Sarreal, Julia. J.S. *The Guarani and Their Missions*, (Stanford: Stanford University Press, 2014).

Thomas, Alfred Barnaby, trans., *Teodoro de Croix and the Northern Frontier of New Spain, 1776–1783* (Norman, OK: University of Oklahoma Press, 1941).

Tuhiwai-Smith, Linda. *Decolonizing Methodologies: Research and Indigenous Peoples* (London: Zed Books, 1999).

Viveiros de Castro, Eduardo. "Cosmological Deities and Amerindian Perspectivism." *The Journal of the Royal Anthropological Institute* 4[3] (September 1998): 469–488.

Weber, David J. *Bárbaros: Spaniards and Their Savages in the Age of Enlightenment* (New Haven, CT: Yale University Press 2005).

White, Richard. *The Middle Ground: Indians, Empires, and Republics in the Great Lakes* Region, *1650–1815* (Cambridge: Cambridge University Press, 1991).

Wilde, Guillermo. "De las crónicas jesuíticas a las 'etnografías estatales': realidades y ficciones del orden misional en las fronteras ibéricas," *Nuevo Mundo Mundos Nuevos* [En ligne], Débats, mis en ligne le 30 novembre 2011, consulté le 27 septembre 2015. Available online at http://nuevomundo.revues.org/62238; DOI:10.4000/nuevomundo.62238

Wilde, Guillermo. "Territorios y Etnogénesis Misional en el Paraguay Del Siglo XVIII," *Revista de História*, Vol. 11, No. 19 (2009): 83–106.

Wilde, Guillermo. *Religion y Poder cu los Misiones Guaranias* (Buenos Aires: Sb. Editorial, 2016).

PART II

Unfree Labor

4
LABOR, EMPIRE, AND THE STATE
The English Imperial Experience in the Seventeenth Century

Abigail L. Swingen

According to the usual story of European exploration and colonization of the Americas, England was a latecomer. The English did not get seriously involved with overseas settlement and colonial exploitation until the late 1500s, nearly 100 years after the Spanish and the Portuguese. In large part, it was jealousy of Iberian wealth and power that eventually pushed the English to seek their own fortunes across the Atlantic.[1] England's initial attempts at settlement did not provide an auspicious beginning, as any scholar of the Roanoke colony can attest. However, despite their "lateness" to the transatlantic imperial game, the English, once they had established successful permanent colonies in the Americas, made up for lost time. Within three decades of the settlement in the colony of Virginia in 1607, the English had permanent settlements throughout New England and the Chesapeake regions of North America and had established growing colonies in the Leeward Islands and Barbados in the eastern Caribbean. Even more remarkably, within a few decades of these developments, the English controlled an immensely profitable transatlantic empire made up of dozens of colonies worked by thousands of coerced laborers, including indentured servants, convicts, and most notably, enslaved Africans. By the turn of the eighteenth century, the English dominated the transatlantic slave trade that provided labor not only to England's colonies, but also to the colonies of other European powers.

This essay explores how and why this happened. In the traditional historical narrative, it tends to be emphasized that early English colonial ventures were designed by religious zealots who hoped to create new Christian societies or freebooting adventurers and maverick merchants and planters who were out for quick profits with little regard for long-term settlement. In this telling, the role of the English state tends to be downplayed or outright ignored. In addition, the development of permanent colonial settlements and the growth of trade in colonial commodities, not to mention servants and slaves, tend to be understood as somewhat accidental. This essay will argue, however, that within a few decades of the establishment of these initial "freebooting" colonial enterprises, the English state inserted itself into colonial affairs and began to develop and articulate a clear imperial agenda. It will also argue that this was a deliberate development, and that a significant reason why the English government got involved with imperial expansion and attempts at regulating colonial trade and governance had to do with transformations in the kinds of labor that were used in the colonies. By the second half of the seventeenth century, the English government espoused a vision of empire that embraced the expansion of colonial settlements, especially those that promoted England's involvement in the transatlantic slave trade from West Africa to the Americas. In addition, the labor regimes established in so many English colonies supported, and were in turn supported by, imperial structures and agendas emerging from the metropolis as well as the colonies.[2]

Part One: The Problem of Labor

In order for colonial settlements, even temporary ones, to work effectively they had to have adequate supplies of labor. This was one of the first problems that faced all European colonies in the Americas, and the English were no exception. Land had to be cleared, shelters had to be built, crops had to be grown for both food and profit, and ships had to be maintained and secured. The story of the Virginia colony's precarious beginnings in the early seventeenth century is a largely familiar one. Roughly 600 men attempted to settle a new colony along the James River in 1607 and within a few years nearly 90 percent of them had perished because of disease, problems of food distribution, and the fact that most of the men who were sent to Jamestown were better prepared for military expeditions than the difficult task of planting a new colony in the American wilderness.[3] But still, settlers continued to come from England, lured by the promises of cheap, abundant land by the Virginia Company, which had been granted a monopoly by King James I on settlement and trade in North America.

What transformed Virginia, of course, was the cultivation of tobacco, which by 1618 made the issue of labor shortages all the more acute. The following year, the Virginia Company under the leadership of Governor Sir Edwin Sandys established a program of sending indentured servants from England, who were either bound to Company lands to work directly or sold to private merchants and planters for a set period of years in exchange for the cost of their transatlantic voyage. In the past, individual settlers had to supply their own laborers. This new system of indentured service corresponded with the early "boom" years of tobacco cultivation, as the English developed a widespread taste for smoking and chewing the exotic plant. This resulted in the creation of a new, brutal labor regime of indentured servitude that swallowed nearly 4,000 people by the early 1620s, including men, women, and children. Most died in the harsh circumstances of an unfamiliar climate, New World diseases, as well as work. The brutality and violence of this regime, in which powerful planters attempted to accumulate as much land and as many laborers as possible with little regard for the long-term consequences, according to Edmund Morgan, laid the foundations for the later acceptance of slavery by North American colonists.[4]

There were two elements that sustained this indentured servant trade that lasted the remainder of the century. The first was a widespread perception that there were too many poor and unemployed people in England and that sending such groups to work in the colonies was a good way to relieve England of its responsibility to care and feed for such people. As a number of historians have shown, this reflected a certain level of reality: England's population grew steadily in the late sixteenth and early seventeenth centuries from roughly 2.8 million in 1541 to approximately 5.1 million a century later.[5] This idea that England had too many of the wrong sorts of people filtered its way into literature encouraging colonization, Virginia in particular. One pamphlet promoting the new colony written in 1609 stated that England was "abounding with swarms of sole persons, which having no means of labour to relieve their misery, do likewise swarm in lewd and naughty practices." To ease these dangerous burdens, urged another pamphlet, England should orchestrate "the transporting of their overflowing multitude into *Virginia*."[6] It is debatable just how much England's unemployed population actually grew in relation to the rest of the populace. But as cities such as London in particular seemed to attract large numbers of these undesirables, the perception was certainly widespread that England had a problem of too many of the wrong sorts of people.[7] The idea that more poor people could always be found in England to labor in the colonies helped create and sustain a violent labor regime that often worked people to death before the end of their terms of service.

The second component that made this labor system function was the participation of a number of colonial merchants who were willing and able to send servants from England to the Chesapeake region and then return to England with cargoes of tobacco and other colonial products. Perhaps most well known was Maurice Thomson, who came to Virginia in 1617 and within a few years not only owned a substantial tobacco farm, but busied himself organizing shiploads of servants from England on behalf of the Virginia Company and eventually on his own. Along with a handful of other colonial merchants such as Martin Noell and Thomas Combes, Thomson was at the forefront of English colonial efforts in the West Indies as well, investing in new plantations in the Leeward Islands and Barbados as early as the 1620s and developing the indentured servant trade to these new colonies.[8] According to historian Hilary Beckles, by the 1630s, between 800 and 1,000 people a year left London for Barbados as indentured servants. By and large these servants were young, male, had probably moved within England, and had some work experience before venturing across the Atlantic. In Barbados they performed a variety of tasks, particularly clearing land and cultivating a variety of crops, including tobacco, indigo, and cotton.[9]

By the middle decades of the seventeenth century, this pattern began to change with the major agricultural transition to the widespread cultivation of sugarcane, first in Barbados and then Antigua in the Leeward Islands. Sugarcane grew well in the Caribbean soil and was in high demand throughout Europe, a market the English hoped to profit from. As a result, English planters in Barbados during the middle decades of the 1600s began turning away from growing other crops and embraced cultivating sugarcane. Growing sugarcane is extremely labor intensive, especially when compared to other cash crops such as tobacco. It requires more time to grow (about 18 months), must be tended to carefully, and timing is of the utmost importance for the cane to be properly harvested and processed. In addition, in order to be profitable, large tracts of land must be devoted to growing the plant. According to one contemporary observer, almost as soon as planters in Barbados turned to growing sugarcane, they began to consolidate their holdings into larger and larger plantations.[10] In addition, planters demanded increasing numbers of laborers to perform these monotonous and often hazardous tasks. One planter who was also a merchant in Barbados, Martin Noell, took advantage of these changes and not only exploited the indentured servant trade, but along with his brothers invested in a number of sugar plantations on the island. In addition, he and his brothers, along with their business associate Maurice Thomson, were at the forefront of delivering another source of coerced labor to West Indies colonies: enslaved Africans. By the end of the 1650s, there were at least 20,000 slaves on the island.[11]

The transition to growing sugarcane and using enslaved Africans as a major source of labor in Barbados did not stem entirely from labor demand in the colonies. It was intimately related to significant political and social upheaval in England. The English Civil War (1642–49), for example, disrupted trade with the home country and made it extremely difficult if not impossible for colonial merchants to deliver the numbers of indentured servants demanded by planters. Not only did war make migration of any kind less likely, historical demographers have noted that by the middle of the 1600s, England's population actually declined, from roughly 5.3 million to about 4.9 million people.[12] This made voluntary emigration from England far less likely as well, because it resulted in higher wages at home for those looking for work, particularly in growing urban areas.[13] As a result, just as demand for labor picked up in Barbados and the Leeward Islands, colonial merchants were unable to meet that demand by relying solely on English servants.

Part Two: Midcentury Turning Point

At this point, the English government was largely out of the picture in terms of direct involvement with colonial settlement and supplying labor to new colonies in the Americas. The Crown had of course usually sanctioned these colonization efforts, either through the granting of a charter to a company (such as the Virginia Company, which was defunct by 1624) or by giving permission to an individual or group of individuals to settle a particular area (such as in the case of Barbados, which had been granted to James Hay, Earl of Carlisle, in a shady deal with King Charles I in 1629). The most direct involvement the English government had in supplying any form of labor to the colonies during the first half of the seventeenth century was in the form of transporting convicts and political prisoners as a form of punishment. From the earliest settlement of Virginia, small numbers of prisoners were sent as bound laborers, often on the orders of the Crown. For example, James I in 1614 granted his Privy Council the authority to sentence convicted felons to transportation to Virginia as a means to ease swelling prisons as well as to provide much-needed labor.[14] But generally speaking in terms of promotion, settlement, resource extraction, and transporting labor to these colonies, the English government was not heavily involved during the first half of the seventeenth century.

This began to change dramatically by the 1650s, when the English state began to develop a systematic imperial agenda, which included providing labor to its growing overseas empire. At the end of the English Civil War in early 1649, King Charles I was put on trial, executed, and the monarchy was abolished. England officially became a republic. Under the leadership of the successful army general Oliver Cromwell, England embarked on an ambitious plan of imperial expansion, beginning first with the conquest and subjugation of Ireland and later Scotland.[15] Cromwell and his allies also had a plan for expanding England's overseas colonies by conquering New World possessions from the Spanish. Cromwell was a notorious anti-Catholic and wanted nothing more than to bring what he perceived to be Europe's biggest Catholic threat to heal by severely diminishing its access to its abundant American wealth.[16]

This agenda was orchestrated and supported not only by Cromwell, but also by a group of colonial merchants who shared his religious prejudices but more importantly had been involved in transatlantic trade in some cases for decades. They felt Spain maintained an unfair advantage in terms of New World trade and colonization, and now that the Civil War was over they wanted to return to expanding their market share in servants and slaves across the Atlantic. This group included such familiar names as Maurice Thomson and Martin Noell; their associates, the merchants and naval captains Henry Hatsell and William Limbery; Secretary of State John Thurloe, who was Noell's brother-in-law; and the colonial merchant William Pennoyer.[17] In 1654, they were appointed to an official planning committee that convinced Cromwell that it was both necessary and realistic to attack and conquer Spanish American territory. This plan, which the government attempted to keep secret, was known as the "Western Design." They appointed two military leaders who had cut their teeth in the Irish conquest, General Robert Venables and General William Penn, to lead the army and navy, respectively.[18]

Venables and Penn and the other officers in charge of the expedition first chose to head to Hispaniola (modern-day Haiti and the Dominican Republic) to attack the city of Santo Domingo. The expedition soon turned into a disaster. After declaring martial law in Barbados and the Leeward Islands in order to recruit more soldiers and sailors without consequence (and meeting a fair amount of resistance from Barbados planters in particular), in April 1655 the fleet set out for Santo Domingo. They landed, however, nearly 30 miles from the city, forcing the poorly trained and ill-equipped regiments to march for days in unforgiving and unfamiliar terrain without adequate food, water, or supplies. According to one contemporary source, nearly

1,000 men died within a few weeks of the landing. Realizing that the conquest of Hispaniola was impossible, Venables and Penn and their fellow commissioners called a war council where they decided to aim for a smaller piece of territory, preferably one without many inhabitants. By the end of April they had landed on Jamaica, located at the center of the Caribbean Sea, and easily took the island from its few hundred residents, including Spanish colonists, enslaved Africans, and escaped former slaves, known as "Maroons."[19]

To many contemporaries the conquest of Jamaica from the Spanish was considered a significant failure. When news of the disaster at Santo Domingo reached England later that summer, Oliver Cromwell reportedly became despondent and convinced himself that the failure was an indication of God's wrath for English sinfulness.[20] News reports and pamphlets circulating in England were highly critical of the expedition, and often placed the blame on Venables and Penn and their failure to properly train and control their men, who were seen as nothing better than "raw Soldiers, Vagabonds, Robbers, and runagate servants."[21] As a result of this string of failures and disappointments, the Western Design and the conquest of Jamaica are often interpreted by historians to be unimportant and only accidentally imperial.[22] But however much Cromwell and his allies might have been disappointed with the conquest of Jamaica, the Western Design had imperial implications and significant long-term consequences. As noted above, before this time, England's colonial projects in the Americas had primarily been orchestrated by groups of individuals or chartered companies, and did not indicate a coherent or cohesive imperial agenda on the part of the government. This changed significantly during the 1650s. The English Commonwealth and Protectorate accomplished more in terms of imperial consolidation and administration than any previous English government had, beginning with the creation of a united Britain that incorporated Ireland and Scotland.[23] And although the plan to capture Hispaniola from the Spanish was a failure, almost immediately Cromwell's merchant allies in London as well as the officers on the ground in Jamaica began to promote the island's commercial as well as military potential, and understood the conquest of Jamaica as a possible new imperial direction for the regime. Observers and critics of the Protectorate government understood both the Western Design in general and the taking of Jamaica in particular as imperial in nature. Some critics even remarked that it was a clear step in the direction of returning to a monarchical form of government, with Cromwell as king or emperor.[24] In fact, rather than abandoning the mission, Cromwell emerged from his despondency in August 1655 and began promoting the settlement of Jamaica with people from England, Ireland, and Scotland as well as from other overseas colonies including Bermuda, the Leeward Islands, and Massachusetts Bay.[25] In addition, beginning in the 1650s, significant numbers of both Irish and Scottish war prisoners were sent to the English colonies in the wake of Cromwell's wars of conquest in those countries. Often colonial merchants familiar with transporting servants, including Martin Noell, were given contracts by the government to deliver such prisoners.[26]

Protectorate imperialism, however, had its limitations. Throughout the late 1650s, Cromwell's merchant allies, some of whom including Noell and his associate Thomas Povey, had been appointed to a committee to oversee the administration of Jamaica, grew increasingly frustrated with what they understood to be a lack of serious effort on the part of the government to promote Jamaica. The government in fact rejected a bold plan on the part of these men to create a joint-stock West India Company, which would have promoted England's commercial interests in the Caribbean at the expense of the Spanish through privateering raids. In addition, the company's projectors, merchants with much experience of the servant trade, proposed that the new company could be charged with sending servants from the hordes of "vagabonds, beggars or condemned persons [in England], & proceed with them to Jamaica."[27] The backers of this scheme hoped that with adequate state support, Jamaica could begin to thrive as a plantation colony much like Barbados and Virginia, and on a much bigger scale. In the end, however, this proposal never got off the ground because of political upheaval in the wake of Oliver Cromwell's death in late 1658. Indeed, despite numerous proclamations and "encouragements," by the end of the decade Jamaica did seem to be languishing from a lack of sustained support from the English government, with only 3,500 total inhabitants, including military officers, privateers, a handful of planters, and about 500 enslaved Africans. Men like Noell and Povey hoped that the demise of the Protectorate might serve as an opportunity to strengthen England's imperial agenda and preserve Jamaica as a worthwhile conquest.

Part Three: The Royal African Company, Colonial Labor as an Interest of the English State

In the spring of 1660, after another year of failed republican governments, the monarchy was restored. King Charles II returned to England amidst widespread celebrations across the country. Within a few months, the king's imperial agenda began to emerge when his government announced two major initiatives. In December 1660, Charles II issued a royal charter creating a new joint-stock trading company, called the "Company of Royal Adventurers into Africa." It was founded by the king's brother, the Duke of York, and his cousin, Prince Rupert of the Palatinate, along with a long list of well-connected courtiers. The company, which had a monopoly on all trade to and from the western coast of Africa, also counted a number of colonial merchants and planters among its founding subscribers, including Martin Noell, Thomas Povey, and others with colonial connections, such as John Colleton, whose brother Peter owned a large sugar plantation in Barbados.[28] There was no explicit mention of the slave trade in the company's first charter, but there is evidence to suggest that those who supported the new undertaking hoped to move the company in that direction. Another subscriber, for example, was Sir Nicholas Crispe, who had worked as a slave trader for decades. In addition, James Ley, third Earl of Marlborough, a naval officer and prominent member of the Council of Trade, the administrative body charged with advising the king on issues of overseas and colonial trade, suggested in a public proposal that the new company could be used to provide enslaved Africans to serve as laborers in Jamaica.[29]

The creation of the African Company was intimately connected to the second initiative that was a key element of the restored monarchy's emerging imperial agenda. The same month that Charles II announced the creation of the African Company, his government also announced its intention to hold onto the colony of Jamaica. Immediately following the Restoration, rumors spread across the Atlantic that the king would in fact return the island to the Spanish, but instead, perhaps convinced that Jamaica could be turned into another profitable sugar plantation colony worked by enslaved Africans, Charles II and his Privy Council chose to maintain the island. This might have owed something to the efforts of men like Noell and Povey, both of whom served on key committees charged with imperial affairs, the Council of Trade and the Council of Foreign Plantations. Together with other prominent merchants and others with colonial connections, they managed to convince the king of Jamaica's potential, and of the possibility for England to profit substantially from the transatlantic slave trade.[30]

The foundation of this African Company, the first of three chartered by Charles II, indicated that the Restoration governments wanted to profit from overseas trade to the colonies and specifically the transatlantic slave trade. Thus slavery and the slave trade were beginning to be understood as key elements of England's imperial designs. The rapid transformation and economic success of Barbados as a sugar and slave colony during the previous two decades served as an illustration of imperial possibilities for many. For example, by 1660, Barbados had a population of approximately 27,000 enslaved Africans; over the course of the decade, this number would increase to about 40,000.[31] There was hope that Jamaica, a much larger island than Barbados (over 4,400 square miles, compared to 166 square miles for Barbados) could become even more profitable through the development of sugar plantations, as well as through the production of other commodities. Colonists and military officers in charge of Jamaica also hoped to encourage the island's transition from a military outpost to a profitable plantation colony. In 1661, Colonel Edward D'Oyley along with the colony's governing council adopted a version of Barbados's slave and servant code, which had been codified the previous year. Although Jamaica had a population of only 500 slaves at this point, this was a clear indication that many hoped to transform the island using larger and larger numbers of enslaved Africans.[32] Dutch traders were also known to surreptitiously land cargoes of African slaves on the island in the early 1660s, indicating a growing demand for forced labor in Jamaica.[33]

The restored monarchy also continued to promote colonies as places where undesirable segments of the population, particularly common criminals and political troublemakers, could be sent for punishment and rehabilitation. Throughout the 1660s a number of laws aimed at religious nonconformists, especially Quakers, included automatic sentences of transportation to the colonies for those caught holding "conventicles" on more than one occasion. Historians of England's criminal justice system have also found that as the century progressed, more judges handed down sentences of transportation for certain crimes by granting convicts a pardon rather than a death sentence.[34] However, convict transportation never became a reliable source of colonial labor during the seventeenth century in large part because there was little systematic regulation of the trade. It was left up to individual merchants to find prisoners to send, and in turn they had to rely on the keepers of England's gaols who were often reluctant to hand over prisoners whose presence provided their income. This drove up the costs of transportation, as one merchant who attempted to bring prisoners as servants to the Leeward Islands lamented in 1682, "The keepers of the prisons oppose us, and must be bribed."[35] Merchants who brought prisoners to the colonies had to employ their own guards and supply their own restraints to move convicts from prisons to dockyards, which also diminished the profitability of the trade. In addition, colonies began to resist being seen as dumping grounds for England's undesirable populations by passing legislation banning the importation of prisoners as bound servants. Owing to these obstacles, it has been estimated that only about 4,500 convicts were sent to England's colonies as bound laborers between 1655 and 1699. This figure does not include war prisoners, who are more difficult to quantify, but it has been estimated that about 10,000 prisoners of war were sent to the colonies during the second half of the 1600s.[36] The system of convict transportation did not become better organized by the government until the passage of the Transportation Act of 1718/19, which gave an exclusive contract for delivering all prisoners to one London-based merchant. Expenses were paid directly by the Treasury.[37]

The Restoration governments, however, continued to promote the transatlantic slave trade. In addition to benefitting from selling enslaved Africans to English planters, merchants involved with the African Companies and the government that supported them, hoped to profit from selling slaves to Spanish merchants in the New World. The Spanish were not direct participants in the slave trade and instead relied on other European traders to supply their American plantations and mines with slave labor from Africa. The Spanish usually issued an exclusive contract, called the *asiento*, to a group of merchants or a trading company to provide them with slaves for a number of years. Unlike English planters, who lacked hard currency and relied heavily on credit to make their purchases, the Spanish could pay for slaves with the bullion thought to be overflowing from their silver and gold mines in Mexico and Peru. This was too tempting for the English Crown, always short of specie, to ignore. When the African Company was reorganized and issued a new royal charter in 1663 (in large part because of outstanding debts from planters and subscribers), one of its official goals was to gain access to the Spanish market for slaves. Almost immediately, the Company petitioned the king requesting permission to trade with the Spanish merchants directly in English colonies. This would require the king to grant special licenses to Spanish merchants, however, because the English Navigation Acts made trade with foreigners in the colonies illegal. The very same day he received this petition, Charles II issued special orders to the governor of Barbados indicating that he had to allow the Spanish to trade freely in the colony despite these laws. Shortly thereafter, he sent the same orders to the governor of Jamaica.[38] This was an indication that Charles II and his government hoped to reap the economic rewards of selling slaves to the Spanish, and also showed his full-scale support for the African Company and its imperial and commercial interests.

This desire to profit from selling slaves to the Spanish, however, put the African Company and the Crown in a difficult position throughout the 1660s. For example, this policy alienated planters who felt that the Company favored Spanish merchants and thus ignored the English planters' needs for coerced labor. In addition, attempting to encourage Spanish merchants to come and trade in English colonies, particularly Jamaica, angered another major colonial constituency, privateers. From its earliest days as an English colony, Jamaica had been a haven for buccaneers who took advantage of the island's location at the center of the Caribbean Sea to plunder ships and Spanish American ports.[39] But in 1663 when the African Company reorganized and adopted a policy of peaceful trade with the Spanish, privateers had to be reined in so Spanish merchants would feel safe coming into English colonial ports to trade. All subsequent governors of Jamaica were given orders to limit the activities of privateers during peacetime. Privateers, of course, usually paid little heed to these official policies and proclamations and regularly pursued their own agendas and continued to attack and plunder Spanish ships and ports, often with the tacit permission of colonial officials.[40] This limited the ability of the African Company to access the Spanish market throughout the 1660s, and bred significant resentment on the part of colonists in Jamaica regarding the Company's monopoly and agenda.

By the early 1670s, the African Company once again was in need of reorganization. The Second Anglo-Dutch War (1665–67) had left many of its outposts in West Africa in ruins and had disrupted its participation in the transatlantic slave trade.[41] Because of outstanding debts owed by planters and subscribers, the Company was dissolved and a new one chartered by Charles II in early 1672. This new Royal African Company was closely governed by the Duke of York and his allies. Its monopoly on all trade to and from West Africa was understood by the Company's backers as essential to ensure that profits made it to England at the expense of other nations. Traditionally, historians have presented the Company as doomed from its inception owing to structural weaknesses, perpetual financial woes, and the persistent success of illegal slave traders, or interlopers, who regularly bypassed the Company's monopoly in Africa and the American colonies. But in reality the Company was commercially successful throughout the 1670s and 1680s in relation to both Dutch slave traders as well as interlopers.[42] According to historian David Eltis, from 1672 to 1680 the Company brought approximately 26,266 slaves to the English West Indies colonies. This was impressive and represented about half of the 51,289 total slaves he estimates were delivered to Jamaica, Barbados, and the Leeward Islands during the same years. This increased to 53,663 during the 1680s, which was about 66 percent of the 81,039 enslaved Africans delivered to those colonies during that decade.[43] The Company was even in a powerful enough position to retaliate against those colonies where planters' debts were high by decreasing supplies of slaves. For example, in 1678 the Company's governing board passed a resolution stating, "That the supplyes of Negroes intended for Jamaica [should] be lessened in regard of the greate debt already owing to the Company in that Island."[44]

Over the course of the 1670s and 1680s, the Royal African Company became even more intertwined with Restoration imperial and political designs. Closely governed by the Duke of York, the Company represented the commercial interests of the Crown in the West Indies colonies. It also came to represent the political ideologies of the later Stuart monarchs and their governments, particularly the firm belief on the part of Charles II and his brother in the absolute authority of the royal prerogative. The Company's charter, granted at the pleasure of the Crown, was a manifestation of this ideology. In other words, the Company owed its existence to the royal prerogative. In addition, according to this ideology, the king held absolute authority over political, diplomatic, and commercial concerns, especially the governance of England's growing empire. This is something that many historians of the Restoration era have failed to recognize. Those who have considered Charles II and his government's imperial policies have tended to argue that it lacked coherence and merely represented the haphazard and chaotic responses of a government with consistent revenue shortages.[45] Looking at Restoration imperialism through the lens of the Royal African Company and England's interests in promoting the slave trade, however, provides a clearer sense of an underlying imperial agenda that emerged over the course of three decades. This agenda was based on profiting from the expansion of slavery and England's involvement in the transatlantic slave trade by promoting and extending the authority of the royal prerogative, and therefore the interests of the African Company, in colonies like Barbados, the Leeward Islands, and Jamaica.

One of the ways imperial authorities in London attempted to promote the interests of the African Company was by reprimanding and even firing colonial officials who failed to support the Company and Crown consistently and completely. For example, Sir Jonathan Atkins, the governor of Barbados for most of the 1670s, regularly confronted both Crown and Company authorities, which eventually lost him his job. In 1675, he authorized the Barbados assembly to petition Charles II with a series of grievances against the Company and its monopoly and he took it upon himself not only to frequently complain about the Company's authority, but to protest and criticize the Navigation Acts and other laws deemed essential for the functioning of the English empire. Both Atkins and the Barbados assembly faced severe written reprimands from the Lords of Trade, the administrative body charged with imperial affairs.[46] Atkins chose not to alter his behavior, however, and continued to ignore attempts on the part of imperial authorities to learn more about the state of affairs in Barbados. He dodged efforts on the part of the Lords of Trade to review the colony's laws for several years, to the point that when he finally sent the laws in 1679, imperial authorities in London were reluctant to trust their contents. He was finally dismissed from office in the summer of 1680. In a private letter to the governor of Jamaica, William Blathwayt, the chief secretary to the Lords of Trade, admitted that consistent complaints about Atkins on the part of the African Company and the Lords of Trade led to the governor's removal.[47]

The attempt on the part of the Lords of Trade to learn more about the laws of Barbados reflected a desire for greater centralization and control of colonial administration on the part of the English government. In general, authorities in London wanted to make sure that colonial laws did not contradict or conflict with English laws. Legal codes governing slaves, however, usually found little precedent in English law, and imperial authorities went to great lengths to better comprehend their place in colonial societies and the empire. Upon receiving the laws of Barbados from Governor Atkins in July 1679, the King-in-Council asked Samuel Baldwin, a lawyer for the Privy Council, to investigate and attest to their validity in relation to English law. The following year Baldwin issued a report in which he remarked that "some of the laws therein contained are not consonant to the Laws of England, as several laws in reference to Negro Slaves who for capital offences are not to be tried by jury, but summarily by two Justices of the Peace and three freeholders neare the place where the said offences are committed." But still he felt they were "reasonable laws," because slaves, "by reason of their numbers they become dangerous, and being a brutish sort of people & reckoned as goods and chattels in that island, it is of necessity or at least convenient to have laws for the government of them different from the laws of England, to prevent the great mischief that otherwise may happen to the planters and inhabitants in that island."[48] The Privy Council and the Lords of Trade agreed, and accepted Barbados's law code governing enslaved people in the colony, despite these obvious deviations from English legal precedent. This acceptance of Barbados's laws governing slaves revealed one of the multiple ways that the English state embraced and supported the development of slave societies in its colonies. What could have remained an area of disconnect and misunderstanding between colony and metropole instead gained legal sanction by the English government. The complete subjugation of slaves was increasingly understood as necessary in order for England and its colonies to profit from slave labor throughout the empire.

This investigation into the laws of Barbados in 1680 was representative of a desire on the part of the government to assert greater control over its colonies through the gathering of information.[49] One of the reasons behind this push for more information was related to growing criticisms at home concerning how colonies were governed and how they fit into the broader polity and economy. In addition to widespread resentment concerning the African Company's monopoly among colonial planters and merchants, beginning in the 1670s and 1680s, a number of economic and political writers in England expressed serious concerns not only about the commercial policies governing the empire, but also about the very existence of England's overseas colonies. For example, the polemicist William Petyt in 1680 lamented, "England was never so populous as it might have been, and undeniably must now be far less populous than ever, having so lately peopled our vast American Plantations." The economic writer Roger Coke admonished in 1670 that, "The Trade of England, and the Fishing Trade, are so much diminished, by how much they have been supplied by those men who are diverted in our American Plantations."[50] This represented a significant change in terms of early modern political economic thought. As we have seen, earlier in the century, colonies had been promoted as dumping grounds for dangerous and undesirable segments of the population. But for many commentators in the later seventeenth century, rather than relieving England of an overabundant population, colonies actually drained England of a precious economic resource: its people. This indicated an intellectual shift in how wealth and wealth creation were understood. Rather than being necessarily limited to tangible things such as land and bullion, and therefore beyond human control or creation, these thinkers instead embraced the idea that wealth could in fact be created by human labor. By this reasoning, England needed the largest possible workforce, and therefore the largest potential population, for infinite economic growth. Colonies, by attracting too many people from England, seemed to hinder this potential.

These ideas not only contributed to the turbulent political atmosphere of the late seventeenth century, but forced the government and others with colonial interests to vigorously defend the empire and the commercial and political interests it represented. Even the African Company got directly involved by trying to take advantage of these sentiments to defend its monopoly. In a pamphlet published in 1680 entitled *Certain Considerations Relating to the Royal African Company of England*, the author argued that because of the Company's involvement in the slave trade to the West Indies, it "hinders the exhausting this Nation of its natural born subjects."[51] In other words, the use of enslaved Africans in the colonies could offer a solution to the "problem" of empire outlined by these political economists.

Not surprisingly, the Royal African Company reached its apogee of power and influence over imperial affairs when its governor the Duke of York ascended the throne as James II in

1685. York had long envisioned a centralized and tightly controlled American empire that relied on slavery and the slave trade to bring profits to the English Crown.[52] The Company's power to seize interloping ships and cargoes, something that it had claimed since 1672 but had remained highly contested, became essentially codified in January 1685, about one month before York became king. The Court of King's Bench decision in the case *East India Company v. Sandys* not only decisively established the authority of the royal prerogative over overseas trade, but it provided clear legal justification for all joint-stock companies with royally granted charters, such as the East India and Royal African Companies, to seize the property of illegal traders because they were deemed to be acting within that prerogative authority.[53] It therefore became all the more necessary to ensure that colonial appointees were loyal to the Company and its interests. During his brief three-year reign, James II tried to ensure that men loyal to the Company and its monopoly were selected to positions of authority in the West Indies colonies. For example, in 1686, the king appointed Edwin Stede as lieutenant governor of Barbados. He had served as the African Company's chief agent on the island for over a decade, and throughout his tenure he remained committed to intercepting interloping slave traders on behalf of the Company, which won him many enemies among the ruling planter class in Barbados. Underscoring his devotion to James II, upon hearing of the king's removal from the throne in late 1688 by William of Orange, he remained hopeful that the "rightful" king would be restored.[54] Similarly, the king secured the appointment of Sir Nathaniel Johnson as governor-general of the Leeward Islands in 1686. Johnson was charged with overhauling that colony's government and purged a number of high-ranking officials from office, many of whom were planters who had been connected either directly or indirectly to the illegal slave trade. Like Stede, Johnson was dismayed at what became known as the "Glorious Revolution" and in 1689 he left his post and headed for Carolina to establish a plantation there.[55] Stede and Johnson were exactly the kind of imperial servants James II wanted running his empire: steadfastly loyal to the Crown and Company, and unwavering in their support for the Crown's imperial policies.

Part Four: Opening of the Slave Trade

Not unexpectedly, after James II's removal from the throne in late 1688, the Royal African Company's position at the center of imperial administration was in serious doubt. All charters that had been granted by the Stuart kings were brought under intense scrutiny, and the Company was no longer able to enforce its monopoly on sure legal footing. As a result, the transatlantic slave trade was effectively opened to all independent traders, many of whom of course had been trading illegally for decades. In addition, a 1689 decision at the King's Bench known as "Nightingale v. Bridges" effectually ended the Company's right to take the private property of suspected interlopers, meaning it could no longer seize the ships or cargoes of those selling slaves illegally.[56] Well aware of its precarious legal and commercial position, not to mention Parliament's new supremacy in the realm of overseas trade in the wake of the Glorious Revolution, the Company throughout the 1690s and early 1700s attempted to have its monopoly restored by an act of Parliament. The Company's directors organized petitioning campaigns and the publication of pamphlets and broadsides defending its monopoly. Enemies of the Company organized themselves as well and did their best to make sure the slave trade remained open, free from monopoly interference. Eventually this group came to be known as the "separate trader" interest.[57] Both sides engaged in a lively pamphlet war, in which the pro-Company position made clear the benefits of monopoly organization, as well as the necessity of maintaining property in the form of forts and castles along the western coast of Africa in order to safely conduct the slave trade. In contrast, the separate traders argued that England

and its colonies would see better profits from an open slave trade, either without any company interference or at least with a regulated rather than a closed joint-stock company. They also did their best to paint the Royal African Company to be a dangerous throwback to the worst of Stuart imperial designs, indelibly marked ideologically by its close relationship to the exiled king and his absolutist tendencies.[58]

These public debates revealed not only clear divisions over the best way to manage the slave trade, but also illustrated the ways in which the slave trade and African slavery in the colonies were imagined to be essential to England's imperial economy and polity by the turn of the eighteenth century. African slavery in the colonies was presented by all sides as a vital part of the imperial economy and a major reason why colonies benefited the entire realm. The Bristol merchant and longtime company critic John Cary, who wrote prolifically on domestic and overseas trade, wrote in 1695 that African slaves, "are the Hands whereby our Plantations are improved, and 'tis by their Labours such great Quantities of Sugar, Tobacco, Cotton, Ginger, and Indigo, are raised." He continued, "our Plantations are an Advantage to this Kingdom ... as they take off our Product and Manufactures, supply us with Commodities ... employ our Poor, and encourage our Navigation; for I take England and all its Plantations to be one great Body."[59] Similarly, another pamphlet declared, "It is well known, that the Riches of the Plantations consists in Slaves chiefly, by whose strength and labour all their Commodities, as Tobacco, Sugar, Cotton, Indigo, Ginger, &c. are produced; and the more Slaves those Plantations are supplyed with, the more Commodities are made."[60] What was remarkable about these debates was that they seemed to indicate a growing agreement that colonies with African slaves were not only beneficial to the imperial economy, but they were integral to it and that slavery was essential for the empire's existence. And of course by relying on enslaved Africans as their main source of labor, the West Indies colonies in particular relied less and less on the migration of people from England.

This was a vision of empire, with the transatlantic slave trade intimately connecting the metropolis to both West African and Caribbean colonies, that the English government wholeheartedly embraced by the 1690s. This was made clear by the fact that in addition to allowing the African Company's monopoly to remain in limbo, the government did not actively promote emigration from England to its overseas colonies. This was despite the fact that throughout the decade, because of the outbreak of the Nine Years' War with France, colonial officials regularly complained to imperial authorities that they desperately needed more white servants to fill their militias in case of foreign attack or slave revolt. Things became so desperate in Jamaica when the French attacked in 1694 that Governor William Beeston and his officers resorted to arming several hundred slaves to help defend the island.[61] But the government in London, too preoccupied with maintaining its own population to fill the armies and navies fighting in Europe, was not forthcoming with any assistance in this regard. For example, in 1696–97, Sir Gilbert Heathcote, a powerful colonial merchant and financier, attempted to send between 500 and 1,000 men to Jamaica, only to be thwarted by the Admiralty and the Board of Trade.[62] In addition, in 1689, Edward Thompson, MP from York, petitioned the new king for a patent on a national office for registering indentured servants. This office existed to make sure that those being sent as indentured servants to the colonies went of their own accord, or at least the accord of their parents or guardians. This effort to regulate the servant trade, however, revealed a certain level of ambivalence regarding early modern population management. This kind of registry served as a potential deterrent to merchants by adding additional fees and layers of bureaucracy to the process, making the servant trade less attractive than it might otherwise have been.[63] Although this attempt to revive a servants' registry in England proved unsuccessful, it provides a further indication that the English state by the 1690s was less interested in promoting the emigration of English people to the colonies, even during war, when those colonies were the most vulnerable.

Despite colonial fears of slave uprisings and foreign invasions, there were few concerted efforts on the part of imperial authorities to send more white servants to the colonies by the turn of the eighteenth century. In general, such endeavors were left up to individual merchants who ultimately had little incentive to provide servants to planters who demanded increasing numbers of African slaves. Indeed, even after the end of hostilities in 1697, when white servants once again began to arrive in small numbers in the West Indies colonies, planters by and large did not purchase their terms of service.[64] The total acceptance of the necessity of slave societies in the West Indies colonies, with all of the dangers they revealed, had spread to the metropolis by the turn of the eighteenth century. This in part helps to explain why despite the Royal African Company's best efforts, its monopoly was never reinstated by Parliament or the Crown. In fact an act passed in 1698 legally opened the slave trade to all merchants paying a 10% duty to the African Company on their goods shipped to Africa. However, this act was poorly enforced and was allowed to expire in 1712. What emerged in the wake of the Glorious Revolution in England was a broadly accepted idea that the empire was beneficial to the home country and that those colonies with slaves were particularly useful to the realm. By the turn of the eighteenth century, slavery in the colonies as well as England's participation in the slave trade came to be understood as key elements of empire that the state had a vested interest in supporting and promoting.

Notes

1 John Appleby, "War, Politics, and Colonization, 1558–1625," *Oxford History of the British Empire*. Vol. 1, *The Origins of Empire*, ed. Nicholas Canny (Oxford: Oxford University Press, 1998), 55–78.
2 For greater elaboration on many of the arguments in this essay, please see my book: Abigail L. Swingen, *Competing Visions of Empire: Labor, Slavery, and the Origins of the British Atlantic Empire* (New Haven: Yale University Press, 2015).
3 Edmund Morgan, "The Labor Problem at Jamestown, 1607–1618," *American Historical Review* 73[3] (June 1971): 595–611; Alison Games, *The Web of Empire: English Cosmopolitans in an Age of Expansion, 1560–1660* (New York: Oxford University Press, 2008), 127–131.
4 Edmund Morgan, "The First American Boom: Virginia 1618 to 1630," *William and Mary Quarterly*, 3rd series, 28[2] (April 1971): 170–198; Wesley Frank Craven, *Dissolution of the Virginia Company: The Failure of a Colonial Experiment* (New York: Oxford University Press, 1932), 96; David Souden, "'Rogues, Whores and Vagabonds'? Indentured Servant Emigrants to North America, and the Case of Mid-Seventeenth-Century Bristol," *Social History* 3[1] (January 1978): 23–41. On tobacco's allure in early modern Europe, see Marcy Norton, *Sacred Gifts, Profane Pleasures: A History of Tobacco and Chocolate in the Atlantic World* (Ithaca, NY: Cornell University Press, 2010).
5 E. A. Wrigley and R. S. Schofield, *The Population History of England, 1541–1870* (London: Edward Arnold, 1981), 208–209 (table 7.8).
6 *Nova Britannia: Offering Most Excellent fruites by Planting in Virginia* (London: Samuel Macham, 1609), D1r, D1v; Patrick Copland and Peter Pope, *Virginia's God be Thanked, or A Sermon of Thanksgiving for the Happie Successe of the Affayres in Virginia this Last Yeare* (London: J. D., 1622), 31.
7 Ted McCormick, "Population: Modes of Seventeenth-Century Demographic Thought," *Mercantilism Reimagined: Political Economy in Early Modern Britain and its Empire*, eds. Philip Stern and Carl Wennerlind (New York: Oxford University Press, 2014), 25–45.
8 Robert Brenner, *Merchants and Revolution: Commercial Change, Political Conflict, and London's Overseas Traders, 1550–1653* (London: Verso, 2003), 115–166, 173–181.
9 Hilary McD. Beckles, "The 'Hub of Empire': The Caribbean and Britain in the Seventeenth Century," *Oxford History of the British Empire*. Vol. 1, *The Origins of Empire*, ed. Nicholas Canny (Oxford: Oxford University Press, 1998), 223; Beckles, *White Servitude and Black Slavery in Barbados, 1627–1715* (Knoxville: University of Tennessee Press, 1989), 15–16, 34 (table 1.6); David Souden, "English Indentured Servants and the Transatlantic Colonial Economy," *International Labour Migration: Historical Perspectives*,

eds. Shula Marks and Peter Richardson (Hounslow, Middlesex: Institute of Commonwealth Studies, 1984), 23–29; Alison Games, "Migration," *The British Atlantic World, 1500–1800*, eds. David Armitage and Michael J. Braddick (New York: Palgrave MacMillan, 2002), 31–50; Richard S. Dunn, *Sugar and Slaves: The Rise of the Planter Class in the English West Indies, 1624–1713* (Chapel Hill: University of North Carolina Press, 1972), 51–57.

10 Richard Ligon, *A True & Exact History of the Island of Barbadoes* (London: Peter Parker, 1673), 94–96.
11 Russell Menard, *Sweet Negotiations: Sugar, Slavery, and Plantation Agriculture in Early Barbados* (Charlottesville: University of Virginia Press, 2006), 25 (table 4), 52–59; Gary A. Puckrein, *Little England: Plantation Society and Anglo-Barbadian Politics, 1627–1700* (New York: New York University Press, 1984), 72.
12 *Population History of England*, 207–215, 208–209 (table 7.8, total calculation mine).
13 Keith Wrightson, *Earthly Necessities: Economic Lives in Early Modern Britain* (New Haven, CT: Yale University Press, 2000), 164–166, 235–236. For more on these trends in a broader context, see *Competing Visions of Empire*, 16–20.
14 Abbot Emerson Smith, *Colonists in Bondage: White Servitude and Convict Labor in America, 1607–1776* (Chapel Hill: University of North Carolina Press, 1947), 93.
15 James Scott Wheeler, *Cromwell in Ireland* (New York: St. Martin's Press, 1999); *Web of Empire*, 263–264; Allan Macinnes, *The British Revolution, 1629–1660* (New York: Palgrave Macmillan, 2005), 190–199.
16 Karen Ordahl Kupperman, "Errand to the Indies: Puritan Colonization from Providence Island through the Western Design," *William and Mary Quarterly*, 3rd series, 45[1] (January 1988): 70–99.
17 *Merchants and Revolution*, Ch. 10; Timothy Venning, *Cromwellian Foreign Policy* (New York: St. Martin's Press, 1995), 72–77.
18 For some discussions among the men involved in planning the Western Design, see *The Clarke Papers. Selections from the Papers of William Clarke*, ed. C. H. Firth. (London: Longmans, Green, 1899), 3: 203–208 (Appendix B).
19 S. A. G. Taylor, *The Western Design* (London: Solstice Productions, 1969); C. H. Firth, ed., *The Narrative of General Venables* (London: Longmans, Green, 1900), 14–39; Anon., "Narrative of the Expedition to San Domingo," *The Clarke Papers*, 3:54–60; I. S., *A Brief and Perfect Journal of The Late Proceedings and Successe of the English Army in the West-Indies* (London, 1655).
20 Blair Worden, "Oliver Cromwell and the Sin of Achan," *History, Society, and the Churches*, eds. Derek Beales and Geoffrey Best (Cambridge: Cambridge University Press, 1985), 135–136.
21 *Brief and Perfect Journal*, 11.
22 Robert Brenner, "The Civil War Politics of London's Merchant Community," *Past and Present*, 58 (February 1973): 106–107; Steven Pincus, "England and the World in the 1650s," *Revolution and Restoration: England in the 1650s*, ed. John Morrill (London: Collins & Brown, 1992), 129–147.
23 *Competing Visions of Empire*, 34–35.
24 *Hypocrisie Discovered* (London, 1655), 14; *The Unparalleld Monarch* (London: T. C., 1656), 77–78.
25 "Proclamation of the Protector Relating to Jamaica," 1655, *A Collection of the State Papers of John Thurloe, Esq.*, 7 vols. (London, 1742), 3: 753; O. Cromwell, *By the Protector. A Proclamation Giving Encouragement to Such as Shall Transplant Themselves to Jamaica* (London: Henry Hills & John Fields, 1655); William Goodson to the Governor of Bermuda, 24 September 1655, in *Thurloe*, 4: 51–52; "Proclamation by Oliver Cromwell, Lord Protector, 25 March 1656," Frank Cundall, *Governors of Jamaica*, plate between pp. xxxii and xxxiii; Lord Broghill to John Thurloe, 18 September 1655, in *Thurloe*, 4:41–42.
26 Mary Anne Everett Green, ed., *Calendar of State Papers Domestic* (London: Longmans, 1882), 1 March 1654/5, 7: 62; 30 March 1655, 7: 107; 30 March 1655, 7: 107–108.
27 "A Proposition for the Erecting of a West India Company, and the Better Securing the Interests of this Commonwealth in America," probably 1657, British Library (BL) Egerton 2395, Folders. 87–88.
28 Cecil T. Carr, ed., *Select Charters of Trading Companies, A.D. 1530–1707*, Publications of the Selden Society, Vol. 28 (London: Bernard Quaritch, 1913), 173–177.
29 "Proposals concerning Jamaica by James Earl of Marlborough," November 1660, The National Archives (TNA), Colonial Office (CO) 1/14, No. 56.
30 Charles M. Andrews, *Johns Hopkins University Studies in Historical and Political Science*. Vol. 26, No. 1 *British Committees, Commissions, and Councils of Trade and Plantations, 1622–1675* (Baltimore, MD: Johns Hopkins University Press, 1908), 67–68; Brian Weiser, *Charles II and the Politics of Access* (Woodbridge, Suffolk: Boydell Press, 2003), 129–130.
31 *Sweet Negotiations*, 25, table 4.
32 Stephen Saunders Webb, *The Governors-General: The English Army and the Definition of Empire, 1569–1681* (Chapel Hill: University of North Carolina Press, 1979), 208; Orders in Council of Jamaica by

D'Oyley, 3 July 1661, TNA, CO 140/1, pp. 17–20; Edward B. Rugemer, "The Development of Mastery and Race in the Comprehensive Slave Codes of the Greater Caribbean during the Seventeenth Century," *William and Mary Quarterly* 70[3] (July 2013): 429–458.

33 "A particular narrative of ye buying & forfeiture of ye ship of Negroes in Jamaica," 14 June 1661, TNA, CO 1/15, No. 63; Richard Whiting to the Navy, 10 March 1661/2, CO 1/16, No. 30.
34 Cynthia Herrup, "Punishing Pardon: Some Thoughts on the Origins of Penal Transportation," *Penal Practice and Culture, 1500–1900: Punishing the English*, eds. Simon Devereax and Paul Griffiths (New York: Palgrave, 2004), 121–137.
35 Christopher Jeaffreson to Capt. Willet, 2 December 1682, *A Young Squire of the Seventeenth Century*, ed. John Cordy Jeaffreson (London: Hurst & Blackett, 1858), 2: 13.
36 David Eltis, *The Rise of African Slavery in the Americas* (Cambridge: Cambridge University Press, 2000), 50, table 2.2; Peter Wilson Coldham, *The Complete Book of Emigrants in Bondage, 1614–1775* (Baltimore, MD: Genealogical Publishing, 1988).
37 J. M. Beattie, *Policing and Punishment in London, 1660–1750* (Oxford: Oxford University Press, 2001), 429–431.
38 Company of Royal Adventurers to the King, 26 February 1662/3, TNA, CO 1/17, No. 4; Charles II to Governor Francis Willoughby of Barbados, 26 February 1662/3, CO 1/17, No. 7; Charles II to the Governor of Jamaica, 13 March 1662/3, CO 1/17, No. 13.
39 Nuala Zahedieh, "'A Frugal, Prudential and Hopeful Trade.' Privateering in Jamaica, 1655–89," *Journal of Imperial and Commonwealth History* 18[2] (1990):145–168; Nuala Zahedieh, "Trade, Plunder, and Economic Development in Early English Jamaica, 1655–89," *Economic History Review*, 2nd series, 39[2] (May 1986): 205–222.
40 Most infamous is the example of Captain Henry Morgan, who had been granted permission by the governor of Jamaica, Sir Thomas Modyford, to attack Spanish ships and ports without the sanction of the Crown throughout the 1660s. *Competing Visions of Empire*, 79–81.
41 Orders of a Council of War on board the *Jersey*, 7 May 1664, TNA, CO 1/18, No. 63; John Callow, *The Making of King James II: The Formative Years of a Fallen King* (Stroud, Gloucestershire: Sutton Publishing, 2000), 247–250; K. G. Davies, *The Royal African Company* (London: Longmans, Green, 1957), 43–44, 57–59.
42 *Royal African Company*; Ann M. Carlos and Jamie Brown Kruse, "The Decline of the Royal African Company: Fringe Firms and the Role of the Charter," *Economic History Review* 49[2] (1996): 291–313.
43 David Eltis, "The British Transatlantic Slave Trade before 1714: Annual Estimates of Volume and Direction," *The Lesser Antilles in the Age of European Expansion*, eds. Robert L. Paquette and Stanley L. Engerman (Gainesville, FL: University Press of Florida, 2001), table 10-1 (total calculation mine); Eltis, *Rise of African Slavery*, 208, table 8.3.
44 Royal African Company Court of Assistants Minute Book, 15 August 1678, TNA, Treasury (T) 70/78, f. 5.
45 Jack Sosin, *English America and the Restoration Monarchy of Charles II: Transatlantic Politics, Commerce, and Kinship* (Lincoln: University of Nebraska Press, 1980), 39, 48–49; Nuala Zahedieh, *The Capital and the Colonies: London and the Atlantic Economy, 1660–1700* (Cambridge: Cambridge University Press, 2010), 35–54; Julian Hoppit, *A Land of Liberty? England 1689–1727* (Oxford: Oxford University Press, 2000), 245–247.
46 Petition of the Barbados Council and Assembly to Charles II, n.d., TNA, CO 1/66, No. 93I; Petition of the Barbados Council and Assembly, 24 November 1675, CO 1/35, No. 45II; Minutes of the Lords of Trade, 26 October 1676, CO 391/1, pp. 234–236.
47 William Blathwayt to the Earl of Carlisle, Governor of Jamaica, 9 July 1680, *The William Blathwayt Papers at Colonial Williamsburg 1631–1722* (Frederick, MD: UPA Academic Editions, 1989), microfilm, Vol. 22, Folder 3, Jamaica.
48 Karen Ordahl Kupperman, John C. Appleby, and Mandy Banton, eds. Order of the King-in-Council, 24 July 1679, *Calendar of State Papers Colonial: North America and the West Indies, 1574–1739* (London: Routledge, 2000), CD-ROM, 10: 401, No. 1075; Samuel Baldwin's report to the Lords of Trade, 14 June 1680, TNA, CO 1/45, No. 13.
49 Matthew Carl Underwood, "Ordering Knowledge, Re-Ordering Empire: Science and State Formation in the English Atlantic World, 1650–1688," (PhD Dissertation, Harvard University, 2010).
50 William Petyt, *Britannia languens, or a Discourse of Trade* (London, 1680), 154; Roger Coke, *A Discourse of Trade* (London, 1670), 7.
51 *Certain Considerations Relating to the Royal African Company of England* (London, 1680), 5.

52 *Competing Visions of Empire*, 121–124.
53 "East India Company v. Sandys," *A Complete Collection of State Trials*, compiler T. B. Howell, Vol. 10 (London: T. C. Hansard, 1816), 532–535; Philip J. Stern, *The Company-State: Corporate Sovereignty and the Early Modern Foundations of the British Empire in India* (New York: Oxford University Press, 2011), 46–58.
54 Edwin Stede to William Blathwayt, 16 March 1688/89, *Blathwayt Papers*, Vol. 32, Folder 5, Barbados.
55 Nathaniel Johnson to the Lords of Trade, 3 March 1687/8, TNA, CO 153/3, pp. 302–317; K. G. Davies, "The Revolutions in America," *The Revolutions of 1688: The Andrew Browning Lectures 1988*, ed. Robert Beddard (Oxford: Clarendon Press, 1991), 251–252; *Sugar and Slaves*, 133–134. Johnson became governor of South Carolina in 1710.
56 W. Darrell Stump, "An Economic Consequence of 1688," *Albion* 6[1] (Spring 1974): 28–29; William A. Pettigrew, "Free to Enslave: Politics and the Escalation of Britain's Transatlantic Slave Trade, 1688–1714," *William and Mary Quarterly*, 3rd series, 64[1] (January 2007): 11.
57 William A. Pettigrew, *Freedom's Debt: The Royal African Company and the Politics of the Atlantic Slave Trade, 1672–1752* (Chapel Hill: University of North Carolina Press, 2013).
58 *Competing Visions of Empire*, 143–147, 151–152.
59 John Cary, *An Essay on the State of England in Relation to its Trade* (Bristol: W. Bonny, 1695), 75, 66–67.
60 *Some considerations humbly offered to demonstrate how prejudicial it would be to the English plantations, revenues of the Crown, the navigation and general good of this Kingdom, that the sole trade for Negroes should be granted to a company with a joynt-stock exclusive to all others* (London: s.n., 1700?), 1.
61 Sir William Beeston to Sir John Trenchard, 23 June 1694, TNA, CO 138/7, pp. 192–196; "A Narrative by Sir William Beeston of the Descent on Jamaica by the French," 23 June 1694, BL Add MS 12430, Folders. 4–13.
62 *Competing Visions of Empire*, 168–170.
63 Petition of Edward Thompson to William III, 1 April 1689, TNA, CO 1/67, No. 68I; David Harris Sacks, *The Widening Gate: Bristol and the Atlantic Economy, 1450–1700* (Berkeley: University of California Press, 1991), 255, 301–302; Dalby Thomas, *An Historical Account of the Rise and Growth of the West-India Collonies* (London: Jo. Hindmarsh, 1690), 41.
64 Proclamation of Governor William Beeston and the Council of Jamaica, 25 February 1697/8, TNA, CO 140/6, pp. 78–79.

References

Andrews, Charles M. *Johns Hopkins University Studies in Historical and Political Science*. Vol. 26, No. 1, *British Committees, Commissions, and Councils of Trade and Plantations, 1622–1675* (Baltimore, MD: Johns Hopkins University Press, 1908).
Appleby, John. "War, Politics, and Colonization, 1558–1625," *Oxford History of the British Empire*. Vol. 1, *The Origins of Empire*, ed. Nicholas Canny (Oxford: Oxford University Press, 1998), 55–78.
Beattie, J. M. *Policing and Punishment in London, 1660–1750* (Oxford: Oxford University Press, 2001), 429–431.
Beckles, Hilary McD. "The 'Hub of Empire': The Caribbean and Britain in the Seventeenth Century," *Oxford History of the British Empire*. Vol. 1, *The Origins of Empire*, ed. Nicholas Canny (Oxford: Oxford University Press, 1998): 218–240.
Beckles, Hilary McD. *White Servitude and Black Slavery in Barbados, 1627–1715* (Knoxville, TN: University of Tennessee Press, 1989).
Brenner, Robert. "The Civil War Politics of London's Merchant Community," *Past and Present*, 58 (February 1973): 106–107.
Brenner, Robert. *Merchants and Revolution: Commercial Change, Political Conflict, and London's Overseas Traders, 1550–1653* (London: Verso, 2003).
Callow, John. *The Making of King James II: The Formative Years of a Fallen King* (Stroud, Gloucestershire: Sutton Publishing, 2000).
Carlos, Ann M., and Jamie Brown Kruse. "The Decline of the Royal African Company: Fringe Firms and the Role of the Charter," *Economic History Review* 49, 2 (1996): 291–313.
Coldham, Peter Wilson. *The Complete Book of Emigrants in Bondage, 1614–1775* (Baltimore, MD: Genealogical Publishing, 1988).
Coke, Roger. *A Discourse of Trade* (London, 1670), 7.
Craven, Wesley Frank. *Dissolution of the Virginia Company: The Failure of a Colonial Experiment* (New York: Oxford University Press, 1932).

Davies, K. G. *The Royal African Company* (London: Longmans, Green, 1957).
Davies, K. G. "The Revolutions in America," *The Revolutions of 1688: The Andrew Browning Lectures 1988*, ed. Robert Beddard (Oxford: Clarendon Press, 1991).
Dunn, Richard S. *Sugar and Slaves: The Rise of the Planter Class in the English West Indies, 1624–1713* (Chapel Hill, NC: University of North Carolina Press, 1972).
Eltis, David. *The Rise of African Slavery in the Americas* (Cambridge: Cambridge University Press, 2000).
Eltis, David. "The British Transatlantic Slave Trade before 1714: Annual Estimates of Volume and Direction," *The Lesser Antiles in the Age of European Expansion*, eds. Robert L. Paquette and Stanley L. Engerman (Gainesville, FL: University Press of Florida, 2001).
Firth, C. H. ed. *The Clarke Papers. Selections from the Papers of William Clarke* (London: Longmans, Green, 1899).
Games, Alison. "Migration," *The British Atlantic World, 1500–1800*, eds. David Armitage and Michael J. Braddick (New York: Palgrave MacMillan, 2002), 31–50.
Games, Alison. *The Web of Empire: English Cosmopolitans in an Age of Expansion, 1560–1660* (New York: Oxford University Press, 2008).
Green, Mary Anne Everett, ed. *Calendar of State Papers Domestic* (London: Longmans, 1882), 1 March 1654/5, 7:62; 30 March 1655, 7: 107; 30 March 1655, 7: 107–108.
Herrup, Cynthia. "Punishing Pardon: Some Thoughts on the Origins of Penal Transportation," *Penal Practice and Culture, 1500–1900: Punishing the English*, eds. Simon Devereax and Paul Griffiths (New York: Palgrave, 2004), 121–137.
Hoppitt, Julian. *A Land of Liberty? England 1689–1727* (Oxford: Oxford University Press, 2000).
Jeaffreson, John Cordy, ed. *A Young Squire of the Seventeenth Century* (London: Hurst & Blackett, 1858).
Kupperman, Karen Ordahl. "Errand to the Indies: Puritan Colonization from Providence Island through the Western Design," *William and Mary Quarterly*, 3rd series, 45, 1 (January 1988): 70–99.
Kupperman, Karen Ordahl, John C. Appleby, and Mandy Banton, eds. Order of the King-in-Council, 24 July 1679, *Calendar of State Papers Colonial: North America and the West Indies, 1574–1739* (London: Routledge, 2000), CD-ROM, 10: 401, No. 1075.
Ligon, Richard. *A True & Exact History of the Island of Barbadoes* (London: Peter Parker, 1673), 94–96.
Macinnes, Allan. *The British Revolution, 1629–1660* (New York: Palgrave Macmillan, 2005).
McCormick, Ted. "Population: Modes of Seventeenth-Century Demographic Thought," *Mercantilism Reimagined: Political Economy in Early Modern Britain and its Empire*, eds. Philip Stern and Carl Wennerlind (New York: Oxford University Press, 2014), 25–45.
Menard, Russell. *Sweet Negotiations: Sugar, Slavery, and Plantation Agriculture in Early Barbados* (Charlottesville, VA: University of Virginia Press, 2006).
Morgan, Edmund. "The First American Boom: Virginia 1618 to 1630," *William and Mary Quarterly*, 3rd series, 28, 2 (April 1971): 170–198.
Morgan, Edmund. "The Labor Problem at Jamestown, 1607–1618," *American Historical Review* 73, 3 (June 1971): 595–611.
Norton, Marcy. *Sacred Gifts, Profane Pleasures: A History of Tobacco and Chocolate in the Atlantic World* (Ithaca, NY: Cornell University Press, 2010).
Pettigrew, William A. "Free to Enslave: Politics and the Escalation of Britain's Transatlantic Slave Trade, 1688–1714," *William and Mary Quarterly*, 3rd series, 64[1] (January 2007).
Pettigrew, William A. *Freedom's Debt: The Royal African Company and the Politics of the Atlantic Slave Trade, 1672–1752* (Chapel Hill, NC: University of North Carolina Press, 2013): 3–38.
Petyt, William. *Britannia languens, or a Discourse of Trade* (London, 1680), 154.
Pincus, Steven. "England and the World in the 1650s," *Revolution and Restoration: England in the 1650s*, ed. John Morrill (London: Collins & Brown, 1992), 129–147.
Puckrein, Gary A. *Little England: Plantation Society and Anglo-Barbadian Politics, 1627–1700* (New York: New York University Press, 1984).
Rugemer, Edward B. "The Development of Mastery and Race in the Comprehensive Slave Codes of the Greater Caribbean during the Seventeenth Century," *William and Mary Quarterly* 70[3] (July 2013): 429–458.
Sacks, David Harris. *The Widening Gate: Bristol and the Atlantic Economy, 1450–1700* (Berkeley, CA: University of California Press, 1991).
Smith, Abbot Emerson. *Colonists in Bondage: White Servitude and Convict Labor in America, 1607–1776* (Chapel Hill, NC: University of North Carolina Press, 1947).
Sosin, Jack. *English America and the Restoration Monarchy of Charles II: Transatlantic Politics, Commerce, and Kinship* (Lincoln, NE: University of Nebraska Press, 1980).

Souden, David. "'Rogues, Whores and Vagabonds'? Indentured Servant Emigrants to North America, and the Case of Mid-Seventeenth-Century Bristol," *Social History* 3[1] (January 1978): 23–41.

Souden, David. "English Indentured Servants and the Transatlantic Colonial Economy," *International Labour Migration: Historical Perspectives*, eds. Shula Marks and Peter Richardson (London: Institute of Commonwealth Studies, 1984): 19–33.

Stern, Philip J. *The Company-State: Corporate Sovereignty and the Early Modern Foundations of the British Empire in India* (New York: Oxford University Press, 2011).

Stump, W. Darrell. "An Economic Consequence of 1688," *Albion* 6[1] (Spring 1974): 28–29.

Swingen, Abigail L. *Competing Visions of Empire: Labor, Slavery, and the Origins of the British Atlantic Empire* (New Haven, CT: Yale University Press, 2015).

Taylor, S. A. G. *The Western Design* (London: Solstice Productions, 1969).

Thomas, Dalby. *An Historical Account of the Rise and Growth of the West-India Collonies* (London: Jo. Hindmarsh, 1690).

Underwood, Matthew Carl. "Ordering Knowledge, Re-Ordering Empire: Science and State Formation in the English Atlantic World, 1650–1688," (Ph.D. dissertation, Harvard University, 2010).

Venning, Timothy. *Cromwellian Foreign Policy* (New York: St. Martin's Press, 1995).

Webb, Stephen Saunders. *The Governors-General: The English Army and the Definition of Empire, 1569–1681* (Chapel Hill, NC: University of North Carolina Press, 1979).

Weiser, Brian. *Charles II and the Politics of Access* (Woodbridge, Suffolk: Boydell Press, 2003), 129–130.

Wheeler, James Scott. *Cromwell in Ireland* (New York: St. Martin's Press, 1999).

Worden, Blair. "Oliver Cromwell and the Sin of Achan," *History, Society, and the Churches*, eds. Derek Beales and Geoffrey Best (Cambridge: Cambridge University Press, 1985), 135–136.

Wrightson, Keith. *Earthly Necessities: Economic Lives in Early Modern Britain* (New Haven, CT: Yale University Press, 2000).

Wrigley, E. A. and Schofield R. S. *The Population History of England, 1541–1870* (London: Edward Arnold, 1981).

Zahedieh, Nuala. "'A Frugal, Prudential and Hopeful Trade.' Privateering in Jamaica, 1655–89," *Journal of Imperial and Commonwealth History* 18, 2 (1990): 145–168.

Zahedieh, Nuala. "Trade, Plunder, and Economic Development in Early English Jamaica, 1655–89," *Economic History Review*, 2nd series, 39, 2 (May 1986): 205–222.

Zahedieh, Nuala. *The Capital and the Colonies: London and the Atlantic Economy, 1660–1700* (Cambridge: Cambridge University Press, 2010).

Figure 5.1 Spanish 1632 Map of the English Island of Barbados.
Source: Nicolás de Cardona/Wikimedia Commons.

5

THE EARLY ENGLISH CARIBBEAN

Conflict, the Census, and Control

Jenny Shaw[1]

On May 28, 1730, Governor William Mathew of the Leeward Islands sent an enumeration of Montserrat's population to London.[2] Entitled "The Political Anatomy of Montserrat," the document reflected the colony's status as a fully fledged slave society with a black population five times as large that of the white community.[3] The census also delineated categories of land, labor, productivity, and control to a degree unseen in any previous accounting of an English Caribbean island. For each of Montserrat's four districts—St. Anthony, St. Patrick, St. George, and St Peter—over 31 columns, including the "names and quality" of each head of household and that person's trade, were painstakingly completed. Additional categories included the kinds of buildings on an estate and the number of men, women, children, servants, and slaves (old and young, men and women, boys and girls). Administrators noted the division of land into acres devoted to sugar, indigo, cotton, or ginger; they also counted some of the livestock. The final two columns recorded the number of "fire armes" and "swords" that could be placed in the hands of loyal subjects at times of internal or external conflict. In this accounting, Montserrat was both a productive colony, sending sugar, cotton, and indigo across the Atlantic, and also one ready to defend itself against potential slave insurrections or an attack from foreign powers.

The title of Montserrat's 1730 census specifically referenced a volume written by one of England's most fervent advocates of "government by demographic manipulation," a hallmark of seventeenth- and eighteenth-century English colonial policy.[4] William Petty, who counted and categorized Ireland's population in the 1650s, later published *The Political Anatomy of Ireland*, a treatise that outlined his plans to improve the Irish and Ireland based on his calculations in political arithmetic.[5] Petty worked to turn the Irish into productive and loyal subjects by focusing on their labor worth, and reducing the potential for perfidy posed by their Catholicism. In the Caribbean, English officials developed policies to manage threats by identifying potentially disruptive populations and mapping their locations.[6] English anxiety about their ability to control the islands shifted focus over the course of the seventeenth century. Officials continued to be worried about Irish Catholics, fearing they would act as a fifth column in the service of their coreligionists, the Catholic European powers of Spain and France, who acted in close proximity and vied for supremacy in the region. As the numbers of enslaved people in the region grew exponentially, English concerns about enslaved uprisings and resistance overtook their fear of Irish Catholics. Like Petty, Caribbean officials hoped that implementing policies based on the numeric landscape of the colonies would improve island populations.

In the English Caribbean, the political arithmetic changed to reflect officials' new priorities. Categories that connoted ethnicity or religious status disappeared over time as their importance waned. At first colonial governors and travel writers sent estimated population figures back to the capital, secure in the knowledge that no one would be able to prove their assessments false.[7] By the 1670s the censuses had become more detailed, including information collected by churchwardens or militia commanders. In Jamaica and Barbados, the primary categories were those of freedom and slavery conflated with skin color: "white" and "negro" featured prominently.[8] When the Leeward Islands' census was taken in 1678, slaves were still "negroes," however landowners were not only "white" but also "English," "Irish," or even, on occasion, "French."[9] By the early eighteenth century, as the numbers of Africans in the English Caribbean surged, "negro" and "white" became the main categories in operation everywhere.[10] The move away from the use of ethnic categories that were also implicitly religious in some enumerations in 1678 to the uniform use of racial categories in the eighteenth century demonstrates another key feature of this changing political arithmetic. English ideas about difference shifted from being primarily based on religion in the seventeenth century to being overwhelmingly understood as rooted in racial distinctions by the eighteenth century.[11]

Examining enumeration shows how the English conceived of their colonial populations, the ways that they employed theories of political arithmetic to govern the islands effectively, and how they responded to the ever-changing challenges to their control through a careful accounting of the people who inhabited the West Indies. The 1730 census, with its clear racial and labor divisions may seem like a logical reflection of a society based on slavery, but its antecedents show that such an outcome was far from preordained. By exploring the inter- and intraimperial context of the seventeenth-century Caribbean, investigating the theoretical connections between counting and improvement that governed English policy, and charting the changing census categories of the late seventeenth and early eighteenth centuries, this chapter demonstrates the multiple ways that demography affected the development of the early modern English Atlantic. Part of the enumeration was the shift toward the dominating racial categories of black and white. This process both created categories that were distinct and immutable and also erased those groups that caused distrust and unease. Moreover, by reducing human bodies to mere numbers on a page, colonial officials made the conceptual move of erasing the humanity of the populations under observation, rendering them less threatening and more easily controlled.

External and Internal Threats

The seventeenth-century Caribbean was a space of fierce interimperial contestation, as religious wars in Europe spilled into the American Mediterranean. Spain, with its claims to the Americas legitimized by Papal Bulls and the Treaty of Tordesillas of 1494, "conquered" the Caribbean in the sixteenth century, and in doing so perfected their model of colonization—displacing the indigenous inhabitants and taking possession of the territory through ceremonial acts.[12] The Spanish focused on urbanization as a way to give structure to colonists, provide security through garrisons, and help colonial officials to control their populations.[13] Building hospitals, universities, administrative buildings, and churches, the Spanish Crown turned these early colonial outposts into replicas of the towns and cities of the Iberian Peninsula, reproducing key markers of Spanish civilization. Spain's imperial ambitions also centered on converting the indigenous populations of the islands and soon Catholic missions became familiar features of the landscape.[14] By the middle of the seventeenth century, as Spain increasingly turned its attention toward South America and the silver that was financing its global aspirations, Hispaniola, Cuba, and Puerto Rico became comparatively restive, while Jamaica became a notorious pirates' haven.[15]

The wealth that Spain was extracting from the Americas was a huge incentive for English imperial ambitions. From 1585 the English Crown sponsored privateering to attack Spanish silver fleets, while providing ad hoc backing to a host of joint-stock companies seeking to establish outposts on the periphery of the Spanish empire.[16] Ignoring Spanish claims to territory, the English built settlements on Barbados, St. Christopher, Nevis, Montserrat, and Antigua by the early 1630s, where they vied with the French for supremacy.[17] Legitimizing their possession through colonization, the islands' settler-oriented populations included large numbers of dispossessed and distressed servants from England, Scotland, and Ireland, as well as a growing number of enslaved Africans. The English model of colonization was very different in scope and form from that of the Spanish as people, not claims to territory, became essential to colonial success.[18]

England's ambitions in the Caribbean took a more expansive turn in the 1650s when Oliver Cromwell, the puritan Lord Protector of the Commonwealth of England, launched his ill-fated Western Design. Believing England's imperial ventures to be providentially inspired, his lofty goals included wresting Jamaica, Hispaniola, and Puerto Rico from the Spanish, and establishing Protestant ascendancy in the Caribbean.[19] Spain rebuffed English invasions on Hispaniola (despite English forces significantly outnumbering the Spanish military presence on the island) and delivered a humiliating defeat to Cromwell's plans. Even the eventual acquisition of Jamaica was not viewed favorably at the time, not least because the English allowed most of the Spanish settlers to escape with their property, including a number of slaves. Others who remained on the island engaged in guerilla warfare with the English until the Restoration in 1660.[20]

As Spanish dominance in the Caribbean waned at midcentury, England and France vied for dominance in the region. Both European powers had settled the eastern Caribbean at virtually the same time, and the islands were divided relatively evenly between the two: the English had control of the Leeward Islands and Barbados, while the French claimed the Windward Islands. Both nations asserted their rights to St. Christopher, splitting its jurisdiction following a joint operation to rid the island of Carib Indians in the 1620s. In the 1660s tensions between the two nations rose: France took full control of St. Christopher, successfully attacked the small English colony of Montserrat, and threatened English supremacy in Antigua and Nevis. Two decades later, during King William's War (1688), these same islands once again came under threat from the French who attempted to take advantage of the conflict between Catholic James II and Protestant William and Mary.[21] The struggle for supremacy in the eastern Caribbean would not be settled until the 1713 Treaty of Utrecht, when England and France eventually made peace.[22]

These external challenges to English control were exacerbated by the internal threat posed by the islands' settlement populations. Irish Catholics were especially feared by the English as a disloyal group who would side with the Spanish or French at times of war rather than remain good imperial subjects. Nervous about the presence of this population, English discussions of Irish Catholics centered in part on their number in an attempt to assess the scope of their threat.[23] During the Western Design, for example, English officials fretted that "12,000 prisoners of war" from Ireland and Scotland had entered Barbados, while 5,000 Protestant English men had been taken "for the invasion of the Indies."[24] More specific reports noted individual shipments of men. In 1652, "liberty" was given to Bristol merchants "Henrie Hazard and Robert Immans … to carrie 200 Irishmen from anie port in Ireland to the Caribean Islands."[25] On October 19, 1654, prisoners of war, including those from Ireland, were ordered to be "sent to the Barbadoes, Bermuda or some other of the English plantations in America."[26] And in 1656, 1,200 men from "Knockfergus in Ireland and Port Patrick in Scotland" were transported to the Americas.[27] Counting those who left Ireland or Scotland for Barbados ultimately meant tracking a potentially disloyal population moving from old European conquests into the heart of England's new American empire.

Irish behavior during the Western Design encouraged English assessments of their allegedly untrustworthy nature. Irish soldiers fought on both sides of this conflict contributing significantly to England's failures. In April 1655 after landing in error some distance from Santo Domingo, one group of English troops came across an "old Irish man" who promised to lead them to safety, but instead guided the weary English into an ambush where "Coll. Murfy an Irishman" led the Spanish attack.[28] And when English soldiers deserted or were taken prisoner, the Spanish used the Irish soldiers among their ranks to interrogate them.[29] Some deserters were Irish Catholics who claimed to have been coerced into fighting for the English in the first place. These men sought sanctuary and assistance from the Spanish in return for the intelligence they could provide about English military maneuvers.[30]

In a similar fashion, Irish Catholics aided the French at moments of interimperial warfare.[31] In the mid-1660s, the Irish were credited with ensuring French control of all of St. Christopher by overthrowing the English-run assembly.[32] As with reluctant Irish troops in Cromwell's army during the Western Design, the Irish serving in the English military failed to provide adequate support in a disastrous attempt to retake St. Christopher. Rather than stand and fight, they betrayed the English by surrendering to the French "whilst most of the English souldiers found graves."[33] Similar events occurred on Montserrat, where the Irish Governor welcomed the French with open arms and turned over jurisdiction of the whole island to the Catholic enemy.[34] And during King William's War, the Irish once again were accused of working in concert with the French on Nevis and St. Christopher. In July 1689 on Anguilla, the French administered "an Oath of Allegiance to King James, and made an Irishman Governour there." Montserrat and Antigua were also said to be in "great danger" from Irish collusion.[35]

Again, numbers told the story of English anxiety. In 1667, fearing that an attack on Barbados was imminent in the wake of French success elsewhere, Governor William Willoughby expressed his concern that of the "4000 fighting men" he had to call on, half were Irish.[36] John Netherway, writing from Nevis in 1689, begged for relief to be sent to Montserrat because the Irish "who are in number three to one to the English" declared "that they will Desert theire Allegiance and Deliver that Island to the French comand."[37] Lieutenant-Governor Christopher Codrington warned of similar trouble on St. Christopher, noting how "the Irish Papists ... being about the number of 150, gathered together in a body declaring openly against their Maj[esties] Authority." In articulating the size and strength of the rebellious Irish populations, the English hoped to better determine how to manage the threat posed by their presence.

By the end of the seventeenth century English officials in the Caribbean were increasingly dealing with a second recalcitrant island population: enslaved Africans. The majority on Jamaica and Barbados by the 1660s, Africans resisted English colonial rule through a variety of means. From the moment England had taken Jamaica from the Spanish, English forces found themselves fighting fugitive Afro-Spanish maroons who sought freedom and autonomy in the mountains of the island.[38] On Barbados there were fewer places to run as the island was almost completely settled by midcentury, but officials nonetheless passed laws indicating that runaways were a problem. In 1657 the council noted the "divers rebellious & runne away negroes" who "lye lurking in the woods and secret places" in the parish of St. Joseph. These runaways were accused of "committinge many violences and attempting to assassinate people to there great Terrour."[39]

Both Jamaica and Barbados experienced a number of slave revolts in the 1670s, 1680s, and early 1690s. On Jamaica, enslaved Africans rose up against their masters in 1673, 1675, and 1678. Militiamen sent to quash these rebellions chased down rebels from some of the islands' most prominent plantations. Executions followed, swift and brutal in all three instances.[40] At roughly the same time, planters on Barbados discovered and foiled a revolt by enslaved Africans. The anonymous author of *Great Newes from the Barbados* explained to metropolitan elites that in 1675 dozens of "*Cormantee* or *Gold Coast Negroes*" had plotted to overthrow the planter hierarchy. Had it not been for intelligence provided by a lone enslaved individual, "Anna, a house Negro Woman belonging to Justice Hall," the plan might have succeeded. Instead, "threescore and odd more" slaves were rounded up, and seventeen were executed for their part in the alleged conspiracy, but elites continued to worry about the threat to colonial security that such a revolt signified.[41]

In the 1680s and 1690s Barbados and Jamaica experienced another flurry of coinciding revolts. The alleged uprising in Barbados in 1686 may well have been more imagined by anxious English officials than real.[42] On Jamaica, however, there was no question about the reality of the enslaved revolt that lasted more than a year, between 1685 and 1686. The uprising began in the north of the island in July 1685 when 150 enslaved runaways obtained guns, killed whites, and fled to the mountains, attacking plantations and causing damage while eluding capture by militia and dogs. In March 1686 the revolt moved south, and in the ensuing pursuit every captured enslaved rebel was burned alive, torn apart by dogs, or drawn and quartered. In 1691 in Jamaica, and 1692 in Barbados slaves attacked the very core of island authorities. On Jamaica, over 300 slaves belonging to the Speaker of the Assembly, Thomas Sutton, took part in a revolt that cost their owner £10,000.[43] And on Barbados, a group of skilled island-born craftsmen planned a revolt with military precision, aiming not only to take control of the island, but styling themselves as the new colonial government in the process.[44]

On occasion, the separate threats posed by island populations overlapped compounding English anxiety. In the winter of 1655 the Barbados Council noted that there were "several Irish servants & negroes out … the Thickets," and branded the act as one of "Rebellion."[45] Irish Catholics found themselves accused of being coconspirators with the "Cormantee Negros" who threatened to take over Barbados in 1675, and were believed to be part of the plots of 1686 and 1692.[46] Just a few years before the 1692 Barbados uprising, English planters on St. Christopher had been terrified by a similar event, this time with French Catholics entering the fray. Edwyn Stede recounted collaboration on St. Christopher between "many of the French, mulattoes … & Negroes that are Imbodyed with the Irish."[47] Clearly the heady mix of cross-racial alliance petrified English colonists who were forced to contend with the realization that their ability to manage their growing island populations was being challenged by the very groups they were trying to control.

The external and internal threats to English colonies posed problems for colonial officials who sought to limit their vulnerability and impose their dominance on the seventeenth-century Caribbean. Across the century the concerns raised by competition between Spain, France, and England for control over the region played out in a series of interimperial wars that pitched Protestants against Catholics. These same wars drew attention to Catholic subjects within England's colonies. With the increasing numbers of enslaved Africans arriving in the second half of the seventeenth century, the challenges to colonial rule increased. English officials, always concerned with legitimizing their claims to Caribbean islands through their settlement and use of land, now became obsessed with enumerating colonial populations. If they knew what kinds of people inhabited the colonies, then they might be able to employ political arithmetic to improve those who could be changed, and to manage those who could not.

Theories of Political Arithmetic

The ideology behind colonial counting was most specifically articulated in Ireland where policies connecting numeracy and the management of the body politic became part of the imperial vision for the island. In the 1650s William Petty created the "Down Survey," an assessment of the island that distinguished between "profitable" and "unprofitable" lands and mapped the population of the country according to political and religious factions in order to improve the island.[48] He used his findings to write *The Political Anatomy of Ireland*, grounding the resulting theory of political arithmetic in assumptions about the inherent connection between numeracy and objectivity. He argued that to make Ireland productive he needed to transform the Irish into good colonial subjects. But rather than focus on the religious or political valences of the population, he instead concentrated on land and labor.[49] Unlike religion and ethnicity, these categories did not have overtly political connotations and could certainly be seen as disinterested.[50] Petty's version of political arithmetic was all the more dangerous for its appearance of neutrality: the connection between land and labor held within Petty's analysis of Ireland would be magnified in the Americas where it would taken on an increasingly racist form.[51]

Petty's ideas about the transmutable nature of the Irish—that they could be turned into good English subjects by intermarriage and transportation—was part of a larger conversation about the improvement of populations that spanned the Atlantic.[52] In the Caribbean, governors frequently received correspondence from London demanding to know the composition of island populations and challenging them to make subjective analyses about the worth of island laborers.[53] In these early years in the context of interimperial warfare and internal dissent the need to know a population so that it could be controlled was paramount. A typical query requested an assessment of the population and the ability of those present to defend the island: "What numbers of Merchants and Planters—English and Forreigners, Servants and Slaves and how many of them are men able to bear armes?" Additional questions pressed for specificity about the European population and for knowledge about African slaves: "What number of English, Scotch, Irish or Forreignors have for these 7 years last past or any other space of tyme come yearly to Plant and Inhabitt within your Government and also what Blacks or slaves have been brought in within the said tyme and what Rates?"[54] As with Petty, hidden in the quantification was a conflation of the desire to know the numeric landscape of each colony with the need to understand how that terrain affected colonial policies. According to contemporary demographic theories, administrators who connected these two elements of enumeration would become more effective imperial officers.

Some Caribbean commentators believed that "people are the foundacon and Improvement of all Plantacons," so that "sending of servants thither" was of utmost importance, but, like Petty, they were also convinced people from less desirable backgrounds could be improved.[55] Richard Ligon hinted at the improvement in status that could be achieved by some European settlers on Barbados "who began upon small fortunes" but were "now risen to very great and vast estates."[56] Implicit in his judgment of the island's European population was the promise of advancement and riches that the Caribbean appeared to offer in such abundance to the right sorts of people. Once they had risen in the Americas through their labor, successful indentures were granted their freedom and given land of their own, a stake in colonial society.

Africans were also discussed from the very first enumerations in terms of their worth to the colonies. In the first surviving questionnaire about Barbados that was remitted to London in 1647, Africans were described as "13,000 Negroes painefull Especially them w[hi]ch come from Angola in color black."[57] "Painefull" connoted the diligence and assiduousness with which these enslaved Africans labored, indicating that this particular group of laborers worked hard to fulfill the demands of the colony. From the security of London, Thomas Povey assumed that these laborers were worth the investment, noting that the "20,000 Negroes who subsist merely of the easye fruits of the Earth who by their labour doe rayse 200000lbs sterl. yearly."[58] For him, Africans could be fed with little effort and cost, especially when their prodigious output was taken into consideration.⁵⁹ Focusing as it did on the production that resulted, rather than on the expense of supporting such a population, Povey's analysis included a positive assessment of the worth of African laborers, an increasingly popular inclusion in dispatches to London in the decades to come.

At the start of the restoration of the Stuart monarchy in England, an anonymous colonial official identified the "severall sorts" of inhabitants of Barbados and arranged them in a hierarchy. "The first and best are the proprietors of the land, whome they call freedhold and who may be effectively five thousand families, the grosse of them are English." Freemen, numbering in the region of 5,000, split equally between English and Scots "and its guessed about one thousand Irish," were listed as the "next sort." They "serve in the country for wages" and "live comfortably." "Christian Servants" followed, numbering around 8,000 men, most of whom, it was alleged, "are Scotts and Irish" sent to Barbados by "the happie success of the Lord Generall Cromwell."⁶⁰ English elites believed these servants to have been transformed by their experience in the colonies. Barbados planters described how those "who were noxious whilest they remained [in England, Scotland and Ireland]" had now been reformed. The "ille wicked and dissolute" prisoners from the civil wars in Great Britain had been turned into a better sort of people in the Caribbean.⁶¹

In this midcentury context, colonial political arithmetic appeared to have worked exceptionally well. Rather than "dangerous consequences" arising from the Irish presence during the "time of wars betwixt the Commonwealth of England & Spain," officials moved swiftly to render them harmless, passing laws targeting "the considerable number of Irish freemen and servants … of the Romish Rule." First, they disarmed all Irish Catholics on Barbados. Next, constables were ordered to whip any Irish women and men found "Wander[ing] up and down from Plantation to Plantation." Finally, the militia was to keep special watch on Irish movement around the island.⁶² In this case, counting the population and surveying and controlling potential malcontents had yielded the desired result, allowing colonial officials to congratulate themselves that their demographic-based policies were having a positive effect.

On closer inspection of the records, it seems that while English officials in the Caribbean hoped to have solved their Irish problem, it was only the Scots they believed to be capable of improvement. The ideas that underpinned parliamentary debates in the metropole hinting that Scots were considered the equal of English indentures appeared to have traversed the Atlantic.⁶³ A 1667 report sang Scottish praises. "Christian Servants" (in particular Scots) were described as "the nerves and sinews" of a plantation, noted for being "excellent Planters & good Souldiers." Nerves and sinews formed essential components in a functioning body; Scottish servants were therefore important signifiers of the island's, and therefore the imperial project's, health and strength. Indeed, the Scots' presence meant that Barbados was now in so "formidable" a position that English colonial officials believed the threat of slave insurrection to be seriously reduced. In 1677, Christopher Jeaffreson, a planter on St. Christopher, concurred, noting that on his island "Scotchmen and Welchmen we esteem the best servants."⁶⁴ Scottish settlement in the colonies also protected the islands against "invasion from a forraigne Enemy."⁶⁵ Unspoken, but crucial to the final part of this calculation, was the Protestantism of the Scots, which would allow these servants to act as a buffer against an internal enemy. "I am for the downright Scot," Governor William Willoughby wrote to Charles II, "who I am certain will fight without a crucifix about his neck," indicating his belief that it was the Catholicism of the Irish that led them to be disloyal.⁶⁶

Indeed, if the Scots contributed to the health of English islands, Irish Catholics threatened to bring disease to the body politic. In a 1667 report to the Privy Council during England's war with France, Governor Willoughby argued that the Lords should "offer a trade with Scotland for transporting people of that nation hither, and prevent any excess of Irish in the future."⁶⁷

Once peace had been restored to the Caribbean, Willoughby wrote to Joseph Williamson, one of Charles II's closest foreign policy advisors and mused that although the Irish did "sweare by Christ they will bee true to his Ma[jesty]," he feared that he could only "believe them till an Enemie appeare."[68] Meanwhile Sir Charles Wheler complained to the colonial office about the "great difference between the English and the Irish [in] their trust and valour."[69] And similar reports arrived in London in the 1680s and 1690s during King William's War. Governor Christopher Codrington noted that the French declared that they gave the Irish protection "on the score of their religion," while from Nevis John Netherway reported similar stories of the French "encouraging and entertaining the Irish Rebells" by referring to the Irish as the "subjects of King James."[70] Codrington worked quickly to disarm the Irish in order to limit their abilities to work with the French rounding up significant numbers, confining them to plantations, or sending them to other Caribbean locations.[71] As in the 1650s, these actions appeared to have the desired effect—the French were ultimately unsuccessful in their attempts to take permanent control of the English Leeward Islands. Codrington could feel confident that if recalcitrant Irish could not be improved, then they could at the very least be controlled.

By creating their discourses of improvement, colonial officials also exposed their concerns about which groups might pose threats to colonial control. As Protestants, the Scots were a prime example of a formerly troublesome population who had been successfully transformed into loyal subjects of the Crown. While there may have been hopes that Irish Catholics would be equally malleable, for the most part, colonial officials worried that they could not be trusted. And enslaved Africans seemed to be the best laborers, but as their number increased, so did English worries about their capacity for revolt. When it came to the more precise enumerations of the late seventeenth and early eighteenth centuries, accounting for these distinctions began to drive political arithmetic. Eventually, however, the ethnic and religious markers faded away, leaving a stark racial dichotomy in their wake.

Accounting for Island Populations

In the early decades of English Caribbean colonization accounting for the people who inhabited the islands was an impressionistic affair, more art than science. Even those charged with communicating population data to the metropole were aware of the difficulties of ensuring the veracity of their reports although this did not stop them making claims of accuracy. Richard Ligon, who included his assessment of Barbados's population in *A True and Exact History of the Island of Barbados* (1657), acknowledged "it were somewhat difficult to give you an exact account of the number of persons upon the Island." Recognizing this fact did not prevent Ligon from trying to account for Barbados inhabitants, passing his estimation off as the "true and exact" figure his title proclaimed. He observed that it "has been conjectur'd by those that are long acquainted [with the island] … that there are no lesse than 50 thousand soules, besides Negroes."[72] "Conjectur'd" was precisely the right verb to describe Ligon's process: he vastly overstated the numbers of Europeans on Barbados, in all likelihood more than doubling the reality of English success.[73] In 1655 Thomas Povey made a similarly inflated assessment of the enslaved population, noting that the English planters of Barbados "are served with more than 20,000 Negroes."[74] Ligon's and Povey's exaggerations (if colonial officials or others knew it) could be forgiven, for they were all engaged in a process that sought to assess the practices and benefits of colonization. Actual figures that might highlight weaknesses were inconvenient truths.

By the final decades of the seventeenth century English approaches to colonial counting took a significant turn toward purported accuracy. In Jamaica, a full accounting of the island was completed in 1673 and Henry Morgan remitted a census of Port Royal's population to London in 1680.[75] Responding to demands from the Lords of Trade and Plantations, William Stapleton ordered a comprehensive census in the Leeward Islands that he returned to London in June 1678.[76] And Governor Jonathan Atkins instructed officials to begin a similar enumeration in Barbados in 1679.[77] As with William Petty's "Down Survey" in Ireland, and earlier estimations from the Caribbean, the accuracy of these censuses was questionable, and the supposed objectivity and exactness they claimed were suspect. But the numbers nonetheless had the effect of persuading census analysts that the population had been counted with some degree of precision.

These censuses reveal what English officials, especially those in the Caribbean, thought were necessary pieces of information to ensure good governance of the islands. In general they focused on three key areas. Each census carefully noted the names of landowners on each island; on Barbados and Jamaica the size of the plantation was also recorded. This assessment allowed officials to see how much land was being used productively and by whom. But how these planters were marked differed depending on location. In Jamaica and Barbados the term used to define planters was "white" and there were no additional markers of ethnicity or religion. Although both colonies had significant numbers of Irish among their European population, they did not choose to number them as such, in much the same way as Quakers were not marked on the Barbados census, despite causing consternation among English officials for their refusals to fight in the militia.[78] Irish landowners with slaves on Barbados included Dermon Mollony in St. Philip, Dermon Conniers in St. Joseph, Patrick Browne and Dennis Murfee in St. Lucy, Daniell Maccoline in St. John, Cornelius Bryan in St. James, and Teague Murfee and Dinis Sullivan in St. Peter.[79] These Irish men, and scores more like them, were absorbed into the planter hierarchy on the island, their number hidden among the English planters, their potential for rebellion reduced as they were counted *for* the defense of the colony and not against it.

In the Leeward Islands landowners were listed under the collective category "white" but individuals had a note beside their entry to connote their ethnicity—"I" (Irish), "E" (English) or, on St. Christopher, "F" (French).[80] Island demography may explain some of the differences—unlike Barbados and Jamaica, all of the Leeward Islands had larger white than black populations, and the proportion of Irish on each was large enough that they would necessarily have to be included in island militias. Irish Catholics accounted for around 25 percent of the white populations of Nevis, St. Christopher, and Antigua, and a dominating 70 percent on Montserrat.[81] By openly counting Irish Catholics, Governor William Stapleton was perhaps making it clear to the Lords of Trade and Plantations that his fellow countrymen had been improved—Irish landowners were now included among the ranks of property holders, and so were responsible and productive colonial subjects. Moreover, as owners of enslaved Africans (the "negroes" carefully counted on their estates), they were part of the emerging racial hierarchy on the islands.[82] Counting landowners proved to officials in London that the colonies were being well managed and productive.

The second area that all censuses focused on was the size and scope of the militia on each island, a category that demonstrated the ability to keep the colonies safe from internal or external threats. The Barbados and Jamaican censuses of 1680 recorded the members of the militia, both foot and horse, as well as a list of officers and soldiers in various army regiments.[83] Of course, taking careful note of militia numbers could backfire. As Governor Atkins discovered, reporting that the number of men available to fight in the militia was only slightly more than half the number expected by the Lords of Trade and Plantations did not instill confidence in his governance in the metropole.[84] Meanwhile the Leeward Islands census was arranged according to military division, not parish, indicating that these colonies were in a permanent state of readiness in case of attack. The militarization of the census provided evidence to London that each colony had a militia ready and able to defend the colony, whether those threats came from domestic laborers or foreign enemies.

The third, and perhaps most significant, group counted in the census was composed of the laborers—enslaved, servant, and free—who could plant, tend, harvest, and process sugar. Here the delineations in Barbados and Jamaica were simple: "white servants," "hired white servants," and "negroes." In the Leeward Islands the category "servant" was not used, but on some of the islands different kinds of white people (men, women, boys, girls) were noted according to household.[85] In other places, only "negroes" were counted. And in yet others the total numbers of enslaved Africans were listed parish-by-parish instead of planter-by-planter. Levels of anxiety about the potential for slave revolts were closely linked to these census reports, which laid out in stark terms how many black bodies were present as a permanent reminder of their threat to the white hierarchy. Indeed island assemblies passed laws encouraging planters to ensure a ratio of one white person for every ten Africans enslaved—on the racial calculation that one white body would be sufficient to control every ten black bodies. Numbers and categories that should have provided comfort could be sources of anxiety if calculations did not add up favorably.

While the census demonstrates what categories English officials thought were important to count, it is equally revealing of what they did not. Often the categories were not delineated by sex, simply listing all enslaved Africans, for example, in the column marked "negroes." The effect was to code almost all categories, or at least categories of importance in the census, as male, whatever the reality. Neither women nor children who made up a significant proportion of the total populations of Caribbean islands were counted as individuals.[86] The inclusion of Honora Burk in the 1678 Montserrat census probably indicated a moment of being between spouses for this Irish woman, who was listed along with two "white children" as residing in Palmetto's Division.[87] The children of European parents (like Burk) were never named and were rarely marked as belonging to a specific household. In fact most European women and their children were listed in bulk numbers for each parish, once the details of the heads of household had been recorded, rendering it impossible to tie them to a particular estate or family. These women were considered as surplus to the categories that really mattered: they could neither be bought nor their offspring sold, they performed no military service, and they did not hold positions of imperial authority. Counting women who worked as servants and slaves was even more unusual, despite the fact female indentures and enslaved women labored in the fields alongside their male counterparts.[88] The disregard for women's labor is all the more surprising when considered alongside their reproductive work. Enslaved women "and their increase" literally grew bonded populations, performing labor so important that it was a defining feature of Atlantic slavery.[89]

Women and children (white or black) may have rarely been counted as individuals by the census takers, but some other groups were completely ignored by colonial officials. The Jamaican, Barbados, and Leeward Islands censuses failed to include categories that recognized mixed race individuals. Children of enslaved African women and their European masters disappeared. In the census, these offspring were hidden in the category "negro children," or perhaps not counted at all.[90] Neither were the children of enslaved African men and indentured or free European women counted.[91] English elites no doubt felt uneasy about recognizing the products of sex between English women and African men, given what such liaisons implied about the quality of the woman involved.[92] Similarly, free people of color were not counted. In St. Michael's Parish on Barbados, John and Hannah Dally and Charles Cuffee and their children were invisible, hidden by a colonial system that sought to deny that the category of "free negro" could exist.[93] The refusal to acknowledge either intimacy across the color line or the presence of free people of color is an example of English officials' reluctance to complicate categories.[94] Moreover, it demonstrates the resistance to include markers that muddied easy divisions between "negro" and "white," identifiers that were becoming increasingly synonymous with "enslaved" and "free."

The lack of consistency in categories in the various seventeenth-century Caribbean censuses changed at the start of the eighteenth century as the documents became more uniform. In 1708, the main categories everywhere were "white" and "black"—ethnicity disappeared in the Leeward Islands as the numbers of enslaved Africans increased rapidly and these former "societies with slaves" became slave societies.[95] Now on all islands Irish Catholics were absorbed into the white population. There were a few exceptions to these binary racial categories. Palmetto Point on St. Christopher included the additional categories of "Mallattoes" and "Indians," but the former did not appear as a separate column, and only three Indian boys were counted.[96] Antigua also noted free people of color, but only seventeen were recorded across the island.[97] Women and children, whether enslaved or free, were still not named in these censuses, but it was becoming increasingly common to include them by household. For example, on St. Christopher, Lieutenant Governor Michael Lambert's estate comprised ten white men, seven white women, two white boys, and six white girls. The census also noted his ownership of 43 enslaved men, 44 enslaved women, 16 enslaved boys, and 15 enslaved girls.[98] Nevis and Antigua also counted households separately in 1708 and the 1715 Barbados census made a similar move. Although the Barbados document only accounted for the white population of the island, the composition of these households was carefully enumerated as officials worked to convey the stability and prosperity of the colony.[99]

In the late 1720s another slew of colonial counting ensued. This time, the census categories broadened to include free blacks, individuals of mixed race, and Indians. But despite this expansion of categories, the numbers demonstrated very clearly that the primary divisions on the islands were between free whites and enslaved Africans. On Jamaica, 90 percent of the population was enslaved; in Barbados and the Leeward Islands the number hovered around 80 percent.[100] Combining these numbers with evidence of the acreage devoted to various cash crops, as on Montserrat in 1730, demonstrated the productivity of the islands, now some of the most profitable in the English Atlantic.[101] English attention shifted from the interimperial concerns of the seventeenth century, to the management of their racially based hierarchies in the eighteenth century, and the census reflected these new priorities.

Conclusion

Colonial counting took many forms in the long seventeenth century. Given the importance of settlements and land use for legitimizing their imperial project, English officials wanted to know how many and what kind of people inhabited the colonies. They also needed to account for enemies, internal and foreign, to know how to protect England's hard won territories. As the imperial challenge brought by Spain and France subsided at the start of the eighteenth century, and as the numbers of enslaved people increased exponentially, who to count and what categories to include changed. These attempts to render populations knowable and therefore controllable were a defining feature of English colonial society.

By the time the 1730 "Political Anatomy of Montserrat" was created, English officials had almost a century of experience of number making and taking in the colonies. The increasing rigidity of census categories coalesced around an accounting that made landowners and laborers, and therefore whites and blacks, the key distinctions that mattered in the colonies; reflecting in that process the ideology in Petty's *Political Anatomy*. Over time, the census also minimized the diversity of island populations as ethnic or religious categories dropped out in favor of those that privileged labor and race. This process was an important articulation of English political arithmetic. Narrowing possible categories allowed officials in the colonies to provide metropolitan authorities with a simple analysis of the populations under their control. It erased potential difficulties caused by the specter of Irish alliances with Catholic European powers and it helped the governments feel confident about their abilities to quash slave revolts. The clean and neat lines of the census gave the impression of control, the numbers themselves providing evidence of good governance and imperial success.

Notes

1 Special thanks to Christian Crouch, Holly Grout, and Heather Kopelson for their comments on this essay, and to Juan Ponce-Vázquez for sharing his work. Some of the source material for this essay appeared in "Subjects Without an Empire: The Irish in a Changing Caribbean," *Past and Present* 219 (2011), 31–60, and *Everyday Life in the Early English Caribbean: Irish, Africans, and the Construction of Difference* (Athens: University of Georgia Press, 2013). The author thanks Kristen Block, Oxford University Press and the University of Georgia Press for permission to use the material here.
2 The National Archives, London (TNA), CO152/18, Board of Trade, Original Correspondence, May 28, 1730. The oversized pages of the "Political Anatomy" must be called separately and can be found under TNA, EXT 1/258. The document is reprinted in full in Vere Langford Oliver, ed., *Caribbeana* (London: Mitchell Hughes and Clarke, 1916), Vol. IV, 302–311. See also Richard B. Sheridan, *Sugar and Slavery, An Economic History of the West Indies, 1623–1775* (Baltimore: Johns Hopkins University Press, 1974), 172–176; Natalie A. Zacek, *Settler Society in the English Leeward Islands, 1670–1776* (Cambridge: Cambridge University Press, 2010), 91–93; Jenny Shaw, *Everyday Life in the Early English Caribbean: Irish, Africans, and the Construction of Difference* (Athens: University of Georgia Press, 2013), 67–68.
3 *Sugar and Slavery*, table on 173. On "slave societies" see Ira Berlin, *Many Thousands Gone: The First Two Centuries of Slavery in North America* (Cambridge: Harvard University Press, 1998), 8–9.
4 Ted McCormick, *William Petty and the Ambitions of Political Arithmetic* (New York: Oxford University Press, 2009), 10. For more on the connections between enumeration and colonial policies see Jennifer L. Morgan, "Demographic Logics and Early Modern English Colonialism," work in progress presented to the Columbia Seminar on Early American History and Culture, February 2011; Mary Poovey, *A History of the Modern Fact: Problems of Knowledge in the Science of Wealth and Society* (Chicago: University of Chicago Press, 1998); McCormick, *William Petty*; Patricia Cline Cohen, *A Calculating People: The Spread of Numeracy in Early America* (Chicago: University of Chicago Press, 1982); Peter Buck, "Seventeenth-Century Political Arithmetic: Civil Strife and Vital Statistics," *Isis* 68, 1 (1977): 67–84; Charlotte Sussman, "The Colonial Afterlife of Political Arithmetic: Swift, Demography, and Mobile Populations," *Cultural Critique* 56 (2004): 92–126.
5 William Petty, *The Political Anatomy of Ireland* (London, 1691). Petty also wrote a tract entitled *Political Arithmetick*, published in 1690.
6 Kathleen Wilson, "Rethinking the Colonial State: Family, Gender, and Governmentality in Eighteenth-Century British Frontiers," *American Historical Review* 116[5] (2011): 1294–1322; Cohen, *A Calculating People*, 44.
7 An exception would be the meticulous records from the 1620s in Virginia, J. C. Hotten, *The Original Lists of Persons of Quality… Who Went From Great Britain to the American Plantations, 1600–1700* (Blowie, MD: Heritage Books, 2006); John F. Dorman, *Adventurers of Purse and Person, Virginia 1607–1624/5* (Baltimore: Genealogical Publishing Company, 2005).
8 For Barbados see TNA CO1/44; for Jamaica see TNA CO1/45.
9 TNA CO1/42.
10 David Eltis, *The Rise of African Slavery in the Americas* (Cambridge: Cambridge University Press, 2000).
11 The literature on the development of racial slavery that investigates the role of religion in this process is vast. Some recent works include, Michael Guasco, *Slaves and Englishmen: Human Bondage in the Early Modern Atlantic World* (Philadelphia: University of Pennsylvania Press, 2014); Heather Miyano Kopelson, *Faithful Bodies: Performing Religion and Race in the Puritan Atlantic* (New York: NYU Press, 2014); Shaw, *Everyday Life*; Katharine R. Gerbner, "Christian Slavery: Protestant Missions and Slave Conversion in the Atlantic World, 1660–1760" (Ph.D. dissertation, Harvard University, 2013); Rebecca A. Goetz, *The Baptism of Early Virginia: How Christianity Created Race* (Johns Hopkins University Press, 2012); Kristin Block, *Ordinary Lives in the Early Caribbean: Religion, Colonial Competition, and the Politics of Profit* (Athens: University of Georgia Press, 2012); Travis Glasson, *Mastering Christianity: Missionary Anglicanism and Slavery in the Atlantic World* (New York: Oxford University Press, 2011).

12 Patricia Seed, "Taking Possession and Reading Texts: Establishing the Authority of Overseas Empires," *William and Mary Quarterly*, 3rd series, 49 (1992): 183–209," 183–209.
13 J. H. Elliot, *Empires of the Atlantic World: Britain and Spain in America, 1492–1830* (New Haven: Yale University Press, 2006), 38–39.
14 *Empires of the Atlantic*, 67–68.
15 Dennis O. Flynn and Arturo Giráldez, "Born with a 'Silver Spoon': The Origin of World Trade in 1571," *Journal of World History* 6[2] (1995): 224–226; Kris E. Lane, *Pillaging the Empire: Piracy in the Americas, 1500–1750* (Armonk, NY: M. E. Sharpe, 1998). The seventeenth-century Spanish Caribbean has recently received more attention from scholars, Molly A. Warsh, "A Political Economy in the Early Spanish Caribbean," *William and Mary Quarterly*, 3rd series, 71[4] (2014): 517–548; Juan Ponce-Vázquez, "Social and Political Survival at the Edge of Empire: Spanish Local Elites in Hispaniola, 1580–1697" (Ph.D. dissertation University of Pennsylvania, 2011); David Wheat, *Atlantic Africa and the Spanish Caribbean, 1570–1640* (Chapel Hill: Omohundro Institute for Early American Culture Imprint, University of North Carolina Press, 2016).
16 On privateering see Kenneth R. Andrews, *Elizabethan Privateering: English Privateering During the Spanish War, 1585–1603* (Cambridge: Cambridge University Press, 1964). Works on English outposts include, Karen Ordahl Kupperman, *Roanoke: The Abandoned Colony* (New York: Rowan and Littlefield, 2007); Karen Ordahl Kupperman, *Providence Island 1630–1641: The Other Puritan Colony* (New York: Cambridge University Press, 1993); Joyce Lorimer, ed., *English and Irish Settlement on the Amazon River, 1500–1640* (London; Hakluyt Society, 1989); James Williamson, *English Colonies in Guiana and on the Amazon, 1604–1668* (Oxford: OUP, 1923).
17 Richard S. Dunn, *Sugar and Slaves: The Rise of the Planter Class in the West Indies, 1624–1713* (Chapel Hill: University of North Carolina Press, 1972), 49–51, 118–119.
18 Seed, "Taking Possession," 185–187.
19 For more on the goals of the Western Design see Carla Gardina Pestana, *The English Atlantic in an Age of Revolution, 1640–1660* (Cambridge: Harvard University Press, 2004), 177–179; Block, *Ordinary Lives*, 110–111, 114–117; Steven C. A. Pincus, *Protestantism and Patriotism: Ideologies and the Making of English Foreign Policy* (New York: Cambridge University Press, 1996), 168–192.
20 Pestana, *English Atlantic*, 180. See also Irene A. Wright, "The Spanish Resistance to the English Occupation of Jamaica, 1655–1660," *Transactions of the Royal Historical Society*, 4th series, 13 (1930): 117–147.
21 Philip C. Boucher, *France and the America Tropics to 1700: Topics of Discontent?* (Baltimore: Johns Hopkins University Press, 2008), 69–70, 181–185, 218–219; Zacek, *Settler Society*, 41–45, 87–88.
22 The French ceded their claim to their parts of St. Christopher at Utrecht, Dunn, *Sugar and Slaves*, 148. For the French perspective see Kenneth J. Banks, *Chasing Empire Across the Sea: Communications and the State in the French Atlantic, 1713–1763* (Montreal: McGill-Queen's University Press, 2002), Ch. 2.
23 Scholars' estimates of the numbers of Irish shipped to the Caribbean vary considerably. Some claim that over 50,000 were "sent beyond the seas" in the 1650s alone; others suggest a range from ten thousand to twenty-five thousand. For the lower figure, see Donald Harman Akenson, *If the Irish Ran the World: Montserrat, 1630–1730* (Toronto: McGill-Queens University Press, 1997), 19. For the higher estimate (which includes Virginia) see William J. Smyth, *Map-Making, Landscapes, and Memory: A Geography of Colonial and Early Modern Ireland, c. 1530–1750* (Cork: Cork University Press, 2006), 161–162.
24 Calendar of State Papers Venetian, Vol. 30, 1655–56 Venetian Ambassador to the Doge and Senate, March 3, 1656; British Library (BL), Add MSS 11,411, Fol. 17, T. Povey, Register of Letters Relating to the West Indies, 1655–61, petition of Barbados planters to Cromwell, n.d. (but likely 1655).
25 TNA, SP 25/31, No. 93, London, August 20, 1652.
26 TNA, SP 25/75, No. 586, London, October 19, 1654.
27 TNA, SP 25/77, No. 141, May 22, 1656.
28 C. F. Firth, ed., *The Narrative of General Venables* (London, 1900), 130–131; Kirstin Block and Jenny Shaw, "Subjects Without an Empire: The Irish in a Changing Caribbean," *Past and Present* 219 (2011): 47.
29 Irene A. Wright, ed., *Spanish Narratives of the English Attack on Santo Domingo, 1655* (London: Camden Miscellany, xiv, 1926), 59–60.
30 Block, *Ordinary Lives*, 131.
31 TNA, CO1/42. See also Dunn, *Sugar and Slaves*, 126–31. For the French perspective see Pritchard, *In Search of*, 47–51.
32 Block and Shaw, "Subjects Without an Empire," 52.
33 TNA, CO1/21 No. 55, "Major Scott's Relation," July 12, 1667.
34 Shaw, *Everyday Life*, 173–174; Zacek, *Settler Society*, 80–81.

35 TNA, CO152/37 No. 41, Codrington to the Lords of Trade and Plantations, Antigua, September 19, 1689.
36 TNA, CO1/21 No. 44, May 27, 1667.
37 TNA, CO152/37 No. 13, June 27, 1689. Zacek discusses the upheaval in the Leewards in 1689, *Settler Society*, 87–88.
38 TNA, CO139/1 Fol. 84, March 16, 1665. See also Susan Dwyer Amussen, *Caribbean Exchanges: Slavery and the Transformation of English Society, 1640–1700* (Chapel Hill: University of North Carolina Press, 2007), 164–167.
39 TNA, PRO31/17/44 p. 231, June 23, 1657.
40 Dunn, *Sugar and Slaves*, 259–261.
41 *Great Newes from the Barbadoes* (London: Printed for L. Curtis in Goat-Court upon Ludgate Hill, 1676), 9 (emphasis in original). For a full analysis of this and the 1692 revolt see Jerome S. Handler, "Slave revolts and conspiracies in seventeenth-century Barbados," *New West Indian Guide/Nieuwe West-Indische Gids* 56 (1982): 5–42; and "The Barbados Slave Conspiracies of 1675 and 1692," *Journal of the Barbados Museum and Historical Society* 36[4] (1982): 312–333. For the role of the enslaved woman Anna see Jennifer L. Morgan, *Laboring Women: Gender and Reproduction in New World Slavery* (Philadelphia: University of Pennsylvania Press, 2004), 175–176; Block, *Ordinary Lives*, 175–178; Shaw, *Everyday Life*, 137–140.
42 Whether the revolt was imagined or not, twenty-two men were executed for their part in the alleged plot, TNA, CO31/1 f. 675, Minutes of the Barbados Council, March 1, 1686.
43 Dunn, *Sugar and Slaves*, 260–261; Amussen, *Caribbean Exchanges*, 170–172.
44 TNA CO28/1, Fols. 203–204, January 20, 1693; Shaw, *Everyday Life*, 129–130, 147–150; Jason T. Sharples, "Discovering Slave Conspiracies: New Fears of Rebellion and Old Paradigms of Plotting in Seventeenth-Century Barbados," *American Historical Review* 120[3] (2015): 811–813; Handler, "Slave Revolts."
45 Bridgetown Public Library (BPL), Lucas MSS, reel 1, fols. 161–162, November 6, 1655; Hilary McD. Beckles, "'A Riotous and Unruly Lot': Irish Indentures Servants and Freemen in the English West Indies, 1644–1713," *William and Mary Quarterly*, 3rd series, 47 (1990): 515–517.
46 On 1675 see: Beckles, "Riotous and Unruly," 517; Handler, "Slave Revolts"; Dunn, *Sugar and Slaves*, 257–258; Amussen, *Caribbean Exchanges*, 159–161; Shaw, *Everyday Life*, 132–140. For 1686 see TNA, CO31/1 f. 675, Minutes of the Barbados Council, March 1, 1686. For 1692 see: TNA, CO28/1, 203–204, Barbados, January 20, 1693; Beckles, "Riotous and Unruly," 518, 521; Handler, "Barbados Slave Conspiracies"; Handler "Slave Revolts"; Shaw, *Everyday Life*, 129–130, 147–152.
47 TNA, CO28/37 No. 11, Barbados, July 16, 1689.
48 William Petty, *The History of the Survey of Ireland, Commonly Called the Down Survey*, ed. Thomas Aiskew Larcom 1851 (Reprint, New York: A.M. Kelly, 1967), 13–14; William Petty, "Survey of Ireland," BL, Add MSS 72875–76.
49 William Petty, *The Economic Writings of William Petty*, ed. Charles Henry Hull (Cambridge: Cambridge University Press, 1899), 561–562.
50 Buck, "Seventeenth-Century Political Arithmetic," 73–74; Petty, *Political Arithmetick*, preface. For a discussion of Petty's philosophical influences and mentors see Poovey, *History of the Modern Fact*, 93–96; McCormick, *William Petty*, especially Ch. 1 and 2.
51 Poovey, *History of the Modern Fact*, 135–137.
52 Petty, *Political Anatomy*, 30–31; Poovey, *History of the Modern Fact*, 136; McCormick, *William Petty*, 199–201; Sussman, "Colonial Afterlife," 103.
53 Cohen, *Calculating People*, 44–45, 69–74. The English approach was in contradistinction to the Spanish Relaciones Geográficas, the royally decreed questionnaires sent by the Spanish crown to their American colonies, Mundy, *The Mapping of New Spain*.
54 TNA, CO153/2, Fols. 176–77, August 19, 1676.
55 BL, Eg 2395, Fol. 277; BL, Add MSS 11,411, Fol. 17.
56 Richard Ligon, *A True and Exact History of the Iland of Barbados* (London, 1657), 43.
57 Ferrar Papers, No. 1117, answers 51 and 3, VCA, Ferrar Papers, 1590–1790, Available online at www.amdigital.co.uk/m-collections/collection/virginia-company-archives. (Accessed October 6, 2008).
58 BL, Add MSS 11,411, Fol. 17.
59 Block notes a similar comment by Henry Whistler during the Western Design, *Ordinary Lives*, 136.
60 BL, Eg 2395, Fol. 625, "An Estimate of the Barbadoes and of the now Inhabitants there."
61 BL, Add MSS 11,411, Fol. 17.
62 BPL, 22. Sept. 1657 Lucas MSS 1. 368, 372. See also Beckles, "Riotous and Unruly," 516–517.
63 Shaw, *Everyday Life*, 25.

64 Jeaffreson, *Young Squire*, 2: 207, cited in Zacek, *Settler Society*, 89; Beckles, "Riotous and Unruly," 511.
65 TNA, CO 1/22, No. 20, 1667, "An Account of the English Sugar Plantations."
66 BL, Stowe MSS, September 16, 1667; Beckles, "Riotous and Unruly," 508–510.
67 TNA, CO1/21, No. 162, December 16, 1667.
68 TNA, CO1/22 No. 60, April 3, 1668.
69 TNA, CO1/29 No. 61, f. 163.
70 TNA, CO153/3 f. 429, Nevis, June 27, 1689.
71 TNA, CO152/37 No. 22, July 31, 1689.
72 Ligon, *True and Exact History*, 43.
73 Dunn, *Sugar and Slaves*, 74–75.
74 BL, Add MSS 11,411, Fol. 17, T. Povey, Register of Letters relating to the West Indies, 1655–1661, n.d., but probably 1655.
75 *Journal of the House of Assembly of Jamaica, 1663–1826* (Jamaica, 1811–1829), I, app., 20, 28, 40, cited in Dunn, *Sugar and Slaves*, 155; TNA CO1/45, No. 1, Fols. i–xiv.
76 TNA, CO 1/42, Fols. 45–59.
77 TNA, CO 1/44, Fols. 142–379. The census was sent to London in April 1680 and is therefore most often referred to as the 1680 census, Dunn, *Sugar and Slaves*, 84.
78 Larry Dale Gragg, *The Quaker Community on Barbados: Challenging the Culture of the Planter Class* (Columbia: University of Missouri Press, 2009), 79–80. Jewish households in Bridgetown were counted, but individual Jews were not, Dunn, *Sugar and Slaves*, 105, 106.
79 TNA, CO1/44, no. 47, x, xii, xv, xvi, xvii, xxi. Wills and deeds from this period demonstrate the presence of Irish men and women on the islands, Barbados Department of Archives (BDA), RB6 (wills), and RB3 (deeds).
80 The categories "S" (Scots) and "D" (Dutch) were also used, but the numbers were very small, Robert V. Wells, *The Population of the British Colonies in America before 1776: A Survey of Census Data* (Princeton: Princeton University Press, 1975), 211–213.
81 TNA, CO1/42. See also Dunn, *Sugar and Slaves*, 126–31.
82 Shaw, *Everyday Life*, Ch. 6.
83 TNA CO1/45, No. 1, fols. (i)–(xiv); TNA, CO 1/44, Fols. 142–379.
84 Dunn, *Sugar and Slaves*, 86–87.
85 Dunn, *Sugar and Slaves*, 126–128.
86 Initially there were as many as nine English men for every English woman in the Caribbean, Dunn, *Sugar and Slaves*, 326. Although more Irish men than women entered the colonies, the proportions were much closer than those for English settlers, Akenson, *If the Irish*, 115. The enslaved African population was even more balanced. Over 40 percent of all Africans who experienced the Middle Passage 1670–1700 were women, about 50 percent were men, and the rest were children, Morgan, *Laboring Women*, 177–79; David Eltis and Stanley Engerman, "Was the Slave Trade Dominated by Men?" *Journal of Interdisciplinary History* 23 (1992): 237–257.
87 TNA, CO1/42, No. 64.
88 Morgan, *Laboring Women*, Ch. 5; Barbara Bush, *Slave Women in Caribbean Society, 1650–1838* (Bloomington: Indiana University Press, 1990), 36–39.
89 Morgan, *Laboring Women*, 82–83.
90 BDA, RL1/17, Fol. 123, August 13, 1683.
91 BDA, RL1/22, Fol. 32, January 1674.
92 Jones, *Engendering Whiteness: White Women and Colonialism in Barbados and North Carolina* (Manchester: Manchester University Press, 2007), 20–23.
93 BDA, RL1/1, Fol. 215, September 9, 1676; RL1/1, Fol. 255, April 3, 1681.
94 For the Spanish approach see Tamar Herzog, *Defining Nations: Immigrants and Citizens in Early Spain and Spanish America* (New Haven: Yale University Press, 2003).
95 Berlin, *Many Thousands Gone*, 8–9; Wells, *The Population*, 211, 224.
96 TNA, CO152/7 No. 47 Fol. v.
97 Wells, *The Population*, 214.
98 TNA, CO152/7 No. 47 Fol. iv.
99 TNA, CO28/16; Dunn, *Sugar and Slaves*, 330–331; Wells, *The Population*, 242–243.
100 Wells, *The Population*, 197, 212.
101 TNA, EXT 1/258.

References

Akenson, Donald Harman. *If the Irish Ran the World: Montserrat, 1630–1730* (Toronto: McGill-Queens University Press, 1997).

Amussen, Susan Dwyer. *Caribbean Exchanges: Slavery and the Transformation of English Society, 1640–1700* (Chapel Hill: University of North Carolina Press, 2007).

Andrews, Kenneth R. *Elizabethan Privateering: English Privateering during the Spanish War, 1585–1603* (Cambridge: Cambridge University Press, 1964).

Banks, Kenneth J. *Chasing Empire Across the Sea: Communications and the State in the French Atlantic, 1713–1763* (Montreal: McGill-Queen's University Press, 2002).

Beckles, Hilary McD. "'A Riotous and Unruly Lot': Irish Indentures Servants and Freemen in the English West Indies, 1644–1713," *William and Mary Quarterly*, 3rd series, 47 (1990): 503–22.

Beckles, Hilary McD. *White Servitude and Black Slavery in Barbados, 1627–1715* (Knoxville: University of Tennessee Press, 1989).

Berleant-Schiller, Riva. "Free Labor and the Economy in Seventeenth-Century Montserrat," *William and Mary Quarterly*, 3rd series 46, 3 (1989): 539–64.

Berlin, Ira. *Many Thousands Gone: The First Two Centuries of Slavery in North America* (Cambridge: Harvard University Press, 1998).

Block, Kristen. *Ordinary Lives in the Early Caribbean: Religion, Colonial Competition, and the Politics of Profit* (Athens: University of Georgia Press, 2012).

Block, Kristen and Jenny Shaw, "Subjects Without an Empire: The Irish in a Changing Caribbean," *Past and Present* 219 (2011): 31–60.

Boucher, Philip P. *France and the American Tropics to 1700: Tropics of Discontent?* (Baltimore: Johns Hopkins University Press, 2008).

Buck, Peter. "Seventeenth-Century Political Arithmetic: Civil Strife and Vital Statistics," *Isis* 68, 1 (1977): 67–84.

Bush, Barbara. *Slave Women in Caribbean Society, 1650–1838* (Bloomington: Indiana University Press, 1990).

Cohen, Patricia Cline. *A Calculating People: The Spread of Numeracy in Early America* (Chicago: University of Chicago Press, 1982).

Dorman, John F. *Adventurers of Purse and Person, Virginia 1607–1624/5* (Baltimore: Genealogical Publishing Company, 2005).

Dunn, Richard S. *Sugar and Slaves: The Rise of the Planter Class in the West Indies, 1624–1713* (Chapel Hill: University of North Carolina Press, 1972).

Elliot, J. H. *Empires of the Atlantic World: Britain and Spain in America, 1492–1830* (New Haven: Yale University Press, 2006).

Eltis, David. *The Rise of African Slavery in the Americas* (Cambridge: Cambridge University Press, 2000).

Eltis, David and Stanley Engerman. "Was the Slave Trade Dominated by Men?" *Journal of Interdisciplinary History* 23 (1992): 237–257.

Firth, C. F., ed., *The Narrative of General Venables* (London, 1900).

Flynn Dennis O. and Arturo Giráldez. "Born with a 'Silver Spoon:' The Origin of World Trade in 1571," *Journal of World History* 6[2] (1995): 201–221.

Gerbner, Katharine R. "Christian Slavery: Protestant Missions and Slave Conversion in the Atlantic World, 1660–1760" (Ph.D. dissertation, Harvard University, 2013).

Glasson, Travis. *Mastering Christianity: Missionary Anglicanism and Slavery in the Atlantic World* (New York: Oxford University Press, 2011).

Goetz, Rebecca A. *The Baptism of Early Virginia: How Christianity Created Race* (Johns Hopkins University Press, 2012).

Gragg, Larry Dale. *The Quaker Community on Barbados: Challenging the Culture of the Planter Class* (Columbia: University of Missouri Press, 2009).

Guasco, Michael. *Slaves and Englishmen: Human Bondage in the Early Modern Atlantic World* (Philadelphia: University of Pennsylvania Press, 2014).

Handler, Jerome S. "Slave revolts and conspiracies in seventeenth-century Barbados," *New West Indian Guide/ Nieuwe West-Indische Gids* 56 (1982): 5–42.

Handler, Jerome S. "The Barbados Slave Conspiracies of 1675 and 1692," *Journal of the Barbados Museum and Historical Society* 36[4] (1982): 312–333.

Herzog, Tamar. *Defining Nations: Immigrants and Citizens in Early Spain and Spanish America* (New Haven: Yale University Press, 2003).

Hotten, J. C. *The Original Lists of Persons of Quality... Who Went From Great Britain to the American Plantations, 1600–1700* (Blowie, MD: Heritage Books, 2006).

John F. Dorman, *Adventurers of Purse and Person, Virginia 1607–1624/5* (Baltimore: Genealogical Publishing Company, 2005).

Jones, Cecily. *Engendering Whiteness: White Women and Colonialism in Barbados and North Carolina* (Manchester: Manchester University Press, 2007).

Kopelson, Heather Miyano. *Faithful Bodies: Performing Religion and Race in the Puritan Atlantic* (New York: NYU Press, 2014).

Kupperman, Karen Ordahl. *Providence Island 1630–1641: The Other Puritan Colony* (New York: Cambridge University Press, 1993).

Kupperman, Karen Ordahl. *Roanoke: The Abandoned Colony* (New York: Rowman & Littlefield, 2007).

Lane, Kris E. *Pillaging the Empire: Piracy in the Americas, 1500–1750* (Armonk: M. E. Sharpe, 1998).

Lorimer, Joyce, ed. *English and Irish Settlement on the Amazon River, 1500–1640* (London; Hakluyt Society, 1989).

McCormick, Ted. *William Petty and the Ambitions of Political Arithmetic* (New York: Oxford University Press, 2009).

Morgan, Jennifer L. *Laboring Women: Gender and Reproduction in New World Slavery* (Philadelphia: University of Pennsylvania Press, 2004).

Morgan, Jennifer L. "Demographic Logics and Early Modern English Colonialism," work in progress presented to the Columbia Seminar on Early American History and Culture, February 2011.

Mundy, Barbara E. *The Mapping of New Spain: Indigenous Cartography and the Maps of the Relaciones Geográficas* (Chicago: Chicago University Press, 1996).

Pestana, Carla Gardina. *The English Atlantic in an Age of Revolution, 1640–1660* (Cambridge: Harvard University Press, 2004).

Petty, William. The Political Anatomy of Ireland (London: D. Brown & W. Rodgers, 1690).

Petty, William. Political Arithmetick (London: R. Clivel, 1691).

Petty, William. *The Economic Writings of William Petty*, ed. Charles Henry Hull (Cambridge: Cambridge University Press, 1899), 561–562.

Petty, William. *The History of the Survey of Ireland, Commonly Called the Down Survey*, ed. Thomas Aiskew Larcom 1851 (Reprint, New York: A.M. Kelly, 1967), 13–14.

Pincus, Steven C. A. *Protestantism and Patriotism: Ideologies and the Making of English Foreign Policy* (New York: Cambridge University Press, 1996).

Ponce-Vázquez, Juan. "Social and Political Survival at the Edge of Empire: Spanish Local Elites in Hispaniola, 1580–1697" (Ph.D. dissertation University of Pennsylvania, 2011).

Poovey, Mary. *A History of the Modern Fact: Problems of Knowledge in the Science of Wealth and Society* (Chicago: University of Chicago Press, 1998).

Pritchard, James. *In Search of Empire: The French in the Americas, 1670–1730* (Cambridge: Cambridge University Press, 2004).

Quinn, David Beers. *Ireland and America: Their Early Associations, 1500–1640* (Liverpool, 1991).

Seed, Patricia. "Taking Possession and Reading Texts: Establishing the Authority of Overseas Empires," *William and Mary Quarterly*, 3rd series, 49 (1992): 183–209.

Sharples, Jason T. "Discovering Slave Conspiracies: New Fears of Rebellion and Old Paradigms of Plotting in Seventeenth-Century Barbados," *American Historical Review* 120[3] (2015): 811–843.

Shaw, Jenny. *Everyday Life in the Early English Caribbean: Irish, Africans, and the Construction of Difference* (Athens: University of Georgia Press, 2013).

Sheridan, Richard B. *Sugar and Slavery: An Economic History of the West Indies, 1623–1775* (Baltimore: Johns Hopkins University Press, 1974).

Smyth, William J. *Map-Making, Landscapes, and Memory: A Geography of Colonial and Early Modern Ireland, c. 1530–1750* (Cork: Cork University Press, 2006).

Sussman, Charlotte. "The Colonial Afterlife of Political Arithmetic: Swift, Demography, and Mobile Populations," *Cultural Critique* 56 (2004): 92–126.

Warsh, Molly A. "A Political Economy in the Early Spanish Caribbean," *William and Mary Quarterly*, 3rd series, 71[4] (2014): 517–548.

Wells, Robert V. *The Population of the British Colonies in America before 1776: A Survey of Census Data* (Princeton: Princeton University Press, 1975).

Wheat, David. *Atlantic Africa and the Spanish Caribbean, 1570–1640* (Chapel Hill: Omohundro Institute for Early American Culture Imprint, University of North Carolina Press, 2016).

Williamson, James. *English Colonies in Guiana and on the Amazon, 1604–1668* (Oxford: OUP, 1923).
Wilson, Kathleen. "Rethinking the Colonial State: Family, Gender, and Governmentality in Eighteenth-Century British Frontiers," *American Historical Review* 116[5] (2011): 1294–1322.
Wright, Irene A., ed. *Spanish Narratives of the English Attack on Santo Domingo, 1655* (London: Camden Miscellany, xiv, 1926).
Wright, Irene A. "The Spanish Resistance to the English Occupation of Jamaica, 1655–1660," *Transactions of the Royal Historical Society*, 4th series, 13 (1930): 117–147.
Zacek, Natalie A. *Settler Society in the English Leeward Islands, 1670–1776* (Cambridge: Cambridge University Press, 2010).

6
THE DEVELOPMENT OF SLAVERY IN THE BRITISH AMERICAS

Justin Roberts

Slavery has been common throughout human history but the form of racially based chattel slavery that had emerged in British America in the middle of the seventeenth century—in which Africans were viewed simply as units of labor—was uniquely exploitative and brutal among slave systems.[1] It became more fully entrenched and dehumanizing and the racial barriers between slave and free became less permeable as slavery expanded and the number of slaves rose in the British Americas from the middle of seventeenth century through the end of the eighteenth century. The majority of slaves in the British Americas toiled in plantation fields producing staple crops for export but slaves also worked in a wide variety of roles throughout the colonies. African slavery existed alongside other forms of coerced labor in the New World, such as indentured servitude or convict labor or the enslavement of the indigenous in the Americas, but it was predominantly enslaved African labor and coerced African migration that drove the settlement and expansion of the British Americas. The majority of the migrants to the Americas were unfree and the vast majority of migrants to the Americas until late in the eighteenth century were African slaves.[2]

Slavery was never a monolithic institution and it took a variety of forms across the British Americas, ranging from societies with slaves, common throughout the northern colonies of North America, in which less than 20 percent of the population consisted of African slaves to slave societies that were fully committed to slavery, such as the deadly slave societies of the Caribbean sugar islands in which African populations came to outnumber whites by ratios of ten to one or more.[3] The economic expansion of the plantation colonies on the southern mainland and in the Caribbean was particularly dependent upon African slaves and these regions were the economic heart of the British Empire. The brutal demands of staple crops such as sugar meant that the enslaved population in the most southern English colonies struggled to achieve natural reproduction and slaveholders required a consistent supply of new African slaves. A combination of economic and territorial expansion and a declining slave population in the Lowcountry until the middle of the eighteenth century (and in the Caribbean sugar islands until emancipation in 1833) meant that the demand for new African slaves grew steadily from the first stages of English settlement in the Americas until the beginning of the nineteenth century.

The enslavement of Africans existed along a continuum as one of many forms of unfree labor in the early modern world.[4] In the British Americas, freedom was certainly a rhetorical concept but most people in the early modern era existed in hierarchical worlds in which they were subject to many restrictions on their freedom.[5] In other words, freedom was relative rather than absolute. In the seventeenth century, the boundaries of enslavement appear to have been quite permeable and the racial divisions between who should be free and who was eligible for bondage were not as strictly defined as they would become. In the first decades of settlement, many Africans could escape enslavement and some whites could be forced to work in brutal labor regimes alongside African slaves. Although chattel slavery and absolute freedom existed along a continuum, there was a trend in the seventeenth and eighteenth-century British Americas toward a more clearly defined slave/free binary that was associated with increasingly stark racial divisions. The populace became divided along color lines into those who were eligible to be exploited through enslavement and for certain kinds of extreme coercive labor practices such as gang labor and those who were not.

Africans would become the most significant labor force in the British Americas, particularly in the Plantation Americas, but the British relied on a variety of coercive labor practices to compel that labor and used many vulnerable populations in some form of coerced labor. They brought indentured white servants (particularly the Irish) to work alongside a gradually growing population of enslaved Africans on early sugar plantations in the Lesser Antilles and on tobacco plantations in the Chesapeake and they banished white convicts from Britain to the Americas as laborers, a practice that would continue deep into the eighteenth century.[6] Michael Guasco has recently argued that slavery was a common enough practice in the sixteenth and seventeenth century world and that the English adoption of a racially based chattel slavery for labor exploitation was not surprising but that the system of indentured servitude or "bound white labor for labor's sake was an innovation of the early seventeenth century."[7] These servants worked in exchange for their passage to the Americas. Their work conditions were brutal compared to most English farm laborers and they often worked alongside enslaved Africans in the same daily tasks but—in contrast to the lifetime and inheritable enslavement of Africans—they served an average of only 53 months as servants before being released. English convicts transported to the Americas were subject to slightly harsher terms with an average of 113 months of labor servitude.[8]

The origins of the racially based enslavement of Africans in the United States have been a longstanding subject of debate for historians and volumes of literature have been produced and continue to be produced to explore those origins. To put it simply, scholars have struggled with the question of whether a deeply ingrained racism before the English settlement of the Americas made the enslavement of Africans, as historian Winthrop Jordan once suggested, "an unthinking decision" or whether racial prejudice developed to legitimate and buttress the institution of slavery, an institution which emerged only slowly and piecemeal in the early colonies and which may have been a way of dividing lower class whites from blacks to solidify the position of elite planters.[9] Much has been made by this latter group of historians of the existence of several notable individuals of African descent, such as Anthony Johnson, who attained freedom at some point in the first decades of the Chesapeake settlement and became property owners and servant masters in their own right.[10] The evidence is thin for studying the status of blacks in the Chesapeake before 1660 but, despite the existence of these free blacks, there is little question now among most historians that the default status for the majority of the blacks in the Chesapeake was enslavement. There were Africans in the colony even before "twenty and odd" African slaves were sold by a Dutch privateer in Virginia in 1619—an oft-cited and hotly debated moment in the history of Africans in early Virginia—and most of this first generation of blacks were almost certainly slaves but their numbers were small.[11] In the few surviving censuses from Virginia from the 1620s, nearly half the Africans in the colony were listed only as "negar" or "negors," adopting the Spanish usage. They were a distinct population and their status as slaves was taken for granted.[12]

The vast majority of that origins debate literature until very recently focused on slavery in the early United States, specifically the Chesapeake but the growth of a broader Atlantic perspective in early American history has led historians in recent years to a new kind of origins of race and slavery debate, refocused on the Caribbean or on the origins of slavery throughout the British Atlantic. Whereas several scholars in the Chesapeake stressed examples of Africans who attained freedom during the first five decades of settlement, much has been made in this new Caribbean-inclusive or Caribbean-focused historiography of the slave-like treatment and the exploitation of the white servants who worked alongside African slaves on the first generation of sugar plantations in the Lesser Antilles. These scholars stress the vulnerability of whites to enslavement in the early modern Atlantic or prejudicial ethnic and religious attitudes toward the Irish that divided whites from the British Isles and made the Irish vulnerable to harsher forms of labor exploitation.[13] This new Atlanticized origins debate emphasizes that in day-to-day life there was little appreciable difference in many cases between the white servants and African slaves on early sugar plantations. Yet, this perspective fails to address a point made most convincingly by historian David Eltis: no whites were ever subject to inheritable lifetime chattel bondage in the Americas and such was the default condition for Africans in English colonies.[14] As early as 1636, before sugar was grown in the island, the Barbados assembly declared that "Negroes and Indians…should serve for life unless a contract was before made to the contrary."[15]

The English used African slaves very quickly after settling colonies in the Americas, albeit in small numbers. The population of African slaves in the English colonies was small enough that there were probably more English slaves in North Africa than there were African slaves in the English colonies in the Caribbean until as late as the 1640s.[16] English colonists would almost certainly have used more slaves if a greater supply had been available or if they could compete with other buyers in the early seventeenth-century market for slaves. The English had no qualms with the institution of slavery. They adopted a system of enslaving Africans that Iberians had brought to the Americas—after earlier experiments on Atlantic islands off the West African Coast—and had used extensively in Brazil, in the Caribbean, and throughout their other South American settlements. The Portuguese had been using African slaves on plantations to cultivate sugar in the fifteenth century in the Atlantic Islands before transferring that plantation system to northeastern Brazil.[17] The English were latecomers to the New World. Along with two other northwestern European powers, the Dutch and the French, the English were part of a second wave of European expansion into the Americas and thus the first English colonies were perched like piratical parasites on the edges of vast and powerful Iberian American empires. Many of the slaves in the early years of English settlement were brought into the English empire through Iberian channels. This may be why a significant number of Africans, like Anthony Johnson, were able to gain freedom from enslavement in peripheral areas of the seventeenth-century Americas such as the Chesapeake. Iberian systems of slavery recognized a slave's legal right to self-purchase or *coartación* and manumission as a tool of social control.[18]

The English were prejudiced against peoples with darker skin before carving out colonies in the Americas. Englishmen associated blackness with the devil and there had been longstanding associations between dark skin and the laboring classes.[19] However, English ideas about race, like the concept of race itself, do need to be historicized. Racism is not a transhistorical attitude. Seventeenth-century notions of racial difference were less essentialist in nature and less clearly articulated than the kind of scientific racism that would emerge in the nineteenth century.[20] In the first half of the seventeenth century in particular, the English saw race as a mutable or malleable characteristic of populations. They were concerned about their own bodies, including the color of their skin, being transformed in the hotter climates of the Americas. Early modern conceptions of difference did not necessarily privilege racial markers of difference. Englishmen were as focused on the Africans' status as non-Christians or "heathens" and their cultural differences as they were on their skin color. Black skin was the most visible marker of African difference in the Americas and English colonists increasingly focused on this difference and essentialized its meaning. They drew support from the biblical story of the Curse of Ham to justify enslavement and to explain the permanence of African skin color. According to this tradition, Ham had seen his father naked and inebriated and his sons had been cursed to be servants of servants. The English believed that African skin color marked them as the descendants of Ham.[21] Skin color had clearly become the marker of a slave in the English Americas by the middle of the seventeenth century when one minister who visited Virginia remarked, "These two words, Negro and Slave" had "by Custom grown Homogenous and Convertible."[22] The stark white/black binaries that evolved in the English Americas, maturing in the eighteenth century, did make slavery in the English Americas distinctive. Slavery in the Latin American world recognized gradations of color. English planters tended to keep lighter skinned slaves from the field, preferring to use them for domestic and skilled labor but they created much firmer boundary lines between blacks and whites, and slaves and free men from the seventeenth through the nineteenth centuries than in the Latin American world.[23]

In the last half of the seventeenth century in particular, the English also drew on native slaves to help feed the rapacious labor demands of their rapidly expanding colonies, especially the budding plantations in the circum-Caribbean world. The English focused less on the physiological differences of enslaved Natives than they did on their enslaved Africans. For the English, it was almost exclusively the Natives' cultural differences and their status as non-Christians that made them eligible for enslavement.[24] Native slaves had been used by Iberian powers before the English settled. The Portuguese, for example, had used native laborers on sugar plantations in Brazil. The practice was eventually banned in 1570.[25] Enslavement was a common practice in Native societies across the Americas and so slaves were easy to acquire from native traders.[26] The English traded for native slaves from the Guianas and from the Carolinas, mainland territories on the periphery of a bustling English Caribbean. One scholar estimates that between 30,000 and 50,000 native slaves were enslaved in the southeastern Lowcountry.[27] They shipped many of these toward the Caribbean sugar colonies. In fact, before 1715, colonists in the Carolinas probably exported more slaves than they imported.[28] The English might have tried to rely more heavily on native labor throughout their colonies if it had been available. As late as the 1650s, Englishmen imagined that large numbers of native laborers would help them settle successful colonies. When Thomas Modyford encouraged parliament to settle the coast of the Guianas in South America in 1654, he described the "infinite number of naked Indians" in the area that the settlers could use for labor.[29] However, disease epidemics that decimated the indigenous populations and rebellions kept the English from exploiting them more fully as a labor source. Nevertheless, there were significant numbers of natives pulled into plantation labor alongside the white servants and Africans. Over time black skin became most prominently associated with the status of slave and the natives who remained amidst African majorities on plantations disappeared from plantation ledgers. They blended into the predominantly enslaved African populations and planters began to simply refer to all their slaves, African and Native alike, as "Negroes."[30]

Slavery emerged as an institution in the English Americas in the absence of any specific legal framework to legitimate or define it or any legal mechanisms of coercion. Until 1661, when the first comprehensive slave code was developed in the English Americas, slaves were held in bondage by custom and there were only a handful of disparate laws regulating the usage of slaves or demarking the status of non-European populations. For example, an Act was passed in 1639 in Virginia that required all colonists "except Negroes" to have weapons.[31] As the population of African slaves in English colonies grew, local assemblies began to pass laws to entrench the system of slavery. The Barbadian assembly passed the first comprehensive English slave code in 1661 and that code became the model for comprehensive slave codes throughout the English plantation colonies. The assembly that passed the Barbadian "Act for the Better Ordering and Governing of Negroes" noted that there was "no Tract to guide Us where to walk, nor any Rule set Us how to Governe such Slaves "in all the "Lawes of England."[32] The Barbadian code of 1661 drew on a variety of influences, including Spanish and French precedents, and they collected several of the acts that had been passed in the island to that point.[33] The comprehensive Barbadian slave code of 1661 became the model for comprehensive slave codes in Jamaica in 1664, South Carolina in 1696, Antigua in 1702, and Virginia in 1705.

The comprehensive Barbadian code was tuned and adapted to new environments but the core principles of the comprehensive codes included limiting slave mobility, limiting interaction with other whites, limiting slave huckstering, and imposing harsh punishments for violence toward whites or for any signs of rebellion.[34] The codes also helped codify skin color as the key marker of enslaved status. Racial divisions became entrenched as colonial assemblies, dominated by elite planters, worked to divide poor white servants from black slaves and to define all African descendants as chattel. The opportunities for manumission began to disappear with the introduction of comprehensive slave codes in each of the plantation colonies, not to remerge until the rise of antislavery sentiments encouraged manumissions in the late eighteenth century.

The English codes were not designed by metropolitan officials but by slaveholders living in the colonies to control the ever-expanding enslaved African populations they lived alongside. Some of the laws passed by colonial assemblies who were inured to the day-to-day violence of the institution were actually draconian enough that they met with disapproval in the metropole. In 1683, the English Crown refused to ratify all of the Jamaican laws. After reviewing the slave laws that had been passed in Jamaica, the Crown noted that the provision of a fine for any man who would "wilfully and wantonly kill a negro" seemed "to encourage the wilful shedding of blood" and they insisted that "[s]ome better provision must be found than a fine to deter men from such acts of cruelty."[35] The English slave laws reflect the degree of dehumanization and beastialization that was occurring as chattel slavery became rooted in the British Americas.[36] The 1696 comprehensive slave codes of South Carolina, for example, had a provision stating that runaways would be gelded after a second offense, a treatment normally reserved for livestock.[37] The codes were more barbaric in colonies with black majorities than in colonies where blacks were a minority population. In eighteenth-century South Carolina, for example, free men could not be executed for killing a slave but "in Virginia, it was at least a theoretical possibility."[38] In contrast to the English slave codes, the French *Code Noir* of 1685 was imposed by Louis XIV in the metropole rather than being created by local assemblies and it showed more recognition of slaves' humanity with provisions such as one that required slaveholders to keep husbands and wives together.[39]

The first permanent and successful English colony began on the North American mainland in Virginia in 1607 but the Chesapeake was slow to develop as a slave society. The Chesapeake had a plantation society and a staple crop before it had a slave society. Tobacco became the staple crop and tobacco plantations began to expand rapidly, albeit unevenly, across the landscape in the 1620s.[40] Most tobacco plantations were small and they were worked by only a handful of laborers, predominantly white servants. Blacks never comprised more than 5 percent of the Chesapeake population in the first five decades after settlement.[41] The English were only able to establish successful colonies on the periphery of most powerful spheres of Iberian control and the Africans who made their way to the Chesapeake usually came via traders to that Iberian world and the slaves had had significant exposure to Iberian powers. Many of the blacks arriving in early Virginia bore names with Iberian origins such as Antonio. Planters in the Chesapeake simply could not compete with wealthier Caribbean planters in the Atlantic market for African slaves for the first half-century after settlement. Ira Berlin argues that this generation of Africans were "Atlantic Creoles" who had more knowledge of Atlantic systems and more bargaining power and thus experienced more agency and opportunities than the later generations of Africans in bondage once a plantation revolution had swept through the southern and Caribbean colonies in the English Americas.[42]

The wealthiest Chesapeake planters began to transition from indentured servants to an African labor force in the 1650s but most planters continued to use a predominantly white servant labor force. In the 1670s, the slow transition to a slave labor force across the Chesapeake began.[43] The timing of the transition to slavery was, in part, an issue of the available labor pool. The total population of England dropped by about 8 percent between the 1650s and 1680s, leading to a decline in white migration to the Americas and by the 1680s there were many more English colonial options.[44] The supply of indentured servants to the Chesapeake had begun to taper off in the 1670s and fell precipitously in the 1680s.[45] A depression in the English Caribbean economy in the 1680s brought the price of African slaves down.[46] By the late 1680s, the price of slaves relative to the price of servants urged planters to begin the transition to slavery and more slave traders began to sell their cargoes in the Chesapeake.[47] By 1720, Virginia and Maryland had finished a long and slow transition toward becoming slave societies.[48]

The Caribbean, however, was the real economic engine of English settlement in the Americas and both black and white migration to the region was much higher than on the North American mainland in the seventeenth century. African slaves were present in significant numbers in the Caribbean even before the English developed large scale plantation agriculture. The first English colonists in the Caribbean to rely on slaves to a significant degree were the puritans who settled Providence Island. The colony became a slave society by 1641 before it was eradicated.[49] The first governor of the colony even brought African slaves with him.[50] The colony, however, never adopted a lucrative staple crop or experienced a plantation revolution and it was destroyed by the Spanish before the transition to sugar unfolded throughout the English Caribbean.[51] The Caribbean was a graveyard for both whites and blacks. From 1661 to 1700, there were three people (including both slaves and free men) arriving in the English Caribbean for every one person migrating to the English colonies on the North American mainland.[52] Yet, the massive importation of African slaves, primarily for sugar plantations, and a flood of white servants and free white men seeking opportunities in the English Caribbean created a population of 148,000 by 1700 among the islands and more than three-quarters of that population was of African descent, almost exclusively enslaved.[53]

Sugar transformed the English Caribbean in the mid-seventeenth century and it led to a much more rapid expansion of the plantation complex and transition to African slavery than in the Chesapeake. Recent literature has questioned how rapidly that process occurred and most historians are no longer willing to call it a "sugar revolution" but at some point this becomes a semantic debate about because there is little doubt that sugar transformed Caribbean societies quickly and that an increasing reliance on African slavery was part of that transformation.[54] Barbadians began to cultivate sugar in the 1640s and plantations spread quickly across the Caribbean in the last fifty years of the seventeenth century. The sugar plantation frontier emanated outward from the Barbadian hub. At first, Barbadian planters used a mix of native, European and African labor in their sugar fields but they transitioned in the 1660s and 1670s to a predominantly African slave labor force.[55] By 1670 there were nearly twice as many African slaves (40,400) as whites (22,400) in Barbados.[56] Sugar cultivation lends itself to economies of scale and the most profitable and efficient way to grow it was with large integrated and consolidated plantations in which the owner of the sugar works also owned the surrounding fields and the labor force. In Brazil, sugar had normally been grown by *lavradores de cana* (cane farmers) around a central mill, owned by a separate mill owner.[57] Barbadians spearheaded the cultivation of sugar in the English world and the development of this new consolidated plantation system.[58] They created a system of sugar cultivation that would prove to be more productive per acre than the sugar grown by the Portuguese in Brazil.[59] Much of this was due to the degree of labor exploitation they employed.

Barbados became and remained the economic powerhouse of the English plantation Americas until the end of the seventeenth century. Migrants, both forced and free, created a bustling and densely populated society. One contemporary noted in 1661 that the island swarmed with people like a hive of bees.[60] The expansion of Barbados from the late 1640s through the 1670s was the key to the rapid growth of plantation slavery in the English Americas in the second half of the seventeenth century. An elite group of Barbadian planters used the spectacular wealth they had gained from sugar production to venture out in person and with capital investments from this Barbadian hub through the circum-Caribbean world. They sought satellite colonies to supply resources such as cattle or timber to the sugar plantations in Barbados and they became the driving force in the expansion of the sugar frontier and the plantation model.[61]

After taking hold in Barbados, the tentacles of the sugar plantation system stretched outward first through the Eastern Caribbean to Surinam and amongst the Lesser Antilles. In the 1650s, vast numbers of Barbadians travelled to the Guianas on the South American mainland to establish a successful sugar colony in Surinam. They brought large numbers of slaves. The combined white and black population by the early 1660s was 5,000 and approximately three-quarters of them were African.[62] Surinam became the next major frontier for Barbadian sugar expansion and there were approximately fifty sugar plantations by the end of the 1660s.[63] This Surinam colony flourished and it seemed to some colonial agents to be poised to rival the riches of Brazil but the English surrendered Surinam to the Dutch in 1667 at the end of the Second Anglo–Dutch war and there was an exodus of English planters from there to Jamaica and Antigua in the next decade, helping to begin a transition to sugar slavery in those islands.[64] Nevis was the first of the Leeward Islands to be developed and Antigua, where many of the planters had Barbadian roots, would become the key producer in the Leewards by the end of the seventeenth century. However, none of the Leeward Islands would ever rival Barbados in sugar production, slave imports, or the size of the slave population on an individual level.[65]

The slave trade to the British Caribbean began either slightly before or followed quickly on the heels of the transition to sugar throughout the region; a regular trade to Barbados, for example, began in the 1640s before sugar took hold; a trade to Surinam began in the mid-1660s after sugar plantations had become entrenched and before the English surrendered it; a regular trade to Jamaica began in the late 1650s when sugar had yet to dominate the economy but many of these slaves were resold on the Spanish Main; and a regular African slave trade to the Leeward Islands began in the second half of the 1670s, shortly after the Barbadian sugar complex had spread there.[66]

Whereas the sugar frontier and its accompanying transition to a predominantly enslaved African labor force spread quickly in Surinam, Jamaica's sugar economy was slow to develop after the English conquered it from Spain in 1655. Jamaica would become the jewel of the British Empire in the Americas in the eighteenth century but for the first two decades it was largely a backwater and a haven for privateers. In the early-to-mid 1660s, there were only slightly fewer settlers in Jamaica (4,200) than in Surinam (5,000) but whereas the sugar growers in Surinam had imported enough slaves that approximately three-quarters of the population was black, Jamaica's population was more than 80 percent white.[67] Sugar and slavery slowly began to transform the Jamaican economy in the 1670s and the pace of that transition to sugar would escalate in the 1680s. The slave trade to Jamaica rose in the 1670s as well and the proportion of slaves in the population steadily grew. A consistent slave trade to Jamaica increased markedly in the late 1670s and early 1680s as sugar expanded.[68] Yet, Jamaica would not become the leading sugar producing colony in the English Caribbean until the 1720s.[69] Moreover, the island's economy—largely because of its topography—remained more diverse throughout its history as a slave society than the smaller sugar islands of the Lesser Antilles.[70]

Barbadians also expanded to the Lowcountry of the North American mainland, bringing a significant number of slaves with them as well as a set of assumptions about how a slave society ought to function. They were the principal architects of a colony in the Carolinas but that colony was too far north to extend the sugar plantation frontier.[71] Barbadian investors, seeking ventures for their capital and outlets for population expansion, began to explore the coast of the Carolinas in the 1660s. Successful and permanent English colonization of the region came in 1670 but the Carolinas would struggle as a colonial frontier until the 1690s. Colonists experimented with a wide range of economic activities but they would finally turn to rice as a staple plantation crop in the 1690s.[72] The supply of white servants to the English Americas had already begun to decline in the 1670s so colonists in the Carolinas had a much larger proportion of African slaves from the outset than there had been in the early years in the Chesapeake. Approximately a quarter of the inhabitants in the early years of the colony were African slaves.[73] Whereas the Chesapeake colony to the north and on the periphery of a Caribbean hub had a staple crop long before it became a slave society, the Carolina colony, within a Caribbean orbit, had a slave society before it had a staple plantation crop. The vast majority of the first slaves in the Carolinas were brought from the Caribbean by investors and colonists with Caribbean connections until the first slaving vessels direct from Africa to South Carolina began to arrive in 1710 after the planters had found a profitable staple crop.[74] The colonists also drew on the already established trade in native slaves for their labor needs and for export to other colonies. The demand for African slaves soared after the adoption of rice and as early as 1708, before the arrival of the first transatlantic slaving vessel, there were more blacks than whites in the colony.[75]

Slaves lived and worked beyond the peripheries of this rapidly developing plantation zone. The middle and northern colonies on the North American mainland had slaves in the seventeenth century but these colonies had no major staple crops and no large-scale plantation enterprise and so they did not embrace African slavery to the extent that the planters south of them had. Demand for slaves outstripped supply through most of the seventeenth century and the colonies outside of the plantation zones simply could not compete for slaves. Many of the slaves who found their way to northern colonies came through Caribbean connections and they were often slaves that were unfit for work in the rapidly expanding Caribbean sugar fields.[76]

Over the course of the eighteenth century, the contrast between slavery in the Caribbean sugar islands and slavery in the Chesapeake became more stark and principally for demographic reasons. The slave population in Virginia and Maryland became naturally reproducing around the 1720s and the population began to grow rapidly over the course of the eighteenth century, creating a surplus slave population. The regular annual supply of African slaves to the Chesapeake ended in 1774, thirty-three years before abolition.[77] Imports were no longer necessary to maintain the population. By the middle of the eighteenth century, approximately 40 percent of all slaves on the North American mainland lived in the Chesapeake.[78] By 1808, there were more slaves in the Chesapeake than there were in Jamaica.[79] The naturally reproducing slave population in the Chesapeake would have a significant impact on the development of the nineteenth-century United States. As cotton spread across the Lower South of the United States and the transatlantic slave trade was abolished, planters in the Lower South would draw slaves for the new cotton frontiers from the abundant and rapidly reproducing Chesapeake population. More than a million slaves would be moved overland south and west in a massive internal migration from the Upper South to the Lower South.[80] In sharp contrast to the rapidly growing Chesapeake slave population, the demographic disaster that came with sugar cultivation meant that Caribbean planters required a regular supply of new laborers and, unlike US slaveholders, they had no access to an internal domestic trade. When the British slave trade closed in 1807, the Caribbean sugar plantations fell into a steady decline and struggled to cultivate sugar with an insufficient and aging labor supply.

Throughout the eighteenth century, the Chesapeake plantation frontier continued to expand and the economy diversified. Land was cleared in the Piedmont for new plantations, driven in part by soil exhaustion from tobacco cultivation on older lands in the Tidewater.[81] The labor involved in clearing the heavier forest covers increased labor demands for the enslaved. As tobacco prices slumped and some of the less fertile lands were no longer able to support tobacco, an increasingly large number of planters in the Chesapeake began to diversify production to increase profits and offset risks, adding corn, wheat, and mixed farming.[82] By the middle of the eighteenth century, more than half of the revenues on big Virginian plantations came from grains and plantations turned into mixed farms.[83] Slaves labored on an increasingly diverse array of activities.[84]

The Lowcountry of the Carolinas became the most committed of the mainland colonies to slave labor in the eighteenth century and the white colonists in the region were wealthier per capita than in any other mainland colony.[85] The African majority that had formed there by the end of the first decade of the eighteenth century continued to grow.[86] In the plantation parishes around Charles Town, blacks outnumbered whites by nearly three to one.[87] The large rice and later indigo plantations of the Lowcountry, the majority black populations, the reliance of planters on the slave trade, and the prevalence of death and disease made the Lowcountry resemble the Caribbean far more than it did the Chesapeake. Unlike the Caribbean, however, the Lowcountry did gain a naturally reproducing slave population by the middle of the eighteenth century.[88]

The frontier of Lowcountry rice plantations expanded to the environmental limits of profitability. Rice cultivation spread into the Lower Cape Fear region of North Carolina but most of the economy of North Carolina and backcountry region was dominated by forest products. Slaves worked in small numbers in such settings and most of the region had a white majority. Georgia was established in 1732 but a ban on slavery in the region slowed the growth of that colony. The ban was lifted in 1750 and South Carolina planters swept into the region with slaves, expanding the Lowcountry plantation frontier yet again and Georgia became a virtual colony of South Carolina. A few Caribbean planters also ventured to Georgia, looking for any available opportunities to continue to expand the plantation frontier.[89]

In the Caribbean, Jamaica overtook the smaller and older islands of the Eastern Caribbean by 1725 as the economic jewel of the English empire in the Americas. The island is thirty times the size of Barbados and the Leeward Islands combined.[90] The expansion of the sugar frontier to Jamaica was due in part to the reduction in shipping costs to and from the island with improvements in shipping and naval technologies.[91] By the late eighteenth century, more than half of the sugar in the British Empire was produced in Jamaica and half the slaves in the British Caribbean lived there.[92] In contrast to Barbadian plantations, which rarely grew larger than 300 slaves, Jamaican sugar estates grew massive in size—often exceeding 500 slaves—with extensive communities, interconnected with other plantations within pockets of plantations or neighborhoods defined by geographic boundaries.[93] The slave population of Jamaica at its height reached 354,000 slaves in 1808 and, although the economy was diverse, approximately 60 percent of

Jamaican slaves lived and worked on sugar plantations.[94] Vastly outnumbered by their slaves, the creole Jamaican planters developed one of the most brutal, violent, and draconian systems of social control of any colony in the English Americas. Violent whipping became commonplace and more disfiguring punishments such as castration, dismemberment, and mutilation occurred often enough that a Jamaican law was passed in 1717 to try to discourage planters from dismembering their slaves by issuing a fine if the master did it on their own authority.[95] White planters and overseers continued to develop sadistic and almost unthinkable tortures to terrorize the enslaved such as a punishment meted out by the Jamaican overseer Thomas Thistlewood called "Derby's Dose" in which he made one slave defecate into another slave's mouth before gagging the slave's mouth.[96]

In 1763, sugar also continued to thrive in the British islands of the Lesser Antilles. The British plantation frontier underwent another significant expansion with the acquisition of the islands of Grenada, St. Vincent, Dominica, and Tobago at the end of the Seven Year War. The slave trade expanded yet again with these new frontiers and the demand for slaves outstripped supply, driving the price of slaves ever upward.[97] Historians have exaggerated the decline of some of the older islands in the Lesser Antilles and it is now clear that Barbados and the older islands continued to prosper throughout the eighteenth century by cutting costs and producing more refined sugars and rum.[98] Many of the slaves on older islands such as Barbados were increasingly creoles, born on the islands, with deep family roots there after more than a hundred years of settlement. The slave population of Barbados did begin to shrink in the late eighteenth century and there were only 75,000 slaves on the island by 1790, a little more than a quarter of the number of slaves in Jamaica at that point.[99] Not all of that population decline was caused by the high mortality or low birth rates that were common to Caribbean slave societies. The fresh soils of the newer islands promised better returns and some slaves were shipped from the older islands of the Lesser Antilles such as Barbados to the Ceded Islands to build the new sugar frontiers.[100]

North of the plantation zones, enslaved Africans continued to be an important labor force in the eighteenth century and they worked in a wide variety of settings but, aside from a few small and select pockets of the north, they never formed a majority of the workforce or of the population. Black slaves populated northern port cities where they worked in maritime trades, as assistants to artisans and as domestics. In most of these cities, the black population was visible but small. In New York, the slave population never rose above 15 percent in the eighteenth century.[101] There were also black slaves working in larger numbers in ironworks and in farms in fertile regions of the north such as the Hudson Valley. Occasionally the number of slaves working in an ironworks factory rose over 50 but the number of slaves working on an agricultural estate was rarely larger than 20.[102] In New England, Rhode Island had the largest number of slaves in the eighteenth century. The evidence suggests that 14 percent of Rhode Island households owned slaves in 1774 on the eve of the revolutionary war.[103] Some people of African descent managed to escape slavery and northern cities also had small communities of free blacks through most of the eighteenth century. There were a few hundred free blacks in the northern mainland colonies in the eighteenth century but that number swelled quickly toward the end of the eighteenth century with the rise of antislavery sentiment and after the American Revolution and by 1810 there were as many as 50,000 free blacks in the north.[104]

The Caribbean sugar plantation remained the archetype of the plantation system throughout the period of slavery in the English colonies and the work regime for sugar was the deadliest for slaves of the major staple crops in the Americas. The only British sugar colony to have a naturally reproducing slave population before the emancipation of slavery in 1833 was Barbados.[105] One of the most significant innovations on English sugar plantations was the development of the brutal organization scheme in the fields of gang labor. The degree of coercive labor extraction in that form of labor was nearly unparalleled. Gangs of slaves worked with a regimented and almost militaristic discipline on the same tasks in fields from dawn to dusk under the close supervision of a driver with a whip. Their physical efforts and their pace were synchronized as they moved across the field and the tasks were monotonous, backbreaking, and constant. The gang system relied on a driver who could ensure a consistent pace and who knew what pace the gang could be pushed to achieve in a single day. Gang labor was physically and psychically exhausting and slaves strove to avoid it. Free laborers have never been consistently and effectively used in the kind of gang labor systems that emerged on sugar plantations.[106] Skilled slaves, supervisors, and domestics were able to avoid the gangs and they had more access to goods, were healthier, and were better able to form successful families because they avoided the field gangs.[107] The archetype of the gang labor system on sugar plantations, stripped slaves of their autonomy and destroyed their health and the vast majority of slaves on large plantations in the Caribbean would become laborers in these gangs at some point in their lives. Women were also more likely than men to be subject to such exhausting labors because planters favored men for skilled and supervisory work. By the end of the eighteenth century, women comprised the majority of most field gangs on sugar plantations, making women vulnerable to greater degrees of exploitation in slavery.[108]

The exhausting demands of gang labor made the already onerous and backbreaking tasks necessary to cultivate sugar much more exhausting. Digging sugar cane holes and bringing the enormous quantities of manure necessary for sugar cultivation to the field to fertilize the holes were the two tasks widely regarded by Caribbean planters as the most physically demanding.[109] The harvest itself required less peak intensity in physical labors but longer hours. The canes were ground in the mill and then boiled immediately after harvesting in factory-like conditions and the work of grinding and boiling lasted through the night, breaking the diurnal patterns of labor common in early modern agriculture.[110] Holing, manuring, and harvesting on sugar plantations were all done using gang labor.

Scholars are still struggling to determine how and when the gang labor system developed. It appears to have evolved piecemeal on sugar plantations in the Lesser Antilles in the second half of the seventeenth century. The English were able to use the system in large part with Africans because the cultural conventions that protected European workers from certain abuses did not seem to apply to Africans. The gang system did not likely fully emerge until planters stopped using indentured white labor in the fields and had transitioned to using almost exclusively African labor.[111] Trevor Burnard has recently suggested that the gang system was forged by seventeenth-century Barbadian planters who had served in European armies and that their experiences helped shape the organization of field labor.[112] The development of the most synchronized and brutal forms of gang labor on sugar plantations may have also been influenced by the introduction in Barbados of a more environmentally sustainable method of digging cane holes at the end of the seventeenth century. To prevent soil erosion, planters began to lay out their cane holes in grid patterns. The grid patterns of holes on the field allowed plantation managers to dictate a steadier and more synchronized labor pace as the slaves worked across the field, allotting an equal share of manuring and holing to each slave. Slaves were divided by physical ability into two or more adult gangs and a children's gang. The first gang was sometimes known as the holing gang because these were the slaves who were physically capable of the demanding task of digging the holes and keeping pace with each other. The chore of holing was destructive enough to slaves' health that, by the late eighteenth century, the wealthiest planters could ameliorate the physical demands on their own slaves by hiring specialized gangs of slaves from poorer whites known as "jobbing gangs" to dig some of these holes.[113]

The majority of slaves in the Americas ended up working in field gangs but planters used a range of systems to organize, deploy, and compel labor across the plantation Americas and task labor systems were also common. Task labor, the opposite of gang labor, is most often associated with rice plantations in the southeastern Lowcountry of the North American mainland but it also appeared in other kinds of agriculture such as Caribbean coffee plantations. Tasking emerged with a staple crop like rice because it did not require as much close supervision as tobacco or as much regimentation or factory-style and synchronized labor patterns as a crop like sugar.[114] In theory, a tasking system could offer slaves more autonomy. Slaves would be given individual or small group tasks and allowed the incentive of free time when the task was completed or punished if the task was not. Free time for the slaves became incentive to labor rather than strictly fear of the lash.[115] Labor organization was driven by the demands of the crop. Such a system might seem preferable to slaves but the balance of power in master–slave relationships was always asymmetrical and planters or overseers could set ever increasing quotas in task systems with a threat of violent retribution always undergirding the whole endeavor.

The British transatlantic slave trade grew alongside the expanding plantation system in the Americas. The English slave trade was dwarfed by the trade of other imperial powers such as the Dutch and the Portuguese until the 1660s.[116] There were, however, limited English efforts to profit from the African slave trade long before English imperial settlers had even established colonies in the Americas. John Hawkins, for example, raided the coast of Africa for slaves to sell in the Iberian colonies in the late 1560s.[117] The need to continually resupply sugar plantations in the Caribbean and, to a lesser extent, rice plantations in the Lowcountry led to a rapid expansion of the English slave trade to the Americas after the 1660s and especially after 1672 with the reformation of the Royal African Company (RAC).[118] The RAC was granted a monopoly on English trade until 1698 when the monopoly was lifted. The British became the dominant imperial power in the eighteenth-century slave trade, particularly after they acquired the *assiento* in 1713 at the end of the War of Spanish Succession. This contract allowed the British to supply slaves to the Spanish Americas because Spain did not have a significant transatlantic slave trade. In 1750 the annual number of slaves the British disembarked in the Americas was more than twice what it had been in 1676 and the number of annual slaves disembarking in 1800 was nearly three times what it had been in 1750.[119] The size of the annual British trade in slaves fell only slightly in the first decade of the nineteenth century before the trade was abolished.[120]

The voyage that Africans took to the Americas was horrific and brutal beyond measure. British slave traders drew slaves from a broad region of the West African coast and, eventually, brought slaves from Madagascar as well. The slaves were not just drawn from coastal societies and so it can be difficult to draw assumptions about their cultural backgrounds based solely on the ports from which they were shipped. Many of the enslaved were drawn from deep in the interior of the continent and as many as one in four of the captives may have died on the overland journey to the coastal ports in Africa. Another 5 to 15 percent likely died on in the open-air pens while waiting to be shipped to the Americas in the middle passage.[121] The average time that slaves spent at sea aboard a British slave ship in this middle passage at the height of the slave trade in the eighteenth century was 63 days.[122] The conditions aboard the slaving vessels were horrific and slave rebellions and uprisings did occur. There were 157 slave insurrections aboard 9,393 British slaving voyages in the eighteenth century, meaning that resistance occurred on board 2 percent of these voyages.[123] The mortality rates for both the crew and the enslaved crammed below deck were very high but the mortality rate for the enslaved fell over the course of the eighteenth century (particularly in the last quarter of the century) as the trade grew and British slavers became more specialized.[124] In the eighteenth century, the mortality rate aboard British ships was 12 percent.[125] Most slaves died of dehydration, usually arising from gastrointestinal disorders.[126]

After arriving in the Americas, the newly arrived Africans faced a series of new horrors. They would be commodified and displayed as people with a price.[127] A portion of these slaves would be shipped yet again to better markets in the Americas in what one scholar has called the "Final Passages."[128] After being sold and reaching their final destination, newly arrived Africans would undergo acclimatization and adaptation to the new disease environments and to the brutal regime of plantation labor that contemporaries labelled as "seasoning." This was a particularly deadly period in the Caribbean. In the second half of the eighteenth century, approximately 15 to 20 percent of the new Africans perished during this period of acclimatization.[129]

The abolition of the slave trade in 1807 brought a sudden end to the expansion of plantation slavery, particularly in the British Caribbean. In the United States, in contrast, a rapidly reproducing slave population ensured the survival of slavery after abolition. As an institution, slavery had seemed repugnant to many contemporaries in the seventeenth and eighteenth centuries, particularly to those living in the metropole but there was no sustained or organized opposition to the institution until the last quarter of the eighteenth century when there was a sharp rise in antislavery and abolitionist sentiment throughout the British Atlantic. It was one of several moral reform projects of the age but it gained the most widespread support and traction. Between 1787 and 1792, approximately 1.5 million people in Britain of a total population of 12 million signed petitions against the slave trade.[130]

Why and how that abolitionist fervor began and spread has been thoroughly debated by generations of historians and the issue has yet to be settled. There was an enormous mix of interconnected cultural, political, religious, and economic factors at play.[131] Before the American Revolution, the Quakers were the most prominent antislavery group. The principles of freedom and resistance to tyranny that were espoused during the American Revolution certainly helped buoy antislavery connections. It was impossible not to see the contradictions of men owning slaves claiming to be enslaved. Samuel Johnson, at the outset of the Revolution, offered a rebuttal to the American Congress, asking "…how is it that we hear the loudest yelps for liberty among the drivers of negroes?"[132] As the American colonists sought to gain their independence, the United States and Britain would compete to gain the moral high ground and claim moral capital in the enlightenment pursuit of moral, social, and economic improvement.[133] This would help push them toward antislavery and abolitionist positions. In the new United States, several of the northern states started to outlaw slavery. Vermont became the first state to abolish slavery in 1777, Massachusetts followed in 1783, and slavery was abolished within the British Empire in Upper Canada in 1793.

Although abolitionist protests were strong in the late 1780s and the new United States Congress and British Parliament began to consider abolition, it would still take 20 years to abolish the slave trade and slaves would not be emancipated in the British colonies until 1833 or in the United States until 1865. The French and Haitian Revolutions caused reactionary fears in the Anglo-American world and created opportunities in the sugar industry that helped to slow the movement toward abolition, particularly in the British Empire, and to dull antislavery protest. Parliament responded to abolitionist protest with a compromise between pro-slave trade and abolitionist pressures, passing the Dolben Act in 1788 as an ameliorative measure to regulate the slave trade and restrict the number of slaves that vessels could carry to try to improve conditions in the middle passage. In fact, the annual number of slaves that the British shipped to the Americas grew significantly during the 1790s after the spike of abolitionist protest and slavery continued to expand rapidly in the British Americas, especially in newly acquired colonies.[134] Some scholars have suggested that the Caribbean sugar plantation system declined and that abolition was economically motivated.[135] There is certainly strong evidence to support some overproduction of sugar in the 1790s that would depress prices immediately before abolition.[136]

However, the most convincing evidence and the dominant historical paradigm suggest that planters in the region successfully adapted to a series of economic challenges such as the disruption of the American Revolution, a series of hurricanes in the 1780s, and soil exhaustion, and that the system was thriving to such an extent that abolition was actually a kind of "econocide" for the British Empire.[137]

Abolition was not necessarily an inevitable consequence of the rise of humanitarian sentiment and changing moral sensibilities during the Enlightenment and proslavery and antislavery convictions in this period were less binary than has often been assumed.[138] Slavery was one of the social institutions that came under criticism during the Enlightenment but not all the critique was aimed at abolishing the institution. Many theorists throughout the British Atlantic began to believe that free labor was superior to slavery and that slavery was an archaic institution that would gradually die.[139] Prominent slaveholders, especially in the Chesapeake, began to manumit hundreds of their slaves after the American Revolution.[140] At the same time, many proslavery theorists argued that slavery as an institution could be rationalized and improved through amelioration and that the route to social reform and improvement lay in the discipline of the unenlightened, such as the enslaved. These proslavery ameliorationists promoted such measures as encouraging slave families, developing pronatalist polices, developing a naturally reproducing slave population, fostering religious instruction among the slaves, and curbing the most brutal physical punishments in favor of other kinds of coercive and incentive measures such as the manipulation of slaves' unsupervised time. As slavery was rationalized, the clock and statistical accounting became key tools in the management of the enslaved populations of large plantations.[141]

In the French Empire, the slave revolt in Saint Domingue (Haiti) overthrew the institution but slaves in the English Americas were never successful at organizing a large-scale revolt that would gain them full liberation. There were several significant attempts at rebellion that were supressed by planters and many more apparent conspiracies to revolt among slaves from the seventeenth through the nineteenth centuries. One of the problems for historians trying to assess the size of those many conspiracies or how organized they were or whether they were at all likely to have been successful is that the sources that describe these revolts were produced by whites; these sources may reflect white paranoia as much as a conspiracy to revolt and, at the least, the size of the revolts may have been exaggerated.[142]

The number of conspiracies and attempted slave rebellions seems to have increased during the Age of Revolution and after the rise of abolitionist sentiment, and some historians have identified a distinct shift in how slaves conceptualized rebellions or freedom in this era. In the earliest stages of rebellion, slaves who were predominantly recent African arrivals ran away to form maroon communities but the increasing number of creole slaves during the Age of Rebellion began to push for full liberation within their societies.[143] Slaves drew on and were inspired by the rhetoric of freedom and natural rights that was so pervasive during the Age of Revolution. They took advantage of the emerging abolitionist impulse that threatened to dismantle slavery and they tried to use it to their advantage and push the cracks in the system. Yet, at the same time, in an age of democratic revolutions in which monarchy was being challenged, the slaves often believed that monarchical power and justice was their best route to freedom.[144]

In the absence of many outright examples of successful rebellion, scholars have unearthed and emphasized many other forms of resistance to the brutal slave regimes in the British colonies, including running away individually or in larger groups to form maroon communities and day-to-day acts of slave resistance such as the sabotage of tools and equipment or shirking work duties. Scholars have even portrayed the survival of African cultural forms and the successful formation of enslaved families in an institution designed to dehumanize slaves as a kind of collective resistance. The assertion of humanity in a dehumanizing system can be seen as a kind of resistance. Slaves were never simply passive victims.[145]

The most common forms of resistance involved slaves taking advantage of opportunities within the system rather than trying to dismantle it altogether or obtain permanent freedom. They negotiated for more autonomy and better working conditions and pushed the envelope of opportunity. For example, it was not uncommon for slaves to abscond from a plantation in groups or organize collective work stoppages at critical points in crop production as a protest to get unpopular white overseers replaced. It was also not uncommon for slaves to leave a plantation to find a greater white authority, such as the plantation attorney, and voice their complaints.[146] The sugar boiler had irreplaceable skills during the time-sensitive sugar harvest and a Jamaican overseer in 1751 observed that "some negroe Sugar Boilers…will make no sugar to get the overseer turn'd out when they don't like him."[147] Slaves also chose sometimes to take the day and be absent from their labors. These were not necessarily protests against the institution itself or efforts to obtain permanent freedom. Managers would overlook the occasional absence from plantation labors. Short-term absences became part of a labor negotiating strategy for the enslaved, a kind of institutionalized pressure valve. When the demands of daily labor became too physically or psychologically taxing or a slave needed more time to travel to visit kin on other estates, the slave could, very occasionally, simply take the day. These short-term absences were far more common than long term runaways and permanent escapes from slavery.[148]

Questions about the extent and nature of resistance dominated the historiography of slavery from the 1970s through the end of the twentieth century but specialists are now asking whether this has led to a much too simplistic understanding of the institution.[149] Within this resistance paradigm, scholars tended to paint caricatures of masters and slaves, casting slaves as political actors battling against the dehumanization and violence of their masters and the European societies that legitimated slavery. This portrayal of slaves as heroic actors battling against evil oppressors has kept historians from fully appreciating the many dimensions of slaves' lives and the range of struggles they faced.[150] There is a tendency to assume that slaves privileged freedom above all other goals rather than weighing a range of competing goals such as individual survival or status within an enslaved community or the maintenance of family ties and community connections. The resistance paradigm has a tendency to depict slaves as struggling only against their masters or the institution. There were hierarchies and often discordant relations within enslaved communities and slaves had to negotiate power relationships with other slaves as well as their masters.[151] There is some evidence for example that creole slaves on sugar plantations demanded forced labor or tribute from new African arrivals. The prominent Jamaican plantation attorney Simon Taylor worried in 1782 that new African slaves should be separated from the slaves already on the estate lest the new ones "be destroyed by the Old Negroes making them their Slaves."[152]

Scholars are now trying to find other conceptual frameworks beyond the resistance paradigm to create richer, more nuanced portrayals of enslaved life. Sidney Mintz, critiquing the emphasis on resistance, argued in the 1990s that "only a tiny fraction of daily life consisted of open resistance. Instead most of life then, like most of life now, was spent living."[153] Randy Browne, borrowing from Vincent Brown, has argued in his groundbreaking dissertation on the experiences of the enslaved in early nineteenth-century Berbice that historians need to focus more on a kind of "politics of survival," recognizing that slaves' first concern was survival in a world in which there was a multifaceted range of power relationships and dynamics. Sometimes slaves struggled against their masters, sometimes against the natural environment and sometimes with each other.[154] Other scholars have suggested that the best way to address the study of slavery is to understand it within the framework of labor history, approaching slavery as one of the many species of labor in the early modern world and focusing on slaves' working environments.[155]

The resistance paradigm has been part of a larger problem of conceptualizing, analyzing, and conveying the tyranny inherent in the quotidian monotony of bondage. Scholars are often focused on extremes in the contest between master and slave: examples of draconian punishments and tyrannical methods of control enacted by masters and forms of clear slave resistance used by the slaves, particularly conspiracies and rebellions. These moments do tend to be highlighted in sources because they were exceptional. The tedious and backbreaking chores of the daily work regime, on the other hand, tend to be buried. While forms of day-to-day resistance among slaves have been teased carefully out of the records by more than one generation of slavery scholars, the counter to this kind of day-to-day resistance has been too often ignored. What has not been emphasized enough is the violence of the mundane in day-to-day plantation operations. Slaves were overworked, malnourished, and deprived of sleep. Their bodies were gradually and incrementally beaten down by day-to-day life, year and after year, in such work regimes and it was this process that murdered slaves, particularly with the most destructive staple crops such as sugar or rice. This violence of the mundane was a constant rather than intermittent occurrence for slaves. Slaves spent the vast majority of their time working and by focusing on what they did in those hours rather than on what they did in the small amount of free time they had away from the masters, scholars can not only gain a better sense of slave life but they can also restore a sense of the violence of the mundane to the study of slave lives. What also gets overlooked when scholars focus on the number and frequency of acts of violence or the number of slaves sexually abused or wrenched from their families and communities by sales is that slaves lived with the fear or threat of such acts every day and it was this constant *threat* as much as the frequency or actuality of such violence that was key to the terror of the institution of slavery.

Slavery drove the development and expansion of the British Americas. The English had no qualms with the institution from its outset or for more than a century after the rise of slave societies in the English colonies. They lacked access to a regular supply of African slaves until the middle of the seventeenth century and they experimented at first with using native slaves and convicts and indentured servants. In the 1640s, the English began to grow sugar, the staple crop that would become the dominant New World export and the engine of English expansion in the New World. The last half of the seventeenth century saw a surge of English expansion in the Americas, particularly in the Plantation Americas, and an African slave trade developed alongside that expansion to support that growth. Slave codes developed to legitimate and entrench the system of racialized chattel slavery. The British would come to dominate the African slave trade to the Americas in the eighteenth century and the lucrative production of staple crops such as sugar, rice, coffee, cotton, and indigo helped encourage a continuous expansion of the frontiers of British settlement. Slaves were subject to increasingly onerous and exhausting labors as planters developed systems of gang labor and more rigorous and exacting work regimes. Slaves resisted complete dehumanization and the absolute control of their masters and they worked to improve their situations and gain as much autonomy as possible but, for the most part, they spent long hours working, battling against disease and exhaustion, against the natural world and sometimes against each other

In the last quarter of the eighteenth century, the institution of slavery and the slave trade came under intense scrutiny. Antislavery and abolitionist sentiments suddenly swelled. Improvement was the buzzword of the Enlightenment and contemporaries began to question whether slavery could be improved or whether it should be eradicated or whether it would simply disappear as society progressed through new stages. Some planters even began to voluntarily manumit their slaves. Others began to insist on an alternative version of modernity and progress in which slavery would remain a central institution. Abolitionist and antislavery sentiment ruled the day as governments asserted their moral capital and freedom and egalitarianism became naturalized as political ideals. The institution of racialized chattel slavery was slowly and gradually dismantled through the nineteenth century, leaving behind an Anglo-American world on which millions of African slaves had left their mark, living, working and dying in bondage in the creation of the British Americas.

Notes

1 Philip Curtin, *The Rise and Fall of the Plantation Complex: Essays in Atlantic History* (New York: Cambridge University Press, 1990), 40.
2 Matthew Mulcahy, *Hubs of Empire: The Southeastern Lowcountry and British Caribbean* (Baltimore: Johns Hopkins University Press, 2014), 112.
3 Historians differentiate between slave societies and societies with slaves and suggest that societies in which people own slaves become slave societies when the enslaved population reaches 20 percent; see Kenneth Morgan, *Slavery and the British Empire from Africa to America* (New York: Oxford University Press, 2007), 28; Ira Berlin, *Many Thousands Gone: The First Two Centuries of Slavery in North America* (Cambridge: The Belknap Press of Harvard University Press, 1998), 7–12.
4 On the pervasiveness of enslavement and English familiarity with it, see Michael Guaso, *Slaves and Englishmen: Human Bondage in the Early Modern Atlantic World* (Philadelphia: University of Pennsylvania Press, 2014).
5 Robert J. Steinfeld, "Changing Legal Conceptions of Free Labor," *Terms of Labor: Slavery, Serfdom and Free Labor*, Stanley Engerman, ed. (Stanford: Stanford University Press, 1999), 137–167; Stanley L. Engerman, "Slavery at Different Times and Places," *American Historical Review* 105[2] (2000): 480–484; Robert J. Steinfeld, *The Invention of Free Labor: The Employment Relation in English and American Law and Culture, 1350–1870* (Chapel Hill: University of North Carolina Press, 1991).
6 For more on indentured servants in the early Caribbean and in North America, see Kenneth Morgan, *Slavery and Servitude in Colonial North America: A Short History* (New York: New York University Press, 2001) and Hilary Beckles, *White Servitude and Black Slavery in Barbados, 1627–1715* (Knoxville: University of Tennessee Press, 1989). For more on Irish servants in particular, see Hilary Beckles, "'A Riotous and Unruly Lot': Irish Indentured Servants and Freemen in the English West Indies, 1644–1713," *William and Mary Quarterly* 47[1] (1990): 3–22 For more on convict laborers in the eighteenth century, see Roger Ekirch, *Bound for America: The Transportation of British Convicts to the Colonies, 1718–1775* (New York: Oxford University Press, 1987).
7 Guasco, *Slaves and Englishmen*, 172.
8 David Eltis, *The Rise of African Slavery in the Americas* (New York: Cambridge University Press, 2000), 73.
9 Winthrop Jordan, *White over Black: American Attitudes toward the Negro, 1550–1812* (Chapel Hill: University of North Carolina Press, 1968), 44–98; Jordan's work is dated but many scholars still find significant merit in it; see, for example, Laurence Shore, "The Enduring Power of Racism: A Reconsideration of Winthrop Jordan's White over Black," *History and Theory* 44[2] (2005): 195–226. For scholars who essentially agree that racism was deeply ingrained at the outset in the early US and that slavery was an "unthinking decision," see Carl N. Degler, "Slavery and the Genesis of American Race Prejudice," *Comparative Studies in Society and History* 2[1] (1959): 49–66; David Eltis, "Europeans and the Rise and Fall of African Slavery in the Americas: An Interpretation," *American Historical Review* 98[5] (1993): 1399–1423 and James H. Sweet, "The Iberian Roots of American Racist Thought," *William and Mary Quarterly* 54[1] (1997): 143–166. The opposing view suggests that slavery and racism emerged more slowly in the US and that it was contingent on key events and on particular demographic and economic forces. Some of these scholars would go so far as to suggest that planters conspired to develop the institution of racial slavery to divide lower class whites from blacks. For examples of this opposing view, see Oscar and Mary F. Handlin, "The Origins of the Southern Labor System," *William and Mary Quarterly* 7[2] (1950): 199–222; Edmund S. Morgan, *American Slavery, American Freedom: The Ordeal of Colonial Virginia* (New York: W.W. Norton & Company, 1975); Berlin, *Many Thousands Gone*; Anthony S. Parent, *Foul Means: The Formation of a Slave Society in Virginia, 1660–1740* (Chapel Hill: University of North Carolina Press, 2003).
10 For an example of how Anthony Johnson has been used as evidence in the origins debate, see J. Douglas Deal, *Race and Class in Colonial Virginia: Indians, Englishmen and Africans on the Eastern Shore of Virginia During the Seventeenth Century* (New York: Garland Publishing, Inc., 1993), 217–250.

11. Lorena Walsh, *Motives of Honour, Pleasure and Profit: Plantation Management in the Colonial Chesapeake, 1607–1763* (Chapel Hill: University of North Carolina Press, 2010),
12. Vaughan, *Roots of American Racism*, 6, 130–131.
13. Hilary Beckles was among the first modern historians to stress—while conceptualizing slavery and freedom as oppositional poles on a continuum—that the Irish servants in Barbados "were nearer slavery than freedom." See Beckles, "A Riotous and Unruly Lot," *William and Mary Quarterly* 47[1] (1990): 511. See also Beckles, *White Servitude and Black Servitude in Barbados, 1627–1715* (Knoxville: University of Tennessee Press, 1989). More recently, Jenny Shaw and Simon Newman have stressed the slave-like conditions for white servants on early sugar plantations. Shaw offers the fullest treatment of the impact of prejudice towards the Irish in the early Caribbean. Michael Guasco has also recently stressed the vulnerability of the English to enslavement in the early modern Atlantic world and the pervasiveness of forms of slavery. See Shaw, *Everyday Life in the Early Caribbean: Irish, Africans and the Construction of Difference* (Athens: University of Georgia Press, 2013); Newman, *A New World of Labor: The Development of Plantation Slavery in the British Atlantic.* (Philadelphia: University of Pennsylvania Press, 2013) and Guasco, *Slaves and Englishmen*. For an example of a work aimed at a more popular audience, see Don Jordan and Michael Walsh, *White Cargo: The Forgotten History of Britain's White Slaves in America* (New York: New York University Press, 2008).
14. David Eltis, "Europeans and the Rise and Fall of African Slavery in the Americas: An Interpretation," *American Historical Review* 98[5] (1993): 1399–1423.
15. As quoted in Lorena Walsh, *Motives of Honour, Pleasure and Profit: Plantation Management in the Colonial Chesapeake, 1607–1763* (Chapel Hill: University of North Carolina Press, 2010), 117.
16. Eltis, *Rise of African Slavery*, 57.
17. Curtin, *Rise and Fall of Plantation Complex*, 9–11, 17–28; David Brion Davis, *Inhuman Bondage: The Rise and Fall of Slavery in the New World* (New York: Oxford University Press, 2006), 103–105.
18. Guasco, *Slaves and Englishmen*, 211; Hubert H. S. Aimes, "Coartación: A Spanish Institution for the Advancement of Slaves into Freedom," *Yale Review* 7 (February, 1909): 412–431.
19. Davis, *Inhuman Bondage*, 50; Morgan, *Slavery and Servitude*, 32.
20. Ivan Hannaford, *Race: The History of an Idea in the West* (Baltimore: Johns Hopkins University Press, 1996).
21. George Frederickson, *Racism: A Short History* (Princeton: Princeton University Press, 2002), 39, 43–44; Davis, *Inhuman Bondage*, 64–69.
22. Morgan Godwyn, *The Negro's and Indians Advocate, suing for their admission to the church, or a persuasive to the instructing and baptizing of the Negro's and Indians in Our Plantations* (London: J.D., 1680), 36.
23. The best broad comparisons of Latin America and the Anglo-American world remain Carl N. Degler, *Neither Black nor White: Slavery and Race Relations in Brazil and the United States* (Madison: University of Wisconsin Press, 1971), and Frank Tannenbaum, *Slave and Citizen: The Negro in the Americas* (New York: Vintage Books, 1946).
24. Alden T. Vaughan, *Roots of American Racism*, 7, 10, 13.
25. Curtin, *Rise and Fall of the Plantation Complex*, 51–52.
26. For more on native slaveries in the Americas, see Rebecca Anne Goetz, "Rethinking the Unthinking Decision: Old Questions and New Problems in the History of Slavery and Race in the Colonial South," *The Journal of Southern History* 25[3] (2009): 599–612; James F. Brooks, *Captives and Cousins: Slavery, Kinship, and Community in the Southwest Borderlands* (Chapel Hill: University of North Carolina Press, 2002); Brett Rushforth, *Bonds of Alliance: Indigenous and Atlantic Slaveries in New France* (Chapel Hill: University of North Carolina Press, 2012).
27. Alan Gallay, *The Indian Slave Trade: The Rise of the English Empire in the American South, 1670–1717* (New Haven: Yale University Press, 2002), 299.
28. Matthew Mulcahy, *Hubs of Empire: The Southeastern Lowcountry and British Caribbean* (Baltimore: Johns Hopkins University Press, 2014), 96.
29. "A Paper of Col. Muddiford Concerning the West Indies," December 1654, *A Collection of the State Papers of John Thurloe*. Vol. 3., ed. Thomas Birch (Burlington: Tanner Ritchie Publishing, 2006), 63.
30. Berlin, *Many Thousands Gone*, 145.
31. "Laws on Slavery," *Virtual Jamestown*. Available online at www.virtualjamestown.org/laws1.html#4 (Accessed November 2015).
32. "An Act for the Better Ordering and Governing of Negroes," September 27, 1661, BL 369, Box 1, mssBL 1-423, William Blathwayt Papers, Huntington Library.

33 Sally Hadden, "The Fragmented Laws of Slavery in the Colonial and Revolutionary Era," *The Cambridge History of Law in America*, Vol. 1, eds. Michael Grossberg and Christopher Tomlins, (New York: Cambridge University Press, 2007), 254, 260.
34 Hadden, "The Fragmented Laws," 262; "An Act for the Better Ordering and Governing of Negroes," 27 September 1661, BL 369, Box 1, mssBL 1-423, William Blathwayt Papers. Some of the provisions against slave huckstering were included in the comprehensive servant codes passed the same year as the slave codes. See Act 21 "An Act for the Good Governing of Servants, and Ordering the Rights Between Masters and Servants" *Acts of Assembly Passed in the Island of Barbadoes, from 1648 to 1718* (London, 1721), 22–29.
35 Lords of Trade and Plantations to Sir Thomas Lynch, 17 February, 1683, No. 948, "America and West Indies: February 1683, 17–28," *Calendar of State Papers Colonial, America and West Indies*, Vol. 11, 1681–1685, ed. J.W. Fortescue (London, 1898), 385–400, British History Online, Available online at www.british-history.ac.uk/cal-state-papers/colonial/america-west-indies/vol11/pp385-400 (Accessed August 2015).
36 For more on beastialization as a key element in New World slavery, see Davis, *Inhuman Bondage*, 30–36.
37 Edward B. Rugemer, "The Development of Mastery and Race in the Comprehensive Slave Codes of the Greater Caribbean during the Seventeenth Century," *William and Mary Quarterly* 70[3] (2013): 455; Philip Morgan, *Slave Counterpoint: Black Culture in Eighteenth-Century Chesapeake and Lowcountry* (Chapel Hill: University of North Carolina Press, 1998), 264.
38 Morgan, *Slave Counterpoint*, 264.
39 Hadden, "Fragmented Laws of Slavery," 268; Morgan, *Slavery in the British Empire*, 114.
40 Walsh, *Motives of Honor, Pleasure, and Profit*, 36–38.
41 Berlin, *Many Thousands Gone*, 29.
42 Berlin, *Many Thousands Gone*, 17–28. Some scholars have now tried to apply the concept of "Atlantic Creoles" to later periods to stress the agency, mobility and bargaining power that some blacks had. See for example, Jane Landers, *Atlantic Creoles in the Age of Revolutions*. (Cambridge: Harvard University Press, 2011).
43 Kenneth Morgan, *Slavery and Servitude in Colonial North America: A Short History* (New York: New York University Press, 2001), 36; John C. Coombs, "The Phases of Conversion: a New Chronology for the Rise of Slavery in Early Virginia," *William and Mary Quarterly* 68[3] (2011); Berlin, *Many Thousands Gone*, 10.
44 Eltis, *Rise of African Slavery*, 43.
45 Morgan, *Slavery and Servitude*, 37.
46 Morgan, *Slavery in the British Empire*, 30.
47 Eltis, *Rise of African Slavery*, 50; Morgan, *Slavery and Servitude*, 37, 39.
48 Coombs, "Phases of Conversion," 334; Morgan, *Slavery and Servitude*, 36.
49 J.H. Elliott, *Empires of the Atlantic World: Britain and Spain in America, 1492–1830* (New Haven: Yale University Press, 2006), 103.
50 Guasco, *Slaves and Englishmen*, 207.
51 For more on the Providence Island Colony, see Karen Ordahl Kupperman, *Providence Island, 1630–1641: The Other Puritan Colony* (New York: Cambridge University Press, 1993).
52 Eltis, *Rise of African Slavery*, 49.
53 Morgan, *Slavery in the British Empire*, 17.
54 B.W. Higman "The Sugar Revolution," *Economic History Review* 53[2] (2000): 213–236; For a critique of the notion of a sugar "revolution," see John J. McCusker and Russell Menard, "The Sugar Industry in the Seventeenth Century: A New Perspective on the Barbadian 'Sugar Revolution,'" *Tropical Babylons: Sugar and the Making of the Atlantic World, 1450–1680*, ed. Stuart B. Schwartz (Chapel Hill: University of North Carolina Press, 2004), 289–330 and Russell R. Menard, *Sweet Negotiations: Sugar, Slavery and Plantation Agriculture in Early Barbados* (Charlottesville: University of Virginia Press, 2006), 18–66.
55 Newman, *A New World of Labor*, 190–195.
56 John J. McCusker and Russell R. Menard, *The Economy of British America, 1607–1789* (Chapel Hill: University of North Carolina Press, 1985), 153–154.
57 Curtin, *Rise and Fall of the Plantation Complex*, 53–55, 83; Eltis, *Rise of African Slavery*, 221–222; Nuala Zahedieh, *The Capital and the Colonies: London and the Atlantic Economy, 1660–1700* (New York: Cambridge University Press, 2010), 216.
58 For the development of the sugar plantation system in Barbados see and Russell R. Menard, *Sweet Negotiations: Sugar, Slavery and Plantation Agriculture in Early Barbados* (Charlottesville: University of Virginia Press, 2006).

59 David Eltis, "New Estimates of Exports from Barbados and Jamaica, 1665–1701," *William and Mary Quarterly*, 3rd series, 52[4] (1995): 647.
60 Edmund Hickeringill said that Barbados was "too small a hive" for the "swarm of people" there. See Hickeringill, *Jamaica Viewed…with several other collateral observations and reflections upon the island*. (London, 1661),17.
61 For more on the Barbadian Diaspora, see Alfred Chandler, "The Expansion of Barbados," *Journal of the Barbados Museum and Historical Society* 12 (May 1946): 106–136. See also Justin Roberts and Ian Beamish, "Venturing Out: The Barbadian Diaspora and the Carolina Colony, 1650–1685," *Creating and Contesting Carolina: Proprietary Era Histories*, eds. Brad Wood and Michelle LeMaster (Charleston: University of South Carolina Press, 2013): 49–72; David Watts, *The West Indies: Patterns of Development, Culture, and Environmental Change since 1492* (New York: Cambridge University Press, 1987), 216–218; Menard, *Sweet Negotiations*, 106–121; Richard Dunn, *Sugar and Slaves: The Rise of the Planter Class in the English West Indies, 1624–1713* (New York: W.W. Norton & Company, 1972), 110–116.
62 Justin Roberts, "Surrendering Surinam: The Barbadian Diaspora and the Expansion of the English Sugar Frontier, 1650–1675," *William and Mary Quarterly* 73[2] (2016): 225–256, esp. 235–236f; See also Alison Games, "Cohabitation, Surinamese-Style: English Inhabitants in Dutch Suriname after 1667," *William and Mary Quarterly*, 72[2] (2015): 202–205, 202f, 217.
63 George Warren, *An Impartial Description of Surinam: Upon The Continent of Guiana in America*. (London: Printed by William Godbid for Nathaniel Brooke at the Angel in Gresham Colledge, 1667), 17.
64 Roberts, "Surrendering Surinam."
65 Eltis, *Rise of African Slavery*, 203–206.
66 *Voyages: The Trans-Atlantic Slave Trade Database* (hereafter cited as *Voyages*). Available online at www.slavevoyages.org/estimates/YXLOYibI (Accessed November 2015).
67 Trevor Burnard, "European Migration to Jamaica, 1655–1780," *William and Mary Quarterly* 53[4] (1996): 771–772; Roberts, "Surrendering Surinam," 235–236f, 240–243.
68 *Voyages*. Available online at www.slavevoyages.org/estimates/YXLOYib (Accessed November 2015); Eltis, *Rise of African Slavery*, 196–197; Nuala Zahedieh, "Trade, Plunder, and Economic Development in Early English Jamaica 1655–1685," *Economic History Review* 39[2] (1986): 205–222. 207; Susan Dwyer Amussen, *Caribbean Exchanges: Slavery and the Transformation of English Society, 1640–1700* (Chapel Hill: University of North Carolina Press, 2007), 80.
69 Richard B. Sheridan, "The Formation of Caribbean Plantation Society, 1689–1748," *The Oxford History of the British Caribbean: The Eighteenth Century*, Vol. II, ed. P. J. Marshall (New York: Oxford University Press, 2001), 395; Verene Shepherd, *Livestock, Sugar and Slavery: Contested Terrain in Colonial Jamaica* (Kingston, Jamaica: Ian Randle Publishers, 2009), 15–16; Roberts, *Slavery and the Enlightenment in the British Atlantic* (New York: Cambridge University Press, 2013), 11–12; Eltis, *Rise of African Slavery*, 193–223.
70 Shepherd, *Livestock, Sugar and Slavery*.
71 Roberts and Beamish, "Venturing Out."
72 Mulcahy, *Hubs of Empire*, 96, 100; Berlin, *Many Thousands Gone*, 71. The origins of rice cultivation in the Americas has been a subject of significant historiographical debate. Some scholars have suggested that Africans from rice-growing regions of Africa were responsible for introducing knowledge about the cultivation of rice whereas others have argued that there is little evidence to support such a contention. For opposing sides of the debate, see Judith Carney, *Black Rice: The African Origins of Rice Cultivation in the Americas* (Cambridge: Harvard University Press, 2002); David Eltis, Philip Morgan and David Richardson, "Agency and Diaspora in Atlantic History: Reassessing the African Contribution to Rice Cultivation in the Americas," *American Historical Review* 112[5] (2007): 1329–1358.
73 Mulcahy, *Hubs of Empire*, 89.
74 Gregory E. O'Malley, "Diversity in the Slave Trade to the Colonial Carolinas," *Creating and Contesting Carolina: Proprietary Era Histories*, eds Michelle LeMaster and Bradford J. Wood (Charleston: University of South Carolina Press, 2013), 236, 237.
75 Mulcahy, *Hubs of Empire*, 101.
76 Berlin, *Many Thousands Gone*, 47–48.
77 There were annual transatlantic slaving voyages to the Chesapeake until 1774 but the trade did not end completely that year. An additional 473 slaves disembarked in the Chesapeake in 1780 and 1781 before another two-decade gap in the trade. Another 68 slaves were disembarked in the Chesapeake in 1801, the last year for the direct trade from Africa to that region. *Voyages*. Available online at www.slavevoyages.org/estimates/PouGDfBi (Accessed November 2015).
78 Morgan, *Slavery in the British Empire*, 28.
79 Roberts, *Slavery and the Enlightenment*, 18.

80 Steven Deyle, "The Domestic Slave Trade in America: The Lifeblood of the Southern Slave System," *The Chattel Principle: Internal Slave Trades in the Americas*, ed. Walter Johnson (New Haven: Yale University Press, 2004), 93.
81 Morgan, *Slavery in the British Empire*, 40.
82 Morgan, *Slave Counterpoint*, 45–49.
83 Walsh, *Motives of Honor*, 601.
84 Roberts, *Slavery and the Enlightenment*, 80–130.
85 Mulcahy, *Hubs of Empire*, 104.
86 Berlin, *Many Thousands Gone*, 142.
87 Berlin, *Many Thousands Gone*, 143–144.
88 Mulcahy, *Hubs of Empire*, 113.
89 Mulcahy, *Hubs of Empire*, 106–111.
90 Richard Sheridan, "The Formation of Caribbean Plantation Society,", *The Oxford History of the British Empire*. Vol. 2: The Eighteenth Century, PJ Marshall, ed (New York: Oxford University Press, 1998), 401.
91 Eltis, *Rise of African Slavery*, 206.
92 David Beck Ryden, *West Indian Slavery and British Abolition, 1783–1807* (New York: Cambridge University Press, 2009), 15.
93 For a description of plantation neighborhoods, see Thomas Barritt to Nathaniel Phillips, April 20, 1791, MS 8372, Slebech Papers, National Library of Wales. Roberts, "The 'Better sort' and The 'Poorer Sort': Wealth Inequalities, Family Formation and the Economy of Energy on British Caribbean Sugar Plantations, 1750–1800," *Slavery & Abolition*, 35[3] (2014): 460–461.
94 BW Higman, *Slave Population and Economy in Jamaica, 1807–1834* (Kingston, Jamaica: Cambridge University Press, 1977), 61; J. R. Ward, "Profitability of Sugar Planting," 206.
95 Diana Paton, "Punishment, Crime and the Bodies of Slaves in Eighteenth-Century Jamaica," *Journal of Social History* 34[4] (2001): 923–954. Corporal punishments continued after slavery ended in Jamaica as a means of state-enforced social control. See Diana Paton, *No Bond but the Law: Punishment, Race, and Gender in Jamaican State Formation, 1780–1870*. (Durham: Duke University Press, 2004).
96 Trevor Burnard, *Mastery, Tyranny and Desire: Thomas Thistlewood and His Slaves in the Anglo-Jamaican World* (Chapel Hill: University of North Carolina Press, 2004), 183.
97 David Eltis, Frank D. Lewis and David Richardson, "Slave Prices, the African Slave Trade, and Productivity in the Caribbean, 1674–1807," *Economic History Review* 58[4] (2005): 679.
98 Roberts, "Uncertain Business"; Sheridan, "Formation of Caribbean Plantation Society," 401.
99 John McCusker, "Economy of the British West Indies, 1763–1790: Growth, Stagnation or Decline," *Essays in the Economic History of the Atlantic World*, ed. J. McCusker (London: Routledge, 1997), 206.
100 "British Sessional Papers, Commons, Accounts and Papers, 1789, Part III" as quoted in Michael Craton, James Walvin and David Wright, eds., *Slavery, Abolition and Emancipation: Black Slaves and the British Empire*, (London: Temple Smith, 1974), 94. For more on the new sugar frontiers of the late eighteenth and early nineteenth centuries in the southern Caribbean, see Kit Candlin, *The Last Caribbean Frontier, 1795–1815* (New York: Palgrave Macmillan, 2012).
101 Berlin, *Many Thousands Gone*, 178.
102 Morgan, *Slavery in the British Empire*, 101–102; Slaves were also used in large ironworks in Virginia; see John Bezis-Selfa, "A Tale of Two Ironworks: Slavery, Free Labor, Work, and Resistance in the Early Republic," *William and Mary Quarterly* 56[4] (1999): 677–700.
103 Berlin, *Many Thousands Gone*, 178.
104 Berlin, *Many Thousands Gone*, 228; For a detailed discussion of the development of free black communities in the North, see Gary B. Nash, *Forging Freedom: The Formation of Philadelphia's Black Community, 1720–1840* (Cambridge: Harvard University Press, 1991).
105 Roberts, *Slavery and the Enlightenment*, 14.
106 For more on gang labor and its development, see Roberts, *Slavery and the Enlightenment*, 131–136, 149–150, 246, 276; Eltis, *Rise of African Slavery*, 220–222.
107 Justin Roberts, "The 'Better sort' and The 'Poorer Sort' 35[3] (2014).
108 Roberts, *Slavery and the Enlightenment*, 180–182; Roberts, "The 'Better Sort' and The 'Poorer Sort'," 464–465; Richard Dunn, "Sugar Production and Slave Women in Jamaica," *Cultivation and Culture: Labor and the Shaping of Slave Life in the Americas*, eds. Ira Berlin and Philip D. Morgan (Richmond: University Press of Virginia, 1993), 49–72; Jennifer Morgan, *Laboring Women: Reproduction and Gender in the New World Slavery* (Philadelphia: University of Pennsylvania Press, 2004).
109 Roberts, *Slavery and the Enlightenment*, 105–110.
110 Roberts, *Slavery and the Enlightenment*, 120–127.

111 Eltis, *Rise of African Slavery*, 220–222.
112 Trevor Burnard, *Planters, Merchants and Slaves: Plantation Societies in British America, 1650–1820* (Chicago: University of Chicago Press, 2015), 55–58.
113 Roberts, *Slavery and the Enlightenment*, 135–136, 148–150.
114 Morgan, *Slave Counterpoint*, 181.
115 Philip D. Morgan, "Task and Gang Systems: The Organization of Labor on New World Plantations," *Work and Labor in Early America*, ed. Stephen Innes (Chapel Hill: University of North Carolina Press, 1988).
116 *Voyages*, www.slavevoyages.org/estimates/et77qt5p (Accessed November 2015).
117 Morgan, *Slavery and the British Empire*, 56.
118 For more on the history of the Royal African Company, see William Pettigrew, *Freedom's Debt: The Royal African Company and the Politics of the Atlantic Slave Trade, 1672–1752* (Chapel Hill: University of North Carolina Press, 2013).
119 *Voyages*, http://www.slavevoyages.org/estimates/AbJEHAYz(Accessed November 2015).
120 *Voyages*, http://www.slavevoyages.org/estimates/zFEyzYlt (Accessed November 2015).
121 Mulcahy, *Hubs of Empire*, 115; Joseph Miller, *Way of Death: Merchant Capitalism and the Angolan Slave Trade, 1730–1830* (Madison: University of Wisconsin Press, 1988), 384–385.
122 *Voyages*, http://www.slavevoyages.org/voyages/2xy2Jhdi (Accessed November 2015).
123 *Voyages*, http://www.slavevoyages.org/voyages/sH9bE4Kv (Accessed November 2015).
124 *Voyages*, http://www.slavevoyages.org/voyages/AIxMrXfD (Accessed November 2015).
125 *Voyages*, http://www.slavevoyages.org/voyages/oDX3xQ7D (Accessed November 2015).
126 Eltis, *Rise of African Slavery*, 186.
127 One of the best discussions of the commodification of human beings in slave markets is in the literature on the internal nineteenth-century US slave trade after the end of the slave trade. See Walter Johnson, *Soul by Soul: Life Inside the Antebellum Slave Market* (Cambridge: Harvard University Press, 2001), 117–134.
128 Gregory E. O'Malley, *Final Passages: The Intercolonial Slave Trade of British America, 1619–1807* (Chapel Hill: University of North Carolina Press, 2014).
129 J. R. Ward, *British West Indian Slavery 1750–1834: The Process of Amelioration* (Oxford: Clarendon Press, 1988), 124–129.
130 Morgan, *Slavery in the British Empire*, 157.
131 The literature on this topic is enormous but for a recent overview of abolition that explores most of the key factors, see Seymour Drescher, *Abolition: A History of Slavery and Antislavery* (Cambridge: Cambridge University Press, 2009). For an older but still useful synthesis, see Robin Blackburn, *The Overthrow of Colonial Slavery, 1776–1848* (London: Verso, 1988). For a classic older work that focuses on the United States, see David Brion Davis. *The Problem of Slavery in the Age of Revolution, 1770–1823* (Ithaca, NY: Cornell University Press, 1975). For an older classic and highly influential work that stresses that the rise of capitalism ended slavery, see Eric Williams. *Capitalism and Slavery* (Chapel Hill: University of North Carolina Press, 1944).
132 Samuel Johnson, "Taxation No Tyranny: An Answer to the Resolutions and Address of the American Congress," [1775], *The Works of Samuel Johnson*, Vol. 8, ed. Arthur Murphy (London, 1801), 203.
133 Christopher Brown, *Moral Capital: Foundations of British Abolitionism* (Chapel Hill: University of North Carolina Press, 2006).
134 *Voyages*, http://www.slavevoyages.org/estimates/28DkUNpv (Accessed November 2015).
135 Lowell Ragatz, *The Fall of the Planter Class in the British Caribbean, 1763–1833* (New York: Octagon Books, 1977 [1928]); Eric Williams, *Capitalism & Slavery* (London: A. Deutsch, 1993 [1944]); David Beck Ryden, "Does Decline Make Sense? The West Indian Economy and the Abolition of the Slave Trade," *Journal of Interdisciplinary History*, 31, 3 (2001): 347–74; Selwyn Carrington, *The Sugar Industry and the Abolition of the Slave Trade, 1775–1810* (Gainesville: University of Florida Press, 2002); David Beck Ryden, *West Indian Slavery and British Abolition, 1783–1807* (New York: Cambridge University Press, 2009).
136 For the best recent work on the overproduction of Caribbean sugar, see Ryden, *West Indian Slavery and British Abolition*.
137 For works that support this thesis, see Seymour Drescher, *Econocide: British Slavery in the Era of Abolition* (Pittsburgh: University of Pittsburgh Press, 1977); J. R. Ward "The profitability of sugar planting in the British West Indies, 1650–1834," *Economic History Review*, 31[2] (1978): 197–213; Ward, *British West Indian Slavery*; Eltis, *Rise of African Slavery*, 193–223. John McCusker, "British West Indies economy, 1763–1790," *Essays in the Economic History of the Atlantic World*, edited by John McCusker (London: Routledge, 1997): 310–30. B. W. Higman, *Plantation Jamaica, 1750–1850: Capital and Control in a Colonial Economy* (King-

ston: University of the West Indies Press, 2005). Justin Roberts, "Uncertain Business: A Case Study of Barbadian Plantation Management, 1770–1793," *Slavery & Abolition*, 32[2] (2011): 247–268.
138 Christa Dierksheide, *Amelioration and Empire: Progress & Slavery in the Plantation Americas* (Charlottesville: University of Virginia Press, 2014).
139 Seymour Drescher, *The Mighty Experiment: Free Labor vs. Slavery in British Emancipation* (New York: Oxford University Press, 2002).
140 Andrew Levy, *The First Emancipator: The Forgotten Story of Robert Carter, the Founding Father Who Freed His Slaves* (New York: Random House, 2005); Melvin Patrick Ely, *Israel on the Appomattox: A Southern Experiment in Black Freedom from the 1790s through the Civil War* (New York: Vintage, 2005).
141 Roberts, *Slavery and the Enlightenment*, 26–79.
142 Michael P. Johnson, "Denmark Vesey and his Co-Conspirators," *William and Mary Quarterly*, 3rd series, 58[4] (2001): 915–976.
143 For the classic work on this subject, see Eugene Genovese, *From Rebellion to Revolution: Afro-American Slave Revolts in the Making of the Modern World* (Louisiana State University Press, 1992).
144 Wim Klooster, "Slave Revolts, Royal Justice, and a Ubiquitous Rumor in the Age of Revolutions," *William and Mary Quarterly* 3rd series, 71[3] (2014): 401–424.
145 For examples of the abundant scholarly work on slave resistance, see Michael Mullin, *Africa in America: Slave Acculturation and Resistance in the American South and the British Caribbean, 1736–1831* (Chicago: University of Illinois Press, 1992); Eric Robert Taylor, *If We Must Die: Shipboard Insurrections in the Era of the Atlantic Slave Trade* (New Orleans: Louisiana State University Press, 2006); James H. Sweet, *Recreating Africa: Culture, Kinship and Religion in the African-Portuguese World, 1441–1770* (Chapel Hill: University of North Carolina Press, 2003).
146 Roberts, *Slavery and the Enlightenment*, 262–263; Randy M. Browne, "Surviving Slavery: Politics, Power, and Authority in the British Caribbean, 1807–1834", (Ph.D. dissertation, University of North Carolina, Chapel Hill, 2012).
147 Thomas Thistlewood Diary, March 18, 1751, Monson 31/2, Thomas Thistlewood Papers, Lincoln County Record Office.
148. Roberts, *Slavery and the Enlightenment*, 263–275.
149. Walter Johnson, "On Agency," *Journal of Social History* 37 (2003): 113–124; "Roberts, *Slavery and the Enlightenment*", 2–5; Sideny Mintz, "Slave Life on Caribbean Sugar Plantations: Some Unanswered Questions," *Slave Cultures and the Cultures of Slavery*, ed. Stephen Palmie (Knoxville: University of Tennessee Press, 1995), 13; Robert William Fogel, *Without Consent or Contract: The Rise and Fall of American Slavery* (New York: Norton, 1989), 154–198.
150 Roberts, *Slavery and the Enlightenment*, 2–5.
151 Roberts, "The 'Better Sort' and the 'Poorer Sort': Wealth Inequalities, Family Formation and the Economy of Energy on British Caribbean Sugar Plantations, 1750–1800," *Slavery & Abolition* 35, 3 (September 2014): 458–473.
152 Simon Taylor to Chalenor Arcedeckne, June 11, 1782, 3A/1782/28, Cambridge University Library.
153 Mintz, "Slave Life on Caribbean Sugar Plantations," 13.
154 Browne, "Surviving Slavery"; Vincent Brown, "Social Death and Political Life in the Study of Slavery," *American Historical Review* 114[5] (2009): 1231–1249, quote on page 1246.
155 For works that approach slavery as a kind of labor history, see Justin Roberts, *Slavery and the Enlightenment*; Newman, *A New World of Labor*; Ira Berlin and Philip D. Morgan, eds. *Cultivation and Culture: Labor and the Shaping of Slave Life in the Americas* (Richmond: University Press of Virginia, 1993).

References

Aimes, Hubert H. S. "Coartación: A Spanish Institution for the Advancement of Slaves into Freedom," *Yale Review* 7 (February 1909): 412–431.
Amussen, Susan Dwyer. *Caribbean Exchanges: Slavery and the Transformation of English Society, 1640–1700* (Chapel Hill: University of North Carolina Press, 2007).
Beckles, Hilary. "A Riotous and Unruly Lot': Irish Indentured Servants and Freemen in the English West Indies, 1644–1713," *William and Mary Quarterly* 47[1] (1990): 3–22.
Beckles, Hilary. *White Servitude and Black Slavery in Barbados, 1627–1715* (Knoxville: University of Tennessee Press, 1989).

Berlin, Ira and Philip D. Morgan, eds. *Cultivation and Culture: Labor and the Shaping of Slave Life in the Americas* (Richmond: University Press of Virginia, 1993).

Berlin, Ira. *Many Thousands Gone: The First Two Centuries of Slavery in North America* (Cambridge: The Belknap Press of Harvard University Press, 1998).

Bezis-Selfa, John. "A Tale of Two Ironworks: Slavery, Free Labor, Work, and Resistance in the Early Republic," *William and Mary Quarterly* 56, 4 (October 1999): 677–700.

Blackburn, Robin. *The Overthrow of Colonial Slavery, 1776–1848* (London: Verso, 1988).

Brion Davis. David. *The Problem of Slavery in the Age of Revolution, 1770–1823* (Ithaca, NY: Cornell University Press, 1975).

Brion Davis, David. *Inhuman Bondage: The Rise and Fall of Slavery in the New World* (New York: Oxford University Press, 2006).

Brooks, James F. *Captives and Cousins: Slavery, Kinship, and Community in the Southwest Borderlands* (Chapel Hill: University of North Carolina Press, 2002).

Brown, Christopher. *Moral Capital: Foundations of British Abolitionism* (Chapel Hill: University of North Carolina Press, 2006).

Brown, Vincent. "Social Death and Political Life in the Study of Slavery," *American Historical Review* 114[5] (2009): 1231–1249.

Browne, Randy M. "Surviving Slavery: Politics, Power, and Authority in the British Caribbean, 1807–1834," (Ph.D. dissertation, University of North Carolina, Chapel Hill, 2012).

Burnard, Trevor. "European Migration to Jamaica, 1655–1780," *William and Mary Quarterly*, 53[4] (1996), 771–772.

Burnard, Trevor. *Mastery, Tyranny and Desire: Thomas Thistlewood and His Slaves in the Anglo-Jamaican World* (Chapel Hill: University of North Carolina Press, 2004).

Burnard, Trevor. *Planters, Merchants and Slaves: Plantation Societies in British America, 1650–1820* (Chicago: University of Chicago Press, 2015).

Candlin, Kit. *The Last Caribbean Frontier, 1795–1815* (New York: Palgrave Macmillan, 2012).

Carney, Judith. *Black Rice: The African Origins of Rice Cultivation in the Americas* (Cambridge: Harvard University Press, 2002).

Carrington, Selwyn. *The Sugar Industry and the Abolition of the Slave Trade, 1775–1810* (Gainesville: University of Florida Press, 2002).

Chandler, Alfred. "The Expansion of Barbados," *Journal of the Barbados Museum and Historical Society* 12 (May 1946), 106–136.

Coombs, John C. "The Phases of Conversion: a New Chronology for the Rise of Slavery in Early Virginia," *William and Mary Quarterly* 68[3] (July, 2011): 332–360.

Craton, Michael, James Walvin, and David Wright, eds. *Slavery, Abolition and Emancipation: Black Slaves and the British Empire*, (London: Temple Smith, 1974).

Curtin, Philip. *The Rise and Fall of the Plantation Complex: Essays in Atlantic History* (New York: Cambridge University Press, 1990).

Deal, J. Douglas. *Race and Class in Colonial Virginia: Indians, Englishmen and Africans on the Eastern Shore of Virginia During the Seventeenth Century* (New York: Garland Publishing, Inc., 1993).

Degler, Carl N. "Slavery and the Genesis of American Race Prejudice," *Comparative Studies in Society and History* 2[1] (October 1959), 49–66.

Degler, Carl N. *Neither Black nor White: Slavery and Race Relations in Brazil and the United States* (Madison: University of Wisconsin Press, 1971).

Deyle, Steven. "The Domestic Slave Trade in America: The Lifeblood of the Southern Slave System," *The Chattel Principle: Internal Slave Trades in the Americas*, ed. Walter Johnson (New Haven: Yale University Press, 2004): 91–117.

Dierksheide, Christa. *Amelioration and Empire: Progress & Slavery in the Plantation Americas* (Charlottesville: University of Virginia Press, 2014).

Drescher, Seymour. *Econocide: British Slavery in the Era of Abolition* (Pittsburgh: University of Pittsburgh Press, 1977).

Drescher, Seymour. *The Mighty Experiment: Free Labor vs. Slavery in British Emancipation* (New York: Oxford University Press, 2002).

Drescher, Seymour. *Abolition: A History of Slavery and Antislavery* (Cambridge: Cambridge University Press, 2009).

Dunn, Richard S. *Sugar and Slaves: The Rise of the Planter Class in the English West Indies, 1624–1713* (New York: W.W. Norton & Company, 1972).

Dunn, Richard S. "Sugar Production and Slave Women in Jamaica," Ira Berlin and Philip D. Morgan, eds. *Cultivation and Culture: Labor and the Shaping of Slave Life in the Americas* (Richmond: University Press of Virginia, 1993): 49–72.

Ekirch, Roger. *Bound for America: The Transportation of British Convicts to the Colonies, 1718–1775* (New York: Oxford University Press, 1987).

Elliott, J. H. *Empires of the Atlantic World: Britain and Spain in America, 1492–1830* (New Haven: Yale University Press, 2006).

Eltis, David, Frank D. Lewis, and David Richardson. "Slave Prices, the African Slave Trade, and Productivity in the Caribbean, 1674–1807," *Economic History Review* 58[4] (2005): 673–700.

Eltis, David, Morgan, Philip, and Richardson, David. "Agency and Diaspora in Atlantic History: Reassessing the African Contribution to Rice Cultivation in the Americas," *American Historical Review* 112[5] (2007): 1329–1358.

Eltis, David. "Europeans and the Rise and Fall of African Slavery in the Americas: An Interpretation," *American Historical Review* 98[5] (1993): 1399–1423.

Eltis, David. "New Estimates of Exports from Barbados and Jamaica, 1665–1701," *William and Mary Quarterly*, 3rd series, 52[4] (1995): 631–648.

Eltis, David. *The Rise of African Slavery in the Americas* (New York: Cambridge University Press, 2000).

Ely, Melvin Patrick. *Israel on the Appomattox: A Southern Experiment in Black Freedom from the 1790s through the Civil War* (New York: Vintage, 2005).

Engerman, Stanley L. "Slavery at Different Times and Places," *American Historical Review* 105[2] (2000), 480–484.

Fogel, Robert William. *Without Consent or Contract: The Rise and Fall of American Slavery* (New York: Norton, 1989).

Frederickson, George. *Racism: A Short History* (Princeton: Princeton University Press, 2002).

Gallay, Alan. *The Indian Slave Trade: The Rise of the English Empire in the American South, 1670–1717* (New Haven: Yale University Press, 2002).

Games, Alison. "Cohabitation, Surinamese-Style: English Inhabitants in Dutch Suriname after 1667," *William and Mary Quarterly*, 72[2] (2015): 195–242.

Genovese, Eugene. *From Rebellion to Revolution: Afro-American Slave Revolts in the Making of the Modern World* (Louisiana State University Press, 1992).

Goetz, Rebecca Anne. "Rethinking the Unthinking Decision: Old Questions and New Problems in the History of Slavery and Race in the Colonial South," *The Journal of Southern History* 25[3] (2009): 599–612.

Guaso, Michael. *Slaves and Englishmen: Human Bondage in the Early Modern Atlantic World* (Philadelphia: University of Pennsylvania Press, 2014).

Hadden, Sally. "The Fragmented Laws of Slavery in the Colonial and Revolutionary Era," eds. Michael Grossberg and Christopher Tomlins, *The Cambridge History of Law in America* Volume 1 (New York: Cambridge University Press, 2007).

Handlin, Oscar and Handlin, Mary F. "The Origins of the Southern Labor System," *William and Mary Quarterly* 7[2] (1950), 199–222.

Hannaford, Ivan. *Race: The History of an Idea in the West* (Baltimore: Johns Hopkins University Press, 1996).

Higman, B. W. "The Sugar Revolution," *Economic History Review* 53[2] (2000), 213–236.

Higman, B. W. *Plantation Jamaica, 1750–1850: Capital and Control in a Colonial Economy* (Kingston: University of the West Indies Press, 2005).

Higman, B. W. *Slave Population and Economy in Jamaica, 1807–1834* (Kingston, Jamaica: Cambridge University Press, 1977).

Johnson, Michael P. "Denmark Vesey and his Co-Conspirators," *William and Mary Quarterly*, 3rd series, 58[4] (2001): 915–976.

Johnson, Walter. "On Agency," *Journal of Social History* 37 (2003): 113–124.

Johnson, Walter. *Soul by Soul: Life Inside the Antebellum Slave Market* (Cambridge: Harvard University Press, 2001).

Jordan, Don and Michael Walsh. *White Cargo: The Forgotten History of Britain's White Slaves in America* (New York: New York University Press, 2008).

Jordan, Winthrop. *White over Black: American Attitudes toward the Negro, 1550–1812* (Chapel Hill: University of North Carolina Press, 1968).

Klooster, Wim. "Slave Revolts, Royal Justice, and a Ubiquitous Rumor in the Age of Revolutions," *William and Mary Quarterly*, 3rd series 71[3] (2014): 401–424.

Kupperman, Karen Ordahl. *Providence Island, 1630–1641: The Other Puritan Colony* (New York: Cambridge University Press, 1993).

Landers, Jane. *Atlantic Creoles in the Age of Revolutions* (Cambridge: Harvard University Press, 2011).

Levy, Andrew. *The First Emancipator: The Forgotten Story of Robert Carter, the Founding Father Who Freed His Slaves* (New York: Random House, 2005).

McCusker, John J. and Russell R. Menard. *The Economy of British America, 1607–1789* (Chapel Hill: University of North Carolina Press, 1985).

McCusker, John J. and Russell Menard. "The Sugar Industry in the Seventeenth Century: A New Perspective on the Barbadian 'Sugar Revolution,'" *Tropical Babylons: Sugar and the Making of the Atlantic World, 1450–1680* ed. Stuart B. Schwartz, (Chapel Hill: University of North Carolina Press, 2004): 289–330.

McCusker, John. "British West Indies economy, 1763–1790," *Essays in the Economic History of the Atlantic World*, ed. John McCusker (London: Routledge, 1997): 310–30.

McCusker, John. "Growth, Stagnation or Decline," *Essays in the Economic History of the Atlantic World*, ed. J. McCusker (London: Routledge, 1997).

Menard, Russell R. *Sweet Negotiations: Sugar, Slavery and Plantation Agriculture in Early Barbados* (Charlottesville: University of Virginia Press, 2006).

Miller, Joseph. *Way of Death: Merchant Capitalism and the Angolan Slave Trade, 1730–1830* (Madison: University of Wisconsin Press, 1988).

Mintz, Sidney. "Slave Life on Caribbean Sugar Plantations: Some Unanswered Questions," *Slave Cultures and the Cultures of Slavery*, ed. Stephen Palmie (Knoxville: University of Tennessee Press, 1995).

Morgan, Edmund S. *American Slavery, American Freedom: The Ordeal of Colonial Virginia* (New York: W. W. Norton & Company, 1975).

Morgan, Jennifer L. *Laboring Women: Reproduction and Gender in the New World Slavery* (Philadelphia: University of Pennsylvania Press, 2004).

Morgan, Kenneth. *Slavery and Servitude in Colonial North America: A Short History* (New York: New York University Press, 2001).

Morgan, Kenneth. *Slavery and the British Empire from Africa to America* (New York: Oxford University Press, 2007).

Morgan, Philip D. "Task and Gang Systems: The Organization of Labor on New World Plantations," *Work and Labor in Early America*, ed. Stephen Innes (Chapel Hill: University of North Carolina Press, 1988).

Morgan, Philip. *Slave Counterpoint: Black Culture in Eighteenth-Century Chesapeake and Lowcountry* (Chapel Hill: University of North Carolina Press, 1998).

Mulcahy, Matthew. *Hubs of Empire: The Southeastern Lowcountry and British Caribbean* (Baltimore: Johns Hopkins University Press, 2014).

Mullin, Michael. *Africa in America: Slave Acculturation and Resistance in the American South and the British Caribbean, 1736–1831* (Chicago: University of Illinois Press, 1992).

Nash, Gary B. *Forging Freedom: The Formation of Philadelphia's Black Community, 1720–1840* (Cambridge, MA: Harvard University Press, 1991).

Newman, Simon. *A New World of Labor: The Development of Plantation Slavery in the British Atlantic*. (Philadelphia: University of Pennsylvania Press, 2013).

O'Malley, Gregory E. "Diversity in the Slave Trade to the Colonial Carolinas," eds. Michelle LeMaster and Bradford J. Wood., *Creating and Contesting Carolina: Proprietary Era Histories* (Charleston: University of South Carolina Press, 2013).

O'Malley, Gregory E. *Final Passages: The Intercolonial Slave Trade of British America, 1619–1807* (Chapel Hill: University of North Carolina Press, 2014).

Parent, Anthony S. *Foul Means: The Formation of a Slave Society in Virginia, 1660–1740* (Chapel Hill: University of North Carolina Press, 2003).

Paton, Diana. "Punishment, Crime and the Bodies of Slaves in Eighteenth-Century Jamaica," *Journal of Social History* 34[4] (2001): 923–954.

Paton, Diana. *No Bond but the Law: Punishment, Race, and Gender in Jamaican State Formation, 1780–1870*. (Durham: Duke University Press, 2004).

Pettigrew, William. *Freedom's Debt: The Royal African Company and the Politics of the Atlantic Slave Trade, 1672–1752* (Chapel Hill: University of North Carolina Press, 2013).

Ragatz, Lowell. *The Fall of the Planter Class in the British Caribbean, 1763–1833* (New York: Octagon Books, 1977 [1928]).

Roberts, Justin and Ian Beamish. "Venturing Out: The Barbadian Diaspora and the Carolina Colony, 1650–1685," eds. Brad Wood and Michelle LeMaster, *Creating and Contesting Carolina: Proprietary Era Histories* (Charleston: University of South Carolina Press, 2013), 49–72.

Roberts, Justin. "Surrendering Surinam: The Barbadian Diaspora and the Expansion of the English Sugar Frontier, 1650–1675," *William and Mary Quarterly* 73[2] (2016): 225–256.

Roberts, Justin. "The 'Better Sort' and The 'Poorer Sort': Wealth Inequalities, Family Formation and the Economy of Energy on British Caribbean Sugar Plantations, 1750–1800," *Slavery & Abolition* 35[3] (2014): 458–473.

Roberts, Justin. "Uncertain Business: A Case Study of Barbadian Plantation Management, 1770–1793," *Slavery & Abolition*, 32[2] (2011): 247–268.

Roberts, Justin. *Slavery and the Enlightenment*; Simon Newman, *A New World of Labor: The Development of Plantation Slavery in the British Atlantic* (Philadelphia: University of Pennsylvania Press, 2013).

Rugemer, Edward B. "The Development of Mastery and Race in the Comprehensive Slave Codes of the Greater Caribbean during the Seventeenth Century," *William and Mary Quarterly* 70[3] (2013).

Rushforth, Brett. *Bonds of Alliance: Indigenous and Atlantic Slaveries in New France* (Chapel Hill: University of North Carolina Press, 2012).

Ryden, David Beck. "Does decline make sense? The West Indian economy and the abolition of the slave trade," *Journal of Interdisciplinary History* 31[3] (2001): 347–74.

Ryden, David Beck. *West Indian Slavery and British Abolition, 1783–1807* (New York: Cambridge University Press, 2009).

Shaw, Jenny. *Everyday Life in the Early Caribbean: Irish, Africans and the Construction of Difference* (Athens: University of Georgia Press, 2013).

Shepherd, Verene. *Livestock, Sugar and Slavery: Contested Terrain in Colonial Jamaica* (Kingston, Jamaica: Ian Randle Publishers, 2009).

Sheridan, Richard B. "The Formation of Caribbean Plantation Society, 1689–1748," *The Oxford History of the British Caribbean: The Eighteenth Century*, Vol. II, ed. PJ Marshall (New York: Oxford University Press, 2001).

Shore, Laurence. "The Enduring Power of Racism: A Reconsideration of Winthrop Jordan's White over Black," *History and Theory* 44[2] (2005): 195–226.

Steinfeld, Robert J. "Changing Legal Conceptions of Free Labor," *Terms of Labor: Slavery, Serfdom and Free Labor*, ed. Stanley Engerman (Stanford: Stanford University Press, 1999), 137–167.

Steinfeld, Robert J. *The Invention of Free Labor: The Employment Relation in English and American Law and Culture, 1350–1870* (Chapel Hill: University of North Carolina Press, 1991).

Sweet, James H. "The Iberian Roots of American Racist Thought," *William and Mary Quarterly* 54[1] (1997): 143–166.

Sweet, James H. *Recreating Africa: Culture, Kinship and Religion in the African-Portuguese World, 1441–1770* (Chapel Hill: University of North Carolina Press, 2003).

Tannenbaum, Frank. *Slave and Citizen: The Negro in the Americas* (New York: Vintage Books, 1946).

Taylor, Eric Robert. *If We Must Die: Shipboard Insurrections in the Era of the Atlantic Slave Trade* (New Orleans: Louisiana State University Press, 2006).

Vaughan, Alden T. *Roots of American Racism: Essays on the Colonial Experience* (New York: Oxford University Press, 1998).

Walsh, Lorena. *Motives of Honour, Pleasure and Profit: Plantation Management in the Colonial Chesapeake, 1607–1763* (Chapel Hill: University of North Carolina Press, 2010).

Ward, J. R. 'The Profitability of Sugar Planting in the British West Indies, 1650–1834', *Economic History Review*, 31[2] (1978): 197–213.

Ward, J. R. *British West Indian Slavery 1750–1834: The Process of Amelioration* (Oxford: Clarendon Press, 1988).

Watts, David. *The West Indies: Patterns of Development, Culture, and Environmental Change since 1492* (New York: Cambridge University Press, 1987).

Williams, Eric. *Capitalism and Slavery* (Chapel Hill: University of North Carolina Press, 1944).

Zahedieh, Nuala. *The Capital and the Colonies: London and the Atlantic Economy, 1660–1700* (New York: Cambridge University Press, 2010).

PART III

British Colonial Developments and the Fates of Indigenous Polities

Figure 7.1 1638 engraving depicting the English massacre of the Pequots at Fort Mystic.
Source: John Underhill. STC 24518, Houghton Library, Harvard University/Wikimedia Commons.

7
SPIRITUAL GIANTS, WORLDLY EMPIRES
Indigenous Peoples and New England to the 1680s

Neal Salisbury

Indigenous peoples inhabited the lands later known as "New England" for millennia before Europeans began arriving in the sixteenth century. Their long presence significantly shaped the colonial region that emerged in the seventeenth century as a Native-European "borderland." As throughout the Atlantic littoral, a regional history constituted one of the myriad blocks upon which an "Atlantic world" was constructed.[1] Drawing on scholarship in history, Indigenous Studies, archaeology, and other fields, this chapter discusses the development over millennia of indigenous spirituality, ways of life, and homelands; the incorporation of early Europeans into Indian exchange networks; and Natives' experiences with, and modes of countering, the trauma of colonization to *c.* 1685.

Before New England

The human history of New England originated in what indigenous studies scholars refer to as "deep time." As measured by Western science, hunting-gathering bands began arriving *c.* 10,000 BC in the aftermath of the last Ice Age. Together the rising sea level and freshly scoured landscape formed a complex coastline, whose inhabitants posited that giant beings emerging from the Atlantic had shaped this environment and ordered relations among the creatures—including themselves—who inhabited it. They understood land and sea, along with sky, not as mutually exclusive categories but as a single space pervaded by spiritual power. Gluskap created the world of Wabanaki peoples in what is now Vermont, New Hampshire, Maine, and the Canadian Maritimes; Maushop figured comparably for those living south of the Wabanakis and east of the Berkshire Mountains. Noncoastal peoples recognized the spiritual power of Gluskap and Maushop while ascribing their local landscapes to giant beavers, bears, and other animals that correspond with early post-Pleistocene species.

Over the next four to five millennia, Gluskap and Maushop raised temperatures and sea level, challenging people to feed, clothe, and otherwise sustain their communities as the environment changed. As Elizabeth Chilton observes, they did so through adaptability and mobility. They burned the forests' underbrush to favor preferred animal and plant species. In carefully calculated seasonal movements through defined homelands, men pursued mammals and fish while women gathered wild plants and shellfish, and prepared all the food. The Atlantic was central to these modifications. The people built weirs for harvesting anadromous fish and dugout canoes for traveling along coasts as well as on rivers to obtain these and other resources. Spring fish runs were especially important social and ceremonial occasions, and remained so into the seventeenth century.[2]

As the climate and environment stabilized, Natives substantially increased food production and, thereby, population growth and density. The most far-reaching developments were women's manufacturing of ceramic vessels for food preparation *c.* 1000 BC, men's adopting the bow and arrow for hunting *c.* AD 700, and—following several centuries of experimentation—women's intensive cultivation of maize, beans, and squash after AD 1000. These women and men adapted techniques passing through long-distance exchange networks (extending across North America and into Siberia and Mesoamerica) to local circumstances. While populations rose and land bases shrank, even groups that focused primarily on farming maintained seasonal subsistence rounds within defined homelands and periodically shifted their fields, enabling soils to replenish.

The networks that brought new materials and techniques also brought spiritual knowledge. Hunters had always ritually addressed the spirits of their prey but their rituals intensified as their weaponry improved. South of Wabanaki country, the most intensive farming societies regarded Cautantowwit as the provider of maize and his southwesterly home as their destination after death. Yet Cautantowwit coexisted with rather than displaced Maushop, who had created the land on which maize grew so abundantly. Natives recognized *manitou* (spiritual power) wherever it originated, and incorporated new sources of it into their complex of beliefs and practices.

Native peoples' most salient contribution to long-distance exchanges was *wampum*—derived from sacred shells and fashioned into discs and beads strung into necklaces, bracelets, and belts. Indians throughout the Northeast regarded *wampum* belts as spiritually potent "words." Demand for wampum escalated during the fourteenth century as five Iroquoian-speaking nations to the west presented wampum belts conveying messages of peace and condolence to one another, enabling them to unite as the League of the Iroquois, or Haudenosaunee. Although Natives as far south as the Chesapeake Bay initially made wampum from a variety of shell species, the most favored became whelks and quahogs, both found in abundance on the shores of Narragansett Bay and Long Island Sound and transformed into wampum by Natives there.

As populations grew in size and complexity, local communities accorded greater political responsibility to male and female *sachems* (or *sagamores*). Sachems allocated family farm plots, resolved intracommunal disputes, and oversaw external relations. Yet communities circumscribed sachems' powers when meeting to make major decisions, including the selection or replacement of councilors and sachems themselves. Beyond the local community, a locus of political identity was the tribe. The power of tribal leaders varied from those who were largely ceremonial to tribute-collecting "great sachems." Kin ties among leading and ordinary lineages provided the foundation for tribes and intertribal alliances centered on great sachems. The production and exchange of wampum undoubtedly enhanced the power of Narragansett and other great sachems. But while few scholars doubt that political centralization under sachems' leadership accelerated during the seventeenth century, they disagree over the extent of sachems' powers before colonization.[3]

The long-distance exchange networks spanning across and beyond North America eventually extended to Europe. The earliest concrete evidence of such linkage is a Norse coin, minted in the eleventh century and uncovered amidst an array of Inuit objects at a site on the Gulf of Maine. The coin's presence is hardly anomalous: from the tenth to fourteenth centuries, Norse colonists in southwestern Greenland interacted extensively with Inuits and Beothuks who in turn maintained ties with Wabanakis and other Algonquian speakers. (The short-lived Norse settlement of Vinland in Newfoundland postdates the minting of the coin.)[4] It is likely that other European objects from this period lie beneath Wabanaki soil, brought not by Europeans but by indigenous intermediaries. From these intermediaries, Wabanakis undoubtedly heard about bearded Europeans and their sailing vessels.

Soon after the last Norse left Greenland, other Europeans began arriving in the Northwest Atlantic. English fishing crews returning from the Grand Banks off Newfoundland inspired a rush for cod and whales while Spain's Caribbean colonization after 1492 brought Iberian, French, and English explorers and slave traders. Through the 1520s the outcomes of several dozen Indian–European interactions in the future New England ranged from friendly exchanges, most notably Giovanni da Verrazzano's 15-day stopover in Narragansett Bay in 1524, to violent encounters like Esteban Gomez' kidnapping of several dozen Penobscot Abenakis in 1525. With European parties consisting solely of adult men, the women of even the most welcoming Native communities remained cautious in their presence. But when visitors observed norms of civility and reciprocity, Indian hosts sealed the relationship and incorporated the newcomers and their manitou into their own social and spiritual world.

Some fishermen quickly realized that Indians could produce abundant quantities of finished beaver and other pelts which they could sell for hefty profits in Europe, where beaver hats were becoming fashionable. By the 1520s Wabanakis held up long sticks hung with furs to signal their interest in trading with coasting fishermen. Specialized traders soon dominated the European side of these exchanges, offering iron tools, copper pots, and glass beads manufactured to suit Native consumers. Favorably located Native partners, particularly Mi'kmaqs on Cape Breton Island and the south shore of the Gulf of St. Lawrence, traded many of these goods to other Wabanaki communities for furs, and the new items soon circulated through exchange networks alongside wampum and other indigenous products. Indians quickly substituted iron axes, knives, and awls for stone or bone counterparts; but they usually reworked copper into ceremonial attire or arrowheads, and they treated glass beads as manitou-charged equivalents of rare minerals such as quartz and mica. While Native peoples understood these exchanges in spiritual terms, their material cultures were significantly modified and the political power of Mi'kmaq and other indigenous intermediaries was enhanced.

By the 1580s, the volume of trade in the Northeast was attracting renewed interest from larger European investors and nation-states. Some hoped to establish posts similar to Tadoussac on the lower St. Lawrence River, frequented annually by French traders. But Tadoussac succeeded because the French carefully cultivated favored Native partners there, whereas intruders on the Atlantic disdained or ignored diplomatic protocols. For example, an Englishman, John Walker, simply stole 300 pelts from a Penobscot Abenaki village in 1580 while a Frenchman, Etienne Bellenger, traded with Penobscots in 1583 before Mi'kmaqs drove him away to prevent his further encroaching on their role as intermediaries.

These patterns intensified after 1600 as Europeans began trying to directly colonize south of the Gulf of St. Lawrence. Driven in part by food shortages arising from an epidemic of French origin, the Mi'kmaqs began sailing French shallops to coastal Abenaki villages, demanding tribute and utilizing metal weaponry when meeting resistance. In this context Abenakis initially welcomed French and English parties offering direct trade ties and peace with the Mi'kmaqs. But French attempts to placate all parties collapsed in 1606 when Mi'kmaqs—some wielding French muskets—and their allies badly defeated an Abenaki coalition at the mouth of the Saco River.

Instead of capitalizing on Natives' resentment of the French, English colonizers aroused even greater hostility by using force against Wampanoags as well as Abenakis. An English expedition in 1602 sparked an Anglo-Wampanoag War that would last for two decades. Particularly offensive was the kidnapping of Indians, many of whom were taken to England. The kidnappers assumed that their captives would recognize English superiority and, upon returning home, persuade their people to accept colonization. Among the first group of captives who lived to return, two Abenakis advised their people to be suspicious of English colonists at Sagadahoc, established in 1607. English factionalism and violence reinforced Abenaki misgivings, and the colony was quickly abandoned. (One English trader maintained ties with nearby Pemaquid Abenakis and their sachem, Samoset.) After Henry Hudson's Dutch-English crew stole furs and other goods from a Penobscot Abenaki village in 1609, the Penobscots halted four years of futile efforts to ally with the English. Meanwhile, Wampanoag resistance reinforced France's decision to focus its colonial efforts on the St. Lawrence, leaving coastal Abenakis to trade and defend against Mi'kmaq raids on their own. An immediate consequence was renewed Mi'kmaq-Abenaki violence that resulted in the death of Bashaba (1614), a revered Penobscot grand sachem.

Although France withdrew from the Atlantic coast, private French traders remained and usually benefited from Anglo-Indian tensions, as former Virginia colonizer John Smith found in 1614. Smith traveled from Penobscot Bay to Cape Cod, familiarizing himself with Native communities, and achieved a truce in the Anglo-Wampanoag War. He believed that with the proper support he could persuade coastal Natives to accept a "New England" in their homeland. After Smith departed, his hopes were dashed when one of his accomplices used the truce to lure 24 to 30 Patuxet and Nauset Wampanoags aboard his vessel and carried them to Málaga to sell as slaves. Days later, Epenow, a Wampanoag sachem who had been captured and taken to England three years earlier, returned home to Noepe (the future Martha's Vineyard), having persuaded his captors that he would lead them to gold. As the ship approached Noepe, Epenow escaped and led his people in driving the English away.[5] These two events further escalated the Anglo-Wampanoag War.

While turning back Europe's colonizers, Wampanoags, Abenakis, and their neighbors were less able to resist its pathogens. From 1616 to 1618, deadly epidemic disease tore through their communities. Whereas earlier European documents portray densely populated, extensively farmed coastal communities, those originating afterward depict empty villages and overgrown fields littered with unburied bodies. European descriptions of symptoms suggest plague, yellow fever, hepatitis, and other possibilities. Scholars have long argued for and against these and other maladies to which indigenous peoples had not previously been exposed. Rejecting several decades of scholarship, David S. Jones asserts that such high Native mortality cannot simply be attributed to a "virgin soil epidemic" in which Natives' immunological defenses were ineffective. Initial survivors were left exposed, malnourished, more vulnerable to other microbes, and emotionally and spiritually traumatized, thereby compounding the mortality and suffering and leaving them politically vulnerable.[6] Yet no European witness fell ill or perished; nor did any of the inland Indians who avoided contact with the victims. Tellingly, the catastrophe of 1616–18 was confined to coastal peoples who had interacted, willingly or unwillingly, with the French and/or English over the preceding decade and a half.

The appearance in spring 1619 of Tisquantum, a Patuxet who was one of those carried to Málaga five years earlier, undoubtedly shocked all Wampanoags. After being redeemed from slavery, Tisquantum lived in Málaga, England, and Newfoundland before finding passage home with a would-be English colonizer. Distrustful of all English, Epenow and his people attacked the party when it reached Noepe and seized Tisquantum.

Beyond the Abenaki-Wampanoag coast, Indians found other ways to interact with Europeans. The establishment of New France in 1608 facilitated Native-French trade ties and an anti-Mohawk alliance along the St. Lawrence as far west as the Richelieu River and Lake Champlain. Dutch traders in 1614 solidified ties with Mohicans and other lower Hudson River Natives as well as Mohawk Iroquois after establishing a colony, New Netherland, and a permanent post where modern Albany now stands. Other Dutch people forged regular ties with Native communities on islands and lower river valleys as far eastward as Narragansett Bay. All these peoples avoided the severe depopulation and traumas experienced by the coastal communities to the east. By 1620 European goods were reaching indigenous communities throughout the future New England from all sides, even interior communities where Europeans had never set foot.

Such was the regional setting when yet another English expedition followed a familiar pattern when landing on Cape Cod in November 1620, stealing corn and robbing graves until Nauset Wampanoags drove them away. But the *Mayflower* differed from earlier European vessels in that most passengers arrived as members of nuclear families intending to settle. They headed on to Patuxet, which they knew was empty and where nearby Wampanoags might be more welcoming. But underfunded and ill prepared for winter, half the 100 settlers died over the next three months as Wampanoags watched. Many Wampanoags wished to drive out the settlers in their weakened state but others, most notably Massasoit, a rising young sachem at Pokanoket, saw the wisdom of admitting them. They would provide a well-armed counterweight to the Dutch-allied Narragansetts and facilitate direct Anglo-Wampanoag trade. The presence of women and children, and the colonists' minimal survival skills, suggested that the two parties would be interdependent, countering the usual English efforts to dominate Natives forcefully. Wampanoag leaders recognized that Tisquantum, with his knowledge of the English language and English ways, could broker a relationship, but his trustworthiness remained questionable. After Epenow transferred his Patuxet captive to Pokanoket, Massasoit asked Samoset, the Pemaquid Abenaki, to initiate contact with Plymouth and, in a second meeting, introduce the colony's leaders to Tisquantum. Taking a huge gamble, the Pokanokets turned Tisquantum over to the English.

Confronting a "Great Migration," 1621–43

"New England" became a political reality, albeit tenuous, when the Pokanoket Wampanoags and Plymouth concluded a treaty, brokered and translated by Tisquantum, in March 1621. Plymouth and numerous smaller English enterprises expanded slowly and unevenly for eight years before a Puritan-dominated "Great Migration" from England poured into Massachusetts Bay and dispersed in all directions, primarily between the lower Merrimack and Connecticut river valleys, disrupting indigenous networks including those which other Europeans had joined. The combination of disease-induced Native depopulation and English immigration undermined the regional balance of people and power, leading in southernmost New England to the massive, violent dislocation of Native peoples and communities. After about 14,000 immigrants had arrived, the influx ended in 1642 when civil war broke out in England.

The Pokanoket-Plymouth Treaty was fraught with ambiguity. Colonists understood it as establishing English sovereignty and Plymouth's authority in Wampanoag country with Pokanoket and its sachem, Massasoit, as supreme among the colony's Native subjects. Pokanokets, on the other hand, assumed that the treaty established an alliance in which Plymouth provided them with trade and military connections in return for tribute—primarily corn and furs—and permission for the colony to collect tribute directly from other Wampanoag communities. But Plymouth reinforced many Wampanoags' anti-English resentments by using force when collecting tribute, showing their arms whenever Native allies were present, and resisting the informal, personal interactions between nonelite Natives and settlers that characterized indigenous understandings of reciprocity. These resentments cooled after 1625 when the colonists finally succeeded in producing their own corn surpluses. Meanwhile other tensions had arisen when Tisquantum mobilized former Patuxets to challenge Massasoit's position as Plymouth's most favored Wampanoag, and ended when Tisquantum suddenly died in 1622. These developments finally replaced the long Anglo-Wampanoag War with peace and solidified Massasoit's claim to the grand Wampanoag sachemship.

Plymouth was unable to establish peace with nearby non-Wampanoags during the 1620s. Although Massachuset and Pawtucket casualties from the epidemics were compounded by escalated Mi'kmaq raiding, both peoples sharply resisted Plymouth's violent efforts to collect tribute from them; instead they traded with scattered English planters who settled nearby and with the Narragansetts. But after about 3,000 settlers—the first wave of the "Great Migration" to Massachusetts Bay —poured into their homelands between 1629 and 1633, the 200 Massachusets and Pawtuckets quickly aligned themselves with the newcomers. The English presence did effectively end Mi'kmaq raids. Several leading sachems declared themselves Christians and permitted the establishment of English towns on portions of their people's lands. Natives also exchanged furs for metal goods, cloth, and (from Plymouth) seed corn to alleviate food shortages. Despite its overwhelming numbers Massachusetts Bay, like Plymouth, banned unregulated gatherings of Natives and feared Natives' close proximity to themselves.

Natives to the west of Massachusetts Bay and Plymouth were drawn to developments emanating from the Hudson River during the 1620s. Expanding Indian-European trade, and the rivalries it generated, heightened Natives' demand for wampum used in diplomatic gatherings. Dutch traders soon realized that they could profit from this demand because most wampum originated in the homelands of their Native trade partners on Long Island Sound and Narragansett Bay. Wampum production escalated in this area as women gathered the shells and, along with men, used Dutch-supplied steel drills to manufacture and string beads and belts. Wampum-producing communities constructed fortified villages as rival alliances, led by the Narragansetts and Pequots, maneuvered to control the movement of wampum, furs, and European goods to and from the Dutch.

The flow of wampum expanded northeastward after 1627 when New Netherland started supplying it to Plymouth. Having recently established a post on the lower Kennebec River, which has long been a regional exchange center, Plymouth traded wampum, maize, and European-made goods to Kennebec Abenakis for furs. That and other English posts on the Maine coast proved attractive to Abenakis, particularly after English troops forced the French from Canada in 1629. By 1632 when the French returned, even more English colonists had arrived, often squatting on Abenaki land or abusing Abenaki trade partners. Meanwhile Abenaki hunters frequently encountered hostile Mohawks in the interior who seized their pelts and wampum. To counter these developments, some Kennebec Abenakis moved to the Christian Innu community of Sillery in New France, where they accepted baptism as Catholics and joined war parties against the Mohawks. The move connected Kennebecs at home with the Franco-Indian alliance against the Iroquois (as seen in the next section, a connection that would broaden in later decades) even as they continued trading with those English who treated them with civility.

The establishment of the Massachusetts Bay Colony strengthened the Narragansetts vis-à-vis the Pequots and provided them with a European counterweight to the Dutch. In 1632 the Narragansetts allied, through the Massachusets and Pawtuckets, with the Bay colony and then, through Puritan dissident Roger Williams, reached a truce with Plymouth and the Wampanoags. Meanwhile the Pequot alliance weakened as some members, most prominently the Mohegans, resisted Pequot domination. Attempting to address Natives' anti-Pequot sentiments, the Dutch West India Company in 1633 established two posts on the Connecticut River at which resident traders circumvented the Pequots by dealing directly with neighboring Native communities. Meanwhile a Narragansett-allied community, farther north on the Connecticut, invited Plymouth traders to locate at their town.

A smallpox epidemic that swept the Northeast in 1633-34 compounded the destabilization of the lower Connecticut River Valley and adjacent regions. While no Native communities were spared, the Massachuset and Pawtucket (again) plus the Connecticut Valley communities suffered mortality rates approximating ninety percent while Narragansett deaths were proportionately fewer. As additional settlers occupied Massachuset and Pawtucket homelands, others defied Massachusetts Bay authorities by moving to the Connecticut. By 1636 three well-armed settlements totaling 800 English were thriving alongside depopulated Native communities. Meanwhile a Dutch-Pequot skirmish at one of the Dutch posts resulted in the death of the Pequot grand sachem, Tatobem, leading several Pequot communities to defect to the Narragansetts. In desperation Tatobem's son, Sassacus, in 1634 signed a treaty with Massachusetts Bay under which the colony collected a heavy tribute in wampum and ordered the Pequots to turn over the alleged killers of an English trader.

With the Pequots severely weakened and isolated, English colonial elites hastened in 1636 to fill the resulting power vacuum. Having established Fort Saybrook on Niantic land at the mouth of the Connecticut, John Winthrop, Jr., son of the Massachusetts governor, was recognized by the settlers upriver as governor of a new colony, Connecticut; Massachusetts Bay merchant William Pynchon arranged with Agawam Indians to found Springfield to the north of Connecticut; and Roger Williams negotiated with the Narragansetts to establish Providence as a settlement for dissenting Puritans on Narragansett Bay. The colonies then blamed the Pequots for the murder of a second Englishman and dispatched an expedition to seek satisfaction. (Neither murder had actually been committed by Pequots.) After a series of provocations on each side, the Pequot War began, pitting Pequots against English, Narragansetts, and Mohegans.

The war turned in May 1637 when an allied expedition attacked a fortified Pequot village on the Mystic River occupied largely by noncombatants. English troops entered at dawn and set the village afire. After they and their allies cut down all but a few who tried to escape, about 700 Pequots lay dead. The scale of the massacre at Mystic surpassed any conflict that had yet occurred in eastern North America. In its aftermath, the remaining Pequots scattered. Some fled to or were captured by Narragansetts, Mohegans, and the English while others sought refuge in swamps or in Native communities westward on Long Island or on the mainland. Some of these communities turned Pequot refugees or their scalps over to the English while others quietly sheltered them. Sassacus offered a substantial wampum payment to some Mohawks who, having already accepted a larger payment from the Narragansetts, instead delivered his scalp and those of six other Pequot sachems to Hartford, thereby ending the war.

Besides the hundreds of Pequots who died or eluded capture, many more survived as captives of the English and their Native allies. Most captives among the English became bonded servants or slaves of wealthy colonists. In 1638 a Massachusetts-commissioned trader, William Peirce, carried 17 Pequots to Providence Island where they entered an enslaved labor force of Africans and indigenous Caribbean peoples. Returning with some Africans, Peirce initiated New England's involvement in the transatlantic slave trade, primarily via the English West Indies.[7] Over the next four decades, enslaved Natives from New England would comprise most of the human cargo in these exchanges.

The power vacuum created by the Pequots' defeat led to intense diplomatic maneuvering by Mohegans, Narragansetts, Massachusetts Bay and Connecticut inhabitants, as well as smaller Native communities. A critical milestone was the Treaty of Hartford, signed by Connecticut, the Mohegans, and the Narragansetts in 1638. Declaring the Pequots dissolved as a political entity, the treaty created a framework for keeping peace between the Narragansetts and the Mohegans, who had supplanted the Pequots as the major Indian power in Connecticut. The agreement also reserved 80 Pequot captives each for the Mohegans and Narragansetts, plus 20 more for the Narragansetts' Niantic allies, in exchange for annual wampum payments to the colonies. The treaty survived its first challenge in 1639 when a Pequot town, Pawcatuck, openly reestablished itself with Narragansett-Niantic support. Connecticut and Mohegan fighters mobilized to crush Pawcatuck but the Narragansetts persuaded them to withdraw.

The treaty enabled a heightened resumption of the movement of land-hungry settlers from Massachusetts Bay to war-torn Indian homelands. By 1643 about 8,000 English had occupied lands in Connecticut and adjacent New Haven (established 1638). Smaller contingents had settled at Narragansett Bay, facilitated by Williams and the Narragansetts, and at Springfield under the auspices of William Pynchon. The fragile balance achieved in the Treaty of Hartford was undermined in 1642 when Massachusetts Bay persuaded a Narragansett tributary, Shawomet, to defect and to deed land for an English settlement.

Recognizing the threat to his own people as well as to the balance of power across southern New England, the Narragansett sachem, Miantonomi, sought to enlist a coalition of indigenous communities extending from the Wampanoags in the east to the Mohawks, Mohegans, and Munsees in the west, to resist or at least contain Massachusetts, Connecticut, and the Mohegans. Among the Munsees, already inflamed by Dutch oppression on the lower Hudson River, Miantonomi's message helped galvanize a united resistance that Dutch and English forces atrociously crushed in Kieft's War (1643–45). Before then a Narragansett-Mohegan skirmish in 1643 ended when the Mohegans captured Miantonomi. In the hands of his rival, Uncas, Miantonomi proposed an anti-English alliance that would link Mohegans, former Pequots, Narragansetts, and Wampanoags. After considering the proposal, Uncas turned Miantonomi over to the just-formed United Colonies of New England, consisting of two commissioners each from Massachusetts, Connecticut, Plymouth, and New Haven and pointedly excluding the Narragansetts' dissident supporters (who would form their own colony, Rhode Island, in 1647). The commissioners' first act was to try and convict Miantonomi for covering up his plot to kill Uncas. Although only Connecticut among the four colonies had signed the Treaty of Hartford, the United Colonies claimed jurisdiction under its terms, thereby transforming it into an instrument of colonial authority.[8] The commissioners turned the condemned sachem over to Uncas, along with English witnesses who subsequently certified that the Mohegans indeed executed Miantonomi and only after reaching Mohegan territory.

Networks, 1640s–1660s

The end of the Great Migration occasioned a shift in relations among Natives and English colonists. The relentless influx of immigrants that spread beyond greater Boston and fueled the Pequot War halted. Even on New England's south-facing coast where the Mohegan-Narragansett rivalry continued to shape political relationships, most of the region's Natives and colonists recognized that whatever their long-range goals, they needed momentarily to stabilize their political and social environments. They did so by strengthening or establishing large-scale networks centered on diplomacy and trade as well as forging more personal intercultural ties among local communities and households. Participants in these exchanges usually communicated in informal pidgins that drew on English and several Native languages, while some on each side became fully multilingual.

Central to the survival strategies of most New England Native peoples during the 1640s–50s were relations between the Mohawk Iroquois and English colonizers. Kennebec Abenakis drew on their Christian kin in Sillery for a solution. The Christians persuaded the Jesuits in 1646 to send Father Gabriel Druillettes to the Kennebec to baptize and preach following a deadly epidemic, many survivors of which declared themselves Catholic. In 1650 Druillettes returned to the Kennebec, accompanied by a powerful Sillery headman, Noel Negabamat, with a more ambitious agenda. The two men sought first to integrate Abenakis, Pocumtucks, and Mohicans into the Franco-Indian alliance against the Iroquois, after which they would proceed to Boston and persuade New England to join a grand anti-Iroquois coalition. Neither part of the plan succeeded: tensions among potential Native allies proved irreparable while the United Colonies Commissioners flatly rejected the proposal, recalling the Mohawks' cooperation in defeating the Pequots.

The Commissioners' memories of friendly Mohawks came not from sentiment but from recognition of the realities of power in midcentury southern New England. Central to the Narragansett-Niantics' strength after becoming the Commissioners' principal enemy was their relationship with the Mohawks, to whom they directly or indirectly supplied much of the wampum reaching Iroquois country. Although the Narragansetts simultaneously avoided paying most of the large wampum "fines" levied by the United Colonies, the Commissioners limited their efforts to collect the wampum by force lest Mohawk warriors intervene against them. Both English and Dutch proceeded carefully because they needed wampum for their own financial transactions in the absence of a hard currency from their home countries. The Narragansetts also reminded colonists that it was they who had gained Mohawk support against the Pequots in 1637, and that Mohawks' former hostility toward the Pequots was now directed at the Commissioners' favored Mohegans. Buttressing the Mohawk-Narragansett connection were the Pocumtucks, who had emerged as the leading community among allied Natives on the Connecticut River in western Massachusetts. These communities traded large volumes of furs to William and (after 1652) John Pynchon at Springfield, as well as wampum that enabled the Pynchons to extend their trading to Mohawks and Mohicans on the Hudson. Pocumtucks and Mohegans constantly provoked one another, and the Pocumtucks often led or joined Narragansetts, Niantics, and other allies in attacking Mohegans. The Mohegans, on the other hand, collected most of their wampum from Natives in areas with a significant English military and political presence.

The Narragansett-Niantics and Mohegans each cultivated significant ties with European supporters. Although self-interested, these Europeans often fused their interests with those of their Native allies. The Mohegans regularly turned to John Mason and other Connecticut leaders, along with Massachusetts Bay, to support their efforts to suppress the Narragansett-Niantics while the latter similarly used Roger Williams and other Rhode Islanders. Williams frequently joined the Pynchons and John Winthrop, Jr., in advocating against the Mohegans. Williams and Richard Smith strengthened their own ties with the Dutch when trading furs obtained from Narragansetts in New Amsterdam. Williams, Samuel Gorton, and other Puritan dissidents directly intervened on several occasions with the English government on behalf of the Narragansett-Niantics, thereby circumventing the Massachusetts Bay and United Colonies' claims to direct authority over these Indian "subjects."

Mohegans and Narragansett-Niantics sought to undermine one another's European ties by attacking, or threatening to attack, each other and by spreading rumors of each other's actions and plots against colonists. The result was several regional war scares, the most notorious of which arose after Ninigret, a Niantic who was now the effective leader of the Narragansett-Niantic alliance, visited New Amsterdam in 1653 during the first Anglo-Dutch War. Mohegans and their tributaries insisted that Ninigret and Governor Pieter Stuyvesant were plotting a massive Indian-Dutch attack on all English colonists. But Stuyvesant (who feared war with English colonists) and Ninigret denied having met at all despite relentless English grilling of Ninigret and his people. So tangled are the multitudinous accounts, there remains no certainty about most of the details surrounding Ninigret's journey.

In the face of Narragansett-Niantic, Mohegan, and European rivalries, smaller Native communities on New England's southward-facing coast maneuvered to maximize opportunities for survival and political autonomy. Most notable were the Pequots, whose very name had been erased under terms of the Treaty of Hartford. Over the next two decades, those Pequots designated by the treaty as captives of Mohegans, Narragansetts, and Niantics augmented their ranks by drawing Pequot survivors from elsewhere, including from English households, and astutely playing Narragansett-Niantics, Mohegans, and various English elites off against one another. By the late 1650s all English leaders agreed that the Pequot communities of Nameag and Pawcatuck should have their own lands and should shift their tribute payments from Narragansetts, Niantics, and Mohegans to Connecticut. While becoming tributaries of Connecticut hardly made the Pequots independent, the outcome strengthened the cultural and political identity that has sustained them ever since.

East and northeast of Narragansett Bay, indigenous polities facing even greater concentrations of English power likewise maneuvered to survive. Distrusted by many English after listening to Miantonomi's appeal in 1642, the grand Wampanoag sachem, Massasoit, retained Plymouth's support by approving sales of vast tracts of tributaries' land to colonists. His sachemship was directly reduced when Noepe Wampanoags began redirecting their tribute to Thomas Mayhew Sr., patriarch of the new colony of Martha's Vineyard. Under intense pressure, Massachusets, Pawtuckets, and some Pennacooks and Nipmucs ostensibly shifted their tribute away from other Natives to Massachusetts Bay. Yet the colony's missionary, John Eliot, who began preaching in 1646—the year that Druillettes first preached on the Kennebec—thereafter competed, with mixed results, with French Jesuits for Pawtucket and Pennacook allegiance.

The central thrusts of missionary work in southern New England revolved around Thomas Mayhew Jr. (succeeded after his death by his father) and Eliot in Massachusetts Bay. The United Colonies Commissioners oversaw their efforts (and several brief, aborted ones) by distributing funds collected in England and by coordinating the missions with larger colonial interests and policies. While the missionaries—particularly the militant ideologue, Eliot—intended to replace Indian "savagery" with English "civilization" and Calvinism, they nevertheless reinforced indigenous identities and communities. Missionaries' initial successes in attracting Native support came in part because they challenged the effectiveness of indigenous *pow-wows* (medicine men) in combating the deadly diseases that continued to kill large numbers of Indians. The preachers assumed that the Natives' renunciation of pow-wows constituted an interest in Christian "conversion" rather than incorporation of a new source of manitou. While "praying Indians' " confessions of personal sin were often deeply heartfelt, they were primarily ritualized acceptances of a revised spiritual and political order. Once a community became predominantly Christian, English authorities recognized it as a "praying town." Remaining holdouts either left for non-Christian towns or joined, often making clear in their confessions that remaining near kin and neighbors was a primary motive. The praying towns provided their residents with a secure land base on which, like the Pequots, they gained a measure of protection from settler encroachments and governed themselves. Some sachems led their followers in engaging with Christianity while others joined praying towns only when realizing that their followers would otherwise abandon them. In the end most towns retained older political structures, with sachems and councilors serving as magistrates and in other official positions. Tellingly, grand sachems presiding over extensive tributary networks—including the otherwise English-friendly Massasoit and Uncas—consistently resisted missionaries' efforts to preach to their people.

Underlying the broad alliances and exchanges connecting indigenous and settler societies, a broad array of ties linked Indian and European individuals, households, and local communities. These ties made clear the extent to which the two peoples—despite fragile, ongoing tensions and misunderstandings—were socially interdependent from the 1640s through the 1660s and often beyond. Indians in autonomous communities with few nearby settlers, such as the Pocumtucks, collected and prepared large volumes of beaver and other furs for annual exchanges with familiar English traders. Members of most other indigenous communities directly exchanged a range of goods and services with neighboring settlers. Indigenous meanings informed Native participation in all these exchanges. European manufacturers fashioned textiles, metal goods, and glass beads according to Indian preferences. Native women sought sewing implements for fashioning garments and jewelry that combined European and indigenous materials in a distinctively "Indian fashion," defying English expectations that "clothing" would demonstrate progress toward "civilization." As mortality remained high, Natives carried "utilitarian" metal tools, glass beads, and musket balls, alongside Jesuit rings, wampum, bows, and mica to their graves whence their souls traveled to Cautantowwit's house. For Natives, animals—"wild" or "domestic" (the boundary between them was indistinct)—embodied manitou. Indians who supplied English traders with pelts also leased grazing lands to nearby settlers, herded their livestock, and shod their horses. After building fences and walls for their neighbors, Natives discovered that the English expected them to enclose their own crops to keep out free-ranging swine. As imported plants, animals, and agricultural practices drove away wild animals, some Indians acquired pigs and other livestock.

While inanimate, firearms too represented a manifestation of English manitou. Although the colonies strictly banned the sale of guns to Natives, flintlocks proliferated among Indians after the Pequot War. Colonial officials blamed the Dutch and French for spreading firearms to Indians, yet it is clear that Indians acquired most such weapons from English colonists. They used guns for hunting as well as to intimidate and sometimes shoot at foes. While guns, shot, and powder originated with Europeans, Indians quickly gained expertise in repairing firearms. Even as Native-English tensions and fears of war sharply escalated in the late 1660s, more English guns than ever were reaching Indians, legally and illegally.[9]

Less amicable Anglo-Indian interactions occurred among those—adults and children—who were neighbors or who resided together in English households (where Indians were day and seasonal laborers, servants, or slaves). Colonists took Natives to English courts for debt, drunkenness, theft, arson, sexual assault, and other offenses that make clear just how close their ties to one another were, even when rooted in hostility. Convicted Indians were most often sentenced to servitude, slavery, or extensions thereof; the most serious offenders were carried to the West Indies. But Natives who appeared in civil or criminal courts as defendants were not invariably convicted. They brought Indian and English witnesses to testify on their behalf before judges and juries, often comprised of other neighbors, who exonerated them. Indians also appeared as accusers and plaintiffs against colonists. Some served warrants and brought in Indian fugitives. As Natives became familiar with colonial judicial practices, many defendants obtained leniency by making formulaic confessions of guilt (comparable to confessions of sin by Christian Indians). Natives built these actions and tactics on their own understandings of law and justice, demanding from courts, as Katherine Hermes notes, "reciprocity."[10]

While some Indians lived in colonists' households, the reverse did not hold. English traders or diplomats might briefly stay with Indians, but a taboo on colonists abandoning "civilization" for life in "savage" communities was more strictly enforced than bans on Indians acquiring firearms, alcohol, or other dangerous commodities. The few recorded occurrences involved English men marrying into Native communities, but no offenders were apprehended before King Philip's War. A well-documented exception united two prominent families on Martha's Vineyard over several generations, beginning in 1666. Although the English husband and Wampanoag wife followed English practice by living in his house, colonists were bitterly divided over the appropriateness of the marriage.[11]

The Martha's Vineyard marriage was potent because the Wampanoag wife thereafter retained membership in her powerful lineage, unlike English women who brought dowries to husbands to whom they became legally subordinated. English documents record few Native women except for some female sachems and women who appeared in court, overlooking women's power within their own communities. At the same time, the continuing crises generated by colonization skewed the gendered balance within Native communities as male warriors and diplomats became a constant rather than occasional presence. Among Indian Christians, missionaries expected wives to defer to their husbands, although their hearing personal confessions from women sometimes cut against that effort. In general, Native wives retained ties to their natal families in spite of rather than because of Christianity.

Eliot and Mayhew proselytized in Wôpanâak, spoken by Wampanoags and Massachusets, rather than English. They relied on Native translators not only to learn the language but to help them convey Christian meanings to their audiences, and employed Native preachers who proved effective in spreading the Christian message. Consequently, that message acquired indigenous inflections that rendered it less than a mirrored reflection of the missionaries' intentions. Indian Christians' continued use of their own language in everyday life, as well as in religious matters, went far toward sustaining indigenous identities and practices in the face of efforts to "civilize" them. Eliot and his collaborators made Wôpanâak a literary language through their Roman-alphabet translations of the Bible and other publications. By the end of the century, many "praying Indians" communicated in written Wôpanâak. Numerous bilingual Indian Christians acquired English literacy when attending colonial grammar schools, and four attended an Indian College inside Harvard. Caleb Cheeshateaumuck, the only graduate of the Indian College, was also literate in classical Greek and Latin.

Empires, Total War, Diaspora, 1660s–1680s

By the 1660s several consequences of colonization were undermining the fragile ties of Anglo-Indian interdependence in New England. One consequence was the transformation of the ecology—including human ecology—wherever colonists situated themselves and their agrarian and commercial endeavors. Another was a heightened imperial rivalry that led England and France to intervene more directly in northeastern North American developments. Together these crises brought about the political isolation of most southern New England Natives followed by all-out warfare. Indigenous mortality and trauma resulting from King Philip's War (1675–76) approximated that of major epidemics, and was compounded by an exodus of Natives as slaves and refugees. The war spread northward into Abenaki country where the English took many Native lives but did not prevail. In the aftermath of war, English imperial officials based at Albany, along with their Mohawk allies, revised the structure of Anglo-Indian relations in New England.

After 1660 it was clear that overhunting had depleted the beaver population accessible to Indians on the Connecticut River and elsewhere in lower New England. Given that English merchants typically advanced Natives with wampum and English goods before each hunting season, they now collected their debts from empty-handed Natives by claiming land as collateral and obliging them to sign deeds that left their lands seriously reduced. New England merchants' accumulation of hard English currency from the sale of pelts (among other endeavors) contributed to the end of colonists' need for wampum as local currency. They traded much of their supply to counterparts in New Netherland where wampum remained legal tender, greatly inflating that colony's economy and leaving merchants holding it unable to supply goods that competed with those that Pynchon and others offered Mohawks and Mohicans. This and other disparities between New England and New Netherland left the latter vulnerable when English forces, aided by English settlers on ostensibly Dutch Long Island, seized New Netherland in 1664 during the Second Anglo-Dutch War.

Renaming its new colony "New York," the victorious English directly challenged France, whose longstanding war with the Iroquois had led it to dispatch French troops to Canada. No longer tied to Pynchon or the Mohawks, the Indians of the middle Connecticut Valley solidified ties with fellow Algonquian speakers to the north who supported the French. Meanwhile New York replaced New Netherland as the Iroquois' prime European ally, supplementing the older commercial link with a military alliance.

Compounding these political shifts was an ever-growing demographic disparity between Natives and settlers. Indigenous mortality due to dietary changes, diminished food sources, and other effects of colonization persisted and now outnumbered births. The most concrete manifestation of this pattern was some tribes' turn after midcentury from small burial plots to large communal cemeteries where the dead from throughout the nation were interred together. The shift reflected a spiritual quest, coinciding with that of Indian Christians, in the face of a strikingly opposite population pattern among the English. Two decades after the Great Migration ended, the adult sons of the first settler generation—one of the healthiest and most fertile in Europe and its diaspora—sought land of their own, often on strikingly different terms from their fathers. Whereas first-generation towns constituted an extension of the English commons to New England, the second inclined away from the commons—especially where original proprietors dominated land distribution—and toward consolidated plots away from town centers or outside their hometowns altogether. Thus began a trend by settlers to move from communal toward individual property holding that would accelerate in later generations.

The settlers' move toward individual land ownership ideologically complemented the entrepreneurial ethos of elite colonial merchants. Along with speculators from England, merchants invested substantial amounts of capital in land to be either marketed to settlers or worked by laborers, bonded or otherwise, including landless Indians. They also used their political power to relentlessly and without scruples escalate pressures on Natives, both antagonists and allies, to cede ever more land. The immediate result was a proliferation in the 1660s–70s of new English settlements that forced some Native communities to relocate altogether while separating residents of other communities from each other and from food and other needed resources.

In this context, heightened fundraising in England enabled the Commissioners to expand missionary efforts to redirect Indians' tributary allegiances toward the colonies, so as to undermine sachems' authority and Natives' ability to retain landholdings. Aided by Indian Christians, missionaries offered material-spiritual sustenance to severely fragmented, demoralized communities. Most sachems resisted these efforts and, at the instigation of Philip (formerly Metacom), the grand Wampanoag sachem, held meetings in 1669 to consider a pan-Indian movement to resist English encroachments. As with Miantonomi's comparable call a quarter-century earlier, rivalries old and new would likely have prevented such a movement from actually forming. But whereas Miantonomi had included the Mohawks as potential supporters, the Mohawks now joined New York against New France and were already at war with former Connecticut Valley and Massachuset allies.

After more than a decade of escalating tensions, a new Anglo-Wampanoag war erupted in June 1675. John Sassamon, a former Christian Wampanoag associate of Philip, had recently informed Plymouth that Philip planned a surprise attack; soon thereafter Sassamon was found dead in Wampanoag territory. Plymouth's trial and execution of three Wampanoag suspects completely ignored Wampanoag authority in such cases as stipulated in the treaty of 1621. Popular outrage among Wampanoags and a racialized determination among neighboring settlers to extirpate them triggered what English authors would later call "King Philip's War." The prospect of war divided Native communities. Because of Ninigret's opposition, the Narragansett-Niantics were initially neutral; but most Narragansetts welcomed Wampanoag refugees (often kin), particularly the powerful Pocasset Wampanoag female sachem, Weetamoo. The Nipmucs were divided between Christians and anti-English militants who began attacking neighboring settlers. Prompted by these events, Connecticut Valley Natives from Springfield northward began attacking English towns in September. Uncas' Mohegans welcomed a chance to fight the Narragansetts while Connecticut secured the support of its Pequot tributaries, although some in each group showed restraint when fighting other Indians (probably kin). Most Indian Christians initially supported their English coreligionists but were deterred by settlers' Indian-hating. Massachusetts Bay and Plymouth confined Christians on offshore islands, particularly Deer Island in Boston's harbor. Lacking food and shelter, most of the thousand or more internees on Deer Island perished over the ensuing winter although some males escaped.

After a month of hard fighting, Plymouth forces drove Philip's Wampanoags from their homeland to Nipmuc country in west-central Massachusetts. In December English, Mohegans, and Pequots moved against the Narragansetts, surprising about 2,000 gathered in the heavily fortified Great Swamp. Comparable but even more deadly than the English assault on Mystic Pequots in 1637, the attackers killed about 1,000, most of them noncombatants, while the English lost 70 soldiers. Except for Ninigret and a few followers, the Narragansetts openly entered the war and most Great Swamp survivors joined other anti-English Indians at encampments in Nipmuc country. From there flintlock-armed Natives killed and captured English people, destroyed their property, and seized food with virtual impunity. Unable to effectively retaliate but regarding all Indians as racial enemies, some colonists enslaved any friendly or neutral Natives they could capture for either personal use or sale abroad.

Despite their military successes, anti-English Natives grew hungry and their leaders recognized the need for external support if they hoped to regain their homelands before the next growing season. In January 1676 Philip led a delegation to Schaghticoke, near the Hudson River north of Albany, and met with Mohicans and French-allied Western Abenakis. The delegates hoped to gain some measure of French support. But disease struck the gathering and Mohawks, armed and encouraged by New York Governor Edmund Andros, attacked and scattered those present. Philip and other survivors rejoined their allies in western Massachusetts. By March it was clear that the colonists were recovering, particularly after they released male internees from Deer Island who assisted them as spies and scouts. Through Nipmuc Christian intermediaries, anti-English Nipmucs returned their English captives in exchange for being allowed to surrender peaceably (and hope for mercy thereafter). Meanwhile Philip and other surviving Wampanoags and Narragansetts dispersed toward their homelands, where many surrendered and some even joined the English.

By August 1676 English troops, aided by Indian supporters, had hunted down and killed Philip, Weetamoo, and other resistance leaders, publicly displaying the heads or bodies of some. Those captured alive, including some Christian Nipmucs, were hanged to great English fanfare. Indian combatants not executed for killing colonists were sold abroad as slaves. In a cruelly forced turn in New England Natives' engagement with the Atlantic, most of the several hundred enslaved during and after the war were carried to Barbados, Jamaica, Bermuda, and other English colonies; smaller numbers went to other European colonies, western Europe, Tangier, and places unknown. Most went to Barbados where, as early as April 1676, their presence was volatile. In combination with measures to prevent an uprising by enslaved Africans, the Barbados assembly prohibited further imports of unruly New England Indians and mandated the export of all those already present. Jamaica banned further imports of enslaved New Englanders in December 1676.[12] Some wives and children of men sent abroad went with them but most noncombatants, along with men found guilty of lesser offenses, were consigned to domestic slavery/servitude, the formal line between the two being indistinct.

The colonies now regarded even the most unwaveringly pro-English Natives as subjects rather than allies. Christian and non-Christian towns were reduced in number and expanse, residents' movements were carefully restricted, and the pressures to cede yet more land intensified. Diminished access to food and other resources left Natives more economically marginalized than ever. Native women expanded their peddling of baskets, brooms, and other wares to English households while men turned to maritime labor, often as debtors, and service in special Native military units that fought Abenakis and other Indian "enemies." Some sachems and others navigated the new terrain more adroitly than others; and for all they had lost, Indian communities sustained residents' connection with a core identity that long antedated the European presence. But the deadliest war yet in North America had cost about 5,000 (c. 40%) indigenous lives, compared to 2,500 (5%) among the colonists. Both peoples were traumatized but the English resumed their expansion and growth within a generation, whereas the subjugation of Natives deepened.

Before, during, and after the war, several hundred Natives left the southern colonies to avoid death, enslavement, or the onerous conditions of racialized colonization. In so doing they became part of the war's northward spread. Some moved westward to Schaghticoke, which offered protection from Mohawk attacks, while others went to Western Abenaki towns or to French-sponsored towns on the St. Lawrence. The largest exodus was to lower Maine, where recently arrived English colonists were generating tensions by encroaching on or stealing Eastern Abenakis' resources. With the outbreak of hostilities to the south, Massachusetts and New Hampshire authorities demanded that Abenakis surrender the firearms they used for hunting as well as fighting. Some communities complied and starved over winter while others refused and joined refugees from the southern war in attacking English forts and settlements with impunity. Native anger was compounded by English wartime practices. In August 1675 the infant child of a powerful sachem, Squando, drowned after English sailors overturned his or her mother's canoe just to see if Indian children swam naturally. In September 1676 Major Richard Waldron summoned 400 Abenakis to a peace conference during which his troops surrounded the attendees, killing some, and enslaving many more. (Abenakis would avenge this and other treacheries of Waldron's in 1689 when capturing and singling him out for extended torture.)

Meanwhile imperial imperatives transformed the New England-New York-Mohawk coalition. Since the Restoration (1660), England had sought to end Massachusetts' defiance of its authority as well as to centralize administrative control of its northeastern colonies. That control was centered at Albany under Andros, to whom New Englanders protested the continued Mohawk attacks and tribute demands on their Indian subjects. In April 1677 Andros called Mohawk, Mohican, Massachusetts, and Connecticut delegates to Albany to resolve this and other issues. The Mohawks agreed not to raid the colonies' Native subjects and to return anti-English Indians to New England, and the colonies agreed to deal with Mohawks and Mohicans only at Albany in Andros' presence. Nevertheless, Mohawks continued to attack the colonies' Massachuset and Mohegan subjects. A second meeting in July 1684 finally prompted the Mohawks to recognize those tribes as the colonies' tributaries. The treaties placed control of Anglo-Indian relations under New York, whose primary allies in England's rivalry with France were the Mohawks and other Iroquois. They were among the Covenant Chain treaties that would eventually link New York and the Iroquois with other tribes and English colonies southward to Virginia.

New York and the Mohawks also intervened to end the war in lower Maine. Although some Eastern Abenakis made peace overtures to Massachusetts, the colony insisted on Abenakis' subordination and disregarded their complaints of abuses by English troops. Andros inserted himself into this stalemate by noting that New York claimed Maine east of Pemaquid, even though most of the fighting occurred on land claimed by Massachusetts. After a New York-Mohawk brokered truce in August 1677, a treaty in April 1678 stipulated that Abenakis would formally recognize settler property rights but not Massachusetts' jurisdiction, and obliged settlers to pay the Abenakis an annual quitrent in corn. The treaty affirmed that the Abenakis had won the war in Maine, but tensions persisted as settlers continued to arrive and threaten their way of life. To avoid this outcome, many more Kennebecs and Abenakis moved to mission towns in New France, engaging with Jesuit Catholicism and joining the anti-English alliance.[13] Conflicts between colonists and Abenakis who remained in Maine persisted until full-scale war between England and France, each supported by indigenous allies, erupted in 1689.

By the 1680s New England was an object of Anglo-French imperial competition in which surviving indigenous peoples were either subjects of the colonies that had emerged thus far or avoided such subjugation, usually by solidifying less coercive ties with less populous New France. But however connected to Europeans, Natives remained more closely tied to kin, communities, and to ancestors in the landed aquatic places that had been home since deep time. Then and now, Maushop and Gluskap define the Native space that others call "New England."

Notes

1 John K. Thornton, *A Cultural History of the Atlantic World, 1250–1820* (Cambridge: Cambridge University Press, 2012), part II; on New England specifically, Bahar (2012), 1–17. Most discussions of indigenous Americans and the Atlantic do not incorporate American history prior to the arrival of Europeans: Paul Cohen, "Was there an Amerindian Atlantic? Reflections on the Limits of a Historiographical Concept," *History of European Ideas*, 34 (2008): 388–410, and works cited therein; Jace Weaver, *The Red Atlantic: American Indigenes and the Making of the Modern World* (Chapel Hill: University of North Carolina Press, 2014), esp. 1–34.
2 Elizabeth Chilton, "New England Algonquians: Navigating 'Backwaters' and Typological Boundaries," ed. Timothy R. Pauketat, *The Oxford Handbook of North American Archaeology* (Oxford University Press, 2012), 3–6.
3 Bragdon (1996), Ch. 5; Elizabeth S. Chilton, "The Archaeology and Ethnohistory of the Contact Period in the Northeastern United States," *Reviews of Anthropology* 29 (2001): 340–41.
4 Bourque, 2001, 93.
5 On Epenow, Tisquantum, and other captives in London, see Coll Thrush, *Indigenous London: Native Travelers at the Heart of Empire* (New Haven: Yale UP, 2016), ch. 2
6 David S. Jones, "Virgin Soils Revisited," *William and Mary Quarterly* 3 series, 60 (2003): 703–742.
7 Newell (2015), 51.
8 Daragh Grant, "The Treaty of Hartford (1638): Reconsidering Jurisdiction in Southern New England," *William and Mary Quarterly*, 3d series, 72 (2015): 461–498.
9 David J. Silverman, *Thundersticks: Firearms and the Violent Transformation of Native America* (Cambridge, MA: Harvard University Press, 2016), Ch. 3.
10 Katherine Hermes, "'Justice Will Be Done Us': Algonquian Demands for Reciprocity in the Courts of European Settlers," *The Many Legalities of Early America*, eds. Christopher L. Tomlin and Bruce H. Mann (Chapel Hill: University of North Carolina Press, 2001), 123–149.
11 Bragdon, (2009), 120–128.
12 Linford D. Fisher, "'Dangerous Designs': The 1676 Act to Prohibit New England Indian Slave Importation," *William and Mary Quarterly* 3 series, 71 (2014), 99–124.
13 Alice Nash, "'La vie des chrétiens': Abenaki Catholicism in the Late Seventeenth Century," *Les systèmes religieux amérindiens et inuit: Perspectives historiques et contemporaines*, eds. Claude Gélinas and Guillaume Teasdale (Quebec: In Situ Press/Paris: L'Harmattan, 2007), 47–71.

References

Anderson, Virginia DeJohn. *Creatures of Empire: How Domestic Animals Transformed Early America* (New York: Oxford University Press, 2004).
Bahar, Matthew R. "'The Sea of Trouble We Are Swimming in': People of the Dawnland and the Enduring Pursuit of a Native Atlantic World" (Ph.D. dissertation, University of Oklahoma, 2012).

Bourque, Bruce J. *Twelve Thousand Years: American Indians in Maine* (Lincoln: University of Nebraska Press, 2001).
Bragdon, Kathleen J. *Native People of Southern New England, 1500–1650* (Norman: University of Oklahoma Press, 1996).
Bragdon, Kathleen J. *Native People of Southern New England, 1650–1775* (Norman: University of Oklahoma Press, 2009).
Brooks, Lisa. *The Common Pot: The Recovery of Native Space in the Northeast* (Minneapolis: University of Minnesota Press, 2008).
Brooks, Lisa. *Our Beloved King: A New History of King Philip's War* (New Haven: Yale University Press, 2017).
Bruchac, Margaret M. "Earthshapers and Placemakers: Algonkian Indian Stories and the Landscape," *Indigenous Archaeologies: Decolonizing Theory and Practice*, eds. Claire Smith and H. Martin Wobst (London and New York: Routledge, 2005), 56–80.
Calloway, Colin. *The Western Abenakis of Vermont, 1600–1800* (Norman: University of Oklahoma Press, 1990).
Cave, Alfred A. *The Pequot War* (Amherst: University of Massachusetts Press, 1996).
Cohen, Paul. "Was there an Amerindian Atlantic? Reflections on the Limits of a Historiographical Concept," *History of European Ideas* 34 (2008): 388–410.
Cronon, William. *Changes in the Land: Indians, Colonists, and the Ecology of New England* (New York: Hill and Wang, 1983).
DeLucia, Christine M. *The Memory Lands: King Philip's War and the Place of Violence in the Northeast* (New Haven, CT: Yale University Press, 2017).
Drake, James D. *King Philip's War: Civil War in New England, 1675–1676* (Amherst: University of Massachusetts Press, 1999).
Fisher, Julie A. and David J. Silverman, *Ninigret: Sachem of the Niantics and Narragansetts* (Ithaca, NY: Cornell University Press, 2014).
Grant, Daragh. "The Treaty of Hartford (1638): Reconsidering Jurisdiction in Southern New England," *William and Mary Quarterly*, 3d series, 72 (2015): 461–498.
Greer, Allan. *Property and Dispossession: Natives, Settlers and Land in North America, 1500–1700* (New York: Cambridge University Press, in press).
Hermes, Katherine. "'Justice Will Be Done Us': Algonquian Demands for Reciprocity in the Courts of European Settlers," *The Many Legalities of Early America*, eds. Christopher L. Tomlin and Bruce H. Mann (Chapel Hill: University of North Carolina Press, 2001), 123–149.
Kupperman, Karen Ordahl. *Indians and English: Facing Off in Early America* (Ithaca, NY: Cornell University Press, 2000).
Lipman, Andrew. *The Saltwater Frontier: Indians and the Contest for the American Coast* (New Haven, CT: Yale University Press, 2015).
Makepeace, Anne. *We Still Live Here: Âs Nutayuneân*. Videorecording, 56:00. Makepeace Productions, 2010. Available online at http://www.makepeaceproductions.com/wampfilm.html.
Morrison, Kenneth M. *The Embattled Northeast: The Elusive Ideal of Alliance in Abenaki-Euramerican Relations* (Berkeley: University of California Press, 1984).
Newell, Margaret Ellen. *Brethren by Nature: Indian Slavery in Colonial New England* (Ithaca, NY: Cornell University Press, 2015).
Oberg, Michael Leroy. *Uncas: First of the Mohegans* (Ithaca, NY: Cornell University Press, 2003).
Pastore, Christopher L. *Between Land and Sea: The Atlantic Coast and the Transformation of New England* (Cambridge, MA: Harvard University Press, 2014).
Plane, Ann Marie. *Colonial Intimacies: Indian Marriage in Colonial New England* (Ithaca, NY: Cornell University Press, 2000).
Pulsipher, Jenny Hale. *Subjects unto the Same King: Indians, English, and the Contest for Authority in Colonial New England* (Philadelphia: University of Pennsylvania Press, 2005).
Rubertone, Patricia E. *Grave Undertakings: An Archaeology of Roger Williams and the Narragansett Indians* (Washington: Smithsonian Institution Press, 2001).
Salisbury, Neal. *Manitou and Providence: Indians, Europeans, and the Making of New England* (New York: Oxford University Press, 1982).
Silverman, David J. *Faith and Boundaries: Colonists, Christianity, and Community among the Wampanoag Indians of Martha's Vineyard, 1600–1871* (New York: Cambridge University Press, 2005).

Simmons, William S. *Spirit of the New England Tribes: Indian History and Folklore, 1620–1984* (Hanover, NH: University Press of New England, 1986).
Thrush, Coll. *Indigenous London: Native Travelers at the Heart of Empire*, (New Haven: Yale UP, 2016).
Weaver, Jace. *The Red Atlantic: American Indigenes and the Making of the Modern World* (Chapel Hill: University of North Carolina Press, 2014), 1–34.
Warren, Wendy. A. *New England Bound: Slavery and Colonization in Early America* (New York: WW Norton, 2016).

8
"VAST AND FURIOUS"
Understanding an Atlantic New England

Wendy Warren

"It hath been deservedly esteemed, one of the great and wonderful Works of God in this *Last Age*," the third-generation New England Puritan minister Cotton Mather began *Magnalia Christi Americana*, his famous retrospective history of the initial colonization of New England, "that the Lord stirred up the Spirits of so many Thousands of his Servants, to Leave the *Pleasant Land* of England, the Land of their *Nativity*, and to transport themselves, and Families, over the *Ocean Sea*, into a *Desert Land*, in *America*." These thousands of English colonists came to North America, he explained, "on the Account of *Pure and Undefiled Religion,* not knowing how they should have their *Daily Bread*, but trusting in God for *That*." And they were right to trust, Mather decided, for "within a few Years a *Wilderness* was subdued before them, and so many *Colonies* Planted, *Towns* Erected, and *Churches* Settled, wherein the true and living God in Christ Jesus, is worshipped, and served, in a place where time out of mind, had been nothing before, but *Heathenism, Idolatry,* and *Devil-worship*."[1] Hard work, piety, and providence, in Mather's telling, facilitated the survival and eventual flourishing of the New England colonies, formed on land conveniently empty, save for those briefly mentioned heathens and devil-worshippers, who were quickly tamed and their lands populated by God's chosen people.

This heroic version of the colonization of New England has retained prominence in the popular understanding of the region's history, at least partly because Mather's description was in some ways accurate. He was right, for example, that many English colonists to the region during the seventeenth century were indeed religiously inspired, and that inspiration did produce an English migrating population that, at least initially, made them distinctive among contemporary colonial endeavors. Many of them, especially in the first decades, were Puritans, seeking a haven where they might worship in their own way. In the first two decades of English colonization, nearly 20,000 of them came to the northeastern coast of North America, where they soon established the colonies that would jointly form New England: Plymouth, Massachusetts Bay, New Haven, Connecticut, and Rhode Island.[2]

Their religiosity made them distinct in other ways. The demographic profile, as Mather insisted, of these New England colonists did look different than, say, the people who initially went to Virginia in the seventeenth century. Those who went to New England came in kin groups (90 percent came in extended families, and 75 percent came with their immediate families), not alone, and they came with some degree of economic stability and resources. "Middling" is a term used often to describe them: neither wealthy, though some were, nor poor, though some were that as well, "middling" captures their social rank well. These migrating families arrived governed by male heads of households, with English servants attached to the household unit. Women and men were close to equally represented amongst the colonial population from the very beginning, whereas in other English colonies outside of New England, there were roughly five men for every woman.[3]

But Mather's broad strokes painted a far from a complete picture of New England. Historians of the region have long questioned other aspects of his characterization of the English colonization of the region. Where Mather emphasized the colonists' piety, many scholars have instead emphasized the material ambitions of New England's colonists, noting that the colonies had more merchants than ministers.[4] Historians have also insisted on the obvious: that those English colonists, Puritan or not, were hardly the only characters in the story. The people Mather dismissively labeled "heathens," actually formed distinct nations, speaking different languages, practicing different religions, and living in elaborate and complicated cultures. Native Americans were active agents in the colonial encounter, gauging how and when the newcomers might be of use, and when they might be a danger. Some used the arrival of Europeans to further local rivalries that long predated European encounters. Others, especially those on the front lines of English encounters, with less to gain and much to lose, fought immediately and hard against colonization.[5] All Indigenous people in the region faced horrendous epidemics throughout the colonial period, brought unwittingly or not by the English. Calculating the decline of the native population is a difficult task. Estimates of the precontact Indigenous population of the region that would be called New England range from 60,000 to 144,000.[6] After King Philip's War in the 1670s, some historians argue that the population fell by 40 percent to around 6,000.[7] By 1750, some estimates have the population as low as just "a few thousand."[8] And by 1780, the Indian population of Massachusetts, Rhode Island, and Connecticut was just over 2,000.[9] Scholars use words like "massive" or "severe" and "precipitous" to describe the population decline, but solid numbers seem impossible to arrive at.[10]

And more recent scholarship also offers a way to complicate the context in which all this happened. Whereas Mather's account had explicitly emphasized the leaving behind of Europe by the original colonists and those who followed, some scholars now emphasize New England's continued ties to the larger English empire, emphasizing that the northern colonies survived and even flourished not only because they were Puritan or hard-working or populated by intact colonial families—though all of that mattered—but also because they were linked extensively to burgeoning European empires fighting and spreading over North America and the Caribbean. For ultimately, the English colonies in New England were tremendously successful *Atlantic* endeavors. In 1650, three decades after the founding of the Plymouth colony, the English population in the region was roughly 22,000; in 1670, it had more than doubled to 50,000; in 1700, it was roughly 90,000; by 1730 it had again more than doubled to over 200,000; by 1750, it had grown to nearly 350,000; and by the time of the American Revolution, the colonial population of New England was nearly 700,000.[11] Atlantic trade was central to that growth; New England's ties to what scholars call the "Atlantic World," fueled New England's development. An Atlantic New England looks far less exceptional than Mather's narrative would suggest, and far more exemplary.

The English Atlantic

In the mid-1950s, the historian George Wilson Pierson read a paper at the annual American Historical Association convention called "The Obstinate Concept of New England." The paper, a meditation on the concept of regionalism, asked thorny questions worth pondering, such as:

"Who is New England? What is New England? Above all, where is New England today?"[12] These questions, rephrased, are relevant to this discussion: where was New England in the colonial period? Where did it begin, and where did it end?

Theorists have long pointed out that names are by their very purpose exclusionary, that they have meaning only insofar as they can effectively delimit what they are not: this is true too of New England. The name "New England" emphasizes the geographically contiguous land mass delineated by colonial political borders, an emphasis with legitimate analytic value. But it also explicitly privileges an identity rooted in political geography, when in fact inhabitants of the region—European, Native American, and African—lived in a world with quite nebulous borders. All inhabitants of New England, Anglo and non-, had friends and family dispersed throughout what scholars call an "Atlantic World," and their own lives were often similarly transcolonial. The political borders of the New England colonies might have meant little to a person living within them.

The idea that political boundaries fail to encompass the lived experience of historical situations is hardly unique to New England. Fernand Braudel, for one, argued for the writing of what he named the "*global* Mediterranean," an entity that went beyond "conventional boundaries." Ignoring those conventional boundaries allowed him to accurately tell the whole story of the Mediterranean, a place and world that required him to "imagine a hundred frontiers, not one, some political, some economic, and some cultural."[13] Influenced by the Braudelian approach, scholars of what is called the "Atlantic World" have insisted on broader borders and frontiers in their own histories of the areas that surrounded that immense ocean.[14] In doing so, these scholars have insisted on the importance of the ties of trade and commerce that bound colonies tightly to each other and to the metropole. No European colony, and certainly no English colony, existed outside of these ties, separate from these networks. They could not have survived without them.

Certainly New England was enmeshed in these circuits of trade—the economic connections that made those northern colonies grow extended far beyond the political borders of the region. Throughout the 17th and 18th centuries, farmers and fishers and merchants traded, bought, and sold wares using the watery networks of commerce that formed the Atlantic World, here understood to be the Atlantic Ocean and the landmasses it touches: the Americas, Western Europe, and Western Africa, with the further understanding that riverine networks of course expanded this world in certain places. Because of its geographic location, New England's interactions with the Atlantic World were largely (but not totally) confined to the North Atlantic, the region north of the equator. But even that limited Atlantic World fostered an economy large enough to make the colonies prosper, mostly because it was centered for so long on the amazingly profitable sugar colonies of the West Indies.

Already in the seventeenth century, colonists in New England and up and down the Americas knew that the West Indies meant money. So did authorities in England. Starting at midcentury, England, following mercantilist principles, passed a series of Navigation Acts; moves designed to create a trade system that excluded other European powers from English markets.[15] Drafted particularly to limit Dutch trade to the English colonies, but never perfectly enforced, the series of Navigation Acts passed over the century nonetheless gradually benefited the growing colonies in New England by increasing their opportunities for trade and restricting their competition. The passage of the Navigation Acts again highlights just how integrally New England's growth was part of a larger imperial design, and also how emphatically the seventeenth century was a time of scrambling for control over, among other things, the Atlantic trade.

This trend toward trading continued throughout the seventeenth and eighteenth centuries, even as later Navigation Acts like the Molasses Act of 1733 threatened rather than strengthened

New England's economy. Even if such eighteenth-century legislation from the metropole suggested the crown cared more about its West Indies holdings than New England, the reality was that smuggling and privateering made the act basically worthless, and that the trade between the regions continued. The leading economic scholars of the New England, particularly but not only of Massachusetts, have described the story of its commerce during the seventeenth and eighteenth centuries as "one of continuity." What New England merchants exported and imported in the seventeenth century, they also exported and imported in the eighteenth century. The region was rich in lumber, tar, fish, and beef throughout the colonial period. In 1665, Samuel Maverick, a royal commissioner to Charles II, described the commodities available from Massachusetts: fish, along with "Pipe-staves, matts, Firr-boards, some Pitch and Tarr, Pork, Beif, Horses and Corne, whch they send to Virginia, Barbados, & take tobacco and Sugar for payment, which they (after) send to England."[16] These products remained constant. Some eighty years later, in 1744, Alexander Hamilton, a physician from Maryland, traveled through the region and noted of Boston, by then a town of more than 20,000 inhabitants, that it was a "considerable place for shipping, [with] now above 100 ships in the harbour, besides a great number of small craft." And the commodities of the country, he observed, were still "shipping, lumber, and fish."[17]

And it wasn't only commodities that were shipped across the Atlantic. Ideas traveled also, via letters and word of mouth, and in that way too a world was formed. Books, pamphlets, sartorial fashions, food practices, domestic decorative fads, and even slang sailed around in ships, packed in next to colonists and enslaved people alike.[18] Even events as famous as the first Great Awakening, were Atlantic revivals, really, experienced around the British colonies from New England to the Caribbean, by Europeans, Africans, and Indians, in all those places.[19]

Black and Red Atlantics

Figure 8.1 shows Boston's hectic and profitable port in the early- to mid-eighteenth century. Its famous long wharf, visible in the center distance, depicts something essential to an understanding of the Atlantic World, and thus to an understanding of seventeenth- and eighteenth-century New England: that neither the former nor the latter were formed exclusively by the sharing of religious ideals. The reason the Atlantic World worked, it perhaps needs to be said early and emphatically, was that it was driven by the profits derived from goods produced by and sold to colonies dominated by the peculiarly grasping institution of chattel slavery. As one scholar has observed, "what moved in the Atlantic in these centuries was predominantly slaves, the output of slaves, the inputs to slave societies, and the goods and services purchased with the earnings of slave products."[20] That this was true benefited even relatively a marginal place like New England, situated on the periphery of the English empire, in an unpromising (for cash crops, anyway) climate.

This reality calls for us to complicate the idea of strict distinctions between the regions, especially regarding the labor system of those island colonies. Moses Finley's distinction between societies with slaves, and slave societies, a framework reinvigorated by Ira Berlin in his masterful *Many Thousands Gone*, has been used to explain the difference between regions like New England, and regions like the West Indies. In a society with slaves, slavery was just one kind of labor system among others. In slave societies, by contrast, slavery was crucial to the entire economy.[21] And yet the two kinds of societies were not so distinct as the division supposes; the New England colonies, for example, grew lockstep with Caribbean colonies, as interconnected parts of the same economic system.

Without enslaved people in the sugar islands growing a crop that could and did bring such phenomenal wealth to the entire Atlantic World, the colonization of North America and the Car-

Figure 8.1 A southeast view of the City of Boston in North America.
Source: Boston Pictorial Archive

ibbean would surely have proceeded quite differently. New England's land, of course, could not grow sugar (or really, any other cash crop, save a few tobacco plantations in Rhode Island in the eighteenth century). But merchants could and did make a living carrying goods to and from those places that could grow such crops. Indeed, those colonies quickly became dependent on food and supplies on mainland colonies. By midcentury, an observer of the West Indies explained that planters there were "so intent upon planting sugar that they had rather buy foode at very deare rates than produce it by labour, soe infinite is the profitt of sugar workes after once accomplished."[22] Such dependence by the island colonies on the northern regions of course gave the New England colonies both real power in the form inflows, and perhaps a feeling of autonomy from the metropole. Certainly representatives of the crown resented both the engrossment of money and the perceived growth of independence. One English captain warned that New England's merchants were losing fear of the crown as their economic clout increased, for "they being the *key of the Indies* without w[hi]ch Jamaica, Barbados & the Caribee Islands are not able to subsist."[23] This man, and others, understood that dominance in Atlantic trade was important to imperial control.

As New England ships plied the rough Atlantic waters, bringing back money and profits to their owners, so too they sometimes brought slaves. Even absent the cash crops that more characteristically called for slave labor in the colonial Americas, New England's colonists still owned slaves. The region's enslaved African population grew steadily over the colonial period. Numbering less than 2,000 in 1700, there were more than 15,000 people of African descent in the region by 1770.[24]

Slavery in New England, except on the tobacco plantations that developed in some parts of eighteenth-century Rhode Island, was different than plantation slavery. Because enslaved people did the same labor as colonists in early New England, they were a useful investment for a variety of households—perhaps a greater variety than in places where slave labor was specialized. In the eighteenth-century south, non-field work was relatively rare, employing only one in six rural enslaved men, rising to one in four by the end of that century. But New England, lacking cash crops, never saw a majority of its enslaved people working in "field work." Instead, from the very beginning, enslaved people in seventeenth-century New England did a variety of jobs. And whereas the larger slave populations that developed in southern colonies meant that slaves generally learned their work from other slaves, enslaved people in early New England, often isolated from others who shared their ethnicity and status, must instead, most commonly, have learned the techniques of specific tasks from their owners.[25] Enslaved women in New England were valued differently than in other regions; their reproductive capacities meant less, it appears, than they would mean in plantation societies; without a community of enslaved people who might help take care of an infant, the presence of a baby only meant that that some woman was hindered in her work. But this situation was never unique to New England—urban slavery elsewhere had these same attributes.

Each new ship that sailed into Boston or Salem or New Haven's harbor with slaves on board, as well as each ship sailing out with captive Indians or slave-produced goods, signified an entrenchment of slavery in the colonies. Perhaps in some ways this decreased the isolation felt by enslaved people in the northern colonies. As more slaves arrived, one palpable change was the existence of a larger community of enslaved Africans in New England, especially for those who lived in port towns. Historian William Pierson has written extensively about an "Afro-American subculture" in eighteenth-century New England, and the roots of this must be found at the end of the seventeenth century.[26] As population numbers increased, some enslaved Africans experienced less isolation and a less dramatic severing of cultural ties. But this experience probably stood in almost direct opposition to that of enslaved Indians exported away from the region.

Port towns in seventeenth-century New England were most likely to have a substantial slave presence. A late-century French observer of Boston noted that "you may also own negroes and negresses; there is not a house in Boston, however small be its means, that has not one or two." He had seen some homes with as many as five or six. He found Africans there to "cost from twenty to forty pistoles … provided they are skilful or robust," thus enacting a value exchange in his head, for the benefit of his readers. And unlike the situation in some other colonies, New England's slave owners, he noted, had little fear that enslaved Africans would escape: "for the moment one is missing from the town, you have only to notify the savages, who provided you promise them something, and describe the man to them, he is right soon found." In any case, he added, such flight happened rarely; enslaved Africans would hardly know where to run "having few trodden roads, and those which are trodden lead to English towns or villages, which, on your writing, will immediately send you back your men."[27] But slaveholding in colonial New England was never merely the province of towns. Probate records and wills from the region even during the first century of colonization confirm that, poor households, middling households, and wealthy households, coastal and inland, all owned human property.

Indeed, even if Atlantic commerce and the concomitant slave trading began on the coast, a secondary economic world consisting of smaller port towns, sometimes upriver from the coast, sometimes in lesser harbors, also helped to create the world. These towns were less imposing in terms of both population and the amount of trade, and their size and relative lack of wealth meant that merchants did not dominate the social scene to the same extent. Nonetheless, these inland market centers also sold their surplus crops throughout the Atlantic, including to the slave societies in the West Indies.[28] In other words, the Atlantic market suffused even inland English communities. By the mid-eighteenth century, one historian has argued that "most of New England was already 'filled-in'" by English colonists who had created a "sprawling network of trade and exchange centered on the region's principal ports."[29] This network of course included the West Indies.

All this was made possible because colonial New England was truly a *colonial* endeavor; a product of aggressive settler colonization with the goal of obtaining land for Europeans, from Indigenous people. Settler colonization is a specific process: in the hopes of better understanding the workings of empire, colonial theorists are increasingly turning their attention away from describing colonialism and postcolonialism as ahistorical entities, and toward differentiating and historicizing forms of colonization. Some of the new distinctions have relevance for the Indian slave trade in New England, in particular the distinction between Extractive Colonies and Settler Colonies. Colonies of exploitation, or extractive colonies are one sort, typified by "indirect control by colonial powers through a relatively small, sojourning group of primarily male administrators, merchants, soldiers, and missionaries." This sort of colonization was and is practiced throughout the globe. In general terms, those extractive colonies require indigenous labor to forward the empire's agenda; in such colonies, indigenous labor is desired and necessary, and colonizers coopt or coerce native peoples into working toward imperial goals. Though it can be violent and destructive to indigenous lives, the process of extractive colonialism attempts to keep colonized bodies in their place, so that they can work toward imperial goals.[30]

In contrast to this kind of colonization, scholars have identified "settler colonialism," in which "the primary object … is the land itself rather than the surplus value to be derived from mixing native labour with it." In settler colonialism, "a much larger settler European population of both sexes for permanent settlement" arrives, less interested in indigenous labor, than in controlling the new territory. This is what happened in New England, a place where indigenous labor was never essential to achieving colonial goals. Rather, colonists wanted the land, so that they could settle it in ways they wanted, according to their priorities. Before that could happen, Indians needed to be removed. Settler colonization, at its foundation, is a "winner-take-all project whose dominant feature is not exploitation but replacement."[31]

In fact, seen from above, the colonization of New England might have looked very much like a process of replacing Native American bodies with English ones. One historian has estimated that New England authorities enslaved over 1,300 Indians in the seventeenth century, mostly exporting them to the West Indies.[32] One reason the English enacted that general policy of Indian removal even in far-flung places like New England was because of the slave-grown crops that were generating such wealth in the West Indies; to grow and harvest that sugar with enslaved Africans required Indian land both in the islands, and in the regions that grew those crops that would feed the enslaved Africans on those islands. The Atlantic slave trade offered to the English a way to remove Indians from the region (for a profit), replacing them with bodies that would work the land in a way meaningful to the colonizers. Replacement and removal was never confined to the early years of colonization: the removal of Indian bodies from land that Europeans wanted was a steady process throughout the eighteenth century, and really throughout United States history.

The Atlantic Chasm

That sense of displacement and entrapment experienced by enslaved bodies is worth pursuing for a bit, because the lived experience of an enslaved person in colonial New England, as attested to by a transient observer of the region, slightly undercuts at least a little bit the idea of a networked Atlantic World. One result of the Atlantic studies movement is that recent scholarly descriptions of the relationship of New England to the Atlantic World have described the region's *connections* to Africa, to the Caribbean, to Europe, to South America, to the rest of the world, all via the convenient ocean that offered the frictionless transportation of goods and people into and out of the colonies. The scholarship on an Atlantic New England as a connected New England is enormous, impressive, and persuasive.

And yet, before rushing to describe these connections, it's worth underscoring that those ties and connections were economic rather than lived. That is to say, we might first take a moment to acknowledge that the Atlantic Ocean was also, literally, a chasm. We might reassert, at least for a moment, the daunting immensity of that ocean, and the gulf it represented to the people living on the continents surrounding it. The Atlantic probably felt like and truly was, to many inhabitants of all the relevant continents, a real and formidable barrier, obstacle, and even a graveyard. In the face of waves of Atlantic scholarship insisting on globalized networks of communication and finance, we might consider the Atlantic World as a means by which people were instead entrapped or imprisoned, a gulf by which they were exiled. We might consider that capital flows more easily than do human bodies, and that the people who lived in New England very possibly experienced the Atlantic not only and possibly not ever as a conduit, but rather as a serious impediment both to communication and to connection. William Bradford, looking back on his Atlantic crossing—a journey he made of his own volition—remembered his crossing of the "vast and furious ocean" as full of "perils and miseries." He was relieved to set his feet back on "the firm and stable earth."[33] The horror and antipathy Bradford felt toward the sea was shared by colonists and others throughout the eighteenth century.

The insistence on the ocean as a barrier rather than a conduit has geographical evidence to support it. Consider size: the Atlantic Ocean consists of 41 million square miles, covering 20 percent of the earth's surface. By way of contrast, Braudel's Mediterranean Sea encompasses less than 1 million square miles; his "world" was less than 1/40 the size of the Atlantic. Such distance meant a lot to those who lived in seventeenth- and eighteenth-century New England. Merchants from the region, of course, among others, traded throughout this entire Atlantic oceanic area (albeit less with that area south of the equator). But not every person in New England was a merchant. Indeed, most were not. Fishers and sailors aside, many colonial New Englanders never set a foot aboard a boat. Even merchants did not often or always sail with their goods; more often, they too stayed put, in their comfortable homes, writing letters to factors and agents abroad, handling their business via letters.

If colonists were hemmed in by the ocean, then enslaved people, whose lives were characterized so often by restrictions on their movement and insistence on a severing of their familial and affective ties, must have been as well. After all, for the first generations of slaves, the Atlantic Ocean was the means by which ships had taken them thousands of miles from family. For subsequent generations of African-Americans, free and not, the ocean very probably loomed as a huge barrier between themselves and a past they could only imagine. Consider the words of Jeffrey Brace, an enslaved boy who spent time in Boston in the 1760s. While there, he recounted, he "became acquainted with many free African descendants, who appeared to be well contented in their situation," and yet still asked the boy "many questions about [his] native country." His description of Africa, he noted, "appeared to gratify them and procure [him] much attention."[34] Here is only one small bit of evidence of a longing for information about Africa, a place foreign in reality but probably not in imagination to Brace's interlocutors. But travel there was simply not possible; the ocean was an impediment to that. And just so was it an impediment to cultural retention in a place like New England, where Africans had arrived in small groups, rather than in large shipments.

As for Native Americans, that ocean in the colonial period, especially as Europeans increasingly controlled coastal travel and trade, was also often a place of exile. We know that prior to European contact, Indians had traveled and traded up and down the coast of North America, and of course all over the riverine networks that flowed into the Atlantic. And recent scholarship has insightfully shown that such travel and trade continued after European colonization commenced. But it is also true that over the course of the seventeenth and eighteenth centuries, such contact was increasingly curtailed.[35] As the English came to dominate the coast, which they did long before they ever came close to dominating the land, Indian access to the ocean became increasingly circumscribed. Jace Weaver has recently and usefully reminded us of the existence of a Red Atlantic.[36] But for many of New England's Indians, over the course of the colonial period, that diasporic community was, like the Black Atlantic, connected more through memory than through actual experience. The more tangible reality of their daily lives was that the ocean served as a means by which families had been sundered.

The power to control enslaved people and their families was crucial to maintaining slavery in the immature colonial setting. We know of course that sustaining the system of chattel slavery practiced throughout the Americas often required an extreme bodily violence; certainly the draconian nature of slave punishments in the sugar plantations of the Caribbean attests to this. A seventeenth-century observer wrote that one of the main reasons slaves in Barbados did not revolt more often was "they are held in such awe and slavery as they are fearful to appear in any daring act; and seeing the mustering of our men, and hearing their Gun-shot (than which nothing is more terrible to them) their spirits are subjugated to so low a condition, as they dare not look up to any bold attempt."[37] In other words, force kept them in line. "To obey is to honour," Thomas Hobbes wrote, "because no man obeys them whom they think have no power to help or hurt them."[38] The obedience of a slave was often achieved with the sharp end of a whip.

But not always. It is also true that when it came to controlling some slaves, the threat of physical violence must have been rivaled in effectiveness by the threat of emotional violence; perhaps the notion of harm to loved ones, or separation from them, prevented as many ideas of rebellion and resistance as the fear of harm to oneself ever did. Physical punishment was painful and debilitating, but often temporary. The sundering of families in the vast Atlantic World was permanent and searing in a completely different way. In many of the seventeenth-century West African societies from which enslaved Africans in North America came, kinship and community were nearly synonymous with identity. The same held true for Native American societies. Estranging a person from their community did violence to their sense of self in a way hardly replicable in today's world of atomized selves and independent lives. "'Tis better to have loved and lost/ Than never to have loved at all," Tennyson wrote centuries after the colonial period of New England ostensibly ended.[39] Perhaps no institution tests that sentiment more than chattel slavery. In the "free" world, people can tell themselves that loss is unusual, unfair, and unlikely, and they can go through life putting off their fears of the worst by assuring themselves that the worst is rare. In contrast, enslaved people in the Atlantic World loved and lived knowing that loss was, almost, a given. This alienation from the right to determine the fate of oneself and one's family has long been at the core of scholarly definitions of slavery. Eugene Genovese described it as a "powerful means of social control," noting that "no threat carried such force as a threat to sell the children, except the threat to separate husband and wife." In that tragic space between potential and certainty lay a cruel means of obtaining obedience from some slaves, even in early New England.[40]

Still, it wasn't only Indians and Africans who felt the immensity of that Atlantic barrier. As evidenced by Braford's words, the English also saw the Atlantic as something impenetrable. Some colonists could not stand the separation and distance from what they considered home, and returned to England.[41] For others, returning home across the ocean was not so easy; some New Englanders found themselves held in bondage in North Africa, Atlantic captives of another sort. The historian David Eltis has noted that "down to the 1640s there were more English slaves in North Africa than there were African slaves under English control in the Caribbean."[42] Another historian estimates that over a million European captives were held in North Africa between 1530 and 1780.[43] And Linda Colley has argued that although England had hopes of controlling the Mediterranean, the repeated kidnapping and capturing of English seamen by North African pirates and soldiers in the sixteenth and seventeenth centuries demonstrated clearly the limits of the British Empire.[44]

New Englanders were aware of North African captivity because it affected them directly and personally. In 1670, the colonist Thomas Hawkins wrote to the General Court for help ransoming his son-in-law, Edward Howard, from "slavery with the Turks." The "Turks" holding Howard had apparently asked for 150 pounds, a sum beyond his wife's and father-in-law's means.[45] In 1680, Martha Dadey petitioned the General Court of Boston for help in raising ransom for her "son in Captivitie with the Turks this Eighteen months past." The frantic mother petitioned the court to consider "[t]he cruelty and Misery he hath Endured, I myself not being able to express, your Petitioner cannot perticularize more than, that it is Turkish." The worst of it, to the ears of New England's authorities, was that he was not alone, "ther being many other with him the like bondage, and that of New England birth."[46] But the Atlantic prevented their redemption. Is it fair to wonder if somewhere in Africa, families of captives held in New England worried and agonized in the same way, albeit without any knowledge of where there own kin had been taken? Can we use English words to recover the experiences of captives of color whose own words were never documented?

Stories of English captives abound in New England's records. In 1681, Boston's Peter Gee, a fisherman, and his wife, Grace, sold their house and land to ransom their "younger son Joshua Gee from out of turkeish slavery in Algier."[47] The following year, in the same town, Elizabeth Purkis sold land, house, and goods to raise money "towards the redeeming of my sd. Husband out of Algier."[48] Dorcas Carver petitioned the governor and General Court for help ransoming Robert Carver, "who was once the Dear, but now if alive, the miserable husband of the Sorrowfull Petitioner." He had sailed with a Boston captain, but had been "carried away into slavery and Captivity, where he hath been for the space of almost two years, under worse than Egyptian Bondage."[49] Perez Savage was taken captive in 1692, on his "voyage from Bilboa to Cadiz and soe hyther to Boston." His brother reported that Perez had undergone "a hard captivity" and "cruel usage." The Savage family could not afford the ransom asked, even though Perez was "the son of one so well knowne to your selves that hath so often served this country both in his person and estate but did also himself serve the publicke against the Indians in a former warr and was sorely wounded and lost the use of his limbs."[50] Not even the sons of respectable Puritans were safe from Atlantic turmoil.

Cotton Mather wrote on the topic of North African captivity more than once. In his 1698 *A Pastoral Letter to the English Captives in Africa,* he addressed English captives held in North Africa, admitting that "when we consider, what a dreadful and what a doleful, and inexpressibly miserable *Captivity* is, that you are gone into, the Lamentations of our *Sorrow,* do indeed become Inexpressible." But, Mather being Mather, he hastened to note that things might be much worse; he reminded the North African captives to keep their Christian faith, promising that New Englanders "should Endure all manner of *Temporal Miseries,* than Incur *Eternal* Ones." After all, corporeal trials might end; spiritual ones would endure. Mather noted that "We had rather a *Turk* or a *Moor* should continually Trample on you, than that the *Devil* should make a *prey* of you." He insisted that "your *slavery* to the *Monsters* of *Africa* will be but short, and you may *Serve God* under it, and *See God* after it."[51] Mather's epistle, though, stood small chance of being delivered to any North African captive. It was in fact a rhetorical sleight-of-hand, because the real captivity that concerned Mather happened far closer to home.

Mather did not say it directly, but the English were frantically worried about the prominence of Native American captivity; that is to say, captivity of English by Indians. It was all around them, and New Englanders did not miss the parallels it had to North African slavery. John Gyles, captured in 1689, repeatedly described the actions of his Indian captors as "barbarities," either consciously or not invoking the enslavement going on across the Atlantic, on the "barbary" coast.[52] The English colonist Nathaniel Saltonstall wrote several narratives about King Philip's War, all intended for consumption by English audiences. He realized that some of the terms in his account would be unfamiliar to his readers, and took pains to explain them. "For the better understanding some Indian Words, which are necessarily used in the following Narrative, the Reader is desired to take Notice," he wrote, "[t]hat a *Swamp* signifies a Moorish Place, overgrown with Woods and Bushes, but soft like a Quagmire or Irish Bogg, over which Horse cannot at all, nor English Foot (without great Difficulty) passe."[53] Notice where his mind went when attempting to explain Native American vocabulary: to things "Moorish," or African, and to Ireland. The former was of course a place of numerous instances of English captivity (that is to say, English captives of North Africans), and more generally the continent from which African slaves came. The latter was an early site of brutal English colonization and enslavement of native peoples, a place seen by many historians as a sort of rehearsal for North American colonization. That Saltonstall would seize upon these places as having explanatory power for describing North American features speaks to the familiarity of various kinds of captivity and bondage to English on both sides of the Atlantic, and to a certain facility of comparative frameworks. Surely Indian captors, who had seen their own family members stolen away and sometimes sold in Atlantic slavery, might have understood the parallels.

The colonist Quentin Stockwell, held captive by New England Indians and taken to New France, described another telling moment as well. Having been struck on the face by an Indian after asking to see a doctor, a French soldier came into his village and "asked where the *Indian* was that struck the *English-man*, and took him and told him he should go the Bilboes, and then be hanged: the *Indians* were much terrified at this, as appeared by their Countenance and Trembling."[54] "Bilboes" were shackles for ankles: two connected, metal, u-shaped loops, connected and locked by a straight bar. The English used them not infrequently as punishment akin to stocks or whippings—the metal chafed a prisoner's skin, and slowed walking to a painful pace. Examples of their use as a punishment appear throughout New England records.[55] But over the century, "bilboes" came to be associated with enslaved Africans. The efficiency of the shackle made them popular among slavers, who would lock two slaves together, one's right ankle shackled to the other's left. In that way, the contraption limited suicide and flight attempts. That the French knew of bilboes of course highlights the existence of their own Caribbean colonies. That the Indians knew of them enough to show fear on the their faces and trembling in their bodies shows how the Atlantic slave trade had penetrated even northeastern North America.[56]

Atlantic New England

In 1857, as signs of an impending civil war seemed ever more ominous, Nathaniel Hawthorne penned a letter to a friend to express his doubts about the reality of national unity. Could anyone really feel a sense of all-encompassing nationalism, he wondered? "New England," he wrote, "is quite as large a lump of earth as my heart can really take in."[57] In writing this, and in disavowing much feeling of kinship with the American South, he implicitly argued for a regional distinctiveness to New England, and a separation from the slave-holding states. But such a separation was never as stark as Hawthorne implied, not in the nineteenth century and surely not in the centuries preceding. Rather, the continuity was one of economic connectivity. Northern states made shoes, and hoes, and clothes for slave states; northern colonies sent fish and tar and lumber south. Opportunities for profit can bridge almost any divide.

Perhaps no region of colonial North America has been so studied and written about as New England, and much of that work was done by some of the greatest historians of the period, almost all of it focused on New England as a bounded entity with a coherent and differentiated identity. Given that solid and deep base, it seems essential to ask: does reframing the region with an Atlantic lens change or challenge this foundational work? Does it really matter that the colonies traded with the Caribbean islands? Does it matter that a relatively small number of enslaved Africans and Indians lived in the region? Does it matter that Atlantic trade offered a way to remove Indians and turn them into profits until there weren't enough to warrant doing so?

The answer to all those different questions is: yes. Writing New England into an Atlantic framework matters, perhaps most of all to the enslaved people of New England, Indian and African, whose stories are seldom told because their numbers have rarely warranted examination. And yet, their numbers were hardly negligible: at times enslaved people formed up to 10 percent of the population of some towns, which means that English colonists saw enslaved people, interacted with them, owned them, read about them being sold, throughout the colonial period. There were enslaved people and slave markets in colonial New England, meaning that even Puritan sermons on topics like the family or salvation need to be reunderstood as happening in the context of a society that knew quite well that some families did not matter, and that some people could not be redeemed or saved. It matters that when New England's colonists spoke of freedom, in the seventeenth century and in the eighteenth century, they had the lived experience of unfreedom in its starkest form in front of their eyes. When a New England farmer grew crops, even far from the coast, a part of his (for they were almost always men) mind was focused on an Atlantic trade—and it matters that even so-called subsistence farmers had part of an eye on an export trade, had a hand in sustaining the Atlantic World.

But there is also a larger understanding to be gained by examining how New England, a small group of colonies at the edge of England's empire, was in fact as implicated as anywhere else in the world of Atlantic trade. In understanding their role in a larger world, we gain an understanding of how local people acting on local stages work according to scripts written elsewhere. We might (and do) read the famed English captive Mary Rowlandson's story as the epitome of a Puritan struggle with the theological and physical difficulties offered by captivity with Native Americans. But that struggle was *more* than that; it was also one more iteration of a colonial conflict waged around the globe, fueled in part by a slave trade. Every generation of historians, it is said, rewrites its predecessors; this essay and the others in this collection are written during what we might call a transnational moment in the writing of history, and they reflect that moment in their insistence on the importance of external influences on a region more often described in insular terms.

Viewed a certain way, the colonization of New England, the wars and strife that bloodied New England's land for so many years, were a local story. At the immediate level, English colonists would have said they were fighting for Christianity, for civilization, or perhaps simply for safety for their families from aggressive Indians who weren't using the land and had no culture to defend anyway. Or perhaps they might have cited the encroaching French, or the Spanish, or even the Dutch, as reasons to defend their scrawny towns and garrisoned trading posts. The Indians of "New England," the Massachusetts, the Narragansetts, the Pequots, and others, might have said they were fighting to defend a way of life and a use of land that predated English arrival; they might have said they were simply protecting their families from encroaching Europeans. And they would have been right—their local, immediate reasons for fighting were those. But the specter of Atlantic trade, of slavery, of sugar, of everything, hovers in the background. New England's local events were embedded in an Atlantic, even global, narrative.

Notes

Portions of the essay also appear in Wendy A. Warren New England Bound: Slavery and Colonization in Early America (New York: WW Norton, 20160.

1. Cotton Mather, *Magnalia Christi Americana, Or, The Ecclesiastical History* (London, 1702), "An Attestation To This Church-History of New England," unpaginated first page.
2. Scholarship that emphasizes the distinctive nature of English colonists to the region and/or their religiosity includes John Demos, *A Little Commonwealth: Family Life in Plymouth Colony* (New York: Oxford University Press, 2000); David D. Hall, *Worlds of Wonder, Days of Judgment: Popular Religious Belief in Early New England* (New York: Alfred A. Knopf, 1989); Carole Karlsen, *Devil in the Shape of a Woman: Witchcraft in Colonial New England* (New York: W.W. Norton, 1987); Kenneth A. Lockridge; *A New England Town: The First Hundred Years: Dedham, Massachusetts, 1636–1736*, rev. ed. (New York: W. W. Norton, 1985); Perry Miller, *The New England Mind: The Seventeenth Century* (New York: The Macmillan Company, 1939); Miller, *The New England Mind: From Colony to Province* (Cambridge, MA: Harvard University Press, 1953); Edmund S. Morgan, *The Puritan Dilemma: The Story of John Winthrop* (Boston: Little, Brown, 1958); Edmund Morgan, *Visible Saints: The History of a Puritan Idea* (Ithaca, NY: Cornell University Press, 1968); Mark A. Peterson, *The Price of Redemption: The Spiritual Economy of Puritan New England* (Stanford, CA: Stanford University Press, 1997); Laurel Thatcher Ulrich, *Good Wives: Image and Reality in the Lives of Women in Northern New England, 1650–1750* (New York: Alfred A. Knopf, 1982); Harry S. Stout, *The New England Soul: Preaching and Religious Culture in Colonial New England* (New York: Oxford University Press, 1986.
3. On the Great Migration's unusual demographics, see Virginia DeJohn Anderson, *New England's Generation: The Great Migration and the Formation of Society and Culture in the Seventeenth Century* (New York: Cambridge University Press, 1991), 21–24, 31; and David Cressy, *Coming Over: Migration and Communication between England and New England in the Seventeenth Century* (New York: Cambridge University Press, 1987), 66–68.
4. See, for example, Bernard Bailyn, *The New England Merchants in the Seventeenth Century* (Cambridge, MA: Harvard University Press, 1955); Stephen Innes, *Creating the Commonwealth: The Economic Culture of Puritan New England* (New York: W. W. Norton, 1995); Mark Valeri, Heavenly Merchandize: How Religion Shaped Commerce in Puritan America (Princeton, NJ: Princeton University Press, 2010); Daniel Vickers, *Farmers and Fishermen: Two Centuries of Work in Essex County, Massachusetts, 1630–1850* (Chapel Hill: University of North Carolina Press, 1994).
5. Examples of scholarship that emphasizes Native American and English encounters includes Katherine Grandjean, *American Passage: The Communications Frontier in Early New England* (Cambridge, MA: Harvard University Press, 2015); Francis Jennings, *The Invasion of America: Indians, Colonialism, and the Cant of Conquest* (New York: W.W. Norton, 1975); Richard W. Cogley, *John Eliot's Mission to the Indians before King Philip's War* (Cambridge, MA: Harvard University Press, 1999); Jill Lepore, *The Name of War: King Philip's War and the Origins of American Identity* (New York: Alfred A. Knopf, 1998); Ann Marie Plane, *Colonial Intimacies: Indian Marriage in early New England* (Ithaca, NY: Cornell University Press, 2000); Jenny Hale Pulsipher, *Subjects unto the Same King: Indians, English, and the Contest for Authority in Colonial New England* (Philadelphia: University of Pennsylvania Press, 2005); Alden T. Vaughan, *New England Frontier: Puritans and Indians, 1620–1675* (Norman: University of Oklahoma Press, 1995).
6. Neal Salisbury, *Manitou and Providence: Indians, Europeans, and the making of New England, 1500–1643* (New York: Oxford University Press, 1982), 24–27; Sherburne Friend Cook, *The Indian Population of New England in the Seventeenth Century* (Berkeley, CA: University of California Press, 1976), 84–85.
7. Margaret Ellen Newell, "Indian Slavery in Colonial New England" *Indian Slavery in Colonial America*, ed. Alan Gallay (Lincoln, NE: University of Nebraska Press, 2009), 45; Pulsipher, *Subjects unto the Same King*, 241.
8. Vaughan, *New England Frontier*, 321–322.
9. Daniel R. Mandell, *Tribe, Race, History: Native Americans in Southern New England, 1780–1880* (Baltimore: Johns Hopkins University Press, 2010), 4.
10. Kathleen J. Bragdon, *Native People of Southern New England, 1650–1775* (Norman, OK: University of Oklahoma Press, 2009), xi, 7, 85; Alden Vaughan, Introduction to *New England Encounters: Indians and Euroamericans ca. 1600–1850* (Boston: Northeastern University Press, 1999), 4; William Cronon, *Changes in the Land: Indians, Colonists, and the Ecology of New England* (New York: Hill and Wang, 1983),

88–89; Salisbury, *Manitou and Providence*, 8. Margaret Ellen Newell, *Brethren by Nature: New England Indians, Colonists, and the Origins of American Slavery* (Ithaca, NY: Cornell University Press, 2015), 22.
11 John J. McCusker and Russell R. Menard, *The Economy of British America, 1607–1789* (Chapel Hill, NC: University of North Carolina Press, 1985), 103.
12 George Wilson Pierson, "The Obstinate Concept of New England: A Study in Denudation," *New England Quarterly* 28[1] (1955): 9.
13 Fernand Braudel, *The Mediterranean and the Mediterranean World in the Age of Philip II* (New York: Harper, 1966), 168–171.
14 On the Atlantic World, see Alison Games, *Migration and the Origins of the English Atlantic World* (Cambridge, MA: Harvard University Press, 1999); David Armitage and Michael J. Braddick, eds., *The British Atlantic World, 1500–1800* (New York: Palgrave, 2002); Nicholas Canny and Anthony Pagden, eds., *Colonial Identity in the Atlantic World, 1500–1800* (Princeton, NJ: Princeton University Press, 1987); April Lee Hatfield, *Atlantic Virginia: Intercolonial Relations in the Seventeenth Century* (Philadelphia: University of Pennsylvania Press, 2004); Karen Ordahl Kupperman, *The Atlantic in World History* (New York: Oxford University Press, 2012); Jack P. Greene and Philip D. Morgan, eds., *Atlantic History: A Critical Appraisal* (New York: Oxford University Press, 2009); John K. Thornton, *A Cultural History of the Atlantic World, 1250–1820* (New York: Cambridge University Press, 2012); and Jeffrey Bolster, *The Mortal Sea: Fishing the Atlantic in the Age of Sail* (Cambridge, MA: Belknap Press, 2012).
15 McCusker and Menard, *The Economy of British America*, 47.
16 "Report of His Majesties Commissioners concerning the MASSACHUSETTS, 1665," Carton 36, Folder 47, Endicott Family Papers, MHS.
17 Alexander Hamilton, *Hamilton's Itinerarium*, ed. Albert Bushnell Hart (St. Louis, MO: William K. Bixby, 1907), 177.
18 On the market economy of the eighteenth-century Atlantic, see T. H. Breen, "Baubles of Britain: The American and Consumer Revolutions of the Eighteenth Century" *Past and Present* 119: (1998) 73–104.
19 On the Great Awakening, see Jon Butler, "Enthusiasm Described and Decried: The Great Awakening as Interpretive Fiction," *The Journal of American History* 69[2] (1982): 305–325; Frank Lambert, *Inventing the "Great Awakening"* (Princeton, NJ: Princeton University Press, 1999); Edwin S. Guastad, *The Great Awakening in New England* (New York: Harper, 1957); Linford D. Fisher, *The Indian Great Awakening: Religion and the Shaping of Native Culture in Early America* (New York: Oxford University Press, 2012).
20 Barbara L. Solow, "Introduction," *Slavery and the Rise of the Atlantic System*, ed. Barbara Solow (New York: Cambridge University Press, 1991), 1.
21 Ira Berlin, *Many Thousands Gone: The First Two Centuries of Slavery in North America* (Cambridge, MA: Belknap Press of Harvard University Press, 1998), 8, 47. Here Berlin draws on the work of Moses Finley, the scholar of slavery in antiquity. See M. I. Finley, *Ancient Slavery and Modern Ideology* (New York: Viking, 1980), 79–80.
22 Richard Vines to John Winthrop, July 19, 1647, *Winthrop Papers* (Boston: The Massachusetts Historical Society, 1947), 5: 172. Vines himself was diving into the business enthusiastically, having bought two adjoining plantations, for a combined total of fifty acres, and an unnamed number of "negroes." The combination of these two purchases, he hoped, would begin making a profit of tobacco in as little as six months; but his real plans involved planting sugar for the next year's harvest.
23 "Captain Bredon's Relation of the State of Affaires in New England at his coming from thence in 1660," Carton 36, Folder 41, Endicott Family Papers, MHS (emphasis added). See also "Clarendon Papers," 16–19. For more on royal commissioners, including Bredon and Maverick, see Pulsipher, *Subjects unto the Same King*, 37–69.
24 John J. McCusker and Russell R. Menard, *The Economy of British America*, 103.
25 On the eighteenth-century South, see Philip D. Morgan, *Slave Counterpoint: Black Culture in the Eighteenth-Century Chesapeake and Lowcountry* (Chapel Hill, NC: University of North Carolina Press, 1998); Wendy A. Warren *New England Bound: Slavery and Colonization in Early America* (New York: WW Norton, 2016), 89-90.
26 William D. Piersen, *Black Yankees: The Development of an Afro-American Subculture in Eighteenth Century New England* (Amherst, MA: University of Massachusetts Press, 1988).
27 "Narrative of a French Protestant Refugee in Boston in 1687," *The Historical Magazine and Note and Queries, Concerning the Antiquities, History and Biography of America* II (Morrisania: Henry B. Dawson, 1867): 296.
28 Bailyn, *The New England Merchants*, 96–98.

29 Richard L. Kagan, "People and Places in the Americas: A Comparative Approach," *The Oxford Handbook of the Atlantic World*, ed. Nicholas Canny and Philip Morgan (New York: Oxford University Press, 2011), 358.
30 Stasiulis and Yuval-Davis, "Introduction: Beyond Dichotomies," 3.
31 Patrick Wolfe, *Settler Colonialism and the Transformation of Anthropology: The Politics and Poetics of an Ethnographic Event* (New York: Cassell, 1999), 163; Stasiulis and Yuval-Davis, "Introduction: Beyond Dichotomies," 3.
32 Newell, "Indian Slavery in Colonial New England," 33.
33 William Bradford, *Of Plymouth Plantation, 1620–1647*, ed. Francis Murphy (New York: Modern Library, 1981), 69.
34 Jeffrey Brace, *The Blind African Slave*, ed. Kari J. Winter (Madison: University of Wisconsin Press, 2004), 152.
35 See Andrew Lipman, *Saltwater Frontier: Indians and the Contest for the American Coast* (New Haven, CT: Yale University Press, 2015).
36 Jace Weaver, *The Red Atlantic: American Indigenes and the Making of the Modern World, 1000–1927* (Chapel Hill, NC: University of North Carolina Press, 2014).
37 Richard Ligon, *A True and Exact History of the Island of Barbados*, ed. Karen Ordhal Kupperman (Indianapolis, IN: Hackett, 2011), 96–97.
38 Thomas Hobbes, *Leviathan*, ed. Richard Tuck (Cambridge, UK: Cambrdige University Press, 1991), 64.
39 Alfred Tennyson, "In Memoriam A. H. H.," *The Major Works*, ed. Adam Roberts (New York: Oxford University Press, 2009), 252.
40 Eugene D. Genovese, *Roll, Jordan, Roll: The World Slaves Made* (New York: Pantheon Books, 1974), 452. Orlando Patterson called the constant experience of this threat to sever familial and cultural ties, and the common practice of actually doing so, a "natal alienation" for enslaved people that led to "social death." Orlando Patterson, *Slavery and Social Death: A Comparative Study* (Cambridge, MA: Harvard University Press, 1982), 5–13, 38–49. Moses Finley noted that a crucial aspect of ancient slavery was that a slave was "denied the most elementary of social bonds, kinship," observing that "there were slave unions and slave families, beyond a doubt, but they counted among the privileges that could be granted unilaterally by a slave owner, and withdrawn unilaterally." Finley, *Ancient Slavery and Modern Ideology*, 75.
41 On homesickness, see David Cressy, *Coming Over*, 191–212.
42 David Eltis, *The Rise of African Slavery in the Americas* (New York: Cambridge University Press, 2000), 57.
43 Robert C. Davis, "Counting European Slaves on the Barbary Coast," *Past & Present* no. 172[1] (2001): 118, cited in Alison Games, *Web of Empire: English Cosmopolitans in an Age of Expansion, 1560–1660* (New York: Oxford University Press, 2008), 68.
44 Linda Colley, *Captives: Britain, Empire, and the World, 1600–1850* (London: Jonathan Cape, 2002), 46–48. See also Nabil Matar, "Introduction: England and Mediterranean Captivity, 1577–1704," *Piracy, Slavery, and Redemption: Barbary Captivity Narratives from Early Modern England*, ed. Daniel J. Vitkus, (New York: Columbia University Press, 2001), 1–54.
45 Petition to the General Court of Boston, October 22, 1670, *Massachusetts Archives Collection* 60: 78.
46 Letter to the General Court of Boston, May 24, 1680, *Massachusetts Archives Collection* 61: 185, 210.
47 Sale of Gee Land, 1681, *Suffolk Deeds*, Book 12 (Boston: Rockwell and Church Press, 1902), 130–131. See also Joshua Gee, *The Narrative of Joshua Gee of Boston, Mass., While He Was Captive in Algeria of the Barbary Pirates, 1680–1687* (Hartford, CT: Connecticut Historical Society, 1943).
48 Contract of Elizabeth Purkis, 1682, *Suffolk Deeds*, Book 12, 229.
49 Dorcas Carver to the General Court of Boston, *Massachusetts Archives Collection* 61: 394.
50 Letter to William Phipps, 1693, *Massachusetts Archives Collection* 61: 393.
51 Cotton Mather, *A Pastoral Letter to the English Captives, in Africa, from New-England* (Boston: B. Green and J. Allen, 1698), 2, 4, 10.
52 John Gyles, "Memoirs of Odd Adventures, Strange Deliverances, etc.," *Puritans Among the Indians: Accounts of Captivity and Redemption, 1676–1724*, ed. Alden T. Vaughan and Edward W. Clark (Cambridge, MA: Belknap Press, 1981), 106.
53 Nathaniel Saltonstall, "A New and Further Narrative of the State of New-England, by N.S., 1676" *Original Narratives of Early American History*, Vol. 14, ed. John Franklin Jameson (New York: Charles Scribner's Sons, 1913), 77. Ironically, though the word became popularized in descriptions of N. America, the OED suggests it was in circulation previously and sources it to a German root (going back way before 1492) meaning "sponge" or "fungus." Saltonstall's false etymological history exoticizes the word.
54 Quentin Stockwell's Account in Increase Mather, *An Essay for the Recording of Illustrious Providences* (Boston, 1684), 54–55.

55 In 1634, for example, the Massachusetts Bay Colony Court noted that, "it is ordered, that Henry Bright shalbe set in the bilbowes for swearing." "Att a Court, holden att Newe Towne, November 7th, 1634," *Records of the Governor and Company of the Massachusetts Bay in New England*, ed. Nathaniel B. Shurtleff (Boston, 1853), 1: 133.
56 For a picture of bilboes and a discussion of general French techniques of slave restraint and torture, see Brett Rushforth, *Bonds of Alliance: Indigenous and Atlantic Slaveries in New France* (Chapel Hill, NC: University of North Carolina Press, 2012), 128–131.
57 Nathaniel Hawthorne to Horatio Bridge, Liverpool, 15 January 1857, *The Centenary Edition of the Works of Nathaniel Hawthorne*, eds. William Charvat, Roy Harvey Pearce, Claude M. Simpson, and Thomas Woodson, Vol. 18, *The Letters: 1857–1864*, eds. Thomas Woodson, James A. Rubino, L. Neal Smith, and Normal Holmes Pearson (Columbus, OH: Ohio State University Press, 1987), 8.

References

Anderson, Virginia DeJohn. *New England's Generation: The Great Migration and the Formation of Society and Culture in the Seventeenth Century* (New York: Cambridge University Press, 1991).

Armitage, David and Michael J. Braddick, eds. *The British Atlantic World, 1500–1800* (New York: Palgrave, 2002).

Bailyn, Bernard. *The New England Merchants in the Seventeenth Century* (Cambridge, MA: Harvard University Press, 1955).

Berlin, Ira. *Many Thousands Gone: The First Two Centuries of Slavery in North America* (Cambridge, MA: Belknap Press of Harvard University Press, 1998).

Bolster, Jeffrey. *The Mortal Sea: Fishing the Atlantic in the Age of Sail* (Cambridge, MA: Belknap Press, 2012).

Brace, Jeffrey. *The Blind African Slave*, ed. Kari J. Winter (Madison: University of Wisconsin Press, 2004).

Bragdon, Kathleen J. *Native People of Southern New England, 1650–1775* (Norman: University of Oklahoma Press, 2009).

Braudel, Fernand. *The Mediterranean and the Mediterranean World in the Age of Philip II* (New York: Harper, 1966).

Breen, T. H. "Baubles of Britain: The American and Consumer Revolutions of the Eighteenth Century" *Past and Present* 119 (1988): 73–104.

Butler, Jon. "Enthusiasm Described and Decried: The Great Awakening as Interpretive Fiction," *The Journal of American History* 69[2] (1982): 305–325.

Canny, Nicholas and Anthony Pagden eds. *Colonial Identity in the Atlantic World, 1500–1800* (Princeton, NJ: Princeton University Press, 1987).

Carver, Dorcas to the General Court of Boston, *Massachusetts Archives Collection* 61: 394.

Cogley, Richard W. *John Eliot's Mission to the Indians before King Philip's War* (Cambridge, MA: Harvard University Press, 1999).

Colley, Linda. *Captives: Britain, Empire, and the World, 1600–1850* (London: Jonathan Cape, 2002).

Cook, Sherburne Friend. *The Indian Population of New England in the Seventeenth Century* (Berkeley, CA: University of California Press, 1976).

Cressy, David. *Coming Over: Migration and Communication between England and New England in the Seventeenth Century* (New York: Cambridge University Press, 1987).

Cronon, William. *Changes in the Land: Indians, Colonists, and the Ecology of New England* (New York: Hill and Wang, 1983).

Davis, Robert C. "Counting European Slaves on the Barbary Coast," *Past & Present* 172[1] (2001).

Demos, John. *A Little Commonwealth: Family Life in Plymouth Colony* (New York: Oxford University Press, 2000): 87–124.

Eltis, David. *The Rise of African Slavery in the Americas* (New York: Cambridge University Press, 2000).

Finley, M. I. *Ancient Slavery and Modern Ideology* (New York: Viking, 1980).

Fisher, Linford D. *The Indian Great Awakening: Religion and the Shaping of Native Culture in Early America* (New York: Oxford University Press, 2012).

Games, Alison. *Migration and the Origins of the English Atlantic World* (Cambridge, MA: Harvard University Press, 1999).

Games, Alison. *Web of Empire: English Cosmopolitans in an Age of Expansion, 1560–1660* (New York: Oxford University Press, 2008).

Gee, Joshua. *The Narrative of Joshua Gee of Boston, Mass., While He Was Captive in Algeria of the Barbary Pirates, 1680–1687* (Hartford, CT: Connecticut Historical Society, 1943).

Genovese, Eugene D. *Roll, Jordan, Roll: The World Slaves Made* (New York: Pantheon Books, 1974).

Grandjean, Katherine. *American Passage: The Communications Frontier in Early New England* (Cambridge, MA: Harvard University Press, 2015).

Greene, Jack P. and Philip D. Morgan, eds. *Atlantic History: A Critical Appraisal* (New York: Oxford University Press, 2009).

Guastad, Edwin S. *The Great Awakening in New England* (New York: Harper, 1957).

Gyles, John. "Memoirs of Odd Adventures, Strange Deliverances, etc.," *Puritans Among the Indians: Accounts of Captivity and Redemption, 1676–1724*, ed. Alden T. Vaughan and Edward W. Clark (Cambridge, MA: Belknap Press, 1981).

Hall, David D. *Worlds of Wonder, Days of Judgment: Popular Religious Belief in Early New England* (New York: Alfred A. Knopf, 1989).

Hamilton, Alexander. *Hamilton's Itinerarium*, ed. Albert Bushnell Hart (St. Louis, MO: William K. Bixby, 1907), 177.

Hatfield, April Lee. *Atlantic Virginia: Intercolonial Relations in the Seventeenth Century* (Philadelphia: University of Pennsylvania Press, 2004).

Hawthorne, Nathaniel to Horatio Bridge, Liverpool, 15 January 1857, in *The Centenary Edition of the Works of Nathaniel Hawthorne*, eds. William Charvat, Roy Harvey Pearce, Claude M. Simpson, and Thomas Woodson, Vol. 18, *The Letters: 1857–1864*, eds. Thomas Woodson, James A. Rubino, L. Neal Smith, and Normal Holmes Pearson (Columbus, OH: Ohio State University Press, 1987), 8.

Hobbes, Thomas. *Leviathan*, ed. Richard Tuck (Cambridge, UK: Cambridge University Press, 1991).

Innes, Stephen. *Creating the Commonwealth: The Economic Culture of Puritan New England* (New York: W. W. Norton, 1995).

Jennings, Francis. *The Invasion of America: Indians, Colonialism, and the Cant of Conquest* (New York: W. W. Norton, 1975).

Kagan, Richard L. "People and Places in the Americas: A Comparative Approach," *The Oxford Handbook of the Atlantic World*, eds. Nicholas Canny and Philip Morgan (New York: Oxford University Press, 2011).

Karlsen, Carole. *Devil in the Shape of a Woman: Witchcraft in Colonial New England* (New York: W. W. Norton, 1987).

Kupperman, Karen Ordahl. *The Atlantic in World History* (New York: Oxford University Press, 2012).

Lambert, Frank. *Inventing the "Great Awakening"* (Princeton, NJ: Princeton University Press, 1999).

Lepore, Jill. *The Name of War: King Philip's War and the Origins of American Identity* (New York: Alfred A. Knopf, 1998).

Ligon, Richard. *A True and Exact History of the Island of Barbados*, ed. Karen Ordhal Kupperman (Indianapolis, IN: Hackett, 2011).

Lipman, Andrew. *Saltwater Frontier: Indians and the Contest for the American Coast* (New Haven, CT: Yale University Press, 2015).

Lockridge, Kenneth A. *A New England Town: The First Hundred Years: Dedham, Massachusetts, 1636–1736*, rev. ed. (New York: W. W. Norton, 1985).

Mandell, Daniel R. *Tribe, Race, History: Native Americans in Southern New England, 1780–1880* (Baltimore: Johns Hopkins University Press, 2010).

Matar, Nabil. "Introduction: England and Mediterranean Captivity, 1577–1704," *Piracy, Slavery, and Redemption: Barbary Captivity Narratives from Early Modern England*, ed. Daniel J. Vitkus (New York: Columbia University Press, 2001), 1–54.

Mather, Cotton. *Magnalia Christi Americana, Or, The Ecclesiastical History* (London, 1702).

McCusker, John J., and Russell R. Menard. *The Economy of British America, 1607–1789* (Chapel Hill, NC: University of North Carolina Press, 1985).

Miller, Perry. *The New England Mind: The Seventeenth Century* (New York: The Macmillan Company, 1939).

Miller, Perry. *The New England Mind: From Colony to Province* (Cambridge, MA: Harvard University Press, 1953).

Morgan, Edmund S. *The Puritan Dilemma: The Story of John Winthrop* (Boston: Little, Brown, 1958).

Morgan, Edmund S. *Visible Saints: The History of a Puritan Idea* (Ithaca, NY: Cornell University Press, 1968).

Morgan, Philip D. *Slave Counterpoint: Black Culture in the Eighteenth-Century Chesapeake and Lowcountry* (Chapel Hill, NC: University of North Carolina Press, 1998).

Newell, Margaret Ellen. "Indian Slavery in Colonial New England" *Indian Slavery in Colonial America*, ed. Alan Gallay (Lincoln: University of Nebraska Press, 2009).

Newell, Margaret Ellen. *Brethren by Nature: New England Indians, Colonists, and the Origins of American Slavery* (Ithaca, NY: Cornell University Press, 2015).

Patterson, Orlando. *Slavery and Social Death: A Comparative Study* (Cambridge, MA: Harvard University Press, 1982).
Peterson, Mark A. *The Price of Redemption: The Spiritual Economy of Puritan New England* (Stanford, CA: Stanford University Press, 1997).
Piersen, William D. *Black Yankees: The Development of an Afro-American Subculture in Eighteenth Century New England* (Amherst: University of Massachusetts Press, 1988).
Plane, Ann Marie. *Colonial Intimacies: Indian Marriage in early New England* (Ithaca, NY: Cornell University Press, 2000).
Pulsipher, Jenny Hale. *Subjects unto the Same King: Indians, English, and the Contest for Authority in Colonial New England* (Philadelphia: University of Pennsylvania Press, 2005).
Rushforth, Brett. *Bonds of Alliance: Indigenous and Atlantic Slaveries in New France* (Chapel Hill, NC: University of North Carolina Press, 2012).
Salisbury, Neal. *Manitou and Providence: Indians, Europeans, and the making of New England, 1500–1643* (New York: Oxford University Press, 1982).
Saltonstall, Nathaniel. "A New and Further Narrative of the State of New-England, by N.S., 1676" in *Original Narratives of Early American History*, Vol. 14, ed. John Franklin Jameson (New York: Charles Scribner's Sons, 1913).
Shurtleff, Nathaniel B., ed. *Records of the Governor and Company of the Massachusetts Bay in New England* (Boston, 1853), 1:133.
Solow, Barbara L. "Introduction," *Slavery and the Rise of the Atlantic System*, ed. Barbara Solow (New York: Cambridge University Press, 1991).
Stasiulis, Daiva and Nira Yuval-Davis. "Introduction: Beyond Dichotomies – Gender, Race, Ethnicity and Class in Settlers Societies" *Unsettling Settler Societies: Articulations of Gender, Race, Ethnicity and Class*, eds. Daiva Stasiulis and Nira Yuval-Davis (Thousand Oaks, CA: Sage, 1995).
Stockwell, Quentin. Account in Increase Mather, *An Essay for the Recording of Illustrious Providences* (Boston, 1684), 54–55.
Stout, Harry S. *The New England Soul: Preaching and Religious Culture in Colonial New England* (New York: Oxford University Press, 1986).
Tennyson, Alfred. "In Memoriam A.H.H.," *The Major Works*, ed. Adam Roberts (New York: Oxford University Press, 2009).
Thornton, John K. *A Cultural History of the Atlantic World, 1250–1820* (New York: Cambridge University Press, 2012).
Ulrich, Laurel Thatcher. *Good Wives: Image and Reality in the Lives of Women in Northern New England, 1650–1750* (New York: Alfred A. Knopf, 1982).
Valeri, Mark. *Heavenly Merchandize: How Religion Shaped Commerce in Puritan America* (Princeton, NJ: Princeton University Press, 2010).
Vaughan, Alden T. *New England Frontier: Puritans and Indians, 1620–1675* (Boston: Little, Brown, 1965).
Vaughan, Alden T. and Edward W. Clark, eds. *Puritans Among the Indians: Accounts of Captivity and Redemption, 1676–1724*, (Cambridge, MA: Belknap Press, 1981).
Vaughan, Alden T. *New England Encounters: Indians and Euroamericans ca. 1600–1850* (Boston: Northeastern University Press, 1999).
Vickers, Daniel. *Farmers and Fishermen: Two Centuries of Work in Essex County, Massachusetts, 1630–1850* (Chapel Hill: University of North Carolina Press, 1994).
Vines, Richard to John Winthrop, July 19, 1647, in *Winthrop Papers* (Boston: The Massachusetts Historical Society, 1947), 5:172.
Weaver, Jace. *The Red Atlantic: American Indigenes and the Making of the Modern World, 1000–1927* (Chapel Hill: University of North Carolina Press, 2014).
Warren, Wendy A.. *New England Bound: Slaery and Colonization in Early America* (New York: WW Norton, 2016).
Wilson Pierson, George. "The Obstinate Concept of New England: A Study in Denudation," *New England Quarterly* 28, 1 (March 1955): 3–17.
Wolfe, Patrick. *Settler Colonialism and the Transformation of Anthropology: The Politics and Poetics of an Ethnographic Event* (New York: Cassell, 1999).

9
THE MIDDLE COLONIES
Region, Restoration, and Imperial Integration

Ned C. Landsman

There was a time not so long ago when the Middle Colonies seemed to be the orphans of early American history, a region whose history was far less examined by historians than those of what were then considered the principal components of colonial America, the earlier-settled New England and Chesapeake regions to the north and to the south. Lacking the celebrated founding moments that were highlighted in the stories of Jamestown or Plymouth, those historians who did write of the Middle Colonies tended to focus instead on the lived experience of diversity itself, along with its attendant culture of toleration, pluralism, factionalism, and individualism, as the truest representation of what American society would eventually become. Exemplifying those descriptions of the region was one historian's famous reference to the Middle Colonies as "America's first plural society."[1]

If only it were that simple. The Middle Colonies can no longer stand in for the general pattern of American development. For one thing, the abundance of historical scholarship on the region produced over the last several decades means that it is no longer possible to claim historical neglect. For another, some of the attributes that had been associated with the mid-Atlantic—diversity, toleration, commercialism, and pluralism—have come to seem less uniform within the region, and less distinctive to it, than they did before. Moreover, given the very different patterns of ethnic, racial, and religious diversity that developed among those colonies, diversity itself now seems less like a shared characteristic of the mid-Atlantic colonies than an indication of the absence thereof. The various mid-Atlantic societies structured heterogeneity and toleration in very different ways.[2]

More fundamentally still, the regional approach itself, until recently almost ubiquitous among colonial historians, has come under challenge. Part of that is the result of two newer approaches to early America that highlight broad connections rather than divisions: an Atlantic focus that principally explores the interrelations among peoples and societies not only in Europe and North America but around the Atlantic basin, and a Continental perspective that puts colonial British America into the larger context of developments far into the American interior, which reverberated a good deal farther than historical narratives previously allowed. Those trends have greatly affected even the conception of regional histories, which now are likely to divide early America into many more than the three or four mainland regions scholars examined earlier, covering a much greater geographical expanse. Yet the burgeoning multiplicity of regions has led some historians to abandon regionalism altogether. The latest articulation by the author of one of the most extensive regional approaches to early America silently omits the Middle Colonies altogether—but not the old standbys of New England, the Chesapeake, or the West Indies—risking an effective return to the older geography of at least the eastern North American continent that mandated the heightened focus on the Middle Colonies in the first place.[3]

Consideration of the Middle Colonies as a region still has much to offer. That is not because they possessed distinctive and timeless traits that extended throughout their territorial borders, nor is it because those traits inevitably evolved into those that would become characteristically American. That would be teleology rather than history. The region matters because of its place within early American development. Emerging within territory that provided close access to a wide North American geography, the Middle Colonies functioned as critical centralizing forces within eastern North America at a time of intense imperial rivalry affecting Europeans and Indians. They helped to consolidate an English and later British presence within lands extending well beyond what are usually defined as the region's borders and did much to reconfigure the worlds of diverse Native American peoples as well as European settlers and traders. The mid-Atlantic colonies provided essential links across a contiguous space of English America and key connections to the world of the British Atlantic. They would constitute a central force in developing and disseminating important aspects of economy, empire, commerce, and culture, extending their influence even to an emerging imperial imaginary.

The Origins of the Middle Colonies

The area commonly known as the "Middle Colonies" comprised what became the four-colony region of New York, New Jersey, Pennsylvania, and Delaware, set within their colonial rather than their modern geographies. The term itself was almost never used at the time, although variations such as "middle settlements" did begin to appear later in the colonial period. In fact European involvement there lagged behind that in the regions immediately to the north and to the south. What drew the region together as a focal point within a zone of Native American and European imperial rivalries was a combination of the topography with the particular historical circumstances. Whatever character it developed as a region emerged over time.

Important attributes in creating what became the Middle Colonies were their topography and setting. A key feature of the mid-Atlantic was that it and its adjoining territories were traversed by extensive river systems that flowed to the Atlantic coast from points deep in the North American interior: the Hudson, the Delaware, the Susquehanna, and the Connecticut. (Two other river systems—the Saint Lawrence and the Ohio—would also play significant roles in regional history, as we shall see.) In the end, what would become the Middle Colonies would not encompass all of the surrounding territory; the Connecticut Valley, of course would end up wholly within New England once final boundaries were established—although not finally until Vermont became the fourteenth state—and the Susquehanna would flow along its outskirts. Nonetheless, together those rivers represented important determinants of the character of the societies that emerged, allowing travel and trade well inland for Indians and Europeans, and facilitating war, conquest, and diplomacy. Those river systems, coupled with excellent early modern harbors, involved the region from the beginning in both Continental and Atlantic affairs. They allowed as well for varied European groups—French, Dutch, English, and more—to make their way into the area.

Other aspects of the geography would also affect regional development. The river valleys and low-lying areas were arable and fertile, suitable for the most basic of European foodstuffs of the early modern world—grain—which brought them into Atlantic commerce early. The presence of valleys surrounded by uplands such as one found along the Hudson River led to substantial interaction among the varied native peoples spread out along those valleys, resulting in a diverse mix of empires and alliances. The arrival of Europeans with competing imperial aims further complicated matters, creating a patchwork of cooperation as well as conflict. Thus in the Hudson Valley, a number of adjacent Indian nations worked together to defend themselves against intrusions by the Dutch of New Netherland and especially the Haudenosaunee, or Five Nations of the Iroquois League. The League was one of cooperation among the adjacent Iroquoian peoples inhabiting the greater Mohawk Valley, and their original aim of precluding bloodshed among themselves extended to the goal of protecting them against rival Indian nations. Iroquois' power in turn prompted the creation of countering alliances from peoples of the Hudson Valley and as far north as the St. Lawrence Valley and the Great Lakes region.[4]

European Arrivals

What became the Middle Colonies sat near the center of several intrusions into the American Northeast by European imperial powers—the French, English, Dutch, and Swedes—in the early years of the seventeenth century. Those powers were themselves involved in a varying pattern of rivalry and alliance that led to a series of Anglo-Dutch wars before 1688 and Anglo-French conflicts—with England's interests aligned with Dutch—thereafter. Their North American rivalries were at least as complicated, leading to competition both over territory and trade. Native peoples witnessing their arrival adapted their own strategic alliances in efforts to take advantage of the opportunities the newcomers provided, to use them against their Indian rivals, and in attempts to defend their own positions against excessive European inroads.

The first Europeans whose presence significantly affected life within the region were the French, who by the early seventeenth century had established themselves in the northern river valley of the Saint Lawrence. They began trading with the local groups of Huron and Algonkian Indians, embedding missionaries and exchanging trade goods, especially seeking furs, which became part of a substantial transatlantic trade. Those relations posed a challenge for the Five Nations, who sat outside of their trade networks, and they fought the Huron and the other French allied Indians in an attempt to force their way into the trade. The French threw in their lot with their opponents, who were already trading partners, and who from their more northerly location had access to more and better pelts. The result was a series of "Beaver Wars," in which French soldiers fought alongside the Huron and other northern Indians against the Iroquois, in wars that decimated the populations of several Indian nations.

The Five Nations were in need of an alternative trading partner, and they found one in the Dutch. The Englishman Henry Hudson's 1609 voyage on behalf of the Dutch East India Company was originally intended to seek an Arctic passage east to Asia, but after being forced to abandon that plan, Hudson wound up instead in the river that would bear his name. That established grounds for a Dutch claim to the adjoining territory. During the succeeding two decades the Dutch West India Company—the trading company chartered for the pursuit of Atlantic interests—established a series of small settlements and trading stations in what they came to call New Netherland, part of a larger effort to build their wealth and commerce in the midst of their eighty-year struggle for independence (1568–1648) from Catholic Spain. The principal stations were at New Amsterdam at the mouth of the North (Hudson) River and Fort Orange and the adjacent town of Beverwyck (Beaver-town) in the vicinity of present day Albany, with additional forts along the South (Delaware) River. From Fort Orange they established trade with the neighboring Mahican Indians, who were eventually pushed out by the more powerful Mohawks, the easternmost of the Five Nations.[5]

New Netherland was never really intended to be a colony of settlers. With the exception of the early planting of a group of French-speaking Walloons to the north of what became New Amsterdam, the company mostly looked for commercial options from their dispersed trading stations along the Hudson and Delaware Valleys and the shores of Long Island Sound. For decades the colony grew only slowly, with an extremely mixed population of European settlers and African slaves arriving from the diverse Dutch trading empire. The settlers they attracted were only nominally "Dutch" and included German speakers, French speaking Huguenots and Walloons, English, Scots, Jews, and Swedes, among others—whomever they could attract from the commercial and refugee center that the Netherlands would become in the seventeenth century. The West India Company's prominence in the slave trade meant that it housed a diverse group of Africans as well, mostly Company servants; they included people of varied African allegiances, many from Portuguese territories, and including at least a few Christians and Muslims.[6] Their early presence would make New Netherland into the central focus of African life in the northern colonies.

Nor was it only the settler population that was diverse; the native peoples of the region were also undergoing significant reconfigurations, as wars and disease spread by the newcomers took their toll on native populations. The Five Nations pushed a number of other nations out beyond their expanding range of influence, westward beyond the Great Lakes, where some of them reformed into new societies. At the same time the Iroquois absorbed members of surrounding nations to uphold their own demographically stressed societies. Thus the establishment of New Netherland altered people's lives in places as far apart as Long Island, the Delaware Bay, the Ohio Country, and what would become Upper Canada.[7]

Among the successful links put together by the Dutch was a complex trade route connecting both ends of the Hudson Valley, acquiring Wampum—rare colorful shells found only on the shores of Long Island Sound—increasing its production through the use of European drills, and using it to trade for furs with the northern Indians at Fort Orange, who valued it for its use in diplomacy—recording the history of agreements and treaties in their lavishly constructed belts—its ritual value, and its trade uses.

The Wampum trade illustrates the manner in which events in one part of the region could influence developments throughout. The demand for wampum encouraged aggressive action by native peoples in the vicinity of the Sound, especially the Pequot Indians, who employed force and intimidation to build an empire along its shores. That trade left New Englanders in Plymouth looking for wampum. The result was a brutal war provoked by New England during the 1630s to decimate the Pequot and engage their rivals. New England's war on the Pequot pushed the Dutch out of their trading stations along the Sound, although Dutch traders kept up business in the region.[8] The Dutch thereafter ceded the Connecticut Valley and the lands to its west to Connecticut.

New Netherland faced another challenge to the south, where a rival fur-trading colony emerged at New Sweden in the Delaware Bay, funded largely by Dutch investors left out of West India Company trading, and populated largely by Finns. It was headed by Peter Minuit, former Director of New Netherland. In the mid-Atlantic friendship and hostility were products of circumstance. Thus in the north, New Netherland aligned with the Mohawk as the leading regional power in what was largely a mutually beneficial relationship, against both the Indians allied with New France and against the Hudson Valley nations. Nearer to New Amsterdam they engaged in brutal conflicts with the surrounding peoples in Kieft's War, in which they employed English veterans of the Pequot War in their own campaign of brutality.[9]

Ultimately, fragmentation gave way to consolidation. The 1650 Treaty of Hartford, although never finally ratified, set a boundary between New Netherland and Connecticut at a line

50 miles west of the Connecticut River. During the 1650s, the New Netherland population finally began to grow, with an influx of people from the Netherlands and beyond. And after a series of competing military maneuvers that nearly cost the Dutch the lower portions of the colony, New Netherland expelled New Sweden from the Delaware Valley in 1655.

New Netherland did not last much longer, giving way to English conquest in 1664 at the outset of the second Anglo-Dutch War, after which the Dutch acquired Surinam from the English while ceding their claim to New Netherland. With the exception of a brief moment during the third Anglo-Dutch war (1672–74), when the Dutch briefly reconquered New Netherland, Dutch rule, though not the activity of Dutch traders in the region, would be no more.

Restoration and Consolidation

The English conquest of New Netherland was a product of the Restoration (1660–88), in which King Charles II, son of the martyred Charles I, was installed on the English and Scottish thrones. After more than two decades of revolution, civil war, and rule by the commoner, Lord Protector Oliver Cromwell, English leaders sought a return to stability. The monarchy was restored. So too was the parliament and the English Church. Those who had been most active in the overthrow of the royal family fled the country or were executed. Independency in religion—the Congregationalist form that the Commonwealth favored—and in governance were rejected. For a royal family trying to avoid a repeat of the breakdown of order of the 1640s, the consolidation of authority was the watchword of the day.[10]

The Restoration regime sought to impose order in the colonial world as well. One of the ways was by establishing a continuous line of English authority from New England in the north, south and west to what had been New Netherland, the Chesapeake, and Carolina. England added the whole of the mid-Atlantic—New York, the Jerseys, and Pennsylvania—as well as Carolina, to its eastern North American possessions during the Restoration years. It worked toward consolidating colonial authority as well. The Restoration Parliament, continuing a process begun under the Commonwealth, enacted a series of Navigation Laws designed to organize colonial commerce to serve English interests. The government also took steps toward consolidating colonial governance, culminating in the 1686 "Dominion of New England," which essentially incorporated the territories of the New England and Middle colonies (other than Pennsylvania) together under a single government.

The key figure in those moves was James, Duke of York and of Albany, Lord High Admiral of England, and younger brother and heir to the king. James cut an imposing figure in the Restoration world, not least because of his uncompromising nature. Where his brother the king was somewhat passive in overseeing the consolidation of authority, James created the most authoritarian system of governance in the English colonial world. Where throughout his reign rumors spread that Charles had converted to Catholicism, James boldly confirmed his new affiliation in public in 1673.[11]

In multiple respects New Netherland was the perfect target. James's interests were extensive, and everywhere it seemed that the Dutch stood as rivals or opponents. James had been raised in France during the Civil War years and he sympathized with that nation—especially after his conversion to Catholicism—in their imperial rivalry with the Protestant Dutch. That was despite the fact that James's nephew, the Dutch protector or *Stadtholder*, William of Orange, would marry James's Protestant daughter Mary. Their interests clashed in Africa, where James was a major player in the Royal African Company. And the Dutch stood in the way of James's plans in North America as well. The conquest of New Netherland at the outset of the second Anglo-Dutch war allowed James to control several things at once. He attacked the commerce of his Dutch rivals. He obtained a territory from which he could rein in the presumptions of the neighboring New England colonists, whose Puritan leanings aligned them with the enemies of the regime; indeed, the New Englanders shielded two of the regicides—those who signed the death warrant for James's father—who fled there during the Restoration. The eventual suppression of New England's colonial charters and their placement under royal governance along with New York and New Jersey further reduced their autonomy. The conquest of New Netherland after the demise of New Sweden reduced the number of European powers engaged in eastern North America, north of Spanish Florida, to two: England and France. And, by creating a contiguous line of English territory along the coast from northern New England as far south as the Carolinas, James was in a position to reorganize and impose order on the whole.[12]

The Duke's charter covered a vast territory, from lands in northern New England and the many islands offshore south to Long Island, to what would become New York, New Jersey, and Delaware. The Duke had only a modest interest in promoting settlement there and instead gave away portions: disputed territory east of the Hudson to John Winthrop, Jr. on behalf of Connecticut, and New Jersey to John Lord Berkeley and Sir George Carteret, both allies of James and Restoration-era politicians. Later he would go along when two groups of Quaker proprietors, led by the prominent figures Robert Barclay and William Penn, took control of East and West Jersey. He accepted it as well when Penn asked for and received the large territory that would become Pennsylvania.

That the new colonies were all proprietary colonies was part of the effort for organization and order. The proprietors individually would have very different goals in mind, ranging from James's notion of hierarchical authority to Penn's vision of a Quaker refuge and holy experiment. Still, they were on the whole prominent men with an interest in establishing and maintaining order. That was of course nowhere more true than in New York. Alone among the English colonies, New York had no legislative assembly; the "Duke's Laws" provided only a governor's council in its stead. As Governor Nicolls remarked, New York's laws were "not contrived soe Democratically" as were those of other colonies.[13] When, after the English reconquest of New York in the third Anglo-Dutch war, settlers on eastern Long Island sought to retain an allegiance to Connecticut rather than New York, Governor Edmund Andros traveled east with a party of soldiers to impose obedience. They got the message.

The existence of New York proved centralizing in two other respects. One was in governance, with the gradual consolidation of colonies leading ultimately to a tightly ruled Dominion of New England under the authority of a military man, Edmund Andros, as governor. The other was diplomatic. In the midst of raging Indian wars with England's colonies to the north and to the south, Governor Andros established a set of working relationships with the Five Nations called the "Covenant Chain." In response to King Philip's War in New England, he persuaded his Mohawk allies to attack Philip's army from the rear and bring that conflict to an end. Similarly, with frontier conflicts including "Bacon's Rebellion" roiling the Virginia and Maryland frontiers, Andros negotiated peace between the Susquehannocks, who had been driven south from their Susquehanna Valley homeland into territories adjoining those colonies, and the Seneca, the westernmost nation of the Iroquois confederacy. Thus New York and the Five Nations functioned as central powers in the territory from western New England and the Hudson and Mohawk Valleys, south and west, to Pennsylvania and the Maryland backcountry.[14]

The covenant chain made the New York capital of Albany and the Central Fire of the Five Nations at Onondaga into the central locations for northeastern diplomacy. Constructed metaphorically, and owing as much to political forms practiced by the Five Nations as those of Europeans, the chain was essentially an agreement to accommodate conflicts by means short of war—through negotiations, reparations, and gifts. It was, like the Iroquois League itself, as much an agreement not to fight one another as a positive alliance. The result was that New York negotiated with the Five Nations on matters concerning other English colonies, while the Five Nations controlled the diplomacy of surrounding Indian nations. It was not an exclusive alliance. A series of defeats at the turn of the century forced the Iroquois to negotiate peace with the leaders of New France, but they negotiated another with the English at the same time. Thereafter they would attempt to use their intermediate status to act as the balance of power and play off one against the other, forcing favors from both sides.[15]

Peaceable Kingdom

The English entered into the mid-Atlantic through an act of war: the conquest of New Netherland. Still, the most often-noted aspect of Middle-Colony diplomacy was William Penn's policy of peace. The proprietor really did intend to deal fairly with his Indian neighbors and resolve disputes through negotiation rather than force, even if some of his own policies would, in the long run, unwittingly undermine those efforts. Nonetheless, for a long time Pennsylvania Indians idealized the name and the legacy of the proprietor—in part as a means of putting pressure on his far less peaceful or fair-minded successors. And for half a century after the founding of Pennsylvania, relations between Indians and settlers in that colony were less violent than those in almost any other.

That was not all the result of Penn's policies. Pennsylvania did not exist in a vacuum, and much that happened there was determined as much by events surrounding Penn's proprietary as within it. Penn's immediate Indian neighbors, the Leni Lenape, or Delawares, had a tenuous relationship with the powerful Five Nations. When Penn arrived, the Pennsylvania Indians were in no position to challenge him and instead eagerly sought an ally. For many years, moreover, the generally peaceful Pennsylvania environment owed a good deal to the *Pax Albania* that James's government had established in New York in the covenant chain the decade before.[16]

Penn's vision consisted of an orderly colony that would attract religious refugees of a spiritualist bent from across Protestant Europe, and he recruited actively not only in England but in Ireland and the European Continent. In drafting his plan for the colony, Penn sought to balance many threads that were influencing the colonies of the Restoration years: a constitutional form of government with a legislative assembly that would provide input for the settlers without (he hoped) taking ultimate authority away from the proprietor; the promise of prosperity for settlers and traders while leaving plenty of room for Penn himself to restore his shaky finances; peaceful relations with the local Indians while allowing for the expansionist ambitions that underlay the essentials of the Quaker community; and a spiritual liberty as great as that found anywhere, except perhaps in the neighboring Quaker colony of West Jersey, while hoping that the new and diverse colonists would not upset the liberties upon which their settlement depended. Reconciling those diverse threads proved a great challenge.

Part of the problem lay in Penn's plan for recruitment. While he invited settlement from spiritualist groups across Europe, the wide toleration he granted meant that non-Quakers from those same nations—from German-speaking lands, and Holland and Ireland—were also attracted by the promise of land and the prospect of being left alone. In the eighteenth century, Pennsylvania would become the principal focus of European migration to North America. Despite a Quaker movement that rivaled the "Great Migration" of Puritans to New England half a century before, it would not be long before Friends were outnumbered in the colony, and even in the Quaker city. Over time, many of those non-Quakers would prove destructive to Penn's experiment.

More immediately, problems came from the Quakers themselves. Quakers—members of the Society of Friends—were an assertive lot: the trouble they caused in England often owed less to any outright challenges to policy than their resistance to approved social norms. Those included showing respect to their social superiors—the reason Friends refused to remove their hats in the presence of men of higher rank—or following policies or laws that conflicted with Quaker conscience. Moreover, Quaker merchants were vested in the idea of bolstering their commercial opportunities, and Friends in general believed in the necessity of adequately supporting their expansive families in order to raise their children at home and keep them within the Quaker fold. Many thought the proprietor too demanding in his insistence upon collecting quitrents, and insufficiently rigorous in honoring his promises in the properties he distributed to First Purchasers and others. After trying unsuccessfully to get the Assembly to go along with his policies, Penn famously asked that his fellow Friends "be not so governmentish!"[17]

Revolution, Empire, and Consolidation

The era of the Restoration came to an abrupt end in 1688, when, at the invitation of a prominent faction of the English political nation worried both by James's Catholicism and his preference for arbitrary rule, William of Orange landed with an army and James fled to the Continent. The crowns then passed to the Protestant William and his wife Mary, James's daughter, in the supposedly bloodless "Glorious Revolution." It was bloodless only in England itself; Scotland and Ireland witnessed considerable violence, and so did England's colonies, especially New York. The revolt began in Boston against the Dominion of New England, as the Puritan leadership of that colony overthrew and imprisoned Governor Andros. In New York the aftermath was far more complicated. There the Lieutenant Governor Francis Nicholson was ousted by the militia led by the merchant Jacob Leisler, a German-speaking veteran of New Netherland, on behalf of William and the Protestant succession.[18]

Unlike the situation in Boston, Leisler confronted significant opposition, both from that part of the elite still loyal to James and others among the English-speaking population, who distrusted Leisler's seeming fanaticism as well as his Dutch connections. In fact the divisions the Revolution reflected overlapped those in the colony: an authoritarian regime appointed by James, with manifestations of pro-Catholic policies and arbitrary rule, was overthrown by a Protestant and largely Dutch movement of Revolution supporters led by veterans of New Netherland. The Leislerians captured New York City and for a time held sway in the province, but they never obtained the support of much of the English-speaking community even among committed Protestants. In the end Leisler was ousted and hanged, and a new government of English speakers, including former supporters of James, returned to office. The result was bitter conflict between the sides for many years.[19]

James's was not the only government that came under attack; the Revolution set off challenges to proprietary authority throughout the mid-Atlantic. James lost New York, along with his kingdom. William Penn was deprived of his colony on suspicion of Jacobitism—favoritism toward James (*Jacobus* in Latin) rather than the new ruling family—and did not regain it until 1694. In East Jersey as in New York, James had many supporters among the most prominent officials; the highest ranking of which, the earls of Perth and Melfort, Catholic members of James's inner circle, went into exile. The proprietors of both Jersey colonies faced so much popular resistance that in 1702 they willingly surrendered their proprietaries to the crown, with the hope of retaining the land. Delaware, the lower six counties of Pennsylvania, established its separation from the Pennsylvania government and legislature, although it continued to share a governor with that colony. Nonetheless, the Williamite government continued the effort at colonial consolidation, albeit in modified form.

The Revolution led to a major diplomatic realignment in Europe that carried over to North America. Where the Restoration monarchs had been raised in France and were sympathetic to that nation and to the Catholic Church, William's takeover put England and Scotland firmly in the Protestant camp on the side of France's rivals in the Netherlands. It also brought Britain into a succession of wars, beginning with the 1688 War of the League of Augsburg. Its colonies were drawn in as well, none more than New York, with its proximity to New France. Central to the American manifestation of that war was the Five Nations, who suffered defeat at the hands of France and, in 1701, agreed to a treaty with that nation and another with Britain at the same time, leaving them as a neutral power with the ability to add their weight to either side should that power impinge on their lands or their position. Still, the Albany/Onondaga axis would long influence war and diplomacy over a large region encompassing most of the mid-Atlantic and beyond.

Wars and Violence

The Revolution of 1688 further absorbed the Middle Colonies into the web of empire. While the new government was less authoritarian than those of the Stuarts, it continued its efforts toward the consolidation of the fiscal-military state in an age of imperial wars. The alliances changed, with Britain now fully aligned with the Netherlands against Catholic France and its aspirations for universal monarchy. New York, with its Dutch roots, its proximity to New France, and its Iroquois connections, moved closer to a central role in the conflicts.

Throughout the eighteenth century, the Five Nations—expanded to six after the addition of the Tuscarora in 1722—continued to play an important role in Middle Colony diplomacy. It was often not a benevolent role, as they used their relative strength to subordinate the interests of weaker neighbors such as the Lenape or Delaware Indians. One result was the infamous "Walking Purchase" of 1737, in which the Penn family, citing a dubious 1686 deed from the Delawares to William Penn, claimed rights to a large tract in eastern Pennsylvania as far as a man could walk in a day and a half. James Logan, on the Penn's behalf, then arranged for runners to cover a cleared path and laid claim to a vastly larger territory than could reasonably have been anticipated, and produced a fraudulent map as well. The Six Nations, involved in their own dealings with Logan and Pennsylvania, compelled the weaker nation to accept the loss. The Delawares dispersed, some to live among the Six Nations, others to western regions. There they would align with the French and join in the attacks on Pennsylvania settlers that began in the region after midcentury.[20]

In the end it is hard to see how Penn's policies could have succeeded. His creation of a colony based on tolerance and peace attracted vast numbers of migrants to Pennsylvania, and Penn's policies encouraged that diversity. The migrants were attracted as well by the promise of land, for themselves and for future generations—a point of particular concern to Quakers and those of other spiritualist religions, who sought ways to raise their families at home removed from the corruptions their children would otherwise encounter. Pennsylvania was an expansive colony. That rate of expansion probably precluded any possibility that local Indians could have remained undisturbed on their lands.[21]

In the middle of the eighteenth century, Pennsylvania went from being the most peaceable colony to probably the most violent. That was in part the result of the French wars and Indian reactions to the Walking Purchase and the other ways that settlement impinged on their territories and their ways of life. On the other side, settlers experiencing Indian raids during the wars and after banded together to attack the alleged perpetrators—or whomever they could conveniently reach. The hatred reached its zenith in 1763, when a group of Scots-Irish frontiersmen from around the town of Paxton launched an attack of their own, against the peaceful Conestoga Indians residing nearby. The Paxton boys raided the Contestoga lodgings at a time when most of the men were away, and slaughtered the women and children inside. That was as much directed against Quaker officials, who refused to provide an aggressive defense for the frontiers, as it was against the Conestoga themselves. The Paxton gang returned later, after the remaining Indians had been moved to the workhouse in Lancaster for their protection, and slaughtered the rest. Pennsylvania thus pioneered a new form of Indian-hating that would be extended beyond its bounds to other British American colonies.[22]

New York, by contrast, kept the peace far longer, as the now Six Nations remained the dominant force in western New York. In the years before the Seven Years' War, Middle-Colony residents led a movement to firm up or "polish" the covenant chain to secure Iroquois support against France. Part of that effort included an intercolonial (and interracial) conference at Albany in 1754, promoted very actively by men from the Middle Colonies, including Benjamin Franklin and such other figures as Archibald Kennedy and James Alexander. It was intended both to placate the Iroquois and unite the colonies in a loose union for defensive purposes. They were not wholly successful in their efforts: the intercolonial union was rejected both by Parliament and by the individual colonies, and the renewal of the Covenant Chain was only partially accomplished, having been neglected for too many years. But under the leadership of New York's Sir William Johnson in the position of superintendent of Indian affairs for the northern colonies, the Covenant grew brighter, with the Mohawk at least. Johnson, a native of Ireland and widower of a German migrant, raised children with his Mohawk common-law wife Molly Brant, sister of a leading chieftain, and kept a house always open to visits by his Mohawk neighbors.[23]

War ensued nonetheless. The Seven Years' War, a global conflagration, began in the western reaches of the mid-Atlantic, at the junction of three rivers in the area of what is now Pittsburgh in western Pennsylvania. The area at the time was claimed variously by Virginia, Connecticut, Pennsylvania, and New France, as well as competing native peoples. Because of their proximity to New France and their Indian allies, western Pennsylvania and the upper Hudson Valley in New York were major focal points of the war. The same rivers and valleys that facilitated communication and trade assisted the movement of armies and Native American attackers. The war saw the negotiation of a major treaty at Easton in Pennsylvania to neutralize Native American groups that had sided originally with the French. The conclusion of the war saw dissatisfaction on the part of Indian groups with the way the treaty was carried out, leading to Pontiac's Rebellion and to the multiple attacks that turned western Pennsylvania into one of the most insecure frontiers.[24]

Commerce and Culture

When they were not at war during the eighteenth century—and sometimes even when they were—the Middle Colonies were developing into the commercial and cultural hubs of British America as well. Merchant networks were extensive within and beyond the region; the colonies were inserting themselves into critical transatlantic cultural networks as well. The mid-Atlantic was becoming a focal point linking British America to places far beyond.

That was predictable from the outset. In or about the year 1661, a former New Englander named Samuel Maverick wrote to a member of the Duke of York's inner circle urging the project of ousting the Dutch from New Netherland. Already, Maverick anticipated a commercial future for the mid-Atlantic. The region had ample possibilities, in his view, and the combination of Continental and Atlantic connections was highly beneficial. The land itself was good, with harbors and navigable rivers that would help provide a market for what it produced. The territory was rich in beaver as well, and the Dutch had developed a profitable trade in skins. Especially important was that the region was "most Commodious for commerce from and wth all parts of the West Indies."[25] Thus even before the English conquest, Maverick envisioned a commercial mid-Atlantic revolving especially around the provisioning trade to the West Indies and the fur trade.

New Yorkers did not originate the region's trading patterns. Maverick was citing commerce already well established by the Dutch of New Netherland and the large group of European merchants the colony attracted. Their activities would not end with conquest. For the West India Company, New Netherland had always been more important as a trading colony than a colony of settlement, and Dutch merchants, with or without a colony, continued to be among the most active traders all along the Atlantic coast, long after their colony's surrender.

More significant than their conveyance of regional produce would be the establishment by Dutch merchants of an entrepôt trade centered in the region, connecting it with other ports in the British Atlantic. While the Duke's interests in the region were more about land and territory than those of the Dutch, the role of the sea was still quite conspicuous in his grant, which gave not only the mainland of what would become New York, but lands to the South (later the Delaware) River, and islands ranging from Manhattan and Long Islands to other islands as far north as what would become Maine.[26]

Within two decades of the English conquest, the trade of New York merchants would be surpassed by those of the newcomers to Philadelphia. The latter had the advantage, among other things, of a more productive hinterland, and a land policy in that colony more suited to establishing a multitude of single-family, grain-growing farms. Just as important was the attraction to that city of Quaker merchants, who—like the Dutch—were also among the more prolific Atlantic traders, working through an extended network of Friends in port cities in England, Ireland, North America, and the Caribbean. The West Indian trade was especially suitable for a grain-growing region such as the mid-Atlantic, which provided foodstuffs and other necessities for those islands' growing slave populations. Quakers from the beginning were a major presence in the West Indian market. Thus during the eighteenth century the Middle Colonies became an important hub of an Atlantic trading world extending from Britain and the European continent to Carolina and the Caribbean, with participation in the African slave trade as well.[27]

The extensiveness of those commercial networks extended outward from the mid-Atlantic cities and their surroundings and created new opportunities for diverse categories of traders. One of the problems confronted by West Indian planters was the desire to leave their plantations in the hands of overseers and retire to healthier climates. The mid-Atlantic was such a place, and prominent families moved to New York, New Jersey, Philadelphia, and Long Island. Some settled on islands, most near harbors, from which they could participate in provisioning their Caribbean holdings.

The commercial culture of the region also allowed for significant participation by women traders. Trading on their own account was a long tradition among Dutch women, who had legal rights to maintain property and maintain businesses that far exceeded those of most other women in Europe. Moreover, Quaker women claimed more assertive spiritual roles under their faith than many others, and some appear to have displayed assertiveness in other areas such as the economic sphere. They even showed a relative propensity toward unmarried life. Both Dutch and Quaker women spread their networks and their influence between the mid-Atlantic and other regions. Still, not all was easy for those traders, and less affluent women traders in particular faced distinctive risks that most of their male counterparts often did not in the underground economy of the cities.[28]

There is of course an irony in the Friends' presence in the West Indian and African trades. Quakers were among the very first in western societies to question the morality of slavery. Yet Quaker merchants brought to the West Indies clothing, foodstuffs, and other things to support their slave societies. Sometimes they brought slaves as well. That reflected a division among Quaker merchants. Some moved slowly toward articulating moral opposition to the trade as rooted in sinful practices such as luxury and violence; the greater number participated in a trade that was beneficial to their Atlantic commercial ambitions. But from the late seventeenth century—far earlier than almost anyone else—a small number of Quakers, mostly in Pennsylvania or New Jersey or Long Island, began to spread ideas about the wrongs of slavery.[29]

Questions about slavery were only one of the cultural trends that connected the settler inhabitants of the mid-Atlantic to others across the Atlantic world. Those included religion much more broadly. The Middle Colonies housed numerous churches and sects, and by the middle of the eighteenth century the region had become the principal North American headquarters of such churches or persuasions as the Presbyterians, Dutch and German Reformed Churches, German and Swedish Lutherans, Quakers, Moravians, Mennonites, and a variety of other spiritualist groups. By the 1760s it would house the most aggressive voices of transatlantic Anglicanism as well. The Middle Colonies would also emerge as a crucial hub in connecting colonial British America to Atlantic trends in philosophy, science, and other ideas we associate with the Enlightenment.

There is no better source for exploring the mid-Atlantic Enlightenment than the memoirs of Benjamin Franklin, which have come down to us as the *Autobiography*; indeed, owing to Franklin's wit and his eye for detail, it has, in some cases, too closely controlled our understanding. The memoirs tell the story of his rise from being a printer's apprentice to becoming a master of his trade, a civic leader in Philadelphia, a renowned scientist and inventor and, finally, political spokesperson, diplomat, and citizen of the world.[30]

Franklin's was, of course, only one life, and it cannot stand in for all the others. What is most useful about the *Autobiography* is the depiction of the abundant enlightened activities involving other citizens of the region, including not only prominent citizens but tradesmen and other middling persons like himself. Franklin's own life was that of the "projector," as described by one of his favorite writers, the Englishman Daniel Defoe.[31] He was an incredibly active promoter of an enormous range and variety of projects—print shops, hospitals, insurance companies, reading and literary societies, libraries, technological projects, and scientific pursuits to name only a few. Many of these, from the post office to the establishment of the American Philosophical Society, extended across colonial boundaries and put the mid-Atlantic at the center of American communications. So also did Franklin's project of establishing partnerships to seed new print shops within and beyond the Middle Colonies.

Many of his projects, such as the societies, libraries, and civic organizations, all suggest another aspect of Franklin's life as an "associator," one who participated in a variety of civic and voluntary associations, as described by Jessica Roney.[32] Here too he was joined by a wide group of other citizens from high to low. Their efforts turned the Philadelphia of Franklin's day into the widely acknowledged and leading Enlightenment city in North America.

There were of course other prominent intellectuals in the mid-Atlantic Enlightenment. Probably the most accomplished was James Logan, a Scottish Quaker who arrived in Pennsylvania in 1699 and served for decades as the principal agent first of William Penn and then of his heirs. Logan worked hard at Pennsylvania politics to protect the family's interests, even at the expense of the Delaware Indians with whom William Penn had tried to deal fairly. Logan was principal architect of the Walking Purchase. He was also a man of the Enlightenment, building what may have been the largest book collection in North America and pursuing interests in science and moral philosophy. Logan was patron to some of the more talented young tradesmen in their pursuit of enlightenment. He was also a key figure in welcoming other prominent men into the Enlightenment circle, such as Cadwallader Colden, another educated Scot and a physician who migrated first to Philadelphia and then to New York, under the patronage of still another Enlightened Scot, the governor Robert Hunter. Hunter and his successor, William Burnet, were also key figures in recruiting educated and Enlightened Scots to settle in the Middle Colonies.[33]

The Enlightenment was largely an urban affair, in the mid-Atlantic as elsewhere. It was also less visible in New York and its surroundings than in greater Philadelphia; in the former the Enlightenment was more closely identified with a group of prominent men, whereas a larger number of tradesmen were associated with the Enlightenment in the latter. In the Philadelphia region and the Jerseys it had important manifestations in several rural areas also, from eastern Pennsylvania to southern and central New Jersey. There one found subscription libraries, literary societies, and, finally, the College of New Jersey, a Presbyterian and largely evangelical institution, which also became probably the most important center of Enlightenment learning in early America. Especially after the appointment of the Scottish minister John Witherspoon to the presidency in 1768, its reach extended through the northern and Middle Colonies and as far south as the British Caribbean.[34]

The Middle Colony Enlightenment also included important roles for women. In and around the College of New Jersey a group of pious and evangelical women initiated their own writing circle, devoted both to the acquisition of knowledge and its use in the promotion of piety and virtue. The women kept up with the latest intellectual trends and awaited the day when men and women could participate together in thoughtful and beneficial discussions. Included in that group were Esther Burr, wife of then College president Aaron Burr and daughter of Jonathan Edwards, and Annis Boudinot, later Annis Boudinot Stockton. Their writings merged intense personal piety with the quest for Enlightenment, perhaps to a degree greater than anywhere else in early America. Their correspondences reached as far as Boston and Philadelphia. In the latter city Boudinot Stockton joined another writing circle out of the home of Elizabeth Graeme Fergusson, which incorporated prominent male visitors as well as a diverse group of reading and writing women.[35]

The involvement of pious persons within Enlightenment culture was another aspect of the mid-Atlantic Enlightenment, well represented in the lifelong friendship between Benjamin Franklin and the celebrated traveling evangelist George Whitefield. There were important practical elements to their friendship. Whitefield's writings were among the most popular publications of the day and were a tremendous boost to Franklin's publishing business; the latter's publication of Whitefield's journals was an important means of drawing crowds to hear the evangelist preach. Still, they shared an appreciation for the streak of benevolence they saw in each other and the impulse to do good for mankind, even if they did not agree on what was the most important work to pursue. While Whitefield's travels were truly transatlantic in scope, he began his major preaching tour in Philadelphia and returned to the city repeatedly, where he attracted some of his greatest crowds. The English evangelist's preaching helped inspire the building of a cosmopolitan meetinghouse open to preachers of all denominations.[36]

Legacies

In his *Letters from an American Farmer* first published in 1782, the French-born writer and New York resident J. Hector St. John de Crèvecoeur famously asked the question, "What is the American?" He offered the answer himself: the American was "this new man," "melted" together out of all nations—or at least all of the nations of Europe—who, leaving behind his "ancient prejudices and manners," forms a new race. His principal representative, fittingly enough, was the farmer in Pennsylvania,[37] who exemplified that character even more than did Crèvecoeur himself in the less cosmopolitan rural New York. By the eve of the American Revolution, Europeans saw no better representative of the American than the printer, inventor, diplomat, and deliberately rustic self-made man in Benjamin Franklin.

Franklin, Crèvecoeur, and the characters the latter created all broadly represented migrants to the region. The history of migration into, from, and through the mid-Atlantic of Indians, Europeans, and Africans, was an important feature that tied many aspects together and to things outside. In the eighteenth century the Middle Colonies, and Pennsylvania in particular, functioned as the migration capital of British America for European settlers, attracting migrants from varied places and funneling them into the whole of the backcountry, from northern New England south to Georgia and Carolina, and beyond. It became the focal point as well of territorial conflicts among British, French, and Native American groups. The scope of that issue extended to the greater mid-Atlantic. In the early days migration to Pennsylvania outpaced that to other places, with liberty and property underwritten by arrangements directed largely from New York. Toward midcentury, as Pennsylvania descended into conflicts and frontier warfare, migration to the relatively underpopulated New York began to grow. The Middle Colonies were central to the process through which Penn's initial plans for peace were permanently undermined.[38]

Notes

1 Michael Zuckerman, ed., *Friends and Neighbors: Group Life in America's First Plural Society* (Philadelphia: Temple University Press, 1982), 3–25; but note also Zuckerman's penetrating discussion of "Regionalism" in Daniel Vickers, ed., *A Companion to Colonial America* (Oxford: Blackwell Publishing, 2003), 311–333.
2 Works that question the concept of the "Middle Colonies" include Robert J. Gough, "The Myth of the 'Middle Colonies': An Analysis of Regionalization in Early America," *Pennsylvania Magazine of History and Biography* 107 (1983): 393–419; and Daniel K Richter, "Mid-Atlantic Colonies. R.I.P.," *Pennsylvania History: A Journal of Mid-Atlantic Studies* 82 (2015): 260–281. See also Wayne Bodle, "The Fabricated Region: On the Insufficiency of 'Colonies' for Understanding American Colonial History," *Early American Studies* 1 (2003): 1–27.
3 Alan Taylor, *Colonial America: A Very Short Introduction* (Oxford: Oxford University Press, 2013); see also Taylor's much longer *American Colonies: The Settling of North America* (New York: Penguin, 2001). The modern emphasis on regionalism may be traced to Jack P. Greene's *Pursuits of Happiness: The Social Development of Early Modern British Colonies and the Formation of American Culture* (Chapel Hill: University of North Carolina Press, 1988). That much of the criticism of David Hackett Fischer's regional approach in *Albion's Seed: Four British Folkways in America* (New York: Oxford University Press, 1989) was itself offered from regional perspectives suggests the hold that that approach attained.
4 Thomas Arne Midtrod, *The Memory of All Ancient Customs: Native American Diplomacy in the Colonial Hudson Valley* (Ithaca, NY: Cornell University Press, 2012); Donna Merwick, *The Shame and the Sorrow: Dutch-Amerindian Encounters in New Netherland* (Philadelphia: University of Pennsylvania Press, 2006); Daniel K. Richter, *The Ordeal of the Longhouse: The Peoples of the Iroquois League in the Era of European Colonization* (Chapel Hill: University of North Carolina Press, 1992).
5 The once-neglected subjects among early American historians of New Netherland, the Dutch West India Company, and the Dutch commercial empire have now sparked expansive literatures. A good starting point is Jaap Jacobs, *The Colony of New Netherland: A Dutch Settlement in Seventeenth-Century America* (Ithaca, NY: Cornell University Press, 2009). A broader view can be gleaned from Christian J. Koot, *Empire at the Periphery: British Colonists, Anglo-Dutch Trade, and the Development of the British Atlantic, 1621–1713* (New York: New York University Press, 2011).
6 Jacobs, *Colony of New Netherland*, Ch. 2 summarizes a now extensive literature on New Netherland diversity. On Africans, see Cynthia J. Van Zandt, *Brothers Among Nations: The Pursuit of Intercultural Alliances in Early America 1580–1660* (New York: Oxford University Press, 2008), Ch. 6.

7 The principal though arguably exaggerated account of the western nations ravaged by the Five Nations is Richard White, *The Middle Ground: Indians, Empires, and Republics in the Great Lakes Region, 1650–1815* (New York: Cambridge University Press, 1991), Ch. 1.
8 Mark Meuwese, "The Dutch Connection: New Netherland, the Pequots, and the Puritans in Southern New England, 1620–1638," *The Worlds of Lion Gardiner, ca. 1599–1663: Crossings and Boundaries*, a special issue of *Early American Studies*, 9 (2011), eds. Ned Landsman and Andrew Newman, 295–323.
9 Katherine Grandjean, "The Long Wake of the Pequot War," *Early American Studies*, 9 (2011), 379–411.
10 Tim Harris, *Restoration: Charles II and his Kingdoms* (London: Penguin Books, 2006).
11 Robert C. Ritchie, *The Duke's Province: A Study of New York Politics and Society, 1664–1691* (Chapel Hill: University of North Carolina Press, 1977).
12 A recent look at James' policies, emphasizing a distinct political economy, is Steven Pincus, *1688: The First Modern Revolution* (New Haven: Yale University Press, 2009).
13 Quoted in Ritchie, *Duke's Province*, 34.
14 Stephen Saunders Webb, *1676: The End of American Independence* (New York: Alfred A. Knopf, 1984); *Beyond the Covenant Chain: the Iroquois and their Neighbors in Indian North America*, ed. Daniel K. Richter and James H. Merrell (Syracuse: Syracuse University Press, 1987).
15 Richard Aquila, *The Iroquois Restoration: Iroquois Diplomacy on the Colonial Frontier, 1701–1754* (Detroit: Wayne State University Press, 1983).
16 Jean R. Soderlund, *Lenape Country: Delaware Valley Society Before William Penn* (Philadelphia: University of Pennsylvania Press, 2015) emphasizes the Lenape role in creating a framework for peace.
17 William Penn to Council, August 19, 1685, quoted in Gary B. Nash, *Quakers and Politics, 1681–1726* (Princeton: Princeton University Press, 1968), 49. John Smolenski, *Friends and Strangers: The Making of Creole Culture in Colonial Pennsylvania* (Philadelphia: University of Pennsylvania Press, 2010) looks at opposition to proprietary authority, as does Jessica Choppin Roney, *Governed By a Spirit of Opposition: The Origins of American Political Practice in Colonial Philadelphia* (Baltimore: Johns Hopkins University Press, 2014).
18 Owen Stanwood, *The Empire Reformed: English America in the Age of the Glorious Revolution* (Philadelphia: University of Pennsylvania Press, 2011).
19 David Voorhees, The 'Fervent Zeale' of Jacob Leisler," *William and Mary Quarterly*, 3rd series, 51 (1994): 447–472.
20 Andrew Newman, *On Records: Delaware Indians, Colonists, and the Media of History and Memory* (Lincoln: University of Nebraska Press, 2012), and see the sources cited in note 22, below.
21 Barry Levy, *Quakers and the American Family: British Settlement in the Delaware Valley* (New York: Oxford University Press, 1992).
22 On Indian-hating, see Peter Silver, *Our Savage Neighbors: How Indian War Transformed Early America* (New York: W.W. Norton, 2008) and Kevin Kenny, *Peaceable Kingdom Lost: The Paxton Boys and the Destruction of William Penn's Holy Experiment* (New York: Oxford University Press, 2011).
23 Timothy J. Shannon, *Indians and Colonists at the Crossroads of Empire: The Albany Congress of 1754* (Ithaca, NY: Cornell University Press, 2002). It was there that Franklin proposed his famous "Albany plan of union," and credits Alexander and Kennedy for their role. See Leonard W. Labaree, et al., eds., *The Autobiography of Benjamin Franklin*, 2nd edition (New Haven: Yale University Press, 2003; first published 1964), 210. Kennedy was the most active promoter of the conference and the Iroquois alliance.
24 Colin Calloway, *The Scratch of a Pen: 1763 and the Transformation of North America* (New York: Oxford University Press, 2006); Fred Anderson, *The War That Made America: A Short History of the French and Indian War* (New York: Penguin Books, 2005).
25 Samuel Maverick to the Earl of Clarendon, *New York State Historical Society Collections* (New York, New York Historical Society, 1811), Vol. 2 (1869), 1–14, 19–22.
26 A copy of the Duke's charter can be accessed at https://en.wikisource.org/wiki/Grant_to_the_Duke_of_York_1664 (Accessed October 17, 2015).
27 On Quakers and Atlantic trading see most recently Jordan Landes, *London Quakers in the Trans-Atlantic World: The Creation of an Early Modern Community* (Houndmills, Basingstoke: Palgrave Macmillan, 2015).
28 Annette M. Cramer van den Bogaart, "The Life of Teuntje Straatmans: A Dutch Woman's Travels in the Seventeenth Century Atlantic World," *Long Island Historical Journal* 15 (2003): 35–53; "Women in the Early Modern Dutch Atlantic World," (Ph.D. dissertation, Stony Brook University, 2013) attempts to sort out the literature on Dutch women. Joan M. Jensen, *Loosening the Bonds: Mid-Atlantic Farm Women, 1750–1850* (New Haven: Yale University Press, 1986) was an early attempt to address the roles of Quaker women; see also Karin Wulf, *Not All Wives: Women of Colonial Philadelphia* (Ithaca, NY: Cornell

University Press, 2000); Serena R. Zabin: *Dangerous Economies: Status and Commerce in Imperial New York* (Philadelphia: University of Pennsylvania Press, 2009).
29 Jean R. Soderlund, *Quakers and Slavery: A Divided Spirit* (Princeton: Princeton University Press, 1985).
30 Labaree, et al., *Autobiography of Benjamin Franklin* New Haven: Yale University Press, 2003; first published 1964
31 Daniel Defoe, *An Essay on Projects* (London: R.R. for Tho Cockerill, 1697).
32 Roney, *Governed By a Spirit of Opposition*.
33 On Logan, see my "James Logan and the Atlantic Enlightenment," Stenton website, http://stenton.org/index.php/history-collections-and-interpretation/the-interpretative-plan/reports/atlantic-enlightenment.(Accessed October 15, 2015). See also John M. Dixon, *The Enlightenment of Cadwallader Colden: Empire, Science, and Intellectual Culture in British New York* (Ithaca, NY: Cornell University Press, 2016 forthcoming) and Mary Lou Lustig, *Robert Hunter 1666–1743: New York's Augustan Statesman* (Syracuse: Syracuse University Press, 1983).
34 Ned C. Landsman, "The American Enlightenment," *Converging Worlds: Communities and Cultures in Colonial America*, ed. Louise A. Breen (New York: Routledge, 2012), 496–523. On New York, see Sara S. Gronim, *Everyday Nature: Knowledge of the Natural World in Colonial New York* (New Brunswick, NJ: Rutgers University Press, 2007); and see Dixon, *Enlightenment of Cadwallader Colden*. On South Jersey see John Fea, *The Way of Improvement Leads Home: Philip Vickers Fithian and the Rural Enlightenment in Early America* (Philadelphia: University of Pennsylvania Press, 2008); on Witherspoon, Gideon Mailer, *John Witherspoon's American Revolution*: : Enlightenment and Religion from the Creation of Britain to the Founding of the United States (Chapel Hill: University of North Carolina Press, 2017).
35 *Milcah Martha Moore's Book: A Commonplace Book From Revolutionary America*, ed. Catherine La Courreye Blecki and Karin A. Wulf (University Park: Penn State University Press, 1997); Susan M. Stabile, *Memory's Daughters: The Material Culture of Remembrance in Eighteenth-Century America* (Ithaca, NY: Cornell University Press, 2004); Sarah Fatherly, *Gentlewomen and Learned Ladies: Women and Elite Formation in Eighteenth-Century Philadelphia* (Bethlehem: Lehigh University Press, 2008).
36 Whitefield's travels are chronicled in his published journals; there is a collected edition published as *George Whitefield's Journals* (London: Banner of Truth Trust, 1960). See also Frank Lambert, *"Pedlar in Divinity": George Whitefield and the Transatlantic Revivals, 1737–1770* (Princeton: Princeton University Press, 1994), Ch. 3.
37 On the tension in Crevecoeur's writing between assimilation and a multicultural stance, see Ned C. Landsman, "Pluralism, Protestantism, and Prosperity: Crevecoeur's American Farmer and the Origins of American Pluralism," *Beyond Pluralism: The Conception of Groups and Group Identities in America*, eds. Wendy F. Katkin, Ned Landsman, and Andrea Tyree (Champagne Urbana: University of Illinois Press, 1998), 105–24.

References

Anderson, Fred. *The War That Made America: A Short History of the French and Indian War* (New York: Penguin Books, 2005).
Aquila, Richard. *The Iroquois Restoration: Iroquois Diplomacy on the Colonial Frontier, 1701–1754* (Detroit: Wayne State University Press, 1983).
Bodle, Wayne. "The Fabricated Region: On the Insufficiency of 'Colonies' for Understanding American Colonial History," *Early American Studies* 1 (2003): 1–27.
Calloway, Colin. *The Scratch of a Pen: 1763 and the Transformation of North America* (New York: Oxford University Press, 2006).
Dixon, John M. *The Enlightenment of Cadwallader Colden: Empire, Science, and Intellectual Culture in British New York* (Ithaca, NY: Cornell University Press, 2016 forthcoming).
Fatherly, Sarah. *Gentlewomen and Learned Ladies: Women and Elite Formation in Eighteenth-Century Philadelphia* (Bethlehem: Lehigh University Press, 2008).
Fea, John. *The Way of Improvement Leads Home: Philip Vickers Fithian and the Rural Enlightenment in Early America* (Philadelphia: University of Pennsylvania Press, 2008).
Fischer, David Hackett. *Albion's Seed: Four British Folkways in America* (New York: Oxford University Press, 1989).
Gough, Robert J. "The Myth of the 'Middle Colonies': An Analysis of Regionalization in Early America," *Pennsylvania Magazine of History and Biography* 107 (1983): 393–419.

Grandjean, Katherine. "The Long Wake of the Pequot War," *The Worlds of Lion Gardiner, ca. 1599–1663: Crossings and Boundaries*, a special issue of *Early American Studies*, 9 (2011), eds. Ned Landsman and Andrew Newman, 379–411.

Greene, Jack P. *Pursuits of Happiness: The Social Development of Early Modern British Colonies and the Formation of American Culture* (Chapel Hill: University of North Carolina Press, 1988).

Gronim, Sara S. *Everyday Nature: Knowledge of the Natural World in Colonial New York* (New Brunswick, N.J.: Rutgers University Press, 2007).

Harris, Tim. *Restoration: Charles II and his Kingdoms* (London: Penguin Books, 2006).

Jacobs, Jaap. *The Colony of New Netherland: A Dutch Settlement in Seventeenth-Century America* (Ithaca, N.Y.: Cornell University Press, 2009).

Jensen, Joan M. *Loosening the Bonds: Mid-Atlantic Farm Women, 1750–1850* (New Haven: Yale University Press, 1986).

Kenny, Kevin. *Peaceable Kingdom Lost: The Paxton Boys and the Destruction of William Penn's Holy Experiment* (New York: Oxford University Press, 2011).

Koot, Christian J. *Empire at the Periphery: British Colonists, Anglo-Dutch Trade, and the Development of the British Atlantic, 1621–1713* (New York: New York University Press, 2011).

La Courreye Blecki, Catherine and Karin A. Wulf, eds. *Milcah Martha Moore's Book: A Commonplace Book From Revolutionary America*, ed. Catherine La Courreye Blecki and Karin A. Wulf (University Park: Penn State University Press, 1997).

Lambert, Frank. *"Pedlar in Divinity": George Whitefield and the Transatlantic Revivals, 1737–1770* (Princeton: Princeton University Press, 1994).

Landes, Jordan. *London Quakers in the Trans-Atlantic World: The Creation of an Early Modern Community* (Houndmills, Basingstoke: Palgrave Macmillan, 2015).

Landsman, Ned C. "Pluralism, Protestantism, and Prosperity: Crevecoeur's American Farmer and the Origins of American Pluralism," *Beyond Pluralism: The Conception of Groups and Group Identities in America*, eds. Wendy F. Katkin, Ned Landsman, and Andrea Tyree (Champagne Urbana: University of Illinois Press, 1998), 105–24.

Landsman, Ned C. "James Logan and the Atlantic Enlightenment," Available online at http://stenton.org/index.php/history-collections-and-interpretation/the-interprative-plan/reports/atlantic-enlightenment (Accessed October 15, 2015).

Landsman, Ned C. "The American Enlightenment," *Converging Worlds: Communities and Cultures in Colonial America*, ed. Louise A. Breen (New York: Routledge, 2012), 496–523.

Levy, Barry. *Quakers and the American Family: British Settlement in the Delaware Valley* (New York: Oxford University Press, 1992).

Lustig, Mary Lou. *Robert Hunter 1666–1743: New York's Augustan Statesman* (Syracuse: Syracuse University Press, 1983).

Mailer, Gideon. *Kirk to Congress: John Witherspoon's American Revolution* (Chapel Hill: University of North Carolina Press, forthcoming).

Maverick Samuel to the Earl of Clarendon, *New York State Historical Society Collections* (New York, New York Historical Society, 1811), Vol. 2 (1869), 1–14, 19–22.

Merwick, Donna. *The Shame and the Sorrow: Dutch-Amerindian Encounters in New Netherland* (Philadelphia: University of Pennsylvania Press, 2006).

Meuwese, Mark. "The Dutch Connection: New Netherland, the Pequots, and the Puritans in Southern New England, 1620–1638," *The Worlds of Lion Gardiner, ca. 1599–1663: Crossings and Boundaries*, a special issue of *Early American Studies*, 9 (2011), ed. Ned Landsman and Andrew Newman, 295–323.

Midtrod, Thomas Arne. *The Memory of All Ancient Customs: Native American Diplomacy in the Colonial Hudson Valley* (Ithaca, NY: Cornell University Press, 2012).

Nash, Gary B. *Quakers and Politics, 1681–1726* (Princeton: Princeton University Press, 1968).

Newman, Andrew. *On Records: Delaware Indians, Colonists, and the Media of History and Memory* (Lincoln: University of Nebraska Press, 2012).

Pincus, Steven. *1688: The First Modern Revolution* (New Haven: Yale University Press, 2009).

Richter, Daniel K. and James H. Merrell, ed. *Beyond the Covenant Chain: the Iroquois and their Neighbors in Indian North America* (Syracuse: Syracuse University Press, 1987).

Richter, Daniel K. *The Ordeal of the Longhouse: The Peoples of the Iroquois League in the Era of European Colonization* (Chapel Hill: University of North Carolina Press, 1992).

Richter, Daniel K. "Mid-Atlantic Colonies. R.I.P.," *Pennsylvania History: A Journal of Mid-Atlantic Studies* 82 (2015): 260–281.

Ritchie, Robert C. *The Duke's Province: A Study of New York Politics and Society, 1664–1691* (Chapel Hill: University of North Carolina Press, 1977).

Roney, Jessica Choppin. *Governed By a Spirit of Opposition: The Origins of American Political Practice in Colonial Philadelphia* (Baltimore: Johns Hopkins University Press, 2014).

Shannon, Timothy J. *Indians and Colonists at the Crossroads of Empire: The Albany Congress of 1754* (Ithaca, NY: Cornell University Press, 2002).

Silver, Peter. *Our Savage Neighbors: How Indian War Transformed Early America* (New York: W.W. Norton, 2008).

Smolenski, John. *Friends and Strangers: The Making of Creole Culture in Colonial Pennsylvania* (Philadelphia: University of Pennsylvania Press, 2010).

Soderlund, Jean R. *Lenape Country: Delaware Valley Society Before William Penn* (Philadelphia: University of Pennsylvania Press, 2015).

Soderlund, Jean R. *Quakers and Slavery: A Divided Spirit* (Princeton: Princeton University Press, 1985).

Stabile, Susan M. *Memory's Daughters: The Material Culture of Remembrance in Eighteenth-Century America* (Ithaca, NY: Cornell University Press, 2004).

Stanwood, Owen. *The Empire Reformed: English America in the Age of the Glorious Revolution* (Philadelphia: University of Pennsylvania Press, 2011).

Taylor, Alan. *American Colonies: The Settling of North America* (New York: Penguin, 2001).

Taylor, Alan. *Colonial America: A Very Short Introduction* (Oxford: Oxford University Press, 2013).

van den Bogaart, Annette M. Cramer. "The Life of Teuntje Straatmans: A Dutch Woman's Travels in the Seventeenth Century Atlantic World," *Long Island Historical Journal* 15 (2003): 35–53.

van den Bogaart, Annette M. Cramer. "Women in the Early Modern Dutch Atlantic World," (Ph.D. dissertation, Stony Brook University, 2013).

Van Zandt, Cynthia J. *Brothers Among Nations: The Pursuit of Intercultural Alliances in Early America 1580–1660* (New York: Oxford University Press, 2008).

Voorhees, David. "The 'Fervent Zeale' of Jacob Leisler," *William and Mary Quarterly*, 3rd series, 51 (1994): 447–472.

Webb, Stephen Saunders. *1676: The End of American Independence* (New York: Alfred A. Knopf, 1984).

White, Richard. *The Middle Ground: Indians, Empires, and Republics in the Great Lakes Region, 1650–1815* (New York: Cambridge University Press, 1991).

Wulf, Karin. *Not All Wives: Women of Colonial Philadelphia* (Ithaca, NY: Cornell University Press, 2000).

Zabin, Serena R. *Dangerous Economies: Status and Commerce in Imperial New York* (Philadelphia: University of Pennsylvania Press, 2009).

Zuckerman, Michael ed. *Friends and Neighbors: Group Life in America's First Plural Society* (Philadelphia: Temple University Press, 1982), 3–25.

Zuckerman, Michael. "Regionalism," *A Companion to Colonial America*, ed. Daniel Vickers (Oxford: Blackwell Publishing, 2003), 311–333.

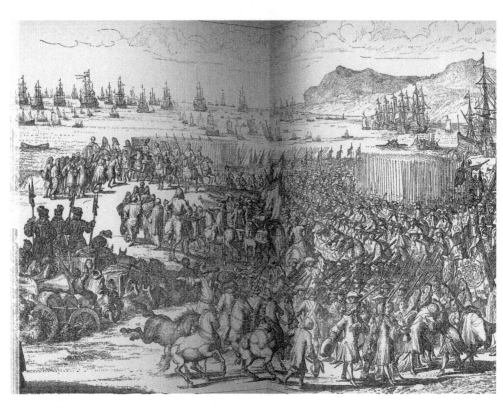

10.1 Glorious Revolution.
Arrival of William III of Orange in England, November 15, 16, 1688.

10
HIS OWN, THEIR OWN
Settler Colonialism, Native Peoples, and Imperial Balances of Power in Eastern North America, 1660–1715

Daniel K. Richter

Contested claims to ownership—of land, of resources, of sovereignty—were central to the world of colonial North America. A growing body of scholarship theorizes these contests in terms of "settler colonialism," which, as its leading theorist Patrick Wolfe bluntly explains, was and is "premised on the elimination of native societies." According to Wolfe, "territorial expropriation was foundational" to settler colonial regimes, in which "the key concept" was "private property." Thus Euro-Americans set out on what another scholar calls "a mission to take command over colonial space, a process that entailed demarcation and control, boundaries, maps, surveys, treaties, seizures, and the commodification of the land."[1] But words like "command" and "control" hardly describe the landscapes of colonial North America in the late seventeenth century, which historians have come to describe as "zones of war, chaos, and brutality," where multiple sovereignties and legal regimes jostled for power.[2] Native and European peoples on both sides of the Atlantic were well aware of the problem of ownership of the disordered continent. Some hints about the complicated ways they understood those problems, and about the limitations of settler colonialism as an explanatory framework for the period, emerge from three scenes in the year 1660.

The first scene occurred on May 25 of that year, when "*Charles Stuart*, the Son of the late King," landed at the English port of Dover, after nine years of exile. During that time, civil wars and rule first by Parliament and then by the deceased Protector Oliver Cromwell had convinced many elite English that "no Government can be so beneficial to this Nation, as to restore it to its ancient Monarchical Government, and to establish the Son of the Old King in his Royal Dignities and Prerogatives." In the same vein, one of many sermons preached to celebrate the king's return asked whether it were "not a favour to the people, to have firm Peace setled in the State upon true Foundations" and to allow "every man to sit under his own Vine, and enjoy his own as well as the King enjoys his own."[3] At home in the metropole, and not just in the colonies, a "key concept" was "private property."

The second scene occurred a little less than three weeks after Charles landed at Dover and a little more than 3,300 miles to the west in New England. It involved another transition from a father to a son concerned about preserving his and his people's "own." Wamsutta, sachem of the Pokanoket Wampanoags and successor to Massasoit, who had forged a mutually beneficial alliance with the Plymouth colony, appeared before the English outpost's leaders. As he and others of his people had done several times during the past decade, Wamsutta complained that swine belonging to the Wampanoags' neighbors of the English town of Rehoboth were destroying Indian crops. After receiving half-hearted assurances of redress and a gift of 12 pounds of gunpowder (along with a stern reminder that it *was* a gift, not a forbidden sale), Wamsutta asked "that the Court would confer an English name upon him." The magistrates "therfore ordered, that for the future hee shalbee called by the name of Allexander Pokanokett," and similarly dubbed his brother and potential successor "Phillip."[4] Whatever was going on here, it was nothing so simple as "the elimination of native societies."

While King Alexander and King Philip puzzled the meanings of their new names, a third scene played out a little over 400 miles to the north in Quebec City, as the Jesuit priest Jérôme Lalemant put the finishing touches on the manuscript of what would soon be published in Paris as the latest installment of *The Jesuit Relations*. Lalemant too felt his own to be under threat, and with it the *Relations*' inspiring narrative of bringing the Roman Catholic version of the true faith to Native people. "The warfare of the Iroquois thwarts all our pleasures, and is the sole affliction of new France, which is in danger of becoming utterly devastated," he wrote. These misfortunes began "when the Dutch took possession of these regions and conceived a fondness for the beavers of the natives, some 30 years ago; and in order to secure them in greater number they furnished those people with firearms." This "rendered them formidable everywhere, and victorious over all the Nations with whom they have been at war."[5] Lalemant, too, longed for a king to intervene and allow him to sit under his vine and enjoy his own, but it would appear to be the Haudenosaunee, not Euro-Americans, who were on "a mission to take command over colonial space."

In 1660, when King Charles recovered his throne, Kings Alexander and Philip received their names, and Père Jérôme pondered his fate, nowhere in eastern North America did people sit securely and enjoy their own, and nowhere could settler colonists or anyone else claim hegemony. After more than a generation of intense interaction among Native people and Europeans, no power—not the supposedly invincible Iroquois and certainly not any Atlantic empire or outpost of European colonists—dominated, much less exerted much control, over the landscape and the direction of affairs. In various locales, Wampanoags and English, Wendats and French, Iroquois and Dutch made political arrangements with each other, sometimes as superiors and inferiors, sometimes as equals, more often as wary contenders for dominance. The English, French, and Dutch colonies were controlled by private corporate bodies, not by anything that could reasonably be called centralized Atlantic empires. After 1660, the restored Charles II and his French counterpart Louis XIV tried to make the outposts founded by their alleged subjects "their own," by elbowing the Dutch out of the way and attempting to manage over the trade and diplomacy of the colonies. Instead of introducing stability, these efforts to create centralized imperial regimes only exacerbated the violence of which Lalemant complained.

Nonetheless, haltingly, painfully, by the early eighteenth century a makeshift system of rival French and English (and Spanish) imperial frameworks emerged to structure relations among the continent's varied European and Native peoples. Within those frameworks, Native allies of the Europeans often held the balance of power and could wield that power to their own advantage. Yet the same metropolitan imperial structures that allowed some Native peoples to maintain their potency and place also allowed English agricultural populations to expand relentlessly and begin to envision clearly an order in which Indians would have no place at all. This vision emerged in a context of multiple Native American and European imperial balances of power that current theorizations of settler colonialism do not adequately explain.

* * *

As historian Fred Hoxie only somewhat unfairly observes, "settler colonialism is a term that scholars often cite but rarely define." Yet most would agree that "settler colonies were not primarily established to extract surplus value from indigenous labour." Instead these formations were "premised on displacing indigenes from (or replacing them on) the land." By these lights, "settler colonialism is routinely and rightly distinguished from imperial expansion undertaken for military advantage or trade." Imperialists dealt "as little as possible with land seizure or internal governance, seeking instead to find and work through reliable indigenous partners." Settler colonialism, by contrast, recognized no such partners, because "settlers came not to exploit the indigenous population for economic gain, but rather to remove them from colonial space."[6] Not to put too fine a point on it, then, imperial colonialism depends on the existence of an indigenous population but settler colonialism depends on its extinction. That extinction can take many forms, from outright genocide to such far more common strategies as those involving education, missionization, or cultural assimilation. Indeed, theorist Lorenzo Veracini identifies 26 such strategies, listed alphabetically from "(A) Necropolitical transfer" to "(Z) Transfer by indigenous/national 'reconciliation.'" Settler colonial theory thus often assumes a totalizing quality evoked by Wolfe's adage that "invasion is a structure not an event."[7]

As a structure—or, as Veracini puts it, a "situation"—settler colonialism is curiously ahistorical even as it tells itself a story of historical progress in which settlers tame a wilderness. Although settlers see themselves as "*founders* of political orders," there is no identifiable historical starting point to their situation, because "they carry their sovereignty and lifestyles with them" when they migrate. "As they transform the land into their image, they settle another place without really moving," construing "their very movement forward as a 'return' to [...] an Edenic condition." By the same token, should they ever *really* "settle" the land by entirely erasing the indigenous presence, they would cease to be settlers. Thus there can be no imagined endpoint; "no matter how much it tries, the settler colonial situation cannot ultimately supersede itself." Nor can settler colonial discourse admit any room for Native historical actors in its atemporal history. As scholar Jodi A. Byrd notes, indigenous peoples "serve primarily as signposts and grave markers along the roads of empire," rather than determiners of historical events. They "are located outside temporality and presence, even in the face of very present and ongoing colonization of indigenous lands, resources, and lives."[8] This emphasis on the intractability of settler colonialism is entirely understandable, because, like Byrd, the vast majority of scholars writing about the topic sit within poststructural, postcolonial, and indigenous studies disciplinary frameworks focused on the twenty-first-century political struggles against regimes that steadfastly deny that they still operate as settler colonizers. By these lights, the particular historical origins of specific colonial structures inspire comparatively little interest. Indeed, scholarly efforts to stress Native agency only become reinscriptions of settler colonial discourse. "The problem is not the recurrent complaint that settler-colonial critique fails to write in Native agency, the notion that it is up to settlers to inscribe Native agency being a contradiction in terms," Wolfe proclaims. "What needs to be written in is not the agency of the colonized but the total context of inscription."[9]

These tendencies of settler colonial studies do not easily survive travel across the disciplinary divide to history, with its predilection for studying individual agency in specific contexts of change over time. "Just when historians were finally attending to the singular experiences and perspectives of some of history's most silenced actors ..." historian Margaret D. Jacobs asks, "might not we risk neglecting the lived experience of historical actors if we subsume their experiences too deeply under the weight of these larger comparative colonial constructs?"[10] The problems multiply with chronological distance from the present. To the extent that settler colonialism is rooted in postcolonial theory, the prepostcolonial, and perhaps even *precolonial* flux of late seventeenth-century North America makes for an uneasy fit, while at the same time raising intriguing questions about how particular settler-colonial structures come into being in realms other than those contained in the imaginary of migrants carrying their sovereignty with them. Historian Lisa Ford thus reminds us that "early colonial North America [. . .] was not a zone of conquest or even of large-scale settlement." It "began and remained a field of cooperation, inter-imperial competition, and increasingly, gradual dispossession." Only after the United States became independent, did dispossession "come to rely on sweeping legal claims about the absence of indigenous rights," because only then was a settler regime able to assert—and indeed define new forms of—sovereignty based on superior assertions of title to land.[11]

As Wolfe insists, "land is settler colonialism's irreducible essence in ways that go well beyond real estate," and "its seizure is not merely a change of ownership but a genesis, the onset of a whole new way of being—for both parties." Thus "setters are not born. They are made in the dispossessing,"[12] Or, as supporters of Charles II might have put it, in the possessing of their "own." Dispossessing and possessing might seem a simple issue of winners and losers in a zone of contestation; as Wolfe declares, "settler colonialism is premised on a zero-sum logic whereby settler societies, for all their internal complexities, uniformly require the elimination of Native alternatives." Nonetheless, a central assumption of settler colonial theory suggests otherwise. As historian John Mack Faragher points out, "in contrast to the binary concept of the frontier, focusing on relationships between indigenes and invaders, settler colonialism posits a ternary model of relations among metropolitan elites, colonial settlers, and aboriginal peoples."[13] The fraught relationship between settlers and metropolitan elites in the postcolonial United States too often gets lost in the settler colonial literature.[14] Yet how much more complicated was the prepostcolonial situation? *Ternary* does not even begin to describe the multipolarity of the struggle over land in seventeenth-century North America, where multiple metropolitan sovereignties contested with multiple Native sovereignties and multiple incipient settler colonial projects. Indeed, borrowing page-folding terms from the period's printers, we might need words as large as *duodecinary* or even *vicesimo-quartinary* to begin to describe the chaos that Charles II, Louis XIV, the rulers of Plymouth, Kings Alexander and Philip, Père Lalemant, and the Haudenosaunee tried to navigate. In this environment, settler colonialism could not yet take coherent form, much less assert hegemony.

★ ★ ★

"It is not so much the vast stretch of seas which separates us from one another, and interposes a great chaos, so to speak, as it is the difference in our conditions," Lalemant explained to his French reading audience in 1660. "Yours is a happy one—you bask in joy, and rest in the bosom of peace; whereas ours is a lamentable one, threatening us with the extreme of misfortune."[15] In reality, however, there was little less chaos in western Europe than in eastern North America. As a boy whose kingdom was ruled by his mother and first minister Cardinal Mazarin, Louis XIV lived through the closing years of the Thirty Years' War and the domestic upheavals known as "the Fronde." At Mazarin's death in 1661, the 23-year-old Louis finally assumed power in his own right, almost simultaneously with England's 31-year-old Charles II (whose formal coronation took place in April 1661). Both sat uneasily on the thrones of unstable kingdoms, and both considered their primary economic rival to be the same Dutch republic that the Jesuit blamed for the miseries of New France.[16] The "firm peace settled in the State upon true Foundations" of which English royalists dreamed prevailed nowhere.

Likewise, in the broader Atlantic and global worlds, neither Dutch, nor English, nor French had anything that could be properly called an empire, much less a stable one, although all three claimed authority over far-flung private colonies. Only the king of Spain—or, to be precise, the king of Castile, another long-time rival of each of the other European powers—could claim a global monarchy. And that was precisely what troubled his rivals. "The Design of *Spain* . . . is to get the Universal Monarchie of Christendom," an English pamphleteer had declared during the

Cromwell regime. "Nor is it a thing less true [...] that our Neighbours [the *Dutch*] [...] have likewise, for som years, aimed to laie a foundation to themselvs for ingrossing the Universal Trade, not onely of Christendom, but indeed, of the greater part of the known world." French people on both sides of the Atlantic shared these fears, as Lalement's comments about Dutch dominance in North America suggest.[17] The Dutch West India Company dominated the transatlantic carrying trade and the African ports that supplied enslaved labor, and the Dutch East India Company wielded even more power east of the Cape of Good Hope. Yet, on the western side of the Atlantic, neither the Dutch nor their Iroquois trading partners wielded anything like the power the priest imagined. The West India Company was, as one historian puts it, "an enfeebled giant," and by 1660 its New Netherland colony was an economic basket case.[18]

So, in neither eastern North America nor western Europe did any nation wield secure power. For a generation, Iroquois people—the Five Nations of the Haudenosaunee—had used their Dutch-supplied firearms and other imported weapons not so much to conquer as to endure in a brutal conflict of all against all not entirely dissimilar to Europe's Thirty Years' War. At the heart of the violence was rapid depopulation and a desperate struggle by those who survived to regroup. For generations, local and regional epidemics of diseases imported from Europe had ravaged Native people, who had had no previous exposure, and thus no "adaptive immunity," to the viruses that caused them. A smallpox pandemic in the mid-1630s was particularly devastating. From New England through Haudenosaunee country to the Great Lakes, and probably the Ohio Valley, roughly half the Native population perished. Smallpox, measles, influenza, and other diseases returned repeatedly over the next few decades. The death toll from disease and related malnutrition and social upheaval was almost unimaginable; on average, populations shrank by 70 to 90 percent during the seventeenth century.[19]

Everywhere, the Native people regrouped with impressive tenacity. Ancient cultural patterns bound scattered survivors together through webs of marriage and kinship, provided experience in incorporating outsiders into communities voluntarily as adoptees or involuntarily as war captives, and structured much of political and economic life around trade and exchange. In almost every case, trade and exchange were key. Leaders and communities who could find reliable European trading partners were able to draw upon kinship ties and the incorporation of outsiders to become the nodes around which populations regrouped. Earlier in the century, for Native communities in closest proximity to colonists—and thus also often suffering most from epidemic depopulation—these efforts often involved formal trade and military alliances with the newcomers. This was a dangerous game, particularly when played with the English. Chiefs who insisted on acting as the superior partners in the alliance—Powhatan and his successor Opechancanough when dealing with Virginians, Sassacus of the Pequots when dealing with New Englanders—could be brutally crushed, as the Powhatans were from 1622 to 1646 and the Pequots from 1636 to 1638. Leaders who could tread a more subtle path, such as Wamsutta's predecessor Massasoit of the Wampanoags, derived great benefits for their people, in large part because the fractious English colonies could be played off against each other. But the fate of the Powhatans and Pequots always threatened. The former lost most of their lands and had to accept tributary status to Virginia; the latter officially lost all of their lands and were either shipped into Atlantic slavery or absorbed by the rival Native nations. Military power resting on access to European firearms and ammunition was a key to avoiding such fates.[20]

When Plymouth officials made clear that Alexander and Philip received gunpowder only at their sufferance, then, the message was ominous. Moreover, the naming ceremony for the two sachems contained within it multiple levels of contested authority. To the Wampanoags, this act was a familiar rite of assuming a new title to mark a new political status. Wamsutta's ability to convince Plymouth officials to bestow a new name on him demonstrated his influence, if not his control, over them, both in terms of the immediate controversy with the people of Rehoboth and in terms of future economic and political benefits. To the English, by contrast, the ceremony clearly put *them* in charge. The particular names they bestowed—Alexander and Philip—recalled the classical tale of the two sons of Philip of Macedon, and, by extension, St. Paul's biblical vision of Macedonians who begged Christian missionaries to "Come over ... and help us." But the ceremony also evoked a widespread English interpretation of who the ancient Alexander and Philip were: the former was Alexander the Great; the latter was the supposed half-wit who presided over the collapse of his brother's empire. Whatever the case, the officials of Plymouth had no intention of allowing the Wampanoags to threaten their political or military dominance, and firearms were both a symbolic and a very real factor in their calculations.[21]

No one understood the importance of weaponry better than the Haudenosaunee, whose homelands were in what would much later be called upstate New York. The epidemics of the mid-1630s coincided with the growth of English and Dutch colonies to the east of Haudenosaunee country, in southern New England and, most important, on the upper Hudson River at Fort Orange and the aptly named *Beverwyck* (later Albany, New York). Iroquois traded beaver and other animal pelts to the Dutch to acquire a substantial arsenal of firearms and on such other weapons such as axes and metal arrowheads. By the mid-1640s, the pragmatic partnership had already yielded at least 300 muskets, with ample ammunition to wage war on less well-armed neighbors in every direction. Haudenosaunee people had no illusions about the nature of this relationship, however. "The Dutch say we are brothers and that we are joined together with chains," a Mohawk spokesman told the magistrates of Fort Orange in 1659, "but that lasts only as long as we have beavers."[22]

In the Haudenosaunee wars, the primary aim was to take captives who could be symbolically or literally adopted into families to replace those who died from epidemics. In the late 1640s, Iroquois warriors destroyed all of the major villages of the Wendat (or Huron) confederacy, who lived on Georgian Bay of Lake Huron and whose Iroquoian language and customs were similar to their own. Having dispersed, killed, or adopted the Wendats, in the 1650s Iroquois war parties turned their guns on other Iroquoian-speaking peoples and other targets all around the Great Lakes, including the Petuns, the Neutrals, and the Eries—nations that seem to have themselves been raiding Anishanabe peoples farther to the west. The yield of enslaved bodies was astonishing; perhaps two-thirds of the people living in Haudenosaunee villages in 1660 may have been adopted captives.[23]

By that year, however, just when Lalemant perceived the Haudeonsaunee to be at the height of their powers, New Netherland's economy was failing and the Iroquois had run out of poorly armed enemies to raid. To their immediate west, lands stood depopulated from the near shores of Lake Huron to the Lakes Ontario and Erie and down through the eastern Ohio Valley. Beyond, in the upper Great Lakes, Anishanabe people welcomed Wendats and others who had escaped the Iroquois and planned to fight another day. In every other direction from Haudenosaunee country, rival Native nations had by 1660 made their own strategic arrangements with European trading partners who, to one degree or another, supplied the weapons and other trade goods necessary for survival. To the east, Alexander, Philip, and other Algonquian leaders relied on their vexed relationship to the southern New England colonies. To the south, the Susquehannocks of what would later be called central Pennsylvania had mirrored Haudenosaunee strategies, purchasing an arsenal from Swedish and Dutch colonists on the Delaware River and English colonists of Maryland that more than matched that of their foes.[24]

Still farther south, survivors from the Great Lakes Iroquoian nations that the Iroquois had dispersed were forging new trading relationships with English colonists. A group of Eries, having probably already incorporated other refugees and captives, settled with a variety of other peoples at the falls of the James River in about 1656. Known by a variety of names—"Richahecrians" to Virginians, "Chichimecos" to Spanish Floridians, "Westos" to others and to historians—this group developed a reputation for ferocity that, if anything, outstripped that of their former northern enemies. The Westos traded with Virginians for firearms, which they turned on the poorly armed Natives of the southern piedmont, whom they enslaved and sold to the English for more guns and trade goods. A few years after the Westos' arrival in the Southeast, an English colonist reported that they "strike a great feare in these Indians haveinge gunns and powder and shott and doe come upon these Indians heere in the tyme of their cropp and destroye all by killinge Caryinge aweay their Corne and Children."[25] But the Westos were hardly alone in trading with Virginians for slaves. Within a few years of their arrival, they were competing with indigenous nations of what is today North Carolina, including the Iroquoian-speaking Tuscaroras and Cherokees, a group the English called "Tomahitans," and, especially, the Siouan-speaking Occaneechis, whose principal town on the Roanoke River dominated major trading paths. Probably to escape these rivals and move closer to unarmed victims farther south, in about 1659 the Westos relocated to present-day Georgia and by 1663 were well ensconced in a village on the Savannah River.[26]

Beyond these bare outlines, historians know little about population trends and warfare in the Southeast during the period in which the slave trade emerged. Still, it is clear that the great Mississippian chiefdoms that Hernan de Soto's Spanish *entrada* had encountered 12 decades earlier had dispersed into much smaller communities. Local and perhaps large-scale epidemics surely played a role in the population decline, but the specifics are hotly contested; indeed a smallpox outbreak in 1696 may have been the first truly region-wide pandemic. Well before that time, however, the entire area became a "shatter zone," where, just as farther north peoples had regrouped in response to war and disease, new communities coalesced. Among the first of these were the Yamasees, a diverse group of people from what is today Georgia who probably came together in response to Westo raids.[27]

Other nodes around which peoples regrouped were more than 30 mission towns nominally supervised by Spanish Catholic priests. Begun in the late sixteenth century and stretching in an arc from today's Savannah through Tallahassee to points west along the Gulf of Mexico, by 1655 these were home to upwards of 25,000 Native people, more than twice the captive-reinforced Haudenosaunee population at the time. The missions were among the Westos' earliest slave-raiding targets and suffered greatly from epidemics; by 1675 their population had shrunk to a little over 13,000. Nonetheless, for most of their residents, the communities provided some defense against attack and at least limited access to imported tools and weapons, along with the spiritual benefits that missionaries promised (and the personal tyrannies they imposed) in a time of relentless death and cultural disruption.[28]

A thousand miles to the north, much the same tenuous benefits accrued to Native people who resettled during the mid-seventeenth-century in such Jesuit mission reserves as Sillery and Lorrette near Quebec and in such Puritan praying towns as Natick in Massachusetts. Much to the chagrin of Alexander and Philip, many of their people joined the "praying Indians," transforming the political protection they sought in the 1660 naming ceremony into something far more threatening to Wampanoag sovereignty. Formally, at least, these Christian communities submitted to the political authority of the French or English colonies, who claimed ultimate title to the lands on which they lived and ultimate credit for their religious salvation. The spiritual conquests thrilled pious audiences in the metropoles who read *The Jesuit Relations* and English equivalents with titles such as *New England's First Fruits*.[29]

★ ★ ★

Spiritual fruits were far less important than temporal ones when the new regimes led by Charles II and Louis XIV expanded their claims to regain what was their "own" from the chaotic landscape of North America. In both cases, crusades against the economic dominance of the Dutch combined with efforts to exert direct control over private colonial entities that had acknowledged too little royal authority and yielded too little royal profit. In 1660, one of the first Parliamentary bills that Charles approved was a Navigation Act, based on Cromwellian legislation in 1651 that had challenged Dutch dominance of transatlantic trade by requiring colonial goods to be transported in English ships. At nearly the same time, decrees from Louis and his chief minister Jean-Baptiste Colbert similarly limited French colonial trade to French ships. Also in 1660, Charles chartered the Company of Royal Adventurers into Africa, reorganized in 1663 as the Royal African Company. Both planned to seize for the royal family and its supporters a share of the Dutch near-monopoly of the slave trade. Likewise, Louis authorized a West India Company in 1663, a Senegal Company in 1673, and a Guinea Company in 1685.[30]

Dutch land and trade in the western hemisphere were targets of both crowns as well. In 1664, Charles granted to his brother, James, duke of York, a charter to the territory occupied by New Netherland, a place whose very existence represented "intollerable disgrace doon to his Majestye [...] by thes bold usurpers" of what rightfully belonged to the English king. The royal commissioners in charge of a fleet that almost without a shot conquered what thus became "New York" also carried instructions to investigate the alleged misdeeds of the private entities that ruled Plymouth, Connecticut, New Haven, Rhode Island, and, most important, Massachusetts Bay.[31] Meantime, a year earlier, Charles had issued a group of his courtiers a charter to what the English had long claimed as "Carolina," a vast tract south of Virginia that the Spanish considered part of Florida. Almost simultaneously, Louis embarked on his own path toward imperial expansion when he revoked the charters of the companies that governed New France and Martinique and Guadeloupe in the West Indies, placing them under direct royal rule. In North America, rather than strike the Dutch directly, the French intended to go after their Haudenosaunee trading partners. The first royal viceroy of New France arrived in 1665 with 1,000 troops and orders to "totally to exterminate" the Iroquois.[32]

These aggressive imperial acts threw an already chaotic North American landscape into further disarray. The English conquest of New Netherland and investigation of New England did not immediately create a centralized royal colossus. Instead, the result was only more fragmentation, as James, duke of York, spun off the separate colony of New Jersey to reward two of the same courtiers who owned Carolina. York's governor meanwhile tried to impose authority on Long Island, Martha's Vineyard, Nantucket, and Maine, which had long been colonized by refractory New Englanders contending with French, Dutch, and Native rivals. The royal commissioners also carved out a new paper colony in Rhode Island called "the King's Province." And, indirectly, the royal commissioners opened yet another contentious front for imperial expansion, when they encountered in Boston two renegade Frenchmen seeking investors for operations in the far north; in 1670, the partnership led to the royal chartering of the Hudson's Bay Company.[33] Meantime, the French army sent to "exterminate" the Haudenosaunee proved amazingly inept, only actually reaching its target once in three attempts during 1666 and then finding villages abandoned by forewarned inhabitants. But the impact of all this activity on Native people who had depended on trade with New Netherland was still profound. Deprived of secure access to Dutch arms, by 1669 the Haudenosaunee had to make peace with the French and to allow Jesuit missionaries to take up residence in all their major villages. As one of those missionaries reported, trade goods were so scarce at Albany, that "our Iroquois resolved to provide themselves with these at Montreal."[34]

The missionary's possessive pronoun was deliberate. In French eyes, the Haudenosaunee and vast numbers of their Native enemies were all being absorbed into an empire that was the

French monarch's own. In 1671, at Sault Sainte Marie, where lakes Superior and Huron meet and in the region where many people who had escaped or resisted Iroquois warriors were coming together among a network of perdurable Anishanabeg kin groups, a French delegation summoned representatives of at least 14 nations to a grand ceremony. Explaining "that he was sent to take possession of that region, receive them under the protection of the great King [...] and to form thenceforth but one land of their territories and ours," he erected a cross, a royal flag, and an iron plate bearing the arms of Louis XIV to mark the imposition of imperial rule. Within a decade, René Robert Cavelier, Sieur de La Sale, sailed down the Mississippi River planting similar crosses and flags to impress Native leaders as he went, convincing himself that each local "chief acknowledged that the village belonged to his Majesty." His final act of possession occurred at the spot of high ground in the Mississippi Delta that La Salle dubbed New Orleans. Like Carolina, this was a locale claimed by Spanish Florida.[35] Everywhere the French soldiers, traders, and missionaries went, they purported to take Native people under their protection. Native leaders said they embraced the protection and the material benefits provided by their French "Father," particularly as it empowered them to join together to resist common enemies like the Iroquois. Yet they seldom gave more than lip service to Louis XIV's sovereignty and mostly went about their lives as if the French served them, not vice versa. So the French established a structure of imperial power that Native people could exploit to achieve their own ends and impose some order on the chaos of the seventeenth century.[36]

But, far from establishing a universal *pax Gallica*—or, as Native people might have put it, a Great Tree of Peace—the result for the rest of the century was only more, and more violent, warfare throughout eastern North America. The Dutch briefly reconquered New York in 1673, before returning it to the English by treaty in 1674. The interlude introduced further uncertainty—and further disruption of transatlantic trade—for Native peoples seeking connections to Europeans. In all these upheavals, the Susquehannocks fared even worse than the Haudenosaunee. Seizing the breathing room provided by French-imposed peace, the Haudenosaunee turned the arms they were again able to acquire at Albany against their old foes to the south, who were not so fortunate in rebuilding their trade connections. "If they went to war, where would they get powder and ball?" a Susquehannock leader reportedly worried during this period.[37] His worry was well founded. The exact circumstances remain obscure, but by early 1675 Susquehannocks had reportedly been "driven from their Habitations" and "utterly defeated" by the Haudenosaunee. Many if not most of the survivors threw themselves at the mercy of the Maryland colony and "desired what part of the Province Should be allotted for them to live upon." As they moved to their assigned homes at an abandoned Piscataway village on the Potomac River, the Susquehannocks seemed to be settling into the same kind of uneasy colonial overlordship as did the inhabitants of praying towns, reserves, and the Powhatan tributaries of Virginia.[38]

Except for the fact that the Susquehannocks resettled on the northern edge of the disease-and-slave-trade shatter zone. If the English conquest of New Netherland was transformative for Native peoples in the north, the second front in England's imperial expansion, the establishment of English Carolina, was equally so for those in the south. Particularly after the establishment of Charles Town in 1670, the Carolina colonists propelled into hyperdrive the Native slave trade that the Virginians, Westos, Occaneechis, and others had created. In 1674, Henry Woodward, the man who controlled South Carolina's official monopoly on the Indian trade, became the Westos' main customer, despite his employers' explicit prohibition on trafficking in enslaved Natives. The entry of Carolina into the scramble appears to have deprived the Virginians who dealt with the Westos of their primary trading partners. These Virginians, many of whom happened to be Governor William Berkeley's inner circle, lost out to competitors dealing with the Occaneechis.[39]

The details of the struggle among Virginians are murky, but it appears that the profits that Berkeley's cronies made from slave trading was one of many grievances among a general colonial population in which, as Berkeley observed, "six parts of seaven at least are Poore Endebted Discontented and Armed."[40] Much of the Virginians' trouble stemmed from the same English imperial moves that sent the Susquehannocks to the James River and the Westos to the Savannah. The conquest of New Netherland and the enforcement of the Navigation Acts closed a formerly profitable New Netherland and Dutch market for Chesapeake tobacco; small planters now received less than half the price they had been able to command before 1664. Rallying around an aristocratic newcomer named Nathaniel Bacon, hard-pressed Virginia colonists turned their rage as much on Indians as on Berkeley's ruling faction. The way out of their economic distress, many concluded, was not to grow less tobacco but to try to grow more by seizing land from the Native people that Berkeley's government was too willing to protect. "The common cry and vogue of the Vulgar was [. . .] wee will have warr with all Indians," a royal commission sent in 1677 to investigate what became known as "Bacon's Rebellion" concluded. "We will spare non, and [if] wee must be hang'd for Rebells for killing those that will destroy us, let them hang us, wee will venture that rather than lye at the mercy of a Barbarous Enemy."[41]

Most prominent among that enemy were none other than the Susquehannocks protected by Virginia's neighbor, the government of Maryland. In the summer of 1675, in a purported case of mistaken identity, Virginia militiamen seeking retaliation against Indians they accused of stealing some hogs shot a number of the Susquehannocks in cold blood. In what was certainly not a case of mistaken identity, a few months later a thousand Virginia and Maryland freelance militiamen surrounded the Susquehannock town and, under cover of peace negotiations, assassinated five chiefs. Later they carried out a similarly perfidious attack on the Occaneechis. Such renegade actions transformed the Anglo-Indian conflicts into a civil war between the supporters of Berkeley and Bacon. By the time Bacon died of dysentery in October 1676, the colonial capital at Jamestown lay in ruins, hundreds of English and Indians had died, and the surviving Susquehannocks, Occaneechis, and others had dispersed in all directions.[42]

As everyone involved knew well, a parallel story was playing out at the same time in New England, in the war associated with the name of Massasoit's and Alexander's successor, King Philip. The roots of New England's Armageddon were as complicated as those of Virginia's; they went far deeper than the English trial and execution of close associates of Philip accused of murdering John Sassamon, a literate Christian who had served as Philip's secretary but been suspected of plotting against him. But weapons and land were at the heart of King Philip's War. In 1662, Plymouth officials had arrested Alexander to answer charges that he was plotting against them. Before he got home after his release, he died of a fever, leaving the sachemship to Philip, who blamed the English for his brother's death. In subsequent years, the English forced Philip to surrender a sizable cache of arms (arms that, significantly, could no longer be purchased from the Dutch). When, in 1671, he resisted complete disarmament, colonial officials summoned him to explain his "insolent carriages and expressions" and forced him to sign a document promising to pay a monetary fine and acknowledging that he and his people were "subjects to his majestie the Kinge of England, etc., and the goverment of New Plymouth, and to theire lawes." Philip later claimed he had agreed to this in hopes of regaining "mani miles square of land" the English had fraudulently acquired. Deprived of firearms, unable to pay the fine, and getting no redress, Philip's people "now [. . .] had not so much land or muny, that thay wear as good get kiled as leave all ther liveflyhode."[43]

In the months of conflict that followed, Philip, his people, and many other southern New England natives lost both their lives and their livelihoods. King Philip's War cut the Native population at least by half. Two thousand died in battle and 3,000 of disease and wartime privation. More than 2,000 more were enslaved; most labored in English households, but several hundred were shipped to Cadiz, Tangier, the Azores, and elsewhere in the Atlantic world. Another 2,000 resettled under Haudenosaunee or French protection. Most of those who remained in New England and escaped slavery or servitude were confined to a few surviving "praying towns." On the English side, less than 1,000 people died, but the physical damage may have been greater than in Virginia. Seventeen towns were completely destroyed and almost every spot more than 20 miles west of Boston was abandoned. The financial burdens of paying for the war, meanwhile, seriously undercut the legitimacy of the region's colonial governments, at the same time that metropolitan authorities redoubled their efforts to rein in what they considered far too independent regimes.[44]

★ ★ ★

The territorial ambitions of ordinary English colonists lay behind both Bacon's Rebellion and King Philip's War. As New England clergyman Increase Mather concluded in the middle of the conflict, "*Land! Land!* hath been the Idol of many in *New-England*."[45] Many a would-be patriarch in both colonies endorsed "warr with all Indians" as the surest way to win the right, like his king, "to sit under his own Vine, and enjoy his own." Bacon's "Manifesto" proclaimed "our Designe not onely to ruine and extirpate all Indians in Generall but all manner of Trade and commerce with them."[46] Such sentiments and behavior no doubt conform to anyone's definition of settler colonialism. Still, for several reasons, they remained an inchoate force in the 1670s. Impersonal abstractions pitting "all Indians" against all colonists simply did not describe the situation. Both Bacon's Rebellion and King Philip's War arose from everyday disputes between people who knew each other well: a controversy over the theft of some hogs, and the murder of a Native man who spoke and wrote English. Personal ties were especially dense in New England. As one historian concludes, the conflict there "was not a war between strangers but rather one between neighbors," who, over the course of two generations "had learned much about each other in the course of trading, working, negotiating, socializing, suing, complaining to their leaders about one another, occasionally fighting, and—in a few cases—attending school and church and even living together."[47]

In such an environment, sweeping calls for ethnic cleansing were more a *result* than a *cause* of the generalized violence that followed, more a cauldron in which settler colonialism was forged than a pot set boiling by it. Moreover, those actually in charge of settler colony governments actually did their best to restrain undifferentiated extermination. Berkeley's government, after all, waged war against the Baconites, the New England magistrates who tried Sassamon's killers thought they were keeping the peace, and, during King Philip's War, a Massachusetts Court actually sentenced four colonists to death for murdering six Indian women and children, while missionary John Eliot raised a lonely voice to remind New Englanders to "indeavour of the Indians conversion, not theire estirpation." But mostly, ineffectual settler governments and military disasters proved the folly of ethnic cleansing. Virginians and New Englanders may have removed thousands of Indians from lands they coveted, yet smoldering English villages and ruined plantations showed that settler colonists were hardly in a position to eliminate indigenous peoples.[48]

Nor were imperial elites yet in a position to play their ternary role in a settler colonial situation, for only in the wake of King Philip's War and Bacon's Rebellion did representatives of Whitehall clearly begin to perceive that the role existed. Those who acted in the name of Charles II and attempted to reboot English royal government in the aftermath of the 1670s carnage understood that settlers (although they did not use the term) were at the root of North America's chaos. Sir Edmund Andros, governor of the king's brother's colony of New York—or rather the governor *at* New York of the vast domains that the English Crown claimed north of the Chesapeake—summed up the lessons in 1678. Strife between colonists and Indians was something "wee must expect and bee lyable to, so long as each pety colony, hath or assumes absolute power of peace and warr, which cannot bee managed by such popular governments as was Evident by the late indian wars in newe England."[49]

The royal commissioners sent to restore order in Virginia agreed that the imperial crown, not the settlers' "popular governments" must take charge. "The sole power of Peace and War are only inherent to his Majesty's Royall Prerogative," they lectured the colony's council and assembly. Ignoring "the putrid homours of our unruly Inhabitants," the commissioners welcomed to Jamestown leaders of Native peoples who professed "their readynesse to enter into a firme League of Peace with the English."[50] That peace was ratified at the Treaty of Middle Plantation, convened purposefully on King Charles's birthday, May 29, 1677. When a copy of the treaty arrived at court, the Privy Council ordered it published and sent back to Virginia for the edification of the king's subjects there. The printed version recounted that, in return for the Natives' acknowledgment of "their immediate Dependency on, and [. . .] Subjection to the Great King of England," the English had pledged that "the said Indian Kings and Queenes and their Subjects shall hold their Lands, and have the same Confirmed to them and their Posterity by Patent under the Seale of this His Majesties Colony."[51]

Andros, meanwhile, extended royal protection to Indians on a grander scale. In 1675—shortly after he took up his post and before the wars in Virginia and New England had begun—he travelled far and wide to collect what he called the "Submissions and Engagements" of Indian people in the Connecticut Valley, in Maine, on Long Island, in New Jersey, in Manhattan, and ultimately at Albany. At that final destination, spokesmen for factions among the Haudenosaunee who were eager to escape the French imperial orbit welcomed the governor. As a result, Andros was able to report that the Native leaders, "declareing there former Allyance [. . .] submitted in an Extraordinary manner, with reitterated promisses." In the winter of 1675–76, the Anglo-Haudenosaunee alliance bore mutually beneficial fruit when Andros supplied arms and encouragement to a party of Mohawks who attacked Philip in his winter encampment north of Albany and forced his army to retreat back toward New England. Andros thus empowered Haudenosaunee people to attack their old eastern Native enemies while at the same time posing as military savior of New England to colonists unlikely otherwise to recognize his authority.[52]

But mostly in the late 1670s Andros mostly posed as peacemaker and protector. After Philip's death, he invited hundreds of Native refugees to resettle under joint New York and Haudenosaunee protection at Schaghticoke, some 20 miles northeast of Albany, a move that happened to expand New York's claims in the direction of both New France and Massachusetts. Meanwhile, he made similar provisions for Susquehannocks migrating northward from the violence in the Chesapeake, brokering peace between longtime Iroquoian-speaking enemies while asserting royal authority far to the south and west of Manhattan. As these people relocated their homelands in the Susquehanna River watershed, they were joined by refugees from southern New England and by Shawnees, Nanticokes, and others who migrated from a variety of directions. At the opposite end of the duke's dominions—in the Maine territory that York disputed with Massachusetts Bay (and New France)—Andros built a fort at Pemaquid in 1677 and convened a peace treaty in 1678 between several local Wabanaki bands and English colonists. These varied transactions created the ad-hoc system of English-Indian alliances known as "the Covenant Chain," through which New York and the Haudenosaunee brokered relationships among the region's English colonies and Indian nations. As one historian puts it, "with Iroquois assistance, Andros demarcated a frontier line between the English and Indians in North America." Or, as a Haudenosaunee orator recalled decades later, "we lodged under the Leaves of the Trees [and] the Christians and We Entered into a Covenant of friendship."[53]

★ ★ ★

Thus came into being an English equivalent to the French system of alliances. Like the Spanish of Florida, local representatives of both crowns now posed as protector to dozens of Native nations, in empires that depended on indigenous partners and thus tried to hold English settler colonialism in check (for that was, in effect, the function of the French as well as English alliances). But England's imperialism no more created a *Pax Britannia* and a Tree of Peace than earlier developments had produced a *Pax Gallica*. Instead, another generation of warfare wracked the North American continent, demonstrating how little control the empires actually exerted over either their Indian partners or their settler colonists.

Almost immediately after the creation of the Covenant Chain, which made peace on their eastern and southern flanks and reopened secure trading connections with Albany, Haudenosaunee warriors picked up where they had left off in the 1660s. War parties waged massive campaigns against the Anishanabeg and others, bringing home hundreds of enslaved captives. By 1684, New France had entered the war openly in defense of its allies. Yet, with the French and English crowns formally still at peace, New York refused to do the same for the Haudenosaunee. In 1688, Andros himself urged his Iroquois friends against retaliation; "You have had notice of the true made by our Great King putting a stop to the French invading this Government, or annoying you further," he pontificated. "Yow may goe and Hunt as formerly, and need have noe other reguard to the French [. . .] then as they are our freinds to doe them noe harme." A few months later, when the Glorious Revolution of 1688–1689 brought William of Orange to the English throne, rebellious colonists deposed Andros, and England entered its new king's ongoing struggle with Louis XIV, Haudenosaunee leaders were ecstatic. Hearing that "there is War betwixt France and England," a Mohawk pledged in 1689 that, "as they are one hand and soul with the English, they will take up the ax with pleasure against the French." But any hopes that an English military proxy would join the fight in a meaningful way were repeatedly disappointed. A series of French invasions and defeats in the Great Lakes region left the Iroquois reeling, particularly after the European crowns made peace in 1697.[54]

Southeastern Native people similarly suffered in the closing years of the seventeenth century. There had been no counterpart of Edmund Andros or the Treaty of Middle Plantation in the southeastern shatter zone, where slaving wars only intensified. The monopoly that Woodward tried to establish with the Westos lasted just a few years. In 1680, a rival faction of planters, immigrants from Barbados known as "the Goose Creek Men," made common cause with the Shawnees or "Savannahs"—like the Westos before them Native people driven southward by war with the Haudenosaunee—to defeat the Westos, enslave most of them, and open the human commerce to all comers, English and Indian alike. Savannahs, Yamasees, Tuscaroras, Cherokees, and others raided far and wide, despite the efforts, or rather rhetoric, of the Carolina proprietors against a trade they proclaimed immoral. Hard statistics are hard to come by, but between 1670 and 1715, perhaps as many as 51,000 Indian slaves passed through the Charles Town market, apparently far more than entered the port from Africa during the same period. The victims came from throughout the region, but particularly from the mission Indians of Florida and, later, from peoples of the lower Mississippi Valley allied with French Louisiana.[55]

Thus, in both north and south, wars largely instigated by Native Americans who traded with the English embroiled England's rival empires and mocked settler colonists' fantasies of extermination. To Europeans (and to many historians since), the conflicts appeared to be global extensions of the conflicts between France and England known in Europe as the War of the League of Augsburg or the Nine Years' War (1688–97) and the War of the Spanish Succession (1701–14). English colonists later dubbed them respectively "King William's" and "Queen Anne's" wars, articulating the exogenous metropolitan, rather than settler colonial, roots of the hostilities. But the turn-of-the-eighteenth-century conflicts might better be considered struggles in which

Native peoples exploited the two imperial systems to attack enemies that happened to be allied with another power. The War of the League of Augsburg, then, was less an Indian proxy war between New York and New England on the one hand and New France on the other than it was a war between the Haudenosaunee and the Anishanabeg and other peoples allied to France, with occasional interventions by the French or English clients. Similarly, the War of the Spanish Succession was less an opportunity for English Carolinians to strike a blow against the French of Louisiana and the Spanish of Florida than it was a chance for their Indian allies to destroy and enslave their various enemies.[56]

Still, in both cases, the results for Native people were disastrous. By 1700 the Haudenosaunee, bereft of meaningful English support, had to make peace with New France, much as they had been forced to do in the 1660s. The surrender was the product of a coup against those who still clung to the English alliance. This act opened space for another faction of leaders to try to develop a consensus around a new relationship to both imperial powers based on neutrality rather than exclusive alliance. In the summer of 1701, a Haudenosaunee delegation met counterparts from more than 30 Indian nations allied to the French to negotiate what became known as "The Great Peace of Montreal." In exchange for a pledge of Iroquois neutrality in future wars between European empires, French Governor Louis-Hector de Callière promised to enforce the peace and to guarantee the right of Iroquois to hunt north of the Great Lakes and to trade at the French post of Detroit. Unbeknownst to Calliére, other Haudenosaunee spokespeople were negotiating at Albany, where they surprised their hosts with a deed conveying ownership of the same Great Lakes lands to the English. The document, the Iroquois diplomats insisted, should be sent to "the great King of England to acquaint how that the French of Canada Incroach upon our Territories […] and to pray that our great King may use all means to prevent itt."[57]

In giving each imperial power a parallel paper claim to the same territory (territory that in fact the Iroquois themselves did not control), this "Grand Settlement of 1701" promised to counter power with power and preserve Haudenosaunee independence. Each empire now had an economic stake in keeping the peace between the Five Nations and their erstwhile Indian enemies. The balance-of-power policy came under considerable stress during the War of the Spanish Succession, but for the most part it held. While not all Haudenosaunee people agreed, factions kept lines of communication and trade open to both imperial powers, playing them off against each other rather than clinging to one or the other as exclusive allies. Concluding that involvement in imperial warfare was suicidal, most Iroquois placed no more trust in the English than they did in the French. As one spokesman explained, "If we should take up the hatchet […] the governor of Canada would look down upon us with indignation, and set the people round about, who are his children, upon us, and that would set all the world on fire."[58]

The lessons the Haudenosaunee (and the Anishanabeg) learned from the War of the League of Augsburg, Southeastern Indians absorbed during the War of the Spanish Succession. Just as Anglo-French rivalry in the north reignited old Native conflicts, so Anglo-Spanish rivalry rejuvenated slave raiding in the south, allowing the Carolina government openly to support attacks on the mission villages of Florida. By the time the European powers made peace in 1713, none of these communities survived, and thousands of their residents had been killed or sold to planters in the West Indies, Carolina, or Virginia. With no more easy targets to the south and with the Chickasaws, Choctaws, and other Mississippi Valley nations proving more formidable foes than formerly, the slave-raiding partners of Carolina turned their attention to each other, while accumulating unpayable debts to English traders whose demands for fresh enslaved bodies could not be met. Those English traders, meanwhile, squabbled among themselves about how to impose some order while grabbing their own slice of the profits.[59]

The Tuscaroras, whose homelands included much of present-day North Carolina, suffered particularly from the squeeze of debts and declining markets. By 1711, their problems were exacerbated by Swiss and German immigrants to Carolina who began settling on their lands without permission. Tuscaroras captured the intruders' leader, Christoph von Graffenried, along with Carolina's provincial surveyor general, John Lawson. At a council of headmen, Graffenried talked his way to freedom, but Lawson was condemned to death. Shortly thereafter, Tuscaroras attacked and killed over 100 Europeans. South Carolina coordinated joint retaliatory expeditions in which it enlisted the Yamasees and other Indian rivals of the Tuscaroras. By 1713, most of the nation's villages had been burned, perhaps 1,000 men, women, and children, had been killed, some 700 others had been enslaved. The 2,500 Tuscaroras who escaped became refugees; only a handful remained in their homeland.[60]

The Yamasees who helped to send them into exile were themselves in desperate straits. Under terms of Carolina legislation passed in 1707 they were confined to a fragment of their former lands on the Savannah River. Even this territory was being overrun by settler planters and their grazing cattle and, as throughout this period, by viral diseases. Like the Tuscaroras before them, many Yamasees were deeply in debt to Carolina traders who routinely enslaved Indians who defaulted. If Yamasees hoped that their service on behalf of the Carolinians in the Tuscarora War would win them some relief, they soon learned otherwise and began building an alliance with similarly oppressed Creeks and others. In April 1715, members of the alliance attacked, destroying Carolina plantations and killing English traders wherever they could find them in Indian country. Even those operating as far away as the lower Mississippi valley were not safe during what became known as the "Yamasee War."[61]

Over the winter of 1715–16, both Creeks and Carolinians sent armed parties into the country of the previously neutral and politically divided Cherokees to pressure that populous nation to take sides. Although the Cherokees were deeply divided, they were as dependent on trade with the English as were their Native neighbors, and the same logic that earlier drove the Yamasees to side with the Carolinians led the dominant Cherokee faction to assassinate a Creek delegation that had come to their country to enlist the nation in their cause. Subsequently, Cherokees "fell upon the Creeks and Yamasees who were in their towns and killed every man of them." The united front of Cherokees and English tipped the military balance, and the Euro-Indian war quickly wound down, although the conflict between Cherokees and Creeks did not. Those Yamasees who avoided death or enslavement relocated to Florida, and many Creeks moved their villages farther west from Carolina, in hopes of establishing trade with the French of Louisiana. When the fighting subsided, vast areas of the Indian southeast were depopulated, some 7 percent of British Carolinians had perished, and the regional economy—including its brutal Native American slave trade—collapsed.[62] The shatter zone itself had been shattered.

There was no Southeastern analogue to the Great Peace of Montreal, but, as in the north a decade and a half earlier, surviving Native people throughout the region seem to have agreed that the mixture of all out war with imperial politics was suicidal, and that some kind of balanced accommodation was the only route to survival. As one historian concludes, "After the Yamasee War, the Chickasaw, Cherokee, and Creek all followed the same basic diplomacy in relation to the Europeans: entangling alliances with none."[63] Everywhere, then, north and south, the Native peoples who survived and even prospered into the eighteenth century capitalized on their geographic position, their economic and military value to European governors, and their decentralized political systems to keep their options open, to maintain connections with more than one imperial power, and thus to maintain their cultural and political autonomy. As a frustrated New York Indian affairs secretary Peter Wraxall put it, "to preserve the balance between us and the French is the great ruling principle of the modern Indian politics."[64]

★ ★ ★

The eighteenth-century continental order, such as it was, required many varieties of balance. "A governor of Virginia has to steer between Scylla and Charybolis, either an Indian or a civil war," concluded Alexander Spotswood, who held that post from 1710 to 1722; "Bacon's Rebellion was occasioned purely by the governor and council refusing to let the people go out against the Indians who at that time annoyed the frontiers."[65] Spotswood described precisely the theoretical indigenous, metropolitan, and settler colonial ternary. But there were far more than three forces involved. Indeed the settler-colonial urge to "go out against the Indians" always simmered in the many provinces of eighteenth-century British America, especially during peacetime, when thousands of immigrants from Europe poured into the continent demanding access to agricultural land. There were many conflicting settler colonies eying the lands of many conflicting Indian nations. Imperfectly cooling the settlers' ardors like stunted trees of peace were the multiple metropolitan imperialisms that traced their roots to the era of Charles II and Louis XIV. Those roots came to entwine with multiple partnerships with indigenous powers, nourishing an imperfect canopy that shaded sources of Native rage against settlers. As Spotswood understood, to allow too little sunlight to reach settler colonialism—to allow Native people to sit under their own vines and enjoy their own—was to risk a civil war with settler colonists who deemed their own vines insufficiently capacious. But the reverse was also true.

Spotswood's nightmare came true in the 1750s, when neither Indians nor settlers were content to sit any longer under imperial arbors. As European settlers increasingly set their minds on lands west of the Appalachians, in 1754 the Indian war that Spotswood prophesied broke out with a vengeance in the Ohio country, and then spread throughout the globe in the great conflict known as the "Seven Years' War." "You may easily see the reason of the gloomy and dark days, they have proceeded from the earth," the Delaware leader Teedyuscung explained to the governor of Pennsylvania in 1757. "The Land is the cause of our Differences[,] that is our being unhappily turned out of the land is the cause, and thô the first settlers might purchase the lands fairly yet they did not act well nor do the Indians justice for they ought to have reserved some place for the Indians."[66] Despite Teedyuscung's indictment of settler colonialism, and despite the ham-fisted effort of the British crown to constrain settlers behind the Proclamation Line of 1763, land remained the colonists' idol. The massive British victory in the Seven Years' War freed settler colonists to believe that they could finally unleash Spotswood's dreaded civil war, a war directed against the entire empire rather than against the government of a single colony. That Atlantic civil war—the American Revolution—had many causes. But for many settler colonists, removing Indians from the land was a central goal. As they saw it, the vines of North America belonged to White men, even if those White men were too busy seizing more real estate to sit still and enjoy the shade.

Notes

1 Patrick Wolfe, *Settler Colonialism and the Transformation of Anthropology: The Politics and Poetics of an Ethnographic Event* (New York: Cassell, 1999), 2; Wolfe, "Land, Labor, and Difference: Elementary Structures of Race," *American Historical Review* 106 (2001): 867–869; Walter L. Hixson, *American Settler Colonialism: A History* (New York: Palgrave Macmillan, 2013), viii.
2 Eliga H. Gould, "Zones of Law, Zones of Violence: The Legal Geography of the British Atlantic, Circa 1772," *William and Mary Quarterly*, 3rd series, 60 (2003): 471–510 (quotation from 475); Lauren A. Benton, *Law and Colonial Cultures: Legal Regimes in World History, 1400–1900* (New York: Cambridge University Press, 2002); Benton, *A Search for Sovereignty: Law and Geography in European Empires, 1400–1900*

(New York: Cambridge University Press, 2010). As Jodi A. Byrd, observes, "For settler sovereignties ... the frontier was not so much lawless as it was in need of law to seize sovereignty and jurisdiction from indigenous peoples and conscript their lands and nations into settler territoriality" ("Follow the Typical Signs: Settler Sovereignty and its Discontents," *Settler Colonial Studies* 4 [2014]: 151–154 [quotation from 152].)

3 Anonymous, *No King but the Old Kings Son. Or, a Vindication of Limited Monarchy, as it Was Established in this Nation, Before the Late War Between the King and Parliament*, broadside (London, 1660) (first and second quotations); Clement Barksdale, *The Kings Return: A Sermon Preached at Winchcomb in Gloucestershire* ... (London, 1660) (third quotation). Barksdale evoked the Royalist civil wars song, *The King Enjoys his Own Again*. In all quotations from period sources, orthography has been modernized and abbreviations expanded.

4 David Pulsifer, ed., *Records of the Colony of New Plymouth in New England*, 12 vols. (Boston: Press of W. White, 1855–1861), Vol. 3, 192. For previous Wampanoag complaints about swine and other domestic animals from Rehoboth, see *Records of the Colony*, vol. 3, 21, 106, 119–120, 167, and for other disputes between the two communities, see *Records of the Colony*, vol. 3, 74, 101, 133–134, 180.

5 Reuben Gold Thwaites, *The Jesuit Relations and Allied Documents: Travels and Explorations of the Jesuit Missionaries in New France, 1610–1791*, 73 vols. (Cleveland, OH: Burrows Brothers, 1896–1901), Vol. 45, 179–213 (quotations from 193, 203–205).

6 Frederick E. Hoxie, "Retrieving the Red Continent: Settler Colonialism and the History of American Indians in the US," *Ethnic and Racial Studies* 31 (2008): 1153–1167 (first quotation from 1158); Patrick Wolfe, *Settler Colonialism and the Transformation of Anthropology*, 1–8 (second quotation from 1); Caroline Elkins and Susan Pedersen, eds., *Settler Colonialism in the Twentieth Century: Projects, Practices, Legacies* (New York: Routledge, 2006), 1–20 (third quotation from 2); Hixson, *American Settler Colonialism*, 1–22 (fourth quotation from 4). For brief definitions of "Settler Colonialism," "Imperial Power Colonialism," and some 10 other variations, see Nancy Shoemaker, "A Typology of Colonialism," *Perspectives on History* 53[7] (2015): 29–30.

7 Lorenzo Veracini, *Settler Colonialism A Theoretical Overview* (New York: Palgrave Macmillan, 2010), 34–49 (first and second quotations); Patrick Wolfe, "After the Frontier: Separation and Absorption in US Indian Policy," *Settler Colonial Studies* 1 (2011), 13–51; Wolfe, *Settler Colonialism and the Transformation of Anthropology*, 2 (third quotation).

8 Veracini, *Settler Colonialism*, 1–6, 49–52, 95–115 (quotations from 1, 2, 98, 51); Lorenzo Veracini, "Introducing," *Settler Colonial Studies* 1 (2011): 1–12; Jodi A. Byrd, *The Transit of Empire: Indigenous Critiques of Colonialism* (Minneapolis: University of Minnesota Press, 2011), 4–46 (quotations from 9–10).

9 Wolfe, *Settler Colonialism and the Transformation of Anthropology*, 214 (first quotation); Wolfe, "Recuperating Binarism: A Heretical Introduction," *Settler Colonial Studies* 3 (2013): 257–279 (second quotation from 274).

10 Margaret D. Jacobs, "Parallel or Intersecting Tracks? The History of the US West and Comparative Settler Colonialism," *Settler Colonial Studies* 4 (2014), 155–161 (quotation from 157). For other thoughtful considerations of these issues, see Erik Altenbernd and Alex Trimble Young, "Introduction: The Significance of the Frontier in an Age of Transnational History," *Settler Colonial Studies* 4 (2014), 127–150; and John Mack Faragher, "Commentary: Settler Colonial Studies and the North American Frontier," *Settler Colonial Studies* 4 (2014), 181–191.

11 Lisa Ford, *Settler Sovereignty: Jurisdiction and Indigenous People in America and Australia, 1788–1836* (Cambridge, MA: Harvard University Press, 2010), 13–29 (quotations from 18). On settler colonialism and post-colonial theory, see Hixson, *American Settler Colonialism*, 1–22; and Bethel Saler, *The Settlers Empire: Colonialism and State Formation in America's Old Northwest* (Philadelphia: University of Pennsylvania Press, 2014), 1–2.

12 Patrick Wolfe, "The Settler Complex: An Introduction," *American Indian Culture and Research Journal* 37 (2013): 1.

13 Wolfe, "Recuperating Binarism," 257; Faragher, "Commentary, 181–182. Veracini posits an even more complicated "system of relations comprising three different agencies: the settler coloniser, the indigenous colonised, and a variety of differently categorised exogenous alterities." The last category includes not just "the European sovereign" but what Byrd calls "arrivants," or "those people forced into the Americas through the violence of European and Anglo-American colonialism," including but not limited to enslaved Africans (Veracini, *Settler Colonialism*, 16; Byrd, *Transit of Empire*, xix).

14 See Jack P. Greene, et al., "Roundtable," *William and Mary Quarterly*, 3d series, 64 (2007): 235–286; and Kariann Akemi Yakota, *Unbecoming British: How Revolutionary America Became a Postcolonial Nation* (New York: Oxford University Press, 2011).

15 Thwaites, *Jesuit Relations*, Vol. 45, 181.
16 Many of the international and domestic issues of the 1650s came to an uneasy resolution in the November 1659 Treaty of the Pyrenees, which provided an important backdrop to the reigns of both Charles II and Louis XIV. See F. J. Routledge, *England and the Treaty of the Pyrenees* (Liverpool: University of Liverpool Press, 1953; and Lucien Bély, "La paix des Pyrénées et les relations internationales au XVIIe siècle," *Hemecht: Zeitschrift für Luxemburger Geschichte/Revue d'Histoire Luxembourgeoise Journal* 62 (2010): 329–343.
17 [Benjamin Worsely,] *The Advocate* (London, 1651), 1–2 (brackets in original).
18 Oliver A. Rink, *Holland on the Hudson: An Economic and Social History of Dutch New York* (Ithaca, NY: Cornell University Press, 1986), 50–68, 94–116, 172–213 (quotation from 62). See also Japp Jacobs, *New Netherland: A Dutch Colony in Seventeenth-Century America* (Leiden: Brill, 2005).
19 David S. Jones, "Virgin Soils Revisited," *William and Mary Quarterly*, 3rd series, 60 (2003), 703–742; (quotation from 733); Paul Kelton, *Epidemics and Enslavement: Biological Catastrophe in the Native Southeast, 1492–1715* (Lincoln: University of Nebraska Press, 2007), 143–158; Daniel K. Richter, *Before the Revolution: America's Ancient Pasts* (Cambridge, MA, Harvard University Press, 2011), 143–151.
20 Richter, *Before the Revolution*, 121–168; Neal Salisbury, *Manitou and Providence: Indians, Europeans, and the Making of New England, 1500–1643* (New York: Oxford University Press, 1982); Michael Leroy Oberg, *Uncas: First of the Mohegans* (Ithaca, NY; Cornell University Press, 2003); Julie A. Fisher and David J. Silverman, *Ninigret. Sachem of the Niantics and Narragansetts: Diplomacy, War, and the Balance of Power in Seventeenth-Century New England and Indian Country* (Ithaca, NY: Cornell University Press, 2014). On the importance of firearms, see David J. Silverman, *Thundersticks: Firearms and the Transformation of Native America* (Cambridge, MA: Harvard University Press, 2016), 21–120).
21 Acts 16:19, King James Version (quotation); Jill Lepore, *The Name of War: King Philip's War and the Origins of American Identity* (New York: Knopf, 1998), xvi–xvii. The company seal of Plymouth's neighbor, the Massachusetts Bay Company, portrayed a Gospel-starved Native American saying "Come over and help us."
22 Daniel K. Richter, *The Ordeal of the Longhouse: The Peoples of the Iroquois League in the Era of European Colonization* (Chapel Hill: University of North Carolina Press, 1992), 75–95; Charles T. Gehring, ed. and trans., *Fort Orange Court Minutes, 1652–1660* (Syracuse: Syracuse University Press, 1990), 453 (quotation).
23 Richter, *Ordeal of the Longhouse*, 50–74; José António Brandão, "'Your fyre shall burn no more': Iroquois Policy toward New France and Its Native Allies to 1701* (Lincoln: University of Nebraska Press, 1997), 72–91; William A. Fox, "Events as Seen from the North: The Iroquois and Colonial Slavery," *Mapping the Mississippian Shatter Zone: The Colonial Indians Slave Trade and Regional Instability in the American South*, eds. Robbie Ethridge and Sheri M. Shuck-Hall (Lincoln: University of Nebraska Press, 2009), 63–80.
24 Richter, *Ordeal of the Longhouse*, 96–104; Francis Jennings, "Glory, Death, and Transfiguration: The Susquehannock Indians in the Seventeenth Century," *Proceedings of the American Philosophical Society* 112 (1968): 17–23.
25 Maureen Meyers, "From Refugees to Slave Traders: The Transformation of the Westo Indians," *Mapping the Mississippian Shatter Zone*, 81–103; Eric E. Bowne, "'Carynge away their Corne and Children': The Effects of Westo Slave Raids on the Indians of the Lower South," *Mapping the Mississippian Shatter Zone*, 104–114; C. S. Everett, "'They shalbe slaves for their lives': Indian Slavery in Colonial Virginia," *Indian Slavery in Colonial America*, ed. Alan Gallay (Lincoln: University of Nebraska Press, 2009), 67–78; Langdon, Cheves, ed., *The Shaftesbury Papers and other Records Relating to Carolina and the First Settlement on the Ashley River prior to the Year 1676* (Charleston: South Carolina Historical Society, 2010 [orig. publ. 1897]), 194 (quotation).
26 James H. Merrell, *The Indians' New World: Catawbas and Their Neighbors from European Contact through the Era of Removal* (Chapel Hill: University of North Carolina Press, 1989), 40–41; April Lee Hatfield, *Atlantic Virginia: Intercolonial Relations in the Seventeenth Century* (Philadelphia; University of Pennsylvania Press, 2004), 32–33; Eric E. Bowne, *The Westo Indians: Slave Traders of the Early Colonial South* (Tuscaloosa: University of Alabama Press, 2005), 72–88.
27 Marvin T. Smith, "Aboriginal Depopulation in the Postcontact Southeast," *The Forgotten Centuries: Indians and Europeans in the American South, 1521–1704*, eds. Charles Hudson and Carmen Chaves Tesser, (Athens: University of Georgia Press, 1994), 257–275; Robbie Ethridge, "Introduction: Mapping the Mississippian Shatter Zone," *Mapping the Mississippian Shatter Zone*, 1–62; Matthew H. Jennings, "Violence in a Shattered World," *Mapping the Mississippian Shatter Zone*, 272–294. The best survey of what is known about regional demography is Peter H. Wood, "The Changing Population of the Colonial

South: An Overview by Race and Region, 1685–1790," *Powhatan's Mantle: Indians in the Colonial Southeast*, rev. ed., eds. Gregory A. Waselkov, Wood, and Tom Hatley (Lincoln: University of Nebraska Press, 2006), 57– 132.

28 Verner W. Crane, *The Southern Frontier, 1670–1732* (New York: W.W. Norton, 1981 [orig. publ. 1928]), 3–15; David J. Weber, *The Spanish Frontier in North America* (New Haven: Yale University Press, 1992), 100–105; Jerald T. Milanich, "Franciscan Missions and Native Peoples in Spanish Florida," *Forgotten Centuries*, 276–303; Paul E. Hoffman, *Florida's Frontiers* (Bloomington: Indiana University Press, 2002), 125–147; Robert C. Galgano, *Feast of Souls: Indians and Spaniards in the Seventeenth-Century Missions of Florida and New Mexico* (Albuquerque: University of New Mexico Press, 2005).

29 James P. Ronda, "The Sillery Experiment: A Jesuit-Indian Village in New France, 1637–1663," *American Indian Culture and Research Journal*[1] (1979): 1–18; Alan Greer, *Mohawk Saint: Catherine Tekakwitha and the Jesuits* (New York: Oxford University Press, 2005); Greer, ed., *The Jesuit Relations: Natives and Missionaries in Seventeenth-Century North America* (Boston: Bedford-St. Martin, 2000), 1–19; Jean M. O'Brien, *Dispossession by Degrees: Indian Land and Identity in Natick, Massachusetts, 1650–1790* (New York: Cambridge University Press, 1997), 1–64; Anonymous, *New Englands First Fruits; in Respect First of the Conversion of Some, Conviction of Divers, Preparation of Sundry of the Indians* (London, 1643); Kristina Bross, *Dry Bones and Indian Sermons: Praying Indians in Colonial America* (Ithaca, NY: Cornell University Press, 2004).

30 Lawrence Averell Harper, *The English Navigation Laws: A Seventeenth-Century Experiment in Social Engineering* (New York: Columbia University Press, 1939), 34–39; Kenneth J. Banks, *Chasing Empire across the Sea* (Montreal: McGill-Queen's University Press, 2002), 22–27.

31 Untitled report, c. 1663, CO 1/17, No. 113, The National Archives (TNA), Kew (quotation); Commission and Instructions to Richard Nicolls, et al., CO 1/18, nos. 48, 51, 53, 54, TNA; Robert C. Ritchie, *The Duke's Province: A Study of New York Politics and Society, 1664–1691* (Chapel Hill: University of North Carolina Press, 1977), 9–46.

32 M. Eugene Sirmans, *Colonial South Carolina: A Political History* (Chapel Hill: University of North Carolina Press, 1966), 3–17; *Documents Relative to the Colonial History of the State of New York*, 15 vols., eds. E.B. O'Callaghan and Berthold Fernow, eds. (Albany, NY, 1853–1887), Vol. 9, 22–29 (quotation from 25).

33 Francis Jennings, *The Invasion of America: Indians, Colonialism, and the Cant of Conquest* (Chapel Hill: University of North Carolina Press, 1975), 280–286; E.E. Rich, *The History of the Hudson's Bay Company, 1670–1870*, 2 vols. (London: Hudson's Bay Record Society, 1958–1959), vol. 1: 21–60.

34 Richter, *Ordeal of the Longhouse*, 99–104; Thwaites, *Jesuit Relations*, Vol. 57, 25 (quotation).

35 Thwaites, *Jesuit Relations*, Vol. 55, 105–113 (first quotation from 111–113); [Claude-Charles] Bacqueville de La Potherie, *Histoire de l'Amerique Septentrionale*, 4 vols. (Paris, [1722]), Vol. 2, 123–130; B. F. French, ed., *Historical Collections of Louisiana, Embracing Many Rare and Valuable Documents Relating to the Natural, Civil and Political History of That State*, Part 1 (New York: Wiley and Putnam, 1846), 45–50 (second quotation from 47).

36 Richard White, *The Middle Ground: Indians, Empires, and Republics in the Great Lakes Region, 1650–1815* (New York: Cambridge University Press, 1991), 1–185; Patricia Galloway, "'The Chief Who Is Your Father': Choctaw and French Views of the Diplomatic Relation," in Waselkov, Wood, and Hatley, eds., *Powhatan's Mantle*, 345–370; Michael Witgen, *An Infinity of Nations: How the Native New World Shaped Early North America* (Philadelphia: University of Pennsylvania Press, 2012); Michael A. McDonnell, *Masters of Empire: Great Lakes Indians and the Making of America* (New York: Hill and Wang, 2015).

37 Daniel K. Richter, "Dutch Dominos: The Fall of New Netherland and the Reshaping of Eastern North America," Richter, *Trade, Land, Power: The Struggle for Eastern North America* (Philadelphia: University of Pennsylvania Press, 2013), 97–112; Victor Hugo Paltsits, ed., *Minutes of the Executive Council of the Province of New York: Administration of Francis Lovelace, 1668–1673*, 2 vols. (Albany: State of New York, 1910), Vol. 2, 502 (quotation).

38 Charles M. Andrews, ed., *Narratives of the Insurrections, 1675–1690* (New York: Charles Scribner's Sons, 1915), 18 (1st quotation); Thwaites, *Jesuit Relations*, Vol. 59, 251 (second quotation); William Hand Browne, et al., eds., *Archives of Maryland*, 72 vols. (Baltimore: Maryland Historical Society, 1883–1972), Vol. 2, 428–429 (third quotation). Francis Jennings, *The Ambiguous Iroquois Empire: The Covenant Chain Confederation of Indian Tribes with English Colonies from its Beginnings to the Lancaster Treaty of 1744* (New York: W.W. Norton, 1984), 135–141.

39 Everett, "'They shalbe slaves for their lives,'" 78–92; James D. Rice, "Bacon's Rebellion in Indian Country," *Journal of American History* 101 (2014), 726–750.

40 Quoted in T. H. Breen, "A Changing Labor Force and Race Relations in Virginia, 1660–1710," *Journal of Social History* 7 (1973–1974): 4.
41 Andrews, ed., *Narratives of the Insurrections*, 113.
42 Matthew Kruer, "'Our Time of Anarchy': Bacon's Rebellion and the Wars of the Susquehannocks, 1675–1682" (Ph.D. dissertation, University of Pennsylvania, 2015).
43 Pulsipher, *Records of the Colony*, Vol. 5, 76, 79 (first and second quotations); Charles H. Lincoln, ed., *Narratives of the Indian Wars, 1675–1699* (New York: Charles Scribner's Sons, 1913), 9 (third quotation); Lepore, *The Name of War*, 21–47.
44 T. H. Breen, "War, Taxes, and Political Brokers: The Ordeal of Massachusetts Bay, 1675–1692," Breen, *Puritans and Adventurers: Change and Persistence in Early America* (New York: Oxford University Press, 1980), 81–105; James D. Drake, *King Philip's War: Civil War in New England, 1675–1676* (Amherst: University of Massachusetts Press, 1999); Jenny Hale Pulsipher, *Subjects unto the Same King: Indians, English, and the Contest for Authority in Colonial New England* (Philadelphia: University of Pennsylvania Press, 2005); Daniel R. Mandell, *King Philip's War: Colonial Expansion, Native Resistance, and the End of Indian Sovereignty* (Baltimore: Johns Hopkins University Press, 2010); Margaret Ellen Newell, *Brethren by Nature: New England Indians, Colonists, and the Origins of American Slavery* (Ithaca, NY: Cornell University Press, 2015), 131–133, 143–159, 174–188, 212.
45 Increase Mather, *An Earnest Exhortation to the Inhabitants of New-England* (Boston, 1676), 9.
46 "Nathaniel Bacon Esq$_r$ his manifesto concerning the Present troubles in Virginia," 1676, CO 1/37, No. 51, TNA.
47 Neal Salisbury, "Introduction: Mary Rowlandson and Her Removes," Mary Rowlandson, *The Sovereignty and Goodness of God, Together with the Faithfulness of His Promises Displayed*, ed. Salisbury (Boston: Bedford Books, 1997), 2 (quotation); Drake, *King Philip's War*:), 35–56.
48 Lepore, *The Name of War*, 158–167 (Eliot quoted on 159); Jenny Hale Pulsipher, "Massacre at Hurtleberry Hill: Christian Indians and English Authority in Metacom's War," *William and Mary Quarterly*, 3d series, 53 (1996): 459–486.
49 Edmund Andros to William Blatwayt, September 16, 1678, CO 1/32, No. 124, TNA.
50 Order of royal commissioners, 1677, CO 5/1371, 116–119, TNA (first quotation from 117); Nicholas Spencer to Charles, Lord Baltimore, May 24, 1677, CO 1/40, No. 89, TNA (second quotation); Commissioners to Henry Coventry, March 27, 1677, CO 5/1371, 145–146, TNA (third quotation).
51 Herbert Jeffreys to Joseph Williamson, June 11, 1677, CO 1/40, No. 104, TNA; Articles of Peace, May 29, 1677, CO 1/40, No. 95, TNA; Order in council, October 19, 1677, CO 1/41, No. 82, TNA; *Articles of Peace between the Most Serene and Mighty Prince Charles II . . . and Several Indian Kings and Queens, etc. . . .* (London, 1677), quotations from 17, 5–6.
52 "A Short accompt of the Generall Concerns of New Yorke, from October 1674, to November 1677," CO 1/41, No. 116, TNA (quotation); Jennings, *Invasion of America*, 313–326.
53 Francis Jennings, "The Constitutional Evolution of the Covenant Chain," *Proceedings of the American Philosophical Society* 115 (1971), 88–96; Michael Leroy Oberg, *Dominion and Civility: English Imperialism and Native America, 1585–1685* (Ithaca, NY: Cornell University Press, 1999), 113–227 (first quotation from 221); O'Callaghan and Fernow, *Documents Relative to Colonial New-York*, 6:106 (second quotation).
54 Thomas Dongan to Earl of Sunderland, September 8, 1687, CO 1/3, No. 29, TNA; Treaty minutes, September 19, 1688, CO 1/65, No. 63IX, TNA (1st quotation from Fol. 229v); Treaty minutes, June 17–18, 1689, Notebook, Indians of North America, Miscellaneous Papers, American Antiquarian Society, Worcester, MA (2d quotation); Richter, *Ordeal of the Longhouse*, 135–189.
55 Alan Gallay, *The Indian Slave Trade: The Rise of the English Empire in the America South, 1670–1717* (New Haven: Yale University Press, 2002), 57–98, 288–314. Direct comparisons of the trades in enslaved Indians and Africans are difficult, but available figures for 1706–1715 show only 1,242 arrivals from Africa. A 1720 census counted a total 11,828 slaves in South Carolina, of whom an undetermined number were Native Americans (Peter Wood, *Black Majority: Negroes in Colonial South Carolina form 1670 through the Stono Rebellion* [New York: W. W. Norton, 1975 (orig. publ. 1974)], 145–151).
56 Daniel K. Richter, *Facing East from Indian Country: A Native History of Early America*, (Cambridge, Mass.: Harvard University Press, 2001), 151–164.
57 Bacqueville de La Potherie, *Histoire*, Vol. 4, 190–266; Treaty Minutes, July 19, 1701, CO 5/1046, No. 33(viii), Folio 289, TNA (quotation); Anthony F. C. Wallace, "Origins of Iroquois Neutrality: The Grand Settlement of 1701," *Pennsylvania History*, 24 (1957): 223–235; Gilles Havard, *The Great Peace of Montreal of 1701: French-Native Diplomacy in the Seventeenth Century*, trans. Phyllis Aronoff and Howard Scott (Montreal: McGill-Queens University Press, 2001); José António Brandão and William A. Starna,

"'Some things may slip out of your memory and be forgott': The 1701 Deed and Map of Iroquois Hunting Territory Revisited," *New York History* 86 (2005), 417–434.
58 Treaty Minutes, August 26–September 28, 1724, Massachusetts Archives Series, Vol. 29, Folio 181, Massachusetts State Archives, Boston (quotation); Richter, *Ordeal of the Longhouse*, 214–235.
59 Gallay, *Indian Slave Trade*, 127–256; John E. Worth, "Razing Florida: The Indian Slave Trade and the Devastation of Spanish Florida, 1659–1715," *Mapping the Mississippian Shatter Zone*, 295–311.
60 Douglas W. Boyce, "'As the Wind Scatters the Smoke': The Tuscaroras in the Eighteenth Century," *Beyond the Covenant Chain: The Iroquois and Their Neighbors in Indian North America, 1600–1800*, eds. Daniel K. Richter and James H. Merrell (Syracuse, NY; Syracuse University Press, 1987), 151–163; Christine Ann Styrna, "The Winds of War and Change: The Impact of the Tuscarora War on Proprietary North Carolina, 1690–1729" (Ph.D. dissertation, College of William and Mary, 1990), 118–178; David La Vere, *The Tuscarora War: Indians, Settlers, and the Fight for the Carolina Colonies* (Chapel Hill: University of North Carolina Press, 2013).
61 Richard L. Haan, The 'Trade Do's Not Flourish as Formerly': The Ecological Origins of the Yamassee War of 1715," *Ethnohistory* 28 (1982): 341–358; Paul Kelton, "Shattered and Infected: Epidemics and the Origins of the Yamasee War, 1696–1715," *Mapping the Mississippian Shatter Zone*, 312–332; Steven J. Oatis, *A Colonial Complex: South Carolina's Frontiers in the Era of the Yamasee War, 1680–1730* (Lincoln: University of Nebraska Press, 2004); William L. Ramsey, *The Yamasee War: A Study of Culture, Economy, and Conflict in the Colonial South* (Lincoln: University of Nebraska Press, 2008).
62 Verner W. Crane, *The Southern Frontier, 1670–1732* (New York: W. W. Norton, 1981 [orig. publ. 1928]), 108–186 (quotation from 182); Christina Snyder, *Slavery in Indian Country: The Changing Face of Captivity in Early America* (Cambridge, MA: Harvard University Press, 2010), 46–79.
63 Tom Hatley, *The Dividing Paths: Cherokees and South Carolinians through the Era of Revolution* (New York; Oxford University Press, 1994), 3–105; Gallay, *Indian Slave Trade*, 340 (quotation); Steven C. Hahn, *The Invention of the Creek Nation, 1670–1763* (Lincoln: University of Nebraska Press, 2004); Joseph M. Hall, *Zamumo's Gifts: Indian-European Exchange in the Colonial Southeast* (Philadelphia: University of Pennsylvania Press, 2009).
64 Peter Wraxall, *An Abridgment of the Indian Affairs Contained in Four Folio Volumes, Transacted in the Colony of New York, from the Year 1678 to the Year 1751*, ed. Charles Howard McIlwain (Cambridge, MA: Harvard University Press, 1915), 219n.
65 Alexander Spotswood to Peter Schuyler, January 25, 1720, Pennsylvania Provincial Council Records, Vol. F, 13–21, Pennsylvania State Archives, Harrisburg.
66 O'Callaghan and Fernow, *Documents Relative to Colonial New-York*, 7: 301.

References

Akemi Yakota, Kariann. *Unbecoming British: How Revolutionary America Became a Postcolonial Nation* (New York: Oxford University Press, 2011).
Altenbernd, Erik and Young, Alex Trimble. "Introduction: The Significance of the Frontier in an Age of Transnational History," *Settler Colonial Studies* 4 (2014), 127–150.
Andrews, Charles M., ed. *Narratives of the Insurrections, 1675–1690* (New York: Charles Scribner's Sons, 1915).
Andros, Edmund to William Blatwayt, September 16, 1678, CO 1/32, No. 124, TNA.
Anonymous, *New Englands First Fruits; in Respect First of the Conversion of Some, Conviction of Divers, Preparation of Sundry of the Indians* (London, 1643).
Anonymous, *No King but the Old Kings Son. Or, a Vindication of Limited Monarchy, as it Was Established in this Nation, Before the Late War Between the King and Parliament*, broadside (London, 1660).
Bacqueville, [Claude-Charles] de La Potherie, *Histoire de l'Amerique Septentrionale*, 4 vols. (Paris, [1722]), Vol. 2, 123–130.
Banks, Kenneth J. *Chasing Empire across the Sea* (Montreal: McGill-Queen's University Press, 2002).
Barksdale, Clement. *The Kings Return: A Sermon Preached at Winchcomb in Gloucestershire...* (London, 1660).
Bély, Lucien. "La paix des Pyrénées et les relations internationales au XVIIe siècle," *Hemecht: Zeitschrift für Luxemburger Geschichte/Revue d'Histoire Luxembourgeoise Journal* 62 (2010), 329–343.
Benton, Lauren A. *Law and Colonial Cultures: Legal Regimes in World History, 1400–1900* (New York: Cambridge University Press, 2002).

Benton, Lauren A. *A Search for Sovereignty: Law and Geography in European Empires, 1400–1900* (New York: Cambridge University Press, 2010).

Bowne, Eric E. "'Caryinge aweay their Corne and Children': The Effects of Westo Slave Raids on the Indians of the Lower South," *Mapping the Mississippian Shatter Zone*, eds. Ethridge and Shuck-Hall, 104–114.

Bowne, Eric E. *The Westo Indians: Slave Traders of the Early Colonial South* (Tuscaloosa: University of Alabama Press, 2005).

Boyce, Douglas W. "'As the Wind Scatters the Smoke': The Tuscaroras in the Eighteenth Century," *Beyond the Covenant Chain: The Iroquois and Their Neighbors in Indian North America, 1600–1800*, eds. Daniel K. Richter and James H. Merrell (Syracuse, NY; Syracuse University Press, 1987), 151–163.

Brandão, José António and Starna, William A. "'Some things may slip out of your memory and be forgott': The 1701 Deed and Map of Iroquois Hunting Territory Revisited," *New York History* 86 (2005): 417–434.

Brandão, José António. *"Your fyre shall burn no more": Iroquois Policy toward New France and Its Native Allies to 1701* (Lincoln: University of Nebraska Press, 1997).

Breen, T. H. "War, Taxes, and Political Brokers: The Ordeal of Massachusetts Bay, 1675–1692," *Puritans and Adventurers: Change and Persistence in Early America* (New York: Oxford University Press, 1980), 81–105.

Bross, Kristina. *Dry Bones and Indian Sermons: Praying Indians in Colonial America* (Ithaca, NY: Cornell University Press, 2004).

Browne, William Hand, et al., eds. *Archives of Maryland*, 72 vols. (Baltimore: Maryland Historical Society, 1883–1972), Vol. 2, 428–429.

Byrd, Jodi A. "Follow the Typical Signs: Settler Sovereignty and its Discontents, *Settler Colonial Studies*, 4 (2014): 151–154.

Byrd, Jodi A. *The Transit of Empire: Indigenous Critiques of Colonialism* (Minneapolis: University of Minnesota Press, 2011).

Cheves, Langdon, ed. *The Shaftesbury Papers and other Records Relating to Carolina and the First Settlement on the Ashley River prior to the Year 1676* (Charleston: South Carolina Historical Society, 2010 [orig. publ. 1897]).

Crane, Verner W. *The Southern Frontier, 1670–1732* (New York: W. W. Norton, 1981 [orig. publ. 1928]).

Dongan, Thomas to Earl of Sunderland, 8 September 1687, CO 1/3, No. 29, TNA.

Drake, James D. *King Philip's War: Civil War in New England, 1675–1676* (Amherst: University of Massachusetts Press, 1999).

Elkins, Caroline and Susan Pedersen, eds. *Settler Colonialism in the Twentieth Century: Projects, Practices, Legacies* (New York: Routledge, 2006).

Ethridge, Robbie. "Introduction: Mapping the Mississippian Shatter Zone," *Mapping the Mississippian Shatter Zone*, Ethridge and Shuck-Hall, eds., 1–62.

Everett, C. S. "'They shalbe slaves for their lives': Indian Slavery in Colonial Virginia," *Indian Slavery in Colonial America*, Alan Gallay, ed. (Lincoln: University of Nebraska Press, 2009), 67–78.

Faragher, John Mack. "Commentary: Settler Colonial Studies and the North American Frontier," *Settler Colonial Studies* 4 (2014): 181–191.

Fisher, Julie A. and David J. Silverman. *Ninigret. Sachem of the Niantics and Narragansetts: Diplomacy, War, and the Balance of Power in Seventeenth-Century New England* and *Indian Country* (Ithaca, NY: Cornell University Press, 2014).

Ford, Lisa. *Settler Sovereignty: Jurisdiction and Indigenous People in America and Australia, 1788–1836* (Cambridge, Mass: Harvard University Press, 2010).

Fox, William A. "Events as Seen from the North: The Iroquois and Colonial Slavery," *Mapping the Mississippian Shatter Zone: The Colonial Indians Slave Trade and Regional Instability in the American South*, eds. Robbie Ethridge and Sheri M. Shuck-Hall (Lincoln: University of Nebraska Press, 2009), 63–80.

French, B. F., ed., *Historical Collections of Louisiana, Embracing Many Rare and Valuable Documents Relating to the Natural, Civil and Political History of That State*, Part 1 (New York: Wiley and Putnam, 1846), 45–50.

Galgano, Robert C. *Feast of Souls: Indians and Spaniards in the Seventeenth-Century Missions of Florida and New Mexico* (Albuquerque: University of New Mexico Press, 2005).

Gallay, Alan. *The Indian Slave Trade: The Rise of the English Empire in the America South, 1670–1717* (New Haven: Yale University Press, 2002).

Galloway, Patricia. "'The Chief Who Is Your Father': Choctaw and French Views of the Diplomatic Relation," *Powhatan's Mantle*, eds. Waselkov, Wood, and Hatley, 345–370.

Gehring, Charles T., ed. and trans., *Fort Orange Court Minutes, 1652–1660* (Syracuse: Syracuse University Press, 1990).

Gould, Eliga H. "Zones of Law, Zones of Violence: The Legal Geography of the British Atlantic, Circa 1772," *William and Mary Quarterly*, 3d series, 60 (2003), 471–510.
Greene, Jack P. et al., "Roundtable," *William and Mary Quarterly*, 3d series, 64 (2007), 235–286.
Greer, Alan, ed., *The Jesuit Relations: Natives and Missionaries in Seventeenth-Century North America* (Boston: Bedford-St. Martin, 2000).
Greer, Alan. *Mohawk Saint: Catherine Tekakwitha and the Jesuits* (New York: Oxford University Press, 2005).
Haan, Richard L. "The 'Trade Do's Not Flourish as Formerly': The Ecological Origins of the Yamassee War of 1715," *Ethnohistory* 28 (1982): 341–358.
Hahn, Steven C. *The Invention of the Creek Nation, 1670–1763* (Lincoln: University of Nebraska Press, 2004).
Hall, Joseph M. *Zamumo's Gifts: Indian-European Exchange in the Colonial Southeast* (Philadelphia: University of Pennsylvania Press, 2009).
Harper, Lawrence Averell. *The English Navigation Laws: A Seventeenth-Century Experiment in Social Engineering* (New York: Columbia University Press, 1939).
Hatfield, April Lee. *Atlantic Virginia: Intercolonial Relations in the Seventeenth Century* (Philadelphia: University of Pennsylvania Press, 2004).
Hatley, Tom. *The Dividing Paths: Cherokees and South Carolinians through the Era of Revolution* (New York: Oxford University Press, 1994).
Havard, Gilles. *The Great Peace of Montreal of 1701: French-Native Diplomacy in the Seventeenth Century*, trans. Phyllis Aronoff and Howard Scott (Montreal: McGill-Queens University Press, 2001).
Hixson, Walter L. *American Settler Colonialism: A History* (New York: Palgrave Macmillan, 2013).
Hoffman, Paul E. *Florida's Frontiers* (Bloomington: Indiana University Press, 2002).
Hoxie, Frederick E. "Retrieving the Red Continent: Settler Colonialism and the History of American Indians in the US," *Ethnic and Racial Studies* 31 (2008): 1153–1167.
Jacobs, Japp. *New Netherland: A Dutch Colony in Seventeenth-Century America* (Leiden: Brill, 2005).
Jacobs, Margaret D. "Parallel or Intersecting Tracks? The History of the US West and Comparative Settler Colonialism," *Settler Colonial Studies* 4 (2014), 155–161.
Jeffreys, Herbert to Joseph Williamson, 11 June 1677, CO 1/40, No. 104, TNA.
Jennings, Francis. "Glory, Death, and Transfiguration: The Susquehannock Indians in the Seventeenth Century," *Proceedings of the American Philosophical Society*, 112 (1968), 17–23.
Jennings, Francis. "The Constitutional Evolution of the Covenant Chain," *Proceedings of the American Philosophical Society* 115 (1971), 88–96.
Jennings, Francis. *The Ambiguous Iroquois Empire: The Covenant Chain Confederation of Indian Tribes with English Colonies from its Beginnings to the Lancaster Treaty of 1744* (New York: W.W. Norton, 1984).
Jennings, Francis. *The Invasion of America: Indians, Colonialism, and the Cant of Conquest* (Chapel Hill: University of North Carolina Press, 1975).
Jennings, Matthew H. "Violence in a Shattered World," Ethridge and Shuck-Hall, eds., *Mapping the Mississippian Shatter Zone*, 272–294.
Jones, David S. "Virgin Soils Revisited," *William and Mary Quarterly*, 3d series, 60 (2003), 703–742. Kelton, Paul. "Shattered and Infected: Epidemics and the Origins of the Yamasee War, 1696–1715," *Mapping the Mississippian Shatter Zone*, eds. Ethridge and Shuck-Hall, 312–332.
Kelton, Paul. *Epidemics and Enslavement: Biological Catastrophe in the Native Southeast, 1492–1715* (Lincoln: University of Nebraska Press, 2007).
Kruer, Matthew. "'Our Time of Anarchy': Bacon's Rebellion and the Wars of the Susquehannocks, 1675–1682" (Ph.D. dissertation, University of Pennsylvania, 2015).
La Vere, David. *The Tuscarora War: Indians, Settlers, and the Fight for the Carolina Colonies* (Chapel Hill: University of North Carolina Press, 2013).
Lepore, Jill. *The Name of War: King Philip's War and the Origins of American Identity* (New York: Knopf, 1998).
McDonnell, Michael A. *Masters of Empire: Great Lakes Indians and the Making of America* (New York: Hill and Wang, 2015).
Mandell, Daniel R. *King Philip's War: Colonial Expansion, Native Resistance, and the End of Indian Sovereignty* (Baltimore; Johns Hopkins University Press, 2010).
Merrell, James H. *The Indians' New World: Catawbas and Their Neighbors from European Contact through the Era of Removal* (Chapel Hill; University of North Carolina Press, 1989).
Meyers, Maureen. "From Refugees to Slave Traders: The Transformation of the Westo Indians," *Mapping the Mississippian Shatter Zone*, eds. Ethridge and Shuck-Hall (Lincoln, NE: University of Nebraska Press, 2009): 81–103.
Milanich, Jerald T. "Franciscan Missions and Native Peoples in Spanish Florida," *Forgotten Centuries*, eds. Hudson and Tesser, 276–303.

Newell, Margaret Ellen. *Brethren by Nature: New England Indians, Colonists, and the Origins of American Slavery* (Ithaca, NY: Cornell University Press, 2015).

O'Brien, Jean M. *Dispossession by Degrees: Indian Land and Identity in* Natick, *Massachusetts, 1650–1790* (New York: Cambridge University Press, 1997).

O'Callaghan, E.B. and Fernow, Berthold, eds., *Documents Relative to the Colonial History of the State of New York*, 15 vols., eds. O'Callaghan and Fernow, Berthold, eds. (Albany, NY, 1853–1887), Vol. 9, 22–29.

Oatis, Steven J. *A Colonial Complex: South Carolina's Frontiers in the Era of the Yamasee War, 1680–1730* (Lincoln: University of Nebraska Press, 2004).

William L. Ramsey, *The Yamasee War: A Study of Culture, Economy, and Conflict in the Colonial South* (Lincoln: University of Nebraska Press, 2008).

Oberg, Michael Leroy. *Dominion and Civility: English Imperialism and Native America, 1585–1685* (Ithaca, NY: Cornell University Press, 1999).

Oberg, Michael Leroy. *Uncas: First of the Mohegans* (Ithaca, NY; Cornell University Press, 2003).

Paltsits, Victor Hugo, ed. *Minutes of the Executive Council of the Province of New York: Administration of Francis Lovelace, 1668–1673*, 2 vols. (Albany: State of New York, 1910)

Pulsipher, Jenny Hale. "Massacre at Hurtleberry Hill: Christian Indians and English Authority in Metacom's War," *William and Mary Quarterly*, 3rd series, 53: (1996) 459–486.

Pulsipher, Jenny Hale. *Subjects unto the Same King: Indians, English, and the Contest for Authority in Colonial New England* (Philadelphia: University of Pennsylvania Press, 2005).

Rice, James D. "Bacon's Rebellion in Indian Country," *Journal of American History* 101 (2014): 726–750.

Rich, E.E. *The History of the Hudson's Bay Company, 1670–1870*, 2 vols. (London: Hudson's Bay Record Society, 1958–1959).

Richter, Daniel K. *The Ordeal of the Longhouse: The Peoples of the Iroquois League in the Era of European Colonization* (Chapel Hill: University of North Carolina Press, 1992).

Richter, Daniel K. *Facing East from Indian Country: A Native History of Early America*, (Cambridge, MA: Harvard University Press, 2001).

Richter, Daniel K. *Before the Revolution: America's Ancient Pasts* (Cambridge, Mass., Harvard University Press, 2011).

Richter, Daniel K. "Dutch Dominos: The Fall of New Netherland and the Reshaping of Eastern North America," *Trade, Land, Power: The Struggle for Eastern North America* (Philadelphia: University of Pennsylvania Press, 2013), 97–112.

Richter, Daniel K. *Trade, Land, Power: The Struggle for Eastern North America* (Philadelphia: University of Pennsylvania Press, 2013), 97–112.

Rink, Oliver A. *Holland on the Hudson: An Economic and Social History of Dutch New York* (Ithaca, NY: Cornell University Press, 1986).

Ritchie, Robert C. *The Duke's Province: A Study of New York Politics and Society, 1664–1691* (Chapel Hill: University of North Carolina Press, 1977), 9–46.

Ronda, James P. "The Sillery Experiment: A Jesuit-Indian Village in New France, 1637–1663," *American Indian Culture and Research Journal* 3, 1 (1979): 1–18.

Routledge, F. J. *England and the Treaty of the Pyrenees* (Liverpool: University of Liverpool Press, 1953).

Rowlandson, Mary. "Introduction: Mary Rowlandson and Her Removes," *The Sovereignty and Goodness of God, Together with the Faithfulness of His Promises Displayed*, Neal Salisbury (Boston: Bedford Books, 1997).

Saler, Bethel. *The Settlers Empire: Colonialism and State Formation in America's Old Northwest* (Philadelphia: University of Pennsylvania Press, 2014).

Salisbury, Neal. *Manitou and Providence: Indians, Europeans, and the Making of New England, 1500–1643* (New York: Oxford University Press, 1982).

Shoemaker, Nancy. "A Typology of Colonialism," *Perspectives on History* 53[7] (October 2015): 29–30.

Silverman, David J. *Thundersticks: Firearms and the Transformation of Native America* (Cambridge, MA: Harvard University Press, 2016).

Sirmans, M. Eugene. *Colonial South Carolina: A Political History* (Chapel Hill: University of North Carolina Press, 1966).

Smith, Marvin T. "Aboriginal Depopulation in the Postcontact Southeast," *The Forgotten Centuries: Indians and Europeans in the American South, 1521–1704*, eds. Charles Hudson and Carmen Chaves Tesser (Athens: University of Georgia Press, 1994), 257–275.

Snyder, Christina. *Slavery in Indian Country: The Changing Face of Captivity in Early America* (Cambridge, Mass.: Harvard University Press, 2010).

Styrna, Christine Ann. "The Winds of War and Change: The Impact of the Tuscarora War on Proprietary North Carolina, 1690–1729" (Ph.D. dissertation, College of William and Mary, 1990).

Thwaites, Reuben Gold ed. *The Jesuit Relations and Allied Documents: Travels and Explorations of the Jesuit Missionaries in New France, 1610–1791*, 73 vols. (Cleveland, OH: Burrows Brothers, 1896–1901).

Veracini, Lorenzo. *Settler Colonialism A Theoretical Overview* (New York: Palgrave Macmillan, 2010).

Wallace, Anthony F. C. "Origins of Iroquois Neutrality: The Grand Settlement of 1701," *Pennsylvania History* 24 (1957): 223–235.

Weber, David J. *The Spanish Frontier in North America* (New Haven: Yale University Press, 1992).

White, Richard. *The Middle Ground: Indians, Empires, and Republics in the Great Lakes Region, 1650–1815* (New York: Cambridge University Press, 1991).

Witgen, Michael. *An Infinity of Nations: How the Native New World Shaped Early North America* (Philadelphia: University of Pennsylvania Press, 2012).

Wolfe, Patrick. "Land, Labor, and Difference: Elementary Structures of Race," *American Historical Review* 106 (2001), 867–869.

Wolfe, Patrick. "After the Frontier: Separation and Absorption in US Indian Policy," *Settler Colonial Studies* 1 (2011), 13–51.

Wolfe, Patrick. "Recuperating Binarism: A Heretical Introduction," *Settler Colonial Studies* 3 (2013): 257–279.

Wolfe, Patrick. "The Settler Complex: An Introduction," *American Indian Culture and Research Journal* 37 (2013): 1.

Wolfe, Patrick. *Settler Colonialism and the Transformation of Anthropology: The Politics and Poetics of an Ethnographic Event* (New York: Cassell, 1999).

Wood, Peter H. "The Changing Population of the Colonial South: An Overview by Race and Region, 1685–1790," *Powhatan's Mantle: Indians in the Colonial Southeast*, rev. ed., eds. Gregory A. Waselkov, Wood, and Tom Hatley (Lincoln: University of Nebraska Press, 2006), 57–132.

Wood, Peter. *Black Majority: Negroes in Colonial South Carolina from 1670 through the Stono Rebellion* (New York: W. W. Norton, 1975 [orig. publ. 1974]).

Worth, John E. "Razing Florida: The Indian Slave Trade and the Devastation of Spanish Florida, 1659–1715," *Mapping the Mississippian Shatter Zone*, eds. Ethridge and Shuck-Hall, 295–311.

Wraxall, Peter. *An Abridgment of the Indian Affairs Contained in Four Folio Volumes, Transacted in the Colony of New York, from the Year 1678 to the Year 1751*, ed. Charles Howard McIlwain (Cambridge, MA: Harvard University Press, 1915).

# 11
THE CHESAPEAKE
Putting Maryland on the Map

Kathleen M. Brown

To judge by John Smith's early seventeenth-century map of the Chesapeake Bay, there was a grain of truth in planter William Byrd's subsequent boastful claim, "in the beginning all America was Virginia." Smith's depiction, completed in 1612, presented the Bay as it appeared to approaching English ships. Surrounding the bay on all sides was land labeled "Virginia," a reflection of Smith's seemingly obtuse failure to recognize Indian inhabitants. Yet in its details, Smith's map revealed his careful observation and engagement with Native Americans, whose place names for rivers, creeks, and villages he carefully recorded. Sponsors of the Maryland colony, founded by proprietary charter in 1633 and settled the following year, struggled to supplant this formative representation of the Chesapeake with one that included their own claims—literally, an effort to put their colony on the map. When, some 50 years after Smith, adventurer Augustin Hermann, originally from Prague, compiled a new map of the region that clearly distinguished Maryland from its southern neighbor, the elated members of the Maryland assembly made him an honorary citizen and bestowed upon him 5000 acres of land.

Although the Virginia colony claimed pride of place and historical preeminence, Virginia and Maryland were linked not only by their geographic and historical proximity, but by their similar topographies, tobacco economies, and early resort to slave labor. The coastal lowlands, known as "the Tidewater" in Virginia and in Maryland as the "Eastern Shore" featured estuarial marshes and expansive fields, many of them former Indian cultivation grounds. After tobacco production proved both feasible and profitable, both colonies turned wholeheartedly to producing for global markets. In both colonies, wealthy tobacco planters began to purchase bound African laborers even before the supply of English servants diminished during the 1660s. Although he failed to recognize this emergent use of slave labor, promotional pamphleteer John Hammond analogized the colonies to the "Two Fruitfull Sisters" of biblical fame, whose fecundity promised prosperity to male immigrants and investors. Like Leah and Rachel, England's two colonies on the North American mainland presented alluring opportunities to the men who exploited the soil to produce tobacco for a global market.[1]

Yet for all these similarities, Maryland and Virginia occupy different places in the historiography of early North America. Distinct political and religious histories and investments in slave labor, among other factors, explain in part how Virginia came to have an outsized significance in the national narrative. Whereas Virginia began as a short-lived company, Maryland became the first proprietary colony; Virginia's embrace of the Anglican establishment at the end of the seventeenth century gave rise to religious revivals of Baptists and Methodists, while Maryland tolerated dissenters, including Catholics, Quakers, and Puritans, and established no parishes until 1692. The independent tributary chiefdom of Powhatan dominated the tidewater peninsulas formed by Virginia's three rivers while the Susquehannocks, Piscataways, Patuxents, and Nanticokes inhabited the region to the north. Aside from these well-known facts, there is also Virginia's place as a prime setting for national mythmaking, including Pocahontas's alleged rescue of John Smith, the fiery speeches of Patrick Henry, Jefferson's articulation of independence, Washington's retirement to Mount Vernon, and the holy triangle of Jamestown, Williamsburg, and Yorktown. Virginia history reveals the deep investments of Americans in a past every bit as mythic as that of Puritans and Wampanoags feasting on turkey together at the first Thanksgiving in Massachusetts Bay. It would take the equivalent of a historiographic bombshell to displace this mythic history, yet to some degree, this is what the concept of the Chesapeake achieved.

How did the historical concept of "the Chesapeake," come into being? What did we gain by adopting this regional approach rather than continuing to focus on individual colonies? Judged by the last twenty years of scholarship, is the Chesapeake still a useful concept for historians?

The historiography of the region we now think of as the Chesapeake reveals three general trends. First, beginning in the late nineteenth century, historians approached Virginia and Maryland as separate colonies with distinct political histories, with Virginia ranking first for the significance of its political history for the national narrative. Second, beginning with the rise of the new social history and quantitative methods during the 1970s, scholars approached the colonies as part of a single Chesapeake region. Political differences between Maryland and Virginia faded in comparison to their common history as "tobacco colonies." Historians found regional coherence in the political economy of slave-produced tobacco, the demography of settlement and slavery, and the ecology and maritime economy of the Chesapeake Bay. In the third and most recent shift, historians of the Atlantic and other revisionist scholars have built upon the insights of the regional approach to analyze each colony's distinctive political and legal history.[2]

Redeeming the South

Much as it dominated early cartographic representations and William Byrd's historical imagination, Virginia also dominated the early historical scholarship on the colonial south. In studies that exhibited an unapologetic southern nationalism, scholars deployed social Darwinist and eugenic logic to explain the evolution of white society in the southern colonies. Historians Philip Bruce, Thomas Wertenbaker, James Ballagh, and Charles Sydnor contended with a Yankee dominated historical profession righteously dedicated to tracing the Puritan roots of a self-conscious American "civilization." Focusing on Virginia rather than on the other southern colonies allowed these scholars to make a dignified retort. In the history of the colony that gave rise to Patrick Henry, George Washington, Thomas Jefferson, and James Madison, they sought redemption for the antebellum, Confederate, and postwar South's racial and political sins. A few located the germ of American character in early Virginia, defining seventeenth century white colonial society as predominantly middle class, democratic, and devoted to liberty. In many ways, their efforts to claim a wholesome, white southern colonial history paralleled the work of their African American activist contemporaries who were engaged in what one historian has dubbed the "politics of respectability."[3]

Philip Bruce, born in Charlotte County, Virginia, in 1856 to one of the largest slaveowning families in the state, trained in law at the University of Virginia and at Harvard. He began his career as a historian with *The Plantation Negro as Freeman* (1889), a study that manifested his family's strong Confederate connections and his own beliefs in white supremacy. During the course of his long career, he wrote many carefully researched volumes on Virginian history—economic, social, and institutional—that made use of newly published primary source material he had helped to make accessible in the *Virginia Magazine of History and Biography*, which he helped to found. He spent a considerable portion of his career writing a history of the University of Virginia that celebrated the vision of Thomas Jefferson. Much as his earlier studies had focused on Virginia's most eminent white male citizens, his *Virginia Plutarch* (1929) offered collective biographies of influential white men with only Pocahontas and Powhatan as exceptions. Bruce's career as a historian was supported after 1907 by his inheritance of 1,400 acres of the family estate in Charlotte County. Ultimately, the labor extracted from slaves built the patrimony that enabled Bruce to write histories denigrating African-Americans and celebrating of the achievements of white Virginians.[4]

Bruce's early work appeared the same year as Jeffrey Richardson Brackett's *Negro in Maryland* (Baltimore, 1889). Born in Massachusetts and educated at Harvard, Brackett subsequently taught at Johns Hopkins where practitioners of so-called scientific history had inaugurated a book series. In keeping with the premises of this approach, Brackett limited the scope of his study to a single colony so as to improve its accuracy. His is a fact-laden chronology of the laws and court cases creating the institution of slavery and an account of the eventual dismantling of that institution through manumission and emancipation. Brackett dutifully observed that the early similarity of the white servant to the African slave gave way to pronounced distinctions as the numbers of slaves increased, but he did not hypothesize the reasons for the change.[5]

Thomas Wertenbaker, born and educated in Virginia, is now remembered mainly for lamenting the arrival of African slaves who, he claimed, undermined the colony's white yeomanry. But in his 1910 doctoral thesis he challenged the widely accepted interpretation that a Cavalier migration had determined the character of white society. Rather, he argued, early seventeenth-century migrants fell into two major categories, merchants and people of low birth, before being repurposed for political virtue by colonial conditions. In Wertenbaker's analysis, the poor laborer, the hunted debtor, the captive rebel, and the criminal had now thrown aside their old characters and become well-to-do and respected citizens. They had been made over—had been created anew by the economic conditions in which they found themselves, as filthy rags are purified and changed into white paper in the hands of the manufacturer. The relentless law of survival of the fittest worked upon them with telling force and thousands that could not stand the severe test imposed upon them by conditions in the New World succumbed to the fever of the tobacco fields, or quitted the colony, leaving to stronger and better hands the upbuilding of the Middle class.

Virginia's merchant migrants experienced a similar transformation owing to the "feudal" character of their large tobacco plantations. Wealth, isolation, and power created the conditions for cultures of chivalry, honor, and pride to blossom. Such conditions also gave rise to the spirit of serving the public good that Wertenbaker found so abundant in the generation of the Founding Fathers, and that accounted for Virginia's preeminence during the Revolution and early national periods.[6]

Two years after Wertenbaker completed his dissertation, Carter G. Woodson, the son of enslaved Virginians, completed his own doctoral thesis, "The Disruption of Virginia." Initially educated at Chicago (he could not attend a still segregated University of Virginia), Woodson began a long career dedicated to African American history. In his doctoral study, which ranged from the early eighteenth century to the beginning of the Civil War, Woodson built on Frederick Jackson Turner's frontier thesis to argue that slavery fomented class conflict between eastern planters and smallholders in the west. He subsequently dedicated his life to professionalizing African American history, launching the *Journal of Negro History* three years later and authoring two books on free African Americans.[7]

Wertenbaker's and Woodson's histories of Virginia appeared just as the Johns Hopkins' book series expanded to subjects beyond Maryland. James Ballagh, trained in the Hopkins research methods, presented evidence that, before the first slavery statutes appeared in 1660, Africans were generally treated like indentured servants. *The History of Slavery in Virginia* (1902), his third book, includes an early chapter on the status of "Negroes and Indians" and emphasizes the relative equality of bound laborers in the colony. His study spawned debates among several other Virginia historians who offered evidence of both difference and similarity in the conditions of the colony's laborers. Among Ballagh's reviewers was Harvard's first African American doctoral student, W. E. B. DuBois, who described Ballagh's study as the "best local study of American slavery," (perhaps a tongue-in-cheek compliment?) but took issue with his romanticized interpretation of slavery as a British institution foisted upon a reluctant colony.[8]

These early studies of Virginia had a wide reach. The leading scholar of southern history in the United States, Ulrich B. Phillips, generally accepted Ballagh's conclusions. Afro-Caribbean historian Eric Williams, meanwhile, was deeply influenced by Ballagh's and Wertenbaker's argument that slavery in Virginia was institutionalized relatively late and motivated by profit rather than by racism. In *Capitalism and Slavery* (1944) Williams ventures a then-controversial critique of British humanitarian motives, arguing that the British abolition modement was actually propelled by the pursuit of profit.[9]

"The Chesapeake" did not figure in these early histories. Scholars focused either on Maryland or Virginia, with an overwhelming number choosing the latter as part of a larger project of redeeming southern history (or of redeeming Virginia from that history). Scholars interested in Maryland, including John Henderson Russell and James M. Wright, in contrast, followed the scientific approach. Their work consisted of detailed, technical, and local studies of voting patterns, property ownership, and office holding. Maryland, furthermore, offered little to southern historians in search of regional political respectability. They could not claim significance for the colony based on its influence upon emergent national political traditions. In addition to producing no presidents, Maryland's most prominent signer of the Declaration was an Irish Catholic, a dubious distinction in an era in which scholars and politicians alike celebrated Anglo-Saxon Protestants and Teutonic superiority and disparaged Catholic immigrants. Writing the history of the Old Dominion, in contrast, offered a chance at dignity, redemption, and restored national significance for the South.[10]

Race, Slavery, Region

Dissent against the Ballagh-Russell interpretation began appearing during the 1940s.[11] Susie M. Ames, a Virginia native who received her Ph.D. from Columbia, found evidence in the court records of Virginia's Eastern Shore that planters classified African laborers as slaves. In *Studies of the Eastern Shore in the Seventeenth Century* (1940), Ames took a fine-grained approach to just one of Virginia's subregions, a set of counties with distinctive migration patterns, politics, and economies. Wesley Frank Craven, author of *Southern Colonies in the Eighteenth Century* (New York, 1949) found Ames's interpretation persuasive. His macro approach to region ("southern" remained undefined but included Maryland, Virginia, the Carolinas, and Georgia) reflected the nineteenth-century divisions of the United States into the "free" North and the slaveholding South.

Charles Sydnor, a well-regarded southern historian and a contemporary of Craven, provides an illuminating example of what attracted scholars to the study of Virginia during this period. More than a generation younger than Ballagh and Dubois, Sydnor, who like Ballagh was educated at Hopkins in the scientific approach to history, initially wrote meticulous empirical studies of the slave South. Like his predecessor, U. B. Phillips, to whom he was often compared, his work on slavery in Mississippi did not challenge the white racial politics of his own time. After a bitter experience with white southern demagoguery at the University of Mississippi during the early 1930s, resulting in purges of an allegedly elitist faculty, he turned from defending slavery and criticizing Reconstruction to skepticism of white southern populism. In *American Revolutionaries in the Making* (1952) Sydnor found a redemptive politics in Washington's Virginia. Revolutionary Virginia, he contended, demonstrated the importance of the political process in selecting educated men to lead. Those serving in the Virginia's House of Burgesses on the eve of Revolution represented a harmonious compromise between the aristocratic tendencies of the wealthy planters and the populist democracy of the voters. It was no wonder that Virginia provided a disproportionate number of exceptional men who founded the nation.[12]

Just a few years later, Iowa-trained Aubrey Land used the family papers of Maryland's founder, Daniel Dulaney, and his son and namesake to offer a counterpoint to the iconic biographies of Virginia's great planters. Dulaney the elder rose from indentured servitude to political prominence as an attorney for Maryland's proprietors. Making good on every advantage of wealth, connection, and education, and writing an important criticism of the Stamp Act, Dulaney the younger decided not join the patriot leadership. This effort at neutrality ultimately cost him the family's vast estate and his political influence. Maryland's prominent founders, in contrast to their Virginia peers, offered little to connect the colonial plantocracy with revolutionary leadership and the political experiments of the new nation.[13]

Beginning in the late 1940s and early 1950s, however, American historians began to abandon questions based on southern nationalism, filiopietism, or the desire to document an American (i.e., Anglo-Saxon and Teutonic) "civilization" to focus instead on what we might recognize as regional cultures. This seemingly "objective" approach owed much to the arduous documentary labors of several female scholars. Susan Myra Kingsbury's decades-long effort resulted in the multivolume *Records of the Virginia Company of London* (1906–33). Attorney and historian Helen Tunnicliff Catterall, compiled *Judicial Cases Concerning American Slavery and the Negro* (Washington, 1926) in five volumes. Elizabeth Donnan, editor of the four-volume *Documents Illustrative of the History of the Slave Trade* (1930–35), made available essential sources about the traffic of enslaved Africans. And Nell Marion Nugent, an archivist with legal training, produced the two-volume *Cavaliers and Pioneers* (1934), a compendium of abstracts of Virginia land patents that includes the names of "headrights;" those family members, servants, and slaves whom land claimants transported to the colony. Maryland scholars continued to resort to the multivolume *Maryland Archives*, which remained the most important source for the colony's history, and to travel to dispersed local archives.

The regions that emerged from the scholarship making use of these newly available sources tended to be larger than a single colony but not always encompassing the entire American South. We can identify three main trends:

1 Historians began to use "Chesapeake" to refer to Maryland and Virginia together as tobacco colonies.
2 Scholarly interest grew in the Chesapeake Bay and its rivers as a bounded and coherent environmental and commercial region.
3 Scholars interested in the history of slavery brought Maryland into the conversation as they turned to statute law and court cases in colonies other than Virginia to expand their understanding of the institution's emergence.

We catch an initial glimpse of the idea of the Chesapeake as a regional culture in Wertenbaker's presidential address to the AHA in 1947 on the connections between democracy in colonial

Virginia and in subsequent settler communities in the trans-Mississippi West. As president of the organization, Wertenbaker urged historians to compare the influence of the tobacco colonies—Maryland, Virginia, and northern North Carolina—with the already acknowledged influence of New England upon the culture and institutions of the Upper Midwest (and, indeed, the nation). "The tobacco civilization of Maryland, Virginia, and northern North Carolina," Wertenbaker observed, "was shaped in a large measure by the soil, climate, and rivers of the Chesapeake Bay region." For Wertenbaker, the political and economic culture of the Chesapeake derived from its environment and suitability for tobacco cultivation, which, in turn, provided livelihoods for small producers. The unique culture of the region became a seedbed for the democratic political institutions of the trans-Mississippi West.

Wertenbaker's suggestion of a tobacco region received fuller treatment from Arthur Pierce Middleton, who eschewed individual colonies to conceptualize the Chesapeake as an ecological and commercial zone. In *Tobacco Coast: A Maritime History of the Chesapeake Bay in the Colonial Era* (1953), Middleton, who received his Ph.D. from Harvard, saw Virginia and Maryland as unified by the Bay itself. The Chesapeake, as he defined it, was both a unique ecosystem and a system of riverine transport that defined agriculture, settlement, and commerce. Borrowing from the European nomenclature that identified West and West Central African coastal regions according to the commodity traded (i.e., Ivory Coast, Gold Coast, and Slave Coast), Middleton imagined British merchants defining the region's geography in terms of its most valuable commodity.

During this initial foray into regional analysis, the dominant focus of debate continued to be political history, which meant that colony rather than region prevailed. Disputing the characterization of early Virginia as having successfully transitioned from Company to colonial government, Bernard Bailyn, in "Politics and Social Structure in Virginia," (1959) emphasized the ungovernable and antisocial features of Virginia's early decades as a Crown colony. Bailyn's interpretation influenced scholars for nearly two decades. Subsequent scholarship on seventeenth-century Maryland identified a similar pattern of turmoil giving way to demographic and institutional stability. The framework of political chaos yielding to order lent support to scholars looking for the causes of Bacon's Rebellion as well as for the deep roots of eighteenth-century political culture.[14]

Perhaps the first notable shift from colony to region appeared in the scholarship on race and slavery, a topic about which little had been written since Ballagh's early effort. Scholars writing during the 1950s and early 1960s were profoundly influenced by Frank Tannenbaum's *Slave and Citizen: The Negro in the Americas* (New York, 1947), an account of the Iberian American slave's legally protected and recognized personhood, and, to a lesser extent, Gilberto Freyre's *The Masters and the Slaves: A Study in the Development of Brazilian Civilization* (1946). Tannenbaum's and Freyre's work distinguished between the harsh slave regimes of the British colonies and the seemingly more humane regimes that emerged elsewhere in Latin America. Different imperial histories and policies, in turn, shaped distinct demographic patterns and institutional supports for slavery.

Informed by Tannenbaum and responding to the Civil Rights activism of their own times, several historians raised new questions about the historical formation of racism and the injustices it spawned. In 1950, Oscar and Mary Handlin embarked on a new analysis of the differences between labor in the North and South. They rejected the Cavalier vs. Roundhead approach to understanding the differences between Virginia and New England, as well as the climatic analysis that made slavery a natural outgrowth of agriculture in tropical weather zones like southern North America. Using sources drawn from Maryland, Virginia, Bermuda, and England, they asked a broad question about the slave South but evidence from Virginia loomed large in their response. How, they asked, had the opposition between free and unfree (with the many gradations of unfreedom owing much to the legacy of English villeinage) become the stark and racially based opposition between free and slave? After considering ancient precedents and conditions for slaves in the Iberian Americas and the British West Indies, the Handlins concluded that slavery did not exist in North America before 1660, only emerging fully by the mid-eighteenth century. The conditions of slavery external to British North America, they contended, could not explain the origins of chattel slavery in North America, where planters (i.e., Virginia planters) preferred white servant laborers and showed no special interest in African slaves until the 1660s:

> The distinctive qualities of the southern labor system were then not the simple products of the plantation. They were rather the complex outcome of a process by which the American environment broke down the traditional European conceptions of servitude. In that process the weight of the plantation had pinned down on the Negro the clearly-defined status of chattel, a status left him as other elements in the population achieved their liberation. (221)

Thus, in their analysis, seventeenth-century vectors of unfreedom clustered along three poles: the labor demands of New World plantations, the rising status of white laborers, and the degradation of Africans.[15]

Although he disagreed with the Handlins' interpretation, Carl Degler also leaned heavily on Tannenbaum's comparative imperial framework. Posing the question differently as, "Which appeared first, slavery or discrimination?" Degler came down on the side of early racial discrimination within the British empire, including Barbados, Somers Island, Providence Island, Virginia, Maryland, and New England. For Degler, the regional distinction that mattered was imperial: Hispanic and Portuguese slave regimes preexisted the actual practice of slavery in the Americas, whereas British colonial slavery built on a history of the degraded status of people of color, African and Indian, well before the legal institutionalization of slavery.[16]

Winthrop Jordan's 1962 "Modern Tensions," provided a dialectical response to the debate staked out by his predecessors and disputed the causal nature of the question posed by Degler. For the purposes of this initial article, Jordan drew mainly upon evidence from Virginia and Maryland. Using "mutual causation" theory, he examined early seventeenth-century examples of the differential and degraded treatment of people of African descent (although in an interesting post-*Brown v. Board* reflection he denied that difference necessarily signified inequality). Not until his subsequent magisterial work, *White Over Black*, did Jordan expand beyond the evidence from Maryland and Virginia to develop his complex rejoinder to the claim, embraced by Ballagh and others, that slavery was simply an economic institution that had little to do with racial prejudice. The truth, he argued, was both more complicated and dynamic; white people's racial views throughout the British colonies encouraged their exploitation of black laborers, and the use of Africans as chattel slaves encouraged racism directed at people of color. In *White Over Black*, Jordan offered as full a discussion of Maryland's laws concerning race and slavery, as he did for Virginia, Barbados, South Carolina, New York, and every other British colony in North America and the Caribbean.[17]

The continuing prominence of Virginia in the "origins debate" reflected both the previous tilt of the historiography toward Virginia and the prominence of Virginia's founding fathers on the nation's subsequent history. All scholars participating in the debate acknowledged Tannenbaum's distinction between British and Iberian slave regimes, yet their work advanced a new concept of region, one in which Maryland and Virginia shared a common history defined not just by proximity to the Chesapeake Bay and tobacco cultivation but by growing investments in slave labor. Jordan's meticulous research on slave law outside of Virginia opened up this view of the Chesapeake as a key region for the subsequent history of slavery in the American South and race in the modern United States. Jordan was ultimately less interested in genuflecting to the mythic status of Virginia's history, although he clearly shared the fascination of earlier scholars with Jefferson's troubled relationship to slavery. Rather, he focused on Virginia as one of many historical contexts in which planters turned to the law and the courts to solidify their claims on human property

The other formative contribution to the regional notion of the Chesapeake came from the prodigious Jacob M. Price, a Harvard-trained economic historian whose early articles and subsequent book-length studies chronicled Maryland's and Virginia's participation in a competitive Atlantic tobacco trade. Price, whose approach incorporated European history, economic history, and quantitative methods, brought new regional and Atlantic perspective to studies of the tobacco economies of North America. Methodologically ahead of his time, he applied quantitative methods to Atlantic capital formation in the eighteenth century. But even more important, although his de facto definition of the Chesapeake was based on its production of tobacco, in his analysis it became a region with a unique credit and capital footprint. Noting that the Chesapeake was "disproportionately capital intensive and credit prone," Price defined the region in terms of the relationships among four groups: the small and middling tobacco farmers who dominated production, the local merchants who facilitated marketing, the mercantile partnerships in London and Scotland who extended credit on long terms, and the British linen drapers and iron mongers who supplied export goods.[18]

At least one scholar revisited Wertenbaker's interpretation of Virginia's role as a crucible of American democracy. In *Virginia 1705–1785: Democracy or Aristocracy?* (1964) Richard Brown found that property ownership and voting among white men in the colony were more widespread than had been previously thought. Indeed, Brown's conclusions about the democratic ways of life available to white men challenged arguments that the most democratic communities in the English-speaking world prevailed in the towns of New England. Brown's conclusions about comparative democracy endured until twenty-first-century critiques pointed to the fallacy of failing to count enslaved people as a disenfranchised population.

Edmund Morgan's *American Slavery, American Freedom: The Ordeal of Colonial Virginia* (New York: Norton, 1975) offered perhaps the fullest conflation of Virginia with modern America and the one with the most profound implications. Morgan was not interested in the political economy of tobacco that united Virginia and Maryland, but in the emergence of populist democracy among white smallholders in Virginia at a time when larger planters were increasing their investment in slave labor. But Morgan's work also reflected the New Left historiography with its interest in Indigenous peoples. Along with Christian Feest, James Axtell, and Nancy Lurie, all of whom wrote about native peoples in Powhatan territory, he depicted a history of the Virginia in which the opening chapters are at least in part based on the response of indigenous peoples to the successive waves of Europeans.[19]

The Chesapeake Emerges

The big shift to approaching the Chesapeake as a coherent region came with the rise of the new social history. Dedicated to producing histories of people poorly represented in historical scholarship (working class people, people of color, women, and others considered to be of little political or intellectual import), social historians created new standards for historical significance. Quantitative analysis was just one of the methodologies that opened up new ways to work with seemingly unpromising sources. When linked to other record groups, including tax lists, inventories, land titles, and other probate documents, even a bare bones source might enable a diligent scholar to piece together the larger patterns of colonial settlers' lives. While these sources provided little basis for making claims about an individual's motives or happiness, they could provide information about entire cohorts of people and reveal patterns of change over time. Armed with quantitative methods, scholars revisited questions about the shift from white indentured to black labor. But they also documented the hardscrabble material lives and unprecedented mortality of early settlers, the absence of so-called natural reproduction among the settler population during the seventeenth century, and the shift from tobacco to grain. Although quantitative methods offered the possibility of empirically based claims about population and economy that would ultimately diminish the differences between Virginia and Maryland, ironically that broader reach came at the cost of undeniable partitioning. The labor intensiveness of gathering data for quantitative analyses led social historians to focus on ever-smaller fractions of colonial society—the county or the parish—even as their claims reflected on the characteristics of an entire region.

Harvard-trained historian Lois Green Carr's pioneering research in the sources at the Maryland Hall of Records (now the Maryland State Archives) and St. Mary's City laid the foundation for Chesapeake studies. For historians trained in quantitative methods, records from the Chesapeake were well suited to illuminating the lives of small and middling tobacco planters. This was especially true of those from Maryland, whose inhabitants had always received short shrift from historians, but whose records were newly convenient for historical research thanks to the efforts of Maryland State Archivist Morris L. Radoff. Beginning with her dissertation in 1968 and her subsequent work as a public historian at Historic St. Mary's City, Carr embarked on a remarkable and sustained project of "record stripping" to compile biographical files of all the colonial residents of St. Mary's City. This approach, based on linking different record groups, influenced an entire generation of scholars, including Russell Menard, Lorena Walsh, Carville Earle, Paul Clemens, Gloria Main, Edward Papenfuse, Ron Hoffman, Richard Beeman, Jean B. Russo, and Allan Kulikoff. Chesapeake scholars following in Carr's wake employed quantitative methods to identify patterns in life expectancy, family size, wealth accumulation, land ownership, and recourse to bound labor. Approached with social-historical methods and from the perspective of the Chesapeake, the disparity in the historical significance of Virginia and Maryland disappeared. Indeed, Maryland's records proved to be better than many of those in Virginia, where entire runs of county and General court records had burned during the Civil War.

If Lois Carr provided the methodological leadership for the Chesapeake school, she together with Lorena Walsh, Russell Menard, and Allan Kulikoff supplied the substance of the new findings in a series of pathbreaking articles published during the 1970s and 1980s. Together, they created a quantitatively demonstrated picture of Maryland tobacco-producing counties that only invested fully in slave labor at the end of the seventeenth century. They described white demography in the Chesapeake as characterized by early mortality, family rupture, and high child mortality throughout most of the seventeenth century. Not until the early eighteenth century did native-born white Marylanders and their children contribute to population growth at a rate greater than immigration. Meanwhile, white servants' numbers and opportunity were declining by the 1670s. Maryland's slave communities were similarly fractured by death and populated by "saltwater" slaves until they, too, began to produce a creole population larger than the proportion of incoming slaves after 1750. This was social history at its finest, and it illuminated a world of servants, slaves, and small planters who had otherwise been big players in the larger nationalist histories.[20]

Influenced by the dynamic intellectual energy of the "Maryland Mafia," a few young historians produced book-length studies using the Maryland records. All three were committed to the goal of discovering the economic logic governing colonial Chesapeake dwellers' decisions about production for the market, investment, consumption, and land allocation. Historical geographer Carville Earle examined 500 inventories in All Hallow's Parish on Maryland's western shore to pursue questions about the Chesapeake's characteristic dispersed settlement patterns. The seeming untidiness of the tobacco landscape, he argued, resulted not from soil exhaustion and economic decay but from the regular rotation of used lands into fallow.[21] Five years later, Paul Clemens also took a microhistorical approach to Maryland's eastern shore to link the conditions of the larger Atlantic economy, especially tobacco prices, to the decisions made by individual householders. Clemens' work echoed that of Menard and others about the decline of white servant opportunity when tobacco prices slumped during the 1680s and larger planters turned increasingly to slave labor. But he also detailed the decisions of an entire cohort of eighteenth-century planters in response to new markets for corn and wheat, to diversify their farms to produce grain.[22] Gloria Main's *Tobacco Colony* followed a few years later with a detailed analysis of 3700 inventories drawn from six quite different Maryland counties. Although her conclusions affirmed those of other Maryland historians about declining opportunity and growing wealth inequality by 1720, she found surprisingly little diversity in the material lives of planters during the 70 years following 1650. Main's planters were not a display-oriented gentry class by 1720, if they were to become one subsequently, and their chances of enjoying prosperity correlated to their longevity and ability to marry, father children who survived, and sustain their own households.[23]

A few scholars employing social history methods used them to ask questions about a world wider than the Chesapeake. Using probate records, Gloria Main compared wealth inequality in Maryland and Massachusetts, concluding that it marked both regions by 1720. In Maryland, the turn to slave labor by the wealthiest planters, the decline in the number of white servants, and the emergence of a native-born elite all exacerbated inequality. Carole Shammas compared the inventories of male decedents in England and Virginia, concluding that region itself was a less significant determinant of wealth than occupation. David Galenson examined the status of the typical English indentured servant headed for North America—a far cry from Wertenbaker's designation "plebian"—and found them to be a cross section of English society's "common sort" rather than representative of a middling order. He also assessed the impact of the shift away from indentured white servant labor and toward slavery in the British Caribbean. In a comparison of two very different slave societies designed to illuminate the impact of different plantation regimes on the lives of enslaved people, Richard S. Dunn revealed the brutality of Jamaican sugar production for family formation and slave mortality but refused to classify Virginia planters as benign. Spared some of the mortal dangers of climate and labor in the cane fields and sugar mills, Virginia slaves were nonetheless vulnerable to family separation and new planter methods for extracting labor.[24]

The Chesapeake school's forays into demography opened up new questions about the lives of women in colonies where they were notoriously few in number. Carr and Walsh teamed up to provide a sketch of the typical white female migrant's experience. They concluded that white women bore fewer children and lived for fewer years than their counterparts in New England. Although they often buried their short-lived husbands and remarried, they died at an earlier age than white male inhabitants of the Chesapeake. Carr's and Walsh's important article endured for decades as the only reliable social history evidence of white women's lives in the Chesapeake.[25] Eight years later, Shammas employed similar methods to shed light on the use of female slaves in Virginia. Disabusing her readers of impressions of female labor allocation based on "Gone With the Wind," she demonstrated the predominant assignment of enslaved women to field work but noted planters' growing investment in domestic and household labor, especially apparent in the employment of young girls in planter households by the last quarter of the eighteenth century.[26]

Maryland starred in the new social histories, often under the rubric of "the Chesapeake," but for those Virginia counties with unbroken sequences of records, quantitative methods also stimulated new interpretations. Darrett and Anita Rutman applied such methods to *A Place in Time* (1984), a narrative history of Middlesex County, Virginia, which they published along with an accompanying explicatus of their data. Rutman and Rutman showed that for one Tidewater county, distinguished by its production of the higher grade sweet-scented tobacco preferred by consumers, the shift to slave labor diminished opportunities for white upward mobility and dispersed social interactions into discreet, class-homogenous networks. Colonial Williamsburg also joined the social history bandwagon. Opened for the first time to the public as an open-air living history museum in the early 1930s and subsequently supported by a National Endowment for the Humanities grant, Colonial Williamsburg hired Carr's coauthor and collaborator Lorena Walsh, to lead its research efforts. One of these, the York County, Virginia Record Project, used record linking methods to produce a wealth of biographies and research reports about life, death, and material conditions in this Virginia tidewater county.[27]

In the decade after the social history turn, a new crop of historians used new methods to address the question of Virginia's relationship to southern culture. Using what he identified as a dramaturgical approach, Rhys Isaac deciphered the eighteenth-century shift from a communal culture of deference to a contract-based, individual culture that had begun to value privacy. Isaac's *Transformation of Virginia* featured Virginians performing social roles in specific material settings: the county courthouse, the planter's great house, and the Anglican Church. The scenes and the culture that captured his imagination include boisterous religious revivals, spirited dances, horse races, and cock fights. As communal culture declined in the face of greater individualism, so, too, did the authority of the larger planters.[28]

Richard Beeman, who had previously authored an account of Virginia's political influence on the early American republic and a biography of Patrick Henry, applied the new social history methods to Lunenberg County in Virginia's Southside. Unlike Isaac's anatomy of gentry culture in the Tidewater, Beeman's Lunenberg emerged beyond the political reach of the Tidewater's gentry and the twin poles of county court and Anglican church. The weak pull of these two institutions combined with the county's economic remoteness from the Tidewater tobacco economy meant that Lunenberg only gradually became a Chesapeake county. Only after evangelical revivals during the 1760s–70s, the disestablishment of the Anglican church after the Revolution, and the region's integration into the Chesapeake tobacco market, did Lunenberg shift from a backcountry to a recognizably southern county. The keys, as Beeman demonstrated, were the absence of any great planter leaders during the first three decades of the county's history, an influx of undeferential Scots-Irish and German residents from western Maryland and Pennsylvania, and the gradual diffusion of slave ownership broadly across the county. This last change gave all white men with property some buy-in to an emergent and militant white southern identity, defensive of the privileges of local belonging and slave owning.[29]

Beeman's work raised important questions about the geographic boundaries of the of the Chesapeake, reminiscent of the east-west divide in Carter Woodson's doctoral thesis; were backcountry counties part of the Chesapeake? Was Virginia's Southside better understood along with North Carolina as part of an emerging, rival tobacco economy late in the eighteenth century? If Beeman's work is suggestive of these larger trends, then the Southside-Carolina tobacco economy was characterized by a flattened white socio-economic hierarchy and a broader diffusion of property and power among small and middling planters—a situation quite different from the pronounced inequality among white people in the Tidewater.

What often went without saying in these works on the Chesapeake was that slavery itself introduced profound inequality, not just among white people, but by producing a racial divide through its creation of a laboring class prohibited from owning land or marrying, two indices of prosperity. A few historians pursued the question of racial inequality by reconstructing the lives of free people of African descent, inadvertently parsing region even more precisely. In this they echoed Ira Berlin, whose influential article "Time, Space, and the Evolution of Afro-American Society in British Mainland North America," urged historians to greater precision about exactly how, where, and in what numbers enslaved people labored.[30] Several of these studies of free people pointed to the unique racial landscape and politics of Virginia's Eastern Shore. Breen and Innes's, *Myne Owne Ground: Race and Freedom on Virginia's Eastern Shore* (1980), offered examples of exceptional free black property holders who were in some cases themselves slave masters, even as Virginia's slave laws made it more difficult for people of African descent to escape slavery. Mechal Sobel's, *The World They Made Together* (1987), which originated as a response to Eugene Genovese's *The World the Slaveholders Made and Roll, Jordan, Roll: The World the Slaves Made* argued that the beliefs of both Africans and English in the supernatural and their resort to similar techniques for fashioning their material worlds created common cultural ground. Together, she concluded, Anglo masters and African-American slaves created a unique and shared spiritual and aesthetic culture. In J. Douglas Deal's, "A Constricted World," free black people on Virginia's Eastern Shore struggled to inhabit that status as new laws circumscribed their access to privileges their white counterparts enjoyed.[31]

A few other historians fell back on de facto colonial boundaries to raise new questions about elite culture and power. Timothy Breen, *Tobacco Culture* (1985) explored the tobacco economy and credit system to track how Virginia planter indebtedness became politicized as a critique of empire and a call for liberty. Both Jan Lewis's *The Pursuit of Happiness* (1986) and Daniel Blake Smith's *Inside the Great House* (1986) portrayed the emotional and domestic lives of Virginia's great planters, arguing for a rise in the ethos of privacy and a shift to a more paternalistic style of power.

Scholars interested in legal and political history were the most likely to hew to colony rather than region. Warren Billings documented the changes in Virginia's legal culture through a series of important judicial decisions, noting that the justices themselves acquired greater fluency with certain of England's legal traditions. Philip Schwartz's *Twice Condemned: Slaves and the Criminal Laws of Virginia* (1988), showed how criminal acts by slaves spurred planter efforts to articulate new regulations, resulting by the eighteenth century in a focus on controlling crime, preserving slavery, and securing white supremacy. In "Order and Chaos" (1985), Jon Kukla challenges the prevailing framework of pre-Restoration chaos in Virginia, citing, among others, the work of James Russell Perry, whose network analysis, which would subsequently appear in *The Formation of Society on Virginia's Eastern Shore* (1990), suggested a more stable society.[32]

Still other signs pointed to the replacement of Virginia with the Chesapeake for engaging larger debates about the national narrative. For Kulikoff, the tobacco-producing regions of the Chesapeake were a seedbed of the Old South's particular class, race, and household dynamics. Influenced by the work of Eugene and Elizabeth Fox-Genovese on political economy and household production, Kulikoff inflected the Chesapeake's school's quantitative methods with an explicit class analysis. He drew upon his own data from the Prince George's County, Maryland but also incorporated quantitative data collected by Beeman and Rutman. Kulikoff defined the Chesapeake as a region, "a group of similar, geographically contiguous places that proceed through similar stages of development." For Kulikoff, the use of enslaved African labor to produce tobacco for an international market distinguished the geographic area surrounding Chesapeake Bay as far west as the Blue Ridge Mountains, as far North as the Patapsco River, and extending South to the Nansemond River in North Carolina. Areas that fell outside of these geographic bounds as well as those in which planters used slave labor to produce wheat were not part of Kulikoff's Chesapeake.[33]

Working with a different definition of region, Jack Greene also found the Chesapeake foundational for the national narrative. In *Pursuits of Happiness* (1988), Greene returned to questions raised by a previous generation of scholars about the relationship between regional cultures and the nation. As a consequence of its diversity, variety, and dependence upon slavery, Greene argued, the colonial Chesapeake, rather than New England, was the prototype for American society.[34]

The implicit Chesapeake school premise—that Maryland could stand in for Virginia under the rubric "Chesapeake"—was put to the test with the publication of *Robert Cole's World* (1991), Carr, Menard, and Walsh's long-awaited study of a mid-seventeenth-century yeoman farm family. Although never wealthy, the Catholic Coles were successful immigrants who left a modest inheritance for their children. Their investment of their own labor to create a plantation established the conditions for Maryland's subsequent development as a tobacco economy run on slave labor. The authors skillfully embedded the Coles in both local and Atlantic commercial networks, revealing the coexistence of community formation with subsistence agriculture and the pursuit of profit.[35]

Perhaps the most original application of the regional approach came with James Horn's *Adapting to a New World: English Society in the Seventeeenth-Century Chesapeake*. Drawing from the records of two English counties, two Virginia counties, and the St. Mary's County, Maryland data, Horn argued for persistent Englishness in the face of the Chesapeake's challenging conditions: demographic ruptures, the grueling demands of plantation labor, and a lower standard of living for the poorest residents compared to their English counterparts. For Horn, the Chesapeake, rather than either colony alone, remained the critical North American region to be studied, even as he concluded that it was but a far-flung English province, where inhabitants remained committed to conducting daily life in English ways.

Region took on yet additional significance in Philip Morgan's comparative *Slave Counterpoint* (1998), a structural analysis of slavery in South Carolina and the Chesapeake. For Morgan, the ecology and requirements of different staple crops—rice in the lowcountry and tobacco in the Chesapeake—accounted for many of the differences in the labor systems and cultures of enslaved people in each region, while the asymmetric power of the master-slave relationship (especially the master's access to economic resources in an agricultural economy) accounted for some of the similarities. In comparison to their counterparts in South Carolina, enslaved people in Virginia were culturally and demographically less African and more creole, more closely supervised and surveilled by white people, but better nourished, longer-lived, and seemingly endowed with greater material comforts. All this came at great cost: less cultural autonomy compared to enslaved people working on rice plantations, who were more likely to be part of a black majority.

Return of the Repressed

A quarter century of Chesapeake Studies not only invigorated early American studies but also put colonial Maryland on the map. Approaching Maryland and Virginia as part of a common region gave us a view of the big structures underpinning the daily lives of people—Native, servant, slave, and planter—in the tobacco economy of British North America. The strengths of the Chesapeake approach, still apparent in a recent benchmark study of the region—Lorena Walsh's *Motives of Honor, Pleasure, and Profit*—lie in the abilities of its practitioners to expose the demographic shifts and economic logics behind patterns of labor, investment, and consumption. We have gained a clearer understanding of the impact of fluctuating tobacco prices, the reasons why planters bought African slaves rather than indentured servants, and the ways enslaved people created family and community.

What the regional approach to the Chesapeake is less suited to, however, is providing explanations for the distinctive political and legal histories of Maryland and Virginia. For that, some scholars have dug deep into their Chesapeake data to account for differences in wealth accumulation, plantation management, and investment. Others have considered the colony as a system of governance with a unique history. Historians continue to be drawn by Virginia's paradigmatic role in the history of North American slavery and race relations, its feudal brand of patriarchy, its entanglement in imperial politics, the path taken by planters to revolution, and the efforts of enslaved people to seize opportunities to rebel. Historians of Maryland, meanwhile, have built on the legacy of Chesapeake studies to illuminate the lives of its great planters and assess the impact of the colony's unique religious history and formative relationships with Native Americans. Even as Chesapeake studies support ever more comprehensive analyses of the tobacco economy's impact on settler society, scholars armed with this new knowledge have returned to investigations of the distinct legal and political trajectories of each individual colony.

As a graduate student, I found Virginia to be a fascinating and fruitful subject for studying patriarchal authority in an emergent slave society. As the first official English experiment with settler colonialism and the first colony in the English-speaking world to pass a statute articulating the matrilineal inheritance of slave status, Virginia appeared to be an ideal place to understand the intersectional nature of that power: the mutual constitution and support of different types of authority including gender privilege, the legal power to regulate sex, the traditions of social hierarchy, and the interests of empire. Working with the records of three counties in the Tidewater, I briefly noted the small group of cosmopolitan planters who took advantage of their Caribbean connections to bring enslaved people to Virginia as early as the 1640s. Under their influence, lawmakers in the colony laid the legal scaffolding for racial distinctions and the slave status, including the principle of maternal inheritance in 1662. Writing in the immediate aftermath of the Chesapeake school's volley of articles about the demography of slavery, I was frequently reminded that, by the standards of the new social history, there simply were not enough enslaved people in the colony to explain these early laws. Indeed, at the time I embarked on my dissertation in 1985, Chesapeake scholars agreed that the shift to slave labor occurred much later. Examining these early laws, however, I found connections between the household head's domestic authority and an emergent public interest in regulating enslaved laborers. Virginia stood out among other societies with slaves for this early statute codifying the legal status of an enslaved woman's child.[36]

This blend of concerns about the capacity of rebels (defined in terms of gender, sex, race, class, and religious terms) to disturb the peace became especially evident in the exclusions elaborated after Bacon's Rebellion. Post-rebellion practices—some in the form of slave regulations—effectively prevented both white women and enslaved people of both sexes from disrupting public order. For enslaved men and women, these exclusions amounted to a disability that was at once legal, social, and economic. Kept from marrying, assuming legal responsibility for children, owning property, or carrying a gun, an enslaved man was legally prevented from achieving the benchmarks of prosperous manhood that so many Chesapeake historians had identified: marriage, fatherhood, and property ownership. An enslaved woman might retain a tenuous connection to her child as a consequence of her master's recognition of the maternal determination of status, but otherwise had less say about her child's welfare than most of her free counterparts.[37]

The particularities of Virginia's laws of entail as well as the rich historiography on this topic also drew Holly Brewer to the Old Dominion. In "Entailing Aristocracy in Colonial Virginia," Brewer subjected Clarence Keim's work on entail to a scrupulous review. Keim's work supported conclusions that entail was but a limited factor in restricting the range of the testatorial choice of Virginia's larger planters. Brewer found, in contrast, that not only was more land tied up in entailed estates than previously thought, but planters seem to have deliberately sought to achieve a feudal order by entailing both land and slaves. Ultimately, market motives and the desire of both testators and nonentail heirs to have greater flexibility led to reform in the aftermath of the Revolution.[38]

Virginia's role during the Revolution prompted Woody Holton to research the colony rather than region. In *Forced Founders* (1999), Holton took on the questions raised by Price and Breen about planter debt and its relationship to their embrace of Revolutionary principles and finds answers in a variety of other internal conflicts that jeopardized the great planters' political legitimacy. Virginia's Revolutionary leaders were less motivated by lofty political principles or a desire for commercial autonomy, Holton argued, than by very real political fears raised by resistant Indians who had made common cause with the British, rebellious enslaved African Americans, and an antagonized white yeomanry. Pushed to lead the colony to rebel against Britain, Virginia's founding fathers embraced revolutionary principles defensively as a means of protecting their estates and their political authority.[39]

For legal historians, too, there was no substituting a Chesapeake approach for a focus upon a particular colony. Anthony Parent traced slave law in Virginia to the purposeful short-term decisions of the colony's planters as well as to the resistance of enslaved people themselves. In *Foul Means*, Parent argued that by the end of the seventeenth century, a powerful planter class had deliberately brought racial slavery to Virginia. According to Parent, enslaved people's acts of mundane resistance as well as more dramatic episodes of rebellion (in 1709 and 1722) all influenced subsequent planter efforts to regulate bound laborers. This included attempts to subvert the rebellious potential of the enslaved through paternalistic management and campaigns to Christianize them.[40]

Perhaps the greatest departure from the Chesapeake school's diligent investigation of local conditions and ordinary people's lives came with the growing interest in Atlantic migration and commerce. Ronald Hoffman and Sally Mason took this innovative approach to reinvent the genre of planter studies. In *Princes of Ireland, Planters of Maryland: A Carroll Saga 1500–1782*, they followed the Carroll family through three generations, from Charles Carroll the Settler (1661–1720) to Charles Carroll of Carrollton (1737–1832), the only Roman Catholic signer of the Declaration of Independence. Carroll the Settler's Catholicism, especially his experience of religious persecution in England and subsequently in Maryland, positioned the Carrolls politically as outside the Chesapeake planter elite. Their stubborn adherence to their faith along with their cleavage to their Irish lineage colored the family's identity and generational strategies for achieving wealth and power. Hoffman and Mason joined the tools of the social historian with an Atlantic perspective, situating this prominent Catholic planter family in an Irish as well as Anglo-Atlantic context. Coming at the topic differently, Trevor Burnard examined Maryland's wealthiest planters to determine their commitments to family, local communities, and Atlantic commercial networks and concluded that, compared to their Virginia counterparts, Maryland's wealthiest were, by the eighteenth century, less immersed in Atlantic trade, less endebted to British merchants, and less involved in county and colony politics. Less encumbered by entail than their Virginian peers, they focused on profiting from agriculture and providing for heirs.[41]

In contrast to Hoffman and Mason, April Hatfield's application of an Atlantic framework to the questions which had animated Virginia's historians for decades, produced vastly different conclusions about colony and region. In Hatfield's *Atlantic Virginia: Intercolonial Relations in the Seventeenth Century*, Virginia assumed porous, dynamic boundaries defined by Native American geography, Atlantic commercial relationships, and migration rather than by static lines on a map. The contours of Powhatan's tributary kingdom, in particular, left a lasting imprint on Anglo-colonial understandings of the Virginia colony's boundaries. Anglo-Indian conflicts, intercolonial networks, and Atlantic circuits of people and trade each created a distinct version of the colony's boundaries. Although in choosing to focus on Virginia, Hatfield clearly intended to engage the historiography on the Chesapeake, she reserved "Chesapeake" for the title of her chapter on the legal history of slavery. Virginia's slave laws, she contended, especially those passed after 1670, were influenced by Barbadian statutes rather than representing an internal development hinging on Bacon's Rebellion, as Edmund Morgan posited. Virginia residents traded, fought, negotiated, and moved to other places. They were influenced by Indian, Atlantic, and colonial others more so than by so-called internal colonial dynamics. Although Hatfield's discussion of slavery was based mainly on Virginia court cases and statute law, her use of "Chesapeake" engaged the demographic and quantitative data about slavery in both Maryland and Virginia. By the conclusion of *Atlantic Virginia*, there was no discreet "Virginia," but perhaps no Chesapeake either; only an area in which residents were as much defined by their links outside of the colony as to each other.

Hatfield's methods represented a departure from the Chesapeake school's focus upon large cohorts of ordinary people whose lives could be extrapolated from county court records. Following leads about Virginian's links to other colonies, including citations from older works like Philip Bruce's to track the movements and business contacts of particular families, Hatfield avoided limiting herself to reading an entire county's court records, inventories, or deeds. But there was a downside. Privileging those with intercolonial connections resulted in a more male-skewed and elite story. Hatfield was also less interested than her predecessors in making an argument based on numbers. She conceived of slavery less as the result of a particular demographic tipping point than of the investments and clout of culturally and politically influential planters with strong connections to Barbados. Could Hatfield have written instead about Atlantic Maryland and come to the same conclusions? Was there an Atlantic Chesapeake? Can Maryland's 1661 slave law, "All Negroes and other slaves shall serve Durante Vita," be traced to Barbados?[42]

A truly Atlantic approach to the Chesapeake, as Lorena Walsh noted in 2001, would require as much diligent research about African origins as about European ones. The claim that, by the mid-seventeenth century, most enslaved Africans in Virginia hailed from the Caribbean rather than directly from West or West-Central Africa appeared to have withstood Walsh's own criticisms. About these Africans' origins, little can be known with any certainty beyond generalizations about the likelihood that they were from West Central Africa, where inhabitants had over a century of contact with the Portuguese. By the 1670s, the beginning of concerted British participation in the Atlantic slave trade, enslaved people carried to the Chesapeake appear to have originated from three main locations: Senegambia, the Gold Coast, and the Bight of Biafra. Slaves who came to the Chesapeake by way of the Caribbean after that date were a shrinking proportion of the total.[43]

Although captives from the Gold Coast were not the dominant population carried to Virginia during Britain's first half century of official slave trafficking, the surviving documents enabled Stephanie Smallwood to craft a searing narrative of the experience of "saltwater slavery."

By the late seventeenth century, employees of the Royal African Company were considering the market for slaves in Virginia as they filled their ships' holds with human cargo. Smallwood tracked 1,735 Gold Coast Africans through the Middle Passage to their fates as plantation laborers in Virginia, detailing the brutalities of commodification. A Gold Coast captive who survived the ordeal of becoming human cargo would be likely to end up in the hands of Virginia planters committed to purchasing slave labor.[44]

Whither the Chesapeake?

The latest wave of research on the Chesapeake situates slavery in a wider world of competing European empires and Native coalitions, strategically managed plantations, and newly compiled slave trade data. Uncoupling the Chesapeake's tobacco colonies has also led to fresh interpretations of the religious and political history of colonial Maryland. The connection of elite Virginia planters to Barbados has taken on even greater significance in these recent works for understanding the early appearance of Virginia's slave laws (although the 1662 law of maternal inheritance remains unexplained by this connection). Meanwhile, Chesapeake plantations have been dissected and shown to be carefully managed economic enterprises that turned profits—even during downturns in tobacco prices—as a result of planters' willingness to extract ever more labor from enslaved people.

Virginia and Maryland were claimed and settled as part of a much larger European movement around the Atlantic and of European plantations throughout the Americas of Dutch, French, English, Swedish, Danish, and Spanish adventurers. Virginia was also the site of the first sustained relationships between Anglo and Indian people who were in the midst of their own tribal reorganization as a consequence of population loss from disease and warfare. During these early years a few Native women, most notably Pocahontas, played important roles in forging Anglo-Native alliances. Anglo-Virginians undoubtedly learned much about tobacco production from Native peoples, but they also brought with their own women's traditions market gardening, in which the main implement was a hoe. It is not clear, however, as several historians have claimed, that Anglo-Virginians adopted the hoe agriculture required for tobacco from their interactions with the Powhatan women who would have been tending the plants.[45]

More important, as Daniel Richter, Hatfield, and Matthew Kruer have shown, region takes on completely different meaning when it is defined by Native American settlement, strategic alliances, and migrations. In response to the land greed of English tobacco growers, Native peoples shifted political alliances and relocated. Some, including the Susquehannocks, cleared out of one English colony and headed to another. This, in turn, had an impact on other Native groups. From the perspective of Native Americans, the region might have been defined by many factors, including the Chesapeake Bay, the Indian roads crisscrossing the region between coast and fall line, and the pressures created by settler land use.[46]

The Chesapeake has also become a topic of interest to environmental historians, who are no longer interested simply in how the climate and topography shaped settlement, but in how settlement itself left its mark on the unique Chesapeake ecosystem. Historic Native land use and subsequent English settlement on the Chesapeake Bay and its river system were themselves a response to soil content, proximity to transportation by water, and access to drinking water. But settlement patterns, the cultivation of tobacco, forest clearance, and water use in turn had an environmental impact which influenced the decisions of Native peoples and English settlers about the dispersal of their habitations, the decision to let tobacco land go fallow, and the movement to new fertile soils.[47]

The Chesapeake was not part of the greater Caribbean like South Carolina, but its connections to Barbados were formative in its wholesale embrace of slavery, the diversification of its economy, and its participation in Atlantic networks. Based on the work of John C. Coombs, Lorena Walsh, Michael Guasco, Russell Menard, and Demetri Debe, it appears that large planters in Virginia and Maryland followed the lead of Barbadian planters and began purchasing enslaved people as early as the 1640s. Even in the absence of positive law defining the status of slaves and their children, settlers in Virginia and Maryland did business in a wider Atlantic world in which the captains of slave ships and merchants made pragmatic decisions about who was and was not a slave. Virginia's large planters, the colony's primary lawmakers and adjudicators were always more connected to the trends in the larger Atlantic. They were the first to buy slaves directly from Africa as early as the 1640s, 50s, and 60s and the first to create novel forms of treatment, legal and punitive, for laborers who were perpetually bound, even after they formed their own families and produced children. Following the lead of these "early adopters" or "early plungers," as Menard has dubbed them, a second wave of planters responded to the declining availability of white indentured servant labor and seized the opportunities presented by the existing laws and institutions to purchase slaves.[48]

As Lorena Walsh has shown in her encyclopedic *Motives of Honor, Pleasure, and Profit* (2010), the largest tobacco planters approached plantation management with a careful calculation of risk and interest in increasing their profit margins. Drawing on the papers of more than thirty wealthy and influential Chesapeake planters, Walsh documented their efforts to improve agricultural efficiency. They accomplished this throughout the eighteenth century but especially after the 1730s by tightening their regulation of enslaved laborers to extract more labor. Planters also responded to seasonal changes and the potential of their own land by devoting portions of it to cultivating wheat and corn.[49]

What is less clear is how Hatfield's Atlantic connects with Walsh's tobacco plantations—or the ways that both relate to the daily politics of labor and domestic life. What did the Atlantic mean for ordinary white men and women in Virginia? To what degree were smallholders and servants living lives more bounded by the local than their elite and cosmopolitan counterparts? Was participation in Atlantic networks a privilege of gender as well as of class? Neither the Atlantic approach nor the focus on plantation management offers many clues about the experiences of enslaved people. What did Barbados represent for enslaved people producing children on the North American mainland? The condition of enslaved men, women, and children clearly declined over time, as Walsh has observed, as whiteness acquired greater legal precision and incorporated numerous exclusive privileges between 1680 and 1730, and planters refined techniques for extracting labor from their slaves.[50]

Curiously, compared to Coombs's seventeenth-century planter lawmakers, Walsh's large tobacco planters were relatively unengaged with the law. Indeed, the difference between Maryland's and Virginia's laws early for inherited slave status do not enter into Walsh's analysis of plantation management. Rather, Walsh summarizes the Virginia maternal inheritance law and never mentions the shift from the paternal principle in Maryland. One wonders about the consequences of treating two different systems for reckoning slave status as part of the same region. Did the difference in laws have any impact on planter decisions during the seventeenth century? Did it encourage Virginia planters to purchase more enslaved women than they might have done, to encourage sexual unions, or to permit enslaved women to engage in "abroad marriages"?[51]

Disaggregated from its fellow Chesapeake colony, Maryland's distinctive demography, economy, and politics have come into view in new ways. As Jean and Elliot Russo have shown, Maryland's history was distinguished by slower population growth and the practice of purchasing land from the Indians rather than warring for it. If the Virginia colony's wealth derived in large measure from its production of sweet-scented tobacco in counties like York and Lancaster, Oronoko-growing Maryland, in comparison, was less of a classic staple crop society and less dependent on fluctuations in tobacco prices. As a consequence of its sweet-scented production, Virginia's slaveowners invested more heavily in slaves, engaged more intensely in land speculation, and steadily expanded the tobacco economy and slavery. In contrast, western movement and expansion happened more slowly in Maryland.[52]

The Atlantic may indeed, be the new Chesapeake. Antoinette Sutto's fresh treatment of politics in colonial Maryland demonstrated the benefits of an Atlantic approach that allows for analysis of unique political histories. In *Loyal Protestants and Dangerous Papists*, Sutto downplayed the importance of slavery to Maryland's political history. Rather, suspicion of the colony's Catholic proprietors in their dealings with Native people and unruly Protestant settlers had a much bigger impact upon debates about political authority. For Sutto, an Atlantic perspective on the English state's relationship to Protestantism revealed the faultlines in Maryland politics on a whole host of issues, including taxes, and relations with Native Americans. The "popery and slavery" refrain, she claimed, did not require the example of African slavery to have resonance for white Marylanders.[53]

Richard Dunn's *A Tale of Two Plantations* (2014), established that certain types of Atlantic history—comparative rather than reconstructive of Atlantic networks—can illuminate the lives of enslaved people. Building on two decades of research and publication as well as on the insights of "many slaveries" approach showcased in Berlin and Morgan, eds., *Cultivation and Culture*, Dunn's study compared slavery in Jamaica and Virginia. Unlike most of the scholars writing about slavery in the Chesapeake from an Atlantic perspective, Dunn was more interested in reconstructing the experiences of the 2000 slaves on the two plantations in his study than he was in plantation management or the trials of the planter class. He offered a view of the catastrophic demography of Jamaica's Mount Airy plantation and the still calculated and destructive use of enslaved labor at the Tayloe plantation in Virginia, where high infant mortality betrayed the cruel impact of slavery in what otherwise appeared to be healthier conditions for labor and nutrition for enslaved women. Taking issue with recent scholarship that represented cotton production as a new threshold of extractive intensity and cruelty, Dunn contended that it was but a variation on Jamaica's sugar regime and the Chesapeake planter's profit calculation.[54]

★ ★ ★

The new social history transformed scholarly approaches to the study of early America in numerous lasting ways, but nowhere more visibly than in its conceptualization of the Chesapeake as a region. Studies of planters, indentured servants, slaves, tobacco production, land ownership, and wealth formation replaced the concerns of an older scholarship about the character of colonial society, its incubation of some presumably American traits, and the relationship of white "democracy" to slavery. Scholars have built on the Chesapeake approach to revisit debates about the turn to slavery, adopt Atlantic perspectives on Virginia and Maryland, and document the lives of enslaved people. They have also gathered voluminous data on how tobacco planters extracted wealth from both the soil of the Chesapeake and the bodies of their enslaved laborers.

The trend to decouple the Chesapeake colonies to reconsider their unique political, imperial, religious and legal histories builds on this previous and crucial work, but it also draws our attention away from the original subjects of Chesapeake studies to focus on colonial power brokers. Although the payoff is yet to be fully realized, one outcome is clear: Chesapeake studies gave us a view of a past both vibrant and cruel, peopled with Native Americans, cosmopolitan planters, servants, enslaved mothers and children, and planters' wives. In doing so, it put Maryland on the map.

Notes

1 John Hammond, *Leah and Rachel, or, the two fruitfull sisters Virginia and Mary-land: their present condition, impartially stated and related: With a removall of such imputations as are scandalously cast on those countries, whereby many deceived souls, chose rather to beg, steal, rot in prison, and come to shamefull deaths, then to better their being by going thither, wherein is plenty of all things necessary for humane subsistence* (London, 1656).
2 In writing this essay, I have consulted, in addition to the actual works discussed here, Thad Tate, "The Seventeenth-Century Chesapeake and its Modern Historians," Tate and Ammerman, eds., *The Chesapeake in the Seventeenth Century* (Chapel Hill: University of N. Carolina [for the Institute for Early American History and Culture], 1979). Tate's careful review of changing methods and approaches took as given that all studies of either Virginia or Maryland were studies of the Chesapeake. In contrast, I emphasize here that, rather than being a natural geographic entity, "the Chesapeake" emerged as a regional approach to colonial history only when historians viewed the common cultivation of tobacco with slave labor as more significant than the distinct political histories of Virginia and Maryland.
3 Evelyn Brooks Higginbotham, *Righteous Discontent: The Women's Movement in the Black Church 1880–1920* (Cambridge, MA: Harvard University Press, 1993).
4 G. Terry Sharrar, *A Kind of Fate: Agricultural Change in Virginia, 1861–1920* (Ames: Iowa State University Press, 2000).
5 Jeffrey Richardson Brackett, *Negro in Maryland: A Study of the Institutionalization of Slavery* (Baltimore: Johns Hopkins University Press, 1889). Brackett later went on to a distinguished career in social work.
6 Thomas Wertenbaker, *Patrician and Plebian in Virginia, or The origin and development of the Social classes of the Old Dominion* (Charlottesville, VA: Michie Co, 1910). Wertenbaker went on to have a distinguished career at Princeton after being hired as a preceptor by Woodrow Wilson in 1910. He wrote about subjects other than colonial Virginia, including regional analyses of the colonial origins of American Civilization, and a multi-volume history of Princeton that occupied the final decades of his career, but he never got early Virginia history out of his system. Most notable for our purposes are his treatments of Bacon's Rebellion (*Torchbearer of the Revolution* [Princeton: Princeton University Press, 1941]), which he represented as a movement for liberty in the tradition of the subsequent American Revolutionaries.
7 Carter Woodson, "The Disruption of Virginia," (Harvard Ph.D, 1912).
8 W.E.B. Dubois, review of James Curtis Ballagh, *The History of Slavery in Virginia, American Historical Review* 8, 2 (1903): 356–357.
9 U.B. Phillips, *American Negro Slavery* (New York, 1918); Eric Williams, *Capitalism and Slavery* (University of North Carolina Press, 1944).
10 John Henderson Russell, *Free Negro in Virginia 1619–1865* (Baltimore, 1913), James M. Wright, Free Negro in Maryland, 1634–1860 (New York: Columbia University Press, 1921).
11 Thad Tate, "The Seventeenth-Century Chesapeake and its Modern Historians," *Chesapeake in Seventeenth Century*, eds. Tate and Ammerman, characterizes this as a period with little new scholarship.
12 Fred Arthur Bailey, "Charles Sydnor's Quest for a Suitable Past," *Reading Southern History: Essays on Interpreters and Interpretation*, ed. Glenn Feldman (University of Alabama Press, 2001), 88–111.
13 Aubrey C. Land, *The Dulanys of Maryland; a biographical study of Daniel Dulany, the Elder (1685–1753) and Daniel Dulany, the Younger (1722–1797)* (Baltimore: Maryland Historical Association, 1955).
14 Sigmund Diamond, "From Organization to Society: Virginia in the Seventeenth Century," *American Journal of Sociology* 63 (1957–1958): 437–75; Bernard Bailyn, "Politics and Social Structure in Virginia," *Seventeenth Century America: Essays in Colonial History*, ed. James Morton Smith (Chapel Hill: University of North Carolina Press [for the Institute of Early American History and Culture], 1959); Jon Kukla, "Order and Chaos in Early America: Political and Social Stability in Pre-Restoration Virginia," *AHR* 90, 2 (April 1985): 275–298.
15 Oscar and Mary Handlin, "Origins of the Southern Labor System," *William and Mary Quarterly* 7 (1950): 199–222.
16 Carl Degler, "Slavery and the Genesis of American Race Prejudice," *Comparative Studies in Society and History* 21[1] (1959): 49–66.
17 Winthrop Jordan, "Modern Tensions and the Origins of American Slavery," Journal of Southern History 28, 1 (1962): 18–30; Jordan, *White over Black: American Attitudes Toward the Negro, 1550–1812* (Chapel Hill: University of North Carolina Press, for the Institute of Early American History and Culture, 1968). Alden Vaughan, "The Origins Debate: Slavery and Racism in Seventeenth Century Virginia," *VMHB* 97, 3 (1989): 311–354.

18 Jacob M. Price "The Economic Growth of the Chesapeake and the European Market," *JEH* 24[4] (1964): 496–511; Jacob M. Price, *France and the Chesapeake: A History of the French Tobacco Monopoly 1674–1791, and Its Relationship to the British and American Tobacco Trades* (Ann Arbor: University of Michigan Press, 1973); Jacob M. Price, *Capital and Credit in British Overseas Trade: The View From the Chesapeake 1700–1776* (Cambridge, MA: Harvard University Press, 1980); Price, "The Market Structure of the Colonial Chesapeake reconsidered," *Tobacco in Atlantic Trade: The Chesapeake, London and Glasgow, 1675–1775* (Brookfield, VT: Aldershot, 1995). Price's enduring commitment to defining a region according to its economic characteristics, rather than privileging historiographic significance based on its political history, was also reflected in his choice of a documentary editing project: in 1979, he edited a London merchant's correspondence with his Maryland partners during the key years of the credit crisis among Chesapeake merchants.
19 Christian Feest, "The Virginia Indian in Pictures," *Smithsonian Journal of History* 21[1] (1967): 1–30, "Notes on the Saponi Settlements in Virginia Prior to 1714," *Quarterly Bulletin, Archaeological Society of Virginia*, 29[3] (1974): 152–155. Among the other important influences were Wesley Frank Craven, *White, Red, and Black: The Seventeenth Century Virginian* (Charlottesville: University of Virginia Press, 1971), Gary Nash, *Red, White, and Black: The Peoples of Early North America* (Prentice-Hall, 1974).
20 Russell Menard, "From Servant to Freeholder: Status Mobility and Property Accumulation in Seventeenth Century Maryland," *WMQ* 30[1] (1973): 37–64; Menard, "From Servant to Slave: The Transformation of the Cheasapeake Labor System," *Southern Studies* 16, 4 (1977): 355; Menard, "Immigrants and their Increase," *Law, Society, and Politics in Early Maryland*, eds. A.C. Land, L. Green Carr, and E.C. Papenfuse (Baltimore: Johns Hopkins University Press, 1977); Walsh and Menard, "Death in the Chesapeake: Two Life Tables for Men in Early Colonial Maryland," *Md Hist Mag* LXIX (1974); Kulikoff, "The Colonial Chesapeake: Seedbed for Southern Culture?" *Journal of Southern History* 45, 4 (1979): 513–540; Kulikoff, "Origins of Afro-American Society in Tidewater Maryland and Virginia, 1700–1790," *WMQ* 35[2] (1979): 226–259; Kulikoff, "A Prolifick People: Black Population Growth in the Chesapeake Colonies 1700–1790" *Southern Studies* 16[4] (1977): 391; Walsh, "Till Death Do Us Part: Marriage and Family in Seventeenth-Century Maryland," *Chesapeake in Seventeenth Century*. Sarah S. Hughes revealed that slave labor influenced more than the households of owners, in "Slaves for Hire: The Allocation of Black Labor in Elizabeth City County Virignia, 1782–1810," *WMQ* 35 (1978): 260–286; Jean B. Lee revealed variation in slave community formation across counties, "The Problem of Community in the Eighteenth Century Chesapeake," *WMQ* 43 (1986): 333–361. Several of the most influential articles appeared in T.W. Tate and D. Ammerman, *Chesapeake in Seventeenth Century*, including those by Shammas, Earle, Kelly, Horn, Walsh, Rutman, and Carr and Menard.
21 Carville Earle, *The Evolution of a Tidewater Settlement System: All Hallow's Parish, Maryland, 1650–1783* (Chicago: University of Chicago Press, 1975).
22 Paul G. E. Clemens, *The Atlantic Economy and Colonial Maryland's Eastern Shore: From Tobacco to Grain* (Ithaca, NY: Cornell University Press, 1980).
23 Gloria L. Main, *Tobacco Colony: Life in Early Maryland 1650–1720* (Princeton: Princeton University Press, 1982).
24 Gloria Main, "Personal Wealth in Colonial America: explorations in the use of probate records from Maryland and Massachusetts 1650–1720," *JEH* 35 (1974): 289–294; Main, "Inequality in Early America: The Evidence from the probate Records of Massachusetts and Maryland," *JIH* 7[4] (1977): 559–581. Carole Shammas, "The Determinants of Personal Wealth in Seventeenth-Century England and America," *JEH* 37 (1977): 675–689. David Galenson, "White Servitude and the Growth of Black Slavery," *Journal of Economic History* 41[1] (1981): 39–47; "Middling People or Common Sort: The Social Origins of Some Early Americans Re-Examined" *WMQ* 35 (1978): 499–524. Richard S. Dunn, *A Tale of Two Plantations: Slave Life at Mesopotamia in Jamaica and Mount Airy in Virginia* (Cambridge, MA: Harvard University Press, 2014).
25 Carr and Walsh "The Planter's Wife: The Experience of White Women in Seventeenth Century Maryland," *WMQ* 34 (1977): 542–571. See also Clara Bowler, "Carted Whores and White Shrouded Apologies: Slander in the County Courts of Seventeenth Century Virginia," *VMHB* 85 (1977): 411–426.
26 Carole Shammas, "Black Women's Work and the Evolution of Plantation Society in Virginia," *Labor History* XXVX (1985): 5–28. See also Joan Gundersen, "The Double Bonds of Race and Sex: Black and White Women in the Colonial Virginia Parish," *Journal of Southern History* 52 (1986): 351–372.
27 Darrett and Anita Rutman, *A Place in Time: Middlesex County, Virginia, 1650–1750* (New York: Norton, 1984).
28 Rhys Isaac, *Transformation of Virginia* (Chapel Hill: University of North Carolina for the Institute of Early American History and Culture, 1982).

29 Richard Beeman, *The Evolution of the Southern Backcountry: A Case Study of Lunenberg County, 1746–1832* (Philadelphia: University of Pennsylvania Press, 1984).
30 Ira Berlin, "Time, Space, and the Evolution of Afro-American Society in British Mainland North America," *AHR* 85 (1980): 44.
31 J. Douglass Deal, "A Constricted World: Free Blacks on Virginia's Eastern Shore," *Colonial Chesapeake Society*, eds. Carr, Morgan, and Russo (Chapel Hill: University of North Carolina Press for the Institute of Early American History and Culture, 1988); Deal, *Race and Class in Colonial Virginia: Indians, Englishmen, and Africans on the Eastern Shore in the Seventeenth Century* (New York: Garland Press, 1993).
32 Billings, *Old Dominion in the Seventeenth Century: A Documentary History* (Chapel Hill: University of North Carolina Press for the Institute of Early American History and Culture, 1975); Philip J. Schwartz, *Twice Condemned: Slaves and the Criminal Laws of Virginia* (Baton Rouge: LSU Press, 1988). See also A.G. Roeber, *Faithful Magistrates and Republican Lawyers: Creators of Virginia Legal Culture, 1680–1810* (Chapel Hill: University of North Carolina Press, 1981); Kukla, "Order and Chaos in Early America: Political and Social Stability in Pre-Restoration Virginia," *AHR* 90 (1985): 275–298; Perry. *The Formation of Society on Virginia's Eastern Shore 1615–1655* (Chapel Hill: University of North Carolina for the Institute of Early American History and Culture, 1990).
33 Kulikoff, *Tobacco and Slaves: The Development of Southern Cultures in the Chesapeake 1680–1800* (Chapel Hill: University of North Carolina for the Institute for Early American History and Culture, 1986), esp. 18–19.
34 Jack Greene, *Pursuits of Happiness: The Social Development of Early Modern British Colonies and the Formation of American Culture* (Chapel Hill: University of North Carolina Press, 1988).
35 Lois Carr, Russell Menard, and Lorena Walsh, *Robert Cole's World: Agriculture and Society in Early Maryland* (Chapel Hill: University of North Carolina Press for the Institute for Early Amerrican History and Culture, 1991); see also G. Terry Sharrar's review for her correction of the soil exhaustion thesis as the reason for rotating crops and allow land to go fallow; *Technology and Culture* 34[3] (1993): 694–696.
36 Kathleen M. Brown, *Good Wives, Nasty Wenches, and Anxious Patriarchs: Gender, Race, and Power in Colonial Virginia* (Chapel Hill: University of North Carolina for the Institute of Early American History and Culture, 1996), 113–114, 133.
37 Brown, *Good Wives, Nasty Wenches*. Several other historians also explored the status of white women in the colony; see Terri Snyder, *Brabbling Women: Disorderly Speech and the Law in Early Virginia* (Ithaca, NY: Cornell University Press, 2003); Linda Sturtz, *Within Her Power: Propertied Women in Early America* (New York: Routledge, 2002); Cynthia Kierner, *Beyond the Household: Women's Place in the Early South, 1700–1835* (Ithaca, NY: Cornell University Press, 1998).
38 Brewer, "Entailing Aristocracy in Colonial Virginia: 'Ancient Feudal Restraints' and Revolutionary Reform," *WMQ* 54 (1997): 307–346.
39 Woody Holton, *Forced Founders: Indians, Debtors, Slaves and the Making of the American Revolution in Virginia* (Chapel Hill: University of North Carolina for the Institute for Early American History and Culture, 1999).
40 Parent, *Foul Means: The Formation of a Slave Society in Virginia, 1660–1740* (Chapel Hill: University of North Carolina for the Institute for Early American History and Culture, 2003). See also Schwartz, *Twice Condemned: Slaves and the Criminal Laws of Virginia, 1705–1865*.
41 Trevor Burnard, *Creole Gentlemen: The Maryland Elite, 1691–1776* (New York: Routledge, 2002).
42 Maryland Archives, I, 526; 533.
43 Lorena S. Walsh, "The Chesapeake Slave Trade: Regional Patterns, African Origins, and Some Implications," *WMQ* 58 (2001): 139–170.
44 Smallwood, *Saltwater Slavery: The Middle Passage from Africa to American Diaspora* (Cambridge: Harvard University Press, 2007).
45 Frederick Gleach, *Powhatan's World and Colonial Virginia: A Conflict of Cultures* (Lincoln: University of Nebraska Press, 1997); Helen Rountree, *Pocahontas, Powhatan, Opechancough: Three Indian Lives Changed by Jamestown* (Charlottesville: University of Virginia Press, 2005).
46 Matthew Kruer, "'Our Time of Anarchy': Bacon's Rebellion and the Wars of the Susquehannocks 1675–1682" (Ph.D. dissertation, University of Pennsylvania, 2015).
47 Philip D. Curtain, Grace Bush, and George Fisher, eds., *Discovering the Chesapeake: The History of an Ecosystem* (Baltimore: Johns Hopkins University Press, 2001).
48 Douglas M. Bradburn and John C. Coombs, "Smoke and Mirrors: Reinterpreting the society and economy of the seventeenth-century Chesapeake," *Atlantic Studies* 3[2] (2006): 131–197; Coombs, "Beyond the Origins Debate: Rethinking the Rise of Virginia Slavery," *Early Modern Virginia: Reconsidering the Old*

Dominion, eds. D. Bradburn and J. C. Coombs (Charlottesville: University of Virginia Press, 2011); Demetri D. Debe and Russell R. Menard, "The Transition to African Slavery in Maryland: A Note on the Barbados Connection," *Slavery and Abolition* 32[1] (2011): 129–141; Russell R. Menard, "Making a 'Popular Slave Society' in Colonial British America," *Journal of Interdisciplinary History* 43[3] (2013): 377–395. Menard, *Sweet Negotiations: Sugar, Slavery, and Plantation Agriculture in Early Barbados* (Charlottesville: University of Virginia, 2006). Michael Guasco, *Slaves and Englishmen: Human Bondage in the Early Modern Atlantic World* (Philadelphia: University of Pennsylvania Press, 2014); John C. Coombs, "The Phases of Conversion: A New Chronology for the Rise of Virginia Slavery," *WMQ* 68 (2011): 332–360. Coombs challenges both E. Morgan's and Menard's previous findings about the timing of the turn to slavery, although the discrepancy appears also to be a consequence of different definitions of "turn." See also John C. Coombs, "Mastering the Chesapeake" *Reviews in American History* 41[1] (2013): 12–18; and Kathleen Brown and Jennifer Spear, "Rethinking the Development of Slave Law in the Atlantic World," (forthcoming).

49 Lorena Walsh, *Motives of Honor, Pleasure, and Profit: Plantation Management in the Colonial Chesapeake 1607–1763*, (Chapel Hill: University of North Carolina for the Institute for Early American History and Culture, 2010).

50 Theodore Allen, *The Invention of White Race*, 2nd edition, 2 vols; Vol. 1: *Racial Oppression and Social Control*, and Vol. 2: *The Origins of Racial Oppression in Anglo-America* (London: Verso, 2012).

51 Walsh, *Motives of Honor, Pleasure, & Profit*, 260–261, 382–383.

52 Jean B. Russo and J. Elliott Russo, *Planting an Empire: The Early Chesapeake in British North America* (Baltimore: Johns Hopkins University Press, 2012).

53 Antoiniette Sutto, *Loyal Protestants and Dangerous Papists: Maryland and the Politics of Religion in the English Atlantic* (Charlottesville: University of Virginia Press, 2015). For another example of how decoupling the Chesapeake colonies frees up a historian's analysis, see Debra Myers, *Common Whores, Vertuous Women, and Loving Wives: Free Will Christian Women in Colonial Maryland* (Bloomington: Indiana University Press, 2003).

54 Dunn, *Tale of Two Plantations*; see also Dunn, "Black Society in the Chesapeake, 1776–1810," *Slavery and Freedom in the Age of American Revolution*, Ira Berlin and Ronald Hoffman (Charlottesville: University of Virginia Press, 1983); and Gary B. Nash, "The Work of Richard Dunn," *Pennsylvania History* 64 (1997): 11–25.

References

Allen, Theodore. *The Invention of White Race*, 2nd edition, 2 vols; Vol 1: *Racial Oppression and Social Control*, and Vol. 2: *The Origins of Racial Oppression in Anglo-America* (London: Verso, 2012).

Ames, Susie M. *Studies of the Virginia Eastern Shore in the Seventeenth Century* (Richmond: The Dietz Press, 1940).

Bailey, Fred Arthur. "Charles Sydnor's Quest for a Suitable Past," *Reading Southern History: Essays on Interpreters and Interpretation*, ed, Glenn Feldman (Tuscaloosa: University of Alabama Press, 2001), 88–111.

Bailyn, Bernard. "Politics and Social Structure in Virginia," *Seventeenth Century America: Essays in Colonial History*, James Morton Smith, ed. (Chapel Hill: University of North Carolina Press for the Institute of Early American History and Culture, 1959).

Ballagh, James C. *A History of Slavery in Virginia* (Baltimore: Johns Hopkins UP, 1902).

Beeman, Richard. *The Evolution of the Southern Backcountry: A Case Study of Lunenberg County, 1746–1832* (Philadelphia: University of Pennsylvania Press, 1984).

Berlin, Ira. "Time, Space, and the Evolution of Afro-American Society in British Mainland North America," *The American Historical Review* 85 (1980): 44.

Billings, Warren M. *The Old Dominion in the Seventeenth Century: A Documentary History* (Chapel Hill: University of North Carolina Press for the Institute of Early American History and Culture, 1975).

Bowler, Clara. "Carted Whores and White Shrouded Apologies: Slander in the County Courts of Seventeenth Century Virginia," *Virginia Magazine of History and Biography* 85 (1977): 411–426.

Brackett, Jeffrey Richardson. *Negro in Maryland: A Study of the Institutionalization of Slavery* (Baltimore: Johns Hopkins University Press, 1889).

Bradburn, Douglas M. and John C. Coombs. "Smoke and Mirrors: Reinterpreting the Society and Economy of the Seventeenth-Century Chesapeake," *Atlantic Studies* 3[2] (2006): 131–197.

Breen, Timothy H. *Tobacco Culture: The Mentality of the Great Tidewater Planters on the Eve of the Revolution* (Princeton: Princeton UP, 1985).

Breen, Timothy H., and Stephen Innes. *'Myne Owne Ground': Race and Freedom on Virginia's Eastern Shore* (New York: Oxford University Press, 1980).

Brewer, Holly. "Entailing Aristocracy in Colonial Virginia: 'Ancient Feudal Restraints' and Revolutionary Reform," *William and Mary Quarterly* 54 (1997): 307–346.

Brown, Kathleen M. *Good Wives, Nasty Wenches, and Anxious Patriarchs: Gender, Race, and Power in Colonial Virginia* (Chapel Hill: University of North Carolina for the Institute for Early American History and Culture, 1996).

Brown, Robert E. *Virginia 1705–1785: Democracy or Aristocracy?* (East Lansing: Michigan State University Press, 1964).

Bruce, Philip A. *The Plantation Negro as a Freeman: Observations on his Character, Condition, and Prospects in Virginia* (New York: Putnam and Sons, 1889).

Burnard, Trevor. *Creole Gentlemen: The Maryland Elite, 1691–1776* (New York: Routledge, 2002).

Carr, L. G. and L. S. Walsh. "The Planter's Wife: The Experience of White Women in Seventeenth Century Maryland," *William and Mary Quarterly* 34 (1977): 542–571.

Carr, Lois, Russell R. Menard, and Lorena S Walsh. *Robert Cole's World: Agriculture and Society in Early Maryland* (Chapel Hill: University of North Carolina Press for the Institute for Early American History and Culture, 1991).

Clemens, Paul G. E. *The Atlantic Economy and Colonial Maryland's Eastern Shore: From Tobacco to Grain* (Ithaca, NY: Cornell University Press, 1980).

Coombs, John C. "The Phases of Conversion: A New Chronology for the Rise of Virginia Slavery," *William and Mary Quarterly* 68 (2011): 332–360.

Coombs, John C. "Beyond the Origins Debate: Rethinking the Rise of Virginia Slavery," *Early Modern Virginia: Reconsidering the Old Dominion*, eds. D. Bradburn and J. C. Coombs (Charlottesville: University of Virginia Press, 2011).

Coombs, John C. "Mastering the Chesapeake," *Reviews in American History* 41[1] (2013): 12–18.

Craven, Wesley Frank. *The Southern Colonies in the Seventeenth Century* (Baton Rouge: Louisiana State University Press, 1949).

Craven, Wesley Frank. *White, Red, and Black: The Seventeenth Century Virginian* (Charlottesville: University of Virginia Press, 1971).

Curtain, Philip D., Grace Bush, and George Fisher, eds. *Discovering the Chesapeake: The History of an Ecosystem* (Baltimore: Johns Hopkins University Press, 2001).

Deal, J. Douglass. "A Constricted World: Free Blacks on Virginia's Eastern Shore," *Colonial Chesapeake Society*, Carr, L.G., Morgan, P., and Russo, J.B. (Chapel Hill: University of North Carolina Press for the Institute of Early American History and Culture, 1988).

Deal, J. Douglass. *Race and Class in Colonial Virginia: Indians, Englishmen, and Africans on the Eastern Shore in the Seventeenth Century* (New York: Garland Press, 1993).

Debe, Demetri D. and Russell R. Menard. "The Transition to African Slavery in Maryland: A Note on the Barbados Connection," *Slavery and Abolition* 32[1] (2011): 129–141.

Degler, Carl. "Slavery and the Genesis of American Race Prejudice," *Comparative Studies in Society and History* 21[1] (1959): 49–66.

Diamond, Sigmund. "From Organization to Society: Virginia in the Seventeenth Century," *American Journal of Sociology* 63 (1957–1958): 437–75.

Dubois, W.E. B. "Review of James Curtis Ballagh, 'The History of Slavery in Virginia'," *American Historical Review* 8[2] (1903): 356–357.

Dunn, Richard S. "Black Society in the Chesapeake, 1776–1810," *Slavery and Freedom in the Age of American Revolution*, eds. Ira Berlin and Ronald Hoffman (Charlottesville: University of Virginia Press, 1983).

Dunn, Richard S. *A Tale of Two Plantations: Slave Life at Mesopotamia in Jamaica and Mount Airy in Virginia* (Cambridge, MA: Harvard University Press, 2014).

Earle, Carville. *The Evolution of a Tidewater Settlement System: All Hallow's Parish, Maryland, 1650–1783* (Chicago: University of Chicago Press, 1975).

Feest, Christian. "Notes on the Saponi Settlements in Virginia Prior to 1714" *Quarterly Bulletin, Archaeological Society of Virginia*, 29[3] (1974): 152–155.

Feest, Christian. "The Virginia Indian in Pictures," *Smithsonian Journal of History* 21[1] (1967): 1–30.

Freyre, Gilberto. *The Masters and the Slaves: A Study in the Development of Brazilian Civilization* (New York: Knopf, 1946).

Galenson, David. "Middling People or Common Sort: The Social Origins of Some Early Americans Re-Examined" *William and Mary Quarterly* 35 (1978): 499–524.

Galenson, David. "White Servitude and the Growth of Black Slavery," *Journal of Economic History* 41[1] (1981): 39–47.

Genovese, Eugene D. *The World the Slaveholders Made: Two Essays in Interpretation*, (New York: Pantheon, 1969).

Genovese, Eugene D. *Roll, Jordan, Roll: The World the Slaves Made* (New York: Pantheon, 1974).

Gleach, Frederick. *Powhatan's World and Colonial Virginia: A Conflict of Cultures* (Lincoln: University of Nebraska Press, 1997).

Greene, Jack. *Pursuits of Happiness: The Social Development of Early Modern British Colonies and the Formation of American Culture* (Chapel Hill: University of North Carolina Press, 1988).

Guasco, Michael. *Slaves and Englishmen: Human Bondage in the Early Modern Atlantic World* (Philadelphia: University of Pennsylvania Press, 2014).

Gundersen, Joan. "The Double Bonds of Race and Sex: Black and White Women in the Colonial Virginia Parish," *Journal of Southern History* 52 (1986): 351–372.

Hammond, John. *Leah and Rachel, or, the two fruitfull sisters Virginia and Mary-land: their present condition, impartially stated and related: With a removall of such imputations as are scandalously cast on those countries, whereby many deceived souls, chose rather to beg, steal, rot in prison, and come to shamefull deaths, then to better their being by going thither, wherein is plenty of all things necessary for humane subsistence.* (London, 1656).

Handlin, Oscar and Mary. "Origins of the Southern Labor System." *William and Mary Quarterly* 7 (1950): 199–222.

Hatfield, April L. *Atlantic Virginia: Intercolonial Relations in the Seventeenth Century* (Philadelphia: University of Pennsylvania Press, 2004).

Higginbotham, Evelyn Brooks. *Righteous Discontent: The Women's Movement in the Black Church 1880–1920* (Cambridge, MA: Harvard University Press, 1993).

Hoffman, Ronald, and Sally D. Mason. *Princes of Ireland, Planters of Maryland: A Carroll Saga 1500–1782* (Chapel Hill: University of North Carolina Press for the Omohundro Institute for Early American History and Culture, 2000).

Holton, Woody. *Forced Founders: Indians, Debtors, Slaves and the Making of the American Revolution in Virginia* (Chapel Hill: University of North Carolina for the Institute for Early American History and Culture, 1999).

Horn, James. *Adapting to a New World: English Society in the Seventeeenth-Century Chesapeake* (Chapel Hill: University of North Carolina Press for the Institute for Early American History and Culture, 1994).

Hughes Sarah S. "Slaves for Hire: The Allocation of Black Labor in Elizabeth City County Virignia, 1782–1810," *William and Mary Quarterly* 35 (1978): 260–286.

Isaac, Rhys. *The Transformation of Virginia* (Chapel Hill: University of North Carolina Press for the Institute of Early American History and Culture, 1982).

Jordan, Winthrop. "Modern Tensions and the Origins of American Slavery," *Journal of Southern History* 28[1] (1962): 18–30.

Jordan, Winthrop. *White over Black: American Attitudes Toward the Negro, 1550–1812* (Chapel Hill: University of North Carolina Press, for the Institute of Early American History and Culture, 1968).

Kierner, Cynthia. *Beyond the Household: Women's Place in the Early South, 1700–1835* (Ithaca: Cornell University Press, 1998).

Kruer, Matthew. "'Our Time of Anarchy': Bacon's Rebellion and the Wars of the Susquehannocks 1675–1682," (Ph.D. dissertation, University of Pennsylvania, 2015).

Kukla, Jon. "Order and Chaos in Early America: Political and Social Stability in Pre-Restoration Virginia," *The American Historical Review* 90 (1985): 275–298.

Kukla, Jon. The Chesapeake Colonies" in Encyclopedia of the North American Colonies. Jacob Ernst Cook et al. eds. vol. 1. (NY: Charles Scribners & Sons, 1998), pp. 188–201.

Kulikoff, Alan. "A Prolifick People: Black Population Growth in the Chesapeake Colonies 1700–1790," *Southern Studies* 16[4] (1977): 391.

Kulikoff, Alan. "Origins of Afro-American Society in Tidewater Maryland and Virginia, 1700–1790," *William and Mary Quarterly* 35[2] (1979): 226–259.

Kulikoff, Alan. "The Colonial Chesapeake: Seedbed for Southern Culture?" *Journal of Southern History* 45[4] (1979): 513–540.

Kulikoff, Alan. *Tobacco and Slaves: The Development of Southern Cultures in the Chesapeake 1680–1800* (Chapel Hill: University of North Carolina for the Institute for Early American History and Culture, 1986).

Land, Aubrey C. *The Dulanys of Maryland: A Biographical Study of Daniel Dulany, the Elder (1685–1753) and Daniel Dulany, the Younger (1722–1797)* (Baltimore: Maryland Historical Association, 1955).

Lee, Jean B. "The Problem of Community in the Eighteenth Century Chesapeake," *William and Mary Quarterly* 43 (1986): 333–361.

Main, Gloria L. "Inequality in Early America: The Evidence from the probate Records of Massachusetts and Maryland," *The Journal of Interdisciplinary History* 7[4] (1977): 559–581.

Main, Gloria L. "Personal Wealth in Colonial America: Explorations in the Use of Probate Records from Maryland and Massachusetts 1650–1720," *The Journal of Economic History* 35 (1974): 289–294.

Main, Gloria L. *Tobacco Colony: Life in Early Maryland 1650–1720* (Princeton: Princeton University Press, 1982).

Menard, Russell R. "From Servant to Freeholder: Status Mobility and Property Accumulation in Seventeenth Century Maryland," *William and Mary Quarterly* 30[1] (1973): 37–64.

Menard, Russell R. "From Servant to Slave: The Transformation of the Chesapeake Labor System," *Southern Studies* 16[4] (1977): 355.

Menard, Russell R. "Immigrants and their Increase," *Law, Society, and Politics in Early Maryland*, eds. A.C. Land, L. Green Carr, and E.C. Papenfuse (Baltimore: Johns Hopkins University Press, 1977).

Menard, Russell R. "Making a 'Popular Slave Society' in Colonial British America," *Journal of Interdisciplinary History*, 43[3] (2013): 377–395.

Menard, Russell R. *Sweet Negotiations: Sugar, Slavery, and Plantation Agriculture in Early Barbados* (Charlottesville: University of Virginia, 2006).

Middleton, Arthur Pierce. *Tobacco Coast: A Maritime History of the Chesapeake Bay in the Colonial Era* (Newport News, VA: Mariner's Museum, 1953).

Morgan, Philip D. *Slave Counterpoint: Black Culture in the Eighteenth-Century Chesapeake and Lowcountry* (Chapel Hill: University of North Carolina Press for the Institute for Early American History and Culture, 1998).

Myers, Debra. *Common Whores, Vertuous Women, and Loveing Wives: Free Will Christian Women in Colonial Maryland* (Bloomington: Indiana University Press, 2003).

Nash, Gary. *Red, White, and Black: The Peoples of Early North America* (Englewood Cliffs, NJ: Prentice-Hall, 1974).

Nash, Gary B. "The Work of Richard Dunn," *Pennsylvania History* 64 (1997): 11–25.

Parent, Anthony S. *Foul Means: The Formation of a Slave Society in Virginia, 1660–1740* (Chapel Hill: University of North Carolina for the Institute for Early American History and Culture, 2003).

Perry, James R. *The Formation of Society on Virginia's Eastern Shore 1615–1655*. (Chapel Hill: University of North Carolina for the Institute of Early American History and Culture, 1990).

Phillips, U.B. *American Negro Slavery* (New York: D. Appleton & Co., 1918).

Price Jacob M. "The Economic Growth of the Chesapeake and the European Market," *Journal of Economic History* 24[4] (1964): 496–511.

Price, Jacob M. "The Market Structure of the Colonial Chesapeake Reconsidered," *Tobacco in Atlantic Trade: The Chesapeake, London and Glasgow, 1675–1775* (Brookfield, VT: Aldershot, 1995).

Price, Jacob M. *Capital and Credit in British Overseas Trade: The View From the Chesapeake 1700–1776* (Cambridge, MA: Harvard University Press, 1980).

Price, Jacob M. *France and the Chesapeake: A History of the French Tobacco Monopoly 1674–1791, and Its Relationship to the British and American Tobacco Trades* (Ann Arbor: University of Michigan Press, 1973).

Roeber, A. G. *Faithful Magistrates and Republican Lawyers: Creators of Virginia Legal Culture, 1680–1810* (Chapel Hill: University of North Carolina Press, 1981).

Rountree, Helen. *Pocahontas, Powhatan, Opechancough: Three Indian Lives Changed by Jamestown* (Charlottesville: University of Virginia Press, 2005).

Russell, John Henderson. *Free Negro in Virginia 1619–1865* (Baltimore: MD: Johns Hopkins University Press, 1913).

Russo, Jean B. and Russo, J. Elliott. *Planting an Empire: The Early Chesapeake in British North America* (Baltimore: Johns Hopkins University Press, 2012).

Rutman, Darrett and Anita. *A Place in Time: Middlesex County, Virginia, 1650–1750* (New York: Norton, 1984).

Schwarz, Philip J. *Twice Condemned: Slaves and the Criminal Laws of Virginia, 1705–1865* (Baton Rouge: Louisiana State University Press, 1998).

Shammas, Carole. "Black Women's Work and the Evolution of Plantation Society in Virginia," *Labor History* XXVX (1985): 5–28.

Shammas, Carole. "The Determinants of Personal Wealth in Seventeenth-Century England and America," *Journal of Economic History* 37 (1977): 675–689.

Sharrar, G. Terry. *A Kind of Fate: Agricultural Change in Virginia, 1861–1920* (Ames: Iowa State University Press, 2000).

Sharrar, G. Terry. "Review," *Technology and Culture* 34[3] (1993): 694–696.

Smallwood, Stephanie. *Saltwater Slavery: The Middle Passage from Africa to American Diaspora* (Cambridge, MA: Harvard University Press, 2007).

Smith, Daniel Blake. *Inside the Great House: Planter Family Life in Eighteenth-Century Chesapeake Society* (Ithaca, NY: Cornell University Press, 1980).

Snyder, Terri. *Brabbling Women: Disorderly Speech and the Law in Early Virginia* (Ithaca, NY: Cornell University Press, 2003).

Sobel, Mechal. *The World They Made Together: Black and White Values in Eighteenth-Century Virginia* (Princeton: Princeton University Press, 1987).

Sturtz, Linda. *Within Her Power: Propertied Women in Early America* (New York: Routledge, 2002).

Sutto, Antoiniette. *Loyal Protestants and Dangerous Papists: Maryland and the Politics of Religion in the English Atlantic* (Charlottesville: University of Virginia Press, 2015).

Sydnor, Charles S. *American Revolutionaries in the Making: Political Practices in Washington's Virginia* (New York: Free Press, 1952).

Tannenbaum, Frank. *Slave and Citizen: The Negro in the Americas* (New York: Knopf, 1946).

Tate, Thad. "The Seventeenth-Century Chesapeake and its Modern Historians." *The Chesapeake in the Seventeenth Century*, eds. Tate and Ammerman (Chapel Hill: University of North Carolina for the Institute for Early American History and Culture, 1979).

Vaughan, Alden. "The Origins Debate: Slavery and Racism in Seventeenth Century Virginia," *The Virginia Magazine of History and Biography* 97[3] (1989): 311–354.

Walsh, Lorena S. "The Chesapeake Slave Trade: Regional Patterns, African Origins, and Some Implications," *William and Mary Quarterly* 58 (2001): 139–170.

Walsh, Lorena, and Russel R Menard. "Death in the Chesapeake: Two Life Tables for Men in Early Colonial Maryland," *Maryland Historical Magazine* LXIX (1974): 211–227.

Walsh, Lorena. *Motives of Honor, Pleasure, and Profit: Plantation Management in the Colonial Chesapeake 1607–1763* (Chapel Hill: University of North Carolina for the Institute for Early American History and Culture, 2010).

Walsh, Lorena. "Till Death Do Us Part: Marriage and Family in Seventeenth-Century Maryland," *Chesapeake in Seventeenth Century*, eds. Tate and Ammerman.

Wertenbaker, Thomas. *Patrician and Plebian in Virginia, or The origin and development of the Social classes of the Old Dominion* (Charlottesville, VA: Michie Co, 1910).

Wertenbaker, Thomas. *Torchbearer of the Revolution* (Princeton: Princeton University Press, 1941).

Williams, Eric. *Capitalism and Slavery* (Chapel Hill, NC: University of North Carolina Press, 1944).

Woodson, Carter. "The Disruption of Virginia" (Harvard Ph.D., 1912).

Wright, James M. *Free Negro in Maryland, 1634–1860* (New York: Columbia University Press, 1921).

12
PROTESTANTISM AS IDEOLOGY IN THE BRITISH ATLANTIC WORLD[1]

Carla Gardina Pestana

Among the various Europeans active in the Atlantic world, the British stood out for their ideological commitment to Protestantism. In their construction, their faith coupled with liberty shaped their forays into the region, benefited participants, and compelled their opposition to the twin foes of Catholicism and tyranny. The quintessential post-Reformation imperial undertaking, the British Atlantic gained its own sense of its distinctiveness from its Protestantism; this self-identification also laid the basis for national identity in the United States. Entering the Atlantic arena belatedly, in the wake of a century of Iberian Catholic activity, the English (along with the Dutch, the French and other more minor actors) framed their role in terms of a common European heritage that guided and justified the taking of new lands and interacting with new peoples. The British, although not unique in their commitment to Protestantism among the latecomers (since the Dutch, the Swedes, and the Danes shared that status), arguably made a more sustained case for the centrality of this religious and cultural identity than any other colonizing power. Protestantism thus joined with other systems for ordering and justifying domination in the Americas, to create a potent conceptualization of membership in a British Atlantic community. Within the context, Protestantism serves as a placeholder for certain understandings of liberty and aversion to Roman Catholic superstition and authoritarianism. It also created a broad category within which a variety of believers—drawn from a panoply of post-Protestant churches and sects—could find common ground. British claims to be Protestant and free proved an enduring legacy that worked to smooth over differences and to obscure disparities between reality and idealism.

Part One: Entry Into the Atlantic World: Shared and Divergent Ideologies

The European entrée into the wider Atlantic world began with the Iberians in the 15th century. The Portuguese sailed south looking for peoples with whom to trade as well as for lands to claim. Until their landing in Brazil in 1500, their Atlantic activity was largely confined to the islands of the Azores, Madeira, and Cape Verde, and to their interactions on the west coast of Africa, where they formed alliances and established trade. The Spanish, exploiting the opportunities afforded them by the voyages of Christopher Columbus, made the first inroads into the Caribbean and the Americas. These Iberians, and particularly the Spanish, set many of the patterns for European thinking about the region, its peoples, and their role in it, employing various tools from the European intellectual and religious tradition to do so. Their control over much of the Americas was justified by the right of discovery, by just war theory, and by the fact that the inhabitants knew nothing of Christianity and therefore required Christianization. Shortly after Columbus's return to Castile where he presented his discovery to the queen, the Portuguese and the Spanish entered into treaties demarcating areas of influence in the newly found lands. They also sought papal authorizations for their activities, gaining control over the conversion of the heathen peoples living in them. Papal donations granted the Spanish Crown not the lands (which they assumed Spain claimed by right of discovery) but rather the responsibility for the souls of the peoples of those lands. Within the Roman Catholic context, papal grants were remarkable for the extent of the authority over the church granted to the Spanish Crown. Within a few years, the Habsburg Holy Roman Emperor married the heir to the thrones of Castile and Aragon, which brought Spain and all its American holdings into the Empire this dynastic change further justified expansion: believing that the Roman heritage of global empire passed to the Habsburgs further supported the incorporation of all of the Americas under the Crown.[2]

These ways of thinking about the Americas shaped Spanish colonization. They first understood their claim as total, making the exception for the Portuguese who held Brazil by treaties signed in the late fifteenth century. Other Europeans had no legitimate place in the hemisphere, and no lands outside of Brazil were open to any but the Spanish (initially more narrowly defined as "the Castilians"). Such was the case regardless of whether they actively occupied those lands. By the 1530s, the Habsburgs prohibited the enslavement of the native peoples of the Americas, who were defined as "vassals" to the king, a legal status that both subjugated and protected them. Missionaries drawn from various religious orders worked among the native inhabitants, with the Church supporting the Spanish conquest as well as working to rein in some of its worst abuses. The Dominican friar Bartolomé de las Casas wrote to expose mistreatment of the Indians, and others later used his writings not to verify the positive role of the Catholic Church but rather the cruelty of the Spaniards.[3] When the conversion of the Indians proved shallow, because many persisted in their traditional ways, the Church responded, at times deploying the Inquisition to police belief and practice, attempting to uncover and punish evidence of older and alternative beliefs.[4] With the special status of the Indians limiting the labor that could be extracted from them, the Spanish tapped into a slave trade that had long existed in West Africa.

The Spanish deployed various common modes of understanding in constructing their Atlantic outposts. Like all Europeans, they believed their Christian religion to be not only superior to all other systems of belief but indeed the one true faith. They similarly believed that both discovery and conquest brought with it certain rights, and that the papacy had conferred responsibility to save the souls of the hemisphere's inhabitants. Especially the many religious personnel among them felt compelled to convert pagans; they understood a failure to embrace Christianity fully in terms of ignorance (in the best case) or heresy (in the worst). The Iberians also drew upon theories of just war.[5] With a long tradition in Iberia of slavery, and an ongoing practice of human bondage in the Mediterranean world, Spanish colonists who could afford to do so purchased enslaved Africans without realizing they were laying the groundwork for a novel system of chattel slavery. The particular constellation of ideas that the Spanish employed and the specific manner in which they utilized them drew on common ideas but suited them to Spanish circumstances: their precedence in the Americas, their Roman Catholicism, the papal donations, and the legal definition of Indians as vassals all distinguished the Spanish case. Their ideas about discovery, conquest, just war and slavery, alternately, they shared with others.

The ideological underpinnings of the English ventures in the Americas overlapped to a great extent with this Spanish mix. They too assumed Christian superiority, thinking of the indigenous inhabitants as either pagans with no idea of the true religion or as heathens devoid of any religion. Although they would prove less energetic as missionaries, the English officially endorsed the view that colonization brought with it an obligation to Christianize native peoples. Every colonial charter made mention of this project, and support for it was periodically apparent (often most passionately in England itself).[6] That the natives were non-Christian also made it possible to contemplate enslaving them, especially when the added impetus of defeat in warfare prevailed.[7] The English also accepted the right of discovery, although they parsed the meaning of Columbus' voyage. Whereas the Spanish interpreted Columbus' landing and limited exploration within the Caribbean region as an endeavor to establish a claim to the entire hemisphere, the English delimited their rights to places they had literally visited and subsequently occupied.[8] Conquest in a just war, they agreed, brought the victor lands certainly and possibly peoples too, especially if other factors (such as pagan status) also pointed in that direction. Like the Spanish, they would rather purchase slaves from others who had already consigned them to that status than take direct responsibility for enslaving them.

While it was possible to counter Spanish claims from within the Roman Catholic fold by drawing on these common ideological underpinnings—as the French would demonstrate—the British foray into the Atlantic was profoundly shaped by English rejection of the Roman Catholic Church. Between the time when Spain laid claim to much of the New World and the moment when the English entered these regions, Western Europe had been splintered by the Reformation.[9] Here too the English were late, among the last to adopt the religious reforms emanating out from Continental Europe. Beginning with Martin Luther's attempt to reform the Church from within, the movement led eventually to the founding of new Christian churches (first of all the Lutheran). This fissure unleashed a process that reconfigured Western Christianity. Luther is often remembered for emphasizing the "priesthood of all believers," a phrase that implies a complete atomization of the faith. Further divisions soon followed in the wake of his critique, yet centripetal influences binding the newly formed church together and bringing believers under the authority of a new leadership countered that centrifugal trend. Hence Lutherans erected a hierarchical structure similar at the lower levels to that of Rome, lopping off only the highest strata of church officials; this outcome was far from the free-for-all that the idea of each person being his or her own priest might suggest. Significant further divisions occurred when Calvinists carved out their own path, reacting to elements within Lutheranism with which they disagreed, and when a Radical Reformation pursued aspects of the critique of the status quo to the extreme represented by the much-maligned "Anabaptism." Despite their differences, these new churches and sects shared a set of devotional practices, such as Bible reading, extemporaneous prayer, and sermons, that focused adherents on their individual relationship to God.[10]

On its own trajectory and in a reformation that began as a top-down affair, England eventually went through a similar process of moderate reformation, internal criticism, and radical extension. The English Reformation arose initially less out of objections to the Roman Catholic Church and more out of Henry VIII's dynastic concerns. Though he intended only a limited reformation, putting the church under his own authority and benefiting from the confiscation of church property, the Church of England shifted gradually toward the Continental Reformation. During his three children's reigns, the church settlement buffeted to and fro, but public opinion galvanized behind the national Church of England by the second half of Elizabeth's long reign. Spain, closely involved in these changes, was understandably antagonistic toward reformed religion in England: first because Henry's discarded wife was the Spanish princess Katherine of Aragon; later because Philip II married Henry and Katherine's daughter Mary and supported her efforts to bring England forcibly back into the Catholic fold; and later still because

Elizabeth's break with both the Roman Church and her erstwhile brother-in-law brought the two monarchies to war.[11] Over the rocky process of fully separating itself from Catholicism, the English battled as much with their powerful Spanish neighbors as they did directly with the papacy in Rome. In the context of these animosities, Elizabeth's subjects made their boldest forays to date into the Spanish Caribbean. As England came to see itself as a champion of international Protestantism against Spanish pretensions to rule the world, anti-Catholic and anti-Spanish sentiment spurred an emerging English identity.[12] Protestantism thus surfaced as an ideology, which guided political discussions and drove policy, distinct from the practice of any particular reformed Christianity. The English would draw on this ideology in their encounters in the Atlantic world.

These developments molded English expansion. By rejecting and vilifying the Roman Catholic Church, the English came to see Spanish proselytizing in a different light. While some commentators acknowledged the energy of the Church's efforts, most joined with George Abbott to lament that "labouring to roote out their infidelity, [they] mingling the *Christian* Religion with much Popish superstition."[13] When English missionary efforts later proved few and fraught with difficulties, advocates such as Cotton Mather asserted that properly teaching the true message of Christianity was necessarily a slow process.[14] Catholicism, in the most extreme English view, brought only superstition and thralldom, not true Christianity. Seeing Catholicism as promoting ignorance and the subjugation of adherents fueled English depictions of their own faith as granting them liberty.[15] From a post-Reformation perspective, too, a Spanish reliance on a papal designation of responsibility for the indigenous inhabitants did little to buttress their case. The English in fact feigned misunderstanding (or literally misunderstood), characterizing the papal bull as denoting the pope's gift of the Americas. The English derided the idea that the pope had the right to give away these territories sight unseen.[16] That enmity was informed by a vehement anti-Catholicism, inflected with envy at Spanish success and joined with criticism of their methods. Well versed in the trope of Spanish cruelty, English colonizers and would-be colonizers often cast themselves as sharing the status of victims with the Indian peoples who had suffered the worst abuses at the hands of the Conquistadors. They entered the Atlantic arrogantly confident that they would improve upon the Spanish record and clung to that belief despite mounting contradictory evidence.

Part Two: Protestantism and Other British Atlantic Ideologies

Protestantism as an ideology came into its own in this context. Despite the ways in which the term was increasingly employed, Protestantism was not a religion or even one specific subset of the larger religion of Christianity. New religious groups that formed as a result of the Protestant Reformation were Lutheran, Reformed, Presbyterian, or Anabaptist/Baptist, not Protestant. As used in the Anglo-Atlantic context, Protestantism functioned as a broad, catch-all category that meant essentially "not Roman Catholic." It served further to smooth over important distinctions among various Christians. Anti-Catholicism was fundamental to its emergence, but the concept's significance had as much to do with its ability to push back against the atomizing nature of Reformation as for its repudiation of Catholicism. Most Christian communities that arose out of the Reformation did so with the confidence that they were creating churches that finally reflected God's wishes, eliminating past errors and corruptions and returning to a pure form of worship.[17] Despite being shaped by well-intentioned men with broadly similar goals, these churches differed in key ways, fragmenting Christendom further. A century after Luther nailed his 95 theses to the Wittenberg church door, numerous new Christian churches existed throughout Northern Europe. Their proliferation dismayed many, but overcoming that dizzying variety to arrive at a common Christian faith that was not Roman Catholic but functioned in a Catholic—that is universal—fashion proved elusive. Protestantism as a category covered all and (hopefully) drew them together.

The history of the term itself illuminates the conundrum. Those who protested the flaws within Roman Catholicism initially bore the label "protestors." For a time Lutherans and Calvinists might be distinguished as Protestants and Reformed Christians (the latter in Calvin's Geneva, the Dutch Reformed Church, the Scottish Presbyterian kirk). Later, once the English government erected the Church of England and fragmentation set in within England as well, the established church was occasionally referred to as "Protestant" to differentiate it from critics within the puritan movement and from more extreme sectarians. Later in a similar vein, Protestants might be opposed to dissenters, meaning those inside or outside the established Church of England.[18] Over time the word ceased to have a narrow meaning associated with a particular subset of post-Reformation Christians and came to work as a capacious term encompassing the variety unleashed by the Reformation and its long aftermath.[19] With Britain increasingly diverse and its American colonies even more so, a vague Protestantism had the potential to bind disparate non-Catholic Christians together.

Still the new churches organized in the wake of Luther's protests countered the divisions of Reformation to emphasize commonalities and seek unity. Churches noted agreement on fundamental matters of doctrine and ascribed differences to minor issues of church organization. Although such claims overstated the level of actual agreement, churches in the Reformed or Calvinist tradition did share much. Churches offered each other mutual aid, and they watched the resurgence of Roman Catholicism in the seventeenth century as a matter of concern for all.[20] A host of authors and activists, starting in England around Samuel Hartlib, worked unsuccessfully toward a union of churches.[21] In the early English Atlantic, New Englanders promoted interchurch cooperation with like-minded Christians, seeking allies across geographical divides. Eighteenth-century evangelicals felt a similar sense of mutuality, especially as revival swept across locations from continental Europe to colonial Connecticut.[22] Moravians pursued a plan for a pan-Protestant union they thought well-suited to the American scene. They believed different Christian faiths shared more than they realized, and that problems of language created false divisions that could be dissolved by a process of "theological translation."[23] A monolithic Protestantism that could stand as the united opposite to Catholicism in a simplified religious landscape had continual appeal.

Despite dreams of unity, the various churches remained separate and diverse. In the Moravian case, their rivals perceived them as attempting to subsume other churches. Most faiths, with the noteworthy exception of Huguenots, resisted incorporation into other communities, fiercely defending their independent existence.[24] The language of Protestantism did not create unity so much as the perception of a shared identity. Protestantism—which becomes generic and broad where it was once narrow and specific—in the colonial context proffered a bond across languages, creeds, and previous geographies. Advocates for religious liberty were few, although beneficiaries of the general acceptance of diversity were everywhere. British colonial America laid the groundwork for an extension of the ideology of liberty to include religious liberty, in large part a practical consequence of the stunning variety within that spiritual landscape. Later the fact of diversity would be perceived as evidence of liberty, but initially the British saw their (vaguely defined) faith as itself signifying liberty. Protestantism as a rhetorically inclusive identity worked more successfully than any actual attempt to unify.

Hence the British claim to be Protestant and free did a variety of work. It made the vast majority of Euro-Americans living in the British colonies into a generic brand of Christians, bound by their status as not Catholic, and obscuring their profound disagreements. It not only coupled this capacious Christian identification with liberty, drawing on the concept of the rights of freeborn Englishmen, it also underlined the ways that being not Catholic meant being free. With Roman Catholicism figuring as thralldom to the priestly caste, to papal authority, and to superstition, the pairing of Protestantism and liberty contained an element of redundancy.[25] The liberties entailed in that claim were broader, however, going beyond the alleged freedoms associated with membership in one of various Christian churches; it referenced in addition the common-law tradition of protected rights. As early as the 1630s, when Providence Island colonists enumerated their demands, they articulated what Karen Ordahl Kupperman later described as the recipe for a successful colonial venture. These rights—to own land, to live under a common-law legal regime rather than martial law, and the like—depended on the common perception of what it meant to live as a freeborn Englishman.[26] In the seventeenth century, with the vast majority of migrants being English, they widely deployed this language; by the eighteenth century it formed the basis of the broad cultural idea of Britishness, which encompassed both liberty and Protestantism.[27]

This cultural ideology made the position of actual Roman Catholics somewhat precarious. Catholics facing this rhetoric hoped to avoid being perceived as hated foes, a challenge they met within England with some success. In the rare instance when Catholics had the upper hand, the problem differed, as opponents could perceive Catholics in authority as bearers of tyranny and a threat to liberty. In the only British colony founded by a Roman Catholic and permitting full participation for Catholics, the Province of Maryland, difficulties abounded. The noble family that held the proprietorship of Maryland grounded its claims on a royal grant of near-feudal authority, appointing elite Catholic men to erect manors, oversee justice, and distribute land to tenant farmers. The approach was highly traditional, and migrants—most of them Protestants—complained that the lords Baltimore intended through it to deprive them of their rights. Various uprisings in seventeenth-century Maryland were invariably framed in terms of defending the rights and religion of the non-Catholics against the threat of a tyrannizing popery.[28] Ultimately the proprietor, Charles Calvert, the third Baron Baltimore, was ousted during the Glorious Revolution—in a case that denied him his property in the interests of defending the liberties and Protestantism of residents. It spoke volumes that his son resumed control of the province in the eighteenth century but only after he converted to the Church of England, becoming again eligible to command authority in an empire defined as Protestant and free. Not coincidentally, the Catholic Calvert family launched the most ambitious missionary campaign in any early English colony, although the work of the Jesuits there paled in comparison to what their coreligionists accomplished in other imperial settings.[29]

The British colonizers considered themselves to be beneficiaries and proponents of liberty, yet they sold or held slaves as soon as they were able to obtain them. The creation of a slave system gave these champions of liberty relatively little pause. Objections to the emerging system were nearly nonexistent. In early Massachusetts Bay a court order released men captured on the coast of Africa and brought to New England for sale, not on the grounds that slavery was wrong but that they had been forced into slavery illegally, through kidnapping. At the same time, the English throughout the Atlantic world bought and sold slaves, both African and Indian, assuring themselves that their enslavement was legal and just, if they considered the matter at all. In fact the designation of English people as carriers of special rights allowed for the creation of a slave system in two ways. First, the Englishness of "freeborn Englishmen" implied alternatives for those not "freeborn" and potentially for those not English as well. Even if the English prided themselves on their own greater commitment to freedom, the early expression of rights in terms that were exclusionary rather than inclusionary arguably opened the way to slavery. In modern terms, these were not framed as human rights.[30] Second, with the protection of property being one highly valued right, slaves defined as property became objects that the freeborn had an inherent right to own. The rhetoric as initially articulated not only excluded slaves, it protected property in slaves.

Slaves for their part saw Protestantism as holding out a promise of freedom, which set the stage for early struggles over the meaning of conversion. Given the long-standing Mediterranean tradition making those of another religion eligible for enslavement (and a related but less robust tradition that conversion brought freedom), the possibility arose that converted slaves would become free. The Spanish easily dispatched this question, requiring conversion of all enslaved persons but closing off the possibility that baptism resulted in liberation. In the Protestant Atlantic, the suspicion that baptism meant emancipation also arose, and in spite of a lack of evidence in support of the theory, it persisted. Masters who feared converted slaves would earn their freedom thwarted those who sought to preach to them, and clergymen advocated laws that stifled such rumors in order that they could set about the work of missions.[31] Fears that Christian conversion would lead slaves to seek freedom ran deeper, however. Masters clearly worried that the message of equality before God would give slaves dangerous aspirations. In addition the ideology of Protestantism as closely bound with liberty (and with Britishness) made enslaved African converts almost an oxymoron. Slaves once they gained access to the Christian message on a wide scale did in fact develop the "liberation theology" component of it, favoring images of exodus and freedom from slavery in their songs and preaching, as Eugene Genovese long ago noted.[32] Although the enslaved pushed back using the tools of Protestantism and liberty, their owners both feared that possible connection—evident when they avoided Christianization—and persuaded themselves to overlook it—when they embraced both slavery for others and liberty for themselves.

Native peoples in the Protestant Atlantic interacted with these European cultural imperatives from their own circumstances. As the inhabitants of the lands that the English and other expansionists expected to seize, they immediately felt the brunt of the European sense of superiority, as unrealistic as that sense proved to be in the early years of settler dependence on indigenous aid and education. America's first inhabitants felt similarly persuaded of their own culture's superiority, as indeed all peoples in ancient and basically functional societies do.[33] In the regions touched first by the English, the residents did not confront highly aggressive and successful conquistadors, they were not subjected to the reading of the *Requerimento* that offered them a choice of conversion or warfare, and they were not subjected to a highly organized missionary campaign. Besides their help and the questions of a few curious intellectuals such as Thomas Harriot or Roger Williams, what the English most sought from the natives was their land, often after an intermediate stage of wishing for their aid, sustenance, and trade goods. The English sent far more people to their colonies (and opened them eventually to many non-English people), introducing a rising tide of settlers who threatened to overwhelm the original inhabitants through land seizures, warfare, disease, and displacement. This settler colonialism shaped the relations of the Indians with those who entered the British Atlantic world.[34]

Looking at the native conversion process from the side of the colonizers' reveals a serious lack of effort for many years, even though Christianity nonetheless gradually became a part of indigenous life. Although the English often framed expansion in terms of replacing Spanish Catholicism with true Christianity, their own missionary campaigns proved modest and belated. Various reasons have been offered for this lag, including institutional, theological, and practical considerations.[35] The most successful efforts allowed the Indians to remain in their own communities, while bringing them Christian instruction and eventual church membership. The biggest project of the seventeenth century, the Praying Indian villages of

New England, fit this model. It separated out those natives willing to learn about Christianity, requiring them to live in an English manner and providing them with teachers, preachers and eventually texts in a written form of the Algonquian language. Proselytes were only admitted to the church when they attained a high level of theological literacy and gave evidence of a saving grace experience (as fitted expectations within the reformed faith). This concerted effort declined markedly as a result of King Philip's War (1675–76) and the death of its major ministerial advocate, John Eliot (1690). The Praying villages, like the later mission to the Mohawk enclaves of eighteenth-century northern New York, worked as weak parallels to the Spanish Republic of the Indians.

Over decades and indeed centuries, the surviving native communities incorporated Christian elements into their belief systems and their worship, often in ways different than missionaries envisioned. Thus by the time a prophet preaching Indian independence from Euro-American domination appeared at the turn of the nineteenth century, his message combined Christian and traditional components even while calling for native separatism. The process of the Christianization of Native America was slow, often partial, and involved not only the work of missionaries but also innumerable individual encounters between Euro-Americans and Native Americans as well as personal choices made by the Indian peoples themselves.[36] The individual and diffused nature of this process signaled the disappointing performance of Protestant missions before 1800 but also made the Indian experience—with its individual and local variation—in some sense prototypically Protestant.

The most striking feature shaping the British Atlantic religiously, however, was not its relative neglect of African or native conversion but its sheer diversity.[37] Arguably this reality was a fundamental trait arising from its Protestantism. Roman Catholic empires erected official barriers to non-Catholics. While the Spanish tried but could not entirely bar individuals of other faiths from entering the Crown's American domains, they succeeded in excluding Jews, Muslims, and "Lutheran heretics" (as they sometimes styled all other Christians) to a remarkable extent. Even as the Church policed Indian backsliding from conversions they had hoped were total, it simultaneously worked to root out intruders (including those whose forced conversion from Judaism or Islam had been less than sincere or complete in previous generations).[38] The French failed to bar Huguenots entirely from their American holdings, although an early policy allowing their presence was officially overturned in the seventeenth century. When compared with the efforts of their Roman Catholic counterparts, the British case stands out for the complexity of the religious mixing that occurred in its Atlantic colonies.

The remarkable diversity of the British Atlantic had three primary causes: the inability of the English Reformation to contain the fragmentation so representative of the Reformation process generally; the creation of a composite monarchy—known as the "Three Kingdoms"—drawing together England and Wales, Ireland, and Scotland, each with its own peculiar religious settlement; and the role of the Atlantic as home to a variety of religious groups from across Northern Europe. By the time England became seriously involved in colonization, James I and VI ruled over three kingdoms, one with a Church of England religious establishment (and a vociferous minority of critics within it known as "puritans" as well as a residual Catholic community); another, his native Scotland, with a Presbyterian establishment and even larger residual Catholic presence; and a third across the Irish Sea that was predominantly Roman Catholic but had an official Church of Ireland patterned on but not identical to the Church of England and a burgeoning community of Scottish Presbyterians in the northern region of Ulster. The fragmentation of religions within England, and to a lesser extent in the other kingdoms, increased dramatically as a result of the midcentury Revolution. The even greater diversity of the Atlantic arose first as a consequence of these circumstances, as individuals from all three kingdoms made their way into the colonies, recreating and compressing this European variety in the British Americas.

Through an uneven and at times contradictory process, the colonies came to welcome numerous additional non-Catholic Christians as well as Jews. At certain times communities within the Three Kingdoms perceived colonies as a likely place to pursue their particular religious vision relatively unmolested. Such expectations animated separatists who left the Netherlands to accept a Virginia Company offer of semiautonomy in the northern reaches of its then more capacious land grant; the Plymouth plantation was settled as a result. Later "puritans" expected greater latitude to organize their religious affairs if they went to Massachusetts Bay and eventually to other colonies in New England; Quakers had similar hopes with regard to Jamaica, the Jerseys, and finally Pennsylvania; and Scots-Irish migrated to the mid-Atlantic mainland for the same reason. Diverse believers from various European points of origin came as well. First Sephardic Jews fleeing temporary residence in Dutch Brazil when the Portuguese retook the colony slipped quietly into many Caribbean and eventually mainland colonies; next the Crown permitted the Huguenots to take refuge in Britain and the colonies after their expulsion from France (1685); and subsequently William Penn recruited German speakers from various churches into his newly founded Pennsylvania.[39] In some of these cases, the opportunities offered fit the later American understanding of the colonies as havens where the religious oppressed could worship freely; but in others migrants pursued a vision of exclusion and intolerance toward difference that upends that cherished narrative. Some, like the puritans, came for freedom to practice their own version of Christianity and to suppress all other variations, while others, like German sectarians, came simply to practice their faiths unmolested. This mix of motives and goals nonetheless created a remarkable level of diversity, which became a hallmark feature of the Protestant Atlantic.[40]

This diversity gave added impetus to the use of the term "Protestant." To the extent that the moniker was broad enough to cover a wide range of cases, it helped to tame the proliferation of religious options. Especially when looking outward toward Catholic enemies (such as France in Quebec or the Spanish in the southeast) a capacious definition of what it meant to belong to the British colonies proved essential. This is not to say that contestation did not roil the waters of a diverse colonial America. In the worst case, authorities imprisoned, exiled, and even in four cases executed Quakers who were initially perceived as outside the boundaries of acceptable belief. Opposition to the Quakers was widespread, but largely ineffective, as the sect made inroads from Barbados to Maine. In better cases, rivals debated and complained, with the Moravians being a particular target for animus. Interestingly, Moravians (known officially as the *Unitas Fratrum*, or Unity of the Brethren) predated the sixteenth-century Protestant Reformation, and their praxis took them far outside the common ground shared by most churches.

Part Three: The Implications of Protestantism as an Ideology

The particular ideological mix in the British Atlantic world not only shaped colonial self-understanding and contributed to later American national mythologies of freedom, it also affected many of the major moments punctuating colonial American history. If colonization started off following the path of least resistance, attempting to avoid confrontation with the Spanish in the Americas, by the time of Oliver Cromwell's Western Design (1655) the English confidently aimed at dismembering the Spanish Atlantic Empire. Unsurprisingly the Design was imbued with the rhetoric of liberty and Protestantism (with Cromwell hailed as the savior of the Protestant cause in Europe as well as its most assertive representative in the Americas). Not only was the Design anti-Catholic to the core, it also indulged the long-standing fantasy that

Africans and Indians in the Americas awaited rescue by the English from their cruel Spanish masters.[41] Although the revolutionary government in England would be displaced in a return to monarchy (1660), the themes of Protestantism and liberty continued to shape England's internal politics and its place in the world.

The Glorious Revolution of 1688–89 reaffirmed this ideological tradition of Protestantism and liberty. As Steven Pincus observes, "The revolutionaries of 1688–9 believed they had saved the English nation—its liberties, its religion, and its culture—from an impending French tyranny."[42] Afterward the state barred succession by any royal person who adhered to the Roman Catholic Church. This outcome pulled the Three Kingdoms, soon to be reconfigured as Great Britain, into a series of wars against the latest most powerful Roman Catholic monarch, the French king; and the rhetoric of Protestantism and liberty formed the basis of an emerging British national identity. In the wider Atlantic, fears of Catholics and of threats to liberty animated a series of coups ostensibly aimed to realign the colonies with the outcome being in Three Kingdoms. As Owen Stanwood has shown, such fears guided the politics and ideology of these developments.[43] The upheaval of this era fueled fear of witchcraft in northern New England, where anxieties over French and Indian papists on the northern frontier combined with a profound angst over the loss of local control over the affairs of both church and state. That the "puritans" of New England indulged in a paroxysm of gendered spiritual violence—in a scare reminiscent of the Continental witchcraft outbreaks of previous centuries—showed both the depth of the crisis and the ways in which even this group of reformed Christians continued to draw upon shared European-wide theological categories. They also struggled to redefine themselves as loyal Protestant Englishmen after having held their region aloof for generations.[44]

The decisive realignment in European alliances brought by the accession of William and Mary furthered the rationalization of English policy toward its empire. Any colonist who hoped that the Glorious Revolution would put an end to Stuart schemes for increased commercial regulation and imperial oversight were disappointed. The new monarchs, partly propelled forward by the demands to build up the state apparatus for waging war against France, continued to augment the state's imperial reach. Invocation of the values of Protestantism and liberty enhanced their ability to do so. That the periodic wars with France could be promoted as defending those ideals against an absolutist monarchy that persecuted Protestants and used native allies (some of them Catholic converts) to attack the northern border of British North America helped enormously both to sell those wars and to make sense of them.[45] While the British union (1707) opened the Atlantic empire to the Scots (who dominated migration from the British Isles in the eighteenth century), their closer incorporation into the polity shifted the language of rights toward Britishness, and the terminology of the rights of freeborn Englishmen was invoked less often, replaced by the broader language of liberty. The ancient constitution remained important, however, because it shaped the English and colonial legal systems, and the commitment to such rights as trial by jury persisted. The accession of the Hanoverians to the throne (1714) illustrated the determination to bar Catholics (agreed in the settlement of 1689), as the Lutheran George jumped over dozens of nearer relations who were Catholic, and signaled the acceptability of the broad category of Protestantism—in that he could head the Church of England by virtue of being outside the Catholic fold.

The religious revivals of the midcentury represented a pan-Protestant movement that bound together various Christian churches as part of a resurgent international Protestantism. Linking continental European, British, and colonial faithful, the Great Awakening foregrounded an evangelical outreach.[46] Revival varied across locations, shaped by local religious geographies, but arguably reached its ultimate expression in British North America. Propelled forward initially by the preaching of George Whitefield, the American revivals cut across numerous different churches. Whitefield himself chose not to promote his own Church of England, making him a poor advocate for the scheme to expand the influence of that ecclesiastical organization, but an excellent symbol of a generic (if evangelical) Protestantism.[47] Other revivalists came out of different traditions—especially Congregationalist, Presbyterian, and Baptist. The Awakening pulled in two directions at once: toward Protestant cooperation on issues of shared concern and a greater proliferation of often hard-fought religious differences. Animus, cooperation, and greater diversity all appeared in its wake. One long-term effect was to bring Christianity decisively into the slave quarters on southern plantations. By the time of the American Revolution, as a result, Christian conversion had made real headway among the enslaved, launching the tradition of black churches as central to the African-American community. After British defeat and Loyalist exile, the process would be extended to the West Indian islands that continued under slavery, the work of enslaved preachers carried by their masters to Jamaica and elsewhere in the British Caribbean.

The American Revolution both culminated and reinvigorated the ideology of Protestantism and liberty. Whether the British government intended to take away rights mattered less than the fact that some colonists perceived such a threat. How deeply committed to this rhetoric the colonials were set them apart from the imperial authorities: although the latter also deployed the idea that Britain was especially Protestant and free, they did not comprehend the depth of the fears that their policies sparked. That the discourse of civic republicanism, with its emphasis on liberty and fear of corruption, persisted so much longer in the colonies than in Britain—which Bernard Bailyn pointed out years ago—followed from the repeated invocations of liberty and Protestantism in the British Atlantic.[48] Certainly the conviction that communities had to be vigilant of their liberties went back to the first decades, when it made no direct reference to classical political theory but rather cited the ancient constitution and freeborn rights. Having clung to these concerns and refined them over the decades, colonists articulated their commitment to and fears for liberty regularly. Hence they were ripe for the message that the authorities meant to revoke their accustomed rights—as well as particularly concerned when similar liberties were granted to the newly conquered Roman Catholic French in Quebec.[49] In this instance, the language of rights crashed into the prejudices of Protestantism. The outrage highlighted the limitations on efforts to extend rights defined as British and Protestant.

The history of Protestantism as an ideology persisted after the fissuring of the British Atlantic world by the American Revolution. Within the British Empire, Protestantism inspired missionary activity at a level unimaginable in the earlier period.[50] Protestantism as a generic category would be called upon to explain the superiority of Britain as a force for modernity, as sociologist Max Weber saw within its Protestant faith a compulsion to work and to save that (he argued) led to capitalist and industrial advances that outstripped the southern European Catholic nations and even his native (largely Lutheran) Germany. Ironically Weber elevated the Quakers—initially perceived as far outside the Protestant pale and never fittingly categorized as Calvinist—as his premier example of the Protestant work ethic striding toward modernity.[51]

In the United States the impact of this ideological heritage mattered profoundly. Later Americans understood their nation as both Christian (by which they meant and generally mean Protestant) as well as free. These convictions remain impervious to corrections that cite the secular nature of the American Revolution, the separation of church and state, and the commitment of many of the founders and their descendants to the institution of slavery. Benjamin Franklin stands as a favored founder: in addition to his many inventions, in the guise of *Poor Richard* he dictated an ethos of hard work and his autobiography charted his personal trajectory as a process of gaining independence from tradition (Boston) to enter a land of liberty and Protestant diversity (Philadelphia). That his own commitment to creedal Christianity was vague and capacious appears beside the larger point that he represents a quintessential American. This imagining of Franklin works precisely because the United States as a Christian nation idea has deep roots not in religion *per se* but in Protestantism as an ideology. He can embody that tradition though he rarely attended any church. [52]

The United States has struggled with this heritage and continues to do so. The first great test came when Irish Catholic immigrants began flooding into the new nation. Both the vicious reaction against them, in which they were subjected to mob violence and deep prejudice, and the creation of a national mythology emphasizing the American commitment to religious liberty owe much to the need to incorporate Roman Catholics into a polity defined by both liberty and Protestantism. Today we mostly forget that Irish Catholics were once seen as unassimilable in part because of their religion, but Americans continue to claim a special status as more Christian and more dedicated to liberty than other nations.

Notes

1 The author thanks Adrian Weimer and Michael Meranze for helpful comments on this essay. Enrique Rivera provided research assistance.
2 Anthony Pagden, *Lords of all the World: Ideologies of Empire in Spain, Britain and France, c. 1500–c.1800* (New Haven: Yale University Press, 1995); Stephanie Kirk and Sarah Rivett, "Introduction," *Religious Transformations in the Early Modern Americas* (Philadelphia: University of Pennsylvania Press, 2014), 6–7.
3 Carla Gardina Pestana, "Cruelty and Religious Justifications for Conquest in the Mid-Seventeenth-Century English Atlantic," *Empires of God: Religious Encounters in the Early Modern Atlantic World*, eds. Linda Gregerson and Susan Juster (Philadelphia: University of Pennsylvania Press, 2010), 37–57; also see Rolena Adorno, *Polemics of Possession in Spanish American Narrative* (New Haven: Yale University Press, 2007).
4 Inga Clendinnen, *Ambivalent Conquests: Maya and Spaniard in Yucatan, 1517–1570* (Cambridge: Cambridge University Press, 1987), 74–82, 117–18.
5 Rolena Adorno, "The Discursive Encounter of Spain and America: The Authority of Eyewitness Testimony in the Writing of History," *William and Mary Quarterly*, 3rd series, 49 (1992): 212–16.
6 Carla Gardina Pestana, *Protestant Empire: Religion and the Making of the British Atlantic World* (Philadelphia: University of Pennsylvania Press, 2009); although the general argument being made here differs to an extent from that of the book (and a related, earlier essay), the book can be consulted for amplification and documentation of the history reviewed here.
7 For an argument that they hesitated somewhat, see Michael Guasco, *Slaves and Englishmen: Human Bondage in the Early Modern Atlantic World* (Philadelphia: University of Pennsylvania Press, 2014).
8 John Elliott, *Britain and Spain in America: Colonists and Colonized* (Reading, England: University of Reading, 1994); also Patricia Seed, "Taking Possession and Reading Texts: Establishing the Authority of Overseas Empires," *William and Mary Quarterly* 49[2] (1992): 183–209.
9 Diarmaid MacCulloch, *The Reformation* (New York: Viking, 2004), provides an excellent overview.
10 Alex Ryrie, *Being Protestant in Reformation Britain* (Oxford: Oxford University Press, 2013).
11 Pauline Croft, "'The State of the World is Marvellously Changed': England, Spain and Europe, 1558–1604," *Tudor England and its Neighbours*, eds. Susan Dorn and Glenn Richardson (New York: Palgrave, 2005), 178–202.
12 Ken Macmillan, "Introduction: Discourse on History, Geography, and Law," *John Dee: The Limits of the British Empire*, eds Macmillan with Jennifer Abeles (Westport, CN: Praeger, 2004), 3, 13, 18–20, 22–3, 27–9. For a helpful discussion of these issues, see Philip S. Gorski, "Premodern Nationalism: An Oxymoron? The Evidence from England," *The SAGE Handbook of Nations and Nationalism*, eds. Gerard Delanty and Krishan Kumar (London: SAGE Publications Ltd., 2006), 143–56.
13 G. Abott, *Briefe Description of the Whole World*, 4th ed. (London: John Brown, 1617), T (irregularly paginated).
14 Evan Haefeli and Owen Stanwood, "Jesuits, Huguenots, and the Apocalypse: The Origins of America's First French Book," *Proceedings of the American Antiquarian Society* 116, 1 (2006): 63, 81; also see Mather's use of "Protestant," 69.

15 Arthur F. Marotti, *Religious Ideology and Cultural Fantasy: Catholic and Anti-Catholic Discourses in Early Modern England* (Notre Dame, IN: University of Notre Dame Press, 2005), Ch. 5.
16 David Armitage, *The Ideological Origins of the British Empire* (New York: Cambridge University Press, 2000), 90–95.
17 What Theodore Bozeman said of the New England migrants was true more broadly, *To Live Ancient Lives: The Primitivist Dimension in Puritanism* (Chapel Hill: University of North Carolina Press, 1988).
18 These shifts in the meaning of the term can be followed in large part in the OED and by searching the term in titles listed in EEBO.
19 It became, in other words, what modern Americans currently mean by the term, which is Christians who are not Roman Catholic (or Orthodox Christians), as in Will Herberg's famed study *Protestant, Catholic, Jew: An Essay in American Religious Sociology* (Garden City, NY: Doubleday, 1955). See also R. L. Moore, *Religious Outsiders and the Making of Americans* (New York: Oxford University Press, 1986), vii–ix, 9–10.
20 Anthony Milton, *Catholic and Reformed: The Roman and Protestant Churches in English Protestant Thought, 1600–1640* (Cambridge: Cambridge University Press, 1994), 377–84. More broadly, see Phillip Benedict, *Christ's Churches More Purely Reformed: A Social History of Calvinism* (New Haven: Yale University Press, 2002), 287–90.
21 Samuel Hartlib, *The Necessity of Some Nearer Conjunction and Correspondence amongst Evangelical Protestants* (London, 1644).
22 W. R. Ward, *Early Evangelicalism: A Global Intellectual History, 1670–1789* (Cambridge: Cambridge University Press, 2006); Susan O'Brien, "A Transatlantic Community of Saints: The Great Awakening and the First Evangelical Network, 1735–1755" *American Historical Review* 91 (1986): 811–32.
23 Patrick M. Erben, *A Harmony of the Spirits: Translation and the Language of Community in Early Pennsylvania* (Chapel Hill: University of North Carolina Press, 2012).
24 This is evident in the material marshalled by Aaron Fogleman in *Jesus Is Female: Moravians and Radical Religion in Early America* (Philadelphia: University of Pennsylvania Press, 2008), although not what he argues.
25 Carla Gardina Pestana, "Whitefield and Empire," *George Whitefield: Life, Context, and Legacy*, eds. Geordan Hammond and David Ceri Jones (Oxford: Oxford University Press, 2016, 82–97.).
26 Karen O. Kupperman, *Providence Island, 1630–1641: The Other Puritan Colony* (Cambridge: Cambridge University Press, 1993).
27 Colin Haydon, "'I Love My King and My Country, but a Roman Catholic I Hate': Anti-Catholicism, Xenophobia and National Identity in Eighteenth-Century England," *Protestantism and National Identity: Britain and Ireland, c. 1650–c. 1850*, eds. Tony Claydon and Ian McBride (Cambridge: Cambridge University Press, 1998), 33–52; Mark Valeri, *Heavenly Merchandise: How Religions Shaped Commerce in Puritan America* (Princeton: Princeton University Press, 2010), 220. Here I differ from Jack P. Greene, who argues for liberty alone, with no reference to Protestantism and no religious context for the concept. See his "Empire and Identity from the Glorious Revolution to the American Revolution," *Oxford History of the British Empire*, Vol. II: *The Eighteenth Century*, ed. P. J. Marshall (Oxford: Oxford University Press, 1998), 215–30.
28 Carla Gardina Pestana, *English Atlantic in an Age of Revolution, 1640–1661* (Cambridge: Harvard University Press, 2007).
29 Antoinette Sutto, "Lord Baltimore, the Society of Jesus, and Caroline Absolutism in Maryland, 1630–1645," *Journal of British Studies*, 48 (2009): 631–52.
30 Laura Doyle, *Freedom's Empire: Race and the Rise of the Novel in Atlantic Modernity, 1640–1940* (Durham, NC: Duke University Press, 2008).
31 Travis Glasson, *Mastering Christianity: Missionary Anglicanism and Slavery in the Atlantic World* (Oxford: Oxford University Press, 2012).
32 Eugene D. Genovese, *Roll, Jordan Roll: The World the Slaves Made* (New York: Pantheon Books, 1974), 248–55.
33 For meeting on common ground with confidence and curiosity, see Karen O. Kupperman, *Indians and English: Facing Off in Early America* (Ithaca: Cornell University Press, 2000).
34 John C. Weaver, *The Great Land Rush and the Making of the Modern World, 1650–1900* (Montreal: McGill-Queen's University Press, 2006).
35 For a review of this issue, see Carla Gardina Pestana, "The Missionary Impulse in the Atlantic world, 1500–1800: Or how Protestants learned to be missionaries," *Social Sciences and Missions* (special issue on Missions and Slavery), 26 (2013): 9–39.

36 Linford D. Fisher, *The Indian Great Awakening: Religion and the Shaping of Native Cultures in Early America* (New York: Oxford University Press, 2012); Edward E. Andrews, *Native Apostles: Black and Indian Missionaries in the British Atlantic World* (Cambridge: Harvard University Press, 2013).
37 The discussion that follows relies heavily on Pestana, *Protestant Empire*, and citations are only provided for more recent works or those that make additional points.
38 Maria Elena Martinez, *Genealogical Fictions: Limpieza de Sangre, Religion, and Gender in Colonial Mexico* (Stanford, CA: Stanford University Press, 2008).
39 Evan Haefeli, "Breaking the Christian Atlantic: The Legacy of Dutch Tolerance in Brazil," *The Legacy of Dutch Brazil*, ed. Michael van Groesen (New York: Cambridge University Press, 2014), 140–45.
40 This generalization also applies in the Dutch colonies, in spite of recent scholarship showing that the established Dutch Reformed Church worked against the proliferation of spiritual options. See Evan Haefeli, *New Netherland and the Dutch Origins of American Religious Liberty* (Philadelphia: University of Pennsylvania Press, 2012).
41 Drawn from my forthcoming *The English Conquest of Jamaica: Oliver Cromwell's Bid for Empire* (Cambridge: Belkusp Press, 2017).
42 Steven Pincus, "'To Protect English Liberties': The English Nationalist Revolution of 1688–1689," *Protestantism and National Identity*, eds. Claydon and McBride (New York: Cambridge University Press, 1986), 78. Pincus's construction, while accurate as far as it goes, dismisses any threat from James II as well as the Atlantic dimension of these conflicts.
43 Owen Stanwood, *The Empire Reformed: English America in the Age of the Glorious Revolution* (Philadelphia: University of Pennsylvania Press, 2011).
44 According to the sensitive reading of Teresa A. Toulouse, they in part used captivity narratives to do so; see *The Captives Position: Female Narrative, Male Identity, and Royal Authority in Colonial New England* (Philadelphia: University of Pennsylvania Press, 2007), 164–65.
45 Thomas S. Kidd, *The Protestant Interest: New England after Puritanism* (New Haven: Yale University Press, 2004), Ch. 2.
46 Thomas S. Kidd, *The Great Awakening: The Roots of Evangelical Christianity in Colonial America* (New Haven: Yale University Press, 2007).
47 Pestana, "Whitefield and Empire."
48 Bernard Bailyn, *Ideological Origins of the American Revolution* (Cambridge: Harvard University Press, 1967).
49 Brendan McConville, *The King's Three Faces: The Rise & Fall of Royal America, 1688–1776* (Chapel Hill: University of North Carolina Press, 2006), 288–89.
50 Rowan Strong, *Anglicanism and the British Empire, c.1700–1850* (Oxford: Oxford University Press, 2007); Andrew Porter, *Religion versus Empire? British Protestant Missionaries and Overseas Expansion, 1700–1914* (New York: Manchester University Press, 2004).
51 Max Weber, *The Protestant Ethic and the Spirit of Capitalism* (New York: Scribner, 1930).
52 John Fea, "Benjamin Franklin and Religion," *A Companion to Benjamin Franklin*, ed. David Waldstreicher (Chichester, West Sussex: Blackwell Publishing Limited, 2011), 129–45, surveys the contradictory scholarship on his religion.

References

Adorno, Rolena. "The Discursive Encounter of Spain and America: The Authority of Eyewitness Testimony in the Writing of History," *William and Mary Quarterly*, 3rd series, 49 (1992): 210–28.

Adorno, Rolena. *The Polemics of Possession in Spanish American Narrative* (New Haven: Yale University Press, 2007).

Andrews, Edward E. *Native Apostles: Black and Indian Missionaries in the British Atlantic World* (Cambridge: Harvard University Press, 2013).

Armitage, David. *The Ideological Origins of the British Empire* (Cambridge: Cambridge University Press, 2000).

Bailyn, Bernard. *Ideological Origins of the American Revolution* (Cambridge: Harvard University Press, 1967).

Benedict, Phillip. *Christ's Churches More Purely Reformed: A Social History of Calvinism* (New Haven: Yale University Press, 2002).

Bozeman, Theodore. *To Live Ancient Lives: The Primitivist Dimension in Puritanism* (Chapel Hill: University of North Carolina Press, 1988).

Bremer, Francis J. *Congregational Communion: Clerical Friendships in the Anglo-American Puritan Community, 1610–1692* (Boston: Northeastern University Press, 1994).

Butler, Jon. *Awash in a Sea of Faith: Christianizing the American People* (Cambridge: Harvard University Press, 1990).

Claydon, Tony and Ian McBride, eds. *Protestantism and National Identity: Britain and Ireland, c. 1650–c. 1850* (Cambridge: Cambridge University Press, 1998).

Clendinnen, Inga. *Ambivalent Conquests: Maya and Spaniard in Yucatan, 1517–1570*, Cambridge Latin American Studies (New York: Cambridge University Press, 1987).

Croft, Pauline. "'The State of the World is Marvellously Changed': England, Spain and Europe, 1558–1604," *Tudor England and its Neighbours*, eds. Susan Dorn and Glenn Richardson. (New York: Palgrave, 2005),178–202.

Doyle, Laura. *Freedom's Empire: Race and the Rise of the Novel in Atlantic Modernity, 1640–1940* (Durham, N.C.: Duke University Press), 2008.

Duffy, Eamon. *The Stripping of the Altars: Traditional Religion in England, C.1400–C.1580* (New Haven: Yale University Press, 1992).

Elliott, John. *Empires of the Atlantic World: Britain and Spain in America, 1492–1830* (New Haven: Yale University Press, 2006).

Erben, Patrick M. *A Harmony of the Spirits: Translation and the Language of Community in Early Pennsylvania* (Chapel Hill: University of North Carolina Press, 2012).

Fea, John. "Benjamin Franklin and Religion," *A Companion to Benjamin Franklin*, ed. David Waldsreicher (Chichester, West Sussex: Blackwell Publishing Limited, 2011), 129–45.

Fisher, Linford D. *The Indians Great Awakening: Religion and the Shaping of Native Cultures in Early America* (New York: Oxford University Press, 2012).

Fogleman, Aaron. *Jesus Is Female: Moravians and Radical Religion in Early America* (Philadelphia: University of Pennsylvania Press, 2007).

Genovese, Eugene D. *Roll, Jordan, Roll: The World the Slaves Made* (New York: Pantheon Books, 1974).

Glasson, Travis. *Mastering Christianity: Missionary Anglicanism and Slavery in the Atlantic World* (Oxford: Oxford University Press, 2012).

Gorski, Philip S. "Premodern Nationalism: An Oxymoron? The Evidence from England," *The SAGE Handbook of Nations and Nationalism*, ed. Gerard Delanty and Krishan Kumar (London: SAGE Publications Ltd., 2006), 143–56.

Greene, Jack P. "Empire and Identity from the Glorious Revolution to the American Revolution," *Oxford History of the British Empire*, Vol. II: *The Eighteenth Century*, ed. P. J. Marshall (Oxford: Oxford University Press, 1998), 215–30.

Greer, Allan and Kenneth Mills, "A Catholic Atlantic," *The Atlantic in Global History, 1500–2000*, eds. Jorge Cañizares-Esguerra and Erik R. Seeman (Upper Saddle River, NJ: Pearson Prentice Hall, 2007), 3–19.

Guasco, Michael. *Slaves and Englishmen: Human Bondage in the Early Modern Atlantic World.* (Philadelphia: University of Pennsylvania Press, 2014).

Haefeli, Evan and Owen Stanwood. "Jesuits, Huguenots, and the Apocalypse: The Origins of America's First French Book," *Proceedings of the American Antiquarian Society* 116: 1 (2006): 59–120.

Haefeli, Evan. *New Netherland and the Dutch Origins of American Religious Liberty.* (Philadelphia: University of Pennsylvania Press, 2012).

Haefeli, Evan. "Breaking the Christian Atlantic: The Legacy of Dutch Tolerance in Brazil," *The Legacy of Dutch Brazil*, ed. Michael van Groesen (New York: Cambridge University Press, 2014), 140–45.

Hartlib, Samuel. *The Necessity of Some Nearer Conjunction and Correspondence amongst Evangelical Protestants* (London, 1644).

Haydon, Colin. "'I Love My King and My Country, but a Roman Catholic I Hate': Anti-Catholicism, Xenophobia and National Identity in Eighteenth-Century England," *Protestantism and National Identity: Britain and Ireland, c. 1650–c. 1850*, eds. Tony Claydon and Ian McBride (Cambridge: Cambridge University Press, 1998), 33–52.

Herberg, Will. *Protestant, Catholic, Jew: An Essay in American Religious Sociology* (Garden City, NY: Doubleday, 1955).

Kidd, Thomas S. *The Great Awakening: The Roots of Evangelical Christianity in Colonial America* (New Haven: Yale University Press, 2007).

Kidd, Thomas S. *The Protestant Interest: New England after Puritanism* (New Haven: Yale University Press, 2004).

Kirk, Stephanie and Sarah Rivett. "Introduction," *Religious Transformations in the Early Modern Americas* (Philadelphia: University of Pennsylvania Press, 2014), 6–7.

Kupperman, Karen O. *Indians and English: Facing Off in Early America* (Ithaca: Cornell University Press, 2000).
Kupperman, Karen O. *Providence Island, 1630–1641: The Other Puritan Colony* (Cambridge: Cambridge University Press, 1993).
McConville, Brendan. *The King's Three Faces: The Rise & Fall of Royal America, 1688–1776* (Chapel Hill: University of North Carolina Press, 2006).
MacCulloch, Diarmaid. *The Reformation* (New York: Viking, 2004).
Macmillan, Ken, with Jennifer Abeles, eds. *John Dee: The Limits of the British Empire.* (Westport, CN: Praeger, 2004).
Marotti, Arthur F. *Religious Ideology and Cultural Fantasy: Catholic and Anti-Catholic Discourses in Early Modern England* (Notre Dame, IN: University of Notre Dame Press, 2005).
Martinez. Maria Elena. *Genealogical Fictions: Limpieza de Sangre, Religion, and Gender in Colonial Mexico* (Stanford, CA: Stanford University Press, 2008).
Milton, Anthony. *Catholic and Reformed: The Roman and Protestant Churches in English Protestant Thought, 1600–1640* (Cambridge: Cambridge University Press, 1994).
Moore, R. L. *Religious Outsiders and the Making of Americans* (New York: Oxford University Press, 1986).
O'Brien, Susan. "A Transatlantic Community of Saints: The Great Awakening and the First Evangelical Network, 1735–1755," *American Historical Review* 91 (1986): 811–32.
Pagden, Anthony. *Lords of All the World: Ideologies of Empire in Spain, Britain and France, 1492–1830* (New Haven: Yale University Press, 1998).
Pestana, Carla Gardina. "Cruelty and Religious Justifications for Conquest in the Mid-Seventeenth-Century English Atlantic," *Empires of God: Religious Encounters in the Early Modern Atlantic World,* eds. Linda Gregerson and Susan Juster (Philadelphia: University of Pennsylvania Press, 2010), 37–57.
Pestana, Carla Gardina. *English Atlantic in an Age of Revolution, 1640–1661* (Cambridge: Harvard University Press, 2007).
Pestana, Carla Gardina. *The English Conquest of Jamaica: Oliver Cromwell's Bid for Empire* (Cambridge: Belkusp Press, 2016) 82–97.
Pestana, Carla Gardina. "The Missionary Impulse in the Atlantic World, 1500–1800: Or How Protestants Learned to be Missionaries," *Social Sciences and Missions* (Special Issue on Missions and Slavery), 26 (2013): 9–39.
Pestana, Carla Gardina. *Protestant Empire: Religion and the Making of the British Atlantic World.* Philadelphia: University of Pennsylvania Press, 2009.
Pestana, Carla Gardina. "Religion," *The British Atlantic World, 1500–1800,* eds. David Armitage and Michael J. Braddick, 2nd edition (New York: Palgrave Macmillan, 2009), 71–91.
Pestana, Carla Gardina. "Whitefield and Empire." In *George Whitefield: Life, Context, and Legacy,* eds. Geordan Hammond and David Ceri Jones (Oxford: Oxford University Press, forthcoming).
Pincus, Steven. "'To Protect English Liberties': The English Nationalist Revolution of 1688–1689," *Protestantism and National Identity: Britain and Ireland, c. 1650–c. 1850,* ed. Tony Claydon and Ian McBride (Cambridge: Cambridge University Press, 1998), 75–104.
Porter, Andrew. *Religion Versus Empire? British Protestant Missionaries and Overseas Expansion, 1700–1914* (New York: Manchester University Press, 2004).
Ryrie, Alec. *Being Protestant in Reformation Britain* (Oxford: Oxford University Press, 2013).
Seed, Patricia. "Taking Possession and Reading Texts: Establishing the Authority of Overseas Empires," *William and Mary Quarterly* 49 (1992): 183–209.
Stanwood, Owen. *The Empire Reformed: English America in the Age of the Glorious Revolution* (Philadelphia: University of Pennsylvania Press, 2011).
Strong, Rowan. *Anglicanism and the British Empire, c. 1700–1850* (Oxford: Oxford University Press, 2007).
Sutto, Antoinette. "Lord Baltimore, the Society of Jesus, and Caroline Absolutism in Maryland, 1630–1645," *Journal of British Studies,* 48 (2009): 631–52.
Toulouse, Teresa A. *The Captives Position: Female Narrative, Male Identity, and Royal Authority in Colonial New England* (Philadelphia: University of Pennsylvania Press, 2007).
Valeri, Mark R. *Heavenly Merchandize: How Religion Shaped Commerce in Puritan America* (Princeton: Princeton University Press, 2010).
Van Ruymbeke, Bertrand. *From New Babylon to Eden: The Huguenots and their Migration to Colonial South Carolina* (Columbia: University of South Carolina Press, 2006).
Ward, W. R. *The Protestant Evangelical Awakening* (Cambridge: Cambridge University Press, 1992).

Ward, W. R. *Early Evangelicalism: A Global Intellectual History, 1670–1789* (Cambridge: Cambridge University Press, 2006).

Weaver, John C. *The Great Land Rush and the Making of the Modern World, 1650–1900*. (McGill: Queen's University Press, 2006).

Weber, Max. *The Protestant Ethic and the Spirit of Capitalism* (New York: Scribner, 1930).

Figure 13.1 1816 Painting by Benjamin West, *Benjamin Franklin Drawing Electricity from the Sky*.

Source: Benjamin West/Philadelphia Museum of Arts/Wikimedia Commons.

13

WAS KNOWLEDGE POWER?

Science in the British Atlantic

Joyce E. Chaplin

The glory of God is to conceal a thing, but the glory of the king is to find it out.
—*Francis Bacon,* The Advancement of Learning, *1605*

The leaves of the Nymphaea nilumbo ... are each upon a green standard, representing the cap of Liberty.
—*William Bartram,* Travels ..., *1791*

It would be extraordinary if anything so complex as science were to elicit universal agreement about its nature and meaning. And thus the rich continuing debate over its role within the European empires that were created in the Americas after 1492, a debate that very much echoes what was argued over at the time. Was science the handmaid of empire, as some claimed it to be, an intrinsic part of discovery and dominion over new lands and naturally coterminous with contemporary forms of social domination? Or was it a subversive tool, useful to discredit and depose distant tyrants, part of the liberating effect of enlightenment, as at least some colonial Americans would insist? The British Atlantic, where the first British empire would take its form *c.* 1607, only to be torn asunder after 1776, is perhaps the best context in which to examine the extent to which modern science was (and is) a form of power—and for whom.

To be sure, the histories of other empires would yield other and valuable information about the problem, but evidence from the English-speaking world is nevertheless distinctively revealing. The key phrase "knowledge is power" is attributed to the early modern English philosopher and jurist Francis Bacon. However spurious, the attribution reveals something characteristically English about science, empire, and state power in the modern era, including an English concern over the optimal nexus among these variables. Bacon's sketch for an institution of learning, Solomon's House, named for the ancient king in scripture, would become a foundation (or at the least a foundation myth) of the Royal Society of London which, chartered 1662, is now the oldest surviving scientific organization in the world. As its regal patronage announced, the society had been configured to be an instrument of the nation-state, meaning monarchical England, as well as a center of calculation for that nation's empire, principally the colonies that lay within North America and the Caribbean. And yet that empire would collapse a century later. Moreover, the science that had been created within it would remain connected to power within the successor state—the United States—that had gained its independence from Great Britain. Above all, it is dismayingly obvious that participation in the activities associated with science, broadly defined as natural knowledge, mirrored colonial social standing, especially the racialized hierarchy at the center of the Atlantic social order, despite multiple efforts to complicate a top-down vision of science.

Some definitions may be helpful here at the outset. This essay considers the topic of science before "science" in its modern incarnation existed. Before 1834, there were no scientists. The word "scientist" would not be put into print until that year, a watershed in recognizing that certain investigations into nature were distinctive and that those who undertook them might even make a living by them. Before then (if not for some time after) the authority to describe the natural world was more explicitly connected to social rank and vocation than to professionally recognized expertise. That connection was particularly apparent at the lower and higher ends of the social scale. Artisans (male and female) who knew how to manipulate physical materials, from working metal to deriving medicaments from plants, were recognized as experts, indeed impressive ones. Some of these individuals might even have been described, by the eighteenth century, as "naturalists," adepts skilled with nature's gifts. But natural philosophy, the theorizing that organized observations of the natural world into patterns and principles, belonged to the learned, typically gentlemen or aristocrats who did not work for a living and could use their wealth to insulate themselves from any pressure to make statements convenient to others; they could afford to speak truth, even to power, even as we today see that they might have embodied power rather than resisted it. Science today has its own compromised connections to politics and society, but they are qualitatively different ones, not those of the early modern world.[1]

To make things even more interesting, this essay considers "science" in the British Atlantic before either "British" or "Atlantic" would have any stable meaning either. There was no Great Britain before 1707, when the Treaty of Union joined Scotland to England and Wales. Before then, the English colonized on their own, including their violent invasions of Ireland and attempts at Scotland, the first Atlantic incursions that presaged and then paralleled forays to the Chesapeake, Caribbean, and greater New England. Nor was "Atlantic" an accepted designation for the ocean the English crossed to claim American territories. Rather, the English tended to call it the "Western Ocean," the water that divided them from the western lands on its opposite side. Only by the end of the period under consideration would "Atlantic" occur frequently in English on maps and charts to designate the water that connected Britain to its empire. That itself was a story of science, representing multiple individuals' contributions in creating intellectual coherence for a certain imperial zone, yet also an end point to its existence just before the American Revolution.[2]

That zone of empire itself has a historiography. Historians of science once explained British America and science in terms of unidirectional, transatlantic diffusion. Diffusionism stressed the centrality of Europe—as birthplace of western science—to scientific activities before the modern period and particularly before the rise of "big science" in the twentieth century, when the United States became a dominant player. Indeed, the use of diffusionism to note the eventual rise of American power endorsed a reading of the United States as exceptional. Together, the narratives of the European diffusion of science and of a terminal American exceptionalism generated a view of the United States as destined to excel in science, another indication of its national splendor and rightfulness in breaking from Great Britain, once owner of a mighty empire but, by the twentieth century, eclipsed by its former colonies. But as historians have questioned the centrality of the nation-state to their analyses, the history of science and the history of America have changed. Atlantic perspectives on new world places have instead traced their connections and similarities, a methodology in which nationalism is less significant and exceptionalism less likely. In that way, historians who have "Atlanticized" science have assessed it either as a component of imperial expansion and Atlantic circulation, or else as part of a postcolonial critique of imperialism.[3]

Even more recently, however, scholars (including the author) have questioned whether new world societies can be adequately explained by imperialism or postcolonialism. Those modes of analysis fail to explain the politics of what were fundamentally settler societies. "Settler colonialism" is a category of analysis for places where the population majority was creole, neither aboriginal nor imperial, but composed of descendants of old world peoples. Colonial in this sense does not imply being ruled from afar, from an empire's center, but instead ruling locally, through formal or informal kinds of home rule; "colonist" retains the ancient Roman meaning of "farmer," tiller of appropriated soil. That appropriation was the foundation of a colonial mindset which, in the United States, handily survived the nation's revolt against empire. Although the United States was a postimperial nation as of 1776, it was not—and still is not—postcolonial. A postcolonial condition requires the withdrawal of an occupying population from land unjustly claimed. But, in the case of the Anglophone Atlantic (as in Australia and New Zealand), the colonizing population, overwhelmingly descended from Europeans, has stayed put. Unlike formerly colonized peoples in Africa and Asia, native Americans and African-Americans have continued to struggle with regimes (and individuals) descended from those established centuries ago, and the struggle over science—who defines it and who is merely defined by it?—remains in place as well.[4]

America the Wonderful

At first, America was a scientific problem, a riot of heretofore unknown phenomena. Astonishing plants, animals, minerals, and peoples either had to be rendered legible, as cognates of what had already been described for other parts of the world, or else explained as so qualitatively different from the known world, particularly Europe, that existing states of knowledge had to be significantly reenvisioned. Some of the earliest scholarship on science in the English colonies, dating from the middle of the twentieth century, documented the painstaking efforts of natural philosophers in England to obtain specimens and descriptions of natural entities from America, a constant flow that planted new information in the old world and constituted half of the Columbian Exchange that relentlessly swapped biota (plants and animals, but also people and diseases) between the two hemispheres.[5]

That scholarly emphasis noted a truth about early Anglo-American science, to be sure, but also supported the old diffusionist version of the history of science, in which raw material flowed east and knowledge, in the form of published and systematized scientific schemas, eventually went west. More recently, there has been a shift toward investigation of how Europeans and colonists shared ways of rendering the Americas as different from the "old world" and yet as entirely legible within old systems of knowledge. Scholars have identified the categories of wonders and marvels, for example, as epistemological containers distinctive to the early modern era and highly relevant to contemporary comprehension of the Americas. To examine the wonderful was to establish the boundless extent of God's creative capacity; it also generated a series of moral warnings about (though sometimes against) normalcy. When it came to information about the "new world," there was plenty of scope for such musing, as with British investigation of the North American opossum. Initial incredulity that female animals could gestate young without sheltering them within internal uteri only slowly gave way—after tortured attempts to get preserved specimens and then living "possums to London—to belief in marsupial animals as natural facts. Even as such, the creatures remained troubling. What did it mean about God's larger design that the ambiguously female animals existed, and how were they to be integrated into ongoing attempts at universal systems of classification?[6]

Whatever the marvels of the new world, difference had been observed elsewhere—the Americas were parts of a global unfolding of information about places unknown or little known to Europeans before 1492. There was a long tradition of exoticizing borderlands, let alone foreign lands. And of course European nations were not expanding uniquely into the Americas. Rather, travelers, settlers, and varied commentators were observing new phenomena in Africa and Asia as well as portions of the Pacific world. A good case in point was the newly global dimension of the European knowledge of plants, pharmacoepia in particular. Confidence in the efficacy (or tastiness) of alien plants built upon the medieval appetite for Asian spices that had led to the "discovery" of the Americas in the first place.[7]

So what was differently different about the Americas? The criteria that would generate the greatest amount of discussion, or controversy, would revolve around questions of weather and climate on the one hand, and blood and soil on the other, though in an era when the human body was considered to be a product of a particular climate, the two concerns overlapped. European observers quickly defined American environments as qualitatively different to Europe's temperate zones. Early encounters with America's tropical regions, in the greater Caribbean, and subsequent ventures to colder climates, as in Canada and Patagonia, reinforced a sense that the Americas had little climatic moderation. Suspicion that American climates were too wet or too dry, too hot or too cold—never quite right, always failing a Eurocentric Goldilocks test—was augmented by the lack of large animals in the Caribbean and South America, the first places settled by Europeans. Where were the American equivalents of the horse, ox, camel, or elephant?[8]

The climatic prejudice was immediately transferred to the new world's human inhabitants. America's lightly bearded native men seemed unmanly, sexually indifferent and unlikely to produce many children; hence, outside of Mexico and the Andes (the prejudice went), the Indians' thin population and brutally treated women. Subsequent epidemics likewise suggested that Indians were innately weak, with their deaths outnumbering births in the very places and circumstances where Europeans might be simultaneously flourishing. From these suspicions, Europeans worried that the new world might transform their own bodies. Because of America's dismaying climates, and the association of them with non-European peoples—at first, Indians, then the Africans forcibly transferred to the colonies—creole white settlers were regarded as different from, and perhaps inferior to, their European ancestors. Systems of ranking peoples proliferated, with Europeans at the top, Indians and Africans far below, and creoles in between, all of these schemas explicitly considered humans as natural, embodied entities.[9]

Even if they granted settlers' superiority to those of non-European stock, the English were quick to assume that colonials might be physically and even mentally inferior to them. After all, the animals native to the Americas were small and timid—why not then the new world's humans, whether indigenous or transplanted? Although the figure who would become most associated with the theory of American degeneracy, Georges Le Clerc, comte de Buffon, would caution against extending the hypothesis to humans (whose rationality enabled them to correct for environmental factors), many others assumed otherwise. To defend themselves, English settlers would pioneer distinctively racialized conclusions about the resistance of certain bodies to American places, whatever the initial conviction that climates guaranteed certain bodily characteristics. Their emphasis on bodily continuity, maintained through certain lineages, was not identical to fully modern theories of race, and yet it would state a racialized belief in the superiority of some bodies over others.[10]

America the Land of Opportunity

To the extent that the English were defining the Americas as places where they could flourish, they also conceived of them as places where they could prosper. Their descriptions of natural resources were therefore almost never neutral assessments but likely to be linked to promotional schemes. The earliest examples now seem ludicrous in their optimism, focusing, as they did, on the possibility that North America harbored the same resources that the Spaniards had found in Central and South America: dense native populations from whom labor could be extracted, mineral wealth, and tropical climates that exploded with vegetation. Belief that climate consisted of stable bands ringing the globe further confused expectations, with English promoters eager to observe that New England lay parallel to France, and therefore should produce its wine. Experts in science advised from afar but a surprising number also went to America. Three early ventures, one to the Canadian Arctic and two to the Chesapeake, included specialists in metals and mining; in expectation that they would need to be on hand when precious minerals were located. It took decades of disappointment to elicit begrudging admission that the zones the English had claimed contained no mines of gold or silver, and seemed with their severe winters not to be exactly like the Mediterranean with which they lay roughly parallel. The closest approximation to Iberian conquistador wealth was achieved in the Caribbean, where sugar plantations yielded the only riches to satisfy the boom fantasies of the earliest colonizing generations.[11]

Elsewhere, agriculture, trade, and resource extraction (particularly of furs) generated slower rates of return but, even in these cases, scientific expertise was often strategic in identifying economic opportunities. Counterintuitive to the earliest fascination with hot climates, much subsequent British investigation focused on the chilly regions of what would later be called Canada, most of it claimed by France, but with English settlements in the Canadian maritimes along the coast. It is astonishing, and still an understudied fact, that the fellows of the Royal Society and the personnel of the early Hudson's Bay Company overlapped extensively, providing a tighter convergence of imperial and scientific efforts than in any other colonial region. The result was a remarkable series of reports and maps about Canada. Preminent among these plans were attempts to find the long-sought Northwest Passage that would conduct English merchants straight to the riches of the Orient. With somewhat more practicality, the later president of the Royal Society, explorer and man of science Sir Joseph Banks, would help to promote wild rice from the Great Lakes. That project presented the Native American staple as a miracle food to rival the so-called Irish potato (actually from the Andes), at a time of British anxiety over the food supply during the Napoleonic Wars.[12]

But as it turned out, the greatest source of colonial wealth lay in the British Atlantic's population, the people who would labor to produce commodities, send them to predominantly British markets, and then consume British goods. The more people to do this, the better—human fecundity was power—which led to questions about how the Americas had been populated in the first place, as well as who bred best there and why. The European discovery of the Americas had challenged the scriptural explanation of how the Earth had been peopled. Had Adam and Eve really sent progeny clear across the Atlantic or the Pacific? The idea of a separate creation of human beings, polygenism, was technically heretical. Native Americans had to come from the same stock as the English and indeed Europeans, which at the least should indicate that the newcomers stood a chance of adapting to these places as well.[13]

The English counted on that possibility—quite literally—in early forms of population science or demography, which would have distinctively British Atlantic foundations. Beginning with some thorough headcounts in the English settlement at Jamestown in Virginia, the first in 1623, population censuses were taken earlier and more often in Anglo-America than in England itself. After several earlier parliamentary attempts to count the English population, England would at last organize its first national census in 1801, whereas in British America, before 1776 there would be 124 colonial censuses, including 21 of the 26 colonies that existed before the American Revolution. Add to that the local histories, governors' letters, militia musters, town bills of mortality, and hundreds of other sources that assessed colonial populations, sometimes with actual enumeration of all persons, and occasionally including Indian populations. The concern to count heads was the result, at least in part, of early fears about the first tiny English settlements, with their notorious "starving times," and then subsequently to determine the military, political, and economic might of the colonies cumulatively or else compared with each other.[14]

Anxiety that the English might not multiply in the Americas quickly gave way to confidence. As early as the first part of the seventeenth century, English colonists claimed "a facultie that God hath given the Brittish Ilanders to beget and bring forth more children than any other nation in the world." That chauvinism was foundational to a racialized theory of population dynamics. Ever since Alfred W. Crosby's analysis of "virgin soil epidemics" in the post-Columbian Americas, scholars have known that such epidemics, disastrous causes of Indian population decline, resulted from lack of native immunity to the contagions that Europeans introduced after 1492—plus settler abuse of Indians. But colonists themselves had a different idea. Starting in the seventeenth century, they hypothesized that the epidemics did not result from their arrival (and introduction of diseases like smallpox) but instead represented outbreaks of endemic maladies. Colonists' superior survival amid these new world hazards thus showed their better and heritable bodily hardiness, a racialized trait that proved their providential ability to live in American environments, compared with Indians. Even in the Caribbean, where Europeans died at appalling rates, colonists pointed out that they out-survived the indigenous populations, some of whom approached extinction. Analysis of these colonial patterns would fundamentally inform the first modern population analyses, true handmaidens of empire.[15]

The relevant pioneer, Englishman William Petty, analyzed populations within an imperial context that included North America. A founding member of the Royal Society of London, Petty coined the term "political arithmetic" to describe population analysis, at this point expressed in terms of empires, including sustained analysis of English, Irish, colonial American, and native American populations. Using a hypothetical unit of 1,000 Pennsylvania Indians who dwindled as settlers increased, he contrasted that differential to Ireland (where he held land). Although the native Irish had been reduced in number during the English reconquest of the 1640s, they were recovering, whereas American Indian populations had shrunk due to natural causes (Petty thought), principally disease and low birthrates, with no signs of recovery. The native Irish remained a source of labor, particularly for agriculture, while native Americans did not. He also thought that Anglo-Irish intermarriage, part of an older pattern of assimilation, might create a strong composite population within England's growing Atlantic empire; in contrast, he offered no scenario of intermarriage for the English and American Indians.[16]

In his *Political Arithmetic* (1690), Petty continued to assess colonial populations and their value to empire. He estimated that Britons doubled in number only every 200 years. Thus the decline of Ireland's population was offset by colonial gains across the Atlantic. "The accession of Negroes to the *American* plantations (being all Men of great Labour and little Expence) is not inconsiderable," he observed, a statement as to slaves' value to empire that many people would eventually contest. There, "few or no Women are Barren, and most have many Children, and people live long and healthfully," which had "produced an increase of as many People, as were destroyed in the late Tumults in Ireland." Small but growing, the American colonies contributed, by Petty's estimate, half a million people to the king's total stock of 10 million subjects.[17]

Experts and Expertise

Amid the much counted peoples of British America, some stood out for their intellectual contributions to science. Their activities have been central to recent scholarly analysis because their ability to affect natural science indicated their power within the British Atlantic, whatever their distance from metropolitan centers of learned activity. Comprehension of their efforts in precisely this way has followed Bruno Latour's definition of a "center of calculation," a site where the more prestigious epistemological work of science took place; this is yet another version of diffusionism, one that recognizes a power differential in the production of knowledge and is applicable to some imperial situations. Which colonials were able to establish connections to English centers of calculation? Which could not?[18]

Although the first recognized experts had also been exports, recruited in England and carefully stocked in the earliest expeditions and fledgling settlements, once the colonies had a permanent and extensive character, men of science began to rally actual settlers, and eventually creole-born British-Americans, to supply specimens and descriptions. Many of these individuals seized the chance to demonstrate that they were minds over matter, different from the American animals whose horns and hides they sent to the cognoscenti, and different yet again from America's "natural" inhabitants, whose customs they detailed and artifacts they collected, but whose bodies they classified as fundamentally different from their own. In the English colonies, schools, colleges, printers, and booksellers all made it credible that the settlements had foundations for knowledge, if spread more thinly than their European counterparts. By 1788, 47 men who had been born or made careers in British America each were able to sign themselves as an "FRS," a Fellow of the Royal Society of London.[19]

Even before the founding of the Royal Society, the most active network of communication ran through individuals associated with Samuel Hartlib, a puritan man of learning, based in England, who solicited information about the natural world. Colonial informants in Ireland and New England corresponded with Hartlib and his associates, for example. It is possible that the "Hartlib Circle" was the basis for the "Invisible College" to which the natural philosopher and chemical experimenter Robert Boyle referred in some of his letters. If so, he meant it as a scientific institution to rival if not outdo the visible colleges of Oxford and Cambridge, representing a way to fulfil Francis Bacon's idea of Solomon's House. At the very least, Hartlib and his correspondents evidenced the quickening of discussion about natural phenomena and the gathering of colonial correspondents into those discussions.[20]

Some of these recruits would be content to act as occasional correspondents, but others wanted reputations to rival those of their metropolitan contacts. The creation of the Royal Society initiated an institutionalized solicitation and publication of information from informants abroad, including the colonies. But they would be in competition with a continuing stream of visitors. In his 1665 "General Heads for a Natural History of a Country, Great or Small," Robert Boyle urged travelers to observe whatever they saw abroad, assuming that they might have the skills to assess natural landscapes that locals would not. (Indeed, Boyle distinguished between the "*Natives*" of a place versus the "*Strangers*, that have been long settled there.") The possibility of being informants to the society set up for colonists three aspirational goals, in ascending order of prestige: publishing in the society's *Philosophical Transactions*, becoming a Fellow of the Royal Society, and winning its Copley Medal for a particularly distinguished contribution to natural knowledge. A great many colonists, and even merchants or ships' captains who did business in the colonies, provided small reports on phenomena that would be little known to the English cognoscenti, from sexually ambiguous possums to Caribbean hurricanes. If read before a meeting of the fellows, and appreciated by them as distinctive contributions to knowledge, such testimonials might then be printed in the *Philosophical Transactions*. Specimens were also welcome.[21]

In this way, New Englander Jonathan Winthrop—first-generation American, son of English founders of the Massachusetts Bay Colony—cultivated the Royal Society carefully, if not relentlessly. He sent multiple natural specimens as well as Native American artifacts (several now displayed in the British Museum). He also gave detailed reports of new world phenomena, as with maize, Indian corn. But to make sure that he was not categorized as a mere informant, unable to generate anything better than empirical observations, he also cultivated an expertise in alchemy. Ancestor of chemistry, alchemy was a highly learned set of semisecret practices, available only to the literate and those with time and means to pursue its exacting experimental procedures. Bermuda-born, Harvard-educated George Starkey, who published alchemical works under the name Eirenaeus Philalethes, was a pioneering American alchemist; dying in 1665, three years after the founding of the Royal Society, Starkey did not become part of England's institutionalized world of science. But his works influenced contemporary alchemists Robert Boyle and Isaac Newton, whose efforts in this area were, at the time, of tremendous intellectual importance. Alchemy also continued to be important to the pursuit of American mineral wealth. For those two reasons, the pursuit of alchemy was an excellent way for Winthrop to establish himself as an independent arbiter on American nature, not as a meek packer of samples for other men. Some of his essays were published in the *Philosophical Transactions* and he became a Fellow of the Royal Society, indeed the first American to achieve this.[22]

But the Royal Society was by no means the only center of calculation for the British Atlantic. Similar institutions existed throughout Europe, as did experimental gardens, menageries, and various other collections; France's Académie royale des sciences always had foreign members, for example, including British members. And collaboration ran across national boundaries. Whatever antagonisms divided Britain and France, particularly in the Second Hundred Years' War that encompassed the Seven Years' War, American War for Independence, and Napoleonic Wars, British and French subjects interested in science found ways to communicate their findings to each other. Prominent figures, of varied nationalities, became foci for correspondence. In the eighteenth century, the Swedish botanist and classifier Carl von Linné, Linnaeus, solicited information and specimens, sent out "apostles," and thereby established a global network of informants that included the British Colonies.[23]

Because of the multiple lines of communication, ever more as time went on, it is impossible to say exactly how much and what information crossed the Atlantic. American animals made their miserable ways across the ocean, sometimes to survive in menageries; Linnaeus had monkeys, parrots, and a raccoon. A wealth of geographic knowledge was put upon manuscript and printed maps, translated into western images and language from original forms as Indians had rendered them in words, upon animal hides, or temporarily on earth or sand. (It is likely that Powhatan's "mantle," the elaborately decorated deerskin now in Oxford's Ashmolean Museum, was not a garment worn by the leader of the Powhatan Indians in Virginia, but instead a pictograph of those people's homeland.) The largest and most easily commodified traffic was in vegetable specimens, particularly dyestuffs and pharmacopeia. The saddest evidence of knowledge of American medicines was represented in the truncated circulation of one particular plant, the "peacock flower" that Caribbean slave women used as an abortifacient in order to prevent further generations being born into alien bondage, far from their original African homeland. European naturalists were reluctant to publicize the fact, including to women in Europe who might, for other reasons, not want to undergo childbirth Knowledge of the peacock flower remained localized on one side of the Atlantic only.[24]

Only very rarely were the people other than free white men named as adept in science. At most, Indians and black people were referred to anonymously; often, their presence can only be inferred from the unlikelihood that a white person would easily come by a certain piece of information. One exception was James Pawpaw, an enslaved man who was set free in Virginia in 1729 for sharing his knowledge of locally derived antidotes to poisonous substances. Free white women fared better, if they were from the wealthier classes, were educated, and belonged to families in which men encouraged such pursuits. Benjamin Franklin's narration of his electrical experiments in Philadelphia, done in the 1730s, indicates that there were female participants, for example. Later, an emergency call for instruments to follow the Transit of Venus across the face of the Sun in 1769 yielded a telescope from one Philadelphia woman, Elizabeth Norris.[25]

The female interest in electricity and astronomy denoted an eighteenth-century shift in scientific effort toward the mechanical philosophy associated, in the English-speaking world, with the work of Isaac Newton. Newtonianism would represent (among other things) an attempt to universalize nature's physical properties; definitions of matter and of its motion would be Newton's central concern. Newton used colonists as data collectors, as for observations of comets visible only on the opposite side of the Atlantic, where New Englanders obligingly sent him their astronomical accounts. But precisely because the nature of a comet, or anything, was supposed to be the same anywhere on Earth, colonists could themselves make claims to help define the universal properties of the physical world.[26]

Indeed, the prominent (if now forgotten) colonial man of science Cadwallader Colden set his sights on outdoing Newton. Born to Scots-Irish parents, educated at the University of Edinburgh and in medicine in London, Colden had lived in Philadelphia but moved to New York in 1718. He had particular skill in botany—Linnaeus praised him as "Summus Perfectus"—but he handed his botanical studies over to his daughter, Jane, and by the early 1740s had moved into Newtonian mechanics. He began to investigate Newton's grand topic of gravitation, not through experiment or observation, but by rational and mathematical analysis of major texts in mechanics. Colden realized his work was speculative. "I have open'd to my self a large Prospect either into Nature or into Fairyland," he confessed to an American friend. He published *An Explication of the First Causes of Action in Matter; and the Cause of Gravitation* in New York in 1745. Although Newton had proposed that aether filled the universe, exerting a force that caused gravitation, Colden said that it was the aether itself, its imponderable particles resisting matter, that created a special force on celestial bodies—it *was* gravity. On the strength of this claim, the book was translated and published all over Europe. Experts tore into it. Swiss mathematician Leonhard Euler wrote a critique, read at the Royal Society, that described it as "an absurdity" to claim "that the Ether between Two of the Coelestial Bodies, has not the same Spring [resistance] as that of the Rest" of matter. The Royal Society declined to read Colden's rebuttal.[27]

The colonist who did establish an international reputation in Newtonian science was Benjamin Franklin. His *Experiments and Observations on Electricity*, first published in 1751 and running through multiple editions, defined electricity as a single material force that exists in two states, positive and negative; this is still how electricity is defined. Franklin had his work published in the Royal Society's *Philosophical Transactions*, became a fellow of the Royal Society, and won its Copley Medal. His work was proof that creoles could become natural philosophers, not mere gatherers of specimens or data. He was, on that level, himself a specimen. The British philosopher David Hume flattered him as such: "America has sent us many good things, Gold, Silver, Sugar, Tobacco, Indigo &c.: But you are the first Philosopher."[28]

Nature and Nation

The scholarly focus on Newtonian science, with concomitant assessment of how colonists could or couldn't participate in it, initially reflected the concerns of the first historians of early American science: they worked at a time—beginning in the 1940s and tapering off in the early 1970—when science enjoyed considerable public prominence and when physics, in particular, was regarded as the paragon of scientific endeavor. These were, after all, the years in which atomic weapons were invented and believed to have won the Second World War in the Pacific, and in which Cold War rivalry encouraged science education at all levels. The reading of early American science as provincial and of physics as the most important of scientific endeavors was apparent in the work of the real pioneer in the field, I. Bernard Cohen. For Cohen, colonists' scientific efforts were commendable in showing an early desire to excel according to the standards laid out within Europe, even as the colonials began to hanker for independence from Britain. Certainly, this was the burden of Cohen's edition of Franklin's *Experiments and Observations on Electricity*, published in 1941, just before US entry into the Second World War. Cohen's intention was to identify an American statesman as a man of science, to forge a link between America's political nationalism and its intellectual prowess.[29]

The designation of physics as the most significant form of modern science clearly marked American science as provincial, as a lesser version of what was done in its original and best form at the center of empire, or as a series of dutiful contributions to projects defined at the center, as with colonial observations of astronomical events not visible in Europe, forwarded to European authorities who would incorporate them in their own calculations about those events. This is a purely contributionist model that marks Britain and not its colonies as the intellectual head of the empire, the source of knowledge diffused.

But some portions of Benjamin Franklin's science could be regarded as substantively American because they examined phenomena distinctive to the new world and were crucial to settler politics at the time. Unlike earlier creole contributions (including Franklin's electrical experiments) these efforts did not necessarily conform to European epistemology. Settler politics were apparent in several maps on which Franklin collaborated, for instance, which showcased colonial authority over nature at least as much as they advised imperial authorities. His political arithmetic was even more overtly pro-settler. In his "Observations Concerning the Increase of Mankind" (written *c.* 1751), Franklin contrasted colonial and European populations in a way intended to challenge the political arithmeticians who had considered only Europeans. He regarded white creoles as natural specimens, far more vigorous than their European counterparts, given their ability to multiply faster. He conjectured that by natural increase alone, free white North Americans doubled their numbers every 20 years.[30]

The essay, first published in 1755, used science to score points about colonial society. Particularly in its first version, the "Increase of Mankind" was explicitly racialized. At no point did Franklin assume any physical difference between Europeans and white colonists; it was the abundance of North American land that elicited greater American fertility by permitting white settlers to marry at younger ages than people in the "old settled" nations of Europe and therefore produce more children. American land was available because, Franklin assumed, Indians used little of it and were doomed to diminish anyway. Nor did he think that the Caribbean's black slaves, the majority of the population, lived under conditions likely to sustain increase. He could have lamented those trends. Instead, he applauded them. In North America, Franklin predicted, "we have so fair an Opportunity, by excluding all Blacks and Tawneys, of increasing the lovely White and Red" complexions of Euro-Americans.[31]

Moreover, Franklin used his racialized analysis to make an anti-imperial point. Colonists, like plants growing on open "ground," would increase immeasurably in the absence of population pressure from Indians and African-Americans, and would eventually outnumber their British overlords. Showcased within the settler conflict with Great Britain, his hypothesis about geometric human increase swirled into general circulation. Via the subsequent work of Thomas Robert Malthus, it would crucially influence the nineteenth century's most important scientific hypothesis, that of natural selection, inciting new debate over humans as racially-defined natural beings.[32]

So too were Franklin's contributions to hydography (ancestor of physical oceanography) done from a colonial perspective, positing the Atlantic as an imperial system about which colonists had distinctive knowledge. As a colonial postmaster, Franklin was puzzled that it took longer for mail to cross the Atlantic going west than east. In 1768, he ventured that the differential resulted from ships' sailing in the middle of the "*Gulph Stream*" which ran from west to east. This simple observation about nature allowed Franklin to make two complicated points about empire: the Gulf Stream was useful to the empire (particularly the postal system), but American mariners knew more about it than their British counterparts. Franklin's source was a maternal cousin, "Captain Folger a very intelligent Mariner of the Island of Nantuckett." Folger knew the Nantucket whalers who knew "that the Whales are found generally near the Edges of the *Gulph Stream*, a strong Current so called which comes out of the Gulph of Florida, passing Northeasterly along the Coast of America, and the[n] turning off most Easterly running at the rate of 4, 3 1/2, 3 and 2 1/2 Miles an Hour." Thus Franklin gave his cousin the authority to define natural facts. The two colonists coauthored the first known chart of the Gulf Stream, produced in 1769 by the British Post Office, complete with Folger's instructions about avoiding the current (if westbound) or using it to slingshot across the Atlantic if bound for England.[33]

No map merely represents what lies in nature. The first chart of the Gulf Stream made a statement about British overseas power, especially the British empire's enlarged territory in North America. But it also indicated a divided sovereignty, simultaneously British and American. It exemplified colonial command over the natural world, command defined both in terms of knowing nature and of using it in ways independent of whatever diffused from the center of empire. But that claim was liberationist only insofar as it upheld white settlers' rights, not necessarily those of anyone else in the colonies.

Atlantic Epistemologies

After 1776, the United States would develop independent scientific interests and institutions that resembled Britain's, whatever the differences that divided the two nations. Science would develop in the new United States in three ways, each making it culturally more similar to Britain (and to Europe). Science became an everyday part of the cultural landscape, it underwent intensive development for specialists, and it was used to express an extensive US dominion over territorial space. In each instance, American science continued to engage, whether positively or disapprovingly, with the colonial politics of racial hierarchy, an expenditure of energy that grew hotter without entirely dissipating. Despite its formal independence, the United States' cultural politics, including its scientific effort, remained profoundly colonial because preoccupied with asserting settler interests.

From the 1790s through the 1820s, science became part of US public culture. Expansion of science curricula in schools and colleges (for male and female students), popular publications in science (including books for children), museums (such as Peale's exhibition space in Philadelphia), libraries, and public lectures and demonstrations (as at Philadelphia's Franklin Institute, opened 1825), all indicated that in the United States, as elsewhere, science was a standard component of the educated person's repertoire of knowledge. The US government indirectly sponsored natural knowledge through its postal system—which was excellent, better, at the time, than any European postal service. (The US Post Office was also indirect evidence of widespread literacy among the nation's free citizens.) Within this context, Yale professor Benjamin Silliman launched the first American scientific journal, the *American Journal of Science and Arts* (1818), intended to interest an educated public.[34]

By the early 1800s, scientific developments were more specialized, and necessarily dependent on what had already occurred within European science, medicine, and technology. The United States Military Academy at West Point, New York (founded 1802), became the foremost site of reception for developments in European engineering and mathematics. Like their British counterparts (including Charles Darwin's father) American physicians sought professional prestige by studying clinical medicine in Paris. Engineers undertook a variety of projects, including surveying and the building of bridges, which depended on state-of-the-art knowledge of cartography and materials science, often as defined abroad rather than within the republic itself.[35]

It would take more time for US citizens to found a scientific organization to rival the Royal Society of London. The American Academy of Arts and Sciences in Massachusetts (1780), had joined Philadelphia's American Philosophical Society as the second learned society in the early republic. But the Association of American Geographers (1840), was the first specialized society, later to be reconfigured as the American Association for the Advancement of Science (1847), the first organization divorced from other branches of learning. Likewise, the *Astronomical Journal* (1849) was the first to be dedicated to specialists, rather than the generally educated readers Silliman had sought for his *American Journal of Science and Arts*. These were counterparts—explicitly conceived as such—to existing European institutions.[36]

It is equally significant that science was used to extend American authority over greater space, to take the measure of the nation and to send its scientific inquiry abroad, in emulation of European scientific expeditions. The first such example was almost comically small, consisting of one man traveling on foot, occasionally by horse or canoe. That solitary traveler was Philadelphia-born William Bartram, a veteran of his father's botanical forays into the southern colonies. (John Bartram had become King's Botanist to North America.) From 1773 to 1777, the younger Bartram traipsed from the Carolinas through Florida and then into western Indian country, collecting specimens and taking notes. The Indian nations of the region welcomed him—and his research. Bartram said that a Creek leader gave "unlimited permission to travel over the country ... & saluting me by the name of PUC PUGGY, or the Flower hunter, recommending me to the friendship and protection of his people."[37]

Bartram's *Travels* (1791) became a bestseller, running through multiple editions into the nineteenth century, prized equally as literature and as science. It was a dissident work, with travel deliberately timed to ignore the colonists' War for Independence, the better to emphasize the peaceful independence of Indian nations within their natural settings—the narrative was profoundly anticolonial. The romantic poets, including Wordsworth and Coleridge, adored Bartram's *Travels*. It is likely that the book prepared the way for Alexander von Humboldt's accounts of his American travels, as well as for John James Audubon's *Birds of America* (1827–38). Charles Darwin would cite it as an authority on American nature.[38]

But Bartram's dissident use of science was not to be the national norm. President Thomas Jefferson (1801–09) wanted his nation to rival Britain or France in sponsoring grander scientific expeditions. The Louisiana Purchase (1803), which added 828,000 square acres to the United States, was a prime opportunity for Americans to add to natural knowledge. Jefferson selected Meriwether Lewis and William Clark to lead the Corps of Discovery Expedition (1804–06), which combined commercial goals with scientific aspirations, and demonstrated that the United States could extend its authority across an entire continent. It was not the case that the United States organized the first documented crossing of the continent—under British sponsorship, Scotsman Alexander Mackenzie, with a small party, had already done that in 1792–93. And the opportunity to publicize Lewis and Clark's discoveries was squandered. Some maps and short accounts were printed. But the specimens were scattered and the expedition's full journals unpublished until the twentieth century, in contrast to publication of James Cook's expeditions into the Pacific and around the world, Jefferson's primary—and British—model for the Corps of Discovery.[39]

If these milestones in the development of science represented some convergence between the United States and Europe, a cultural narrowing of the transatlantic space, the character of

American society was nevertheless qualitatively different. Because of its combative relations with Indian nations, and due to the continuation of slavery in the South, the United States resembled the British empire, not Great Britain itself. Within Europe, the question of classifying non-European peoples as citizens would be deferred to the twentieth century, after decolonization. But that issue was always present in the nineteenth-century United States, as in other parts of the Americas. The spread of literacy, the circulation of written materials, and the creation of scientific institutions were all, explicitly or de facto, restricted to the population defined as citizens, overwhelmingly white. Benjamin Banneker, the free African-American almanac maker, was for this reason the object of controversy, with potential patrons, including Thomas Jefferson, questioning whether a black person could actually do the astronomical observations necessary to compose an ephemeris, the calendrical foundation of any almanac.[40]

Within an expanding national territory, debates over US citizenship openly used discourse on race. The decennial US Census, defined in 1789, did this (notoriously) in the clauses that enumerated slaves as three-fifths of their actual numbers for the purposes of taxation and the distribution of representatives in Congress, and in the refusal to count (let alone enfranchise) any Indians who did not pay taxes. Starting with the second census, of 1800, Franklin's hypothesis that the free population would double every 20 years was vindicated. So was his prophecy that the indigenous population would dwindle. After Georges Cuvier hypothesized the concept of species extinction, the British geologist Charles Lyell extended that possibility to certain "races," predicting that American Indians and Australian aborigines were doomed. Many white Americans found that prospect attractive, even though Indian suffering had manifestly unnatural causes. Wars against the Indian nations of the Ohio Valley in the 1790s and the removal of southern Indian nations to Oklahoma Territory on the "Trail of Tears" in the 1830s guaranteed their decline. So did US indifference to their health. Spain had begun to inoculate Indians against smallpox in the eighteenth century, the British implemented vaccinations in Canada in the 1820s, but the United States had no such policy until the 1830s. Meanwhile, not only had the institution of slavery continued, but slaves multiplied even after the trade in African captives ended in 1808.[41]

The problem of slavery was a problem for science—on both sides of the Atlantic. Scientifically educated individuals used physiological criteria to differentiate "races," as Edward Long did in his erudite yet poisonously racist *History of Jamaica* (1774). On both sides of the argument over the Atlantic slave trade in the United States and Great Britain, abolitionists and proslavery advocates deployed statistics and in particular political arithmetic to argue for the ability of an enslaved labor force to reproduce in the absence of new infusions from Africa. It must frankly be said that the matter was not solved by science—religious opponents of the slave trade were, in the end, far more convincing in making a moral argument against enslavement. At this point, in the United States, settler interests were in fact divided, and people in slave versus nonslave states thought accordingly, even about natural science.[42]

Although the politics of racial exploitation would be proximate within the United States, distant (for the moment) in Great Britain, they had resulted from the same nexus of interests that had bound the British Atlantic together and created a settler colonialism that dominated new world places, Canadian, US, or Caribbean. Once transplanted to colonized zones, that ideology was difficult to uproot, even once European nations began to relinquish their Atlantic colonies, beginning in 1776 and continuing through the Haitian Revolution and the Wars of Independence in Latin America. Although this essay focuses on the English-speaking portions of the Americas, its analysis is appropriate for other American zones in the Atlantic world, as well for as Pacific spaces dominated by settler colonialism, most obviously New Zealand and Australia. Colonial epistemologies of science are not unique to the British Atlantic, but they were developed first and most intensively there.

Notes

1. Steven Shapin, *A Social History of Truth: Civility and Science in Seventeenth-Century England* (Chicago: University of Chicago Press, 1994); Laurel Thatcher Ulrich, *A Midwife's Tale: The Life of Martha Ballard, Based on Her Diary, 1785–1812* (New York: Knopf, 1990).
2. Joyce E. Chaplin, "Knowing the Ocean: Benjamin Franklin and the Circulation of Atlantic Knowledge," *Science and Empire in the Atlantic World*, eds. Delbourgo and Dew, 2008).
3. George Basalla, "The Spread of Western Science," *Science* n. s., 156, 3775 (1987), 611–22; Michael Adas, *Machines As the Measure of Men: Science, Technology, and Ideologies of Western Dominance* (Ithaca, NY: Cornell University Press, 1989); James Delbourgo and Nicholas Dew, *Science and Empire in the Atlantic World* (New York: Routledge, 2008); Suman Seth, "Putting Knowledge in Its Place: Science, Colonialism, and the Postcolonial," *Postcolonial Studies*, 12[4] (2009), 373–88; Ian Tyrrell, "American Exceptionalism in an Age of International History," *American Historical Review*, 96[4] (1991): 1031–55.
4. Joyce E. Chaplin, Expansion and Exceptionalism in Early American History," *Journal of American History* 89, 4 (2003): 1431–1455; Eliga H. Gould, "Entangled Atlantic Histories: A Response from the Anglo-American Periphery," *American Historical Review*, 112, 3 (2007): 1416; James Belich, *Replenishing the Earth: The Settler Revolution and the Rise of the Anglo-American World, 1783–1939* (New York, Oxford University Press, 2009).
5. Raymond Phineas Stearns, *Science in the British Colonies of America* (Urbana: University of Illinois Press, 1970), 44–83; Alfred W. Crosby, *The Columbian Exchange: Biological and Cultural Consequences of 1492* (Westport, CT: Greenwood Press, 1972).
6. Stephen Greenblatt, *Marvelous Possessions: The Wonder of the New World* (Chicago: University of Chicago Press, 1991); Anthony Grafton, with April Shelford and Nancy Siraisi, *New Worlds, Ancient Texts: The Power of Tradition and the Shock of Discovery* (Cambridge, MA: Harvard University Press, 1993); Deborah Harkness, *The Jewel House: Elizabethan London and the Scientific Revolution* (New Haven, CT: Yale University Press, 2007); Susan Scott Parrish, "The Female Opossum and the Nature of the New World," *William and Mary Quarterly*, 3rd series 54[3] (1997), 475–514.
7. Harold J. Cook, *Matters of Exchange: Commerce, Medicine, and Science in the Dutch Golden Age* (New Haven, CT: Yale University Press, 2007).
8. Suman Seth, "Putting Knowledge in Its Place: Science, Colonialism, and the Postcolonial," *Postcolonial Studies*, 12, 4 (2009): 373–88; Antonello Gerbi, *The Dispute of the New World: The History of a Polemic, 1750–1900*, trans. Jeremy Moyle (Pittsburgh, PA: University of Pittsburgh Press, 1973); Antonello Gerbi, *Nature in the New World: From Christopher Columbus to Gonzalo Fernandez de Oviedo*, trans. Moyle (Pittsburgh, PA: University of Pittsburgh Press, 1985).
9. Joyce E. Chaplin, *Subject Matter: Technology, the Body, and Science on the Anglo-American Frontier, 1500–1676* (Cambridge, MA: Harvard University Press, 2001); Nicolás Wey-Gómez, *The Tropics of Empire: Why Columbus Sailed South to the Indies.* (Cambridge, MA: MIT, 2008).
10. Gerbi, 1973; Gerbi, 1985; Chaplin, 2001.
11. Karen Kupperman, "Fear of Hot Climates in the Anglo-American Colonial Experience," *William and Mary Quarterly*, 3rd series, 41[2] (1984): 213–40; Chaplin, 2001.
12. Stearns, 1970, 247–57; Glyndwr Williams, *Arctic Labyrinth: The Quest for the Northwest Passage* (Berkeley, University of California Press, 2009); Anya Zilberstein, "Inured to Empire: Wild Rice and Climate Change," *William and Mary Quarterly*, 72[1] (2015): 127–58.
13. Grafton, *New Worlds, Ancient Texts*, 2007, 11–58, 95–158.
14. Robert V. Wells, *The Population of the British Colonies in America before 1776: A Survey of Census Data* (Princeton: Princeton University Press, 1975), 5, 8–11, 13–23.
15. [Philip Vincent], *A True Relation of the Late Battell*. London, 1637, [1], 21; Chaplin, 1997; David S. Jones, *Rationalizing Epidemics: Meanings and Uses of American Indian Mortality since 1600* (Cambridge, MA, Harvard University Press 2004), 21–67.
16. Joyce E. Chaplin, *Subject Matter: Technology, the Body, and Science on the Anglo-American Frontier, 1500–1676* (Cambridge, MA, Harvard University Press, 2001), 318–20; Ted McCormick, *William Petty and the Ambitions of Political Arithmetic* (New York: Oxford University Press, 2010).
17. William Petty, *Political Arithmetick*. London, 1751, 66, 80–81, 83.
18. Bruno Latour, *Science in Action: How to Follow Scientists and Engineers through Society.* (Cambridge, MA: Harvard University Press, 1988).
19. Londa L. Schiebinger, *Plants and Empire: Colonial Bioprospecting in the Atlantic World* (Cambridge, MA: Harvard University Press, 2004); James Delbourgo et al., *The Brokered World: Go-Betweens and Global*

Intelligence, 1770–1820 (Sagamore Beach, MA: Science History Publications, 2009); Raymond Phineas Stearns, "Colonial Fellows of the Royal Society of London, 1661–1788," *WMQ*, 3[2] (1946): 208–68.
20 Charles Webster, ed., *Samuel Hartlib and the Advancement of Learning* (Cambridge, Cambridge University Press, 1971).
21 Robert Boyle, "General Heads for a Natural History of a Country, Great or Small," *Philosophical Transactions* 1 (January 1665), 188.
22 Stearns, 1970, 118–39; Lawrence M. Principe, *The Secrets of Alchemy* (Chicago: University of Chicago Press, 2013); William R. Newman, *Gehennical Fire: The Lives of George Starkey, an American Alchemist in the Scientific Revolution* (Cambridge: Harvard University Press, 1994); Walter W. Woodward, *Prospero's America: John Winthrop, Jr., Alchemy, and the Creation of New England Culture, 1606–1676* (Chapel Hill, University of North Carolina Press, 2010).
23 Pascale Brioist, "The Royal Society and the Académie des Sciences in the First Half of the Eighteenth Century," *Anglo-French Attitudes*, eds. Charle et al, 2007; Lisbet Koerner, *Linnaeus: Nature and Nation* (Cambridge, MA: Harvard University Press, 1999).
24 Koerner, 1999; Delbourgo, et al., 2009, pp. 271–320; Schiebinger, 2004.
25 Susan Scott Parrish, *American Curiosity: Cultures of Natural History in the Colonial British Atlantic World* (Chapel Hill, NC: University of North Carolina Press, 2006), 287; James Delbourgo, *A. Most Amazing Scene of Wonders: Electricity and Enlightenment in Early America* (Cambridge, MA: Harvard University Press, 2006), 109–19; Joyce E. Chaplin, *The First Scientific American: Benjamin Franklin and the Pursuit of Genius* (New York: Basic Books, 2006), 220.
26 Stearns, 1970, p. 153; Schaffer, 1987.
27 Leonard Labaree, et al., 1959–, Vol. 2, 416; Stearns, 1970, 494–97, 559–75; John Dixon, *The Enlightenment of Cadwallader Colden: Useful Knowledge and Unreasonable Politics in British New York* (Ithaca, NY: Cornell University Press, 2015).
28 Bernard I. Cohen, *Franklin and Newton: An Inquiry into Speculative Newtonian Experimental Science and Franklin's Work in Electricity as an Example Thereof* (Philadelphia: American Philosophical Society, 1956); Chaplin, 2006); Labaree, et al., 1959–, Vol. 10, 81.
29 Bernard I. Cohen, *Benjamin Franklin's Experiments: A New Edition of Franklin's Experiments and Observations on Electricity* (Cambridge, MA: Harvard University Press, 1941), 3–12; Chaplin, 2006, pp. XX.
30 Chaplin, 2006, 117–22, 196–200, 319–24; Joyce E. Chaplin, *Benjamin Franklin's Political Arithmetic: A Materialist View of Humanity*. (Washington, DC: Smithsonian Institution, 2009); Labaree, et al., 1959, Vol. 4, 227–28.
31 Labaree, et al., 228, 232–34; Chaplin, 2009).
32 Chaplin, 2009.
33 Labaree, et al., 1959–), Vol. 15, 246–47; Chaplin, 2008.
34 Stanley M. Guralnick, *Science and the Ante-bellum American College* (Philadelphia: American Philosophical Society, 1975); McFarland and Bennett, 1997; Kohlstedt, 1999; Richard R. John, *Spreading the News: The American Postal System from Franklin to Morse.* (Cambridge, MA: Harvard University Press, 1995); Simon Baatz, "Squinting at Silliman": Scientific Periodicals in the Early American Republic, 1810–1833," *Isis* 82, 2 (1991): 223–44.
35 Alexandra Oleson and Sanborn C. Brown, *The Pursuit of Knowledge in the Early American Republic: American Scientific and Learned Societies from Colonial Times to the Civil War* (Baltimore: Johns Hopkins University Press, 1976); Bruce, 1987; John Hartley Warner, *Against the Spirit of System: The French Impulse in Nineteenth-Century American Medicine* (Princeton: Princeton University Press, 1998); Ann Johnson, "Material Experiments : Environment and Engineering Institutions in the Early American Republic," *National Identity: The Role of Science and Technology*, eds. C. E. Harrison and A. Johnson (Chicago, University of Chicago Press, 2009).
36 Daniels, 1967; Sally Gregory Kohlstedt, *The Formation of the American Scientific Community: The American Association for the Advancement of Science, 1848–1860* (Urbana, University of Illinois Press, 1976); Paul Lucier, "The Professional and the Scientist in Nineteenth-Century America," *Isis* 100, 4 (2009): 699–732.
37 Bartram, 1996, 163.
38 Thomas P. Slaughter, *The Natures of John and William Bartram* (New York: Alfred A. Knopf, 1996).
39 Thomas P. Slaughter, *Exploring Lewis and Clark: Reflections on Men and Wilderness* (New York: Alfred A. Knopf, 2003); Andrew J. Lewis, Nineteenth-Century Scientific Opinion of Lewis and Clark," R. S. Cox (ed.). *The Shortest and Most Convenient Route: Lewis and Clark in Context* (Philadelphia: American Philosophical Society, 2004), 236–50.

40 William L. Andrews, "Benjamin Banneker's Revision of Thomas Jefferson: Conscience versus Science in the Early American Antislavery Debate," *Genius in Bondage: Literature of the Early Black Atlantic*, eds.V. Carretta and P. Gould (Lexington, KY, University of Kentucky Press, 2001), 218–41.

41 Conway Zirkle, "Benjamin Franklin,Thomas Malthus and the United States Census," *Isis* 48, 1 (1957): 58–62; Paul Semonin, *American Monster: How the Nation's First Prehistoric Creature Became a Symbol of National Identity* (New York: New York University Press, 2000); David S. Jones, *Rationalizing Epidemics: Meanings and Uses of American Indian Mortality since 1600*(Cambridge, MA, Harvard University Press, 2004), 112–16.

42 Suman Seth, "Materialism, Slavery, and *The History of Jamaica*," *Isis* 105, 4 (2014): 764–72; Christopher P. Iannini, *Fatal Revolutions: Natural History, West Indian Slavery, and the Routes of American Literature* (Chapel Hill, Omohundro Institute of Early American History and Culture, 2012); Katherine Paugh, "The Politics of Childbearing in the British Caribbean and the Atlantic World during the Age of Abolition, 1776–1838," *Past & Present* 221 (2013): 119–160; Christopher Leslie Brown, *Moral Capital: Foundations of British Abolitionism* (Chapel Hill: Omohundro Institute of Early American History and Culture, 2006).

References

Adas, Michael. *Machines As the Measure of Men: Science, Technology, and Ideologies of Western Dominance*. (Ithaca, NY: Cornell University Press, 1989).

Andrews, William L. "Benjamin Banneker's Revision of Thomas Jefferson: Conscience versus Science in the Early American Antislavery Debate," *Genius in Bondage: Literature of the Early Black Atlantic*, eds. Vincent Carretta and Philip Gould (Lexington: University of Kentucky Press, 2001).

Baatz, Simon. "Squinting at Silliman": Scientific Periodicals in the Early American Republic, 1810–1833," *Isis* 82, 2 (1991): 223–44.

Bartram,William. 1791. *Travels* … (NewYork: Penguin, 1997).

Basalla, George. "The Spread of Western Science," *Science* n. s., 156, 3775 (1986), 611–22.

Belich, James. *Replenishing the Earth: The Settler Revolution and the Rise of the Anglo-American World, 1783–1939* (NewYork, Oxford University Press, 2009).

Boyle, Robert. "General Heads for a Natural History of a Country, Great or Small," *Philosophical Transactions* 1 (January 1665): 188–91.

Brioist, Pascale. "The Royal Society and the Académie des Sciences in the First Half of the Eighteenth Century," *Anglo-French Attitudes*, eds. Charle et al. (Manchester: Manchester University Press, 2007).

Brown, Christopher Leslie. *Moral Capital: Foundations of British Abolitionism* (Chapel Hill: Omohundro Institute of Early American History and Culture, 2006).

Bruce, Robert V.. *The Launching of Modern American Science, 1846–1876* ((NewYork: Alfred W Knopf, 1987).

Brückner, Martin. *The Geographic Revolution in Early America: Maps, Literacy, and National Identity* (Chapel Hill for the Omokundro Institute of Early American History and Culture: University of North Carolina Press, 2006).

Chaplin, Joyce E. *Subject Matter: Technology, the Body, and Science on the Anglo-American Frontier, 1500–1676* (Cambridge, MA: Harvard University Press, 2001).

Chaplin, Joyce E. "Expansion and Exceptionalism in Early American History," *Journal of American History* 89[4] (2003): 1431–1455.

Chaplin, Joyce E. "Natural Philosophy and an Early Racist Idiom in North America: Comparing English and Indian Bodies," *William and Mary Quarterly* 54[1] (1997): 229–52.

Chaplin, Joyce E. *The First Scientific American: Benjamin Franklin and the Pursuit of Genius* (NewYork: Basic Books, 2006).

Chaplin, Joyce E. "Knowing the Ocean: Benjamin Franklin and the Circulation of Atlantic Knowledge," *Science and Empire in the Atlantic World*, eds. Delbourgo and Dew, (NewYork: Routledge, 2008), 71–97.

Chaplin, Joyce E. *Benjamin Franklin's Political Arithmetic: A Materialist View of Humanity*. (Washington, DC: Smithsonian Institution, 2009)

Charle, Christopher, Julien Vincent, and Jay Winter, eds. *Anglo-French Attitudes: Comparisons and Transfers between English and French Intellectuals since the Eighteenth Century* (Manchester: Manchester University Press, 2007).

Clark,William, Jan Golinski, and Simon Schaffer, eds. *The Sciences in Enlightened Europe* (Chicago: University of Chicago Press, 1999).

Cohen, I. Bernard. *Benjamin Franklin's Experiments: A New Edition of Franklin's Experiments and Observations on Electricity* (Cambridge, MA: Harvard University Press, 1941).

Cohen, I. Bernard. *Franklin and Newton: An Inquiry into Speculative Newtonian Experimental Science and Franklin's Work in Electricity as an Example Thereof* (Philadelphia: American Philosophical Society, 1956).

Cook, Harold J. *Matters of Exchange: Commerce, Medicine, and Science in the Dutch Golden Age* (New Haven, CT: Yale University Press, 2007).

Crosby, Alfred W. *The Columbian Exchange: Biological and Cultural Consequences of 1492* (Westport, CT: Greenwood Press, 1972).

Crosby, Alfred W. *Ecological Imperialism: The Biological Expansion of Europe, 900–1900* (New York: Cambridge University Press, 1986).

Daniels, George H., "The Process of Professionalism in American Science: The Emergent Periods, 1820–1860," *Isis* 58[2] (1967): 150–66.

Daston, Lorraine J., and Katherine Park. *Wonders and the Order of Nature, 1150–1750* (Cambridge, MA: MIT Press, 1998).

Delbourgo, James. *A Most Amazing Scene of Wonders: Electricity and Enlightenment in Early America* (Cambridge, MA: Harvard University Press, 2006).

Delbourgo, James, and Nicholas Dew, eds. *Science and Empire in the Atlantic World* (New York: Routledge, 2008).

Delbourgo, James, Kapil Raj, Lissa Roberts, and Simon Schaffer, eds. *The Brokered World: Go-Betweens and Global Intelligence, 1770–1820* (Sagamore Beach, MA: Science History Publications, 2009).

Dixon, John. *The Enlightenment of Cadwallader Colden: Empire Science and Intellectual Culture in British New York* (Ithaca, NY: Cornell University Press, 2016).

Drayton, Richard. *Nature's Government: Science, Imperial Britain and the 'Improvement' of the World* (New Haven: Yale University Press, 2000).

Gascoigne, John. *Science in the Service of Empire: Joseph Banks, the British State, and the Uses of Science in the Age of Revolution* (New York: Cambridge University Press, 1998).

Gerbi, Antonello. *The Dispute of the New World: The History of a Polemic, 1750–1900*, trans. Jeremy Moyle (Pittsburgh, PA: University of Pittsburgh Press, 1973).

Gerbi, Antonello. *Nature in the New World: From Christopher Columbus to Gonzalo Fernandez de Oviedo*, trans. Moyle (Pittsburgh, PA: University of Pittsburgh Press, 1985).

Gould, Eliga H. "Entangled Atlantic Histories: A Response from the Anglo-American Periphery," *American Historical Review*, 112, 3 (2007): 1415–1422.

Grafton, Anthony, with April Shelford and Nancy Siraisi. *New Worlds, Ancient Texts: The Power of Tradition and the Shock of Discovery* (Cambridge, MA: Harvard University Press, 1992).

Greenblatt, Stephen. *Marvelous Possessions: The Wonder of the New World* (Chicago: University of Chicago Press, 1991).

Greene, John C. *American Science in the Age of Jefferson* (Ames, Iowa: Iowa State University Press, 1984).

Gronim, Sara Stidstone. *Everyday Nature: Knowledge of the Natural World in Colonial New York* (New Brunswick, NJ: Rutgers University Press, 2007).

Grove, Richard H. *Green Imperialism: Colonial Expansion, Tropical Island Edens and the Origins of Environmentalism 1600–1860* (Cambridge: Cambridge University Press, 1995).

Guralnick, Stanley M. *Science and the Ante-bellum American College* (Philadelphia: American Philosophical Society, 1975).

Harkness, Deborah. *The Jewel House: Elizabethan London and the Scientific Revolution* (New Haven, CT: Yale University Press, 2007).

Hindle, Brooke. *The Pursuit of Science in Revolutionary America, 1735–1789* (Chapel Hill for the Institute of Early American History and Culture, University of North Carolina Press, 1956.).

Iannini, Christopher P. *Fatal Revolutions: Natural History, West Indian Slavery, and the Routes of American Literature* (Chapel Hill, NC: Omohundro Institute of Early American History and Culture, 2012).

John, Richard R. *Spreading the News: The American Postal System from Franklin to Morse.* (Cambridge, MA: Harvard University Press, 1995).

Johnson, Ann. "Material Experiments: Environment and Engineering Institutions in the Early American Republic," *National Identity: The Role of Science and Technology*, eds. C. E. Harrison and A. Johnson (Chicago: University of Chicago Press, 2009).

Jones, David S. *Rationalizing Epidemics: Meanings and Uses of American Indian Mortality since 1600* (Cambridge, MA: Harvard University Press, 2004).

Koerner, Lisbet. *Linnaeus: Nature and Nation* (Cambridge, MA: Harvard University Press, 1999).

Kohlstedt, Sally Gregory. *The Formation of the American Scientific Community: The American Association for the Advancement of Science, 1848–1860* (Urbana: University of Illinois Press, 1976).

Kohlstedt, Sally Gregory. "Parlors, Primers, and Public Schooling: Education for Science in Nineteenth-Century America," *Isis*, 81[3] (1990), 424–45.

Kupperman, Karen. "Fear of Hot Climates in the Anglo-American Colonial Experience," *William and Mary Quarterly*, 3rd series, 41[2] (1984), 213–40.

Labaree, Leonard, W. et al., eds. *The Papers of Benjamin Franklin*. 46 vols. to date (New Haven: Yale University Press, 1959–).

Latour, Bruno. *Science in Action: How to Follow Scientists and Engineers through Society*. (Cambridge, MA: Harvard University Press, 1987).

Lewis, Andrew J. *A Democracy of Facts: Natural History in the Early Republic* ed. R. S. Cox (Philadelphia: University of Pennsylvania Press, 2011).

Lewis, Andrew J. "Nineteenth-Century Scientific Opinion of Lewis and Clark," R. S. Cox (ed.). *The Shortest and Most Convenient Route: Lewis and Clark in Context* (Philadelphia: American Philosophical Society, 2004).

Lucier, Paul. "The Professional and the Scientist in Nineteenth-Century America," *Isis*, 100, 4 (2009), 699–732.

McCormick, Ted. *William Petty and the Ambitions of Political Arithmetic* (New York: Oxford University Press, 2009).

Meyers, Amy R. W., and Margaret Beck Pritchard, eds. *Empire's Nature: Mark Catesby's New World Vision* (Chapel Hill: University of North Carolina Press for the Omokundro Institute for Early American History and Culture, 1998).

Newman, William R. *Gehennical Fire: The Lives of George Starkey, an American Alchemist in the Scientific Revolution* (Cambridge: Harvard University Press, 1994).

Nye, Mary Jo. *Before Big Science: The Pursuit of Modern Chemistry and Physics, 1800–1940* (Cambridge, MA: Harvard University Press, 1996).

Oleson, Alexandra, and Sanborn C. Brown, eds. *The Pursuit of Knowledge in the Early American Republic: American Scientific and Learned Societies from Colonial Times to the Civil War* (Baltimore: Johns Hopkins University Press, 1976).

Parrish, Susan Scott. "The Female Opossum and the Nature of the New World," *William and Mary Quarterly*, 3rd series. 54[3] (1997), 475–514.

Parrish, Susan Scott. *American Curiosity: Cultures of Natural History in the Colonial British Atlantic World* (Chapel Hill, NC: University of North Carolina Press for the Omokundro Institute of Early American History and Culture, 2006).

Paugh, Katherine. "The Politics of Childbearing in the British Caribbean and the Atlantic World during the Age of Abolition, 1776–1838," *Past & Present* 221 (2013): 119–160.

Petty, William. 1751. *Political Arithmetic*. London 1690.

Porter, Roy, ed. *The Cambridge History of Science* vol. 4: *Eighteenth-Century Science* (Cambridge: Cambridge University Press, 2003).

Principe, Lawrence M. *The Secrets of Alchemy* (Chicago: University of Chicago Press, 2013).

Schaffer, Simon. "Newton's Comets and the Transformation of Astrology," *Astrology, Science and Society; Historical Essays*, ed. Patrick Curry (Woodbridge, Suffolk: Boydell Press, 1987).

Schiebinger, Londa L. *Plants and Empire: Colonial Bioprospecting in the Atlantic World* (Cambridge, MA: Harvard University Press, 2004).

Semonin, Paul. *American Monster: How the Nation's First Prehistoric Creature Became a Symbol of National Identity* (New York: New York University Press, 2000).

Seth, Suman. "Putting Knowledge in Its Place: Science, Colonialism, and the Postcolonial," *Postcolonial Studies*, 12[4] (2009), 373–88.

Seth, Suman. "Materialism, Slavery, and *The History of Jamaica*," *Isis* 105[4] (2014): 764–72.

Shapin, Steven. *A Social History of Truth: Civility and Science in Seventeenth-Century England* (Chicago: University of Chicago Press, 1995).

Sheridan, Richard B. *Doctors and Slaves: A Medical and Demographic History of Slavery in the British West Indies, 1680–1834* (New York: Cambridge University Press, 1985).

Slaughter, Thomas P. *The Natures of John and William Bartram* (New York: Alfred A. Knopf, 1996).

Slaughter, Thomas P. *Exploring Lewis and Clark: Reflections on Men and Wilderness* (New York: Alfred A. Knopf, 2003).

Stearns, Raymond Phineas. "Colonial Fellows of the Royal Society of London, 1661–1788," *William and Mary Quarterly*, 3[2] (1946): 208–68.

Stearns, Raymond Phineas. *Science in the British Colonies of America* (Urbana: University of Illinois Press, 1970).

Tyrrell, Ian. "American Exceptionalism in an Age of International History," *American Historical Review*, 96[4] (1991): 1031–55.

Ulrich, Laurel Thatcher. *A Midwife's Tale: The Life of Martha Ballard, Based on Her Diary, 1785–1812* (New York: Knopf, 1990).

Vincent, Philip. *A True Relation of the Late Battell*. London, 1637.

Warner, John Harley. *Against the Spirit of System: The French Impulse in Nineteenth-Century American Medicine*. (Princeton: Princeton University Press, 1998).

Webster, Charles, ed. *Samuel Hartlib and the Advancement of Learning* (Cambridge: Cambridge University Press, 1971).

Wells, Robert V. *The Population of the British Colonies in America before 1776: A Survey of Census Data* (Princeton: Princeton University Press, 1975).

Wey-Gómez, Nicolás. *The Tropics of Empire: Why Columbus Sailed South to the Indies*. (Cambridge, MA, MIT, 2008).

Williams, Glyndwr. *Arctic Labyrinth: The Quest for the Northwest Passage* (Berkeley: University of California Press, 2010).

Woodward, Walter W. *Prospero's America: John Winthrop, Jr., Alchemy, and the Creation of New England Culture, 1606–1676* (Chapel Hill: University of North Carolina Press for the Omokundro Institute of Early American History and Culture, 2010).

Zilberstein, Anya. "Inured to Empire: Wild Rice and Climate Change," *William and Mary Quarterly*, 72[1] (2015), 127–58.

Zirkle, Conway. "Benjamin Franklin, Thomas Malthus and the United States Census," *Isis* 48[1] (1957), 58–62.

PART IV

Competition and Imperial Frontiers

Figure 14.1 1662 Painting of the Portuguese Palace in Olinda, Present-Day Brazil.
Source: Rijksmuseum Amsterdam, SK-A-742/Wikimedia Commons.

14
DEFYING MERCANTILISM
Dutch Interimperial Trade in the Atlantic World

Willem Klooster

The seventeenth and eighteenth centuries saw the Dutch build a global empire. The East India Company (the Vereenigde Oost-Indische Compagnie or VOC, founded in 1602) developed into a commercial giant in the Indian Ocean, overseeing a network of factories from Indonesia to Japan and from Siam to Ceylon, linked by a regular exchange of information and commodities. The company derived its strength in part from its commercial monopolies, including cinnamon, nutmeg, and cloves. Its Atlantic counterpart, the West India Company (WIC, founded in 1621) started out on the same footing, conquering strategic places on either side of the Atlantic: Elmina, Luanda, northern Brazil, and Curaçao. Eventually, however, it was ousted from most of the lands it had occupied, and no new colonies were captured after Suriname was wrested from England in 1667. The Dutch contribution to the early modern Atlantic was, therefore, not primarily an imperial, but a commercial one. As this essay will show, the Dutch were actually the interimperial traders *par excellence* in the Atlantic world.

War and Trade

In the 1590s, Dutch merchants began to explore the wider world. All of a sudden, ships left for the Mediterranean, the Indian Ocean, and the Atlantic world. While Africa was the main destination for Dutch ships during the first decades of Dutch global expansion, trade with the New World flourished around the turn of the century, partly as an outgrowth of the activities of Dutch salt collectors on the Araya peninsula on the Spanish Main. The Dutch had traditionally obtained most of their salt in Andalusia, but the war with Spain, which had begun in 1568, induced Spanish King Philip II to issue economic embargoes against enemy vessels visiting the Iberian Peninsula. His son and successor, Philip III, forbade all Dutch trade in Iberian ports in 1598, forcing Dutch salt collectors to go a quest for alternative sources, which led them to Araya. After six years of intensive collection (1599–1605), they were expelled by a Spanish expedition. During that brief window, salt traders returning to Europe as well as larger ships joined French and English merchants in a lively trade with Cuba and Hispaniola, exchanging linen and silk for hides and dyewood.[1]

Dutch entrepreneurs could also tap Spain's overseas markets by way of Seville, the terminal point of Spain's transatlantic trade system. Since much of this trade was illegal, little is known of its scope and value, but the discovery by Spanish officials of one secret deal reveals the way in which the Dutch were involved. The plan was for a Spanish captain to load nets and mats in Amsterdam, sail with a Flemish crew (who must have been conversant in Spanish) to Havana, exchange the cargo for gold, silver, dyewood, hides, sugar, and tobacco, and return to Europe by joining the Spanish treasure fleet of 1619.[2] Such elaborate schemes must have been unusual. More common was the dispatch of goods intended for the Spanish colonies to Seville or Cádiz, where they were sold to Spaniards or resident Flemings involved in the Indies trade.[3]

The resumption of the Spanish war in 1621, after a 12-year truce expired, effectively closed the door to direct Dutch trade with Spanish America until peace arrived in 1648. Meanwhile, Dutch trade throughout the Atlantic world became the monopoly of the WIC, a single joint-stock company, modeled on the Dutch East India Company. The WIC may have been its namesake, but in practice the two organizations were very different. While commerce was paramount for the VOC, war was the driving force behind the WIC, a distinction that was clear to investors from the outset. If merchants who had traded in the East Indies before 1602 did not hesitate to help the VOC get up and running, those who had been active in the Atlantic world prior to 1621 refused by and large to pour their capital into the WIC.[4] The general public also lacked enthusiasm, in particular because the Company's stated objective of harming the enemy and seizing its overseas strongholds were viewed as high-risk ventures against a mighty and well-defended empire.[5] Earning profit was not what motivated most investors. They were rather swayed by patriotism.[6]

When presented with the choice between trade and bellicose pursuits, many a shipowner opted for the latter by fitting out privateers. They considered privateering simply another, faster way to obtain riches from the New World, especially silver from Mexico or Peru and Brazilian sugar. Privateering and trade were, however, not mutually exclusive, and there was no lack of merchant vessels plying the Atlantic who seized the opportunity to capture an enemy ship. That occurred in the 1630s, but especially in the 1640s, after the commercial monopolies of the WIC had been dismantled in quick succession.[7] The last monopoly the Company relinquished was that of the slave trade in 1648.

Although the WIC failed in most attempts to capture ports and provinces in Ibero-America, the Company's war machine did spawn the establishment of colonies in Brazil and Curaçao and trading posts along the West African coast, including Elmina and the short-lived Dutch "factory" at Luanda. In the 1620s and 1630s, private initiatives added colonies in other parts of the Americas, including Berbice, Essequibo, New Netherland, Saba, St. Eustatius, St. Martin, and Tobago. From then onward, Dutch trade in the Atlantic would be bifurcated. While some transatlantic vessels were active in colonial commerce, others took part in interimperial trade, which was more important for much of the seventeenth century.

An enormously wide array of goods was exported to the Dutch colonies in the seventeenth century. The staple goods were manufactured such as silk, wool, and linen, but most striking are the innumerable victuals sent to some colonies. Salted meat, fish, bacon, bread, dried cod, beans, peas, butter, cheese, salt, oil, wine, beer, vinegar, and train oil filled the holds of each ship leaving for Dutch Brazil. Contrary to New Netherland, where cereal subsistence farming took off soon after the Dutch first arrived, the settlers' dependence on food supplies from the United Provinces continued beyond the stage of exploration in Brazil, Suriname, and Essequibo. Warfare with rival European nations and uncertain relationships with Amerindians help explain this dependence, but cultural factors must also have kept the overseas Dutch from procuring reliable food sources in the colonies.[8] In return for European supplies, Brazil—the foremost Dutch colony in the Americas—sent tropical products to the Netherlands. Johannes de Laet, WIC director and the Company's first historian, wrote that the value of sugar and dyewood exports from Brazil alone amounted to almost 28 million guilders in the years 1637–44, almost three-quarters of which were shipped by private merchants outside the WIC.[9] That was the boom period of Dutch Brazil. A colonial revolt that started in 1645 reduced the colony's sugar area significantly.

Suriname, a Dutch colony since 1667, took over from Brazil as the leading Dutch overseas purveyor of sugar. From the 1720s through the end of the eighteenth century, the colonists sent 15 to 20 million pounds of sugar to the metropolis, valued at 2.5–3 million guilders in most years. In value, Suriname's sugar was overtaken by locally grown coffee in the 1750s, while minor crops shipped back to the Republic were cacao and cotton.[10] The same four crops arrived in the Dutch Republic from Essequibo and Demerara, two colonies situated further west on the Guiana coast that developed in spectacular fashion in the last quarter of the eighteenth century. In the 1780s, their coffee exports accounted for half a million guilders per year.[11] By contrast with Suriname, however, many of these exports did not end up in Dutch ports, but foreign ones.

Connections with French and English America

The multiple foreign ties were the distinguishing mark of the Dutch Atlantic. They show the limits of studying Atlantic history within purely national frameworks. Dutch merchants sold goods to residents of all non-Dutch empires and absorbed their crops and other colonial products. The low prices they asked for their cargoes, their willingness to extend credit and to carry the products themselves made them valued trading partners in many parts of the New World.[12] Some of the earliest samples of English colonial produce left the Americas on Dutch ships bound for the United Provinces. Barbados tobacco, for example, was sold in Rotterdam less than two years after the first crop had been grown on the island.[13] Dutch merchants also frequented the English colonies on Providence Island and the small Leeward Islands of St. Christopher and Montserrat, where they soon posted commercial agents.[14] Dutch traders also discovered the tobacco industry in Virginia, where they became major customers.[15] West India Company ships rarely took part in these transactions, which were largely the domain of private merchants.

The Dutch conquest of northeastern Brazil stimulated commercial contacts with foreign Caribbean islands. Many a transatlantic voyage combined a visit to Brazil with stops at English colonies. The route of the *Blauwe Haen* in 1644 was Brazil-Barbados-St. Kitts-New Netherland-United Provinces, while *Hoop Casteel van Sluys* was to sail from Rotterdam to Barbados, St. Kitts, and Virginia before returning to Rotterdam.[16] The contractor of the latter voyage was Aelbrecht Cockx (1616–56), a private trader who personified Rotterdam's close ties to the English colonies. In the year 1644 alone, Cockx was involved in five voyages to Virginia and the West Indies, and imported more tobacco than any other Rotterdam merchant. Cockx conducted a brisk trade with Barbados, where an Amsterdam ship's captain looked after his interests, and St. Christopher, where he maintained an agent. He also traveled to those colonies himself on a few occasions.[17] Transport of passengers was an additional source of income for Cockx. He sent several ships to English colonies with European settlers on board, such as the 11 planters and their servants who were disembarked in Barbados and St. Christopher or the 8 servants who were transported to Virginia.[18]

In the early 1630s, tobacco planters from recently founded French colonies in the Caribbean also traveled repeatedly to the United Provinces to cultivate ties with Dutch merchants.[19] Due in part to these initiatives Dutch merchants came to dominate, and at times monopolize, the import-export trade of St. Christophe (the French settlement on St. Christopher), Guadeloupe, and Martinique. The commercial services provided by the Dutch contributed enormously to the development of the sugar industry. According to a remark by Guadeloupe's governor in 1665, many of the best sugar plantations owed their existence to Dutch credit. As many as 637 colonists were indebted to these foreign merchants, almost all of whom were based in the province of Zeeland.[20] Horses in St. Christophe that could drive the sugar mills and transport the crops often came off of Dutch ships, while French settlers learned many technical details about sugar production from Dutch artisans who left Brazil after the Dutch surrendered their colony in 1654.[21] Finally, the Dutch supplied virtually all African slaves that arrived to the French sugar islands in the 1660s. All of this adds up to the conclusion that the Dutch, albeit not deliberately, enabled the French Caribbean sugar plantations to take off.

Historians of English colonialism have argued for many years that the Dutch played a similar role in Barbados, where they are said to have created the right conditions for the sugar revolution to take place. It is certainly true that Dutch provisions saved starving settlers more than once and that Dutch trade flourished, at least until the First Anglo-Dutch War (1652–54).[22] Likewise, the furnaces used in boiling cane juice seem to have been built of Dutch bricks, which were often used on Dutch ships as ballast.[23] But it is hard to agree with the widespread notion that the Dutch, having become experienced sugar cultivators, almost singlehandedly introduced all the ingredients for a successful sugar industry, from loaning capital and capital goods to furnishing know-how and supplying slaves. Archives in the Netherlands reveal that textiles and provisions were the staples sent to Barbados, not sugar cauldrons or other capital goods.[24] Nor is there evidence that the Dutch sold many enslaved Africans that would work the plantations.

It may seem plausible that the Dutch transatlantic slave trade was redirected to Barbados after a revolt against Dutch rule in Brazil in 1645 reduced this once-prosperous colony to a small area where little sugar would be cultivated.[25] There are even some indications that plans were made to that effect. Instead of abandoning the slave trade altogether, the authorities in Dutch Brazil instructed local commissioners to sell newly arrived slaves first in Barbados ("at which island they fetch the best market and will be worth most") and then in St. Kitts.[26] A few months later, the Dutch director general in Elmina suggested making Barbados an alternative destination for slaves.[27] Such designs were, however, not translated into action. Only three Dutch slave trade voyages to Barbados have been documented for the mid-1640s.[28] The restructuring of the Dutch slave trade benefited the Spanish and French colonies, not the English ones.[29] Resident English merchants and planters, not the Dutch, launched the sugar boom that started around 1640. The capital they generated producing cotton and tobacco was invested in the incipient sugar industry.[30] Moreover, English slave shipments to Barbados must have been numerous, even though archival proof is missing.[31]

The virtual free trade the Dutch enjoyed with the young colonies of England and France was not to last. Once these countries had each closed a domestic chapter marked by major political upheaval, they turned their attention to overseas provinces. Mercantilist measures, intended to cut the Dutch out of colonial trade, were introduced, first by England in the form of Navigation Acts in 1651 and 1660. The first act targeted the Dutch by stipulating that goods could only be shipped to English ports directly from the place of manufacture and that colonial produce was to be transported to England or other English domains only in English-owned ships.[32] The act was implemented immediately to the detriment of Dutch traders, nineteen of whom were captured at or near Barbados by English war ships and armed merchantmen. Four years later, an English squadron seized another two Dutch ships off of Barbados.[33] Although local supporters of the Dutch rejected the new laws, as in Montserrat, where they petitioned the governor of the Leeward Islands to restore free trade so that it "be restored to their pristine happiness," Dutch traders were bound to lose out in the long term.[34] Merchants in Amsterdam therefore opted for an indirect trade with Barbados, contracting with Englishmen, Irishmen, and Scots to transfer their cargoes to the Caribbean island.[35]

French authorities were not far behind in introducing restrictions on colonial trade in their empire. The chief instrument to oust the Dutch was the royally decreed Compagnie des Indes

Occidentales, founded in 1664, "in little time to withdraw trade from the hands of foreigners and bring it to our ports for the benefit of the subjects of our kingdom." The Compagnie aroused high expectations that it failed to meet. The quality and quantity of the goods it supplied left much to be desired. Within two years, Dutch ships were allowed to return and conduct trade, albeit only after paying a 5 percent duty.[36] By the late 1660s, Dutch trade was made virtually impossible by the imposition of a 10 percent tax on all imports and exports.[37] These discriminatory practices, combined with the *Compagnie*'s monopoly, produced large-scale revolts, first in Martinique (1665–67) and then Saint-Domingue (1670–71). These protests however, could not prevent the termination of Dutch control of France's colonial trade. Ships from France now carried the necessities to the islands and shipped back colonial produce, allowing the French to build 28 sugar refineries in the metropole before 1683.[38]

Exploring Spanish America

The heyday of Dutch "free" trade with the French colonies coincided with a renewed Dutch commercial interest in Spanish America. Immediately after the United Provinces had signed a peace treaty with Spain in 1648, Dutch merchants extended their commercial interests to Spanish America. They worked around the clock to carve out a place for themselves in the *carrera de Indias*, Spain's transatlantic trade system. Focusing on Cádiz, which had succeeded Seville as the port from which Spain's ocean fleets left and to which they returned, the Dutch loaded impressive amounts of cargo as they worked through Spanish freighters. Their imports were worth 6 million pesos by the fall of 1649.[39]

At the same time, Amsterdam merchants began to explore the markets in the Spanish colonies themselves. The ships they fitted out often engaged in "cruising," sailing through the Caribbean in hopes of being admitted to one or more ports. The items carried on board were of great variety, usually destined for specific ports. Since the voyages were always risky, wealthy merchants tended to be the main investors, men such as Henrico Mathias (1609–76) and Philips van Hulten (c. 1631–92). Mathias was one of the merchants chartering the *Liefde*, which conducted trade in several Cuban ports before sailing to the Spanish Main, exchanging goods in Caracas (La Guaira), Maracaibo, and Río Hacha. After a successful Atlantic crossing, the ship anchored, completing its voyage in 1665 with 4,000 hides, 3,000 canisters of tobacco, and 30,000 pesos. One day before, the *San Pedro* had returned to Dutch shores, a ship that had probably sailed with the *Liefde*. Also freighted by Amsterdam merchants, its outgoing cargo worth 150,000 guilders was exchanged in Santiago de Cuba, Puerto del Príncipe, Campeche, Caracas, and Maracaibo for 30,000 pesos, 200 canisters of Barinas tobacco, 2.5 million pounds of Campeche dyewood, 4,000 hides, some indigo, and other produce.[40]

Van Hulten was among a group of Amsterdam merchants who started corresponding with residents of the Canary Islands in 1653 in order to tap the riches of Spanish America.[41] They sent ships that were allowed to do business upon the payment of a bribe, exchanging their cargoes for products from the Spanish colonies. The Canaries also served as a gateway to direct Dutch trade in the Indies, as Dutch merchants secured registers (or licenses) in the name of Canary residents. These registers usually permitted navigation with Canary wine to Havana, where a new license for trade in other parts of Spanish America could be obtained.[42] Residents of the Spanish empire—from the Iberian Peninsula, the Canary Islands, as well as the Spanish West Indies—were as much part of these commercial schemes as Dutch natives. Captain Antonio de Vasconcelos from the Canaries, for example, traveled to Amsterdam in 1658 to strike a partnership with local merchants Jan Broersz and Isaacq Hermans and send a ship to the Spanish Caribbean by way of the Canary Islands. The cargo would be sent under Vasconcelos' name.[43]

Voyages through the Canary Islands came to an end around 1670. Merchants based in Amsterdam must have concluded that the expeditions involving multiple stops across the Atlantic were too risky. Confiscation of both the ship and its cargo was a distinct possibility, given the illegal nature of the trade in the eyes of Spanish officials. Besides, an attractive alternative was available in the form of Curaçao, the island the Dutch had conquered during the war with Spain. Since it was a barren place that could not produce cash crops, the WIC considered abandoning it, but Curaçao sprang into life in the mid-1650s, when Amsterdam merchants forged commercial ties with the Spanish Main. Their ships started carrying Venezuelan cacao to Europe by way of Curaçao, where they claimed the crop had been grown.[44] As increasing numbers of merchants settled on Curaçao, trade relations with both Venezuela and the southwestern corner of the Caribbean flourished. The availability of an entrepôt reduced the risk of Spanish American commerce for metropolitan Dutch merchants, who henceforth directed their ships to Curaçao instead of ports in the Spanish Caribbean. Small, maneuverable vessels that could outwit Spanish coastguard ships now left the island with cargoes that originated in Amsterdam or Middelburg. The Curaçaoans, moreover, could respond quickly to the demand of their customers.[45]

The years around 1670, which featured the rise of Curaçao as an entrepôt and the conquest of Suriname, set the tone for Dutch America in the long eighteenth century (1688–1815). On the one hand, the Dutch continued their role as interlopers in other empires from their bases in Curaçao and Statia. On the other hand, and more in line with the general pattern of the European colonization of the Greater Caribbean, they engaged in the production of cash crops, not only in Suriname, but other parts of Guiana (Berbice, Demerara, and Essequibo), and to a much lesser extent in Statia and St. Martin. Still, even the plantation colonies were deeply involved in trade with other parts of the Americas, in particular the Caribbean and British North America. Another distinction, which no historian has made, is that between the active Dutch interimperial traders and those on the receiving end. During the first 70 years of the seventeenth century, Dutch merchants, most of them based in the metropole, took the initiative for multiple forms of interimperial Atlantic trade. In the "Second Dutch Atlantic" (1680–1815), interimperial trade remained a hallmark, but the Dutch role was usually a passive one, as trade by foreign merchants in the ports and roadsteads of St. Eustatius, St. Martin, Suriname, and the other Guiana colonies eclipsed interimperial commerce initiated by Dutch colonial traders. Until the late eighteenth century, Curaçao proved the exception to this rule.

Curaçao

The merchants and petty traders of Curaçao were imbued with the same entrepreneurial drive that had marked the Dutch Golden Age. Each week, their sloops and schooners departed in all directions to conduct trade with French, British, and especially Spanish colonies. Since in normal years, any transactions by foreigners in Spanish America were illegal, the Curaçaoan developed some methods to camouflage their actions. They bribed guards, used watchwords, and engaged in offshore mock battles with Spanish American vessels before unloading their goods and taking local produce in payment. In the Greater Caribbean, Curaçao fulfilled an important commercial function, supplying silk, woolen, and linen fabrics; as well as lace, cotton, muslins, ironware, naval supplies, brandy, and spices to non-Dutch customers.[46] From the early days of the island's emergence as a commercial center, Curaçao was also a major transit port in the intra-American slave trade. Dutch slavers disembarked 100 slaves on Curaçao in the years 1656–1730, when the island functioned as a slave depot for Spanish America, legalized by contracts signed by the WIC with the holders of the *asiento*, the legal monopoly of the Spanish slave trade.

In return for their goods, the Curaçaoans obtained tobacco, hides, and especially cacao, of which Venezuela was the world's largest producer until the early nineteenth century. Venezuela was the main destination for Curaçaoan vessels, accounting for over 80 percent of Curaçao's shipping in 1785–86.[47] While Curaçaoans dominated commerce on the Venezuelan coast, Jamaican traders reigned supreme on the adjacent littoral of New Granada, although merchants from Curaçao were also active there, establishing close ties with the independent Guajiro natives, from whom they bought brazilwood, cows, mules, and goats in exchange for firearms, gunpowder, cannonballs, muslins, coarse cotton cloth, machetes, and spoons.[48]

The sight of a Curaçaoan vessel was also welcomed in Puerto Rico and the French and Spanish parts of Hispaniola. In Santo Domingo, half all exported hides left the colony legally in Curaçaoan holds, a share that must have been higher given the ubiquity of smuggling.[49] Ties with New York were equally close, at least from the 1680s onward. One British eyewitness reported in 1709–10 that the inhabitants of the Dutch island "have all sorts of provision both for eating and drinking, as bread, flower, butter, cheese, peas, rice, beef, pork, and corn, from Pennsylvania and New York strong and small beer, for Carolina and New England pitch and tar, from Charribbee islands and Jamaica, rum, sugar, cotton, ginger, indico, and tobacco."[50] By midcentury, Curaçao was New York's main connection after Jamaica. Much money was made in this trade, a pamphleteer wrote in the mid-eighteenth century: "The merchants of New York have gotten their estates by the Curesaw Trade."[51]

One important branch of Curaçao's economy, which historians have hardly acknowledged, was the mule trade. Throughout the eighteenth century, the Curaçaoans operated as go-betweens between dealers on the Spanish Main and sugar planters on the French islands and Jamaica.[52] French colonial merchants often relied on the Curaçaoan merchants with their time-honored contacts not only in Ríohacha, but everywhere on the Spanish Main.[53] After midcentury, Saint-Domingue, with its flourishing sugar industry, became the main destination for mules from the Spanish Main, until the Haitian Revolution led to the collapse of the local sugar industry.

Statia and St. Martin

Although it was settled by Dutch natives in 1636 for its tobacco prospects and boasted 35 sugar and cotton plantations a century later, the main economic role of St. Eustatius, or "Statia," was that of an entrepôt like Curaçao. Vessels from the nearby French islands of Guadeloupe and Martinique arrived in large numbers to conduct business, usually with sugar from these colonies in their holds (Table 14.1). Ships from Spanish colonies were rarely spotted on Statia's roadstead, but there was a regular presence of bottoms from British North America and the Danish islands of St. John, St. Croix, and St. Thomas. The British West Indies were also prominent trading partners. In some years, such as 1744, on average one vessel sailed from British St. Kitts each day. Ships from British colonies did not often supply plantations' produce, but instead offered a variety of foodstuffs for sale. In 1733, provisions came off ships from Antigua, Barbados, Bermuda, Montserrat, Nevis, Maryland, New York, and Virginia.[54] Indeed, foodstuffs were the main import items from North America, especially cheese and fish from New England and bread and flour from New York and Philadelphia. Building materials were another North American staple, including planks, shingles, hoops, staves, bricks, turpentine, and tar.[55] Rum and molasses were the main items the Statians exchanged for British supplies, while customers from the French islands were more interested in European manufactures that had been shipped from Dutch metropolitan ports, including printed cotton and linen in different varieties, such as fine white linen and rough linen from Osnabrück in Germany.[56]

Table 14.1 Statia's American trade, 1733–1785

	1733	1744	1762	1768	1776	1785	Average
British WI	20.4	44.1	32.0	27.6	39.3	23.3	31.1
Dutch WI	3.6	33.7	42.4	11.0	26.7	43.5	26.8
French WI	56.9	13.1	9.1	31.9	16.4	15.0	23.7
BNA/USA	17.5	3.3	0.9	16.8	3.3	6.2	8.0
Danish WI	0.0	5.0	7.8	4.9	11.4	10.7	5.9
Spanish WI	0.7	0.9	7.8	7.8	2.9	1.2	3.6

The figures represent arriving vessels. The category "Dutch West Indies" includes Berbice, Demerara, Essequibo, and Suriname. "BNA" stands for British North America. Adapted from Goslinga, *Dutch in Caribbean and Guianas*, 204–5, Knappert, *Geschiedenis*, 219, and Menkman, "Sint Eustatius' gouden tijd," 394–5.

Trade increased tenfold between the 1730s and the 1770s, when between 1,000 and 3,000 ships touched at Statia each year. As a colony in an empire that maintained its neutrality after the War of the Spanish Succession (1702–13), Statia's trade blossomed during the season of war. In 1744, during the War of Jenkins' Ear, British privateers deprived the French Caribbean islands of their metropolitan connections. Statia's commander Johan Heyliger used the situation to the island's advantage by commissioning over 50 French vessels to ship provisions and war material to the French islands.[57] Statia was also used by the French for provisioning during the early part of the Seven Years' War (1756–63), which again pitted France against Britain. Vessels based in Statia were at times even escorted by French men-of-war to Martinique and St. Domingue.[58] Those vessels that sailed unprotected were at great risk of seizure by the British, paralyzing the resident merchant class. In 1758 alone, losses for the island in terms of goods and vessels amounted to over 1 million guilders.[59]

In the late 1770s and early 1780s, Statia emerged as a major transfer point in the shipment of war material to the Continental Congress, in exchange of course for Chesapeake tobacco, South Carolina indigo, and other produce. In 1781, a British naval force took revenge for Statia's commercial support of the American Revolution by confiscating 200 ships at anchor and emptying all the warehouses. Total costs of this raid amounted to more than 7 million pound sterling.[60] Although they were a devastating blow to Statia's economy, these actions did not prove lethal. And yet, it was only a matter of time before the entrepôt did collapse, never to rise again.[61]

If Statia was connected to British ports throughout the Americas, but also to British merchants based in Madeira and Irish ports such as Cork and Waterford, the neighboring Dutch colony of St. Martin—which shared an island with the French—was likewise incorporated into British commercial networks during the course of the eighteenth century. Three out of four foreign vessels arriving there in 1735–36 originated from the British islands, while ships from the British mainland colonies began to include St. Martin in their Caribbean voyages during the midcentury. Despite the proximity of French soil, trade with the French islands was not very significant in the 1730s, nor 50 years later when the local volume of trade had multiplied by a factor of eight.[62]

Suriname and Essequibo

Barbados had been Suriname's earliest trading partner under English rule, and the commercial ties between the two colonies survived both the Dutch takeover of 1667 and the Third Anglo-Dutch War (1672–74).[63] The typical exchange was timber from Suriname's forests for

"Barbadian" foodstuffs, although the most entrepreneurial resident of Suriname, Samuel Cohen Nassy combined the export of timber to Barbados with the import of provisions and horses from North America. Thus began the horse trade from New England and New York, which was to last for many decades.[64] Eventually, North American competition put an end to the Barbadian connection. Suriname preferred receiving foodstuffs directly from the North instead of those reexported from Barbados, while Barbados came to see Suriname as a commercial rival once the island became a major customer of wood from New York and New England.[65] Barbados' governor complained in 1707 about New England's massive imports of rum, sugar, and molasses from the Dutch colony. Indeed, before North American merchants discovered French rum and molasses, they obtained it in Suriname.[66] Around the turn of the century, New England merchants increased their trade to Suriname. While one or two New England ships arrived at Paramaribo in 1682–92, in the years 1713–17 an average of 10 vessels left there for Boston each year and probably even more were based in Rhode Island.[67] When New England merchants entered trade relations with the French Caribbean, Suriname was not abandoned. Well into the eighteenth century, it remained the main stop on their Caribbean voyages, where the New Englanders could exchange cargoes of fish, flour, bread, butter, and building materials for sugar, rum, and molasses.[68] Rum and molasses, byproducts of the sugar industry, were in great demand in North America. By 1715, Boston alone imported annually more than 100,000 gallons of Dutch colonial rum.[69] The volume of this traffic was not affected by the Molasses Act in 1733, which British Parliament had adopted to obtain a monopoly on the sales of British West Indian sugar and molasses on the North American mainland, but the law was evaded on an enormous scale. Suriname's governors did what they could to make this evasion possible, signing the statements of New England or New York skippers that listed Madeira as the destination.[70]

The North American connection was for Suriname nothing less than a lifeline. Almost 90 percent of the 4,478 ships that historian Johannes Postma has counted as anchoring at Paramaribo from 1667 through 1795 hailed from North America. They shipped more than 30,000 horses, including a type of horse apparently bred specifically for export to the Dutch colony.[71] The maritime link between the two regions was firmly controlled by the North Americans. Their skippers negotiated purchases with local merchants, used local intermediaries, and sent agents to buy molasses at the plantations.[72] It did happen that molasses was carried to North America on board Surinamese ships, when merchants and planters were keen on overseeing the sale and organizing return cargoes, but this remained illegal from the Dutch colonial vantage point until 1783. Only then did the colony's owner, the Sociëteit van Suriname, give in to settler demands and authorize it.[73] At this juncture, US entrepreneurs also discovered the profitability of trading African slaves to Paramaribo. They would soon eclipse the Dutch slave trade.[74]

Essequibo's foreign trade resembled that of Suriname, with one exception: its traders actively engaged in commerce with Spanish settlers in the nearby Orinoco region. From there, annatto dye was imported, as well as mules and horses that were needed to propel the mills on Essequibo's sugar plantations. From the early eighteenth century onward, horses were also disembarked on ships from New England. Like in Suriname, the New Englanders sought to secure a cargoes of rum and molasses, although they could only do so legally against payment of high export duties.[75]

Merchants from the Thirteen Colonies regularly carried foodstuffs to Essequibo, saving the colony from starvation more than once. Besides, African slaves were carried to Essequibo in large numbers on North American ships in spite of a ban on foreign slave supplies. Planters preferred dealing with British slavers, who were willing to extend long-term credit, unlike their Dutch colleagues, an interesting reversal of seventeenth-century practices.[76] Enslaved Africans also came along with immigrant British planters, who relocated to Essequibo primarily from

Barbados and Antigua, and had the right to introduce their own slaves. Attracted by fertile soil, free land, and a 10-year tax exemption offered by the WIC, these British settlers changed Essequibo beyond recognition.[77] The Essequibo frontier kept its allure for residents of the British Caribbean throughout the eighteenth century, although a large number also moved to the adjacent Dutch colonies of Berbice and Demerara. By 1803, 5,000 of the 7,000 whites in Demerara and Essequibo were British subjects.[78]

The immigration of Britons unleashed a productive revolution, especially in cotton and coffee. The number of plantations grew at breakneck speed and the introduction of African slaves changed the demographic profile of the three Dutch colonies, and there was no lack of shipping to absorb the vast growth in production. Apart from Dutch and British ships, those from North America were a fixture on the roadsteads of Essequibo and Demerara. In 1781–91, a total of 581 vessels from North America, for example, entered Demerara, making up 3 out of every 10 arrivals.[79] What was not clear to the Dutch at the time is that the three Dutch Guiana colonies were gradually becoming part of the British empire, accelerated by several British occupations between 1781 and 1802 and assisted by 10 million pound sterling in credit extended by merchants in London, Liverpool, Bristol, and Glasgow. By the end of the Napoleonic wars, Dutch Guiana was swallowed for good by the British empire, which refused to return the colony to Dutch rule.[80]

Dutch Home Ports and the Foreign Americas

The Dutch-based trading firms that had been involved in direct New World trade before 1670 did not all abandon the Americas. The establishment and consolidation of Curaçao and Statia as entrepôts reduced these companies' risk, allowing them to work with agents in the colonies who could see to the sale of their manufactures and the purchase of return goods.[81] Nonetheless, some companies avoided the Dutch colonies in their quest for American riches. One example is the Middelburgse Commercie Compagnie, which was not only the largest Dutch slaving firm in the eighteenth century, but was also active in commerce outside the slave trade in Spanish America from the 1720s through the 1740s. The company's expeditions resembled the cruising voyages of old, as the ships touched at numerous ports, including Margarita, Cumaná, Portobelo, Santo Domingo, and Cuba.[82]

Most Dutch-American trade was, however, with British North America and later the United States. Amsterdam and New York had very close ties, kept alive by contraband trade. Amsterdam merchants frequently bypassed New York and steered their ships to a place south of the city named "Sandy Hook" or even further afield to avoid detection by customs officers.[83] These firms, who maintained factors in the city, undersold their British colleagues in textiles, guns, gunpowder, and tea, and imported fur, lumber, dyewood, tobacco, wine, and fish.[84] Amsterdam was also an important market for New York merchants, although increasingly came to be used to complement their trade with England and not as their main destination.[85]

Rotterdam had always been involved with British America, especially Virginia, but starting in the late seventeenth century, the initiative in this trade passed to the North Americans. Their ships started to sail to Rotterdam in growing numbers, some in flagrant breach of the Navigation Laws, others after first having cleared a British home port. In the six years preceding the Seven Years' War (1750–55), 78 ships arrived from South Carolina—26 from Maryland, 26 from Virginia, and 12 from New York—carrying rice, tobacco, and dyewood.[86] Rotterdam did not become a mere recipient of Atlantic shipping. Two firms from the Maas town, along with one from Amsterdam, dominated the shipment of German migrants to the British colonies.[87]

Free Trade Under Fire

In spite of the obvious advantage to the Dutch Atlantic economy of free trade, its premise did not always go unchallenged among the Dutch themselves. A debate broke out in the early years of the eighteenth century about the wisdom of admitting foreign ships to Suriname. The Sociëteit van Suriname first insisted on a total ban, but eventually made concessions after corresponding with the colonial council, which had rejected the Sociëteit's proposal to limit foreign trade to the import of horses and to confiscate both cargo and ship when other goods were introduced. The compromise reached in 1704 stipulated that Suriname's inhabitants were allowed to trade with ships from New England and New York and those from nearby islands. Foreign ships were not at freedom to sell slaves, European manufactures, East Indies goods or rye, barley, oats, and meat. Ships bound for North America were also forbidden to load sugar. These regulations were enlightened compared to those approved by the WIC's Zeeland Camber regarding Essequibo in the same year. No trade was permitted to take place there with New York or Barbados, other than in cases of great need.[88]

In practice, this policy was routinely circumvented, leading the same Chamber to complain in 1748 about British ships trading in Essequibo without paying any duties. In this colony, the traditional roles were reversed. Whereas Dutch traders active in foreign colonies had often compensated for the lack of imperial (and therefore legal) shipping, here Dutch ships supplied too few manufactures to satisfy local demand, leaving a niche for British merchants. Ignoring the protests of local officials, Dutch metropolitan authorities acted similar to their foreign counterparts, the WIC board in 1773 banning the import of European manufactures while also prohibiting foreign slave deliveries. "Alien" ships could only take in molasses, rum, and wood.[89]

In the 1750s, the issue of free trade also surfaced regarding Statia. The bone of contention was sugar supplied by the French that was purchased by English merchants as if it were an English colonial product. This practice had existed for decades and showed no signs of diminishing.[90] Contending that these transactions were harmful for the Dutch sugar trade and refinery, some merchants in the Dutch Republic advocated a prohibition of free trade in sugar at Statia and sugar refining on the island. A group of 81 Statians involved in local refining reacted in a letter to the island's commander by pointing out that the French sugar supplies were of great value and that a prohibition would scare away the French merchants. The WIC directors, however, were persuaded by metropolitan merchants and decided that sugar could not be sold to foreigners. For all products shipped in from foreign colonies, in addition to the usual 2 percent weighage, an additional 3 percent duty had to be paid. The measure made some merchants pack up and leave Statia, while the governor and council feared that English traders would move their business to the Danish islands. The French would then follow suit, given their interest in the cash, fish, meat, flour, and horses the English sold on the island. This argument probably made the Company directors change their minds, because they soon rescinded the new duty.[91]

Conclusion

Dutch commercial expansion in the seventeenth century was largely carried out by merchants based in the metropole, who engaged in often risky ventures to numerous parts of the Americas. The way in which interimperial trade was organized changed once the entrepôts of Curaçao and Statia had matured in the third quarter of the seventeenth century. Cargoes from the Dutch Republic were henceforth reexported from these islands to foreign parts of the New World. Continuing the tradition of their metropolitan colleagues, Curaçao's traders sailed with their vast cargoes of manufactures and other European wares to numerous ports, coves, and inlets in

Atlantic America. Statia's role in the eighteenth century was more passive, as foreigners seeking Dutch goods anchored at Oranjestad. Nor did the Dutch plantation colonies in Guiana use a fleet of vessels that swarmed to North America or the Greater Caribbean. Instead, foreigners, and almost exclusively British merchants, sought out these colonies for commercial ends. What enabled their trade was both the supply of rum and molasses and the perennial need of the Dutch colonies for foodstuffs.

Notes

1 Wim Klooster, *Illicit Riches: Dutch Trade in the Caribbean, 1648–1795* (Leiden: KITLV Press, 1998), 24–8.
2 Eddy Stols, "Gens des Pays-Bas en Amérique Espagnole aux premiers siècles de la colonization" *Bulletin de l'Institut Historique Belge de Rome* 44 (1974): 580.
3 Eufemio Lorenzo Sanz, *Comercio de España con América en la época de Felipe II*, 2 vols. (Valladolid: Servicio de Publicaciones de la Diputación Provincial de Valladolid, 1980), 2: 157.
4 Oscar Gelderblom, *Zuid-Nederlandse kooplieden kooplieden en de opkomst van de Amsterdamse stapelmarkt (1578–1630)* (Hilversum: Verloren, 2000), 237–8.
5 Ewout Teellinck, *De tweede wachter brengende tijdinghe vande nacht, dat is, Van het overgaen vande Bahia, met Eenen heylsamen raedt, wat daer over te doen staet* ('s-Graven-haghe: Aert Meurs, 1625), Ch. 3.
6 *De Portogysen goeden buurman.*
7 Hermann Wätjen, *Das holländische Kolonialreich in Brasilien: Ein Kapitel aus der Kolonialgeschichte des 17. Jahrhunderts* ('s-Gravenhage: Martinus Nijhoff, Gotha: Perthes, 1921), 337, 344. E. B. O'Callaghan, ed., *Documents Relative to the Colonial History of the State of New-York; Procured in Holland, England and France by John Romeyn Brodhead, Vol. I* (Albany, NY: Weed, Parsons, 1856), 245. Franz Binder, "Die zeeländische Kaperfahrt 1654–1662," *Archief: Mededelingen van het Zeeuwsch Genootschap der Wetenschappen* (1976): 40–92.
8 Wätjen, *Das holländische Kolonialreich*, 305–6.
9 Johannes De Laet, *Iaerlyck Verhael van de Verrichtinghen der Gheoctroyeerde West-Indische Compagnie in derthien Boecken*, eds. S.P. l'Honoré Naber and J.C.M. Warnsinck, 4 vols. ('s-Gravenhage: Martinus Nijhoff, 1931–1937), 4: 298.
10 Johannes Postma, "Suriname and its Atlantic Connections 1667–1795," *Riches from Atlantic Commerce*, eds. Postma and Enthoven, 314–7.
11 Eric Willem Van der Oest, "Forgotten Colonies of Essequibo and Demerara, 1700–1814," *Riches from Atlantic Commerce: Dutch Trans-Atlantic Trade and Shipping, 1585–1817*, eds. Johannes Postma and Victor Enthoven (Leiden and Boston: Brill, 2003), 350–1.
12 Christian J. Koot, *Empire at the Periphery: British Colonists, Anglo-Dutch Trade, and the Development of the British Atlantic, 1621–1713* (New York and London: New York University Press, 2011), 36–37. Klarenbeek, "Grutters op de Antillen Particuliere kooplieden uit de Republiek op het eiland Sint Christoffel in de zeventiende eeuw," *Tijdschrift voor Zeegeschiedenis* 32[2] (2013): 27.
13 Gemeentearchief Rotterdam [GAR], Oud Notarieel Archief [ONA] 141: 140/212, act of June 22, 1630.
14 Karen Ordahl Kupperman, *Providence Island 1630–1641: The Other Puritan Colony* (Cambridge: Cambridge University Press, 1993), 133; Kopperman, "Ambivalent allies," 62–63.
15 Victor Enthoven and Wim Klooster, "Contours of Virginia-Dutch Trade in the Long Seventeenth Century," In *Early Modern Virginia: New Essays on the Old Dominion*, eds. Douglas Bradburn and John Coombs (Charlottesville: University of Virginia Press, 2011).
16 Stadsarchief Amsterdam [SAA], Notarieel Archief [NA] 1861/462–463, act of October 21, 1644.
17 GAR, ONA 95, 205/332, act of August 4, 1643, 96, 23/34, act of March 17, 1645, 96: 144/232, act of January 31, 1648. R. Bijlsma, "Rotterdam's Amerika-vaart in de eerste helft der 17de eeuw," *Bijdragen voor Vaderlandsche Geschiedenis en Oudheidkunde*, 5th series, 3 (1916): 129, 132. W. G. D. Murray, "De Rotterdamsche toeback-coopers," *Rotterdamsch jaarboekje*, 5th series, 1 (1943): 33.
18 GAR, ONA 86, 307/585, act of January 13, 1644.
19 Pierre Pluchon, *Histoire des Antilles et de la Guyane* (Toulouse: Edouard Privat, 1982), 71, 89.
20 Gérard Lafleur, "Relations avec l'étranger des minorités religieuses aux Antilles françaises (XVIIe–XVIIIe s.)," *Bulletin de la Société d'Histoire de la Guadeloupe* 57–58 (1983): 29, 34.
21 Stewart L. Mims, *Colbert's West India Policy* (New Haven: Yale University Press, 1912). 326–7. Paul Butel, *Histoire des Antilles françaises XVIIe–XXe siècle* (s.l.: Perrin, 2002), 70. Philip P. Boucher, *France*

and the American Tropics to 1700: Tropics of Discontent? (Baltimore: The Johns Hopkins University Press, 2008), 157.

22 Vincent T. Harlow, *History of Barbados 1625–1685* (New York: Negro Universities Press, 1926), 38. See for a list of 138 Dutch ships trading at Barbados in the years 1634–1669: Yda Schreuder, "Evidence from the Notarial Protocols in the Amsterdam Municipal Archives about Trade Relationships between Amsterdam and Barbados in the Seventeenth Century," *Journal of the Barbados Museum and Historical Society* 52 (2006): 73–7.

23 Nicholas Darnell Davis, *The Cavaliers and Roundheads of Barbados, 1650–1652* (Demerara: "Argosy" Press, 1883), 49.

24 Ernst van den Van den Boogaart et al., *La expansión holandesa en el Atlántico* (Madrid: Mapfre, 1992), 163.

25 See for this thesis, for example, Yda Schreuder, "The Influence of the Dutch Colonial Trade in Barbados in the Seventeenth Century," *Journal of the Barbados Museum and Historical Society* 48 (2002): 53 and Matthew Parker, *The Sugar Barons: Family, Corruption, Empire, and War in the West Indies.* (New York: Walker & Company, 2011), 57.

26 Nationaal Archief, the Netherlands [NAN], Oude West-Indische Compagnie 60, Fol. 89: instructions of the High Council in Brazil for commissioners Walien Jorisz and Laurens van Heusden, December 30, 1645.

27 Porter, "European activity," 263.

28 These were the *St. Jacob* (captured by English in 1644), the *Seerobbe* (1646), and the *Tamandare*. See the Trans-Atlantic Slave Trade Database and Klass Ratelband, *Nederlanders in West-Afrika 1600–1650: Angola, Kongo en São Tomé* (Zutphen: Walburg Pers, 2000), 259, 278.

29 Binder, "Zeeländische Kaperfahrt," 53.

30 John J. McCusker and Russel R. Menard, "The Sugar Industry in the Seventeenth Century: A New Perspective on the Barbadian "Sugar Revolution," *Sugar and the Making of the Atlantic World, 1450–1680*, ed. Stuart B. Schwartz (Chapel Hill & London: The University of North Carolina Press, 2004), 301–303.

31 Larry Gragg, "To Procure Negroes," The English Slave Trade to Barbados, 1627–60," *Slavery and Abolition* 16 (1995): 65–84. Van den Boogaart et al., *La expansión holandesa*, 161.

32 Charles M. Andrews, *The Colonial Period of American History*, 4 vols. (New Haven: Yale University Press, 1938), 4: 36–37, 61–62.

33 NAN, Staten-Generaal 4846, resolutions of the States General, February 18, 1651. Charles Wilson, *Profit and Power: A Study of England and the Dutch Wars* (London, New York and Toronto: Longmans, Green, 1957), 87. Cornelius Ch. Goslinga, *Dutch in the Caribbean and on the Wild Coast, 1580–1680* (Assen: Van Gorcum, 1971), 330. Claudia Schnurmann, *Atlantische Welten: Engländer und Niederländer im amerikanisch-atlantischen Raum 1648–1713* (Köln: Böhlau Verlag, 1998), 182–4.

34 Donald Harman Akenson, *If the Irish Ran the World: Montserrat, 1630–1730* (Montreal: McGill-Queen's University Press, 1997), 67.

35 Schreuder, "Evidence," 68.

36 Boucher, *France and the American Tropics*, 172, 181.

37 SAA, NA 2230, Fols. 998–999, act of August 1, 1669, depositions of Claes Carstensz and Hendrick Breijhaen.

38 Alain Ph. Blérald, *Histoire économique économique de la Guadeloupe et de la Martinique: du XVIIe siècle à nos jours* (Paris: Karthala, 1986), 20.

39 Archivo General de Simancas [AGS], Estado 2070, the Count of Peñaranda to King Philip IV, November 13, 1649.

40 Archivo General de Indias [AGI], Seville, Indiferente General, 1668, memorandum of Esteban Gamarra, November 1665.

41 AGI, Indiferente General 1668, Esteban de Gamarra to the Spanish Crown, November 27, 1663.

42 Fernando Serrano Mangas, *Armadas y flotas de la plata (1620–1648)* (Madrid: Banco de España, 1990), 367. Jonathan I. Israel, *Diasporas within a Diaspora: Jews, Crypto-Jews and the World Maritime Empires (1540–1740)* (Leiden: Brill, 2002), 275–276. Lutgardo García Fuentes, *El comercio español con América.* Sevilla: Excma (Diputación Provincial de Sevilla, 1980), 96–99.

43 SAA, NA 2859, Fol. 248, deposition of Antonio de Vasconcelos, May 29, 1658.

44 AGS, Estado 8383, fol. 61, report of Spain's consul Jacques Richard, Amsterdam, March 4, 1656.

45 Klooster, *Illicit Riches*, 54–5.

46 Hartog, *Curaçao*, I: 365.

47 Klooster, *Illicit Riches*, 74.

48 Klooster, *Illicit Riches*, 76. Grahn, *The Political Economy of Smuggling: Regional Informal Economies in Early Bourbon New Granada* (Boulder, Colorado: Westview Press, 1997), 41. Miguel Izard, "Contrabandistas, comerciantes e ilustrados," *Boletín Americanista* 20, 28 (1978): 59.
49 Klooster, *Illicit Riches*, 77–8.
50 Schnurmann, *Atlantische Welten*, 287, 289.
51 Thomas M. Truxes, "Transnational Trade in the Wartime North Atlantic: The Voyage of the Snow 'Recovery'," *The Business History Review* 79[4] (2005): 751–780.
52 NAN, Nieuwe West-Indische Compagnie [NWIC], 609, Fol. 556, Governor Jean Rodier and Council to the WIC, March 14, 1774.
53 Jean Tarrade, "Le commerce entre les Antilles françaises et les possessions espagnoles d'Amérique à la fin du XVIIIe siècle," *Commerce et plantation dans la Caraïbe XVIIIe et XIXe siècles: Actes du Colloque de Bordeaux, 15–16 mars 1991*, ed. Paul Butel (Bordeaux: Maison des Pays Ibériques, 1992), 30, 36.
54 Goslinga, *Dutch in Caribbean and Guianas 1680–1791* (Assen: Van Gorcum, 1985), 204–5. L. Knappert, *Geschiedenis van de Nederlandsche Bovenwindsche eilanden in de 18de eeuw* ('s-Gravenhage: Martinus Nijhoff, 1932), 219.
55 Victor Enthoven, "That Abominable Nest of Pirates,": St. Eustatius and the North Americans, 1680–1780," *Early American Studies: An Interdisciplinary Journal* 1[2] (2012): 260.
56 Knappert, *Geschiedenis*, 221.
57 Frank Wesley Pitman, *The Development of the British West Indies, 1700–1763* (New Haven: Yale University Press, 1917), 291–2.
58 Klooster, *Illicit Riches*, 93.
59 Klooster, *Illicit Riches*, 103.
60 Spooner, *Risks at Sea: Amsterdam Insurance and Maritime Europe, 1766–1780* (Cambridge: Cambridge University Press, 1983), 100–1. Klooster, *Illicit Riches*, 95–6. Enthoven, "That Abominable Nest of Pirates," 288–93.
61 Han Jordaan and Victor Wilson, "Eighteenth-Century Danish, Dutch and Swedish Free Ports in the Northeastern Caribbean: Continuity and Change," *Dutch Atlantic Connections, 1680–1815: Linking Empires, Bridging Borders*, eds. Gert Oostindie and Jessica Roitman. (Leiden: Brill, 2014), 297. De Hullu, "St. Eustatius, St. Martin en Saba," 390.
62 In 1735–36, a total of 175 vessels anchored at Dutch St. Martin. In 1785 alone, 694 vessels arrived. Knappert, *Geschiedenis*, 224.
63 Karwan Fatah-Black, *White Lies and Black Markets: Evading Metropolitan Authority in Colonial Suriname* (Leiden: Brill, 2015), 42–7, 62. Zeeuws Archief, Archief van de Staten van Zeeland, 2035/22, Johan Tressy to the States of Zeeland, c. June 1668.
64 Schnurmann, *Atlantische Welten*, 240–4.
65 Fatah-Black, "Suriname and the Atlantic World, 1650–1800" (Ph.D. dissertation, University of Leiden, 2013). 94–5.
66 Pitman, *Development*, 197, 203.
67 Fatah-Black, *White Lies and Black Markets*, 49. Bernstein, *Origins of Inter-American Interest*, 17.
68 David S. Lovejoy, *Rhode Island Politics and the American Revolution, 1760–1776* (Providence, R.I.: Brown University Press, 1958), 19.
69 Gilman M. Ostrander, "Colonial Molasses Trade," *Agricultural History* 30 (1956): 79.
70 Fatah-Black, *White Lies and Black Markets*, 60–1.
71 Johannes Postma, "Breaching the Mercantile Barriers of the Dutch Colonial Empire: North American Trade with Surinam during the Eighteenth Century," *Merchant Organization and Maritime Trade in the North Atlantic, 1660–1815*, ed. Olaf Uwe Janzen (St. John's, Newfoundland: International Maritime Economic History Association, 1998), 114–5. Postma, "Suriname and its Atlantic Connections," 300–4. Fatah-Black, *White Lies and Black Markets*, 48. William Douglass, *A Summary, Historical and Political, of the First Planting, Progressive Improvements, and Present State of the British Settlements in North-America* (Boston, 1755), 108. Suriname's demand for horses declined after 1750, due to the relocation of many sugar estates to the coastal lowlands, where water mills could be used instead of animal mills. Postma, "Suriname and its Atlantic Connections," 301, 303.
72 Richard Pares, *Yankees and Creoles: The trade between North America and the West Indies before the American Revolution* (Cambridge, MA: Harvard University Press, 1956), 106–7.
73 Fatah-Black, *White Lies and Black Markets*, 179–80.
74 Fatah-Black, *White Lies and Black Markets*, 166.
75 Van der Oest, "Forgotten Colonies," 357.

76 Bram Hoonhout, "De noodzaak van smokkelhandel in Essequebo and Demerary, 1750–1800." *Tijdschrift voor Zeegeschiedenis* 32, 2 (2013): 65.
77 Gert Oostindie, "'British Capital, Industry and Perseverance' versus Dutch 'Old School'? The Dutch Atlantic and the Takeover of Berbice, Demerara and Essequibo, 1750–1815," *BMGN – Low Countries Historical Review* 127[4] (2012): 36. Frank van de Kreeke, "Essequebo en Demerary, 1741–1781: beginfase van de Britse overname" (Master's thesis, University of Leiden, 2013), 57.
78 Rawle Farley, "The Economic Circumstances of the British Annexation of British Guiana (1795–1815)," *Revista de Historia de América*, 39 (1955): 38.
79 Hoonhout, "De noodzaak van smokkelhandel," 62. Van der Oest, "Forgotten Colonies," 353.
80 McGowan, "French Revolutionary Period," 12–4. Farley, "Economic Circumstances," 31. Oostindie, "British Capital, Industry and Perseverance," 49.
81 Klooster, "Curaçao as a Transit Center to the Spanish Main and the French West Indies." *Dutch Atlantic Connections*, eds. Oostindie and Roitman, 40–2.
82 Klooster, *Illicit Riches*, 84–6. Reinders Folmer-Van Prooijen, *Van goederenhandel naar slavenhandel*. After 1744, when France entered the War of Jenkins' Ear, the same company sent ships to Statia with china, furniture, sailcloth, and specie intended for the trade-starved French Caribbean. Enthoven, "Atlantic Shipping," 333.
83 Governor the Earl of Bellomont to Council of Trade and Plantations, New York, November 7, 1698, in J.W. Fortescue, *Calendar of State Papers, Colonial Series, Colonial Series, America and West Indies*, Vol. 16: 1697–1698 (London: Her Majesty's Stationery Office, 1905). Vol. 16: 531. Virginia D. Harrington, *The New York Merchant on the Eve of the Revolution* (New York: Columbia University Press, 1935), 255, 268.
84 Cathy Matson, *Merchants and Empire: Trading in Colonial New York*. (Baltimore: The Johns Hopkins University Press, 1998), 146–9, 208–11.
85 Schnurmann, *Atlantische Welten*, 350–3. Koot, *Empire at the Periphery*, 153, 203.
86 Universiteitsbibliotheek Leiden, Stukken betreffende de West-Indische Compagnie, "Lijst der scheepen, welke uit de Engelsche Colonien eenige goederen over Engeland of Schotland te Rotterdam hebben aangebragt," January 1750–January 9, 1759, appendix in a letter from the Maze Admiralty, October 19, 1759.
87 Marianne S. Wokeck, *Trade in Strangers: The Beginnings of Mass Migration to North America* (University Park: The Pennsylvania State University Press, 1999).
88 Fatah-Black, *White Lies and Black Markets*, 47–54.
89 Van de Kreeke, "Essequebo en Demerary," 29, 30, 43.
90 Pitman, *Development*, 211, 278–9. The amount of sugar from the French islands that was sold on Statia to English merchants was actually modest, at least in the period 1768–79. Of all sugar that left Statia – a small portion of which was locally produced – only an average of 11.6 percent was shipped to destinations in the British empire, while the remainder was largely transported to the Dutch Republic. The percentage sent to British destinations fluctuated from 13.9 (1768) to 19.4 (1770) to 1.4 (1779), while the percentage shipped to the Dutch Republic went from 85.1 (1768) via 79.3 (1770) to 97.9 (1779). Calculated on the basis of Menkman, "Sint Eustatius' gouden tijd," 383.
91 NAN, NWIC 1188, Simon de Graaff et al. to Commander Jan de Windt. St. Eustatius, March 30, 1754. Knappert, *Geschiedenis*, 255–8. Goslinga, *Dutch in the Caribbean and Guianas*, 212.

References

Akenson, Donald Harman. *If the Irish Ran the World: Montserrat, 1630–1730* (Montreal: McGill-Queen's University Press, 1997).

Andrews, Charles M. *The Colonial Period of American History*, 4 vols. (New Haven: Yale University Press, 1938).

Bernstein, Harry. *Origins of Inter-American Interest, 1700–1812* (Philadelphia: University of Pennsylvania Press, 1945).

Bijlsma, R. "Rotterdam's Amerika-vaart in de eerste helft der 17de eeuw," *Bijdragen voor Vaderlandsche Geschiedenis en Oudheidkunde*, 5th series, 3 (1916): 97–142.

Binder, Franz. "Die zeeländische Kaperfahrt 1654–1662," *Archief: Mededelingen van het Zeeuwsch Genootschap der Wetenschappen* (1976): 40–92.

Blérald, Alain Ph. *Histoire économique de la Guadeloupe et de la Martinique: du XVIIe siècle à nos jours* (Paris: Karthala, 1986).

Boogaart, Ernst van den, Pieter Emmer, Peter Klein & Kees Zandvliet, *La expansión holandesa en el Atlántico* (Madrid: Mapfre, 1992).

Boucher, Philip P. *France and the American Tropics to 1700: Tropics of Discontent?* (Baltimore: The Johns Hopkins University Press, 2008).

Butel, Paul. *Histoire des Antilles françaises, XVIIe–XXe siècle* (s.l.: Perrin, 2002). The Count of Peñaranda to King Philip IV. Archivo General de Simancas [AGS], Estado 2070, November 13, 1649.

Davis, Nicholas Darnell. *The Cavaliers and Roundheads of Barbados, 1650–1652* (Demerara: "Argosy" Press, 1883).

de Graaff, Simon et al. to Commander Jan de Windt, NAN, NWIC 1188. St. Eustatius, March 30, 1754.

De Portogysen goeden buurman: Ghetrocken uyt de Registers van syn goet Gebuerschap gehouden in Lisbona, Maringan, Caep Sint Augustijn, Sint Paulo de Loando, en Sant Tomée. Dienende tot Antwoort op het ongefondeerde Brasyls-Schuyt-praetjen, Weest onnosel als de Duyven, En voorsichtich als de Slangen. 1649.

de Vasconcelos, Antonio, deposition, SAA, NA 2859, Fol. 248, May 29, 1658.

Douglass, William. *A Summary, Historical and Political, of the First Planting, Progressive Improvements, and Present State of the British Settlements in North-America* (Boston: R. Baldwin, 1755).

Enthoven, Victor. "That Abominable Nest of Pirates": St. Eustatius and the North Americans, 1680–1780," *Early American Studies: An Interdisciplinary Journal* 1[2] (2012): 239–301.

Enthoven, Victor and Wim Klooster, "Contours of Virginia-Dutch Trade in the Long Seventeenth Century," In *Early Modern Virginia: New Essays on the Old Dominion*, eds. Douglas Bradburn and John Coombs (Charlottesville: University of Virginia Press, 2011).

Enthoven, Victor. In *Mercantilism Reimagined: Political Economy in Early Modern Britain and Its Empire*, eds. Philip J. Stern and Carl Wennerlind (Oxford: Oxford University Press, 2014).

Farley, Rawle. "The Economic Circumstances of the British Annexation of British Guiana (1795–1815)," *Revista de Historia de América*, 39 (1955): 21–59.

Fatah-Black, Karwan Jalal. "Suriname and the Atlantic World, 1650–1800" (Ph.D. dissertation, University of Leiden, 2013).

Fatah-Black, Karwan. *White Lies and Black Markets: Evading Metropolitan Authority in Colonial Suriname* (Leiden: Brill, 2015).

Fortescue, J. W., ed., *Calendar of State Papers, Colonial Series, America and West Indies*, Vol. 16: 1697–1698 (London: Her Majesty's Stationery Office, 1905).

Gelderblom, Oscar. *Zuid-Nederlandse kooplieden en de opkomst van de Amsterdamse stapelmarkt (1578–1630)* (Hilversum: Verloren, 2000).

García Fuentes, Lutgardo. *El comercio español con América*. Sevilla: Excma (Diputación Provincial de Sevilla, 1980).

Goslinga, Cornelis Ch. *The Dutch in the Caribbean and on the Wild Coast, 1580–1680* (Assen: Van Gorcum, 1971).

Goslinga, Cornelis Ch. *The Dutch in the Caribbean and in the Guianas 1680–1791* (Assen: Van Gorcum, 1985).

Gragg, Larry. "'To Procure Negroes': The English Slave Trade to Barbados, 1627–60," *Slavery and Abolition* 16 (1995): 65–84.

Grahn, Lance. *The Political Economy of Smuggling: Regional Informal Economies in Early Bourbon New Granada* (Boulder, Colorado: Westview Press, 1997).

Harlow, Vincent T. *A History of Barbados, 1625–1685* (New York: Negro Universities Press, 1926).

Harrington, Virginia D. *The New York Merchant on the Eve of the Revolution* (New York: Columbia University Press, 1935).

Hoonhout, Bram. "De noodzaak van smokkelhandel in Essequebo and Demerary, 1750–1800." *Tijdschrift voor Zeegeschiedenis* 32[2] (2013): 54–70.

Hullu, J. de. "St. Eustatius, St. Martin en Saba op het laatst van de 18de eeuw" *West-Indische Gids* 1 (1919): 385–93.

Israel, Jonathan I. *Diasporas within a Diaspora: Jews, Crypto-Jews and the World Maritime Empires (1540–1740)* (Leiden: Brill, 2002).

Izard, Miguel. "Contrabandistas, comerciantes e ilustrados," *Boletín Americanista* 20, 28 (1978): 23–86.

Jordaan, Han and Victor Wilson, "The Eighteenth-Century Danish, Dutch and Swedish Free Ports in the Northeastern Caribbean: Continuity and Change," *Dutch Atlantic Connections, 1680–1815: Linking Empires, Bridging Borders*, eds. Gert Oostindie and Jessica Roitman. (Leiden: Brill, 2014), 275–305.

Klarenbeek, Monique. "Grutters op de Antillen: Particuliere kooplieden uit de Republiek op het eiland Sint Christoffel in de zeventiende eeuw," *Tijdschrift voor Zeegeschiedenis* 32[2] (2013): 20–37.

Klooster, Wim. *Illicit Riches: Dutch Trade in the Caribbean, 1648–1795* (Leiden: KITLV Press, 1998).

Klooster, Wim. "Curaçao as a Transit Center to the Spanish Main and the French West Indies." *Dutch Atlantic Connections*, eds. Oostindie and Roitman (Leiden: Brill, 2014), 25–52.

Knappert, L. *Geschiedenis van de Nederlandsche Bovenwindsche eilanden in de 18de eeuw* ('s-Gravenhage: Martinus Nijhoff, 1932).

Koot, Christian J. *Empire at the Periphery: British Colonists, Anglo-Dutch Trade, and the Development of the British Atlantic, 1621–1713* (New York and London: New York University Press, 2011).

Kopperman, Paul E. "Ambivalent allies: Anglo-Dutch relations and the struggle against the Spanish empire in the Caribbean, 1621–1641," *The Journal of Caribbean History* 21[1] (1987): 55–77.

Kreeke, Frank van de. "Essequebo en Demerary, 1741–1781: beginfase van de Britse overname" (Master's thesis, University of Leiden, 2013).

Kupperman, Karen Ordahl. *Providence Island, 1630–1641: The Other Puritan Colony*. (Cambridge: Cambridge University Press, 1993).

Laet, Johannes de. *Iaerlyck Verhael van de Verrichtinghen der Gheoctroyeerde West-Indische Compagnie in derthien Boecken*, eds. S.P. l'Honoré Naber and J.C.M. Warnsinck, 4 vols. ('s-Gravenhage: Martinus Nijhoff, 1931–1937).

Lafleur, Gérard. "Relations avec l'étranger des minorités religieuses aux Antilles françaises (XVIIe–XVIIIe s.)," *Bulletin de la Société d'Histoire de la Guadeloupe* 57–58 (1983): 27–44.

Lovejoy, David S. *Rhode Island Politics and the American Revolution, 1760–1776* (Providence, R.I.: Brown University Press, 1958).

Matson, Cathy. *Merchants and Empire: Trading in Colonial New York*. (Baltimore: The Johns Hopkins University Press, 1998).

McCusker, John J. and Russell R. Menard, "The Sugar Industry in the Seventeenth Century: A New Perspective on the Barbadian "Sugar Revolution," *Sugar and the Making of the Atlantic World, 1450–1680*, ed. Stuart B. Schwartz (Chapel Hill & London: The University of North Carolina Press, 2004), 289–331.

McGowan, Winston F. "The French Revolutionary Period in Demerara-Essequibo, 1793–1802," *History Gazette* [Guyana] 55 (April 1993): 1–18.

Menkman, W. R. "Sint Eustatius' gouden tijd," *West-Indische Gids* 14 (1932–33): 369–96.

Mims, Stewart L. *Colbert's West India Policy* (New Haven: Yale University Press, 1912).

Murray, W. G. D. "De Rotterdamsche toeback-coopers," *Rotterdamsch jaarboekje*, 5th series, 1 (1943): 18–83.

O'Callaghan, E.B., ed., *Documents Relative to the Colonial History of the State of New-York; Procured in Holland, England and France by John Romeyn Brodhead, Vol. I* (Albany, NY: Weed, Parsons, 1856).

Oest, Eric Willem van der. "The Forgotten Colonies of Essequibo and Demerara, 1700–1814," *Riches from Atlantic Commerce: Dutch Trans-Atlantic Trade and Shipping, 1585–1817*, eds. Johannes Postma and Victor Enthoven (Leiden and Boston: Brill, 2003), 323–361.

Oostindie, Gert. "'British Capital, Industry and Perseverance" versus Dutch 'Old School'? The Dutch Atlantic and the Takeover of Berbice, Demera and Essequibo, 1750–1815," *BMGN – Low Countries Historical Review* 127[4] (2012): 28–55.

Ostrander, Gilman M. "The Colonial Molasses Trade," *Agricultural History* 30 (1956): 77–84.

Pares, Richard. *Yankees and Creoles: The trade between North America and the West Indies before the American Revolution* (Cambridge, MA: Harvard University Press, 1956).

Parker, Matthew. *The Sugar Barons: Family, Corruption, Empire, and War in the West Indies*. (New York: Walker & Company, 2011).

Pitman, Frank Wesley. *The Development of the British West Indies, 1700–1763* (New Haven: Yale University Press, 1917).

Pluchon, Pierre. *Histoire des Antilles et de la Guyane* (Toulouse: Edouard Privat, 1982).

Porter, Robert D. "European activity on the Gold Coast, 1620–1667" (Ph.D. dissertation, University of South Africa, 1975).

Postma, Johannes. "Breaching the Mercantile Barriers of the Dutch Colonial Empire: North American Trade with Surinam during the Eighteenth Century," *Merchant Organization and Maritime Trade in the North Atlantic, 1660–1815*, ed. Olaf Uwe Janzen (St. John's, Newfoundland: International Maritime Economic History Association, 1998), 107–131.

Postma, Johannes. "Suriname and its Atlantic Connections, 1667–1795," *Riches from Atlantic Commerce*, eds. Postma and Enthoven (Leiden: Brill, 2003), 287–322.

Ratelband, Klaas. *Nederlanders in West-Afrika 1600–1650: Angola, Kongo en São Tomé* (Zutphen: Walburg Pers, 2000).

Reinders Folmer-Van Prooijen, C. *Van goederenhandel naar slavenhandel: De Middelburgse Commercie Compagnie, 1720–1755* (Middelburg: Koninklijk Zeeuwsch Genootschap der Wetenschappen, 2000).
Sanz, Eufemio Lorenzo. *Comercio de España con América en la época de Felipe II*, 2 vols. (Valladolid: Servicio de Publicaciones de la Diputación Provincial de Valladolid, 1980).
Schnurmann, Claudia. *Atlantische Welten: Engländer und Niederländer im amerikanisch-atlantischen Raum 1648–1713* (Köln: Böhlau Verlag, 1998).
Schreuder, Yda. "The Influence of the Dutch Colonial Trade in Barbados in the Seventeenth Century," *Journal of the Barbados Museum and Historical Society* 48 (2002): 43–63.
Schreuder, Yda. "Evidence from the Notarial Protocols in the Amsterdam Municipal Archives about Trade Relationships between Amsterdam and Barbados in the Seventeenth Century," *Journal of the Barbados Museum and Historical Society* 52 (2006): 54–83.
Serrano Mangas, Fernando. *Armadas y flotas de la plata (1620–1648)* (Madrid: Banco de España, 1990).
Spooner, Frank C. *Risks at Sea: Amsterdam Insurance and Maritime Europe, 1766–1780* (Cambridge: Cambridge University Press, 1983).
Stols, Eddy. "Gens des Pays-Bas en Amérique Espagnole aux premiers siècles de la colonization" *Bulletin de l'Institut Historique Belge de Rome* 44 (1974): 565–99.
Tarrade, Jean. "Le commerce entre les Antilles françaises et les possessions espagnoles d'Amérique à la fin du XVIIIe siècle," *Commerce et plantation dans la Caraïbe XVIIIe et XIXe siècles: Actes du Colloque de Bordeaux, 15–16 mars 1991*, ed. Paul Butel (Bordeaux: Maison des Pays Ibériques, 1992).
Teellinck, Ewout. *De tweede wachter, brengende tijdinghe vande nacht, dat is, Van het overgaen vande Bahia, met Eenen heylsamen raedt, wat daer over te doen staet* ('s-Graven-haghe: Aert Meurs, 1625).
Truxes, Thomas M. "Transnational Trade in the Wartime North Atlantic: The Voyage of the Snow 'Recovery'," *The Business History Review* 79, 4 (2005): 751–780.
Wätjen, Hermann. *Das holländische Kolonialreich in Brasilien: Ein Kapitel aus der Kolonialgeschichte des 17. Jahrhunderts* ('s-Gravenhage: Martinus Nijhoff, Gotha: Perthes, 1921).
Wilson, Charles. *Profit and Power: A Study of England and the Dutch Wars* (London, New York and Toronto: Longmans, Green, 1957).
Wokeck, Marianne S. *Trade in Strangers: The Beginnings of Mass Migration to North America* (University Park: The Pennsylvania State University Press, 1999).

15
ATLANTIC, WESTERN, AND CONTINENTAL EARLY AMERICA[1]

Paul W. Mapp

How best to approach the history of early America is always a matter of discussion. In classrooms, it has often been a case of studying the colonies that gave rise to modern nations like the United States, Canada, and Mexico. Imperial schools of early American history have called more attention to the dynamics of the empires of which these colonies were a part. An alternative hemispheric paradigm, articulated classically by Herbert Bolton in 1932, has seen the Americas, north and south, as having a common history.[2] More recently, Atlantic history, with its emphasis on the myriad interactions among the diverse peoples, empires, and economies ringing the Atlantic Basin has been intellectually ascendant. Alongside Atlantic history, what we might call "North American continental history" has tried to treat not just the British colonies, French America, the Spanish Borderlands, or the extraimperial Amerindian West in isolation, but rather all of these regions and polities together. A shorthand way of thinking of the continental paradigm is as the addition of the North American West to the early American East.

Continental history, like all the approaches to early American history, has its detractors. For the paradigm of Atlantic history, and from the perspectives of the great Atlantic empires, a continental view of early American history has often seemed less than appealing because the early modern North American West has traditionally been considered of limited historical importance. Before the late eighteenth century, the Spanish, French, and British Empires seemingly had little to do with and, in fact, little information about large parts of western North America. Those parts of the West they were concerned with were literally and often figuratively marginal to the Atlantic world.

The British Empire offers the most extreme case of limited interest and involvement in the Far West. Before the Seven Years' War, Britain's empire was, in large part, a maritime affair of the Atlantic seaboard and Caribbean islands. During the first century-and-a-half of British settlement in mainland North America, the Appalachians, New France, Louisiana, France's Indian allies, and perhaps a certain want of inland initiative confined a substantial British presence to lands within reach of the Atlantic.

There were exceptions. Francis Drake sailed up the Pacific Coast at least as far as northern California in 1579, part of a spectacular but singular circumnavigation. Carolina trader Thomas Welch reached the Mississippi in 1698, and other Carolinians moved west from Charles Town in the decades that followed. By the mid-eighteenth century, Virginia and Pennsylvania land speculators were coveting the Ohio Country and traders and hunters were pushing into it. But Drake was a fleeting presence, and he left so little evidence at the bay where he spent five weeks that its exact location remains a matter of sometimes fanciful controversy. The Carolinians were checked by Louisiana; and it would take a global war to secure the British claim to the Ohio Valley and another half-century of conflict to overwhelm indigenous opposition to Anglo-American settlement. The center of mass of Britain's prerevolutionary mainland American colonies lay east of the Appalachians—a long way from Drake's Bay.

The more significant exception to the limited extent of British involvement in the West was not Drake, Carolina traders, or the Ohio Country, but the Hudson's Bay Company and its fur trading posts along the great maritime indentation of the North. Hudson Bay was, along with the Mississippi and St. Lawrence Rivers, one of the three main water routes into the North American interior. Its forts along the bay gave the Hudson's Bay Company the opportunity to push explorers and enterprise far to the west, as the company would do in the nineteenth century. From its founding in 1670 until after the Seven Years' War, however, the company largely preferred, in the words of a 1752 critic, to remain asleep "at the edge of a frozen sea." As the eminent historian of American exploration Glyndwr Williams has so well established, before mid-eighteenth opponents challenged its chartered monopoly of the Hudson Bay trade, the company generally preferred to restrict its activities to its bayside forts, having Indians bring furs to its traders rather than sending traders and goods inland to the Indians. Exploration in the northern interior was dangerous and expensive, profits from the littoral trading posts relatively small, but also relatively reliable. It was from 1754 and the journey of Anthony Henday that the company began serious efforts at exploration, and only in the 1770s that it began establishing inland posts and launching frequent and productive expeditions.[3]

If Britain's was the North American Empire with the most negligible western presence, France's trading, proselytizing, and alliance-making, centered in the Great Lakes, Illinois Country, and lower Mississippi Valley, offers the best example of European dynamism in the early West. Although French traders, missionaries, and explorers made it farther west than their pre-Seven Years' War British counterparts, even their intrepidity was limited in reach and left much for late eighteenth- and early nineteenth-century British and Anglo-American successors like Alexander Mackenzie, Meriwether Lewis, and William Clark to accomplish. In 1739, an expedition under the brothers Pierre and Paul Mallet made it from the Illinois Country to Santa Fe, but Spanish authorities had no desire to let them go further. On the contrary, Spanish officials were apprehensive about the possibility of French trade with what were supposed to be exclusively Spanish markets. They were alarmed by the French provision of guns to plains Indians, many of whom had already acquired Spanish horses. They worried about French alliance with Indian nations like the Comanches and Wichitas, and feared that traders like the Mallets might be harbingers of a French invasion not just of penurious New Mexico, but also of silver-rich New Spain.

Farther north, members of the La Vérendrye family pushed west to Lake Winnipeg and into what are now the Dakotas. In 1738–39, Pierre Gaultier de Varennes et de la Vérendrye led an expedition from Fort La Reine on the Assiniboine River south of Lake Manitoba to the Mandan Villages of the upper Missouri River. In 1743, his sons Louis-Joseph and François espied what were probably the Black Hills before their "Bow Indian" hosts' fear of mounted "Snake" Indian raiders forced a halt. Whoever these Snakes may have been, perhaps the ancestors of the Shoshones later encountered by the Lewis and Clark Expedition, the most substantial obstacle to French expansion on the Northern Plains were the Sioux. In a superb recent book on Indian slavery in New France, Brett Rushforth has offered a forceful explanation of why this was the case. He contends that enemies of the Sioux like the Crees, Assiniboines, and Monsonis gave and sold Sioux captives to French traders, who in turn had them sold in Montreal. The La Vérendryes were active in this trade. The presence of Sioux slaves in Montreal, as one particularly vivid 1742 account demonstrates, did not endear the French Empire to the Sioux emissaries who saw them. The Sioux might have been, as some Frenchmen proposed, the most desirable allies and trading partners in the West, but the machinations of their enemies and the French demand for slaves ensured that the Sioux would oppose rather than aid French projects. The Missouri route west that Lewis and Clark would later—just—succeed in using was largely closed to their eighteenth-century French predecessors.[4]

North of the Sioux barrier, on the other hand, moving west from Lake Winnipeg and up the Saskatchewan River Valley, French explorers continued toward the Pacific into the early 1750s. The evidence is inconclusive, but, in 1751, a party dispatched by Jacques Legardeur de Saint-Pierre may have glimpsed the Canadian Rockies. The Seven Years' War, however, interrupted French expeditions in what are now Saskatchewan and Alberta. St. Pierre died fighting the British at New York's Lake George in 1755.

French traders and explorers made it far, but they never found an inland western sea, a Northwest Passage, the Columbia or Colorado Rivers, the Pacific Coast, or the fortune-making trade with wealthy New Spain they sought. Instead, Virginians Meriwether Lewis and William Clark led the Euro-American expedition that first succeeded in descending the great river of the West; and another Virginian, William Becknell, played a key role in establishing the Santa Fe Trail in the 1820s.

What of the western Spanish colonies to which the Santa Fe Trail and the dreams of French, British, and Anglo-American avarice so often led? Spain established an earlier and more westerly presence in occidental North America than did France and Britain. These Spanish outposts were one goal of westering French explorers and traders—and indeed of a handful of British mariners pushing toward and sometimes around Cape Horn to the Pacific. Given the undeniable historical importance of the Spanish Empire and the durable allure of Spanish imperial wealth to Spain's European rivals, Spain's western establishments might seem an irrefutable claim to the early significance of western North America. Like France and Britain, however, early modern Spain's limited reach left most of the West untouched. Despite the extraordinary voyages of Spanish mariners, the arduous journeys of Spanish conquistadors, and the persistent efforts of Spanish missionaries, most of the North American West was beyond rather than within the range of Spanish control, or even Spanish cognizance. From the 1520s to the first decade of the seventeenth century, Spanish expeditions discovered—in the sense of making familiar to Spanish outsiders—a good part of the Southwest. From 1528 to 1536, Alvar Núñez Cabeza de Vaca trekked from coastal Florida and Texas to what is now northwestern Mexico. In 1540–42, Vásquez de Coronado pushed north up the Rio Grande Valley and west across the southern Plains into what is now Kansas. The Juan de Oñate *entrada* of 1598–1605 included a reconnaissance of the Grand Canyon as well as another foray onto the Southern Plains, this one stymied by hostile "Escanxaques." In this same period one Spanish naval expedition under Hernando de Alarcón made it up the Colorado to its junction with the Gila in 1540, and another under Bartolomé Ferrelo may have reached as far north as Cape Blanco on the southern Oregon Coast in 1543.

Of the most lasting significance for the Southwest was the establishment by Oñate and his successors of a precarious, but lasting Spanish colony in New Mexico. New Mexico, along with the British Hudson Bay forts and the French fur traders and missionaries of the Great Lakes region, was one of the three major European western salients. How great New Mexico's influence on the larger West was is difficult to ascertain, but it certainly, as Ned Blackhawk has recently and eloquently argued, extended European diseases and the Spanish demand for Indian slave labor into the Great Basin and onto the Southern Plains.[5] The colony provided, moreover, especially after the 1680 Pueblo Revolt temporarily drove Spanish New Mexicans south to El Paso, the escaped and captured horses that would thrive on the Plains, allow for an equestrian revolution there, and become so iconic a feature of the West that it can be difficult to remember that horses had been extinct in North America for millennia before the Spanish reintroduced them.

An important salient, New Mexico was still only a salient. After the first decade of the seventeenth century, Spanish exploration of and expansion into North America stalled. The Pacific Coast had turned out to be a nightmare of rocks, fog, cold, and contrary currents, and nothing seen there justified the risk or cost of sending returning Manila Galleons or specially commissioned exploratory vessels along these hazardous shores. It was true that the existence of a Northwest Passage remained a possibility, and a chronicler of Sebastian Vizcaíno's 1602–03 expedition even claimed that one of its ships had reached the passage's entrance, but possible was not probable. Moreover, Spanish officials were aware that if Spanish ships did locate such a passage, it might be French and British vessels that would use it to open an illicit trade with Spanish Pacific ports. Inland, Spanish expeditions like Coronado's and Onate's had encountered the arid and featureless southern Plains, the rugged mountains and deserts of the Southwest, a host of Indian peoples quite capable of killing Spaniards, but nothing like the civilizations, empires, and riches of Mexico and Peru that would justify substantial efforts to extend Spanish dominion beyond the settled and moderately prosperous peoples of the Rio Grande Valley. It was only in the 1680s, in response to rumors of René-Robert, Cavalier de La Salle's 1682 descent of the Mississippi, and again after the 1699 establishment of a French presence in Louisiana that the Spanish Empire began a halting, mission-based push into Texas. And it was only in the 1760s, impelled in part by imperial concerns about Russian and British moves into the Pacific, that the Franciscans launched their missionary efforts in upper California. Even the precocious and world-spanning Spanish Empire was largely external to most of the North American West.

Moreover, as intriguing as these early modern western historical developments were, nineteenth-century events sometimes made it appear as though they did not much matter, as though they did little to shape the modern continent: the early West was seemingly overwhelmed by the modern East. The United States deprived the Spanish Empire's Mexican successor state of its northern territories and the territories' varied inhabitants of much of their land. Farther north, despite determined resistance, Indian peoples were repeatedly vanquished by disease, famine, and warfare. Western Indians did not vanish, as their descendants have been more and more effectively pointing out, but they became a small enough percentage of the population in much of the West that scholars could write for decades as though they had. Having had the modern United States and Canada imposed upon it, the early modern West appeared to many scholars to be a historical dead end, another stage on which developments originating in the East could unfold. Why bother with the early West if the really decisive history came from the early East? And why bother with early modern continental history if the contours of modern North America were determined by Atlantic and eastern America?

Atlantic and early American scholars should extend their attention to include the early West, and indeed the North American continent as a whole, most simply because the temporal depth, geographic connections, and cultural interaction the continent's western reaches place before the eyes of historians offer so much more of the kinds of material investigators are currently and rightly interested in. Inclusion of the West puts peoples like the Sioux, Apaches, Mandans, and the Spanish-Puebloan population of New Mexico on the historical stage much longer than is the case if they are merely fringe characters of Latin American history or foils for the nineteenth-century United States. They become, literally, the actors they actually were, as much so as the Anglo-American interlopers who have dominated so much of the traditional historiography. As it puts Western peoples on the stage longer, a continental approach to early America also expands the stage, not just because it means encompassing a larger part of North America, but more because consideration of the West inevitably leads to contemplation of the region's connections to the Spanish Empire and the many worlds of the early modern Pacific. Including the West aids the transition from American to global history.

As attention to the continent as a whole highlights global connections, it also brings into sharper relief the human contacts—sometimes gentle, often brutal—that were creating hybrid American populations and cultures. The early West points to, it is increasingly clear from recent scholarship, a "mestizo America," in the sense that the tendency of the region before Anglo-American dominance and exclusivism imposed themselves was toward the mixing of Indigenousand Old World peoples. What this temporal depth and these geographic and human connections really add up to is the argument that adding a chunk of western territory to early American and Atlantic history enables scholars to satisfy our inclusive and culturally variegated twenty-first-century sense of humanity.

It is usually best to place grand claims within precise definitions, and, having thrown around terms like "the West" and "continental history," it would be a good idea at this point to say what they mean. The definition of continental is fairly straightforward. A continental approach to early American history generally includes all of the continent north of Mesoamerica and its near borderlands, and usually treats the Caribbean islands as well. The common practice is to take the different regions of North America in succession, but a noteworthy feature in the recent work of some intrepid scholars—Elizabeth Fenn and Pekka Hämäläinen are good examples—is the ability to see American historical patterns on a continental scale.[6]

Delimiting the North American West and distinguishing it from the North American East and Mesoamerica is trickier. A good working definition of the early West is those parts of North America west of Hudson Bay, the Great Lakes, and the Mississippi River; north of the Rio Grande to around El Paso, and then north of a line running roughly west from El Paso to the Pacific. Generally speaking, these areas were at some distance from the Atlantic Ocean—and usually even from its Hudson Bay and Gulf of Mexico extensions—and thus removed from the centers of Atlantic commerce and colonization. Much of the West was hard to get to from the Atlantic Basin, by land or water.

Beyond this geographically defining feature of remoteness, a politically defining feature of the West was the absence of a large-scale, rich, urbanized, socially complex, centralized, and lettered empire like the Aztec Empire encountered by Cortés. There were many Western polities, perhaps, if we accept Pekka Hämäläinen's grand claims about the Comanches, a kind of brigand empire had taken shape on the Southern Plains by the early nineteenth century.[7] The imposing Amerindian community that scholars have called "Cahokia"—its still prominent mounds a kind of argument in relief for the significance of the pre-Columbian cultures of the Mississippi Valley—was very possibly a hegemon of the area around its location at the junction of the Missouri and Mississippi Rivers during the city's heyday from the eleventh to thirteenth centuries. Such cases notwithstanding, there was no early modern or pre-Columbian emperor of the West, no capital of a really vast part of the region, no corps of administrators. Following from this political decentralization was the difficulty for early modern outsiders and, consequently, later scholars, of obtaining information about the region, because such information does not seem to have been gathered and organized by an empire as was the case in Mexico and Peru. Moreover, the lack of a centralized transportation system like the famous roads of the Inca Empire meant that it was relatively difficult to move around much of the West's difficult terrain. The West was not easily accessible to outsiders.

In fact, many of the cultures of the transmontane West appear to have been somewhat isolated from those of other parts of the Americas. Some of the key Western tongues belonged to language families like Salish/Salishan that were not found outside the Western parts of the continent. Upper California, the Columbia Basin, and the northern Pacific Coast seem almost to have been on different planets than the eastern woodlands. (We might even ask, inspired by Franz Boas's 1897 Jesup North Pacific Expedition and its consideration of cultural commonalities among peoples on both sides of the Bering Strait, if the maritime Pacific Northwest, behind successive mountain ranges—supporting wealthy and complex cultures on a foundation of salmon rather than corn, washed by an ocean current that touches Japan—wasn't as much part of a North Pacific world as a North American continent.) Such mention of distinctive cultures, or perhaps simply a diversity of cultures, shouldn't cause us to discount the trade connections and movements of peoples and customs that connected distant parts of North America. Well-trodden paths crossed Northwestern mountain ranges, Indians from across the Rockies traded at the Mandan villages on the upper Missouri. The Puebloan communities of New Mexico and what is now southern Arizona seem to have been tied to Mesoamerica by trade routes and cultural influence, as indicated by ball courts in the Southwest and turquoise moving south from the region in exchange for feathers and bells. Much of the West was remote from much of North America and most of the world, but none of it was hermetically sealed.

What all of the West was before the Spanish started describing it in writing, and most of it was even after European expeditions started investigating the region, was poor in documents. Early modern Spanish, French, British, and Russian authors wrote relatively little about the West and knew relatively little about most of the region. The Indian peoples of the West did not leave behind a corpus of sources comparable to those in languages like Nahuatl that can inform scholars about early and premodern Mexico. This paucity of written records is one of the main reasons historians long kept their distance from the early modern West: their sources didn't allow them to do much with it. This is enormously frustrating, because we know enough to know that there was a lot worth knowing. What could historians do with an early account of the Columbia River's Dalles trading site comparable to Bernal Díaz del Castillo's description of Tenochtitlán?

There are a number of possible responses to this evidentiary difficulty, responses other than giving up, that is. If the early West was one of those parts of the world, like interior Africa, that outsiders didn't know much about, we can make a virtue of that ignorance by using it to raise the question of what about region or outside investigators made it so difficult to apprehend. This question becomes more interesting when posed in comparative terms. Early modern Europeans came to know a good deal about Mexico, Peru, large parts of China, and even Siberia. What made the one set of areas relatively accessible to European inquiry while the West frustrated outsiders for centuries? In short, we can make the difficulty of investigation a subject of inquiry. Long inability to see the West becomes a reason to look at it.

Or, we can think of the early West and the continent of which it was a part as a kind of incipient character in global history. If one defining feature of continental North America was the absence of the kind of imperial governance and cultural complexity evident in Mesoamerica, someone, a Jared Diamond or William McNeill, for instance, might very well ask where they were.[8] One way to get at this question is to recall a question from McNeill's seminal 1963 *Rise of the West*. In one of those suggestive digressions that makes McNeill's writing so fascinating, he remarked at one point that archaeologists had only unearthed evidence of the Indus Valley Civilization in the 1920s, and he wondered whether and where other such lost civilizations might be found. He mentioned the Oxus and Jaxartes river valleys. Given the prominence of the Tigris-Euphrates, Nile, Yellow, and Ganges rivers in McNeill's global history and in so many histories of early developments around the world, he might just as well have looked at early modern locales closer to his University of Chicago base, like the Rio Grande and Mississippi-Missouri valleys, where cultivation of the great trinity of corn, beans, and squash was laying a foundation for the towns, social hierarchy, and refined craft production that have marked the development of complex societies around the world. The sites of some of these developments are almost visible from the tops of Chicago's skyscrapers. Fifty years ago in *Rise of the West*, McNeill wasn't much interested in the early Americas, but the kinds of historical change so crucial to global history were taking place there. McNeill's successors, today's world and global history textbooks, aided by a half-century of scholarly research, are attentive to the kind of historical and prehistorical dynamism characterizing the African, Austronesian, and American areas once invisible in so much of the scholarly big picture.[9]

Another way we can make something of the maddening nescience of European sources is to treat comparatively the purposes benightedness could serve. Brett Rushforth's study of Indian slavery in New France offers an illustrative example. In the African interior, south of the Sahara and north of what seventeenth-century French writers called "Guinea," was the convenient fiction of Nigritie: a powerful, distant, ill-defined kingdom allegedly enslaving and trading in human beings. Apologists for French involvement in the African slave trade could claim that Nigritie justified French purchase of slaves because the origin of their bondage lay with a political other. The North American equivalent was the remote, ill-defined Panis nation somewhere in the obscurity of the upper Missouri West, its members enslaved by other Indians and sold to Frenchmen whose distant hands remained theoretically clean. Uncertain, unverifiable ideas about human and political geography could be employed to rationalize involvement in slavery. Those shifting forms on the edges of European maps and consciousness were a little like the ink blots of a Rorschach Test, hinting at the cultural logic that made certain justifications for slavery seem necessary or persuasive.[10]

There are now, however, easier ways to enter early Western and continental American history than through the interpretation of absence, ignorance, and errant conceptions; for geographical barriers like the imposing Rockies and forbidding Plains don't necessarily separate the Far West from Atlantic history. Paradoxically, though the West was defined in many respects by its remoteness from the Atlantic Ocean, Atlantic history leads naturally to the inclusion of the region in the story of early America. One reason has to do with the geography of North America and the multi-imperial interests of Atlantic history. In the past, for a scholar specializing in traditional fashion on the history of the Spanish, French, or British Empires, the West was a peripheral subject, a matter of the lands and peoples mostly beyond his or her immediate field of study. The West was studied in the language of frontiers and marches, borders and hinterlands. Many Atlantic historians still concentrate on one of the great Atlantic empires, but many consider more than one, and it is fair to say that even specialists now are cognizant of the importance and interaction of the multiple polities—imperial and otherwise—of the Atlantic world. This is important, because when a contemporary Atlantic historian sees North America from the vantage point not of the Spanish, French, or British empires separately, but of the Spanish, French, and British (and even Russian) empires simultaneously, the West goes from being peripheral to one empire to being central to three or four of them.

This is more than one of those geographic statements that captures attention without addressing a question; for it is directly relevant to the evidentiary issues mentioned above. The great problem for the study of those Western areas beyond or even at the edge of the literate empires, it almost goes without saying, is written evidence. Historians would love to say more about the early modern Columbia Basin, but it is difficult to do so when a key site like the Dalles has left us more fish bones than written records. Atlantic history cannot pen the documents that were never written, but the Atlantic historian's habit of casting wide the evidentiary net does tend to multiply the available documents. Three or four literate empires have more to say than one. Looking at Western evidence penned in New Mexico and the Missouri Valley, or Hudson

Bay and the western Great Lakes starts to fill in some blanks left by an examination solely of Spanish, French, or British records. We can use the La Vérendryes' Northern Plains interrogations of western Indians to learn about the cultural reach of Spanish New Mexico, or 1720s New Mexico hide paintings to raise questions about the presence of Frenchmen at the 1720 defeat of the Spanish Villasur Expedition in what is now Nebraska, or the testimony of Hudson Bay Company factors to trace the transmission of Spanish trade goods. In some cases, Spanish, French, and British sources allow for a kind of evidentiary triangulation.

An interesting example of this kind of triangulation comes from a collection of what might, at first glance, seem simply to be fabulous rumors of distant Western peoples. The party Pierre and Paul Mallet led from the Illinois country to New Mexico in 1739 spent nine months in the Spanish colony. In an abstract of their journal, the Mallets reported having heard in New Mexico of a "tradition" concerning a country of large seaside towns inhabited by silk-wearing white men and lying three months to the west.[11] Given the commercial and strategic importance that Chinese or Japanese settlements on the North American coast would have held for the French Empire, it is tempting to write this report off as the wishful thinking of gullible French traders or an effort to write what French officials wanted to hear. But it's best to accompany a healthy skepticism with an open mind. The Mallets were, after all, not the only authors hinting at some kind of wealthy, sophisticated, extra-American people on the Pacific Coast. In 1721, Father Pierre-Francois-Xavier de Charlevoix wrote of having "met at la Baye (Green Bay) some Sioux, whom I closely questioned about the Regions which are West and North-West of Canada." Charlevoix averred that he had "every reason to believe, in comparing what they have related to me with what I have heard from several other sources, that there are on this Continent Spanish or other European Colonies—far more to the North than those of which we have knowledge in New Mexico or California."[12]

Earlier than Charlevoix and the Mallets, Spanish explorer Antonio de Espejo wrote of hearing at Zuni Pueblo in 1583 about "a large lake where the natives claimed there were many towns. These people told us that there was gold in the lake region, that the inhabitants wore clothes, with gold bracelets and earrings, that they dwelt at a distance of a sixty days' journey from the place where we were."[13] All of these reports may be fanciful, they may be invented, or they may simply be misunderstandings. If rooted in accounts of real places, they may have been different places. But it is at least worth mentioning that late eighteenth-century Spanish, French, British, and United States visitors to the Pacific Northwest wrote of large villages around Puget Sound and the Inside Passage between Vancouver Island and the mainland inhabited by people wearing splendid cedar bark clothing, journeying in large ornately carved canoes, exhibiting copper ornaments, and having what some observers referred to as fair skin. These peoples enjoyed material abundance and displayed remarkable artistic sophistication. It is at least conceivable that reports of these Northwest Coast cultures reached places like Green Bay and New Mexico and made their way into reports like those of Espejo, Charlevoix, and the Mallets. If so, we begin to get a sense of the range of reports in Western America and of the place of one of the region's most remote cultures in the mental geographies of peoples far to the east and south. In isolation, various early European accounts are easily dismissed, and the later observations of Pacific navigators passed over without remark, but when multiple sources from many empires and nations and different angles and times are combined, intriguing questions arise. There is no simple connection of report and referent, and I suspect Espejo was hearing about an area closer to New Mexico than Puget Sound, but simply opening the possibility that disparate reports were referring to a common set of peoples and places stimulates thinking about the circulation of goods, information, and people among the communities of the early modern West. Looking in to the West from multiple evidentiary directions allows for tentative arguments that would be much more difficult if based solely on evidence looking out from a single empire. None of this will make the early Northwest the evidentiary equivalent of the Northeast, but it at least helps us make the most of the documents we have.

As the configuration of North American lands and Atlantic empires makes the West central, the navigational logic of the world's oceans connected the West's Pacific face to Atlantic history. One of the essential features of Atlantic history is that the South Atlantic is stormily joined to rather than impassably separated from the southern Indian and Pacific Oceans. Bartolomeu Dias had figured out how to round Africa before Columbus traversed the Atlantic, and Magellan managed to get into and across the Pacific less than three decades after Columbus sailed the Caribbean. From its earliest days, Atlantic history was maritime history. Moreover, having found only long and dangerous ways of getting around southern Africa and South America, Europeans remained interested in finding shorter and safer ways of getting to the Pacific and Indian Oceans. It took three centuries after Columbus and the meticulous navigation and charting of figures like James Cook and George Vancouver to accept that the Northwest Passage was a chimera. A not entirely inaccurate way of thinking about canals like that of Panama and Suez is simply as the inevitable holes left by four centuries of Europeans banging their heads against walls in their efforts to find easier access to the Indian and Pacific Oceans.

And with good reason, for while the Northwest Passage proved to be a dangerous fantasy—at least before global warming has begun to make it an ominous reality—the importance of the Pacific was both an early modern fact and an accurate prediction of modernity. One of the two founding Atlantic empires was also a Pacific power, with Spanish-American cities stretching from Chile up the west coast of Mexico, and with Spanish galleons laden alternately with silver and silk sailing annually from Acapulco to Manila and back. French and British explorers wanted a Northwest Passage so badly, and French and British navigators naval stations in the South Atlantic and Pacific so intently, not just because of interest in the fabled markets of China and Japan, but also because of a desire to get direct access to the Spanish-American silver crossing the Atlantic or glinting in the markets of Chile and Peru. While the 1529 Luso-Spanish Treaty of Saragossa made the Pacific, in European diplomatic theory, a Spanish Lake, Iberian concords did not stop Dutch, French, and British mariners from craving access to the South Sea and its charted and uncharted shores. Consequently, the Pacific coast of the North American West, whether as the possible site of a Northwest Passage, as the bitter end for a storm-tossed Spanish galleon, as a refuge for Francis Drake or late-seventeenth-century Caribbean pirates trying their luck on the other side of the Isthmus of Panama, or even as the supposed site of East Asian outposts or still undiscovered Amerindian civilizations, was a matter of interest to Atlantic history. Atlantic waters and maritime ambitions flowed to the lands of the American West.

More generally, it is worth remarking on how, in so many of these cases, questions about the West lead logically to comparisons or connections with other parts of the world. This is sometimes a matter of geography, with Pacific currents connecting the American and Asian shores and southern capes of the worlds oceans; sometimes a matter of simultaneous imperial enterprise, France being an affair of Africa and America, as Spain was an empire of the Atlantic and the Pacific; and sometimes a matter of the ratio of subject to evidence, scholars naturally posing big questions about the vast time and space of the West and looking for similar questions about other times and spaces to aid them through comparison. The West points to the world.

If, in a general way, the early American West is a subject made more central, accessible, and interesting by Atlantic history, and more exciting by the easy transition from it to global history, we are still left with the question of what we gain by looking at this rather large chunk of North America. A good place to begin is with the signal benefit of a more sustained engagement with a good part of North America's indigenous peoples.

One emphasis of recent scholarship is on the enduring power of the West's Indian nations, power which lingered long into what is often called the "European colonial period," and, indeed, in the case of particular peoples like the Comanches and Sioux, may have increased in both absolute and relative terms after the arrival of Europeans and the dispersal of their horses and guns. Distinguished recent works by scholars such as Juliana Barr, Kathleen Duval, and Michael Witgen speak of parts of Texas dominated by Caddoan peoples, of the Arkansas River Valley by Quapaws and Osages, of the western Great Lakes by the Ojibway, and of vast stretches of the southern Plains by the Comanches; they speak of Middle Grounds, Native Grounds, Native New Worlds, and Indian cores. The least exciting formulation of these intriguing arguments is to aver that centuries after Columbus reached the Americas, Amerindians held sway over the large parts of South and North America not yet controlled by Europeans. Who has argued the contrary? How could they? Recent historians have gone beyond the mere observation of lingering Indian might, however, using arguments about indigenous power to address historical questions or arrive at surprising explanations. One example is when they assert a higher degree and longer duration of Indian power than expected, as Pekka Hämäläinen contends was the case with the nineteenth-century Comanches, or Michael Witgen claims for the seventeenth-to-twenty-first-century Anishinaabeg (Ojibway).[14]

Another promising tack is to define precisely what is meant by power or control, as Juliana Barr has done with her arguments about clearly defined territorial claims in the case of the Caddos and other southwestern Indian peoples, or Hämäläinen has with his affirmation of a nineteenth-century Comanche empire.[15] Broadly speaking, however, I think that most of these claims of indigenous power still run into the historiographical problem of the relative superiority of the nineteenth-century Euro-American states. However impressive the Comanches, Apaches, Sioux, Osages, Blackfeet, and Caddos may have been, they ended up on the unfortunate side of a nineteenth- and twentieth-century divide between complex industrial societies and everybody else. The old argument that the westward sweep of the United States and Canada renders the prior history of the West relatively inconsequential remains potent even if you argue that Indian peoples were dominant 20 minutes before that sweep occurred.

More rewarding than asserting indigenous power is making the most of Indian longevity; for when scholars take on more Western space, they gain Amerindian time. One way to see this is to begin with one of the classic problems of the classic east-to-west version of North American history: that most individual Indian nations do not stay on the historical stage very long. Powhatans, Pequots, Delawares, Shawnees, or Mohicans, appear, interact with Britons or Americans, alternate between peaceful relations and intense hostilities, end up in a decisive war, lose, and are overwhelmed or pushed onto a reservation. Their tale is a matter of decades.

Including the West in early American and Atlantic history puts many Indian peoples in view for a much longer time. If Cabeza de Vaca and Coronado's Southwest is a part of Atlantic history, the document-based history of the Puebloan peoples conquered by the United States in the Mexican War of the 1840s goes back to the 1530s. If we push our early modern scholarly interest beyond the Great Lakes, the Sioux who defeated Custer have a history of western might dating back at least to the Dakotas' alliance with the Ojibway in the 1660s. If the Southern Plains are included in early American history, the Comanches tantalizing John Wayne in *The Searchers* have ancestors who entered the historical record in 1706—they fit more descriptions than he. If our early America stretches west to the upper Missouri, the Mandan villages visited by Lewis and Clark in 1804–05 are notably similar to those visited by La Vérendrye in 1738–39.

The Mandans are as good an example of temporal depth as any the early West has to offer. In a classic United States history course, the Mandans rise out of their earth lodges, greet Lewis and Clark, turn out not to be Welsh, and Lewis and Clark continue to the mouth of the Columbia.

Later, the Mandans pose for a few portraits before being obliterated by smallpox. Lewis and Clark have traceable roots in Virginia history, and represent a bridge between the history of the modern West and old Virginia—and even old England. Their achievements and place in the narrative of United States expansion make them nearly immortal. The Mandans are temporary curiosities, poignant examples of the vanishing Indian, beautiful portraits, but off the stage too quickly to be appreciated as characters. On the other hand, if the West is a part of early American and Atlantic history, so is La Vérendrye's 1738–39 visit with the Mandans and his description of them as "very industrious," "skillful in dressing leather," and working "very delicately in hair and feathers." One of the Mandan towns had "about one hundred and thirty" "cabins"; "the streets and open spaces" were "very clean," "the ramparts" were "smooth and wide," impregnable to savages"; "their fortification indeed," had "nothing savage about it."[16] It is not just that 1730s Mandans sound quite a bit more urbane than many 1730s Virginians, but that the early 1800s Mandans clearly have a backstory rivaling that of Jefferson's emissaries.

Indeed, one great advantage of taking the early modern West into account is that doing so pulls the brain back into the more distant past. Part of what made the Mandans so striking to La Vérendrye and Lewis and Clark was that the Mandans were taking full advantage of the possibilities opened up by growing corn. This corn is therefore a serious matter, as important as wheat or rice in Eurasia. Was it ahistorical? Had the Mandans' ancestors or had those of other upper Missouri people been cultivating maize since the creation of the world, as some Plains Indian creation stories would seem to indicate? No, at least not in a conventional chronological sense. Archaeological evidence indicates that cultivation of forms of corn came to the upper Missouri by the centuries around ad 1000; for that matter, to the Southwest centuries before Christ. If we take the corn back to its literal and figurative roots in Mexico, the story goes back farther still. In short, the Mandan culture Lewis and Clark and La Vérendrye observed was a product of long-term historical developments, and thinking about that stretch of time between 1738 and 1804 impels the mind to think about those long-term changes that gave rise to the agricultural society glimpsed by Franco and Anglo-American explorers in 1738 and 1804. The recognition of temporal extension leads to the search for greater extension.

The same tendency is evident when we start putting the Puebloan peoples ravaged by Coronado and the southwestern cliff houses visited by National Park enthusiasts on a common timeline: the mind naturally pushes farther back on the timeline to the ancient past of the Americas. The Mandans are a good example because of their association with iconic figures in US history—not to mention their position at the center of a northern Plains trading network, connecting people from the Columbia Basin, Great Lakes, Hudson Bay, and New Mexico. Southwestern communities like the Puebloans are critical because those adobe structures from Mesa Verde to Chaco Canyon are an undeniable physical indicator of a deeper story. Combining a three-century early modern American historical narrative with premodern archaeological and material evidence starts to redress the temporal imbalance of early American history. Europeans coming to the Americas arrived with the Tigris and Euphrates, Stonehenge, Lascaux, and Mycenae in their historical baggage; the Western Amerindians meeting them carried the Colorado, Rio Grande, and Mississippi-Missouri River system, Chaco Canyon, Mesa Verde, the ancient canals of modern Phoenix, the residual northern warmth from Mesoamerican culture hearths, the still visible outlines of ancient Mandan towns. Including the West extends the American story into the past.

And a lost future is as crucial as the gained past, for this consideration of indigenous antiquities suggests not just the significance of what was, but also the importance of what might have been. An evocative way of thinking about this lost future is by way of the nascent complex societies of the West. The earliest European observers of what is now Arizona, New Mexico, and northern Mexico, of the Missouri and other Western tributaries of the Mississippi system, and of the Northwest Coast commented about an awful lot of people harvesting corn, beans, squash, and salmon. Many of these people lived in imposing fortified towns. These communities were connected to one another by various forms of cultural and social affiliation and long-ranging trade routes. Some of these towns and their environs were graced by earthen mounds or even pyramids, adobe-building complexes, and beautifully sculpted wooden poles. Within many of these towns, and among these cultivated fields or harvested waters, there seem to have been marked differences of social status. In some communities, such as those around Nootka Sound during Cook's visit in 1778, there was sufficient leisure time for the "ingenious" sculpting of humans and animals, often "with a degree of accuracy in proportion, and neatness in execution"; and for the placing on garments of images that suggested to one observer that "though there be no appearance of the knowledge of letters amongst them, they have some notion of commemorating and representing actions, in a lasting way, independently of what may be recorded in their songs and traditions."[17] It is not just that these Indians differed from the iconic wandering hunter of John Winthrop, Thomas Jefferson, and James Fennimore Cooper, or from the mounted warrior of Hollywood films, but that they differed from what had gone before. Indians who grew corn, lived in towns, and crossed the Columbia in ocean-worthy canoes had ancestors who did none of these things. Along the Rio Grande and Missouri, communities went from not eating corn to growing it. In the Pacific Northwest, peoples went from fishing and gathering—and living really well—to fishing and gathering and producing forests of sculpture exceeding in artistry and rivaling in beauty the forests around. And as these societies differed from their predecessors, their successors would have differed from them. Historical change would have continued. And that's the key point: the dynamism of so many of the indigenous peoples of the early and premodern West is a reminder that the encounter with the Old World not only devastated many New World peoples, but it also interrupted the historical trajectory of the Americas. The world lost not just what Europeans and their viral and animal companions destroyed, but all those alternative futures cut off by the collision of continents. The early modern West, with its adobe cliff houses, irrigation ditches, trading sites now submerged by dams, mounds now leveled by ploughs, and urban outlines now visible only from the sky, offers us not just evidence of the lost worlds of American antiquity, but of the world lost because of blocked historical developments. Go for a walk on a beautiful western spring day and with the imagination prompted by historical reflection, you can see not just the region's famous natural beauty, not just the undeniable achievements of the United States and Canada, but also hazy outlines of the West that might have taken shape if the Atlantic were wider.

Walking today, one might also see a revival of a key feature of large parts of the early modern West: the blending of cultures and peoples of distant and distinct origins. One theme of some of the most insightful recent books about the region is the increasing prominence in the late eighteenth and early nineteenth centuries of something that had been apparent in the West from the beginnings of European and African contact with the region: the blending of Old and New World peoples, indeed the creation of new peoples combining the cultures and physical materials of the many communities coming together in the early West; "Métis America." This metissage or mestizaje was submerged, overshadowed, and not infrequently suppressed, excluded, or expelled for much of the nineteenth and twentieth centuries. It began to return to prominence, for reasons very different from those prevailing in the early modern period, in the second half of the twentieth century. Indeed, with the early West in view, modern diversity looks more like a return to North American history and less a departure from United States and Canadian history.

The Spanish-Indian borderlands are a good place to begin because they encompassed so much of the West in the late eighteenth and nineteenth centuries and because the mixing of peoples was so evident there. This was, in part, a result of the nature of the Spanish Empire. Like many empires, that of Spain had proved quite adept at holding together many seemingly incongruous parts. Unburdened by a commitment to equality, not having a democracy's need to create a single demos—to go from pluribus to unum, confident in the ultimate victory of Christianity and Spanish culture over what Spanish observers deemed indigenous barbarism, the late Spanish Empire was quite flexible in its dealings with the West's indigenous peoples. There were Puebloan villages in New Mexico separated from Spanish communities and subject to Spanish authority; Franciscan missions in California imposing Christianity and Spanish culture on Indians stunned by the catastrophic effects of European diseases and livestock; and Southern Plains Comanches nominally subordinate to Spain, sometimes allied with it, and effectively independent of it. Spanish officials pursued different policies for different Indians in different parts of the Americas.

This was a matter of practicality, even of necessity. As David Weber has elegantly argued, by the late eighteenth century, many Spanish officials had come to terms with the Spanish Empire's limited ability to impose Spanish dominion on many of the peoples of the Americas—including many living on what was ostensibly Spanish territory. From Araucania in southern Chile to the Southern Plains of North America and beyond, Spanish governors, soldiers, and missionaries were dealing simultaneously with peoples who needed and wanted Spanish help, with peoples interested in Spanish goods but contemptuous of Spanish authority, and with peoples more likely to impose themselves on putatively Spanish territory than be imposed upon by scanty Spanish force. Nor was Spain confronting Indians alone, nor, in many cases, facing isolated Indians. After the Seven Years' War forced France out of North America, Spain no longer had to worry about one of its traditional North American rivals, but it did have to cope with a British Empire and then a separate American republic of burgeoning population, commercial dynamism, and westward inclination. Spain and North American Indians might share Anglo-American enemies, or Indian peoples might make use of alternative British and Anglo-American sources of goods, weapons, and allies to undermine Spanish intentions. The limits of Spanish power and the presence of foreign threats did not prevent the extension of Spanish dominion everywhere in North America—the late eighteenth century was the period of Spanish expansion into upper California, for example—but they certainly constrained Spanish officials to think of Indian peoples as possible allies or partners as well as subjects or enemies. The beleaguered Spanish Empire had to adapt.[18]

A good example of this adaptation is a set of 1785–86 Spanish treaties with the Navajos, Utes, and Eastern and Western Comanches. These treaties tried to limit hostilities between Navajos and New Mexicans, make peace between New Mexico's Ute allies and the Western Comanche *rancherías* that had threatened both Utes and New Mexico with destruction, end or reduce eastern Comanche assaults on Spanish Texas, and isolate the Apache raiders against whom Spanish officials had been conducting an on-again off-again policy of destruction since 1772. The Ute-Comanche peace did not last, but Navajo-New Mexican hostilities were at least contained by both the 1786 treaty and by developing practices of targeted warfare and recurring negotiation. The New Mexico peace furnished the Comanches with the trade goods they wanted and had been increasingly unable to get after Spain cut off trade from what had been French Louisiana, and it also gave them the breathing space they needed after a particularly lethal 1779 Spanish campaign against them and the ravages of an early 1780s smallpox epidemic. New Mexico, freed from Comanche raids, saw its trade extend eastward onto the Plains and its population grow. Spanish Texas, too, was largely freed from Comanche assaults until the Mexican independence movement in the 1810s disrupted the supply of gifts that had helped sustain the Comanche peace. Spanish officials might consider Comanches, Navajos, and Utes as subordinates, perhaps as eventual subjects, but the treaties hinted at a recognition of effective independence, and, in the case of the Comanches, perhaps even of at least temporary dominance of the Southern Plains.

In contrast, the treaties threatened to make good on Spanish threats of extermination of the Apaches. Frustrated by decades of increasingly destructive Apache raids across the Southwest—conducted in some cases by Apaches fleeing Comanche attacks on the Southern Plains—Spanish officials had experimented with offensive policies against the Apaches from 1772–1779. Such repeated Spanish campaigns could be effective against peoples like the Apaches, particularly when the Spanish and their allies were able to destroy the herds or devastate the crops on which peoples like the Apaches depended. The Spanish and Comanches launched another wave of such attacks after 1786. But, though Spain conducted for a time a seemingly merciless war against Apaches, even sent Apache captives into slavery in Mexico City or Cuba, by the 1790s Spanish officials were moving some Apaches groups into *establecimientos* (reservations) south of the frontier. The Apaches going to these *establecimientos* were hoping for a respite from Spanish attacks, the Spanish were hoping for the eventual acculturation—rather than annihilation—of their foes.

More generally, the kind of offensive strategy pursued against the Apaches in the 1770s and 1780s was giving way to a different approach. Such campaigns were expensive, and therefore subject to interruption when conflicts in Europe and eastern North America, such as those stemming from the American Revolution, drew away Spanish governmental attention and resources. Interruption prevented the persistence that made the campaigns effective in the first place. There was, moreover, the problem of the more hinter hinterland. How far beyond Spanish outposts could Apaches, or Comanches for that matter, safely be pursued? It was increasingly coming to seem better to many Spanish officials to build forts, make treaties, and exchange goods. The 1785–86 treaties were an example of this kind of thinking, as were the Apache *estableciemientos*. Enemies could be accommodated, incorporated, and even allied with. The Spanish Empire had room for many arrangements.

It made such arrangements even in stretches of the borderlands more favorable for Spanish domination. Even in upper California, where Spain was able to extend a chain of missions from 1769, to induce or coerce Indians ravaged by the spread of European diseases and the disruptions of Spanish livestock to come to and even stay at the sites of religious and cultural conversion. As can be seen in Steve Hackel's wonderful book about Mission San Carolos Borromeo, Spain was cooperating with Indian peoples as well as commanding them. Upper California's Indians had not made the transition to mounted hunting and raiding that rendered Plains Indians like the Comanches and Sioux so formidable, nor did they have the large-scale confederations and councils that enabled a people like the Comanches to mass against hapless Spanish outposts. Those in the missions often needed the food and protection the Franciscans could offer. So inhospitable had California outside the missions become that the discipline, disease environment, cultural disdain, and corporal punishments of the Franciscan establishments seemed to some Indians, at least some of the time, better than the alternative. But even here, the Spanish Franciscans tried to set up traditional Spanish forms of town government to organize their charges, and it was Indians who were elected as town councilmen and *alcaldes*. In many cases the Indians elected drew their authority also from their existing status as leaders of indigenous communities. Accepting Spanish office meant formally placing their community under Spanish rule, but it also gave these Indian officers a not inconsiderable voice in Spanish administration. Even where subordinate, Indians could use a system of ranks to their advantage.[19]

The Spanish Empire was a kind of hybrid entity, composed of many different peoples governed, or treated, in all manner of ways, and this hybridity went well beyond treaties and negotiations. For when we talk of Spaniards and Indians in the northern borderlands, we are speaking loosely, for many thousands of people in the region combined elements of both populations. As scholars like James Brooks and David Weber have suggested, by the nineteenth century, centuries of living near one another, of Spaniards raiding Indian communities for slaves or buying the captives taken by Indian parties; of Indian parties raiding Spanish outposts and adopting those born Spanish into Indian communities; of Spanish traders living in Indian communities, learning their languages, and finding marriage partners there; of mission Indians picking up Catholic doctrine, the Spanish tongue, and European crops and livestock; centuries of intermingling meant that Indian and Spanish communities knew a lot about each other, indeed, to a certain extent, were each other. A Comanche Indian might have a Spanish mother and a fair acquaintance with his mother's language. New Mexico included Pueblo towns living apart from their neighbors, and *genízaro* communities made up of the descendants of slaves of many Indian origins and of the Spanish masters of these slaves. A Spanish New Mexican might have an Indian grandparent.[20] Ramón Gutiérrez has argued that, in eighteenth-century New Mexico, even as consciousness of racial categories became more marked, the incidence of marriage across racial lines was increasing.[21] In some cases, the blending effects of cross-cultural Eros, in others, the most brutal aspects of kidnapping, capture, enslavement, and rape were obscuring the lines between neighboring peoples. Had there been a J. Hector St. John de Crèvecoeur in New Mexico, he might very well have written the ode to this new person of the northern frontier, as Mexican intellectuals like Francisco Javier Clavijero did for the offspring of the great encounter farther south.

Nor was this tendency of the Indo-Spanish borderlands unique. New France and, less famously, Louisiana were also characterized by hybrid populations. The fur traders moving west from Montreal often found wives among the Indian peoples with whom they lived and worked. Indeed, it was marrying into indigenous communities that often made it possible for Frenchmen to live and work. The Métis descendants of these marriages would form a substantial population with a collective identity into the nineteenth century and beyond. As there were French fur traders with Indian wives and Métis offspring throughout the Great Lakes region, in the hinterlands of French Louisiana one could find small farmers of French origin and Indian marriage using Indian farming techniques well into the nineteenth century. And from Michilimackinac, Fort Saint Joseph, and Detroit to Quebec, and especially in Montreal, one could find Sioux, Fox, Plains Apache, and other Indian slaves working on French farms and in French households. Some were the gifts of Indian peoples seeking to tie France into alliances against the nations from whom the slaves were taken; some were brought into French communities by Frenchmen whose western businesses included human bondage as well as animal pelts. Throughout the eighteenth century, New France and the French outposts in the Great Lakes held hundreds of Indian slaves from the West. And in those Franco-Indian Great Lakes settlements, the full implications of the mixing of cultures would have been evident. Some female captives are likely best understood as sex slaves, others became wives and perhaps free members of the community. Many slaves were baptized, many of the males took names like Jean-Baptiste, Pierre, and Joseph. Many of the Indian women gave birth to the children of French fathers. In these mixed towns one would have heard Romance, Algonquian, Siouxan, and Athabascan tongues, and seen lust and love, rape and marriage, coercion and consent, Catholic rituals and Indian beliefs, servitude, freedom, and either having given way to the other: in short, a world of many brutalities and many joinings.[22]

Moving later in time and farther north in space, Gwenn Miller has showed how the Russian-American Company and Russian Orthodox Church were trying in the outpost on Kodiak Island by the early nineteenth century to use the offspring of Russian men and Alutiiq women—Kodiak Kreols—as agents of Russian power in Alaska; as missionaries, company clerks, sailors, and artisans for example. Ethnic blending had characterized Russian expansion across Siberia, and such reliance on children of mixed descent was a natural practice at the imperial edges where there were few Russians (and those Russians there were often looked down on by officials) to sustain an empire of seemingly infinite space. In 1821, the new charter for the Russian-American Company recognized company-educated children of Russian and indigenous Alaskan women who completed 10 years of service for the company as a distinct class of "colonial citizens" different from Russians or aboriginal Alaskans and crucial for the continuation of the Russian colonial project.[23] Similar tendencies towards ethnic intermixing were evident from the heart of the continent to its arctic edges.

What unified these varied North American borderlands comprised of peoples of disparate European, African, and American origins? In Spanish, French, and Russian cases, there were a relatively small number of men of European descent in the proximity of a greater number of indigenous women. In all of these borderlands in this preindustrial world, societies needed human labor and were familiar—and often quite comfortable—with taking it by force. All of this put Euro-Americans and Amerindians in the close and sustained contact that generated, by force or consent, children of European and Indian descent and some mixture of European and Indian culture. We should also emphasize, as a recent essay by Pekka Hämäläinen so astutely has, that borderlands communities in the neighborhood of the great indigenous power centers like the Iroquois, Dakotas and, over the course of the eighteenth and into the nineteenth century, the Comanches, lived a precarious and fearful existence, and consequently were in need of the kind of friends that intermarriage could help generate and sustain.[24] In short, many features of the early West pushed many of its peoples toward hybridity.

This tendency calls to mind Gary Nash's suggestive 1995 essay "The Hidden History of Mestizo America." Well aware of leading features of United States history such as racial discrimination, segregation, and exclusion, Nash called attention in this essay to the many less prominent cases of and tendencies toward racial and cultural *mestizaje* in colonial American and United States history. He wrote of obscure theorists of union such as Randolph Bourne, of iconic Anglo-American frontiersmen like Sam Houston and Kit Carson who, by adoption or marriage, were also Indian or Hispano-American. He mentioned Sikh male immigrants to early twentieth-century California who married Hispanic women, and escaped African American slaves who found refuge and spouses in American Indian communities.[25] Nash was trying to identify an obscured American history, perhaps less characteristic of the United States from 1776 to about 1965 than were racial prejudice, exclusion, and segregation, but not uncharacteristic. When Atlantic and early American history include the early modern West—roughly two-thirds of North America for roughly three centuries, and its many instances of *mestizaje*, perhaps its inclination toward hybridity, the examples Nash cites start to seem more typical than atypical. Racial exclusionism and homogeneity start to look more exceptional and ephemeral. America starts to look more like America. Adding western territory to early American and Atlantic history, making early American history continental, gives us a subject more in keeping with our twenty-first century sense of a deeply rooted, globally connected, multifarious humanity.

Notes

1 I tried out some of the ideas in this essay in an unpublished paper, "Interpretive Implications of a Continental Approach," presented at a May 2009 *William and Mary Quarterly-Early Modern Studies Institute* workshop at the Huntington Library. Eric Hinderaker and Rebecca Horn refer to the paper in "Territorial Crossings: Histories and Historiographies of the Early Americas," *William and Mary Quarterly* 67 (2010): 405–406. My thanks to all the workshop participants for helping me develop my ideas.
2 Herbert Bolton, "The Epic of Greater America," *American Historical Review* 38 (1933): 448–474.
3 Glyn Williams, *Voyages of Delusion: The Search for the Northwest Passage in the Age of Reason* (London: Harper Collins Publishers, 2002), xvii, 5–7, 18–30, 67–70, 189–236.
4 Brett Rushforth, *Bonds of Alliance: Indigenous and Atlantic Slaveries in New France* (Chapel Hill: University of North Carolina Press, 2012), 193–237.

5 Ned Blackhawk, *Violence over the Land: Indians and Empires in the Early American West* (Cambridge, MA: Harvard University Press, 2006), 6–54.
6 Elizabeth A. Fenn, *Pox Americana: The Great Smallpox Epidemic of 1775–82* (New York: Hill and Wang, 2001); Pekka Hämäläinen, "The Shapes of Power: Indians, Europeans, and North American Worlds from the Seventeenth to the Nineteenth Century," *Contested Spaces of Early America*, eds. Juliana Barr and Edward Countryman, (Philadelphia: University of Pennsylvania Press, 2014), 31–68.
7 Pekka Hämäläinen, *The Comanche Empire* (New Haven: Yale University Press, 2008).
8 For an example of Diamond's way of asking questions, see Jared Diamond, *Guns, Germs, and Steel: The Fates of Human Societies* (New York: W.W. Norton & Company, 1997).
9 On the Oxus and Jaxartes, see William McNeill, *The Rise of the West: A History of the Human Community* (Chicago: University of Chicago Press, 1963), 66.
10 Rushforth, *Bonds of Alliance*, 102–104, 165–173.
11 "Extrait du journal de Voyage des frères Mallet à Santa Fé," in Donald J. Blakeslee, *Along Ancient Trails: The Mallet Expedition of 1739* (Boulder: University Press of Colorado, 1995), 218.
12 Charlevoix quotation from "Charlevoix Visits Wisconsin: His Description of the Tribes," in *Collections of the State Historical Society of Wisconsin*, vol. 16, *The French Regime in Wisconsin—I, 1634–1727*, eds. Reuben Gold Thwaites (Madison: Wisconsin State Historical Society, 1902), 417–418.
13 "Report of Antonio de Espejo," *The Rediscovery of New Mexico, 1580–1594: The Explorations of Chamuscado, Espejo, Castaño de Sosa, Morlete, and Leyva de Bonilla and Humaña*, ed. and trans. George P. Hammond and Agapito Rey (Albuquerque: University of New Mexico Press, 1966), 225, 227.
14 Juliana Barr, *Peace Came in the Form of a Woman: Indians and Spaniards in the Texas Borderlands* (Chapel Hill: University of North Carolina Press, 2007); Kathleen DuVal, *The Native Ground: Indians and Colonists in the Heart of the Continent* (Philadelphia: University of Pennsylvania Press, 2006). Hämäläinen, *Comanche Empire*; Michael Witgen, *An Infinity of Nations: How the Native New World Shaped Early North America* (Philadelphia: University of Pennsylvania Press, 2011).
15 Juliana Barr, "Geographies of Power: Mapping Indian Borders in the 'Borderlands' of the Early Southwest," *William and Mary Quarterly* 68 (2011): 5–46; Hämäläinen, *Comanche Empire*.
16 "Journal in the Form of a Letter," *Journals and Letters of Pierre Gaultier de Varennes de la Vérendrye and His Sons*, ed. Lawrence J. Burpee (Toronto: Champlain Society, 1927), 332, 339–343.
17 James Cook (and William Anderson), *A Voyage to the Pacific Ocean* (London, 1784), Vol. 2, 313–318, 326–327.
18 David J. Weber, *Bárbaros: Spaniards and Their Savages in the Age of Enlightenment* (New Haven: Yale University Press, 2005), 2, 151–220.
19 Steven W. Hackel, *Children of Coyote, Missionaries of Saint Francis: Indian-Spanish Relations in Colonial California, 1769–1850* (Chapel Hill: University of North Carolina Press, 2005), 228–271.
20 James F. Brooks, *Captives and Cousins: Slavery, Kinship, and Community in the Southwest Borderlands* (Chapel Hill: University of North Carolina Press, 2002), 99, 103, 107–108, 124–148, 162–164, 195–197, 208, 239, 291–2, 321–322, 342, 363–365; Weber, *Bárbaros*, 221–256.
21 Ramón A. Gutiérrez, *When Jesus Came, the Corn Mothers Went Away, 1500–1846* (Stanford, CA: Stanford University Press, 1991), 327–336.
22 On enslaved Indians in New France, see Rushforth, *Bonds of Alliance*, 253–347.
23 Gwenn A. Miller, *Kodiak Kreol: Communities of Empire in Early Russian America* (Ithaca, New York: Cornell University Press, 2010), 14–19, 137–146.
24 Hämäläinen, "The Shapes of Power."
25 Gary Nash, "The Hidden History of Mestizo America," *Journal of American History* 82 (1995): 941–964. It was Gwenn Miller who first called this essay to my attention.

References

Anderson, Gary Clayton. *The Indian Southwest, 1580–1830: Ethnogenesis and Reinvention* (Norman: University of Oklahoma Press, 1999).
Barr, Juliana. *Peace Came in the Form of a Woman: Indians and Spaniards in the Texas Borderlands* (Chapel Hill: University of North Carolina Press, 2007).
Barr, Juliana. "Geographies of Power: Mapping Indian Borders in the 'Borderlands' of the Early Southwest," *William and Mary Quarterly* 68 (2011): 5–46.
Barr, Juliana and Edward Countryman. *Contested Spaces of Early America* (Philadelphia: University of Pennsylvania Press, 2014).

Blackhawk, Ned. *Violence over the Land: Indians and Empires in the Early American West*. (Cambridge, MA: Harvard University Press, 2006).

Blakeslee, Donald J. *Along Ancient Trails: The Mallet Expedition of 1739* (Boulder: Univ. Press of Colorado, 1995), 218.

Bolton, Herbert. "The Epic of Greater America." *American Historical Review* 38 (1933): 448–474.

Brooks, James F. *Captives and Cousins: Slavery, Kinship, and Community in the Southwest Borderlands*. (Chapel Hill: University of North Carolina Press, 2002).

Burpee, Lawrence J. ed., *Journals and Letters of Pierre Gaultier de Varennes de la Vérendrye and His Sons* (Toronto: Champlain Society, 1927), 332, 339–343.

Calloway, Colin. *One Vast Winter Count: The Native American West before Lewis and Clark* (Lincoln: University of Nebraska Press, 2003).

Cook, James. *A Voyage to the Pacific Ocean*. Vol. 2. London, 1784.

de Charlevoix, Father Pierre-Francois-Xavier, "Charlevoix Visits Wisconsin: His Description of the Tribes," *Collections of the State Historical Society of Wisconsin*, vol. 16, *The French Regime in Wisconsin—I, 1634–1727*, ed. Reuben Gold Thwaites (Madison: Wisconsin State Historical Society, 1902), 417–418.

DeVoto, Bernard. *The Course of Empire* (Boston: Mariner Books, 1998).

Diamond, Jared. *Guns, Germs, and Steel: The Fates of Human Societies* (New York: W.W. Norton & Company, 1997).

DuVal, Kathleen. *The Native Ground: Indians and Colonists in the Heart of the Continent* (Philadelphia: University of Pennsylvania Press, 2006).

Eccles, W. J. *The Canadian Frontier, 1534–1760*. Rev. ed. (Albuquerque: University of New Mexico Press, 1992).

Fenn, Elizabeth A. *Pox Americana: The Great Smallpox Epidemic of 1775–82* (New York: Hill and Wang, 2001).

Fenn, Elizabeth A. *Encounters at the Heart of the World: A History of the Mandan People*. (New York: Hill and Wang, 2014).

Gutiérrez, Ramón A. *When Jesus Came, the Corn Mothers Went Away, 1500–1846*. (Stanford, CA: Stanford University Press, 1991).

Hackel, Steven W. *Children of Coyote, Missionaries of Saint Francis: Indian-Spanish Relations in Colonial California, 1769–1850* (Chapel Hill: University of North Carolina Press, 2005).

Hämäläinen, Pekka. *The Comanche Empire*. (New Haven: Yale University Press, 2008).

Hämäläinen, Pekka. "The Shapes of Power: Indians, Europeans, and North American Worlds from the Seventeenth to the Nineteenth Century," Juliana Barr and Edward Countryman, eds., *Contested Spaces of Early America* (Philadelphia: University of Pennsylvania Press, 2014).

Hammond, George P. and Agapito Rey, ed. and trans., *The Rediscovery of New Mexico, 1580–1594: The Explorations of Chamuscado, Espejo, Castaño de Sosa, Morlete, and Levyva de Bonilla and Humaña*, (Albuquerque: Univ. of New Mexico Press, 1966).

Igler, David. *The Great Ocean: Pacific Worlds from Captain Cook to the Gold Rush* (Oxford: Oxford University Press, 2013).

Mapp, Paul. *The Elusive West and the Contest for Empire, 1713–1763* (Chapel Hill: University of North Carolina Press, 2011).

McNeill, William. *The Rise of the West: A History of the Human Community* (Chicago: University of Chicago Press, 1963).

Miller, Gwenn A. *Kodiak Kreol: Communities of Empire in Early Russian America* (Ithaca, NY: Cornell University Press, 2010).

Nash, Gary. "The Hidden History of Mestizo America." *Journal of American History* 82 (1995): 941–964.

Rushforth, Brett. *Bonds of Alliance: Indigenous and Atlantic Slaveries in New France* (Chapel Hill: University of North Carolina Press, 2012).

Saunt, Claudio. *West of the Revolution: An Uncommon History of 1776* (New York: W.W. Norton, 2014).

Usner, Daniel H., Jr. *Indians, Settlers, &Slaves in a Frontier Exchange Economy: The Lower Mississippi Valley before 1783* (Chapel Hill: University of North Carolina Press, 1992).

Weber, David. *The Spanish Frontier in North America* (New Haven: Yale University Press, 1992).

Weber, David. *Bárbaros: Spaniards and Their Savages in the Age of Enlightenment* (New Haven: Yale University Press, 2005).

White, Richard. *The Middle Ground: Indians, Empires, and Republics in the Great Lakes Region, 1650–1815* (Cambridge: Cambridge University Press, 1991).

Williams, Glyn. *Voyages of Delusion: The Search for the Northwest Passage in the Age of Reason* (London: Harper Collins Publishers, 2002).

Witgen, Michael. *An Infinity of Nations: How the Native New World Shaped Early North America* (Philadelphia: University of Pennsylvania Press, 2011).

16
NATIVE–EUROPEAN INTERACTIONS IN NORTH AMERICA AND THE TRADE IN FURS

Ann M. Carlos and Frank D. Lewis

Introduction: The Place of Commerce in Native–European Interactions

The literature on the early interactions between North American Aboriginals and Europeans is often dominated by the negative effects the newcomers had on native society. Europeans brought diseases against which the isolated populations had few defences, while in later years, as colonial and later US settlement expanded, conflict and the loss of hunting grounds further reduced their numbers.[1] There is at the same time a parallel narrative, equally important, if we are to understand the development of Native societies after European contact. That literature focuses on the commercial interactions between natives and Europeans.[2]

In this chapter we explore the trade that became central to why Europeans and natives initiated and then maintained contact. What made trade between Native Americans and Europeans almost seamless, even from the earliest days, was the development of native society prior to contact. Anthropologists and archaeologists have discovered that, throughout North America, natives had been engaging in trade even over long distances. Moreover, in areas with high population densities, trade was an important part of the native economy. In large areas of the northern half of North America evidence has been found of trade in silver, silica, copper, and obsidian (Carlson 1987). Like the other materials, obsidian, a dark glass-like volcanic rock, valued for cutting, has been discovered at widely dispersed sites. These scarce, high value goods speak of interconnected exchange that took place over great distances. More intensive geographically confined trade arrangements have been found among the Chumash of southern California and neighboring tribes. The Chumash specialized in a variety of activities including the "minting" of money from the shells of sea snails.[3]

There is also evidence of trade in food, despite the fact that most native groups prior to contact were hunters. Natives hunted bison on the Great Plains almost from their arrival in the Americas. Most hunting was on a limited scale, the killing of small numbers of animals at varied locations to meet the food requirements of the individual groups. But starting about 2,000 years ago, there is evidence of the production of meat for trade. At Head-Squashed-In, an area in southern Alberta, there was intensive hunting and processing of bison.[4] The area contains "over a million projectile points, hundreds of thousands of potsherds, and millions of kilograms of rocks" that were carried several kilometers and "used in stone boiling to render bone grease," which was a highly labor-intensive activity (Bamforth 2011, 8). The bone grease was used to produce pemmican, a nutritious mixture of powdered meat mixed with melted fat that was lightweight, storable, and easy to carry over long distances. Indeed, the output at Head-Squashed-In far exceeded what was required to meet local demand. This industrial level of production coincided with the expansion of exchange networks on the Plains. There is also evidence of trade in pottery that extended from Illinois and Ohio to the Rocky Mountains (Bamforth 2011, 10).

Trading with Europeans, nevertheless, represented a major shift from the more limited exchange that had been part of native society. With the arrival of Europeans, Native American trade increased by orders of magnitude both in volume and variety. The nature of the goods depended on the region, the resources available to the natives, and their consumption demands; but throughout the northern part of the continent the trade on the Native side was dominated by furs, especially beaver pelts. The Dutch had some involvement in the fur trade in the early years, but the North American fur trade, indeed all trade with the Indians, ultimately became the preserve of the English and French, with the French playing the much larger role. In establishing an effective mechanism, Europeans faced the challenges of distance, time, language, and culture. Trade was taking place thousands of miles from the markets where the furs were ultimately sold. Transport included not only ocean shipping from Europe to North America, but also the movement of European goods and furs within the continent. How the Europeans and natives developed a trading system in the face of these barriers is the theme of this chapter.

Origins of the North American Trade in Beaver Pelts

The earliest interactions between Europeans and the native groups who occupied the northern half of North America had elements that were social, cultural, and religious, but theirs was primarily a commercial relationship. From the isolated exchanges between natives offering pelts to European fishermen, who, in turn, beckoned the same individuals with metal items, there grew a broadly based trade. Native Americans had raw materials that were valued in Europe, and Europeans traders could supply a wide variety of goods not available in America. This bilateral exchange not only provided new technologies that improved the natives' ability to meet their basic needs of food and clothing, but it also gave them access to a wide range of new consumer goods. In exchange Europeans received a steady supply of furs, most importantly beaver, which were used primarily in the European felting and hatting industries.[5]

From as early as the twelfth century and into the twentieth century, hoods and then hats, caps, and bonnets were part of everyday dress for both women and men. Over the centuries, men's hats expanded and contracted, brims increased and decreased, crowns rose and fell, but what remained invariant was the raw material: wool felt. As a fabric, felt is stronger than woven cloth. It does not tear or unravel in a straight line, it is lightweight but warm, it is resistant to water and, with a sufficient level of beaver wool content, it will hold its shape even when wet. These characteristics made beaver-wool felt the prime material for hatters, especially when the hat had to be large enough to be worn over a wig or when fashion called for hats with large brims. The quality of a felt hat was determined largely by the amount of beaver wool used. "Beavers," as the top-of-the-line hats were called, had the most beaver wool, but also included varying amounts of hare or rabbit. Less expensive "castors" had a greater proportion of lower-cost fur, while "felts" had no beaver wool at all (Ginsberg 2008; Lawson 1943).

Over the seventeenth and eighteenth centuries, the felting and hatting industry in England and France was growing. This expansion was due in large part to taste and fashion. But taste and fashion could take the industry only so far. Ultimately, the industry was dependent upon a supply of beaver pelts, the raw material from which these hats were made. For centuries beaver pelts had come from northern Europe, especially the Baltic region, but, by the seventeenth century, with depletion of the European beaver, known as "castor fiber," a new supply was needed. That supply came to be filled by Native Americans. In fact by the middle of the seventeenth century most of the beaver pelts imported to Europe originated in North America. Had they not been fashionable, beaver hats would not have been produced; but, at the same time, had there not been a demand by Native Americans for the commodities that Europeans had to offer in exchange for furs, beaver hats could not have been produced for lack of the essential raw material.

Structure of the Fur Trade

With the end of Dutch authority on the North American mainland, the European side of the fur trade was carried on exclusively by Britain and France.[6] The French came first to the fur trade and, until the end of the Seven Years' War in 1763 when control of New France shifted to the British, they conducted most of the trade. The French operated through various monopolies, while the main English player in the interior of the continent was the Hudson's Bay Company. New France had begun participating in the fur trade in the sixteenth century, and during the first half of the eighteenth century the French were the Hudson's Bay Company's main rivals, and also the main rivals of the English merchants operating out of Albany. In 1700 control of the French trade passed from the Northern Company, a joint French-Canadian venture, to the Colony Company, whose board of directors was exclusively Canadian. Perhaps through mismanagement, disruptions in the fur market, or lack of capital, the company was unsuccessful; it was only in 1718 with the formation of the Compagnie des Indes that French trade increased (Miquelon 1987). English trade was carried on by the Hudson's Bay Company, which was chartered in 1670, and by English merchants operating out of Albany.

The trade of the Compagnie des Indes far surpassed not only that of the Hudson's Bay Company, it exceeded all of the English trade. Over the period from 1720 to 1760, London was receiving on average 70,000 beaver pelts per year of which 51,000 pelts were brought in by the Hudson's Bay Company; while in Paris, beaver pelts received by the Compagnie des Indes averaged 166,000 (Wien 1990, 309). The greater trade, twice that of the English and three times that of the Hudson's Bay Company, reflected its much larger trading area. The French operated not just in the Northeast and Great Lakes regions, but also in areas that extended down the Mississippi River basin.

The Compagnie des Indes exported far more furs than the Hudson's Bay Company, but it had a much smaller presence in North America, employing just two or three receivers, a few clerks, and an agent in Quebec City.[7] The company was really little more than a wholesaler. It brought in European goods on hired merchants ships; sold the goods to independent French fur traders, called *voyageurs*; purchased the furs that the voyageurs obtained through trade with the Indians; and transported the furs to France, where it sold them at auction. The prices the company paid to voyageurs were based on a fixed scale that was periodically adjusted according to market conditions. Thus, the voyageurs knew in advance what they would be receiving for their furs and could determine the appropriate rates of exchange to offer the Indians and how far inland they could afford to travel. In contrast to the Hudson's Bay Company, which conducted all trading along the bay coast for most of the eighteenth century, the voyageurs went to the Indians, locating their trading posts in the interior. The French, therefore, reduced the distance the Indians needed to travel, and this was reflected in the market. In areas where the voyageurs and the Hudson's Bay Company competed, the French paid the Indians lower prices for their furs.

Following the British conquest in the Seven Years' War, control of the St. Lawrence fur trade passed from the French to mainly Scottish merchants operating out of Montreal. The structure of the interior trade, however, remained much the same, as the voyageurs continued to be the ones who dealt directly with native traders. In 1779 the Montreal companies formed an association, the North West Company, built new posts, and greatly extended their trading network, even reaching the Rocky Mountains. In response, the Hudson's Bay Company, which previously had done all its trading along the bay coast, set up posts in the interior. In 1821, after 40 years of competition, the Hudson's Bay Company and the North West Company merged.[8] With Jay's Treaty and the delineation of the border between the United States and Canada, the North West Company's Mississippi operation was sold to John Jacob Astor's American Fur Company, which became a major competitor.

In contrast to the organization of the Compagnie des Indes and the other French companies, the Hudson's Bay Company was a hierarchical joint-stock company with paid employees, trading posts around Hudson Bay, and a headquarters in London with a board of directors elected by stockholders. The governor and the board of directors, known as the "Court of Assistants," ran the company. They organized the purchase of goods, hired men to go to Hudson Bay, and arranged fur sales in England. Most importantly, they established trading posts or "factories" around the bay and employed salaried managers or "factors" to run them, along with accountants, skilled tradesmen, and laborers, who were known as the company's "servants."

The great distance separating the directors in London from the managers in Canada led to problems of information and control.[9] The managers at the posts had better information than London about many aspects of the trade because they were the ones who dealt directly with natives. On the other hand, the directors in London had much better knowledge of the European market. Recognizing that they could not micromanage their factories, the directors in London set up systems that informed them about the trade and the actions of their employees. Central were detailed accounting records along with journals, diaries, and letters. These records, an extraordinary trove of documents, allow us to explore the commercial interactions of the Hudson's Bay Company in amazing detail.[10]

Organization of the Trade at Hudson Bay

The Hudson's Bay Company's operation was, thus, based on centralized control. The company established trading posts along the coast of Hudson Bay at the mouths of major rivers, and sent men to operate the posts and conduct the trading. Trade goods were delivered to the posts by ship, once a year, in late July or early August. Native traders, however, arrived during the early summer to trade furs for the European goods that had been delivered to the posts the previous year. The furs were transported to England on the next ship to arrive. In England, the company auctioned the pelts to furriers and hatters.

The company's head office in London made the key decisions concerning the number of men to send to Hudson Bay and the quality and types of goods to deliver to the posts. But these decisions were not made in isolation. Reports on native preferences were central to these decisions.[11] The head office also gave guidance to the post traders about the rates of exchange between trade goods and furs. All correspondence between the post governors and the company officials in London was carried on the annual ship, which meant that the company was effectively operating in an extended futures market. The furs sold in London were exchanged in North America for trade goods that the company had purchased at least 18 months earlier.

The correspondence between each post and the head office in London had to be maintained according to specifications set by the head office. This included a format for letters, accounts, and the keeping of a daily journal kept by the chief factor (Carlos and Hejeebu 2007). James Isham's journal for the 1740–41 trading year at York Factory provides a picture of life at the post and a description of how the trade was conducted. York Factory and the other bayside trading posts (Moose Factory, Fort Albany, and Fort Churchill) were designed to be self-sufficient.[12] Each had a doctor, armorer, tailor, carpenter, blacksmith, cooper, bricklayer, and other men, mainly laborers. The full complement at York Factory was between 36 and 50, although in 1740–41 there were fewer than 30 men at the post.

The post journal notes that in 1740 the annual ship arrived from London in the latter half of July and left York Factory on August 1, carrying its cargo of furs, pelts, timber, men returning home, and all the correspondence and account books. The departure of the annual ship represents the end of the trading year. A few canoes arrived in August and September, but no natives came to trade furs. Those natives who did come to the post were the "home guard" Indians, who spent the year in the general vicinity of the post, supplying the men with meat and fish. Their presence helped make the trade viable, but their direct contribution in terms of furs was limited. On September 29, Isham reported the river "full of ice" and other than the occasional native who came on foot there was little further contact with the natives until April.

The trading posts provided not just new trading opportunities but also new economic opportunities. In addition to other home guard Indians who visited the post, 26bfamilies (130 individuals) came in April for the goose hunt. It was not until the end of May that Native groups began arriving with pelts and furs. This marked the start of the fur-trading season, which was very short and hectic, occupying less than a month. In fact, nearly all the trade that year was conducted during the week of June 12. On Monday 85 canoes arrived, representing at least 4 different native groups. The following day another 13 canoes came; and on June 17, 30 canoes. The Indians who came to trade spent very little time at York Factory. Some stayed as little as one day, and others just a few days. The journey to the trading post was long, the rivers were navigable for a short period, and the natives needed to return to hunting. In fact by June 20, all those who had arrived on or after June 12 had left. Another 30 canoes came to the post on June 22, but by the end of the month the trading season was effectively over. So even though the company men spent the entire year at Hudson Bay, the fur trading itself took less than a month, and in 1741, nearly all of that trade was concentrated in just one week.

With trading largely over by the end of June, company men spent the summer preparing for the arrival of the ship from England. The furs were sorted, counted, packed into bundles, and placed in casks. In late July, buoys were readied, and on August 2, 1741, the *Churchill* arrived along with a sloop. By August 6, the vessels were unloaded, and over the next three days the homeward cargoes of furs and timber were loaded. On August 12, having spent just 10 days at the post, the vessels weighed anchor and the next day set sail for London.

The annual cycle of trade at York Factory, developed over many years, required coordination between the head office in London and the post governor. This was achieved entirely through the extensive and detailed correspondence that accompanied the ship. But even though communication was infrequent, the company was able to conduct a profitable business. Indeed, for native groups in the region, a commercial fur trade provided a new range of economic options to which they adapted, even specializing in activities related to the trade.

The Exchange Process at the Hudson's Bay Company Trading Posts

A striking feature of the Native American and European traders was their ability to overcome their cultural, ethnic, and linguistic differences. A potentially serious barrier was language. In some circumstance, such as typified by the informal and much simpler trade of the sixteenth century between natives and fishermen on the East Coast, gestures or a basic pidgin were sufficient. These brief, one-off exchanges were conducted with very little use of language. But the complex nature of a permanent commercial fur trade, which involved many European goods and a variety of pelts, required sophisticated verbal communication. Very quickly, Cree emerged as the language of the trade, used by both the English and French. Decisions concerning language were made early in the Hudson's Bay Company's operation, when it produced a Cree-English dictionary for use by its traders (Carlos and Lewis 2010, 75–78). The company was clearly aware that it had to deal effectively with its customers. The French voyageurs also recognized the essential role of good communication and they too spoke Cree.

Trade at the Hudson's Bay posts was a two-part process. The company directors became aware, as had the French, that if they were to attract significant numbers of native traders to its posts, it would be necessary to adopt aspects of native practice. An "ethic of generosity" was an important element of native society, not just in the region of Hudson Bay but throughout the Americas, and a component of this ethic was gift giving. Accordingly, the trade began with an elaborate gift exchange ceremony between natives and their trading captain on one side, and the governor and post factors on the other. The ceremony typically was announced by the discharge of guns by the Indians on their arrival at the post. This was met by a response from the fort cannons and the flying of the company flag. Then the two sides would meet outside the post and exchange gifts. In one ceremony, the governor and factors presented the trading captain with a suit of clothes, stockings, shoes, sash, handkerchief and a decorated hat, while the whole group was given bread, prunes, tobacco and brandy. Often, the governor would be presented with some furs and pelts. There would also be ceremonial drinking and pipe smoking. The second stage was the actual trading of furs for European goods. Although the trading captain was allowed in the post warehouse, other natives traded through an opening or window. Given the concentrated nature of the trading season, the men at the post would have been trading and holding gift exchanges almost continuously, activities that were facilitated by the long period of daylight during the northern summer.

Bargaining and the Price of Furs

Beaver pelts were the cornerstone of the trade on the native side, although other furs and pelts were involved to some degree, while the Hudson's Bay Company offered in exchange more than 60 varieties of goods.[13] Table 16.1 lists all the goods the natives received in trade in 1740 from York Factory, the largest of the posts. In the post accounts, the goods are listed alphabetically. In Table 16.1, we have grouped them into four categories: producer goods, household goods, tobacco and alcohol, and other luxuries. Included in the table is the price and value of each good, but in an unusual monetary unit.

To help company traders determine the rates of exchange between beaver pelts and the more than 60 European trade goods, the company established a unit of account that they called the "made beaver" (mb). A single prime beaver pelt was assigned a price of 1 made beaver, and the price of every trade good was based on that measure. The entire price list was called the "official standard." The price of each good, in terms of "made beaver" is given in Table 16.1. For example the price of a gun, included under producer goods, was 14 made beavers. Since the price of a beaver pelt was 1 made beaver, it follows that at the official rate it took 14 beaver pelts to buy 1 gun. Table 16.1 also reports the value of guns, which in 1740 was 3,500 made beavers. This means that the natives received 250 guns (3,500/14) in the trading phase. They received an additional 18 guns during the gift-giving ceremony. Alcohol was a trade item whose official price was 4 made beavers per gallon. The brandy and "strong water" obtained thorough trade was 1,646 made beavers or 412 gallons, and natives received a further 82 gallons as gifts.

Table 16.1 Goods purchased by native traders at York Factory, 1740 (values in made beaver)

Purchased in trade	Price mb/unit	Value mb	Purchased in trade	Price mb/unit	Value mb
Producer goods			*Other luxuries*		
Files	1	308	Bayonets	1	150
Fishhooks	0.071		Beads (lb)	2	318
Flints	0.083	192	Cloth (yd)	3.5	3,454
Guns	14	3,500	Combs	1	346
Hatchets	1	762	Egg boxes	0.333	47
Ice chizzles	1	472	Flannel (yd)	1.5	29
Knives	0.25	828	Gartering (yd)	0.667	244
Net lines	1	218	Hats	4	140
Powder horns	1	181	Hawkbells (pair)	0.083	42
Powder (lb)	1	3,360	Lace (yd)	0.667	123
Scrapers	0.5	108	Looking glasses	1	108
Shot (lb)	0.25	1,847	Needles	0.083	34
Twine (skein)	1	114	Pistols	7	182
Total		11,974	Rings	.12–.33	106
Household goods			Sashes	1.5	72
Blankets	7	1,323	Scissors	0.5	28
Kettles	1.5	1,018	Shirts	2.5	226
Total		2,540	Stockings	2.5	64
Tobacco and alcohol			Thimbles, thread		53
Brandy (gal.)	4	1,514	Trunks	4	148
Rundlets	1	350	Vermillion (lb)	16	296
Tobacco (lb)	2	4,543	Worsted (yd)	.5.67	59
Tobacco boxes	1	162	Total		6,418
Water, strong (gal.)	4	132	Total received in trade		27,633
Total		6,701	Total received as gifts		2,024
			Grand total		29,657

Source: Carlos and Lewis (2010, 81–85).

The directors in London initially expected their post factors to adhere rigidly to the "official standard," but it soon became apparent that the company could earn more by permitting the post traders more discretion. Post managers needed to respond to changing market conditions in Europe and to competition from the French. Increased latitude over pricing thus allowed the trading mechanisms of the company to mesh more seamlessly with native trade practices; for example, facilitating the exchange of ceremonial gifts at the opening of the trade. Accordingly, toward the end of the seventeenth century, the pricing structure was made more flexible, although all exchange continued to be underpinned by the official standard. Post factors were now permitted and ultimately encouraged to bargain with the Indians over specific furs and European goods. For example, in 1716 the official standard price of a pound of Brazil tobacco at Fort Albany was 1mb. In his annual letter to the head office, Richard Staunton, the chief factor at Fort Albany, reported that during the summer of 1716 he had traded Brazil tobacco at 1/2 pound per made beaver, half the official rate. Other examples included shot at 3 1/4 pounds per pelt as compared with the official standard of 5 pounds; vermillion, 3/4 ounces per pelt rather than 1 1/2 ounces; and blankets, 7 rather than 6 beaver pelts per blanket. These comparisons are typical of the period before 1750 in that post factors were exchanging European goods for furs at rates far less than the official standard. For example, in 1740 at York Factory, the total value of goods the natives received both in trade and as gifts was 29,657 made beavers (see Table 16.1), but the furs they gave up in exchange had a value of 39,128 made beavers. This means natives obtained just 75.8 percent of the value of their furs, based on the official standard. Taking the official standard as 100, the price of furs, therefore, was 75.8. With increased market power, largely due to greater competition from the French, native traders were able to obtain higher prices for their furs; sometimes generating an price index of furs that went above 100 or higher than the official standard.

In Figure 16.1, we illustrate how interrelated the markets were for beaver pelts in Europe and at the Hudson's Bay Company trading posts. During the first half of the eighteenth century, strong demand in Europe for hats made with beaver wool, combined with advances in felting technology, dramatically increased the prices of beaver at the fur auctions both in London and Paris. Until 1720 the price in London was about 5 shillings per pelt; but as a result of the changing market demand, the price started increasing, ultimately reaching 15 shillings in the 1760s, or three times the 1720 level. The French traders, the voyageurs, were also affected by the higher prices. It now paid them to trade further into the interior of the continent, where they began competing with Hudson's Bay Company. In the 1730s La Vérendrye and his men started setting up trading posts in region of Hudson Bay; and in 1738 he built Fort Maurepas, a post that competed directly with York Factory. The effect on the English post was immediate. Until 1738 the price of furs at York Factory, as measured by our price index, was hovering around 68, but in 1739 it jumped to 75 and continued to increase, rising to over 100 in the 1750s (see Figure 16.1). It should be emphasized that, although the European fur market and French competition made higher prices at the posts possible, it was the bargaining ability of the natives, who played off the English and French, that actually brought about the better rate of exchange.

Evidence of bargaining by natives appears throughout the correspondence between the post governors and the head office in London. In fact James Isham, who was governor at York

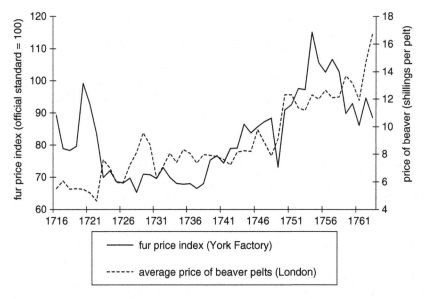

Figure 16.1 Fur price index at York Factory and the price of beaver pelts in London, 1716–63.
Source: Carlos and lewis (2010, 65).

Factory from 1737 to 1741, gave an example of the sorts of exchanges that traders might expect. The following, from his *Observations on Hudson Bay, 1743* (Rich 1949), was likely for instructional purposes and presents in phonetic Cree and English the possible give and take between a company trader (E) and two native traders (B and F):

B	I will trade a Long gun small and handy with a Red gun case	parskasigan wekawtaway Cawkenaworsquck na = howock misquock u' Spikanawgan
E	here is a very good gunn itt will not freese in the winter	mawkane methoshasit parskasigan nema cutta = miskowatin pepunnoack
F	how many Long Beads for a Beaver	tantarto norto menuck piuc aurtie
E	Ten	metartut
F	that's hard I will not trade them	addaman nema weder Kokawtaway

In this illustration native trader, B, will likely purchase the gun, but trader E will not accept the offer of 10 long beads for his beaver pelt. In fact, natives regularly threatened to trade with the French if the company didn't offer them attractive deals.[14]

European Goods Purchased by Native Traders

The Cree, Assiniboine, Dakota, and Ojibwa traders who made the journey downriver to York Factory and the other trading posts came to buy European goods. Trade provided natives with access to new technologies. Iron pots, awls, blankets, twine, and knives were all superior to the stone, bone, and wood implements that they replaced. What Kathryn Braund (1993, 130) has noted in the context of a more southerly trade held equally in the Hudson Bay region: the new tools improved the natives' ability to complete traditional tasks as "metal replaced stone, bone, and shell." Of course, not all European technologies were superior to native practice. The bow and arrow, for example, continued to be used for hunting many decades after natives had access to firearms.

In addition to making new technologies available, the commercial trade allowed Indians access to a wide variety of goods. Some items, such as kettles, guns, and blankets, came in different sizes and weights, while beads came in a wide range of colors and shapes. Even ignoring size variations, native traders could typically select from among 60 to 70 different goods. This variety helped attract natives to the posts. In Table 16.1, we organized the goods into a few broad categories based on their function: producer goods, household goods, tobacco and alcohol, and other luxury items. One advantage of the account books, from which Table 16.1 is derived, is that they allow us to determine how the natives were allocating their income from the fur trade across the various goods and categories of goods.

Producer goods were those items that helped natives meet their subsistence needs. Most goods in this category were metal products: files, fish hooks, ice chisels, hatchets, and scrapers, but the group was dominated by guns and related supplies, including flints, gun worms, shot, and powder. In 1740, of the 27,600 made beavers worth of goods received in trade, producer goods accounted for 12,000 made beavers or 43 percent; and of the producer goods, guns and related items made up 75 percent. But despite the importance of firearms in the overall trade, they were not used to hunt beaver. No felter, hatter, or furrier wanted a pelt full of shot holes.[15] During the winter when most beaver were hunted, twine and ice chisels were of more use: twine for traps that were set under water, and ice chisels to break open the beaver lodges.

Producer and household goods were an important part of the trade. Many of the goods in these categories were the metal equivalent of native technologies but, depending on the specific item, they dramatically reduced the time needed for hunting and household tasks. For example, a metal pot could be hung directly above a fire to boil water; whereas to heat water in a traditional pot, hot stones were placed in the water. In the years leading up to 1720, producer goods accounted for more than 60 percent of the total value of commodities purchased. However, during the next two decades, the share of producer goods in total trade fell to between 40 and 50 percent. Then, beginning in the early 1740s through to 1770, the share fell further to just 30 percent of native expenditure (see Figure 16.2). The share of native expenditure on blankets and kettles, the main items in the household goods category, also fell: from about 10 percent to roughly 6 percent. These declines were part of significant changes that were taking place in native consumption patterns.

Since the share of native expenditure on both producer and household goods declined, the share of expenditure on the remaining category, luxury goods, must have increased. We have defined everything not in the producer or household category as a luxury item and have subdivided these into three broad product groups: tobacco and related goods; alcohol and related goods; and other luxuries, including beads, cloth, lace, jewelry, and vermillion, among many others. Despite the lack of attention paid to tobacco in much of the literature, it was the most important luxury good for much of the period. Tobacco had an official price of 2 made beavers per pound. In 1740, traders purchased 2,271 pounds of tobacco with an official value of 4,543mb (see Table 16.1). They also received 96 pounds of tobacco as gifts. In total, tobacco and related goods accounted for 16 percent of native expenditure. The pattern over time is described in Figure 16.3. There were several large year-to-year fluctuations, but for the most part consumption of tobacco as a share of total expenditure remained in the 15 to 20 percent range.

The Hudson's Bay Company shipped two types of tobacco to their posts: Brazilian roll tobacco and Virginia roll tobacco.[16] Brazilian roll was of decidedly higher quality than the Virginia tobacco. Brazilian roll tobacco was produced in South America and shipped to Lisbon. In Lisbon, the company purchased the tobacco through agents who sent it on to

Figure 16.2 Share of native expenditure on producer and household goods: york factory, 1716–70.
Source: Carlos and lewis (2010, 87).

Figure 16.3 Share of native expenditure on tobacco and alcohol: York Factory, 1716–70.
Source: Carlos and lewis (2010, 88).

London, where it was reexported on company ships for the final journey to Hudson Bay. This single trade item was thus part of a transoceanic transport network that typified global trade in the eighteenth century. Obtaining Brazilian tobacco was sometimes a problem since the long delivery chain could be broken, usually as a result of war or the loss of a ship due to weather. In the annual letter of 1730 to Anthony Beale, governor of Fort Churchill, the head office wrote that it had sent everything that he had asked for "except Brazil tobacco, having not this year been able to procure so much as one roll, therefore have sent a greater quantity of English [Virginia] roll (quoted in Carlos and Lewis 2010, 89)." Natives, however, regarded this product as inferior.

In contrast to purchases of tobacco, which remained relatively constant after 1725, consumption of alcohol increased markedly, albeit from a very low level (see Figure 16.3). In fact, in the early years of the trade, there were no purchases of alcohol, and even in 1730 alcohol was still a relatively minor item with a share of about 5 percent. However, with the rise in fur prices beginning in the mid-1730s, alcohol expenditures increased, and from 1750 to the end of the period, alcohol equaled or surpassed tobacco in value. Nonetheless, as late as the 1740s natives spent more than twice as much on tobacco as they did on alcohol. The consumption of both tobacco and alcohol mirrored a phenomenon noted by Carole Shammas (1993, 178) in her work on European consumption patterns: "Probably the most striking development in consumer buying during the early modern period was the mass adoption by the English and the colonials of certain non-European groceries," among them tobacco, tea, sugar, and rum.

Much has been written about the influence of alcohol on native society. The literature on the more southerly trade intimates that vast quantities of alcohol were traded, and even suggests that some natives were addicted to the point of trading furs only for alcohol. Peter Mancall (1995) documents a long history of the destructive effect of alcohol on natives. As he characterizes it, alcohol in the more southerly trade was a "deadly medicine," often destroying individuals as well as the native social fabric. Daniel Usner (1987, 178) writes that the "English government in Pensacola attempted to restrict Indian traders to fifteen gallons every three months, which was considered a necessary amount for their purchase of food from Indian villagers," while in 1772 several Choctaw chiefs complained that rum "pours in upon our nation like a great Sea from Mobille and from all the Plantations and Settlements round about."

The trade accounts from York Factory, although involving different native groups, offer another perspective on the place of alcohol in native society. In 1740, as we noted, natives received 412 gallons of alcohol in trade and another 82 gallons in the gift-giving ceremonies. The total, 494 gallons, for the approximately 8,600 natives in the York Factory hinterland, translates to 0.06 gallons per person or four two-ounce drinks per year. Limiting the comparison to adult males, and even more restrictively to those who were directly involved with the fur trade, still gives a picture of natives who drank far less than the British and, even more so, than the American colonists. In the 1740s English per capita consumption was 1.4 gallons, and in 1770 North American colonists were consuming 4.2 gallons (Carlos and Lewis 2010, 93). Thus, by the standards of the time the natives of the Hudson Bay region were practically abstemious. Alcohol may be a serious problem in many Native American communities today, but in the Hudson Bay region during the early days of the fur trade, alcohol had little impact on native society. The evidence on alcohol is a piece of the overall composition of the trade and the response of natives to prices. The fur trade was a mechanism for improving their condition.

Trade and the Living Standards of Native Americans

The fur trade gave natives access to goods they could not produce themselves—goods that had a great impact on native life. Now, rather than relying exclusively on implements of stone, bone, and wood, they could substitute guns, knives, ice chisels, kettles, and other metal products. And the European technology embodied in these goods made daily activities easier. Iron kettles, knives, awls, and needles all improved the daily round of women's work. Cooking was easier with kettles, especially since women were able to specify the characteristics of the kettles that were sent over, and knives made food easier to prepare. But perhaps for the women awls and needles were even more exciting. Awls allowed women to punch holes in leather that was being used for clothing, and metal needles were a big improvement over bone or animal quills. Beads, that sometimes disparaged trade item, allowed for greater creative expression. The Cree had always decorated their clothing. Dyed porcupine quills, for example, adorned moccasins, but beads allowed greater color, variety, and texture.

Knives, ice chisels, twine, nets, hatchets, and firearms raised the men's productivity in hunting and other activities. Ice chisels allowed them to break into the beaver lodges in winter, and with twine nets it was easier to capture the beaver as they tried to escape underwater. Firearms greatly increased the catch during the bird migrations and were increasingly used to hunt large game animals. Hatchets helped the Indians gather firewood. The trade also provided cloth, lace, and other textiles, which changed the material culture of native society as traders purchased these goods in trade. Indeed, from the 1730s, when a strong market in Europe led to higher fur prices at the trading posts, natives began purchasing many more luxury items. Tobacco and alcohol, especially, became an increasing part of the social and spiritual life of native communities. At the same time, and despite the greater use of alcohol, the Cree and other natives living in the region remained moderate drinkers. But to what extent did the fur trade allow natives a material condition of life equivalent to that of Europeans? We address this issue of comparative living standards by combining the goods produced in the traditional native economy with the new goods that the fur trade made available to them, using as our basis of comparison the low-wage English worker of the mid-eighteenth century.[17]

Richard Steckel and Joseph Prince (2001) argue that the traditional native economy made possible a biological standard of living higher than in Europe. The Indians of the Great Plains, including the Assiniboin, who lived much of the year in the boreal forest south of Hudson Bay, were among the "tallest in the world," a clear indication that they were better nourished. Health-based measures are one approach to living standards, but a comprehensive method requires that we take account of all consumption. In the case of the natives of the Hudson Bay region this includes the variety of goods that they obtained through trade.

The great advantage of Native Americans over Europeans in nutrition is illustrated in Table 16.2, which compares the diets of low-wage English workers in the mid-eighteenth century with the diets of the natives of the boreal forest. Daily caloric intake was much greater, 3,500 kilocalories versus 2,500 kilocalories for adult males, but this gap is a reflection of different energy demands. More revealing is the composition of the diets. Because of the greater meat component, natives consumed much more protein, close to 500 grams per day versus 100 grams per day by the English. English workers derived just 5 percent of their calories from meat, 14 percent if dairy products are included. Their diet was mainly grain-based. In contrast, Native Americans obtained nearly all their calories from meat and fish, and most of that came from the flesh of large ungulates, the highest-priced type of food in Europe. This means that a measure of living standards based on food gives natives a decided advantage.

Native clothing, which was made from animal skins that were often decorated, was superior to the low-quality cloth worn by English workers. Budget studies reveal that the cost of English workers' clothing was far less than the value of the deer, caribou, beaver, and other skins that were used in native clothing. On the other hand, natives, because of their nomadic lifestyle, had inferior housing; living in tipis or wigwams in the winter and communal log houses in the summer. And despite the volume of luxury goods they received from the fur trade, native purchases of luxuries, especially alcohol, were much less than in England.

Arriving at an overall comparison of living standards requires weighting the categories of consumption goods. Weights can be derived from the choices of these eighteenth-century consumers. Where weights corresponding to English budgets are used, natives in the Hudson Bay region are derived to have real incomes between 10 and 25 percent less than English workers. But if native weights are used, the positions are reversed. The real income of natives is 10 to 20

Table 16.2 Calorie and protein content of the eighteenth-century diet of English workers and Native Americans (adult males)

English Workers	Budget share %	Price per calorie Meat = 1	Calories	Protein grams	Native Americans	Calories	Protein grams
Bread	22.2	0.34	555	22	Big Game	2,500	375
Wheat flour	30.0	0.33	775	32	Other meat and fish	750	100
Oatmeal	14.4	0.22	572	19	Vegetal products	250	
Potatoes	5.6	0.19	249	5			
Beef	3.3	1	29	4			
Mutton	3.3	1	29	4			
Pork	7.8	1	67	5			
Milk	5.6	0.43	110	6			
Butter	4.4	0.59	65	0			
Cheese	3.3	0.59	49	6			
Total	100	0.34	2,500	103		3,500	475

Source: Carlos and Lewis (2010, 172).

percent higher. The implication is that in the mid-eighteenth century Native Americans and low-wage English workers had similar living standards.

Our comparison for natives in the Hudson Bay region may, in fact, be understating their relative incomes. Native Americans certainly had inferior housing as measured on a cost basis, but natives, being nomadic, did not require the more substantial structures of the Europeans. Moreover, the fact that they spent more time outdoors, and their population densities were very much less, likely led to a healthier environment. The European diseases, such as smallpox, did not arrive until the late eighteenth century and may not have been as serious as generally reported (Carlos and Lewis 2012). It might also be noted that the greater consumption of luxuries by Europeans, an important element in the comparison, was largely due to their greater use of alcohol. Furthermore, the Hudson Bay region did not include the natives with the highest living standards. Although taller than Europeans, the Assiniboin were shorter on average than Indians of the Great Plains (Steckel and Prince 2001, 289). The natives of the Pacific Northwest had even higher living standards as judged by their plentiful supply of fish and their elaborate clothing and artifacts.

Beginning in the late eighteenth century, however, the position of nearly all natives relative to Europeans declined. In the Hudson Bay region dwindling fur and game resources contributed to an absolute decline. But more importantly, a commercial trade based on furs rather than agriculture or manufacturing could not promote long-run economic growth, especially the modern economic growth of Europe and colonial North America. The number of fur-bearing animals was limited by the capacity of their habitat, and so the fur trade could offer no more than the constraints dictated by that habitat.

Conclusion

Modern economies are underpinned by markets, but trade and exchange central to preindustrial Europe also played an important role in the aboriginal societies of North America. Prior to contact with Europeans, Native Americans had developed exchange mechanisms that allowed them to better deal with their environment. But in most of North America the options and advantages of trade were limited. Natives were mainly hunter-gatherers, possibly supplementing their food sources with small-scale farming. They produced similar goods in similar ways, and as a result there was little scope for the comparative advantage that is fundamental to trade. Nevertheless, the archaeological evidence reveals long-distance trading among aboriginals in some goods, especially those used for hunting. But it was in the areas of high population density, such as the area of southern California occupied by the Chumash, that trade was most fully developed.

The arrival of Europeans led to conflict in some regions, but in many areas, including the Hudson Bay hinterlands, there was little violence. Rather, the trade with Europeans offered natives access to new hunting technologies and more consumption options. Meanwhile the Europeans, both English and French, had opened up a new source of furs. They responded with arrangements for transporting the trade goods, and they established effective trading mechanisms that adapted to native practices. These included the introduction of gift giving and the learning of native languages. The aboriginals also adjusted, becoming effective bargainers and traders. Trade between aboriginals and Europeans was responsive to the potential for mutual gain. The goods they consumed were different, their technologies were different, and their institutional arrangements were different; but the nature of the exchanges and the ways the groups responded to their opportunities were, fundamentally, very much the same.

Notes

1 See Fenn (2001) for a discussion of the 1775–82 smallpox epidemic and Hackett (2002) on epidemics in the Hudson Bay region from 1670–1846. Other diseases of particular significance included measles, tuberculosis, whooping cough, and influenza.
2 Portions of this chapter are based on Carlos and Lewis (2010) and Carlos and Lewis (2014). See also Rich (1958), Ray (1974), and Ray and Freeman (1978).
3 See King (1971) and Gamble (2008).
4 www.history.alberta.ca/headsmashedin/.
5 Where the harsh subarctic winters produced furs of exceptional quality, beaver pelts could also be used in garments.
6 The Treaty of Breda, signed in 1667, marked the end of the Second Anglo-Dutch War and saw the transfer of Dutch territory including New Amsterdam (renamed New York) to the English.
7 In addition to paying the salaries of the workers, the company hired guards to curtail smuggling and was required to pay a tax on its beaver receipts of about 4 percent (Wien 1990, 299). Each Hudson's Bay Company post, by contrast, had a complement of roughly 30 to 50 men. With four major posts in the first half of the eighteenth century, Hudson's Bay Company employed more than 100 on the Canadian side of its operation (Carlos and Lewis 2010, 47).
8 See Carlos (1986) and Carlos and Hoffman (1986).
9 For a discussion of agency issues see Carlos and Nicholas (1988, 1990, 1993).
10 The original material is kept by the Hudson's Bay Company Archives in Winnipeg, Manitoba. Nearly all of the records have been available on microfilm for many years, and more recently some it has been placed online, available at www.gov.mb.ca/chc/archives/hbca/.
11 See Carlos and Lewis (2010, Ch.3) for a detailed discussion of how Native consumers determined the quality and type of European goods that were sent.
12 At this time the other main trading posts were Moose Factory, Fort Albany, and Fort Churchill. See Carlos and Lewis (2010, 41).
13 Beaver accounted for more than 80 percent of the trade with marten at about 10 percent.
14 The ability of the natives to bargain is captured in the title of Ray and Freeman's (1978) book, *Give Us Good Measure*.
15 Neither were guns in this region used for hunting large game or for warfare. The 3-foot gun that natives purchased were not suited for either purpose. Instead firearms were for hunting small game and, more importantly, waterfowl.
16 Wimmer (1998) fully recognizes the importance of tobacco.
17 In the mid-eighteenth century English workers were among the highest paid in the world (Allen 2000).

References

Allen, Robert C. "The Great Divergence in European Wages and Prices from the Middle Ages to the First World War," *Explorations in Economic History* 38 (2000): 411–47.
Bamforth, Douglas B. "Origin Stories, Archaeological Evidence and Post-Clovis Paleoindian Bison Hunting on the Great Plains"., *American Antiquity* 76 (2011): 24–40.
Carlos, Ann M., and Stephen Nicholas "Giants of an Earlier Capitalism: The Chartered Trading Companies & Multinationals," *Business History Review* 62 (1988): 398–419.
Carlos, Ann M., and Stephen Nicholas "Agency Problems in Early Chartered Companies: The Case of the Hudson's Big Company," *Economic History* 50 (1990): 853–875.
Carlos, Ann M., and Stephen Nicholas "Managing the Manager: An Application of the Principal Agent Model to the Hudson's Big Company," *Oxford Economic Papers New Series* (1993), 45(2): 243–256.
Carlos, Ann M., and Elizabeth Hoffman "The North American Fur Trade: Bargaining to a Joint Profit Maximum Under Incomplete Information, 1804–1821," *Journal of Economic History* 46 (1986): 967–86.
Carlos, Ann M., and Santhi Hejeebu "The Timing and Quality of Information: The Case of the Long-Distance Trading Companies, 1650–1750," *Information Flows: New Approaches in the Historical Study of Business Information*, eds. J. Ojala and J. McCusker (Helsinki: Studia Historica, 2007) 139–168.
Carlos, Ann M., and Frank D. Lewis. *Commerce by a Frozen Sea: Native Americans and the European Fur Trade* (Philadelphia: University of Pennsylvania Press, 2010).
Carlos, Ann M., and Frank D. Lewis. "Smallpox and Native American Mortality: The 1780s Epidemic in the Hudson Bay Region." *Explorations in Economic History* 49 (2012): 277–90.

Carlos, Ann M., and Frank D. Lewis. "Native Americans and Exchange: Strategies and Interactions before 1800," *The Cambridge History of Capitalism*, Vol. 1, eds. L. Neal and J. Williamson (New York: Cambridge University Press 2014), 455–90.

Carlson, Roy L. "Prehistoric Trade," *Historical Atlas of Canada*, Vol. 1, ed. R. Cole Harris, plate 14 (Toronto: University of Toronto Press, 1987).

Clark, Fiona. *Hats* (London: Anchor Press, 1982).

Fenn, Elizabeth A. *Pox America: The Great Smallpox Epidemic of 1775–82* (New York: Hill and Wang, 2001).

Gamble, L. H. *The Chumash World at European Contact: Power, Trade, and Feasting among Complex Hunter-Gatherers* (Berkeley: University of California Press, 2008).

Ginsberg, Madeleine. *The Hat: Trends and Traditions* (London: Studio Editions, 1988).

Hackett, Paul. *A Very Remarkable Sickness: Epidemics in the Petit Nord, 1670–1846* (Winnipeg, Manitoba: University of Manitoba, 2002).

King, C.D. "Chumash Inter-village Economic Exchange," *The Indian Historian* 4 (1971): 31–43. Reprinted in L. Bean and T. Blackburn, eds., *Native Californians: A Theoretical Retrospective*. Ramona (CA: Ballena Press, 1976), 289–318.

Lawson, Murray G. *Fur: A Study in English Mercantilism, 1700–1775* (Toronto: University of Toronto Press, 1943).

Mancall, Peter C. *Deadly Medicine: Indians and Alcohol in Early America* (Ithaca, NY: Cornell University Press, 1995).

Miquelon, Dale. *New France, 1701–1744: "A Supplement to Europe,"* The Canadian Centenary Series (Toronto: McClelland and Stewart, 1987).

Ray, Arthur J. *Indians in the Fur Trade: Their role as Hunters, Trappers and Middlemen in the Lands Southwest of Hudson Bay, 1660–1870* (Toronto: University of Toronto Press, 1980).

Ray, Arthur J. and Donald Freeman. *"Give Us Good Measure": An Economic Analysis of Relations Between the Indians the Hudson's Bay Company Before 1763* (Toronto: University of Toronto Press, 1978).

Rich, E. E., ed. *James Isham's Observations on Hudson Bay, 1743* (Toronto: Champlain Society 1949).

Rich, E. E. *Hudson's Bay Company, 1670–1870*. 2 vols. (London: Hudson's Bay Record Society, 1958).

Shammas, Carole. "Changes in English and Anglo-American Consumption from 1550–1800," *Consumption and the World of Goods*, eds. J. Brewer and R. Porter (London: Routledge, 1993) 177–205.

Steckel, Richard H., and Joseph M. Prince. "Tallest in the World: Native Americans of the Great Plains in the Nineteenth Century," *American Economic Review* 91 (2001): 287–94.

Usner, Daniel H., Jr. "The Frontier Exchange Economy of the Lower Mississippi Valley in the Eighteenth Century," *William and Mary Quarterly*, 3rd Series, 44 (1987): 165–92.

Wien, Thomas. "Selling Beaver Skins in North America and Europe, 1720–1760: The Uses of Fur-Trade Imperialism," *Journal of the Canadian Historical Association*, new series 1 (1990): 293–317.

Wimmer, Linda. "'To Encourage a Trade with the Indians': Brazilian Tobacco and Cross-Cultural Relations in the Hudson's Bay Company Fur Trade, 1690–1750." Working Paper No. 98–22 (1998). Presented at the International Seminar on the History of the Atlantic World, 1500–1800, Harvard University.

17

DISMANTLING THE DREAM OF "FRANCE'S PERU"

Indian and African Influence on the Development of Early Colonial Louisiana

Elizabeth Ellis

On March 5, 1731 three African captives, French lieutenant Regis du Roullet, and the influential Choctaw leader Alibamon Mingo found themselves at a diplomatic impasse. The men were deep in Choctaw territory, and Regis du Roullet was on a mission to reaffirm French Louisiana's alliance with the Choctaw nation and secure the return of several African captives in the Choctaws' possession. Roullet was scrambling to negotiate a satisfactory price for the return of African captives from the Choctaws when the captives themselves barged into the meeting and demanded to speak with Roullet.

The three African prisoners had been looking for an avenue to escape their Choctaw captors and they hoped to negotiate with Roullet to facilitate these ends. For weeks they had been severely abused by the Choctaws and forced to perform grueling labor, and they feared for their lives. As they poured forth their proposition to the French official, they explained that their Choctaw captors "exhaust (sic) us, mistreat us, and have taken from us our clothing," and Roullet noticed that one of these captives indeed had "a tomahawk wound on the head which went as far as the bone." The three captives implored Roullet to personally escort them out of Choctaw territory and said they were willing to return to the French settlements. Additionally, they convinced Roullet that if he did this, they promised to persuade the other African captives in Choctaw possession to return to the French as well.[1]

Roullet needed a solution that balanced Choctaw, French, and African desires. Alabamon Mingo refused to part with these captives for less than two horses as payment. He also reminded Roullet that many of the Choctaws were suggesting that the English colonists to the east would compensate the Choctaws more generously for their services if their southern French neighbors failed to do so. The Lieutenant recognized that Louisiana desperately needed the alliance of the Choctaws and that if Louisiana lost Choctaw support the colony was destined for failure. Thus he could not afford to alienate as powerful of a leader as Alabamon Mingo. As a representative of the French colony, Roullet also could not simply give up the African captives to the Choctaws. By 1731 Louisiana had extremely limited access to the transatlantic slave trade, and therefore Roullet could not count on the arrival of additional enslaved Africans to replenish the labor force. Finally, if he did not act fast, these Africans would likely die or run away as so many of their comrades had in the last several weeks, and that would leave furious parties on all sides. Thus, Roullet found himself forced to negotiate a solution on both African and Choctaw terms. He would send Alabamon Mingo to Mobile where he could receive two horses from another official, and he would send a French escort along with the party to protect the captives from further abuse.[2]

As Roullet simultaneously negotiated with Alabamon Mingo and the African captives, he was forced to consider the limits of French authority, the extent of Choctaw power, and the desires of enslaved Africans. Like so many exchanges in the eighteenth-century Lower Mississippi Valley, this negotiation involved peoples of varied linguistic and ethnic backgrounds, took place in a contested territory, and involved both free and unfree actors. In this borderland both Natives and newcomers had to learn to negotiate across cultures and sovereignties and to rely on their connections with others to navigate a tumultuous geopolitical landscape. As Roullet demonstrated by weighing Louisiana's lack of access to the transatlantic slave trade, English imperial ambitions, and the fraught politics of Choctaw diplomacy in 1731, navigating life in the Lower Mississippi Valley required attention to both continental and Atlantic networks. Although France formally asserted control of the vast region from the Gulf Coast to the Canadian interior, on the ground this was an Indian-dominated borderland that was shaped by the fluid interactions among African, European, and Native peoples. Colonial success or failure, the ability to find liberty or freedom from abuse, and the geopolitical aspirations of nations of all sizes depended upon inhabitants' abilities to forge relationships with the multiethnic inhabitants of the Lower Mississippi Valley and to consider both the region's internal and external politics and economies.

The French settlers who arrived in this densely Indigenous borderland at the end of the seventeenth century brought with them goals of establishing a prosperous plantation economy and politically dominating the Lower Mississippi Valley. Louisiana officials looked to the roaring successes of the Spanish empire in Mexico and Peru, and of the English in Virginia and thus desired their own wildly lucrative North American enterprise. Yet, by the 1730s it was evident that this dream would never be permitted to come to fruition. By examining the first half of the French colonial era, it becomes clear that while imperial policy and transatlantic logistical challenges certainly hindered the development of this French colony, the initiatives and actions of enslaved Africans and powerful Native peoples were largely responsible for stymieing the growth of Louisiana. Thus, although many historians have considered French Louisiana to be a story of the failure of French administration in a peripheral colony, it is better understood as a tale of negotiated outcomes in a contested borderland. The tenuousness of Louisiana's Atlantic connections and the powerful bonds of interdependency that linked Native, African, and European peoples in the Lower Mississippi Valley fundamentally shaped the colonial reality that emerged within the Native southeast.

Securing a Toehold Along the Gulf Coast

In 1699 a French expeditionary force led by Pierre Le Moyne d'Iberville washed ashore on the beaches of Biloxi Bay. These men were part of a reconnaissance voyage sent to explore the region and claim the territory for the French King Louis XIV. Their mission was to set up a chain of defensive posts that could halt British expansion across North America from the east, assess the region's natural resources, establish diplomatic alliances with the region's Native peoples, and determine if colonization would be a worthwhile venture for the French crown. Over the course of the seventeenth century, British settlements along the eastern seaboard had expanded steadily westward toward the Appalachian Mountains. As English settlements grew, British officials and merchants forged connections with the Native peoples who controlled these trans-Appalachian territories, thereby expanding their economic and political networks from the Atlantic Ocean into the continental interior. French officials feared that with this expansion of influence the British were poised to claim control of a large swath of the North American continent and might ultimately block France's territorial claims and trade networks in Canada. Therefore, they hoped that a French settlement in the Lower Mississippi Valley might be able to curb British expansion and possibly generate a lucrative trade economy of its own.[3]

Yet regardless of these grand imperial designs, when Iberville and his men arrived in the Lower Mississippi Valley in 1699, they faced a starkly different reality. Most urgently, these newcomers needed to establish a base of operations, secure provisions, and find allies who could provide them with geographic and political intelligence. Thus, the bulk of French activity during the first decade of colonization in the Lower Mississippi Valley was focused on building relationships with local Indian nations. These Indigenous peoples would supply the newcomers with the food, guides, protection, and labor that helped the French assert their claims to the region.

French explorers' first relationships in the Lower Mississippi Valley were with the petites nations. At the turn of the century the region was home to more than 35 small Native polities, each of which ranged in size from 50 to 2,000 people. Collectively the French called these small polities the "petites nations," in order to distinguish them from the larger inland nations like the Chickasaws or the Choctaws. The petites nations each controlled discrete pieces of territory along the Gulf Coast and Mississippi, and they spoke more than four different languages and were of a variety of ethnic and cultural backgrounds. By forming relationships with these diverse, small polities the settlers who claimed Louisiana began to make inroads along the Gulf Coast.[4]

Among the very first petites nations to establish an alliance with the French newcomers were the Biloxis. When Iberville and his men disembarked from their ships they crossed into Biloxi territory near present day Biloxi, Mississippi.[5] The Biloxis initially fled the French, fearing that this heavily armed, all-male attachment was a war party, but upon further observation the Biloxis ascertained that these newcomers might make appealing allies. After engaging the explorers in a calumet ceremony, the essential peace-making ritual that enabled diplomacy among foreign nations, the Biloxis agreed to a partnership with the Frenchmen. The Biloxis fed and sheltered the hungry French travelers, offered to serve as their diplomatic emissaries in the region, and permitted the French to build a small fort on their land from which they could base their operations. Biloxi guides also provided Iberville and his men with directions and diplomatic introductions to neighboring native nations, thereby connecting the French into the regional political networks.[6]

During the first decade of French presence in the Lower Mississippi Valley Louisiana settlers and soldiers resided almost exclusively in settlements alongside or within very close proximity to petites nations villages, and they depended on their partnerships with these communities for their survival. Both Biloxi and Mobile, the first two major settlements in colonial Louisiana, were located alongside petites nations villages. In 1702 French officials accepted an offer from the petite nation of Mobilians to relocate to Mobile Bay from their outpost at Biloxi in order to live within a cluster of petites nations settlements. This new location offered the French better protection from the continual floods that inundated their meager fort at Biloxi and gave them access to the Mobilians, Naniabas, Tohomes, and Capinans.[7] In addition to acting as their diplomatic emissaries, these nations furnished the Louisiana settlers with corn, fish, and game. By 1702 there were only 140 French settlers enmeshed within a Native population of more than 1,225 at Mobile. Including the region surrounding Mobile, there were about 3,500 petites nations peoples, and thus they were able to accommodate the needs of these few settlers fairly easily.[8]

These partnerships among petites nations and the French worked in large part because both the Louisiana settlers and local Native populations were in dire straits at the turn of the century. When Iberville and his men landed in Louisiana in 1699, they entered a geopolitical world that had been thrown into chaos by the expansion of the Southeastern Indian slave trade. By the 1690s the Chickasaws and the Upper Creek polities of the Alabamas, Abihkas, and Talapoosas began conducting frequent raids against the small nations of the Gulf Coast and lower Mississippi River.[9] During the 1680s the Chickasaws and Upper Creeks had formed trade partnerships with the English at Carolina in order to protect their own people from slave raiders. The Chickasaws' position in present-day northern Mississippi and the Upper Creeks location north and east of Mobile in present-day Georgia meant that all these polities were located on the peripheries of British settlement. They quickly discovered that Charleston merchants were willing to pay handsomely in guns, munitions, cloth, and metal tools for Indian captives and so they sought to capitalize on this market opportunity. Charleston merchants saw promise in the trade in Indian captives to fulfill labor shortages not just in South Carolina, but within English colonies across the Atlantic world.[10]

The Chickasaws, Abihkas, Talapoosas, and Alabamas' access to guns gave them a substantial military advantage and enhanced both the efficacy and range of their raids. Although the Chickasaws numbered only about 7,000 people in 1700, this advantage in weapons technology enabled them to strike Choctaw villages that collectively totaled 17,500 and the more than 20,000 petites nations peoples. During the first two decades of the eighteenth century these warriors hammered the Lower Mississippi Valley, enslaved more than 3,000 Native people, and killed untold numbers more in the process. Thus, when the French arrived bearing weapons and promises of trade in the 1700s, nations like the Biloxis saw great potential for these alliances to help them better defend their people from Native slave raids.[11]

French settlers also faced their own sets of internal and external challenges during the early years of settlement. Much as the French feared the growth of English settlements along the East coast, the English felt threatened by French attempts to claim territory in the continental interior that could halt English expansion and undermine their partnerships with their Indian allies. Thus, English officials hoped to use their partnerships with their Native allies to frustrate the development of colonial Louisiana. French settlement also threatened the regional dominance of the Chicaksaws, Abihkas, Alabamas, and Talapoosas. These nations recognized that if their enemies, the Choctaws, formed an alliance with the French, this would provide the Choctaws with steady access to Atlantic networks and to guns, which they could then turn on Upper Creek and Chickasaw raiders. Therefore, during the first decade of the eighteenth century Chickasaw and Upper Creek warriors not only attacked the petites nations and Choctaws, but also assaulted French settlers near Mobile. In 1704 several Alabamas killed a French trader who was trespassing into their territory, and in 1708 the Chickasaws threatened to attack the tiny French settlement at Mobile and "eat up a village of white men."[12]

To combat threats from these powerful Indian polities, French officials sought to cultivate an extensive Indian alliance network that could shield Louisiana settlers from these raids. This defensive strategy required the support of both large and small Indian nations in the region. For example, in 1704 the French requested help from the petites nations of the Tohomes and Mobilians as well as from the Choctaws to mount a punitive expedition against the Alabamas and for their murder of the French trader. Staunch resistance from newly armed Choctaws also helped repulse Chickasaw incursions into the region. While the French crown claimed dominance of the Mississippi River Valley, on the ground Louisiana officials were acutely aware of the frailty of their imperial establishment. As French Governor Jean Baptist Le Moyne de Bienville recognized in 1711, without the support of the Choctaws, whom he described as "the key to this country," the French could not expect to hold Louisiana.[13]

In addition to securing an alliance with the powerful Choctaws and trade relationships with the petites nations, a shift in Upper Creek policy during the 1710s was perhaps the third most critical factor in ensuring the viability of the Louisiana polity. After a decade of conflict with the French in Louisiana, the Abihkas, Talapoosas, and Alabamas tired of the ongoing bloodshed and of French-orchestrated assaults against their villages. By 1712 many within these polities had decided it would be more advantageous for them to form an alliance with the French settlers at Mobile rather than continue to fight these colonists. This new political connection would both provide the Upper Creeks with access to European trade goods without having to travel to Carolina, and enable them to engage in "play-off diplomacy." By holding competing alliances with imperial polities, Upper Creek diplomats were able to gain leverage for better trade terms by "playing-off" these competing offers. Additionally, these alliances would afford their people protection from the Indian nations allied with both European powers, at least in theory.[14] Although chronic supply shortages prevented the French from ever having enough trade goods to sustain strong economic ties or close political alliances with the Alabamas, Abhikas, and Talapoosas, this loose alliance at least halted Creek attacks on Mobile and Biloxi and allowed the French settlements to develop in greater safety.[15]

While the French officials worked to strengthen their bonds with Native nations along the Gulf during the first years of settlement, their Atlantic networks remained feeble, and the Louisiana settlers found themselves desperately isolated from the rest of the French empire at this critical time. In 1700 the King of Spain, Charles II, died without an heir and left his throne to the grandson of French King Louis XV. If the English were already concerned about France's attempts to carve out territories in North America and growing French influence in Europe, the ascent of a French King to the Spanish throne seemed to confirm their fears that the Catholic monarchies were joining forces to dominate both Europe and the Americas. To prevent this consolidation of power, in 1702 England declared war against Spain and France. The War of Spanish Succession, as this conflict became known, sapped enormous resources from the Dutch, English, Spanish, and Austrian belligerents. In the North American theater, British, Spanish, and French troops fought across Florida, New England, and Canada, until the Peace of Utrecht finally concluded the war in 1713.[16]

While France was embroiled in this massive conflict, the French crown had very few resources to devote to the colonies, and thus Louisiana, a fledgling backwater of minimal value, was largely neglected during the first decade of colonization. The few colonists at Mobile and Biloxi languished while they waited for the arrival of ships carrying critical provisions like grain, livestock, clothing, millstones, and gifts for Indians. Without regular supply lines to France, the colonists in Louisiana faced shortages of nearly everything. Between 1708 and 1711 not one supply ship arrived in Louisiana to aid the few hundred settlers and this led to one of the periods of most abject hunger and dependency for the stranded Louisiana colonists.[17]

Colonial administrators sent repeated desperate requests for supplies, hard currency, food, and laborers, but because of the War of Spanish Succession their requests went largely unanswered. In 1702 Governor Bienville sent an urgent plea for women and for African laborers to help support the colony. Bienville reasoned that in addition to the provisions, the French needed laborers to support the settlements and cultivate the lands. Bienville believed that 100 young women of good quality and strong moral character would be an adequate amount to support the colony at Mobile and alleviate some of the labor shortage. The first ships of explorers had not included any women, and colonial officials were concerned about the deleterious effects of the lack of female presence, specifically the lack of a labor force to do the feminine work of washing and cooking.[18] Yet the first group of French women did not arrive in Louisiana until 1704, and then only 21 women came, rather than the requested 100.[19] Similarly, by 1706 Louisiana settlers were vociferously demanding that the French government send African slaves to the colony to help clear the land and establish plantations. Much as these French officials reasoned that they needed women to do domestic work, French settlers believed that African bodies were more suited to the grueling labor of clearing fields and establishing farms. Again, the French crown processed their requests slowly and incompletely. The first Africans did not arrive in Louisiana until 1709 and they remained extremely scarce until the 1720s.[20]

The shortages of laborers and provision meant that the French remained heavily dependent on their Native allies. In addition to trading and providing military support and services to the settlers, the petites nations near Mobile also offered French soldiers refuge for months at a time. During the winter of 1706 the garrison at Fort Mobile ran out of provisions and Governor Bienville was forced to send the soldiers to petites nations villages while he awaited the arrival of supplies. Andre Penicaut, one French carpenter who found refuge with the petites nations of the Acolapissas and Nassitoches during that long winter, reported that the French were warmly welcomed into these Native villages. He explained that the French entertained themselves through the cold months teaching the Indian men and women to dance minuets, and bumbling their way through Acolapissa and Nassitoches dances. When a French ship bearing provisions finally arrived in 1707 and Penicaut had to return to the stark life at colonial Mobile, he wistfully remarked that he was sorry to leave and that only "the wine consoled us for the loss of favors of [the Nassitoches and Acolapissa] girls."[21]

The close connections that linked French settlers to Native villages and sustained colonial settlement during the early years of French Louisiana deeply troubled some colonial officials, who believed these relationships threatened to destabilize the colony. Although most French men in the Lower Mississippi Valley did not marry into Native communities as they did in Canada or in Illinois, administrators worried that intimate bonds and personal relationships with Indian men and women endangered the loyalty of men like Penicaut to France. Yet it was not just French settlers' ties to the petites nations that troubled colonial officials, but also their intimacy with Indian slaves within French settlements.[22]

Enslaved Native men, women, and children labored in colonial Mobile and Biloxi from the earliest years of European arrival, and by 1708 there were 80 Indian slaves in the colony. Given that there were only 279 French colonists in the imperial settlements, that meant that enslaved Indians comprised nearly a third of the total colonial population.[23] Native men performed the backbreaking work needed to build the infrastructure of colonial Mobile and New Orleans and labored on the plantations as the French attempted to scrape a living out of the muddy delta. Both enslaved Native men and women played crucial roles in sustaining the nascent French settlements around Mobile. Enslaved women washed, cleaned, mended clothes, and prepared food for French men. In addition to expecting enslaved Native women to perform this multitude of household chores, many French men also expected them to perform all of the duties of French wives including sex. Indian women enslaved at French settlements were coerced to have sex with their French masters so often that early observers labeled them as the "wives" or "concubines" of their French masters.[24]

In 1718 two key developments, one continental and one Atlantic, altered the demography and labor system of Louisiana. The first was the conclusion of the Yamasee War in Carolina. During the years between 1690 and 1715 many Native nations in alliance with Carolina benefited enormously from trade in deerskins and Indian slaves with the English settlers. Yet by the 1710s, nations including the Yamasees, Catawbas, and Choctaws were furious with Carolina traders for their unscrupulous trade practices. English traders had gained reputations for shorting their customers, physically abusing Native women, and impounding the families and property of Indian peoples who held outstanding debts. Additionally, Southeastern groups critiqued the English for failing to distinguish between allied and enemy captives and for selling the kin of their Native business partners. Thus in 1715 the Yamasees and their Native allies attacked English settlers in Carolina and English traders across the Southeast. Although the Yamasee coalition failed to wipe out the English presence in Carolina, their assault did convince the English that trading in Indian slaves was too dangerous of a prospect for the colony. Likewise, the shockwaves of the Yamasee War encouraged French officials to curtail their own efforts to acquire Indian slaves from local nations.[25]

Meanwhile, in France, King Louis XIV transferred exclusive property rights to Louisiana to the Scottish financier John Law. Louisiana was not only unprofitable but a serious drain on French coffers, and so King Louis was eager to free himself of this fiscal burden. In 1718 the King transferred control of the colony to John Law. Law proposed a colonization scheme for the Lower Mississippi Valley that would be funded by a joint stock company, the Company of the Indies, and he promised he would finally make this territory profitable.[26] The company aimed to provide the colony with the financial support it so desperately needed, but they failed to account for the power of continental politics and economies.[27] In 1718 the Lower Mississippi Valley was a Native-dominated space that was home to several small French outposts and feckless transatlantic networks. Thus, even as the company dumped funding into the Louisiana venture they found their efforts stymied by the power of the region's Native peoples.

Colonial Schemes and Popular Protest

In 1718 the French newspaper the *Nouveau Mercure* published a letter that was allegedly from a French colonist in Louisiana written to a "woman of quality" in Paris. In this letter the colonist extoled the many virtues of Louisiana. He prophesied that the colony "may one day become France's Peru" and generate tremendous wealth from the numerous "gold and silver mines," silk production, and through the labor of friendly Indians who would be so eager to support these projects that for "just a few trinkets, we could get from them the most valuable merchandise in Europe."[28] Between 1717 and 1719 John Law commissioned a wave of advertisements and propaganda pieces, like this letter, to generate interest and investment in his Louisiana venture and to recruit prospective settlers.

Throughout the 1720s, the Company of the Indies strove to realize this idyllic vision of Louisiana and to convert a destitute backwater into a profitable hub of Atlantic exchange. Rather than striving to follow France's North American settlement model of dispersed settlements and an economy fueled by the fur trade, the Company sought to develop a society that was more Caribbean than Canadian in structure and that was centered on plantation production.[29] Thus in addition to recruiting French and German settlers, the Company imported thousands of enslaved Africans into Louisiana. However, despite Law's grand ambitions, Louisiana did not become a plantation-based slave society. Rather, during the 1720s staunch resistance from enslaved Africans on slave ships on the coasts of West Africa, Indian attacks on French settlements along the Mississippi, and French men and women's protests in the streets of Paris all dismantled Law's vision for "France's Peru."

The critical first step for the Company of the Indies' revitalization plan for Louisiana would be to secure settlers for the colony. In 1717, nearly 20 years after the French arrival, there were only 400 French inhabitants in Lower Louisiana.[30] The propaganda pieces did generate some interest in Europe and between 1717 and 1721 119 French planters, 2,462 indentured laborers and artisans, and 2,600 German, Alsacian, and Swiss immigrants boarded ships for transport to Louisiana.[31] To supplement this dismal voluntary turnout, the Company enacted what amounted to penal colonization. They took convicts, deserters, vagabonds, and disorderly men and women out of the jails and off the hands of the government.[32] More than 1,200 French subjects were forcibly sent to Louisiana between 1717 and 1720.[33]

Prison may have been a preferable option for many of both the voluntary and involuntary settlers who arrived in Louisiana during these years. The ships that bore these colonists arrived along Mobile Bay desperately underprovisioned. While the Biloxis and Mobilians had been able to support a few hundred Frenchmen and they continued to take soldiers into their villages during hard winters, neither they nor the other petites nations were equipped to feed the thousands of migrants who poured into the region. Left without food, medicine, wine, and adequate clothing along the sandy, humid coast, these settlers experienced brutal famine during the winter of 1718–1719. Colonists quickly devoured the livestock that was intended to breed herds for the colony and attempted to subsist on shellfish and wild herbs. Surviving settlers reported eating weevil infested wheat and finding the bodies of Germans next to heaps of oyster shells along the water's edge.[34] Not surprisingly, many of these colonists returned to France at the first opportunity and about 1,000 of these colonists made the voyage back to Europe between 1719 and 1722. They brought stories of suffering and rumors of bloodthirsty Indians that effectively stemmed interest in voluntary migration and struck terror into those slated for penal deportation.[35] In January 1720, 50 inmates in a Paris prison orchestrated a jailbreak in order to escape shipment to Louisiana, and in early summer there were riots in the streets of a Parisian suburb against the injustice of this involuntary relocation.[36] The tenor of this protest reached such a fever pitch that in May the King formally forbade the deportation of any more prisoners to Louisiana.[37]

While the forced migration of French subjects to Louisiana stopped by 1720, thousands more enslaved Africans were taken from their homelands and deposited into the colony. During 1717 and 1718 the Company of the Indies sent 1,284 enslaved Africans from the Bight of Benin, 323 from Senegal, and 294 from West Africa to Biloxi and Mobile. Then, between 1719 and 1723 an additional 2,083 enslaved Africans arrived in Louisiana. After the initial voyages in 1717 and 1718 the majority of these enslaved Africans came on ships from Senegambia, and many of these slaves had been captured during the wars that forged the Segu empire among the Bambara kingdoms in Africa.[38] The African men and women who survived this voyage then languished in underprovisioned holdings in the Lower Mississippi Valley where many of them died of thirst and hunger. Of the first 2,000 enslaved Africans imported into Louisiana less than 700 survived to 1720 and by 1726 the census of the colony reports that there were only 1,540 enslaved Africans still living in the colony. All told, between 1719 and 1731, 5,761 enslaved Africans were sent to colonial Louisiana, and yet by 1731 only 2,529 of these captives were still alive.[39]

The Africans who arrived along the Gulf Coast in the late 1710s and 1720s sustained and revitalized the destitute French settlements in the Lower Mississippi Valley. Enslaved Africans helped construct colonial settlements at Mobile and New Orleans. In 1718 repeated flooding once again encouraged Louisiana officials to relocate the capital, and they established a small settlement on the old Bayagoula territory along a bend in the Mississippi, which they christened New Orleans. This settlement provided key access to both the Mississippi River and the Gulf of Mexico, but like Biloxi and Mobile, it was also prone to flooding. Enslaved African men toiled in the Mississippi mud to construct the levee that protected New Orleans from the swollen Mississippi currents. On the outskirts of this new colonial capital African laborers cleared brush and planted the indigo, tobacco, and corn designated for overseas markets. Enslaved Africans also brought with them their expertise cultivating rice, an ideal crop for the swampy Lower Mississippi Valley. Not until the 1730s did the Lower Louisiana settlements begin to receive regular shipments of flour from French farms in the Illinois River Valley, and even then these deliveries were insufficient to supply the colony. Therefore, in addition to the corn and meat produced and sold by Indian traders, African grown rice provided a staple of the Louisiana diet.[40]

By the late 1720s Louisiana seemed to be well on the way to becoming a successful slave society. By 1726 there were 1,952 French subjects and 276 European servants within the colony.[41] Massive epidemics has devastated many of the petites nations peoples during the 1700s and 1710s. Some nations, like the Mobilians, lost more than 90 percent of their populations during these decades, and thus the ratios of Native to white to black inhabitants shifted at the multiethnic settlements of Mobile and New Orleans. While Native populations collapsed, a steady supply of enslaved African streamed into Mobile and New Orleans, and their cultivation of indigo promised to convert Louisiana's dismal financial prospects into a lucrative cash-crop economy. Echoing this optimism in 1726, Governor Bienville proclaimed that "It can no longer be doubted now that indigo will successes in Louisiana … The harvests of rice that have been grown there for three years have been abundant" and that the Company "would not fail to make profit" on the timber commerce. Further up river French colonists residing alongside the Natchez Indian nation had discovered that the fertile terrain was ideal for growing tobacco "of a good quality" and suspected that this would enable Louisiana to compete with English tobacco from Virginia on the global market. Bienville credited the stagnation of the colony during the first two decades to the neglect of the French crown and, now that the colony was receiving firmer support and thousands of enslaved Africans from the Company of the Indies, he saw prosperity on the horizon.[42]

For all of Bienville's optimism, Native and African peoples' resistance hindered his rosy dreams. From its inception, the transatlantic trade that carried enslaved Africans to the Gulf Coast faced a multitude of problems. Louisiana was considerably further from Senegal than were the West Indies, and ships often stopped through Caribbean ports first and where they were able to sell most of their cargo. This deterred slave traders from making the longer journey north and meant fewer slaves reached Louisiana. For company-funded vessels destined for Louisiana, the difficult ports at Biloxi, Mobile, and New Orleans presented logistical problems, as did the lack of sufficient food and water available in the colony, which the slave ships needed to restock for the return journey. Within the markets themselves, Louisiana settlers were often short on hard currency, and so ended up paying for slaves on credit from the company. Yet it was not just logistical issues that ultimately stifled the slave trade in Louisiana. Rather, as Gwendolyn Midlo Hall has argued, it was also the direct resistance of enslaved Africans themselves that stymied the growth of a slave society in Louisiana.[43]

In 1729 a group of captive Africans on board *L'Annibal*, a ship bound for Louisiana, led an uprising that brought the slave trade from West Africa to Louisiana to a grinding halt. In April of 1729 slave traders loaded a Company ship with African captives from Goreé and than headed to Gambia to collect additional captives. The Africans onboard this ill-fated ship had already been in captivity at Goreé for months, and had been subject to malnourishment, unhygienic conditions, and other abuse. The brutal onboard conditions compounded with this long period of suffering meant that captive Africans began to die almost immediately. In May, as the boat pitched and churned while the crew waited at the mouth of the Gambia River, the African captives rose up and attacked the crew. They stormed the supply rooms, grabbed lances, pikes, and pistols and fired on their captors. For eight hours they waged battle before the crew was able to suppress the revolt. By the end of the fight there were 45 black men missing (likely jumped into the sea), 3 women and 2 babies dead, 47 wounded African captives, and 9 wounded or killed crewmembers. While the captive African passengers did not succeed in gaining their freedom, their resistance thwarted the ship's voyage to Louisiana and it made other slave traders extremely hesitant to commit to the long voyage to Louisiana. After 1731 only one more slave ship arrived in Louisiana during the French era of colonization, and that one did not arrive until 1743.[44] While logistical difficulties and African resistance plagued Louisiana's Atlantic networks and challenged French dreams of a slave-labor driven economy, pressure from Native groups within the Lower Mississippi Valley was ultimately responsible for the collapse of the Louisiana's plantation fortunes.

In 1714 the Natchez Indians welcomed a few French settlers and soldiers onto their fertile lands as part of a diplomatic partnership. The Natchez were a larger and more socially stratified polity than the surrounding petites nations. Located south and west of the Choctaws near the present day location of Natchez Mississippi, the Natchez nation was organized along a strict social and political hierarchy with strong centralized, theocratic leadership. The Natchez were governed by a class of ruling elite who they called the great "Suns," in reference to their celestial heritage and power. Yet like so many of the other nations of the region, the Natchez suffered from the devastating spread of disease in the region beginning in the 1690s, and by 1698 the nation was comprised of just five villages with a total population of 3,500. To ameliorate this population drop and rebuild their regional power, the Natchez incorporated refugee groups and forged new connections with other southeastern polities. By the second decade of the eighteenth century, the Natchez had formed close partnerships with both the Chickasaws and their English allies. These connections provided the Natchez with access to English trade goods, and it also protected their nation from English-allied slave traders. Yet, much as the War of Spanish Succession sapped resources from the Louisiana colonists and left them without a supply line, English preoccupation with the war also meant that fewer trade goods made it far west from Carolina and into the Lower Mississippi Valley. Cut off from access to English trade networks, the Natchez were therefore eager to gain access to French trade goods and were looking to expand their extensive political alliance network during the 1710s.[45]

Although the Natchez saw great potential in the incorporation of these refugee Frenchmen into their polity, within a decade the relationship between the French and Natchez soured. The French were greatly impressed by the elite Natchez and they saw echoes of their own "Sun King" in the way that the Natchez revered their divine leaders. Yet they struggled to conform to Natchez social norms and they committed continual cultural and political blunders. The French planters who settled at Natchez in the 1720s were interested in exploiting the land and laborers to make profit, and their treatment of both Native and African people deeply troubled the Natchez villagers. Within Natchez society women had considerable economic liberty and sexual freedom and the Natchez recognized both men and women as diplomatic leaders. French mistreatment of Native women, their tendency to permit their livestock to trample Natchez crops, and their failure to comply with Natchez norms of economic exchange strained the relationship between these neighboring peoples.[46]

Coupled with these blunders, French attempts to establish a plantation society within Natchez territory fueled resentment and gradually dismantled Natchez hopes for a partnership with the French. In addition to being frustrated by the colonists' cows and horses and the French inhabitants' ever-expanding requests for land, the Natchez were deeply disturbed by the gross exploitation of enslaved Africans on these plantations. Between 1726 and 1729 the population of French settlers and enslaved Africans within Natchez territory nearly quadrupled. In 1726 there were a 105 French settlers and 74 African slaves living beside a Natchez population of roughly 1,750. By 1729 there were 400 French settlers and 280 African slaves within the Natchez settlements.[47] While the Natchez and other Indians in the Lower Mississippi Valley certainly held slaves and lived in highly stratified societies, French settlers' exploitation and physical abuse of African slaves violated Natchez cultural norms. George Milne has recently argued that by watching the French exploit African laborers Natchez people had come to understand themselves as fundamentally different from and incompatible with their French neighbors, and came to rely upon a racial ideology to articulate their desire to rid themselves of these "impudent immigrants."[48]

Although Natchez resentment had simmered for years, the final blow that severed the Natchez's relationship with the French came in November of 1729. Earlier that year, the commandant of the French fort at Natchez, Sieur de Chepart, asked the Natchez village of White Apple to relocate in order to make space for his plantation. The White Apple villagers were shocked by this obtuse request to relocate their entire village, and this move served to buttress rumors that the French planned to dispossess and enslave all Natchez along with the Africans. During the summer of 1729 Natchez village leaders met to discuss their options. Given the settlers' lust for Natchez land and concurrent expansion of African slavery, these leaders concluded that it was impossible for Natchez and French societies to coexist. As one Natchez leader explained,

> Before the French came amongst us, we were men, content with what we had and that was sufficient: we walked with boldness every road, because we were our own masters; but now we go groping, afraid of meeting thorns, we walk like slaves, which we shall soon be, since the French already treat us as such. When they are sufficiently strong they will no longer dissemble…Shall we suffer the French to multiply, till we are no longer in a condition to oppose their efforts?[49]

Thus during the November of 1729 they launched a surprise mass attack against the French soldiers and inhabitants in their territory that they hoped would completely wipe out these invasive newcomers. On November 28, Natchez warriors from White Apple attacked French settlements and killed at least 229 colonists, and captured 50 French women and children and 300 African slaves. The sudden attack on French settlers by their Natchez allies induced a state of panic throughout the colony. In New Orleans, rumors circulated of a pan-Indian revolt. In April of 1730 colonists in New Orleans unleashed their terror and rage on Natchez captives that had been brought to the capital by a French-allied petites nation and French colonists stabbed, burned, and tortured these French captives in the public square. It appeared that Louisiana was on the verge of complete destruction.[50]

Fortunately for the French, the Choctaws decided to support the Louisiana colonists against the Natchez.[51] In January of 1730 the Choctaws sent 800 warriors to support the Louisiana militia. In December of 1729 Louisiana had no more than 325 soldiers in the colony and many of these soldiers were so ill and malnourished as to be effectively useless in combat. By comparison, in the mid-1720s the Natchez had about 500 warriors, and thus would have easily defeated the French forces. Thus, the assistance of Choctaw troops proved vital in securing French victory.[52]

For three bloody years the Natchez fought the French and their Choctaw and petites nations allies. Most of the Natchez who survived and were able to escape this onslaught fled east to their Chickasaw, Catawba, and Cherokee allies, although some remained in hiding in the lands north of Natchez. Those who could not escape were taken captive by the French, and most were sold as slaves in the French Caribbean.[53]

Choctaw assistance did not come without a price, and the Natchez conflict underscored the weakness and dependency of Louisiana on their alliances with the Lower Mississippi Valley nations. French officials spent the better part of 1730–31 recovering captives from the Choctaws. With their meager resources depleted from the war, they were in an especially difficult position as officials like Regis du Roullet sought to negotiate the return of not just African captives but also of the French settlers who had been seized by the Natchez. French officials were especially upset to find that the Choctaws were holding the French women and children that they had captured from the Natchez as bound laborers, but they could do little more than plead for the captives' return. This struck the Choctaws as an especially obtuse set of requests.[54] As the Chief of the Yellow Canes excoriated in 1730, the Choctaws had lost many loved ones in this war, and in return the French "had given them nothing…" and "had robbed them by having left with the slaves both French and negroes whom they had taken from the Natchez without giving them goods or notes." Hence when Roullet visited Alabamon Mingo to reclaim some of these African captives in 1731, the Choctaw leader was sure to exact generous payment for the prisoners.[55]

Although the Natchez War failed to eradicate the French presence in the Lower Mississippi Valley, it did halt the growth of a plantation-based society in the region. While the Natchez polity was all but dismantled by 1731, their resistance forcefully reminded French settlers of the dangers of living in a colony surrounded by powerful and numerous Native people. Through their attacks on French plantations and their execution of French slave owners, they made clear that the Louisiana settlers could not expect unfettered access to Indian lands. The combination of enslaved African revolts at sea, Natchez assaults on land, and the difficult logistics of acquiring sufficient laborers and settlers to populate the colony prevented the crown and Company of the Indies from realizing the goals of creating a plantation society in the Lower Mississippi Valley.

In the wake of the Natchez War, French settlers in Louisiana were forced to confront both the precariousness of their hold on Louisiana and their continued dependency on their Native allies. While the French did not entirely give up on Louisiana—it remained an important colonial possession to act as a buffer against British and Spanish expansion—these resistance movements effectively ensured that Louisiana was destined to remain a colonial backwater within a Native-dominated borderland. Without a steady influx of slaves, immigrants, or capital, Louisiana grew slowly and by the end of French tenure in 1763, the colonial population of the Lower Mississippi Valley was comprised of only 4,000 Europeans, 5,000 black slaves, 200 mulatto slaves, 100 Indian slaves, and 100 free people of color.[56] Thus, the pressure that Natchez, Choctaw, and African peoples exerted critically obstructed the development of colonial Louisiana.

Conclusion

If Louisiana never became France's Peru, it was not singularly or perhaps even primarily due to colonial administrative failures. During the late 1710s and 1720s the Company of the Indies injected tremendous resources into this imperial outpost at the edge of the Atlantic world. Yet at each turn, the Company's schemes were thwarted. Rioters in France, African resistors on board slave ships, and Natchez warriors within Louisiana dismantled its imperial endeavors. While the logistics of transporting slaves, settlers, and provisions to the Gulf Coast challenged the French crown and the proprietary company, the development of French colonial Louisiana was shaped not only by its tenuous connections to the Atlantic world, but by the power that Native people held over its continental ones. Natchez violence, Choctaw coercion, and Upper Creek polities formatively shaped and limited the Louisiana colony's diplomatic endeavors, and the petites nations peoples wrought its economic networks. The restraints imposed by powerful Native nations and strained Atlantic supply networks fostered a society that was defined by the limitations of imperial power, dependence on its Native allies, and characterized by fluid labor relationships. When we consider the goals of Native nations and enslaved Africans alongside those of French settlers, the story of Louisiana becomes not one of failure, but rather a narrative of negotiated outcomes and of the contested convergence of black, white, and red networks in the muddy Mississippi delta.

Notes

1 Regis du Roullet to Perier 4 3/16/1731, *Mississippi Provincial Archives: French Dominion, 1729–1740* Translated and edited by Dunbar Rowland and A. G. Sanders (Jackson: Press of the Mississippi Department of Archives and History, 1927), 1: 65–66. (Hereafter cited as MPA: FD).
2 Regis du Roullet to Perier, 3/16/1731, MPA:FD 1: 65–67.

3 Giraud, Marcel. *A History of French Louisiana, 1698–1715: The Reign of Louis XIV.* Vol. 1. (Baton Rouge: Louisiana State University Press, 1974), 14–15, 58–59; Mathé Allain, "*Not Worth a Straw*": *French Colonial Policy and the Early Years of Louisiana,* (Lafayette, University of Southwestern Louisiana, 1988), 47–54; Peter H. Wood, "The Changing Population of the Colonial South: An Overview by Race and Region, 1685–1790," *Powhatan's Mantle: Indians in the Southeast* ed. Peter H. Wood, Gregory A. Waselkov, and M. Thomas Hatley (Lincoln: University of Nebraska Press, 1989), 60–64.

4 Wood, "Changing Population of the Colonial South," 38–39, 73–75; John R. Swanton, *Indian Tribes of the Lower Mississippi Valley and the Adjacent Coast of the Gulf of Mexico* Bureau of American Ethnology, Bulletin 43 (Washington D.C.: Smithsonian, 1911), 17–20; Daniel H. Usner, *Indians Settlers and Slaves in a Frontier Exchange Economy: The Lower Mississippi Valley Before 1783* (Chapel Hill: University of North Carolina Press, 1992), 18, 44–45.

5 Guillaume de L'Isle, *Carte des Environs du Missisipi*, 1701, Louis C. Karpinski Map Collection, Newberry Library; N. de Fer, *Les Costes aux Environs de la Riviere de Misisipi*, 1701, Louis C. Karpinski Map Collections, Newberry Library; Pierre Le Moyne d'Iberville, *Iberville's Gulf Journals* Ed. Richebourg Gaillard McWilliams (Tuscaloosa: University of Alabama Press, 1981), 5–7, 44–49.

6 Jean-Baptiste Bénard de La Harpe, *The Historical Journal of the Establishment of the French in Louisiana.* Ed. Glenn R. Conrad, Trans. Joan Cain and Virginia Koenig (Lafayette: University of Southwestern Louisiana, 1971), 9–10; Pierre Le Moyne Iberville, "Journal of the Badine," *Iberville's Gulf Journals*, trans. and ed. Richebourg Gaillard McWilliams (Tuscaloosa: University of Alabama Press, 1981) 44–56.

7 Sauvole de Villantray, *The Journal of Sauvole: Historical Journal of the Establishment of the French in Louisiana*, ed. Jay Higginbotham (Mobile: Griffin Printing Co. Alabama, 1969), 45–46, 48.

8 Daniel H. Usner, *American Indians in the Lower Mississippi Valley: Social and Economic Histories* (Lincoln: University of Nebraska Press, 1998), 35; Usner, *Indians, Settlers, and Slaves*, 31; Marcel Giraud, *A History of French Louisiana*, 1:101; Kathleen DuVal, "Interconnectedness and Diversity in French Louisiana," *Powhatan's Mantle*, 138–142.

9 The Talapoosas, Abihkas, and Alabamas were polities that would later become part of the Creek nation and together collectively form the Upper Creek division. Kathryn E. Holland Braund, *Deerskins and Duffels: The Creek Indian Trade with Anglo-America: 1685–1815* (Lincoln: University of Nebraska Press, 1993), 5–8; Robbie Ethridge, *From Chicaza to Chickasaw: The European Invasion and the Transformation of the Mississippian World 1540–1715* (Chapel Hill: University of North Carolina Press, 2010), 174.

10 Robbie Ethridge, "Introduction: Mapping the Mississippian Shatter Zone," *Mapping the Mississippian Shatter Zone*, ed. Robbie Ethridge and Sheri M. Shuck-Hall (Lincoln: University of Nebraska Press, 2009), 11–2, 9–12.

11 Ethridge, *Chicaza to Chickasaw*, 91; Eric E. Bowne, *The Westo Indians: Slave Traders of the Early Colonial South* (Tuscaloosa: University of Alabama Press, 2005), 37–38; James R. Atkinson, *Splendid Land Splendid People: The Chickasaw Indians to Removal* (Tuscaloosa: University of Alabama Press, 2004), 11–29; Marvin D. Jeter, "Ripe for Colonial Exploitation: Ancient Traditions of Violence and Enmity as Preludes to the Indian Slave Trade," *Native American Adoption, Captivity and Slavery in Changing Contexts*, ed. Max Carocci and Stephanie Pratt (New York: Palgrave MacMillan, 2012), 39–42; Usner, *Social and Economic Histories*, 35; Alan Gallay, *The Indian Slave Trade: The Rise of the English Empire in the American South, 1607–1717* (New Haven: Yale University Press, 2002), 150, 296–297.

12 Jean Baptiste Le Moyne, Sieur de Bienville, to Jérôme de Pontchartrain, 2/25/1708, *Mississippi Provincial Archives: French Dominion*, ed. Dunbar Rowland and A. G. Sanders (Jackson: Press of the Mississippi Department of Archives and History, 1932), 3:113–114; Duclos to Pontchartrain 6/17/1716, MPA: FD, 3: 205–211.

13 Bienville to Pontchartrain, 10/27/1711, MPA: FD, 3:159; Usner, *Indians, Settlers, and Slaves*, 77–81; Bienville to Pontchartrain, 6/6/1704, MPA: FD 3: 19–22.

14 Braund, *Deerskins and Duffels*, 34–37; Michael James Forêt, "Red Over White: Indians, Deserters, and French Colonial Louisiana" *Proceedings of the Meeting of the French Colonial Historical Society*, 17 (1993): 79–80; Bienville to Pontchartrain, 6/6/1704, MPA: FD 3: 19–25; Pontchartrain to Bienville, 5/10/1710, MPA: FD 3: 139; Bienville to Pontchartrain, 10/27/1711, MPA: FD, 3:160–162.

15 De La Chaise to the Directors of the Company of the Indies 9/6/1723, Mississippi Provincial Archives: French Dominion ed. Dunbar Rowland and A. G. Sanders (Jackson: Press of the Mississippi Department of Archives and History, 1929), 2; 312–314; Hubert to the Council, 10/26/1717, MPA: FD, 2:238–240.

16 Alan Taylor, *The American Colonies* (New York: Viking, 2001): 292–293; Evan Haefli and Kevin Sweeney, *Captives and Captors: The 1704 French and Indian Raid on Deerfield* (Amherst: University of Massachusetts Press, 2005), 35.

17 In 1708 the entire population of French colonial Louisiana was comprised of 180 men bearing arms, 27 French families, and 60 French men living dispersed among Indian nations in the backcountry. Gregory A. Waselkov, "French Colonial Archaeology at Old Mobile: An Introduction" *Historical Archaeology* 36, 1, French Colonial Archaeology at Old Mobile: Selected Studies (2002); André Penicaut, *Fleur de Lys and Calumet: Being the Penicaut Narrative of French Adventure in Louisiana*, Trans. and ed. by Richebourg McWilliams (Tuscaloosa: University of Alabama Press, 1988), 106; Bienville to Pontchartrain 6/6/1704, *MPA: FD*, 3:25; Savole to Pontchartrain, 8/1/1701, MPA:FD 2:12; Hamilton, *Colonial Mobile*, 65; Usner, *Indians, Settlers, and Slaves*, 25–27; "Census of Louisiana by Nicolas de la Salle," 1708, MPA: FD, 2: 19.

18 Jennifer M. Spear, *Race, Sex, and Social Order in Early New Orleans* (Baltimore: Johns Hopkins University Press, 2009), 20.

19 Allain, *Not Worth a Straw*, 84–87; Jay Higginbotham, *Old Mobile Fort St. Louis de la Louisiane*. (Tuscaloosa: University of Alabama Press, 1991),143, 163.

20 Daniel H. Usner Jr., "From African Captivity to American Slavery: The Introduction of Black Laborers to Colonial Louisiana," *The Louisiana Purchase Bicentennial Series in Louisiana History: The French Experience in Louisiana* (Lafayette, University of Southwestern Louisiana, 1995), 183–197; Spear, *Race, Sex, and Social Order*, 54–57.

21 Penicaut, *Fleur de Lys and Calumet*, 106–115.

22 Kathleen DuVal, "Indian Intermarriage and Métissage in Colonial Louisiana." *The William and Mary Quarterly* 65[2] (2008): 267–268.

23 Gallay, *The Indian Slave Trade*, 310–311; "Census of Louisiana by Nicolas de la Salle," 1708, MPA: FD, 2: 19–20.

24 Waselkov, *Old Mobile Archaeology, 38, 46;* La Mothe Cadillac to Pontchartrain 10/26/1713, MPA: FD 2: 169; Bienville to Pontchartrain 2/25/1708, MPA:FD, 3:124; Abstracts of letter from Cadillac, Diron, and Bienville to Crozat 10/1713, MPA:FD, 3:176–178; Carl J. Ekberg, *Stealing Indian Women: Native Slavery in the Illinois Country*. Urbana: University of Illinois Press, 2007. 29; Sophie Burton and F. Todd Smith, "Slavery in the Colonial Louisiana Backcountry: Natchitoches, 1714–1803," *Louisiana History* 52[2] (2011), 140–146.

25 William L. Ramsey, "Something Cloudy in Their Looks: The Origins of the Yamasee War Reconsidered" *The Journal of American History* (2003) 90[1], 44–57; Bienville to Pontchartrain, 9/1/1715, MPA:FD, 3:188–189; la Harpe, *Historic Journal*, 65: Gregory A. Waselkov and Bonnie L. Gums, *Plantation Archaeology at Rivière aux Chiens ca. 1725–1848* (Mobile, University of South Alabama Center for Archaeological Studies, 2000), 19; Braund, *Deerskins and Duffels*, 28–35.

26 In 1712 the French king had transferred control of Louisiana to Antoine Cruzat, a wealthy Paris financier, with the agreement that Cruzat would manage the colony for 15 years. Like the imperial French administration before him, Cruzat had also failed to make a profit off of Louisiana and so he eagerly resigned this position in 1718. This joint stock company was initially called the Company of the West after the company was expanded in 1720 it was retitled the Company of the Indies.

27 Emily Clark, *Masterless Mistresses: The New Orleans Ursulines and the Development of a New World Society, 1724–1834* (Chapel Hill, University of North Carolina Press, 2007), 36–37; Mathé Allain, "In Search of a Policy," *The Louisiana Purchase Bicentennial Series in Louisiana History: The French Experience in Louisiana* ed. Glenn R. Conrad (Lafayette: University of Southwestern Louisiana, 1995), 91–92.

28 "A Letter about Louisiana, Also Called Mississippi [written to a woman of quality], Nouveau Mercure February 1718," *Le Plus Beau Païs du Monde*, ed. May Rush Gwin Waggoner (Lafayette: Center for Louisiana Studies, 2005), 57, 75–77.

29 Paul LaChance, "The Growth of Free and Slave Populations in the French Colonial Louisiana," *French Colonial Louisiana and the Atlantic World* (Baton Rouge: Louisiana State University Press, 2005), 105–107; Ira Berlin, *Many Thousands Gone: The First Two Centuries of Slavery in North America* (Cambridge: Harvard University Press, 1998): 77–81.

30 Emily Clark, *Masterless Mistresses*, 36.

31 Carl A. Brasseaux, "The Image of Louisiana and the Failure of Voluntary French Emigration, 1683–1731," *The Louisiana Purchase Bicentennial Series in Louisiana History: The French Experience in Louisiana*, ed. Glenn R. Conrad (Lafayette: Center for Louisiana Studies, 1995), 158, Clark, *Masterless Mistresses*, 37.

32 Gwendolyn Midlo Hall, *Africans in Colonial Louisiana: The Development of Afro-Creole Culture in the Eighteenth Century* (Baton Rouge: Louisiana State University Press, 1992), 5; James D. Hardy, "The Transportation of Convicts to Colonial Louisiana," *Louisiana History* 7, 3 (1996): 208–212.

33 Hall, *Africans in Colonial Louisiana*, 7; Clark, *Masterless Mistresses*, 38.

34 Usner, *Indians, Settlers, and Slaves*, 35–36; Thomas N. Ingersoll, *Mammon and Manon in Early New Orleans: The First Slave Society in the Deep South, 1718–1819* (Knoxville: University of Tennessee Press, 1999), 9.
35 Brasseaux, "The Image of Louisiana," 159.
36 Brasseaux, "The Image of Louisiana," 159, Hall. 6.
37 Hall, *Africans in Colonial Louisiana*, 6.
38 Hall, *Africans in Colonial Louisiana*, 43.
39 3,396 or nearly two-thirds of these men, women, and children came from Senegambia where the company's main concession lay. Ibrahima Seck, "St Louis of Senegal, Its Hinterlands, and Colonial Louisiana," *French Colonial Louisiana and the Atlantic World*, ed. Bradley G. Bond (Baton Rouge: Louisiana State University Press, 2005), 269–270; Hall, *Africans in Colonial Louisiana*, 60–63; Charles, Maduell, *The Census Tables for the French Colony of Louisiana from 1699–1732* (Baltimore: Genealogical Publishing Co. Inc., 1972), 50, 113; Ira Berlin, *Many Thousands Gone*, 82–83.
40 Carl J. Ekberg, "The Flour Trade in French Louisiana," *Louisiana History* 37[3] (1996), 262, 266; Spear, *Race, Sex, and Social Order*, 58–59; Usner "From African Captivity," 30–32.
41 Maduell, *The Census Tables*, 50.
42 "Bienville's memoir of Louisiana 1725–1726," MFA: FD, 3: 519–521, 524, 537; Berlin, *Many Thousands Gone*, 84–86; Higginbotham, *Old Mobile Fort*, 201; Carl J. Ekberg, "The Flour Trade in French Louisiana," 262–270.
43 Spear, *Race, Sex, and Social Order*, 58; Hall, *Africans in Colonial Louisiana*, 58–63; Thomas N. Ingersoll, "The Slave Trade and the Ethnic Diversity of Louisiana's Slave Community," *Louisiana History* 37[2] (1996), 136.
44 The Africans about *L'Annibal* were sold at St. Domingue. When the ship arrived in the port on the island to reload, a port official decided that given the danger of a further mutiny it made more sense to sell the surviving cargo. Hall, *Africans in Colonial Louisiana*, 60, 87–95.
45 Ian W. Brown, "An Archaeological Study of Culture Contact and Change in the Natchez Bluffs Region," *La Salle and His Legacy* (Jackson: University Press of Mississippi), 179–184; George Edward Milne, *Natchez Country: Indians, Colonists, and the Landscapes of Race in French Louisiana* (Athens: University of Georgia Press, 2015), 15–44; Usner, *Indians Settlers and Slaves*, 28.
46 Milne, *Natchez Country*, 16–17, 100, 106; Usner, *Social and Economic Histories*, 25; Swanton, *Indian Tribes of the Lower Mississippi Valley*, 215–216; Bienville, "Minutes of the Superior Council of Louisiana," 7/23/1723, MPA: FD, 3: 359–360.
47 Usner, *Indians Settlers and Slaves*, 66, 113; Paul LaChance, "The Growth of Free and Slave Populations in the French Colonial Louisiana," *French Colonial Louisiana and the Atlantic World*, 212, 215–216; Giraud, *History of French Louisiana* 5: 390; Maduell, "*Census Tables*," 26.
48 Milne, *Natchez Country*, 79, 156–172.
49 Speech from a Natchez village chief calling for war with the French at a council meeting in 1729. Du Pratz, *A History of Louisiana*, 83; Usner, *Social and Economic Histories*, 25; Swanton, *Indian Tribes of the Lower Mississippi Valley*, 215–216; James F. Barnett Jr. *The Natchez Indians: A History to 1735* (Jackson: University Press of Mississippi, 2007), 99–105.
50 Milne, *Natchez Country*, 198; Sophie White, "Massacre, Mardi Gras, and Torture in Early New Orleans" *The William and Mary Quarterly* 70[3] (2013), 497, 519–530; Caillot, *A Company Man: The Remarkable French-Atlantic Voyage of a Clerk for the Company of the Indies: A Memoir*, ed. Erin M. Greenwald (New Orleans: The Historic New Orleans Collection, 2013), plate 6, 146–148; Barnett Jr. *The Natchez Indians*, 105; Usner, *Indians, Settlers, and Slaves*, 27.
51 Like most southeastern Indian groups during the eighteenth century, the Choctaw polity was actually comprised of a number of smaller political groups. Among the Choctaws there were for main divisions; the Eastern, the Western, the Chickasawhays, and the Sixtowns. Each of these divisions had its own set of relationships with outside nations and made their own decisions about whether to engage in war. Given that the Sixtowns Division had historically maintained relationships with the Natchez it is unlikely that they participated in this campaign. Thus to say that the "Choctaws" backed the French is a generalization and should not suggest that all Choctaw towns and divisions supported the French in this conflict. Patricia K. Galloway "'So Many Little Republics': British Negotiations with the Choctaw Confederacy, 1765" *Ethnohistory*, 41[4] (1994): 516–517; Galloway, *Practicing Ethnohistory*, 264; Lusser to Maurepas, 1/25/1730, MPA: FD, 1: 94; Milne, *Natchez Country*, 188.
52 Giraud *A History of French Louisiana* 5:403–404, 409; Broutin to the Company, 8/7/1730, MPA: FD, 1: 131–132.
53 Despite French claims of victory and the total destruction of the nation, Natchez people remained in the southeast and even in the Lower Mississippi Valley in the decades after the war. Their continued

presence in the region plagued the French, as they burned plantations, attacked livestock, and continued to harass the settlers. Throughout the 1730s the French continued to send petites nations patrols into the woods around Natchez to capture the remaining Natchez. The French did not know how many Natchez remained in the lands around Natchez after the war, but they were convinced that the nation was still fairly large. Bienville, "On the Indians," 5/15/1733, MPA: FD 1: 196–197; Caillot, *A Company Man,* 154; La Chance, *French Colonial Louisiana and the Atlantic World,* 242; Midlo Hall, *Africans in Colonial Louisiana,* 245–247; Giraud, *History of French Louisiana,* 5:409, 428; Bienville to Maurepas 1/28/1733 MPA: FD, 3:580–581; Broutin to the Company, 8/7/1730, MPA:FD, 1: 131–132.
54 Lusser to Maurepas, 1/25/1730 MPA: FD 1: 100–106.
55 Journal of Lusser, 1/12/1730–3/23/1730, MPA: FD 1: 105.
56 Usner, *Indians, Settlers, and Slaves,* 108.

References

Allain, Mathé. *"Not Worth a Straw": French Colonial Policy and the Early Years of Louisiana* (Lafayette, University of Southwestern Louisiana, 1988), 47–54.
Allain, Mathé. "In Search of a Policy," *The Louisiana Purchase Bicentennial Series in Louisiana History: The French Experience in Louisiana* ed. Glenn R. Conrad (Lafayette: University of Southwestern Louisiana, 1995).
Atkinson, James R. *Splendid Land Splendid People: The Chickasaw Indians to Removal* (Tuscaloosa: University of Alabama Press, 2004).
Barnett Jr., James F. *The Natchez Indians: A History to 1735* (Jackson: University Press of Mississippi, 2007).
Berlin, Ira. *Many Thousands Gone: The First Two Centuries of Slavery in North America* (Cambridge: Harvard University Press, 1998).
de Bienville, Jean Baptiste Le Moyne Sieur. "Bienville's memoir of Louisiana 1725–1726," the Mississippi Department of Archives and History: FD, 3: 519–521, 524, 537.
de Bienville, Jean Baptiste Le Moyne Sieur. "Minutes of the Superior Council of Louisiana," 7/23/1723, the Mississippi Department of Archives and History: FD, 3: 359–360.
de Bienville, Jean Baptiste Le Moyne Sieur to Maurepas 1/28/1733 the Mississippi Department of Archives and History: FD, 3: 580–581.
de Bienville, Jean Baptiste Le Moyne Sieur to Jérôme de Pontchartrain, 2/25/1708, *Mississippi Provincial Archives: French Dominion,* ed. Dunbar Rowland and A. G. Sanders (Jackson: Press of the Mississippi Department of Archives and History, 1932), 3: 113–114.
de Bienville, Jean Baptiste Le Moyne Sieur to Pontchartrain, 6/6/1704, the Mississippi Department of Archives and History: FD 3: 19–22.
de Bienville, Jean Baptiste Le Moyne Sieur to Pontchartrain, 10/27/1711, the Mississippi Department of Archives and History: FD, 3: 159.
de Bienville, Jean Baptiste Le Moyne Sieur to Pontchartrain, 10/27/1711, the Mississippi Department of Archives and History: FD, 3: 160–162.
de Bienville, Jean Baptiste Le Moyne Sieur to Pontchartrain 2/25/1708, the Mississippi Department of Archives and History: FD, 3: 124.
de Bienville, Jean Baptiste Le Moyne Sieur to Pontchartrain, 9/1/1715, the Mississippi Department of Archives and History: FD, 3: 188–189.
de Fer, N. *Les Costes aux Environs de la Riviere de Misisipi,* 1701, Louis C. Karpinski Map Collections, Newberry Library.
d'Iberville, Pierre Le Moyne. *Iberville's Gulf Journals* Ed. Richebourg Gaillard McWilliams (Tuscaloosa: University of Alabama Press, 1981), 5–7, 44–49.
de La Chaise to the Directors of the Company of the Indies 9/6/1723, Mississippi Provincial Archives: French Dominion ed. Dunbar Rowland and A. G. Sanders (Jackson: Press of the Mississippi Department of Archives and History, 1929), 2; 312–314.
de La Harpe, Jean-Baptiste Bénard. *The Historical Journal of the Establishment of the French in Louisiana.* Ed. Glenn R. Conrad, Trans. Joan Cain and Virginia Koenig (Lafayette: University of Southwestern Louisiana, 1971), 9–10.
de la Salle, Nicholas. "Census of Louisiana by Nicolas de la Salle," 1708, the Mississippi Department of Archives and History: FD, 2: 19
de L'Isle, Guillaume. *Carte des Environs du Missisipi,* 1701, Louis C. Karpinski Map Collection, Newberry Library.

Duclos to Pontchartrain 6/17/1716, the Mississippi Department of Archives and History: FD, 3: 205–211.

du Roullet, Regis to Perier 4 3/16/1731, *Mississippi Provincial Archives: French Dominion, 1729–1740* Translated and edited by Dunbar Rowland and A. G. Sanders (Jackson: Press of the Mississippi Department of Archives and History, 1927).

DuVal, Kathleen. "Indian Intermarriage and Métissage in Colonial Louisiana." *The William and Mary Quarterly* 65[2] (2008): 267–268.

DuVal, Kathleen. "Interconnectedness and Diversity in French Louisiana," *Powhatan's Mantle*, 138–142.

Bowne, Eric E. *The Westo Indians: Slave Traders of the Early Colonial South* (Tuscaloosa: University of Alabama Press, 2005).

Brasseaux, Carl A. "The Image of Louisiana and the Failure of Voluntary French Emigration, 1683–1731," *The Louisiana Purchase Bicentennial Series in Louisiana History: The French Experience in Louisiana,* ed. Glenn R. Conrad (Lafayette: Center for Louisiana Studies, 1995).

Braund, Kathryn E. Holland. *Deerskins and Duffels: The Creek Indian Trade with Anglo-America: 1685–1815* (Lincoln: University of Nebraska Press, 1993).

Brown, Ian W. "An Archaeological Study of Culture Contact and Change in the Natchez Bluffs Region," *La Salle and His Legacy* (Jackson: University Press of Mississippi).

Burton, Sophie and Smith, F. Todd. "Slavery in the Colonial Louisiana Backcountry: Natchitoches, 1714–1803," *Louisiana History* 52, 2 (2011): 133–188.

Caillot, Marc-Antoine. *A Company Man: The Remarkable French-Atlantic Voyage of a Clerk for the Company of the Indies: A Memoir*, ed. Erin M. Greenwald (New Orleans: The Historic New Orleans Collection, 2013).

Clark, Emily. *Masterless Mistresses: The New Orleans Ursulines and the Development of a New World Society, 1724–1834* (Chapel Hill: University of North Carolina Press, 2007).

Ekberg, Carl J. "The Flour Trade in French Louisiana," *Louisiana History* 37, 3 (1996): 262–270.

Ekberg, Carl J. *Stealing Indian Women: Native Slavery in the Illinois Country* (Urbana: University of Illinois Press, 2007).

Ethridge, Robbie. "Introduction: Mapping the Mississippian Shatter Zone," *Mapping the Mississippian Shatter Zone*, ed. Robbie Ethridge and Sheri M. Shuck-Hall (Lincoln: University of Nebraska Press, 2009).

Ethridge, Robbie. *From Chicaza to Chickasaw: The European Invasion and the Transformation of the Mississippian World 1540–1715* (Chapel Hill: University of North Carolina Press, 2010).

Forêt, Michael James. "Red Over White: Indians, Deserters, and French Colonial Louisiana" *Proceedings of the Meeting of the French Colonial Historical Society*, Vol. 17 (1993).

Gallay, Alan. *The Indian Slave Trade: The Rise of the English Empire in the American South, 1607–1717* (New Haven: Yale University Press, 2002).

Galloway Patricia K. "'So Many Little Republics': British Negotiations with the Choctaw Confederacy, 1765" *Ethnohistory* 41[4] (1994): 513–537.

Galloway, Patricia K. *Practicing Ethnohistory*, (Lincoln, NE: University of Nebraska, 2006).

Giraud, Marcel. *A History of French Louisiana, 1698–1715: The Reign of Louis XIV.* Vol. 1 (Baton Rouge: Louisiana State University Press, 1974).

Haefli, Evan and Kevin Sweeney. *Captives and Captors: The 1704 French and Indian Raid on Deerfield* (Amherst: University of Massachusetts Press, 2005).

Hall, Gwendolyn Midlo. *Africans in Colonial Louisiana: The Development of Afro-Creole Culture in the Eighteenth Century* (Baton Rouge: Louisiana State University Press, 1992).

Hardy, James D. "The Transportation of Convicts to Colonial Louisiana," *Louisiana History* 7[3], (1996): 208–212.

Higginbotham, Jay. *Old Mobile Fort St. Louis de la Louisiane* (Tuscaloosa: University of Alabama Press, 1991).

Iberville, Pierre Le Moyne. "Journal of the Badine," *Iberville's Gulf Journals*, trans. and ed. Richebourg Gaillard McWilliams (Tuscaloosa: University of Alabama Press, 1981), 44–56.

Ingersoll, Thomas N. "The Slave Trade and the Ethnic Diversity of Louisiana's Slave Community," *Louisiana History* 37[2] (1996).

Ingersoll, Thomas N. *Mammon and Manon in Early New Orleans: The First Slave Society in the Deep South, 1718–1819* (Knoxville: University of Tennessee Press, 1999).

Jeter, Marvin D. "Ripe for Colonial Exploitation: Ancient Traditions of Violence and Enmity as Preludes to the Indian Slave Trade," *Native American Adoption, Captivity and Slavery in Changing Contexts*, ed. Max Carocci and Stephanie Pratt (New York: Palgrave MacMillan, 2012).

LaChance, Paul. "The Growth of Free and Slave Populations in the French Colonial Louisiana," *French Colonial Louisiana and the Atlantic World* (Baton Rouge: Louisiana State University Press, 2005).

Maduell, Charles. *The Census Tables for the French Colony of Louisiana from 1699–1732* (Baltimore: Genealogical Publishing Co. Inc., 1972).

Milne, George Edward. *Natchez Country: Indians, Colonists, and the Landscapes of Race in French Louisiana* (Athens: University of Georgia Press, 2015).

Penicaut, André. *Fleur de Lys and Calumet: Being the Penicaut Narrative of French Adventure in Louisiana*, Trans. and ed. by Richebourg McWilliams (Tuscaloosa: University of Alabama Press, 1988).

Ramsey, William L. "Something Cloudy in Their Looks: The Origins of the Yamasee War Reconsidered" *The Journal of American History* 90[1] (2003): 44–57.

Savole to Pontchartrain, 8/1/1701, the Mississippi Department of Archives and History: FD 2: 12.

Seck, Ibrahima. "St Louis of Senegal, Its Hinterlands, and Colonial Louisiana," *French Colonial Louisiana and the Atlantic World*, ed. Bradley G. Bond (Baton Rouge: Louisiana State University Press, 2005).

Spear, Jennifer M. *Race, Sex, and Social Order in Early New Orleans* (Baltimore: Johns Hopkins University Press, 2009).

Swanton, John R. "Indian Tribes of the Lower Mississippi Valley and the Adjacent Coast of the Gulf of Mexico," *Bureau of American Ethnology*, Bulletin 43 (Washington DC: Smithsonian, 1911).

Taylor, Alan. *The American Colonies* (New York: Viking, 2001).

Usner Jr., Daniel H. "From African Captivity to American Slavery: The Introduction of Black Laborers to Colonial Louisiana," *The Louisiana Purchase Bicentennial Series in Louisiana History: The French Experience in Louisiana* (Lafayette: University of Southwestern Louisiana, 1995).

Usner, Daniel H. "From African Captivity to American Slavery: The Introduction of Black Laborers to Colonial Louisiana," *Louisiana History*, 20[1] (1979).

Usner, Daniel H. *American Indians in the Lower Mississippi Valley: Social and Economic Histories* (Lincoln: University of Nebraska Press, 1998).

Usner, Daniel H. *Indians Settlers and Slaves in a Frontier Exchange Economy: The Lower Mississippi Valley Before 1783* (Chapel Hill: University of North Carolina Press, 1992).

de Villantray, Sauvole. *The Journal of Sauvole: Historical Journal of the Establishment of the French in Louisiana*, ed. Jay Higginbotham (Mobile: Griffin Printing Co. Alabama, 1969), 45–46, 48.

Waselkov, Gregory A. "French Colonial Archaeology at Old Mobile: An Introduction" *Historical Archaeology*, 36, 1, French Colonial Archaeology at Old Mobile: Selected Studies (2002).

Waselkov, Gregory A. and Bonnie L. Gums. *Plantation Archaeology at Rivière aux Chiens ca. 1725–1848* (Mobile: University of South Alabama Center for Archaeological Studies, 2000).

Waselkov, *Old Mobile Archaeology* (University of Alabama Press, 2005).

White, Sophie. "Massacre, Mardi Gras, and Torture in Early New Orleans" *The William and Mary Quarterly* 70[3] (2013).

Wood, Peter H. "The Changing Population of the Colonial South: An Overview by Race and Region, 1685–1790," *Powhatan's Mantle: Indians in the Southeast*, ed. Peter H. Wood, Gregory A. Waselkov, and M. Thomas Hatley (Lincoln: University of Nebraska Press, 1989).

PART V
Revolutions

18
HOW TO LOSE AN EMPIRE
British Misperceptions of the Sinews of the Transatlantic System

Andrew Shankman and Ignacio Gallup-Diaz

By the middle of the eighteenth century, the British American colonies had achieved an unprecedented level of economic and political integration with Great Britain. This process coincided with a significant shift in the home country's turbulent politics—the persistent levels of violent conflict that bedeviled the Stuart monarchs in the seventeenth century were transformed into a politics of consensus that followed the Glorious Revolution settlement, which ensured that a Protestant monarch would be constrained to rule through (and in partnership with) the nation's Parliament. However, the development and practice of a politics within parameters—which incorporated regular elections for Parliament and the control of the king's income and the actions of his ministers by the legislative body—did not necessarily erase all conflict.[1]

Hard-fought elections and bruising parliamentary politics coincided with the removal of restrictions on the press and printers, and oversight of the government's policies led to the not-infrequent use of impeachment to remove or chastise state officials. The stakes were high as the political nation—a body which included government ministers, members of Parliament (MPs), lenders, investors, financiers, and pamphleteers—engaged in the processes of managing and commenting upon a costly and contentious international conflict, as England confronted Louis XIV's France in Europe and the Americas almost continuously between 1689 and 1715.

A Court interest gathered around the crown and its representatives in Parliament in London—power-wielding secretaries of state, directors of the Bank of England, and financiers—and emerged as a center of power and patronage. Opposition to this Court affinity was voiced by political outsiders who articulated a Country ideology that eschewed the lure of London, and depicted its nexus of institutions, stock exchanges, coffee houses, Parliament, and palaces as a circle of corruption. These factions competed fiercely with one another, but the regularization of politics in Parliament meant neither resorted to violence against the state.

The attainment of political stability in the home country was bound to exert an influential effect upon the colonies, providing a fertile ground for transatlantic integration. Having noted that, however, developments in British America were not *entirely* integrative. While developing closer ties to the mother country and reflecting its political culture, the colonies were at the same time affected by strong nonintegrative forces. Beyond the Atlantic coastline, removed from their legislative capital cities and towns, each colony was bounded by a frontier zone at which relationships with indigenous polities were of crucial importance.

As the century progressed and the populations of the colonies increased continuously, conflict between settlers and Indians became increasingly more regularized, racialized, and acrimonious. In addition, social inequality—especially in urban environments such as Boston, New York, and Philadelphia—created situations in which colonials engaged in conflict over wages, living conditions, and political representation. More importantly, slavery, an institution that underpinned the social systems of the Caribbean and the Chesapeake, could never entirely be brought into line with the mother country's socioeconomic system.

This chapter will explore the mechanisms through which the colonies were integrated into the society, economy, and politics of the imperial center, with the end goal being to provide an explanation for the countercyclical process that sundered the First British Empire. Part One of the chapter has three sections. The first discusses colonial political cultures, and how they reflected the Court versus Country binary that operated in Great Britain after the Glorious Revolution; the second examines a system of raw material procuration that became intertwined with political patronage in New Hampshire; and the third discusses the empire's halting but ultimately successful efforts to manage colonial manpower in North America during the Seven Years' War. The imperial crises that followed the home country's attempts to deal with the financial costs of the War are the subjects of Part Two.

Part One. A Federal Empire: Imperial Regulation, Local Elites, and Voluntarism

J. H. Elliott, E. H. Koenigsberger have written about the complex nature of early modern states and monarchies, and early modern England was a decidedly composite state.[2] As diplomatic marriages and processes of conquest and incorporation brought together previously independent realms, the newly enlarged entities contained overlapping—and in some cases contradictory—layers of administrative authority and sovereignty. The sixteenth-century Hapsburg system is the archetypal entity through which to grasp this insight, as Spain, the Low Countries, Sicily, and German-speaking parts of central Europe were united under the rule of a single house. Local nobilities, councils, legislatures, urban elites, and guilds were brought together in such a way that the central rulers needed to acknowledge local nodes of authority while at the same time subordinating them to their own.

As the rulers of medieval England extended their hegemony over the other realms of the British Isles, a similar system of overlapping and composite sovereignties emerged.[3] Cornwall and Wales were integrated into the realm of England, while Ireland and Scotland—realms over which English sovereignty was claimed—became persistent areas of conflict. As England exerted its hegemony over other realms, the rule and administration of border marches were delegated to loyal grandees. Given the limited nature of the monarch's power and the lack of an extensive bureaucracy, important state functions, such as the gathering of the crown's taxes and customs were placed in the hands of syndicates of merchants or other powerful individuals.[4]

During Elizabeth's reign, the gathering of an army and navy for the defense of the realm, activities typical of the modern nation-state, were reliant upon the mustering activities of county-level grandees in their various localities.[5] The defeat of the Spanish Armada in 1588, to which a prior generation of historians credited the 'birth of the British navy,' in fact illustrated the absence of centralized power and the Tudor state's reliance upon the actions of individuals willing to offer their services to the state in a time of danger and need.[6]

The early history of English expansion displayed the same pattern, as the crown devolved upon individuals and companies that it chartered the power to claim lands, treat with indigenous polities and their rulers, and, in effect, to establish an empire in its name. In what might appear paradoxical, the sixteenth-century monarchies that acquired overseas empires were composite states that lacked many of the attributes commonly associated with central state power. So, rather than centralized states expanding and establishing empire, composite and disarticulated states attained empire (through a variety of means), which forced rulers to centralize in order to better reap and manage the benefits of expansion—they then acquired powers they had previously lacked.

The companies that carried out the processes of early English expansion were not only chartered agents of the composite state, their far-flung activities also embodied the functions associated with states.[7] Systematic attempts by the crown itself to rationalize colonial affairs would await the efforts of the bureaucratizing Stuart monarchs and their reliance upon experts. Charles II and James II centralized royal power after the Restoration in order that the crown might reap the rewards of empire and rule for extended periods of time without Parliamentary assent.[8] These actions sparked violent conflict and, in the end, rebellion. The Glorious Revolution, and the Protestant settlement effected (and protected) by Parliament that followed it, were the necessary elements for the English political nation to accept and fund the levels of state debt and taxation necessary to support standing military forces in England.[9]

In an illustration of how deeply ingrained the composite reality was as a component of English administrative thought and practice, elements of the system were simply transferred to the Americas. The charters granted by the crown to the Calvert family in Maryland and the Carolina proprietors conferred upon them the powers exercised by the Bishop of Durham in "his county palatine." The representatives of the Penn family sought these powers as they lobbied the crown as the charter for their colony was in preparation. The clause appeared in drafts for the charter, but it did not appear in the final version.[10]

Context: Colonial Political Culture(s)

In his essay "Political Development," John M. Murrin explored the ways in which the British colonies became better integrated with the empire in the decades following the Glorious Revolution of 1688.[11] While colonies as diverse as Massachusetts, New York, and Virginia each experienced the pull of integration with London, they did so through mechanisms that reflected their particular economic and social trajectories. As elites in the colonies balanced royal authority with their locally elected legislatures, they expressed the North American variant of the political settlement that had produced the crown-in-Parliament in the home country.

Robert Walpole, who emerged as the king's chief minister, managed the nation's politics in the era that followed the close of the War of Spanish Succession in 1715 and the collapse of the South Sea Company in 1720.[12] His peacetime ministry worked to manage the nation's finances and consolidate its debt while stabilizing and building upon the gains made by the defeat of France and the eclipse of Spain. Walpole established a governing strategy through which MPs who supported his policies were rewarded with a variety of inducements: safe parliament seats, places on the boards of chartered companies, and access to important political and financial decision makers.

Walpole's opponents criticized this powerful nexus of the king's ministers, loyal MPs, and rewards for services as "the Robinocracy." Characterizing the system as hopelessly corrupt, they saw London as the necessary problematic site at which MPs, projectors, financiers, directors, and investors all had undue access and influence upon one another. Using classical figures as their models, they pictured London as the new Rome, and viewed themselves as the heirs of honorable ancient politicians who had either been exiled from the center of power or had absented themselves to their rural estates in order to escape corruption and the dissolution of their ideals.

The Court versus Country dynamic predated "Robin's reign," as the later Stuart monarchs Charles II and James II relied upon and rewarded their supporters in London and ruled without

Parliaments for extended periods—forcing "men of virtue" to literally retire to their country estates. (The Catholicism of the two later Stuart kings also fed and strengthened the place that corruption had in the equation.)[13] As Bernard Bailyn has argued in his study of Bacon's rebellion, the Court versus Country dynamic was also deeply embedded in Virginia politics, as planter elites in the colony were disquieted in the 1670s by Governor Berkeley's practice of surrounding himself with a circle of favorites whom he rewarded with offices and favors.[14]

However, the war with France that followed the Glorious Revolution, coupled with regular elections and the increased scope of the state's domestic, economic, financial, and international activity, cemented a new kind of Court interest. The financial revolution, through which the government established reliable systems of taxation, the Bank of England, and a funded national debt, heightened the scope of the spoils available for distribution as well as the frame of Parliament's activities while raising the stakes for Parliamentary politics. In building a Court faction, Walpole had inducements at his disposal that previous English politicians and monarchs quite simply lacked.[15]

Following the Restoration, the crown had chartered new colonies (New York, Pennsylvania, the Carolinas) and created new administrative units (the Dominion of New England; which grouped together New York and the New England colonies) in order to exert greater control over the North American colonies. However, the Glorious Revolution in England was accompanied by rebellions in the Americas, with royal officials overthrown in New York, Boston, and Maryland.[16] The Revolution settlement, which established Parliamentary supremacy, had resulted in the universal acceptance of a mixed and balanced constitution, and this politics constrained by parameters found its expression in the colonies. The crown recognized the authority of legislative assemblies, while colonial elites accepted that their local governments included unelected councils, and that their governors were appointed by the crown.

Colonial subjects, like Britons in the home country, came to recognize the value of their inclusion in a polity managed and protected by a powerful fiscal-military state. Although the state was large, and was not shy in taxing its subjects, it was Protestant, and wielded those taxes in order to field armies against France, and after 1720 to enforce the parameters of the hegemony the British state had attained. While there were notable differences between colonies—differences which were the result of the interplay between distinct kinds of economic, demographic, and social experiences—the colonies did become integrated into the wider British polity in ways that would have made the later Stuart kings quite envious.

In Virginia and the Carolinas, royal governors learned to work in concert with the legislatures, resulting in a politics in which all professed to work in harmony out of a mutual concern for the common good. Rather than representing a Court interest, governors like Spotiswood and Gooch in Virginia were subsumed into the Country.[17] In northern colonies, on the other hand, governors deployed methods derived from Robert Walpole's perfection of the Court politics system of patronage and rewards. The Wentworths' management of materiel provisioning under the White Pines Act is a soon-to-be-discussed example; another is Massachusetts governors who granted commissions to militia units and appointments to offices such as the Justice of the Peace in order to reward those who supported their policies.[18]

The discussion that follows will show the processes by which the eighteenth-century British Imperial State, in this case king-in-parliament, could govern distant colonies powerfully and effectively, and also the real limits of this often effective state's capacity to govern. Those limits were shaped far more by the reality of the features of British North America—distance of the governors from the governed, widespread ownership of productive property, and a widely dispersed population—than they were by ideological antipathy. Those features would continue to shape political culture, political institutions, and the capacity of the nation-state to act throughout the early American Republic.[19]

A Representative Policy: The White Pines Act

First enacted in 1711, then again in 1722 and 1729, the White Pines Act required owners of these pines, abundant especially in New Hampshire, to meet the needs of the British navy before they could sell to other buyers. The act angered those affected by it, but not nearly as much as we might think, because the act was patently unenforceable.[20] During the first three decades of the eighteenth century it became clear that the British fiscal-military state of limited constitutional monarchy that emerged from the Glorious Revolution settlement could enforce a certain amount of its imperial policies more effectively than ever before.[21] The Navigation Acts had been essentially meaningless before the eighteenth century. Yet by 1730 they had truly come to shape imperial commerce. During the 1720s, while the White Pines Act was proving unenforceable, the Navigation Acts were becoming the strong and effective spine of the rising commercial British Empire.

The difference in the fate of these acts was that the Navigation Acts sought to regulate external behavior—what the colonists did on ships on the oceans—while the White Pines Act sought to regulate internal behavior—what they did on their own land in dense forests far from any state presence. The British fiscal-military state was developing an enormous (certainly relative to its competitors) capacity to use coercive power to regulate colonial behavior in the external realm of the oceans. But coercive power to enforce diminished rapidly the farther from the coastline and into the interior of British North America a policy had to travel. On land there was no coercive power equivalent to the British navy, and colonists could usually act as they liked with little fear of punishment. The coastline was the single most important feature for determining whether imperial policy could be relatively easily enforced. Externally, the British state could usually enforce its policies; internally enforcement was a tremendous challenge.

But it was not an impossible one. Ultimately the White Pines Act proved a great success for the empire. This development is discussed in more detail elsewhere.[22] In brief, from the 1730s through the 1760s the oligarchic Wentworth family that governed New Hampshire organized the lumber market as part of a vast patronage network that included the sale and distribution of land and public offices as well.[23] The Wentworth royal governors essentially bought white pines continuously, paying top price, and always had a ready supply to meet imperial needs. Their management changed potentially hated figures, the surveyors of the king's woods, into, of all things, popular imperial office holders. Surveyors earmarked the best white pines for the navy. But under the Wentworths' management, property owners coveted their endorsement; it guaranteed sale at top price. Indeed, the Wentworths, following the management methods of Robert Walpole, gave the position of surveyor to members of the New Hampshire legislature who proved they could continue to win elections. Accepting the office in no way jeopardized the surveyors' popularity with voters. In fact, it enhanced it.[24]

This episode helps us to understand how a distant central government, facing real practical limits to its coercive power, could, nevertheless, successfully uphold its governing authority in British North America. The White Pines Act could not have been enforced had the residents of New Hampshire refused to comply with it. Indeed, between 1711 and the late 1720s they did refuse, which is why the act had to be continually reenacted. Governor Benning Wentworth figured out how to elicit the colonists' voluntary cooperation with the act. He organized enforcement so that it went with the grain of a people who largely lived on land that they owned, and who could, for the most part, determine what would happen and what would not be allowed to happen on that land. Was this episode an example of a weak or a strong state? It was certainly an example of an effective state. A policy conceived in Whitehall worked pretty much as its authors intended 3,000 miles and an ocean away in the middle of a dense forest. But it worked because shrewd middlemen largely hid from the highest-level policymakers how they were administering the policy. And part of their shrewdness was to understand the real limitations of their coercive authority. They understood quite intimately how to convince those they were being told to govern to actually want to be governed.

The White Pines Act helps us to see the tremendous practical difference regarding governance between the internal and external realms. What happened when the stakes were raised beyond a lumber act, when the imperial state asked colonists to risk their lives in war? The demands the British made of the colonists during the French and Indian War occurred in the internal realm, the location where Britain had the least amount of coercive power and was least capable of using force to govern. For the war to work, policymakers, or at the very least shrewd intermediaries, would need to figure out how to elicit voluntary cooperation on a much more massive scale, and under much more difficult conditions, than the Wentworth royal governors had faced in New Hampshire.

Practical Knowledge: The Keys to Success in North America

In the initial years of the French and Indian War, prior to William Pitt's appointment as first minister, Britain suffered embarrassing and potentially disastrous defeat.[25] Then from late 1758 to 1761 Pitt managed the empire as effectively as it had ever been managed. He successfully negotiated the challenges and complexities produced by the organic federal system that divided power along the internal/external axis of the coastline, the system in which British policymakers and British North American colonial subjects lived.

Prior to 1759, especially under the regime of the hated Lord Loudon, British policymakers tried coercive measures that could only work on an unwilling population if they were backed by the sort of force the British simply did not possess inside their North American colonies. Essentially, the British state wanted three things from its colonies, primarily Massachusetts: funds to supplement war costs, funds to quarter troops, and obedience to a military chain of command dominated by the British officer corps. Under Loudon this last expectation meant requiring every provincial officer, regardless of rank, to obey the orders of even the most junior British officer.

In 1757 and 1758 Loudon sought to accomplish these three objectives with coercive dictates to the Massachusetts General Court, and the result was near disaster. The military effort stalled and, taking an extraordinary step in 1758, the Massachusetts legislature refused to vote any funds for the coming campaign.[26] This decision was an extreme and dramatic consequence of the failure to understand the organic imperial federal reality, and of the need for voluntary cooperation when governing the interior of North America from a great distance. Certainly in this instance the British fiscal military state, which all historians comfortably identify as strong, was exposed as profoundly weak. Yet it was the same state that could enforce the Navigation and White Pines Acts. The difference between the Navigation Acts and Loudon's efforts was one of location. And the differences between the White Pines Act and Loudon's methods were the conditions created by the policies' enforcers, the methods chosen by those enforcers in relation to the conditions they created, and the resulting and very different attitudes of those willing to be governed in New Hampshire and those refusing to be governed in Massachusetts.

Yet Pitt's success after removing Loudon was as complete as had been Loudon's failure. Pitt quickly mastered the lessons of voluntary cooperation necessitated by the organic imperial federal reality. He set aside a fund of specie and provided partial reimbursement for taxes and expenditures that colonial legislatures voluntarily undertook to pay for the war and quarter troops. The incentive of getting much-needed specie into colonial economies caused the legislatures to compete with each other in seeking who could tax the most to pay for the war.

Massachusetts voluntarily taxed itself at unprecedented levels in 1759–60. To resolve conflicts among British and Provincial officers, Pitt raised every British officer in a command position (that is, the highest ranking British officer within a unit dealing with Provincial officers) to the newly created rank of colonel in America Only. Since the highest rank Provincial officers could attain was that of Colonel, they would now only have to receive orders from British officers of equal or greater rank. But the new rank disappeared as soon as the British officer left North America, preserving the British military command structure going forward.

These ingenious solutions came from a careful understanding of precise and particular problems. Pitt's methods for eliciting voluntary cooperation led the way to the spectacular military successes of 1759–61, successes in which colonists enthusiastically played a major role. Consider that the core grievances of the great imperial crisis of 1764–76 centered around whether colonists would be taxed to contribute to the costs of empire, whether they would bear the cost of quartering troops, and whether they would obey, respect, and work with the British military. Pitt managed to get colonist elites in the years immediately preceding that crisis, to voluntarily and cooperatively do all three. Did his methods suggest a weak or a strong state? Again, they certainly suggested a highly effective one. But effective only because of a keen awareness of where coercive power could work and where it could not. Policymakers such as Pitt developed this awareness from a sensible, practical, and reasonable acceptance of the situation in which they found themselves. Coercive power could not work in those spaces where the governed really could impose limits on their governors.

Part Two. The (Mis-)Management of Imperial Crises
The Stamp Act

The organic federal imperial reality also shaped the Stamp Act Crisis. This crisis demonstrated that some British policymakers and colonials had come to understand the significance of the coastline as the key axis for determining policymaking and the appropriate methods for governing in the empire. They had come to understand even though neither Parliament's claim of absolute sovereignty, nor the colonists' insistence that Parliament's sovereignty did not include taxing the colonies, explained, or even recognized, the true features of the organic imperial federal reality.

Colonists such as James Otis, who perceived correctly the 1764 external Sugar Act as a tax, had no difficulty denouncing it for the same ideological and constitutional reasons that provoked opposition to the Stamp Act of 1765. Yet the Sugar Act was an effective revenue maker from the start, and especially in its amended 1766 form. That year Parliament reduced the tax so that it was cheaper than most of the bribes colonial merchants had been paying to avoid the prohibitive duty of the 1733 Molasses Act. Colonists could nullify the internal Stamp Act because, as with all internal measures, to work it required their voluntary cooperation. Potential stamp distributors were vulnerable to their neighbors, the stamps themselves and the property associated with them could easily be destroyed. But collected in distant ports, or in British North America's coastal ports, by customs collectors protected by the royal navy, the Sugar Act was not vulnerable to direct action and physical resistance. Though colonists subjected both acts to the same powerful ideological critique, the external Sugar Act succeeded while the internal Stamp Act failed. In 1765 the Grenville ministry collapsed due to the Stamp Act debacle, and the question emerged: Could this empire, a federal system without a federal ideology to explain and justify it, survive a crisis this grave?

It could, primarily because of the same shrewd awareness of realities and limits to power that Pitt had exhibited. The Marquis of Rockingham, in close consultation with, among others, intelligent and loyal empire men such as Benjamin Franklin, managed to resolve the Stamp Act crisis by working within the organic imperial federal reality, and by accepting the limitations it imposed. His tripartite legislation of early 1766 resolved the crisis along the coastal axis that actually mattered, despite its not figuring in any explanation of the imperial-colonial relationship that had emerged during the crisis. First, under Rockingham's direction, Parliament passed the Declaratory Act, a seemingly all-inclusive and complete assertion of parliamentary sovereignty. But Rockingham rejected the suggestion coming from within his ministry to clearly state Parliament's authority over all "cases of Taxation, and in all other cases whatsoever," leaving out any references to the power to tax.[27]

MPs believed the power to legislate included the power to tax, and so heard in the Declaratory Act what they needed to hear. Colonists had just spent the last year explaining the distinction between the power to legislate and to tax, and so heard what they needed to hear in the act as well. Next Rockingham repealed the Stamp Act, leaving it as the first and only time that Parliament sought to tax the colonists internally. Franklin had helped Rockingham to see that he could never force the colonists to do something in the internal realm that they truly did not want to do. And finally, Rockingham amended the Sugar Act reducing the duty so that it was cheaper than most of the bribes. As Franklin had told MPs during a thorough questioning arranged by Rockingham, "the oceans are yours." He was careful to avoid saying explicitly that the colonists accepted his statement ideologically for purposes of taxation. Rather, he was stating a practical fact of the organic federal imperial reality, and suggesting that Parliament should pursue potentially troublesome policies in the arena where its claim to power and its actual power, for the most part, overlapped.[28]

When the Sons of Liberty disbanded in 1766, a year of peace and relief followed months of tumult and anxiety.[29] Few stopped to consider that the crisis had been resolved along the internal/external axis. That axis had tremendous practical significance for how the empire actually worked, and for how the imperial state had to approach governance. But no available belief system recognized it or could account for it. Yet the policies of the White Pines Act, the French and Indian War, and the Stamp Act crisis each showed a clear pattern of governance for a state claiming dominion over the vast territory that would become the United States. The coercive authority that early modern political theorists associated with state sovereignty was present on the oceans and the coast. The farther into the interior a policy traveled, a gulf widened between the claim to power and actual power. That gulf could be bridged only by imagining policies the governed would accept. Policies were likely to be thwarted, even nullified, once the governed decided to withhold their voluntary cooperation. These patterns were the result of distance, the independence that came with widespread property ownership, and the limits of state formation—the lack of institutional development, presence of state personnel, and bureaucratic structure—faced by even highly developed and effective states such as eighteenth-century Britain's. In other words, the patterns and conditions that caused British subjects to create the imperial federal reality did not disappear with independence and the formation of the early American Republic. Instead, they intensified.

The Crises and the Revolution: A Failure of Vision

Thus the onset of imperial conflict, and eventually the American Revolution, "was a countercyclical event. It ran against the prevailing integrative tendencies of the century."[30] Yet this countercyclical event emerged from what began as a very British conflict and, initially, a very British revolution. Between 1764 and 1776 all of the British North American colonies grew frustrated by the post-1763 attempts on the part of the crown's ministers to reorganize and more forcefully integrate and govern the colonies. The British West Indies did not try to join the independence movement. These colonies, with much smaller populations of white Anglophone subjects deeply jealous of their British liberties, much less differentiated social relations among whites, and less diverse economies (economies the least like Britain's), fit closest the classic colonial model of producing what they did not consume and consuming what they did not produce. They did not seek to leave the empire.[31] The North American colonies, on the other hand, replicated or imitated British culture, politics, social relations, and values and had growing local populations that increasingly identified as British. They went from frustrated to furious as they discovered that Britain did not view them as the British subjects they believed they were.[32]

Between 1763 and 1765 the ministry of George Grenville refused to learn the lesson of imperial federalism and voluntary cooperation put to such impressive use by William Pitt in 1759 and 1760. In the decade after 1763 the empire would break apart over the colonists' refusal to fund imperial projects in North America, quarter British troops, and respect and follow British military commanders. In the previous decade Pitt had shown that they could be convinced to do each of those things, and during far more trying circumstances than those of the postwar period. Under Grenville subsidy and voluntary cooperation were replaced by the Sugar and Stamp Acts. A policy that had brought specie to the colonies, stabilizing colonial currencies, was replaced by the Currency Act. Grenville subscribed to a narrative of the war that ignored Pitt's achievements. Any who wished to point to problems of governance within the empire over the course of the eighteenth century certainly could find problems to make their point. Colonists had initially disobeyed the White Pines Act, Massachusetts had refused to fund troops during wartime, and certain colonial governors (who did not learn the appropriate methods for governing their colonies) could and did report horror stories. Indeed, there was a small industry of deep thinkers producing a stream of pamphlets focusing on all that was wrong with the empire and suggesting the reforms that were necessary to keep it intact.[33]

Yet virtually none of those contributing to these discussions was a colonial figure, and many had never even set foot in the colonies. Would-be imperial reformers seemed always to be seeking to correct problems that had already been solved and were incessantly fighting the last war. As the British provoked conflicts beginning in 1764–65, over the next decade they proved less and less capable of responding to the actual challenges they faced. Instead they resorted to earlier ways of thinking and to solutions that had been conceived to resolve problems that no longer existed. For example, in 1765 General Thomas Gates asked for a quartering act that would allow him to place soldiers in private homes if necessary. Gates was thinking of the challenges of policing the new proclamation line established in 1763, far to the west in the Appalachians, where there were no quarters for his soldiers. Rather than respond to the problem of 1763, the Quartering Act of 1765 sought to deal with problems that had arisen during the years of defeat in the French and Indian War, the years prior to Pitt's taking office. The Act compelled legislatures to pay for the quartering of troops, ignoring that legislatures had shown a cheerful and voluntary willingness to provide the funds once Pitt figured out how to work with them. All the 1765 Act did was to needlessly antagonize colonial legislatures in order to solve a problem that had once been solved. The Act did not, however, give Gage authority to quarter troops in private homes. Thus the problem of 1765 went unmet as Parliament reached back to solve a problem of 1757–58 that did not need solving.

The more famous legislation of 1764–75, the Sugar and Stamp Acts, resulted from similar thinking. The Sugar Act was meant to end the smuggling of French molasses that had so angered Parliament during the French and Indian War. Yet smuggling had been in steep decline after 1758 as Britain had come to dominate North America and much of the Caribbean. Yet again this was a problem that was not in need of a solution. The Stamp Act was a response to colonial legislatures' refusal to vote funds for troops in 1758. Parliament ignored the highly successful ways in which the colonists had voted funds for troops after 1758 choosing to focus on failure, and enact policy to deal with it, rather than success. The result, once again, was the unnecessary alienation of the colonists. As John Murrin has written "with amazing consistency Britain's imperial policies of 1764-66 carefully addressed the specific problems of 1754-57, most of which were well on their way to resolving themselves through various informal mechanisms."[34]

Yet as imperial relations worsened after 1765, Parliament reacted by reaching deeper into the past for solutions rather than focusing on the actual problems it was causing, and thinking creatively as Pitt had done about how to solve them. The Townshend Acts Crisis of 1767–70 began when Charles Townshend proposed extensive external taxes in order to pay royal governors' salaries directly (rather than have colonial legislatures vote the funds). Townshend recalled that royal governors dependent on colonial legislatures had been believed to be a serious problem when he was a young man on the Board of Trade just beginning his career in 1748. Yet by 1767 paying the governors' salaries had long since ceased to be a problem. Virtually all royal colonies made a show of loyalty and enthusiasm by voting a new governor his salary for life upon appointment. Even Massachusetts, with its reputation for willfulness, had long developed a tradition of deferentially voting the governor his salary at the start of each new year's legislative session before proceeding to other business. Seeking to solve a problem, instead Townshend provoked one and once again needlessly angered the colonists and provoked suspicion of his motives and those of the royal governors, suspicion that had not been there before the Townshend Acts.

In 1765 Parliament had looked back about eight years to solve problems long solved. In 1767 it moved back about two decades to grapple with the problems of the late 1740s, problems that had long been resolved. In the final and most severe crisis, the Coercive Acts Crisis of 1774–76, Parliament responded to the Boston Tea Party by reviving an idea of the empire that was by that point 75 years old, that it could forcibly alter a colony's charter, in this case that of Massachusetts. At the beginning of the eighteenth century the Board of Trade had considered the possibility of using an act of Parliament to change colonial charters. The idea had merit in 1701 when the colonies were weak and unformed polities just emerging from a period of shock and crisis. It was a foolish notion in 1774 given the complexity and sophistication experienced by the British North American colonies in the ensuing 75 years, and given the enormous pride they took in their charters, which they saw as key expressions of the British liberty rendered safe by the Glorious Revolution settlement. In the space of a decade Parliament's thinking went from being about eight years behind to being almost a century out of date. As John Murrin tartly explains, "this time the empire came apart with the charter, possibly a fitting response when a policy of 1701 had emerged as Britain's brightest idea for 1774."[35]

This brief description suggests a clear narrative path to understand the linkages between the events from 1763 to the Battle of Lexington and Concord. The narrative reinforces the lessons of imperial federalism and Anglicization and connects them to the real, but less than insurmountable, complexities of governing the British Empire. The British, on the whole, lurched from what had worked to what did not, never really focusing on what they had achieved and why. As they grew more desperate to address problems, many of their own making, they revealed ever more clearly their inability to celebrate their achievement of 1763: "Britain may actually have lost her colonies because, in the last analysis, the English simply did not know how to think triumphantly."[36]

Instead they thought defensively. Taxation by an unrepresentative body provoked colonial fears for liberty and property, fears easily articulated by self-identified British subjects of King-in-Parliament. Yet the colonists quite effectively nullified the internal Stamp Act, while the external Sugar Act, in its modified 1766 form, functioned as a revenue-maker. Parliament could impose its will on the oceans and could not govern internally without voluntary cooperation, a lesson both the Marquis of Rockingham (who had ultimately replaced George Grenville) and Benjamin Franklin understood.[37]

The first imperial crisis exposed that Parliament's claim to sovereignty everywhere was not enforceable and also that the colonists' distinction between legislation and taxation, while it had enormous ideological significance for them, had far less practical impact than the axis of imperial federalism: the coastline. The tax on French West Indian molasses was equally ideologically obnoxious to colonists as was the tax on stamps, while the Stamp Act was equally within Parliament's claim to sovereignty. The difference was that oceanic measures did not require voluntary cooperation. Neither Parliament's nor the colonists' understanding of the distribution of power in the empire explained how the empire actually functioned.

In late 1765 and early 1766 Rockingham, the London merchants, and loyal empire men such as Franklin actively cooperated.[38] Before he heard news of the colonial boycott, Rockingham organized a merchants' campaign to portray the Stamp Act as disastrous to trade. The campaign gave Parliament a reason to repeal that did not have to acknowledge the colonists' ideological position. Franklin, publicly questioned before the House of Commons, made as cogent a presentation of imperial federalism as one could ask for. Stating to Parliament that "the oceans are yours," he conveyed clearly that Parliament alienated the colonists internally at its peril and that it should pursue potentially controversial policy needs on the oceans where its sovereignty was both theoretical and real.[39] Often lost in discussions of the Stamp Act Crisis is that when it ended in 1766, and with nearly universal rejoicing in the colonies and the voluntary disbanding of the Sons of Liberty, Parliament had in fact augmented its power.[40] Parliament was taxing the colonies with the amended and external Sugar Act, something it had never done before. Franklin's performance is an excellent illustration of the practical ways in which the shrewdest men could manage the empire and make it function, even in the aftermath of the Stamp Act riots.

In the decade after 1766 the perspective represented by Grenville won out over the lessons offered by the achievements of Pitt, Rockingham, and Franklin. Imperial policymakers could look at 13 separate polities, in at least three distinct and differentiated regions, and see one homogenous unit increasingly unwilling to be governed. At a distance they did not see a reality that was much more visible up close. Each of these regions was producing subjects who identified with many imperial goals. Problems of the past had been resolved, were manageable, or were less significant than the empire's considerable achievements. However, British imperial policy makers had come to identify one distinct "America" when few colonists did so. They acted on this "America" simultaneously and in uniform ways guaranteed to terrify and infuriate colonial subjects who felt that British liberty applied to them in their separate colonial units. By doing so, they provided a common enemy that could drive the different colonies together. British actions did more for nascent American nationalism than any of the naturally arising trends developing within the 13 colonies.

As the colonists reacted to the Townshend and Coercive Acts crises, the Country ideology, which urged subjects to be highly suspicious of power and hypervigilant in protection of liberty, did seem to depict the British state accurately. A language that had been marginal in many colonies and manageable and conducive to a politics of harmony in many others rapidly began to function in the incendiary ways. Yet until very late in the process, the colonists clung to their idea of British liberty and the imperial constitution. The solution was to go back to the situation they thought had existed in 1763: an empire that honored the distinction between taxation and legislation.[41]

The Townshend Acts crisis severely escalated tensions and caused far more people to rely on the Country language of opposition to understand British actions.[42] The Coercive Acts crisis destroyed the colonists' sense of their place and liberties within the empire, for these acts were pieces of legislation, not measures to raise revenue. Having always denied Parliament's right to tax them, the colonists came to the conclusion from the Coercive Acts that Parliament's legislation was an even greater threat to liberty than the right it claimed to tax. If Parliament could not tax or legislate, it could do nothing, making the colonists independent of Parliament.

Yet that conclusion came only after a decade of escalating crisis and, from the colonial viewpoint, extreme provocation. Between 1689 and 1764 the integration of the empire created conditions that gave imperial policy makers a decade or so to come up with a solution to the empire's problems once they became manifest. The problems in the end were not solved. But considering how and why they might have been and with ideas, approaches, and policies that were available and that, at times, were actually in use, allows us to see the colonial period on its own terms.

It was, among many other things, a period that produced provincial British societies in North America and an empire that achieved most of its key objectives, almost in spite of the men who ended up running it. Integration provided imperial policy makers a real margin for error (over a decade's worth), while also providing the colonists with the mentality, identity, and language that led them to conclude that what was being done to them was wrong, to interpret what they believed were the reasons for British actions, and gave them a program for how to respond.

The events of 1764 to 1776 produced a unique situation in the Anglophone world: in the 13 colonies the Country ideology became the dominant political idiom, even for a time in those colonies where it made little organic sense for it to be so. But Country ideology was now mixed with the values produced by the radicalizing upheaval of prerevolutionary and revolutionary conflict. Internal social conflict did not necessarily unify the colonists or lead directly to the movement for independence (after all, social conflict was more likely to divide colonists than to unite them). But the external actions of the British did create a large political movement that swept up hundreds of thousands into it, people who were also quite interested in how revolutionary politics might address internal social concerns.

The Revolution was, in part, a movement for independence that resulted from the final contours of a long and complex process of integration that has been termed "Anglicization." It was also a sustained hegemonic breakdown and an assault on one form of authority that could quickly spread to assaults on other forms. As challenges to British authority, and ultimately demands for home rule, overawed existing structures of authority, a space opened up to articulate social and economic grievances. In this fluid and raucous context, the social and economic inequalities of colonial America encouraged further assaults on authority, which began to threaten colonial elites who would have liked to limit the challenge to the authority of British policy makers.[43]

The Revolution made governance in the new Republic it created highly challenging, both in the short and long terms. Much of this challenge resulted from the remnant of political ideology that remained credible to the bulk of an Anglicized people who had turned against mainstream British political and cultural forms. What remained as the most dominant surviving example of Anglicization was a widespread belief in the Country ideology. But this belief was now expressed on a political terrain shaped by revolution, a terrain where virtually all examples of authority and hierarchy, both public and private, were being challenged and shaken.[44]

In many ways the revolutionary United States sought to make itself the anti-Britain. The Articles of Confederation government was about as complete a rejection of the fiscal-military state that a people could make and yet still claim to have a central government. This repudiation of the mainstream processes of eighteenth-century state formation fit with the general and more bottom-up rejections of authority. Those advocating the bottom-up rejections generally sought to place governance in much more local institutions. Potentially even more subversively, challenges to authority from revolutionary impulses could often develop within private spaces, within household walls, affecting the intimate relations of husbands and wives, parents and children, and masters, servants, and slaves. Revolutionary possibilities for change had real, profound, and deeply unfortunate limits. But those limits were measurable primarily because of the sharp challenge to authority that followed the repudiation of British authority and the Anglicizing mainstream.[45]

Notes

1 For examinations of how a polity that had attained stability and consensus could still harbor a raucous political culture, see J.H. Plumb, *The Growth of Political Stability in England, 1675–1725* (London: Macmillan Press, 1967); and Tim Harris, *Politics Under the Later Stuarts: Party Conflict in a Divided Society 1660–1715*, (New York and London: Routledge, 1993).
2 H.G. Koenigsberger, "Monarchies and Parliaments in Early Modern Europe: *Dominium Regale* or *Dominium et Regale*," *Theory and Society* 5[2] (1978): 191–217; and J.H. Elliott, "A Europe of Composite Monarchies," *Past and Present* No. 137 (1992): 48–71; and P. Cardin et al. Polycentric Monarchies: How Did Early Modern Spain and Portugal Achieve and Maintain a Global Hegemony? (Sussex: Sussex Academic Press, 2012)..
3 For an examination of this process, see R.R. Davies, *The First English Empire: Power and Identity in the British Isles 1093–1343*, (Oxford UP, 2000).
4 Michael Braddick, *State Formation in Early Modern England, c. 1550–1700*, (Cambridge UP, 2000), explores the processes through which England developed into a fiscal-military state.
5 For the complexities of this process, see L.O.J. Boynton, *The Elizabethan Militia, 1558–1638*, (London: Routledge, 1967).
6 For the argument that Drake and his contemporaries comprised the state's naval force, see Julian Corbett, *Drake and the Tudor Navy, with a History of the Rise of England as a Maritime Power*, 2 volumes, (London: Longmans, 1898). A corrective is provided by N.A.M. Rodger, *The Safeguard of the Sea: A Naval History of Britain, 660–1649*, (Harper Collins, 1997).
7 Philip J. Stern, *The Company-State: Corporate Sovereignty and the Early Modern Foundations of the British Empire in India*, (Oxford [England]: Oxford UP, 2011), explores the way in which chartered companies did more than merely serve as agents of the state; he argues that they embodied state functions as they carried them out.
8 For studies of how careers could be made through service to the centralizing crown, see Michael G. Hall, *Edward Randolph and the American Colonies 1676–1703*, (University of North Carolina Press [for the Institute of Early American Studies], 1960); and Barbara C. Murison, "The Talented Mr Blathwayt: His Empire Revisited," in Nancy L. Rhoden, (ed.), *English Atlantics Revisited: Essays in Honoring Ian K. Steele*, (McGill-Queens University Press, 2007): 33–58.
9 For the nature of politics in England after the Restoration, see Harris, *Politics Under the Later Stuarts*; and W.A. Speck, *The Birth of Britain: A New Nation 1700–1710*, (New York: Wiley, 1994).
10 Richard S. Dunn and Mary Maples Dunn, eds., *The Papers of William Penn, Volume 2: 1680–1684*, (Philadelphia: University of Pennsylvania Press, 1982), 19–79.
11 John M. Murrin, "Political Development," in Jack P. Greene and J.R. Pole, (eds.), *Colonial British America: Essays in the New History of the Early Modern Era*, (Baltimore: Johns Hopkins University Press, 1984): 408–456.
12 For treatments of Walpolean political management, see Paul Langford, *A Polite and Commercial People: England, 1727–1783*, (The Clarendon Press, Oxford: Oxford UP, 1989), esp. chapter 2, "Robin's Reign, 1727–1742", 9–58; and J.H. Plumb, *Sir Robert Walpole: The Making of a Statesman*, (Cresset Press, 1956); and Plumb, *Sir Robert Walpole: The King's Minister*, (Cresset, 1960).
13 For a discussion of the opposition to the crown (and London) through the lens of the introduction of civic humanist thought into English politics, see J.G.A. Pocock, "Machiavelli, Harrington, and English Political Ideologies in the Eighteenth Century," *William and Mary Quarterly* 22 (1965): 549–583; and Pocock, *The Machiavellian Moment: Florentine Political Thought and the Atlantic Republican Tradition*, new edition, (Princeton: Princeton University Press, 2003; orig. pub. 1975).

14 Bernard Bailyn, "Politics and Social Structure in Virginia," in James Morton Smith, ed., *Seventeenth Century America* (Chapel Hill, NC: University of North Carolina Press, 1959): 90–115.
15 For discussions of the enhanced power and capabilities of the post-Glorious Revolution British state, see John Brewer, *The Sinews of Power: War, Money, and the English State 1688–1783*, (New York: Knopf, 1989); and Lawrence Stone, (ed.), *An Imperial State at War: Britain from 1689 to 1815*, (London: Routledge, 1994).
16 For studies of the process in the colonies, see Michael G. Hall, *The Glorious Revolution in America: Documents on the Colonial Crisis of 1689*, (Williamsburg, VA: Institute for Early American History and Culture, 1964); David S. Lovejoy, *The Glorious Revolution in America*, new edition, (Wesleyan University Press, 1987; orig. pub. 1972); and Robert M. Bliss, *Revolution and Empire: English Politics and the American Colonies in the Seventeenth Century*, (Manchester and New York: Manchester UP, 1990).
17 See Stacy L. Lorenz, "Policy and Patronage: Governor William Gooch and Anglo-Virginia Politics, 1727–1749," in Rhoden, *English Atlantics Revisited*, pp. 81–106.
18 This process of gubernatorial patronage-wielding is discussed by John M. Murrin, in his "Review Essay," *History and Theory* 11 (1972) 226–275; 260–270.
19 Much of what follows is a distillation of two recent essays by Andrew Shankman: "A Synthesis Useful and Compelling: Anglicization and the Achievement of John M. Murrin," in Ignacio Gallup Diaz, Andrew Shankman, and David J. Silverman eds., *Anglicizing America: Empire, Revolution, Republic* (Philadelphia: University of Pennsylvania Press, 2015) 20–56; and Shankman, "Conflict for A Continent: Land, Labor, and the State in the First American Republic," in Andrew Shankman ed., *The World of the Revolutionary American Republic: Land, Labor, and the Conflict for a Continent* (London: Routledge, 2014) 1–24.
20 Pauline Maier, *From Resistance to Revolution: Colonial Radicals and the Development of an American Opposition to Britain, 1765–1776* (New York: W.W. Norton, 1972) 6, 9.
21 Steve Pincus, *1688: The First Modern Revolution* (New Haven, CT: Yale University Press, 2009); Brewer, *The Sinews of Power*; Patrick O'Brien, "Inseparable Connections: Trade, Economy, Fiscal State, and Expansion of Empire, 1688–1815," in P.J. Marshall ed., *The Oxford History of the British Empire: The Eighteenth Century* (New York: Oxford University Press, 1998) 53–77; Jacob Price, "The Imperial Economy," in Marshall ed., *The Oxford History of the British Empire*, 78–104.
22 Shankman, "A Synthesis Useful and Compelling," 30–33.
23 Jere Daniell, "Politics in New Hampshire under Governor Benning Wentworth, 1741–1767," *William and Mary Quarterly* 23 (1966) 76–105.
24 J.H. Plumb, *The Growth of Political Stability*; for a similar process in eighteenth-century Massachusetts, see Murrin, "Review Essay."
25 Fred Anderson, *A People's Army: Massachusetts Soldiers and Society in the Seven Years War* (Chapel Hill, NC: University of North Carolina Press, 1984); and *Crucible of War: The Seven Years' War and the Fate of Empire in British North America, 1754–1766* (New York: Vintage, 2000).
26 Anderson, *A People's Army*, 14.
27 Edmund S. Morgan and Helen M. Morgan, *The Stamp Act Crisis: Prologue to Revolution* (Chapel Hill, NC: University of North Carolina Press, 1995) 288–289.
28 A lengthy portion of Franklin's examination is reprinted in Jack P. Greene ed., *Colonies to Nation, 1763–1789: A Documentary History of the American Revolution* (New York: W.W. Norton, 1975) 72–78.
29 Maier, *Resistance to Revolution*, 112.
30 John M. Murrin, "1776: The Countercyclical Revolution," in Michael A. Morrison and Melinda Zook, eds., *Revolutionary Currents: Nation Building in the Transatlantic World* (New York: Rowman & Littlefield, 2004), 65–90, 67.
31 Andrew Jackson O'Shaughnessy, *An Empire Divided: The American Revolution and the British Caribbean* (Philadelphia: University of Pennsylvania Press, 2000).
32 Jack P. Greene, "Empire and Identity from the Glorious Revolution to the American Revolution," in Marshall, ed., *Oxford History of the British Empire*, 208–30; Julie Flavell, *When London Was Capital of America* (New Haven, CT: Yale University Press, 2010).
33 J.M. Bumsted, "'Things in the Womb of Time': Ideas of American Independence, 1633–1763," *William and Mary Quarterly*, 3rd ser., 31 (1974): 534–64; John Shy, "The Spectrum of Imperial Possibilities: Henry Ellis and Thomas Pownall, 1763–1775," in Shy, *A People Numerous and Armed: Reflections on the Military Struggle for the American Revolution* (Ann Arbor: University of Michigan Press, 1990), 43–80; LaCroix, *Ideological Origins of American Federalism*, chap. 2.

34 John M. Murrin, "The French and Indian War, the American Revolution, and the Counterfactual Hypothesis: Reflections on Lawrence Henry Gipson and John Shy," *Reviews in American History* 1 (1973): 307–318, 315.
35 Murrin, "French and Indian War," 313–15.
36 Ibid., 316.
37 Murrin, *Liberty, Equality, and Power*, 167–68.
38 Morgan and Morgan, *Stamp Act Crisis*; John L. Bullion, "British Ministers and American Resistance to the Stamp Act, October–December 1765," *William and Mary Quarterly*, 3rd ser., 49 (1992): 89–107; Wood, *Americanization of Benjamin Franklin*.
39 A good portion of Franklin's session is reprinted in Jack P. Greene, ed., *Colonies to Nation: A Documentary History of the American Revolution* (New York: W. W. Norton, 1975), 72–78.
40 For the Sons of Liberty, see Maier, *From Resistance to Revolution*, 112.
41 Murrin, "1776: The Countercyclical Revolution," esp. 76–78.
42 For a complete narrative of events in Massachusetts, see Jeremy A. Stern, "The Overflowings of Liberty: Massachusetts, the Townshend Acts Crisis, and the Reconception of Freedom, 1766–1770" (Ph.D. diss., Princeton University, 2010).
43 John M. Murrin, "In the Land of the Free and the Home of the Slave, Maybe There Was Room Even for Deference," *Journal of American History* 85 (1998): 86–91.
44 See Jackson Turner Main, "Government by the People: The American Revolution and the Democratization of the Legislatures," *William and Mary Quarterly*, 3rd ser., 23 (1966): 391–407; Wood, *Radicalism of the American Revolution*; Jay Fliegelman, *Prodigals and Pilgrims: The American Revolution Against Patriarchal Authority, 1750–1800* (Cambridge: Cambridge University Press, 1992); W. J. Rorbaugh, "'I Thought I Should Liberate Myself from the Thraldom of Others': Apprentices, Masters, and the Revolution," in Young, ed., *Beyond the American Revolution*, 185–217; Allan Kulikoff, "The American Revolution, Capitalism, and the Formation of the Yeoman Classes," in Young, ed., *Beyond the American Revolution*, 80–119; Mary Beth Norton, *Liberty's Daughters: The Revolutionary Experience of American Women, 1750–1800* (Boston: Little, Brown, 1980); and David Brion Davis, *The Problem of Slavery in the Age of Revolution, 1770–1823* (Oxford: Oxford University Press, 1975), for the merest sampling of a vast literature.
45 Douglas R. Egerton, *Death or Liberty: African Americans and Revolutionary America* (Oxford: Oxford University Press, 2009); Eva Sheppard Wolf, *Race and Liberty in the New Nation: Emancipation in Virginia from the Revolution to Nat Turner's Rebellion* (Baton Rouge: Louisiana State University Press, 2006); George William Van Cleve, *A Slaveholders' Union: Slavery, Politics, and the Construction of the Early American Republic* (Chicago: University of Chicago Press, 2010); Trevor Burnard, "Freedom, Migration, and the American Revolution," in Eliga H. Gould and Peter S. Onuf, eds., *Empire and Nation: The American Revolution in the Atlantic World* (Baltimore: Johns Hopkins University Press, 2005), 295–314; Gregory Evans Dowd, *A Spirited Resistance: The North American Indian Struggle for Unity, 1745–1815* (Baltimore: Johns Hopkins University Press, 1992); James H. Merrell, "Declarations of Independence: Indian-White Relations in the New Nation," in Jack P. Greene, ed., *The American Revolution: Its Character and Limits* (New York: New York University Press, 1987), 197–223; Rosemarie Zagarri, *Revolutionary Backlash: Women and Politics in the Early American Republic* (Philadelphia: University of Pennsylvania Press, 2007); Linda K. Kerber, *Women of the Republic: Intellect and Ideology in Revolutionary America* (Chapel Hill: University of North Carolina Press, 1980).

References

Anderson, Fred. *A People's Army: Massachusetts Soldiers and Society in the Seven Years War* (Chapel Hill, NC: University of North Carolina Press, 1984).
Anderson, Fred. *Crucible of War: The Seven Years' War and the Fate of Empire in British North America, 1754–1766* (New York: Vintage, 2000).
Bailyn, Bernard. "Politics and Social Structure in Virginia," in James Morton Smith, ed., *Seventeenth Century America* (Chapel Hill, NC: University of North Carolina Press, 1959): 90–115.
Bliss, Robert M. *Revolution and Empire: English Politics and the American Colonies in the Seventeenth Century*, (Manchester and New York: Manchester UP, 1990).
Boynton, L.O.J. *The Elizabethan Militia, 1558–1638*, (London: Routledge, 1967).

Braddick, Michael. *State Formation in Early Modern England, c. 1550–1700*, (Cambridge UP, 2000).
Brewer, John. *The Sinews of Power: War, Money, and the English State 1688–1783*, (New York: Knopf, 1989).
Bullion, John L. "British Ministers and American Resistance to the Stamp Act, October–December 1765," *William and Mary Quarterly*, 3rd ser., 49 (1992): 89–107; Wood, Americanization of Benjamin Franklin.
Bumsted, J. M. "'Things in the Womb of Time': Ideas of American Independence, 1633–1763," *William and Mary Quarterly*, 3rd ser., 31 (1974): 534–64.
Burnard, Trevor. "Freedom, Migration, and the American Revolution," in Eliga H. Gould and Peter S. Onuf, eds., *Empire and Nation: The American Revolution in the Atlantic World* (Baltimore: Johns Hopkins University Press, 2005), 295–314.
Cardin, P., Herzog, T., Ibáñez, J. R. and Sabatini, G. Polycentric Monarchies: How Did Early Modern Spain and Portugal Achieve and Maintain a Global Hegemony? (Sussex: Sussex Academic Press, 2012).
Corbett, Julian. *Drake and the Tudor Navy, with a History of the Rise of England as a Maritime Power*, 2 volumes, (London: Longmans, 1898).
Daniell, Jere. "Politics in New Hampshire under Governor Benning Wentworth, 1741–1767," *William and Mary Quarterly* 23 (1966) 76–105.
Davies, R.R. *The First English Empire: Power and Identity in the British Isles 1093–1343*, (Oxford UP, 2000).
Diaz, Andrew Shankman, and David J. Silverman (Philadelphia: University of Pennsylvania Press, 2015) 20–56.
Dowd, Gregory Evans. *A Spirited Resistance: The North American Indian Struggle for Unity, 1745–1815* (Baltimore: Johns Hopkins University Press, 1992).
Dunn, Richard S. and Mary Maples Dunn, eds. *The Papers of William Penn, Volume 2: 1680–1684*, (Philadelphia: University of Pennsylvania Press, 1982), pp. 19–79.
Egerton, Douglas R. *Death or Liberty: African Americans and Revolutionary America* (Oxford: Oxford University Press, 2009).
Elliott, J.H. "A Europe of Composite Monarchies," *Past and Present* No. 137 (1992): 48–71.
Fliegelman, Jay. *Prodigals and Pilgrims: The American Revolution Against Patriarchal Authority, 1750–1800* (Cambridge: Cambridge University Press, 1992).
Greene, Jack P. ed., *Colonies to Nation, 1763–1789: A Documentary History of the American Revolution* (New York: W.W. Norton, 1975) 72–78.
Greene, Jack P. "Empire and Identity from the Glorious Revolution to the American Revolution," in Marshall, ed., *Oxford History of the British Empire*, 208–30; Julie Flavell, *When London Was Capital of America* (New Haven, CT: Yale University Press, 2010).
Hall, Michael G. *Edward Randolph and the American Colonies 1676–1703*, (University of North Carolina Press [for the Institute of Early American Studies], 1960).
Hall, Michael G. *The Glorious Revolution in America: Documents on the Colonial Crisis of 1689*, (Williamsburg, VA: Institute for Early American History and Culture, 1964).
Harris, Tim. *Politics Under the Later Stuarts: Party Conflict in a Divided Society 1660–1715*, (New York and London: Routledge, 1993).
Kerber, Linda K. *Women of the Republic: Intellect and Ideology in Revolutionary America* (Chapel Hill: University of North Carolina Press, 1980).
Koenigsberger, H.G. "Monarchies and Parliaments in Early Modern Europe: *Dominium Regale* or *Dominium et Regale*," *Theory and Society* 5[2] (1978): 191–217.
Kulikoff, Allan. "The American Revolution, Capitalism, and the Formation of the Yeoman Classes," in Young, ed., *Beyond the American Revolution*, 80–119; Mary Beth Norton, *Liberty's Daughters: The Revolutionary Experience of American Women, 1750–1800* (Boston: Little, Brown, 1980).
Langford, Paul. *A Polite and Commercial People: England, 1727–1783*, (The Clarendon Press, Oxford: Oxford UP, 1989), esp. Ch. 2, "Robin's Reign, 1727–1742," 9–58.
Lorenz, Stacy L. "Policy and Patronage: Governor William Gooch and Anglo-Virginia Politics, 1727–1749," in Rhoden, *English Atlantics Revisited*, pp. 81–106.
Lovejoy, David S. *The Glorious Revolution in America*, new edition, (Wesleyan University Press, 1987; orig. pub. 1972).
Maier, Pauline. *From Resistance to Revolution: Colonial Radicals and the Development of an American Opposition to Britain, 1765–1776* (New York: W.W. Norton, 1972) 6, 9.

Main, Jackson Turner. "Government by the People: The American Revolution and the Democratization of the Legislatures," *William and Mary Quarterly*, 3rd ser., 23 (1966): 391–407.

Merrell, James H. "Declarations of Independence: Indian-White Relations in the New Nation," in Jack P. Greene, ed., *The American Revolution: Its Character and Limits* (New York: New York University Press, 1987), 197–223.

Morgan, Edmund S. and Helen M. Morgan, *The Stamp Act Crisis: Prologue to Revolution* (Chapel Hill, NC: University of North Carolina Press, 1995) 288–289.

Murison, Barbara C. "The Talented Mr Blathwayt: His Empire Revisited," in Nancy L. Rhoden, (ed.), *English Atlantics Revisited: Essays in* Honoring Ian K. Steele, (McGill-Queens University Press, 2007): 33–58.

Murrin, John M. "In the Land of the Free and the Home of the Slave, Maybe There Was Room Even for Deference," *Journal of American History* 85 (1998): 86–91.

Murrin, John M. "Political Development," in Jack P. Greene and J.R. Pole, (eds.), *Colonial British America: Essays in the New History of the Early Modern Era*, (Baltimore: Johns Hopkins University Press, 1984): 408–456.

Murrin, John M. in his "Review Essay," *History and Theory* 11 (1972) 226–275; pp. 260–270.

Murrin, John M. "1776: The Countercyclical Revolution," in Michael A. Morrison and Melinda Zook, eds., *Revolutionary Currents: Nation Building in the Transatlantic World* (New York: Rowman & Littlefield, 2004), 65–90, 67.

Murrin, John M. "The French and Indian War, the American Revolution, and the Counterfactual Hypothesis: Reflections on Lawrence Henry Gipson and John Shy," *Reviews in American History* 1 (1973): 307–318, p. 315.

O'Brien, Patrick. "Inseparable Connections: Trade, Economy, Fiscal State, and Expansion of Empire, 1688–1815," *The Oxford History of the British Empire: The Eighteenth Century*, ed. P.J. Marshall (New York: Oxford University Press, 1998) 53–77.

O'Shaughnessy, Andrew Jackson. *An Empire Divided: The American Revolution and the British Caribbean* (Philadelphia: University of Pennsylvania Press, 2000).

Pincus, Steve. *1688: The First Modern Revolution* (New Haven, CT: Yale University Press, 2009).

Plumb, J.H. *The Growth of Political Stability;* for a similar process in eighteenth-century Massachusetts, see Murrin, "Review Essay."

Plumb, J.H. *Sir Robert Walpole: The Making of a Statesman*, (Cresset Press, 1956).

Plumb, J.H. *Sir Robert Walpole: The King's Minister*, (Cresset, 1960).

Plumb, J.H. *The Growth of Political Stability in England, 1675–1725* (London: Macmillan Press, 1967).

Pocock, J.G.A. *The Machiavellian Moment: Florentine Political Thought and the Atlantic Republican Tradition*, new edition, (Princeton: Princeton University Press, 2003; orig. pub. 1975).

Pocock, J.G.A. "Machiavelli, Harrington, and English Political Ideologies in the Eighteenth Century," *William and Mary Quarterly* 22 (1965): 549–583.

Price, Jacob. "The Imperial Economy," in Marshall ed., *The Oxford History of the British Empire*, 78–104.

Rodger, N.A.M. *The Safeguard of the Sea: A Naval History of Britain, 660–1649*, (Harper Collins, 1997).

Rorbaugh, W.J. "'I Thought I Should Liberate Myself from the Thraldom of Others': Apprentices, Masters, and the Revolution," in Young, ed., *Beyond the American Revolution*, 185–217.

Shankman, Andrew. "A Synthesis Useful and Compelling: Anglicization and the Achievement of John M. Murrin," *Anglicizing America: Empire, Revolution, Republic*, eds. Ignacio Gallup Diaz, Andrew Shankman, and David J. Silverman (Philadelphia: University of Pennsylvania Press, 2015) 20–56.

Shankman, Andrew. "Conflict for A Continent: Land, Labor, and the State in the First American Republic," in ed., *The World of the Revolutionary American Republic: Land, Labor, and the Conflict for a Continent*, ed. Andrew Shankman (London: Routledge, 2014) 1–24.

Shy, John. "The Spectrum of Imperial Possibilities: Henry Ellis and Thomas Pownall, 1763–1775," in Shy, *A People Numerous and Armed: Reflections on the Military Struggle for the American Revolution* (Ann Arbor: University of Michigan Press, 1990), 43–80.

Speck, W.A. *The Birth of Britain: A New Nation 1700–1710*, (New York: Wiley, 1994).

Stern, Philip J. *The Company-State: Corporate Sovereignty and the Early Modern Foundations of the British Empire in India*, (Oxford [England]: Oxford UP, 2011).

Stern, Jeremy A. "The Overflowings of Liberty: Massachusetts, the Townshend Acts Crisis, and the Reconception of Freedom, 1766–1770" (Ph.D. diss., Princeton University, 2010).

Stone, Lawrence, ed. *An Imperial State at War: Britain from 1689 to 1815*, (London: Routledge, 1994).

Van Cleve, George William. *A Slaveholders' Union: Slavery, Politics, and the Construction of the Early American Republic* (Chicago: University of Chicago Press, 2010).
Wolf, Eva Sheppard. *Race and Liberty in the New Nation: Emancipation in Virginia from the Revolution to Nat Turner's Rebellion* (Baton Rouge: Louisiana State University Press, 2006).
Zagarri, Rosemarie. *Revolutionary Backlash: Women and Politics in the Early American Republic* (Philadelphia: University of Pennsylvania Press, 2007).

19

THE REVOLUTIONARY BLACK ATLANTIC

From Royalists to Revolutionaries

Jane Landers

The Black Atlantic was born not in the eighteenth century but in the mid-fifteenth century, when Portuguese factors reached the Upper Guinea Coast and began a trade with local rulers for luxury goods, including the enslaved.[1] Free and enslaved Africans had long formed important segments of the urban populations of southern Portugal and Spain, and they became cultural brokers in the Upper Guinea trade.[2] By the early sixteenth century, Africans were also key to the success of Portuguese settlements in the Madeira, Canary, and Cape Verde Islands, where the free worked in urban and domestic labor, small-scale trade and sailing, as they had in Portugal, and the enslaved produced foodstuffs and worked on cotton and sugar plantations.[3] Together, Portuguese and Africans would later develop the earliest Atlantic slave trade to the Americas.[4]

While Portugal concentrated on developing trade and colonies in Africa, Spain focused on the Americas and Africans participated in each of Spain's exploratory voyages across the Atlantic and their wars of conquest.[5] Once the Indian wars on Hispaniola waned and colonization was underway, small groups of battle-tested Africans joined in new Caribbean campaigns and in the spectacular conquest of the Aztec empire. As Frederick Bowser and James Lockhart have shown, free and enslaved Africans participated in even more significant numbers in the conquest of the great Inca empire of Peru and in the subsequent Indian and civil wars which wracked the region.[6] These engagements allowed "black conquistadors," as Matthew Restall has called them, to petition for rewards for their *meritos y servicio* (merits and services), and thus, leave a documentary trail of their exploits. Spanish chronicles and ecclesiastical records also document the African among the Spanish expeditions and in the earliest Spanish settlements.[7]

Chronically short-handed Spanish officials in the Americas very early began to include both free and enslaved Africans in their military forces. Slaves commonly appeared on militia rolls as drummers and fifes in their owner's units and also served as interpreters on Indian frontiers. They also served as coastal sentinels and sailors on locally organized patrol boats throughout the Spanish Caribbean, as French and English pirates challenged Spanish hegemony in the region.[8] When France and Spain went to war in 1552 "the Caribbean became for the first time a significant theater of international warfare" and soon Spanish officials were complaining that Caribbean waters were "as full of French as New Rochelle."[9] During a French pirate attack on Havana in 1555, some 100 blacks (most of whom were probably enslaved) and an equal number of Indians joined 40 Spaniards in an unsuccessful defense of the city. Despite the best efforts of this multiracial force, the city fell, and Havana's governor hastily raised an additional force of over 200 black slaves from the countryside to help battle the French pirates.[10] Enslaved blacks also helped defend Puerto Rico in 1557, Cartagena in 1560 and 1572, and Santo Domingo in 1583. Cartagena's officials reported in the same period they had 200 to 300 slaves whom they could arm for service and Santo Domingo's officials estimated an available slave force of about 400–500.[11] The *pardo* (mulatto) company of Puebla helped defend the Crown's interests repeatedly in Veracruz, Campeche, and Mexico City. In the unhealthy coastal city of Veracruz, New Spain's main Atlantic port, almost the entire military force, the Corps of Lancers, consisted of persons of color.[12]

Despite the efforts of such men, Spain began losing both treasure fleets and territory in the "Spanish lake." The Dutch seized Curaçao in 1634 and by midcentury French smugglers and buccaneers had occupied the western third of Hispaniola and the island of Tortuga off its north coast.[13] Soon after, in 1655, English forces attacked Jamaica as part of Oliver Cromwell's Western Design. In this contest, many slaves joined the Spanish forces trying to hold the island, and in defeat, many departed with the Spanish to Cuba. Other black warriors stayed behind to join the maroons in Jamaican mountains, from whence they continued to harry the English.[14] By mid-seventeenth century (Spain's century of depression), the Dutch, the French, and the English had established economic and military bases across the Caribbean from which to attack Spanish fleets and settlements.[15]

Recognizing that Spain could not respond quickly enough with metropolitan troops to these escalating foreign threats, the King ordered the creation of more black military units, noting that the blacks and mulattos who defended his realms were "persons of valor" who fought with "vigor and reputation".[16] By mid-seventeenth century then, the Spanish Crown had fully accepted that free men of color could be brave and honorable, and this important metropolitan acknowledgment apparently encouraged enlistments. Free *pardo* militias were established in Lima as early as 1615 and in Chile by 1643.[17] Similar units were organized in Guatemala, Nicaragua, Costa Rica, and Panama.[18] A Central American roster from 1673 listed almost 2,000 *pardos* serving in infantry units throughout the isthmus.[19] Local units of free black men were also organized in Hispaniola, Vera Cruz, Campeche, Puerto Rico, Panama, Caracas, Cartagena, and Florida, among other locales.[20]

Other men of African descent took to the Atlantic, serving whatever European power offered them the best opportunities. The interrogation of a black corsair captured in a raid on St. Augustine in 1687 adds to our understanding of this little known black experience. Diego testified he was born in Tortuga, the infamous pirate haven off the northern coast of Hispaniola. As a young man he grew tobacco that he sold to the buccaneers and he later joined the French corsair named "Sanbo" who sailed for the Mosquito Coast. Diego caught turtles for the crew and participated in the capture of two Spanish prizes from Cartagena, thereby earning a share of the take. Later he joined a Captain Cahrebon on a second corsairing expedition to Cartagena, where he cut wood for some time before canoeing back to the Mosquito Coast. His last captain, the Frenchman, Nicholas Grammont, sacked Campeche, capturing black slaves whom he sold at San Jorge (present-day Charleston), before heading for Florida, where Diego and a mulatto translator named Thomas joined Grammont in attacking St. Augustine. After several days of pitched battles against the Spaniards and their black and Indian militias, Diego was finally captured, being one of only two pirates to have survived the attack.[21]

In his circum-Atlantic travels, Diego may have met another, more famous, black corsair, Capitán Diego Martín (alias Diego *el Mulatto*). Born a slave in Havana, he escaped to join Dutch privateers, capturing many prizes and prisoners in raids on Campeche and Veracruz. In 1638 Diego Martín offered his service to Spain in a letter delivered to Spanish officials. Martín expressed his great desire to serve as a "valiant soldier of the King, our lord" (Valeroso

Soldado del Rey nuestro Señor), making appropriate references to the King's championship of the Catholic faith. He promised that if the King agreed, no Dutch ship or any other enemy would any longer stop along Cuba's coasts, "especially knowing that I am here very few would dare pass on to the Indies, for they certainly fear me." Captain Martín's boast must have been well founded for Havana officials sent the offer to Spain with a recommendation of royal pardon and a salary equivalent to that of an admiral, making no derogatory mention of his color or class.[22] The testimony of the first Diego and the boast of the second confirm the geopolitical, economic, and military capital that accrued to at least some black men in the Atlantic world of the seventeenth century.

For their service to Spain, black men across the Atlantic also won grants of land (which the Crown had to spare). Former maroons and free blacks across the Spanish empire were also rewarded with land and formally recognized and self-governing towns of their own, in return for peace and military service. Thus were born free black towns like Nirgua, in modern Venezuela, San Lorenzo de Cerralvo (also known as San Lorenzo de los Negros) outside Orizaba, New Spain and Gracia Real de Santa Teresa de Mose, outside San Agustín, Florida, among others. By establishing, and defending, "well-governed" towns, freed blacks earned another corporate identity and at least a measure of respectability as *vecinos* (townspeople) and *pobladores* (settlers) who lived a *vida política* (civil life).[23]

The Black Atlantic was almost three centuries in the making when Bourbon Reformers won the Spanish Crown in the War of Spanish Succession (1700–1713) and created formal Disciplined Militias across the Atlantic. Military men of African descent now elected their own officers, designed their unit's uniforms and received the *fuero militar*, a corporate charter that exempted them from tribute and prosecution in civilian courts and granted them equal juridical status with white militiamen. The *fuero* also granted black soldiers military, hospitalization, retirement, and death benefits, all major protections never before available to them.[24] Formal membership in the military corporation also granted these men and their families higher status in a status-obsessed world. The juridical and social benefits of militia membership were clearly appreciated by men of African descent across Spain's Atlantic holdings and they developed traditions of multigenerational service.[25] The military service of free men of color also redounded to the benefit of their wives and children who could inherit pensions and property, as well as a certain social status, from their husbands and fathers.[26]

The Bourbon creation of black battalions was not met with universal acclaim across the Spanish Atlantic. Christon Archer and Ben Vinson have analyzed the racist attitudes of the Conde de Revillagigedo, Viceroy of New Spain (Mexico). Alan Kuethe found similar resistance and resentment among Spanish officials in New Granada (Colombia) as well as in Cuba where Captain General Luis de las Casas allowed Spanish units to change their uniform so as not to wear the same as black and mulatto troops.[27] At the same time, recognizing his need, the Spanish King enjoined his subjects not to disparage or insult Havana's black troops, "because it is my royal will that they be treated well and with love and that they not suffer the least outrage or insult."[28] The men of the Pardo and Moreno Battalions of Cuba, in turn, seized every opportunity to demonstrate their loyalty, their service to the Crown and the community, their devotion to the Catholic Church and their civility. During drills and for public occasions, they marched on the Plaza dressed in uniforms of their own design and led by their own elected officers, under banners such as that of the Pardo battalion that read "Always Onward to Glory."[29].

Spain needed every hand it could take during the seemingly endless wars of the eighteenth century—the Spanish War of Succession or Queen Anne's War (1700–13), the War of Jenkins' Ear (1739–43) which became the War of Austrian Succession (1739–48), King George's War (1744–48) and the Seven Years' War (1759–63)—and its new Disciplined Militias served around the Atlantic as needed. Meanwhile, free black civilians continued to serve in local militias and as sailors and corsairs on Spanish ships, attacking English ships and settlements across the Atlantic. These chronic conflicts further connected the black Atlantic.

Men of African descent formed a significant part of Spain's military forces during the War of Jenkins' Ear (1739–43). England imagined that it would easily trounce the Spaniards when Admiral Edward Vernon commanded a fleet of English warships attacking Spanish ports around the Atlantic but Porto Bello (Panama) was Vernon's only success and free black militias helped Spain hold all the others.[30] In 1740 the free blacks of Gracia Real de Santa Teresa de Mose also helped Spain hold Florida when a Royal Fleet from Jamaica bombarded Spanish St. Augustine for a month and Georgia's Governor James Oglethorpe and a combined force of Georgians, Carolinians, and allied Indians besieged the colony by land. Governor Manuel de Montiano formally commended the black troops to the Crown and Mose's Captain Francisco Menéndez also wrote several letters to the King detailing his service in the siege and asking for a promotion. When the King failed to respond to his two written requests, Menéndez decided to become a corsair and make his way to "old Spain" to speak to the King in person.[31]

As Julius Scott's important work showed, black sailors and corsairs like Menéndez formed critical social networks across key Atlantic ports and served as conduits of political news. Scholars such as Marcus Rediker and Jeffrey Bolster have argued that even the English maritime culture of the eighteenth and nineteenth centuries, "while by no means either color-blind or without internal prejudice" created its own institutions and its own stratifications, which could work to the relative advantage of black men." Bolster contends that merchants judged crews based on their strength, ability, and experience rather than skin color, with black and white crewmen earning equal pay for equal jobs, and many sailors, in fact, earning more than whites.[32]

Reduced social distinctions and hoped-for pay may well have been reasons for Spanish blacks to take to the sea, just as they had to the militias, but when captured by the English they were presumed by their color to be slaves, and thus fair prizes of war. In 1746 New York's Admiralty Court considered the fate of 20 "Indians Mollattoes & Negroes" captured aboard two Spanish prizes the year before. Although Spanish officials from Havana presented proof that 17 were, in fact, free men, by the time the New York court finally met and ordered freedom for 4 of the men, only 3 could be located.[33] Nor was this an isolated incident. On August 16, 1748, the British corsair, *Ester*, captained by Robert Troup, seized the *Nuestra Señora del Carmen* after it left Havana and claimed as part of the prize 45 black corsairs. Of the 45 captives, 20 were members of the Batallones de Pardos y Morenos Libres de Havana and carried certificates from their commander. The recently concluded Treaty of Aix-la-Chapelle guaranteed that all men captured after August 9 of that year would be returned.[34] Despite the treaty provisions, repeated efforts by the Spanish governors to recover their black subjects met with failure and Florida's governor, Fulgencio García de Solis, warned "without those of 'broken' color (*color quebrado*, a term for anyone of mixed race, usually meaning *mulatto*), blacks and Indians, which abound in our towns in America, I do not know if we could arm a single corsair with Spaniards alone."[35]

Despite such dangers, the juridical and social benefits of militia membership were clearly appreciated by men of African descent in the Spanish circum-Caribbean who developed traditions of long-term family service.[36] The military service of free men of color also redounded to the benefit of their wives and children who could inherit pensions and property, as well as a certain social status, from their husbands and fathers.[37]

It is not surprising then, that many blacks adopted a royalist position, ardently supporting in word and deed the monarchs who rewarded and honored them. During the Seven Years' War (1759–63) the British captured Havana in a surprise attack, despite the bravery of both free and enslaved black Cubans.[38] The British gave no quarter to those black men they captured but despite that knowledge a group of 20 Cuban slaves, armed only with machetes and acting totally independently, launched their own offensive against a superior English force at Cuba's great Morro Castle, killing some of the English enemy and capturing seven more. The "ladies of Havana" described the slaves' heroism in a letter to the King who freed them and awarded their leader, Andrés Gutiérrez, the title of Captain. The compensation claims of their owners document other slaves who fought and died fighting the British.[39] During the English invasion, free Cubans of color, like the barber Gabriel Dorotea Barba, spent their own funds to raise units of volunteers to defend their "homeland."[40] By the terms of the 1763 Treaty of Paris that ended this conflict, Spain recovered Havana but it also had to cede Florida to the British. In the exodus that followed, black militiamen from Pensacola and St. Augustine evacuated with the Spanish and made new lives for themselves and their families in Cuba and New Spain. There they were integrated into the local black militia networks. By 1770 Cuba's Disciplined Black militias numbered more than 3,000 men and they constituted more than one-fourth of the island's armed forces.[41]

Men of African descent, of different ethnic backgrounds, languages, and loyalties served in all of the Atlantic Revolutions. As an ally of the French and an enemy of Great Britain, Spain supported the Patriots in the American Revolution, the first to erupt in the so-called Age of Revolutions. Cuba's black militiamen fought in the Gulf and Mississippi River campaigns, serving with distinction in Manchac, Baton Rouge, Mobile, and Pensacola.[42] Governor Bernardo de Gálvez nominated a number of his black troops for royal commendations and the Crown acknowledged the importance of their contribution with silver medals and promotions. Some of these troops later went on to fight the English again at Providence in the Bahamas. Most of these men had at least some infantry training but, as already noted, they also equipped themselves well as corsairs in naval campaigns in Atlantic and Caribbean waters.[43]

In 1779 another group of black troops also crossed the Atlantic to fight in the American Revolution. The service of the Chasseurs-Voluntaires de Saint-Domingue who left Le Cap to assist American Patriots in Savannah is acknowledged today by a sculpture in the city square.[44] Meanwhile, other men of African descent joined the British as Black Loyalists. Captain Tye, formerly Titus Corlies, gained fame attacking Patriot planters and their forces in Monmouth New Jersey.[45] In South Carolina, one of the bloodiest of the American theaters, enslaved men fought on both Patriot and Loyalist sides. Some former slaves fought alongside the famed "Swamp Fox," Francis Marion, while others like Thomas Johnston joined the Loyalists and departed with them for London at war's end.[46] Others who survived the carnage in South Carolina ended up escaping across the southern border to claim religious sanctuary in Spanish Florida, where the men joined the colony's black militia. In that unit, African fugitives from Carolina slavery like Big Prince (Juan Bautista Whitten) later rose to positions of relative status in the Spanish community, defending St. Augustine from a series of enemies, including Georgian forces recruited by Citizen Edmund Genêt (1795), Seminole Indians (1800), and US Marines (1812). Fighting alongside Witten in St. Augustine's polyglot and multiethnic black militia were former slaves like the Congo man Felipe Edimboro, who had earned his freedom through self-purchase (*coartación*).[47]

Ironically, Spain's dependence upon former slaves reached new heights as a result of the slave revolt that erupted in Saint Domingue in 1791. The former slaves who led the revolution in Saint Domingue and made themselves and their followers free were simultaneously feared and courted by France, Spain, and Britain.[48] After more than two hard years of fighting and low on supplies, in 1793 the three main leaders of the revolt Georges Biassou, Jean-François Papillon, and Toussaint Louverture decided to accept the Spanish offer of alliance, declaring in a rhetorical flourish that they would "rather be slaves of the Spaniards than free with the French."[49] In fact, they never intended to return to slavery under any regime and were determined to cut the best deal possible for themselves, their kin, and their troops.

Spain designated its newly recruited armies of risen slaves the "Black Auxiliaries of Charles IV," a much more formal title and affiliation than any earlier or later black militias ever received. To celebrate the new alliance, Captain General Joaquín García, Governor of Santo Domingo, ceremoniously decorated Jean-François, Georges Biassou, and Toussaint with gold medals bearing the likeness of the king, and presented them with documents expressing the gratitude and confidence of the Spanish government. Twelve other subchiefs also received silver medals and documents attesting to their meritorious service.[50] Jean-François later decorated himself with the Cross of Saint Louis, and Biassou titled himself the "Viceroy of the Conquered Territories" while the subsequently more famous Toussaint Louverture more modestly came on board as aide and physician to Biassou's large army.[51] While Toussaint later switched his allegiance to the French Republic, Jean-François and Biassou and large numbers of their troops remained committed to Spain.[52]

The alliance Spain struck with Saint Domingue's black rebels was an uneasy one, marked by distrust on both sides. Although Spanish officials generally complied with the Crown's promises of freedom and support, they also watched the former slaves with fear and suspicion and tried to isolate them and the dangerous ideas they represented. And although it is clear that Spain's black allies were later embittered by the graceless way some Spanish officials treated them and never anticipated the diaspora they would experience at the end of the war, Jean-François and George Biassou did not die betrayed in a French jail as did Toussaint.

In 1795 Spain and the Directory of the French Republic finally concluded the Treaty of Basle and Spain agreed to cede western Hispaniola to the French and to disband the Black Auxiliaries of Carlos IV. David Geggus, Jorge Victor Ojeda, Matt Childs, and I have all written about the diaspora of Spain's Black Auxiliaries following their trails to Florida, Cuba, Mexico, and Spain and Miriam Martin Erickson is now tracking the large group of "Negros franceses" commanded by Jean François's lieutenant, Jean Jacques (Juan Santiago), that were finally resettled in the Kingdom of Guatemala. She has found a letter Jean François wrote Juan Santiago from exile in Cádiz in which he shows he hoped to reunite the Black Auxiliaries that had been dispersed across the Atlantic.[53]

Meanwhile, in Florida, Generalissimo Jorge Biassou, as he now called himself, was also struggling to maintain intact his "family" of relatives and troops, as well as the military status and authority granted him by King Carlos IV.[54] Biassou's group of revolutionaries turned royalists expanded their "family" when only three months after arriving in Florida, Biassou's brother-in-law and military heir, Sergeant Juan Jorge Jacobo, married Rafaela Witten in St. Augustine's cathedral.[55] This union had important political implications for the bride was the daughter of Juan Bautista (Big Prince) Witten, who only the year before had served with distinction against an invasion mounted by the French radical and Minister Plenipotentiary to the United States, Citizen Genêt. The marriage of Biassou's heir, Jorge, and Witten's daughter, Rafaela, thus united the leading families of both groups of blacks who had allied with the cause of the Spanish king against the forces of French republicanism. Subsequent marriages and baptisms added new layers of connection, as the refugees from Saint Domingue and the Anglo South used the structures of the Catholic Church to strengthen their blended community. The overlapping military and personal relationships and creation of extended fictive families among these Atlantic figures can be traced up to 1821 when, once again, Spain evacuated Florida, this time having sold the colony to the young American nation it helped create. And they continued in Cuba.[56]

Cuba prided itself on being "the ever faithful Isle" and it was the most important, and most heavily fortified, of Spain's Atlantic holdings.[57] But with the destruction of sugar plantations in Saint Domingue, Cuban planters invested heavily in that crop and in the African slave trade on which it depended. With the rise of a so-called second slavery in Cuba (which American capital helped) came the "Africanization" of Cuba. Neither the British embargo of 1807, nor the US embargo of 1808, nor the Mixed Commissions for the Suppression of the Slave Trade Britain—established in Havana, Rio de Janeiro, Suriname, and Sierra Leone to decide whether captured ships were illegally slaving—deterred Cuban slave traders. Between 1790 and 1820 Cuban planters imported approximately 325,000 slaves, a three-fold increase in slave imports in only 30 years.[58] In the same period, the social position of Cuba's free black population declined and Cuba was wracked by a series of slave revolts and conspiracies plotted jointly by free and enslaved Cubans. The terrible repressions that followed such events largely destroyed Cuba's free black class and in a new Atlantic Diaspora, many free people of color fled the island for Mexico, Brazil, Europe, Jamaica, and the United States, once again to remake lives in new locales.[59]

Meanwhile, the revolutionary principles and examples emanating from the United States, France, and Saint Domingue triggered a series of independence movements across the Atlantic World: in the French colonies of Guadeloupe and Martinique and in Spanish colonies such as New Granada and La Plata, among others. In each of these examples, persons of African descent had to decide whether to remain loyal subjects of the metropole or to risk all to become citizens of new nations. Royal black militias were deployed across the Atlantic again, to some of the bloodiest battlegrounds of South America, while black revolutionaries also took to the seas as corsairs for ephemeral new states.[60] Meanwhile, in a better-known diaspora, large groups of Black Loyalists from the American Revolution were also scattered across the Atlantic to such disparate locales as the Bahamas, Nova Scotia, Sierra Leone, and Liberia.[61] As this essay has demonstrated, the Revolutionary Black Atlantic was created over three centuries by persons of many diverse African ethnicities and their descendants, who found themselves dispersed across at least four continents, and many of whom reshaped their lives multiple times in course of their Atlantic crossings.

Notes

1 Paul Gilroy, *The Black Atlantic: Modernity and Double Consciousness* (Cambridge, MA: Harvard University Press, 1993); Peter Mark and José da Silva Horta, "Trade and Trading Networks in the Greater Senegambia: An Introductory Essay," Trade, Traders and Cross-Cultural Relationships in Greater Senegambia, *Mande Studies* (2007): 1–8.
2 Toby Green, *The Rise of the Trans-Atlantic Slave Trade in Western Africa, 1300–1599* (NY: Cambridge University Press, 2012); A.C. de C.M. Saunders, *A Social history of Black Slaves and Freedmen in Portugal, 1441–1555* (NY: Cambridge University Press, 1982), Ch. 1.
3 Toby Green, "Building Slavery in the Atlantic World: Atlantic Connections and the Changing Slavery in Cabo Verde, Fifteenth-Sixteenth Centuries, *Slavery & Abolition* 32[2] (2011): 227–245; Alberto Vieira, "Sugar Islands: The Sugar Economy of Madeira and the Canary Islands, 1455–1650," *Tropical Babylons: Sugar and the Making of the Atlantic World, 1450–1680*, ed. Stuart B. Schwartz (Chapel Hill: University of North Carolina Press, 2004), 42–84.
4 David Wheat, *Atlantic Africa and the Spanish Caribbean, 1570–1640* (Chapel Hill: University of North Carolina Press, 2016); *Before Middle Passage: Translated Portuguese Manuscripts of Atlantic Slave Trading from West Africa to Iberian Territories, 1513–26*, trans. and ed. Trevor P. Hall (Farnham, Surrey: Routledge, 2015); Marc Eagle, "Chasing the Avença: An Investigation of Illicit Slave Trading in Santo Domingo at the End of the Portuguese Asiento Period," *Slavery & Abolition* 35[1] (2014): 99–120; Maria Manuel Ferraz Torrão, "Os portugueses e o trato de escravos de Cabo Verde com a América Espanhola," *Portugal na Monarquia Hispânica. Dinâmicas de integração e conflito*, eds. Pedro Cardim, Leonor Freire Costa, and Mafalda Soares da Cunha (Lisbon: CHAM-Red Columnaria, 2013), 93–106.
5 Jane Landers, *Black Society in Spanish Florida* (Urbana: University of Illinois Press, 1999), Ch. 1. The West African Juan Garrido sailed from Seville to help conquer Hispaniola in 1496 and thereafter participated in the conquest of Puerto Rico, the exploration of Florida, and the conquest of the Aztec

empire. Ricardo E. Alegría, *Juan Garrido, el Conquistador Negro en Las Antillas, Florida, México y California, C. 1503–1540* (San Juan de Puerto Rico, 1990), 17, 20, 30. Several Aztec codices depict Juan Garrido at Cortes' side and the African joined his patron on one final, and unsuccessful, expedition in search of black Amazons in what came to be California. Peter Gerhard, "A Black Conquistador in Mexico," *Hispanic American Historical Review* 58 (1978): 451–59; Alegría, *Juan Garrido*, 114, 116, 119, 127–38.

6   With promises of freedom, the rebel Francisco Hernández Girón raised an army of 300–400 slaves for his unsuccessful bid to wrest Peru from Spain in 1554. Frederick P. Bowser, *The African Slave in Colonial Peru, 1524–1650* (Stanford: Stanford University Press, 1974); James Lockhart, *Spanish Peru, 1532–1560: A Social History* (Madison: University of Wisconsin Press, 1994), 193–224.

7   Matthew Restall, "Black Conquistadors: Armed Africans in Early Spanish America," *The Americas*, 57[2] (200): 171–205.

8   Landers, *Black Society*, Ch. 1.

9   Kenneth Andrews, *The Spanish Caribbean: Trade and Plunder, 1530–1630* (New Haven: Yale University Press, 1978), 82.

10 Información hecha por Diego de Mazariegos sobre la toma de La Habana por Jacques de Sores, 1555, Patronato 267, Archivo General de Indias (hereafter cited as AGI), cited in *Documentos para la historia colonial de Cuba: Siglos XVI, XVII, XVIII, XIX*, ed. César García del Pino and Alicia Melis Cappa (Havana: Editorial de Ciencias Sociales, 1988), 4–40; Alejandro De la Fuente, *Havana and the Atlantic in the Sixteenth Century* (Chapel Hill: University of North Carolina Press, 2008); Irene A. Wright, *Historia documentada de San Cristóbal de La Habana en el siglo XVI* (Havana: Impresora El Siglo XX, 1927).

11 Paul E. Hoffman, *The Spanish Crown and the Defense of the Caribbean, 1535–1585: Precedent, Patrimonialism and Royal Parsimony* (Baton Rouge: Louisiana State University Press, 1980), appendix II.

12 Christon I. Archer, "Pardos, Indians and the Army of New Spain: Inter-Relationships and Conflicts, 1780–1810," *Journal of Latin American Studies* 6[2] (1974): 231–55 and "Militares," *Ciudades y Sociedad en Latinoamerica colonial*, eds. Louisa S. Hoberman and Susan Socolow (Mexico City: Fonde de Cultura Económica, 1993).

13 Kris E. Lane, *Pillaging the Empire: Piracy in the Americas, 1500–1750* (Armonk, NY: Me. E. Sharpe, 1998).

14 Francisco Morales Padrón, *Spanish Jamaica* (Kingston: Ian Randall Publishers, 2003); Irene Aloha Wright, trans., Julian de Castilla, *The English conquest of Jamaica; an account of what happened in the island of Jamaica, from May 20 of the year 1655, when the English laid siege to it, up to July 3 of the year 1656* (London: Offices of the Royal Historical Society, 1923).

15 Lane, *Pillaging the Empire*, 103–05.

16 Royal order to the Viceroy of New Spain, July 6, 1663, México 1070, AGI, cited in *Colección de documentos para la historia de la formación social de hispanoamérica 1493–1810*, ed. Richard Konetzke (3 vols. Madrid: Consejo Superior de Investigaciones Cientificas, 1953–1962), Vol., III, 510–1.

17 Hugo Contreras Cruces, "Las milicias de pardos y morenos libres de Santiago de Chile en el siglo XVIII, 1760–1800," *Cuadernos de Historia*, 25 (Santiago: Universidad de Chile, 2006): 93–117.

18 Rina Cáceres, *Negros, mulatos, esclavos y libertos en la Costa Rica del siglo XVII* (Mexico City: Instituto Panamericano de Geografía e Historia, 2000).

19 Stephen Weber, "Las compañías de milicia y la defensa del istmo centroamericano en el siglo XVII: el alistamiento general de 1673," *Mesoamérica* 14 (December 1987): 511–528; Santiago Gerardo Suarez, *Las milicias: instituciones militares hispanoamericanas* (Caracas: Academia Nacional de la Historia, 1984), 90–5; Paul Lokken, "Useful Enemies: Seventeenth-Century Piracy and the Rise of Pardo Militias in Spanish Central America," *Journal of Colonialism and Colonial History* 5[2] (2004).

20 Herbert S. Klein, "The Colored Militia of Cuba: 1568–1868," *Caribbean Studies* 6 (July 1966): 17–27; Pedro Deschamps Chapeaux, *Los Batallones de Pardos y Morenos Libres* (La Habana: Editorial Arte y Literatura, 1978); Allan J. Kuethe, *Cuba, 1753–1815, Crown, Military and Society* (Gainesville: University of Florida Press, 1957), *Military Reform and Society in New Granada, 1773–1808* (Gainesville: University of Florida Press, 1978) and "The Status of the Free Pardo in the Disciplined Militia of New Granada," *Journal of Negro History* 56 (April 1971): 105–15. On Santo Domingo see Margarita Gascon, "The Military in Santo Domingo, 1720–1764," *Hispanic American Historical Review* 73 (August 1993): 431–452 and Christine Rivas, "The Santo Domingo Militia, 1701–1770," *The Americas* 60[2] (2003): 249–272. Pardo and Moreno Militia of St. Augustine, 1683, Santo Domingo (hereafter SD) 226, AGI, cited in Landers, *Black Society*, appendix 1; Jane Landers, "Transforming Bondsmen into Vassals: Arming the Slaves in Colonial Spanish America," *Arming Slaves in World History*, ed. Philip Morgan and Christopher Brown (New Haven: Yale University Press, 2006), 120–45.

21 Interrogation of the black corsair, Diego, by Governor Don Juan Márques Cabrera, St. Augustine, Florida, 1686, in the John Tate Lanning papers, 13–18. The mulatto translator, Thomas, had also participated in the 1683 attack on St. Augustine. I am indebted to John H. Hann, of the San Luis Archaeological and Historical Site, in Tallahassee, Florida, for this reference and his generosity. For more see Luis Arana, "Grammont's Landing at Little Matanzas Inlet, 1686," *El Escribano*, 107–112.
22 Documentos relacionado con el ofrecimiento del Capitán Diego Martín, Diego El Mulato, de pasar al servicio de España, in García del Pino, et al., *Documentos*, 139–140.
23 Jane Landers, "*Cimarrón* and Citizen: African Ethnicity, Corporate Identity and the Evolution of Free Black Towns in the Spanish Circum-Caribbean," *Slaves, Subjects and Subversives: Blacks in Colonial Latin America*, eds. Jane G. Landers and Barry M. Robinson (Albuquerque: University of New Mexico Press, 2006), 111–145.
24 Scholars such as Lyle N. McAlister and Christon I. Archer analyzed how Spaniards in New Spain protested these changes and the resulting blurring of racial boundaries in Spain's oldest viceroyalty. Lyle N. McAlister, *El fuero militar en la Nueva España (1764–1800)* (Mexico City: Universidad Nacional Autónoma de México, 1982); Christon I. Archer, *The Army in Bourbon Mexico, 1760–1810* (Albuquerque, NM: University of New Mexico Press, 1977) and "Pardos, Indians and the Army of New Spain." Also see Joseph P. Sánchez, "African Freedmen and the Fuero Militar: A Historical Overview of Pardo and Moreno Militias in the Late Spanish Empire," *Colonial Latin American Historical Review* 3[2] (1994) and Leon Campbell, "The Changing Racial and Administrative Structure of the Peruvian Military under the Later Bourbons," *Americas* 32 (1975): 117–33. Ben Vinson's more recent study confirms that officials in New Spain resisted the social advancement of black militiamen and sought to abridge the benefits of their fuero, generally limiting its enjoyment to officers in active service. Ben Vinson III, *Bearing Arms for His Majesty: The Free Colored Militia in Colonial* Mexico (Stanford: Stanford University Press, 2001), 25.
25 Scholars working on other Spanish colonies have found similar patterns of social advancement, family linkages, and multigenerational patterns of service among free black militiamen. María del Carmen Bárcia, *Los ilustres apellidos: Negros en la Habana colonial* (La Habana: Ediciones Boloña, 2009); George Reid Andrews, "The Afro-Argentine Officers of Buenos Aires Province, 1800–1860," *Journal of Negro History* 64 (1979): 85–100 and Deschamps Chapeaux, *Batallones de pardos y morenos libres* 56–62.
26 Jane G. Landers, "Free Black Plantations and Economy in East Florida, 1784–1821," *Colonial Plantation and Economy in Florida*, ed. Jane G. Landers (Gainesville: University Press of Florida, 200), 121–135 and "Acquisition and Loss on a Spanish Frontier: the Free Black Homesteaders of Florida, 1784–1821," *Slavery & Abolition: A Journal of Slave and Post-Slave Studies* 17[1] (1996): 85–101.
27 Luis de las Casas to Campo de Alange, Cuba, 1487, AGI, cited in Archer, "Pardos, Indians and the Army of New Spain."
28 Philip V to the royal officials of Havana, May 20, 1714, SD 337, AGI, cited in Klein, "Colored Militia of Cuba," 18.
29 Jane Landers, *Atlantic Creoles in the Age of Revolutions* (Cambridge, MA: Harvard University Press, 2014), Ch. 6. The colorful and diverse uniforms of black units posted around the Spanish Empire, from the Philippines to Santo Domingo, can be accessed via the Mapas y Planos section of PARES, Spain's online digital archive. Available online at http://pares.mcu.es/.
30 Spanish forces defeated the English at La Guaira and Cartagena de Indias (Colombia) and Cuba.
31 Manuel de Montiano to Juan Francisco Güemes y Horcasitas, March 31, 1742, SD2593, AGI; Memorial of Francisco Menéndez, November 21, 1740, SD 2658, AGI; Jane Landers, "The Atlantic Transformations of Francisco Menéndez," *Biography and the Black Atlantic*, eds. Lisa A. Lindsay and John Wood Sweet (Philadelphia: University of Pennsylvania Press, 2014), 209–223.
32 Julius Sherrard Scott, III, "The Common Wind: Currents of Afro-American Communication in the Era of the Haitian Revolution,' PhD Thesis, Duke University, 1986 and "Criss-Crossing Empires: Ships, Sailors and Resistance in the Lesser Antilles in the Eighteenth Century," *The Lesser Antilles in the Age of European Empires*, eds. Stanley Engerman and Robert Paquette (Gainesville: University Press of Florida, 1996), 280–301; Markus Rediker, *Between the Devil and the Deep Blue Sea: Merchant Seamen, Pirates and the Anglo- .American Maritime World* (Cambridge, MA: Harvard University Press, 1987), 286; W. Jeffrey Bolster, "To Feel like a Man: Black Seamen in the Northern States, 1800–1860," *Journal of American History* 76 (March 1990): 79, 83 and *Black Jacks: African American Seamen in the Age of Sail* (Cambridge, MA: Harvard University Press, 1997).
33 "Ex Parte Seventeen Indians Molattos & Negroes," *Report of Cases in the Vice Admiralty of the Province of New York and in the Court of Admiralty of the State of New York, 1717–1788*, ed. Charles Merrill Hough (New Haven, CT: Yale University Press, 1925), 29–31.

34 Florida's governor, Melchor de Navarrete, permitted the *Carmen*'s captain, Francisco de Laguna, to travel to New York and try to recover his ship and crew. Report of Captain Fernando Laguna, Oct. 7, 1752, SD 2584, AGI.
35 Florida's Governor, Fulgencio García de Solís, wrote letters to the governors of Havana, Cartagena, Santa Marta, and Margarita, and to the lieutenant of the Cuban village of Bayamo, asking their prompt assistance in determining the free status of the black captives. Fulgencio García de Solís to Ferdinand VI, August 25, 1752, SD 845 Melchor de Navarrete to Francisco Cagigal, July 7, 1750, SD 2584, AGI.
36 Scholars working on other Spanish colonies have found similar patterns of social advancement, family linkages, and multigenerational patterns of service among free black militiamen. María del Carmen Bárcia, *Los ilustres apellidos*; George Reid Andrews, "The Afro-Argentine Officers of Buenos Aires Province, 1800–1860," *Journal of Negro History* 64 (1979): 85–100 and Deschamps Chapeaux, *Batallones de pardos*, 56–62.
37 Jane G. Landers, "Free Black Plantations and Economy in East Florida, 1784–1821," *Colonial Plantation and Economy in Florida*, ed. Jane G. Landers (Gainesville: University Press of Florida 200), 121–135 and "Acquisition and Loss on a Spanish Frontier: the Free Black Homesteaders of Florida, 1784–1821, *Slavery & Abolition: A Journal of Slave and Post-Slave Studies* 17[1] (1996): 85–101.
38 Elena Schneider, "African Slavery and Spanish Empire: Imperial Imaginings and Bourbon Reform in Eighteenth-century Cuba and Beyond," *The Journal of Early American History* 5[1] (2015): 3–29.
39 Deschamps Chapeux, *Los Batallones de Pardos*, 29–30.
40 Landers, *Atlantic Creoles*, Ch. 6.
41 The *Reglamento para las milicias de infantería y caballería de la Isla de Cuba* governed these new units as well as military reorganizations in Florida, Puerto Rico, Louisiana, and Panama, where blacks also enlisted in large numbers. Klein, "Colored Militia of Cuba."
42 Landers, *Atlantic Creoles*; Kimberly S. Hanger, *Bounded Lives, Bounded Places: Free Black Society in Colonial Louisiana, 1769–1803* (Durham: Duke University Press, 1998), 119–21.
43 Again, their service records detail where black servicemen served, their merits and services, the battles in which they engaged and the ships they seized as Spanish corsairs. Landers, *Black Society*, 61–8, 246–8.
44 French officials had followed the Spanish example and organized black troops on Saint Domingue whose main function was to track maroons. In 1695 several hundred enslaved and free men in these black militias accompanied French buccaneers that assaulted Cartagena. Stewart R. King, *Blue Coat or Powdered Wig: Free People of Color in Pre-Revolutionary Saint Domingue* (Athens: University of Georgia Press, 2001), Ch. 4; John Garrigus, "Vincent Ogé Jeune (1757–91): Social Class and Free Colored Mobilization on the Eve of the Haitian Revolution," *The Americas* 68[1] (July 2011): 33–62.
45 Graham Russell Gao Hodges, "African Americans in the Revolution," *Encyclopedia of the American Revolution: Library of Military History*, ed. Harold E. Selesky (Detroit: Charles Scribner's Sons, 2006), 10–15.
46 Claims and Memorial Petition of Thomas Johnston, London, July 21,1786, British Public Records Office (hereafter BPRO), Audit Office, Class 13, Vol. 70b, Part 1, Folios 301–302 cited in *The On-Line Institute for Advanced Loyalist Studies*, www.royalprovincial.com/military/mems/sc/clmjohnston.htm and Black Dragoons Abstract of Pay, 1782, cited in ibid. http://www.royalprovincial.com/military/rhist/scmil/scmpay.htm (accessed 6/1/2016); Landers, *Atlantic Creoles*, 29, 31–32.
47 Landers, *Atlantic Creoles*, Ch. 1 and Appendix 2.
48 Madison Smartt Bell, *Toussaint Louverture: A Biography* (New York: Pantheon Books, 2007). King, *Blue Coat or Powdered Wig*; Graham Nessler, *Islandwide Struggle for Freedom: Revolution, Emancipation and Reenslavement on Hispaniola. 1789–1800* (Chapel Hill: University of North Carolina Press. 2016); Ada Ferrer, *Freedom's Mirror: Cuba and Haiti in the Age of Revolution* (New York: Cambridge University Press, 2014).
49 The three chiefs swore submission and vassalage to the Spanish king in the house of Don Matias de Armona on November 8, 1793. Estado (hereafter cited as ES) 13, AGI; Captain General Joaquín García to the Duque de la Alcudia, February 18, 1794, ES 14, doc. 86, AGI; Captain General Joaquín García to the Duque de Alcudia, December 12, 1795, cited in Emilio Rodríguez Demorizi, *Cesión de Santo Domingo a Francia* (Ciudad Trujillo, 1958), 46–48.
50 Landers, *Atlantic Creoles*, 51–55.
51 C. L. R. James, *Black Jacobins: Toussaint L'Ouverture and the San Domingo Revolution* (New York, 1963), 103–106; David Patrick Geggus and Norman Fiering, eds. *The World of the Haitian Revolution* (Bloomington: Indiana University Press, 2009) and David Patrick Geggus, *Haitian Revolutionary Studies* (Bloomington: Indiana University Press, 2002); Laurent Dubois, *Avengers of the New World: The Story of the Haitian Revolution* (Cambridge, Mass.: Harvard University Press, 2004).

52 Landers, *Atlantic Creoles*, Ch. 2.
53 Landers, *Atlantic Creoles*, Ch. 6.
54 Biassou sought to return to Saint Domingue to search for his mother left behind, but Spanish officials rejected his petition. Biassou finally sent his wife and sisters to the more important port of Havana, perhaps hoping to join them there since his offer to go to Spain to fight for his king had been rejected. Landers, *Atlantic Creoles*, Ch. 4.
55 Witnesses at the marriage of Jorge Jacobo and María Rafaela Kenty included the groom's sister and Biassou's wife, Romana, and the bride's brother, Francisco. Marriage of Jorge Jacobo and María Rafaela Kenty, April 12, 1796, Black Marriages, Catholic Parish Registers (hereafter CPR), microfilm reel 284 L, P. K. Yonge Library of Florida History, University of Florida, Gainesville, FL. (hereafter PKY). When the couple's children were born, the maternal grandfather, Juan Bautista (Prince) Witten, and the paternal grandmother, Ana Gran Pres, served as godparents for María del Carmen and the maternal uncle, Francisco Witten, and the paternal aunt, Barbara Gran Pres, served as godparents for the next child, Julian. Another militiaman from Saint Domingue, Benjamín Seguí, was Catalina Melchora Jacobo's godfather. Black Baptisms, vol. 2, CPR, microfilm reel 284 J, entries no. 176, 563, 670, 799, and Vol. 3, microfilm reel 284 J, entry no. 31, PKY. When Francisco Witten married on January 26, 1799, his marriage sponsors were Felipe Edimboro and Romana Jacobo (aka Biassou), who had also served the same roles at his parents' wedding the previous year. Marriage of Juan Bautista Witten and María Rafaela Kenty, July 7, 1798, Black Marriages, CPR, microfilm reel 284, PKY.
56 Jane Landers, "An Eighteenth-Century Community in Exile: the Floridanos of Cuba," *New West Indian Guide* 70, 1 and 2 (Spring 1996): 39–58 and *Atlantic Creoles*, Ch. 4.
57 Sherry Johnson, *The Social Transformation of Eighteenth-Century Cuba* (Gainesville: University Press of Florida, 2001). David Sartorius, *Ever Faithful: Race, Loyalty, and the Ends of Empire in Spanish Cuba* (Durham: Duke University Press, 2013).
58 Jane Landers, "Slavery in the Spanish Caribbean and the Failure of Abolition," *REVIEW, A Journal of the Fernand Braudel Center,* special issue, "The Second Slavery: Mass Slavery, World-Economy, and Comparative Microhistories, Part II", eds. Dale Tomich & Michael Zeuske (XXXI-3-2008); David Murray, *Odious Commerce: Britain, Spain and the Abolition of the Cuban Slave Trade* (Cambridge, 1980); Robert Francis Jameson, *Letters from the Havana: During the Year 1820, Containing an Account of the Present State of the Island of Cuba* (London, 1821), 23–37; Luis Martínez-Fernández, *Fighting Slavery in the Caribbean: the Life and Times of a British Family in Nineteenth-Century Cuba* (Armonk, NY, 1998); Laird W. Bergad, Fe Iglesias García, and María del Carmen Barcia, *The Cuban Slave Market, 1790–1880* (Cambridge, MA: Cambridge University Press, 1995), 23–37.
59 Matt D. Childs, *The Aponte Rebellion in Cuba and the Struggle against Atlantic Slavery* (Chapel Hill: University of North Carolina Press, 2006); Manuel Bárcia, (Baton Rouge: Louisiana State University Press, 2012) and Seeds of Insurrection: Domination and Slave Resistance on Cuban Plantations (Baton Rouge: Louisiana State University Press, 2008); Michele Reid-Vazquez, *The Year of the Lash: Free People of Color and the Nineteenth-Century Atlantic World* (Athens: University of Georgia Press, 2011); Aisha Finch, *Rethinking Slave Rebellion in Cuba: La Escalera and the Insurgencies of 1841–1844* (Chapel Hill: University of North Carolina Press, 2015); Jane Landers, "Catholic Conspirators? Religious Rebels in Nineteenth-Century Cuba," Special Issue, New Sources and New Findings: Slavery and Abolition in the Atlantic World, *Slavery and Abolition*, 36[3] (2015): 495–520; Landers, *Atlantic Creoles*, Ch. 6 and Epilogue.
60 Laurent Dubois, *A Colony of Citizens: Revolution and Slave Emancipation in the French Caribbean 1787–1804* (Chapel Hill: University of North Carolina Press, 2004); Sartorius, *Ever Faithful;* Aline Helg, *Liberty and Equality in Caribbean Colombia, 1779–1835* (Chapel Hill: University of North Carolina Press, 2004); Marixa Lasso, *Myths of Harmony: Race and Republicanism during the Age of Revolution, Colombia, 1795–1831* (Pittsburgh: University of Pittsburgh Press, 2007); Marcela Echeverri, "Race, Citizenship, and the Cádiz Constitution in Popayán (New Granada)" *The Rise of Constitutional Government in the Iberian Atlantic World: The Impact of the Cádiz Constitution of 1812, eds.* Scott Eastman and Natalia Sobrevilla Perea (Tuscaloosa: University of Alabama Press, 2015) 91–110; Lyman L. Johnson, *Workshop of Revolution: Plebeian Buenos Aires and the Atlantic World, 1776–1810* (Durham: Duke University Press, 2011).
61 Cassandra Pybus, *Epic Journeys of Freedom: Runaway Slaves of the American Revolution and their Global Quest for Liberty* (Boston: Beacon Press, 2006); Simon Schama, *Rough Crossings: Britain, the Slaves, and the American Revolution* (London: BBC Books, 2005); *Slavery, Abolition and the Transition to Colonialism in Sierra Leone,* eds. Paul E. Lovejoy and Suzanne Schwartz (Trenton, NJ: Africa World Press, 2014).

References

Alegría, Ricardo E. *Juan Garrido, el Conquistador Negro en Las Antillas, Florida, México y California, C. 1503–1540* (San Juan de Puerto Rico, 1990).

Andrews, George Reid. "The Afro-Argentine Officers of Buenos Aires Province, 1800–1860," *Journal of Negro History* 64 (1979): 85–100.

Andrews, Kenneth. *The Spanish Caribbean: Trade and Plunder, 1530–1630* (New Haven: Yale University Press, 1973).

Arana, Luis. "Grammont's Landing at Little Matanzas Inlet, 1686," *El Escribano*, 107–112.

Arana, Luis. "Militares," *Ciudades y Sociedad en Latinaomerica colonial*, eds. Louisa S. Hoberman and Susan Socolow (Mexico City: Fonde de Cultura Económica, 1993).

Arana, Luis. "Pardos, Indians and the Army of New Spain: Inter-Relationships and Conflicts, 1780–1810," *Journal of Latin American Studies* 6[2] (1974): 231–55.

Archer, Christon I. *The Army in Bourbon Mexico, 1760–1810* (Albuquerque, NM: University of New Mexico Press, 1977).

Bárcia, Manuel. *Seeds of Insurrection: Domination and Slave Resistance on Cuban Plantations* (Baton Rouge: Louisiana State University Press, 2008).

Bárcia, Manuel. *The Great African Slave Revolt of 1825: Cuba and the Fight for Freedom in Matanzas* (Baton Rouge: Louisiana State University Press, 2012).

Bárcia, María del Carmen. *Los ilustres apellidos: Negros en la Habana colonial* (La Habana: Ediciones Boloña, 2009).

Bell, Madison Smartt. *Toussaint Louverture: A Biography* (NY: Pantheon Books, 2007).

Bergad, Laird W., Fe Iglesias García, and María del Carmen Barcia, *The Cuban Slave Market, 1790–1880* (Cambridge, MA: Cambridge University Press, 1995).

Bolster, W. Jeffrey. "To Feel like a Man: Black Seamen in the Northern States, 1800–1860," *Journal of American History* 76 (March 1990).

Bolster, W. Jeffrey. *Black Jacks: African American Seamen in the Age of Sail* (Cambridge: Harvard University Press, 1997), 1173–1199.

Bowser, Frederick P. *The African Slave in Colonial Peru, 1524–1650* (Stanford: Stanford University Press, 1974).

Cáceres, Rina. *Negros, mulatos, esclavos y libertos en la Costa Rica del siglo XVII* (Mexico City: Instituto Panamericano de Geografía e Historia, 2000).

Campbell, Leon. "The Changing Racial and Administrative Structure of the Peruvian Military under the Later Bourbons," *Americas* 32 (1975): 117–133.

Childs, Matt D. *The Aponte Rebellion in Cuba and the Struggle against Atlantic Slavery* (Chapel Hill: University of North Carolina Press, 2006).

Contreras Cruces, Hugo. "Las milicias de pardos y morenos libres de Santiago de Chile en el siglo XVIII, 1760–1800," *Cuadernos de Historia*, no, 25 (Santiago: Universidad de Chile, 2006): 93–117.

De la Fuente, Alejandro. *Havana and the Atlantic in the Sixteenth Century* (Chapel Hill, University of North Carolina Press, 2008).

de Montiano, Manuel to Juan Francisco Güemes y Horcasitas. March 31, 1742, SD2593, AGI.

Deschamps Chapeaux, Pedro. *Los Batallones de Pardos y Morenos Libres* (La Habana: Editorial Arte y Literatura, 1978).

Dubois, Laurent. *Avengers of the New World: The Story of the Haitian Revolution* (Cambridge, Mass.: Harvard University Press, 2004).

Dubois, Laurent. *A Colony of Citizens: Revolution and Slave Emancipation in the French Caribbean 1787–1804* (Chapel Hill: University of North Carolina Press, 2004).

Eagle, Marc. "Chasing the Avença: An Investigation of Illicit Slave Trading in Santo Domingo at the End of the Portuguese Asiento Period," *Slavery & Abolition* 35[1] (2014): 99–120.

Echeverri, Marcela. "Race, Citizenship, and the Cádiz Constitution in Popayán (New Granada)" *The Rise of Constitutional Government in the Iberian Atlantic World: The Impact of the Cádiz Constitution of 1812*, eds. Scott Eastman and Natalia Sobrevilla Perea (Tuscaloosa: University of Alabama Press, 2015).

Ferrer, Ada. *Freedom's Mirror: Cuba and Haiti in the Age of Revolution* (NY: Cambridge University Press, 2014).

Finch, Aisha. *Rethinking Slave Rebellion in Cuba: La Escalera and the Insurgencies of 1841–1844* (Chapel Hill: University of North Carolina Press, 2015).

García del Pino, César and Alicia Melis Cappa, eds. *Documentos para la historia colonial de Cuba: Siglos XVI, XVII, XVIII, XIX*, (Havana: Editorial de Ciencias Sociales, 1988).

Garrigus, John. "Vincent Ogé Jeune (1757–91): Social Class and Free Colored Mobilization on the Eve of the Haitian Revolution," *The Americas*, Vol. 68, NO. 1 (2011): 33–62.

Gascon, Margarita. "The Military in Santo Domingo, 1720–1764," *Hispanic American Historical Review* 73 (1993): 431–452.

Geggus, David Patrick, *Haitian Revolutionary Studies* (Bloomington: Indiana University Press, 2002).

Geggus, David Patrick and Norman Fiering, eds. *The World of the Haitian Revolution* (Bloomington: Indiana University Press, 2009).

Gilroy, Paul. *The Black Atlantic: Modernity and Double Consciousness* (Cambridge, MA: Harvard University Press, 1993).

Green, Toby. "Building Slavery in the Atlantic World: Atlantic Connections and the Changing Slavery in Cabo Verde, Fifteenth-Sixteenth Centuries," *Slavery & Abolition* 32[2] (2011): 227–245.

Green, Toby. *The Rise of the Trans-Atlantic Slave Trade in Western Africa, 1300–1599* (NY: Cambridge University Press, 2012).

Hall, Trevor P. trans. and ed. *Before Middle Passage: Translated Portuguese Manuscripts of Atlantic Slave Trading from West Africa to Iberian Territories, 1513–26*, (Farnham, Surrey: Routledge, 2015).

Hanger, Kimberly S. *Bounded Lives, Bounded Places: Free Black Society in Colonial Louisiana, 1769–1803* (Durham: Duke University Press, 1998).

Helg, Aline. *Liberty and Equality in Caribbean Colombia, 1779–1835* (Chapel Hill: University of North Carolina Press, 2004).

Hodges, Graham Russell Gao. "African Americans in the Revolution," *Encyclopedia of the American Revolution: Library of Military History*, ed. Harold E. Selesky (Detroit: Charles Scribner's Sons, 2006).

Hoffman, Paul E. *The Spanish Crown and the Defense of the Caribbean, 1535–1585: Precedent, Patrimonialism and Royal Parsimony* (Baton Rouge: Louisiana State University Press, 1980).

James, C. L. R. *Black Jacobins: Toussaint L'Ouverture and the San Domingo Revolution* (New York: Vintage Books, 1963).

Jameson, Robert Francis. *Letters from the Havana: During the Year 1820, Containing an Account of the Present State of the Island of Cuba* (London, 1821).

Johnson, Lyman L. *Workshop of Revolution: Plebeian Buenos Aires and the Atlantic World, 1776–1810* (Durham: Duke University Press, 2011).

Johnson, Sherry. *The Social Transformation of Eighteenth-Century Cuba* (Gainesville: University Press of Florida, 2001).

King, Stewart R. *Blue Coat or Powdered Wig: Free People of Color in Pre-Revolutionary Saint Domingue* (Athens: University of Georgia Press, 2001).

Klein, Herbert S. "The Colored Militia of Cuba: 1568–1868," *Caribbean Studies* 6 (July 1966): 17–27.

Kontezke, Richard, ed. *Colección de documentos para la historia de la formación social de hispanoamérica 1493–1810*, 3 vols. (Madrid: Consejo Superior de Investigaciones Cientificas, 1953–1962).

Kuethe, Allan J. "The Status of the Free Pardo in the Disciplined Militia of New Granada," *Journal of Negro History* 56 (April 1971): 105–15.

Kuethe, Allan J. *Cuba, 1753–1815, Crown, Military and Society* (Gainesville: University of Florida Press, 1957).

Kuethe, Allan J. *Military Reform and Society in New Granada, 1773–1808* (Gainesville: University of Florida Press, 1978).

Landers, Jane. "Acquisition and Loss on a Spanish Frontier: the Free Black Homesteaders of Florida, 1784–1821," *Slavery & Abolition: A Journal of Slave and Post-Slave Studies* 17, 1 (1996): 85–101.

Landers, Jane. "An Eighteenth-Century Community in Exile: the Floridanos of Cuba," *New West Indian Guide* 70, 1 and 2 (Spring 1996): 39–58.

Landers, Jane. *Black Society in Spanish Florida*, (University of Illinois Press, 1999).

Landers, Jane. "Free Black Plantations and Economy in East Florida, 1784–1821," *Colonial Plantation and Economy in Florida*, ed. Jane G. Landers (Gainesville: University Press of Florida 200), 121–135.

Landers, Jane. "*Cimarrón* and Citizen: African Ethnicity, Corporate Identity and the Evolution of Free Black Towns in the Spanish Circum-Caribbean," *Slaves, Subjects and Subversives: Blacks in Colonial Latin America*, eds. Jane G. Landers and Barry M. Robinson (Albuquerque: University of New Mexico Press, 2006), 111–145.

Landers, Jane. "Transforming Bondsmen into Vassals: Arming the Slaves in Colonial Spanish America," *Arming Slaves in World History*, eds. Philip Morgan and Christopher Brown (New Haven: Yale University Press, 2006), 120–45.

Landers, Jane. "Slavery in the Spanish Caribbean and the Failure of Abolition," *REVIEW, A Journal of the Fernand Braudel Center*, special issue, "The Second Slavery: Mass Slavery, World-Economy, and Comparative Microhistories, Part II," eds. Dale Tomich & Michael Zeuske (XXXI-3-2008).

Landers, Jane. "Catholic Conspirators? Religious Rebels in Nineteenth-Century Cuba," Special Issue, New Sources and New Findings: Slavery and Abolition in the Atlantic World, *Slavery and Abolition* 36, 3 (September 2015): 495–520.

Landers, Jane. "The Atlantic Transformations of Francisco Menéndez," *Biography and the Black Atlantic*, eds. Lisa A. Lindsay and John Wood Sweet (Philadelphia: University of Pennsylvania Press, 2014), 209–223.

Landers, Jane. *Atlantic Creoles in the Age of Revolutions* (Cambridge, MA: Harvard University Press, 2014).

Lane, Kris E. *Pillaging the Empire: Piracy in the Americas, 1500–1750* (Armonk, NY: Me. E. Sharpe, 1998).

Lockhart, James. *Spanish Peru, 1532–1560: A Social History* (Madison: University of Wisconsin Press, 1994).

Lokken, Paul. "Useful Enemies: Seventeenth-Century Piracy and the Rise of Pardo Militias in Spanish Central America," *Journal of Colonialism and Colonial History* 5[2] (2004).

Lovejoy, Paul E. and Suzanne Schwartz, eds. *Slavery, Abolition and the Transition to Colonialism in Sierra Leone* (Trenton, NJ: Africa World Press, 2014).

Mark, Peter and José da Silva Horta, "Trade and Trading Networks in the Greater Senegambia: An Introductory Essay," Trade, Traders and Cross-Cultural Relationships in Greater Senegambia, *Mande Studies* (2007): 1–8.

Martínez-Fernández, Luis. *Fighting Slavery in the Caribbean: the Life and Times of a British Family in Nineteenth-Century Cuba* (Armonk, NY: Sharpe, 1998).

McAlister, Lyle N. *El fuero militar en la Nueva España (1764–1800)* (Mexico City: Universidad Nacional Autónoma de México, 1982).

Murray, David. *Odious Commerce: Britain, Spain and the Abolition of the Cuban Slave Trade* (Cambridge: Cambridge University Press, 1980).

Nessler, Graham. *Islandwide Struggle for Freedom: Revolution, Emancipation and Reenslavement on Hispaniola. 1789–1800* (Chapel Hill: University of North Carolina Press. 2016).

Pybus, Cassandra. *Epic Journeys of Freedom: Runaway Slaves of the American Revolution and their Global Quest for Liberty* (Boston: Beacon Press, 2006).

Rediker, Markus. *Between the Devil and the Deep Blue Sea: Merchant Seamen, Pirates and the Anglo-. American Maritime World* (Cambridge, 1987).

Reid-Vazquez, Michele. *The Year of the Lash: Free People of Color and the Nineteenth-Century Atlantic World* (Athens: University of Georgia Press, 2011).

Report of Cases in the Vice Admiralty of the Province of New York and in the Court of Admiralty of the State of New York, 1717–I788, ed. Charles Merrill Hough (New Haven, CT: Yale University Press, 1925).

Restall, Matthew. "Black Conquistadors: Armed Africans in Early Spanish America," *The Americas* 57[2] (2000): 171–205.

Rivas, Christine. "The Santo Domingo Militia, 1701–1770," *The Americas* 60[2] (2003): 249–272.

Rodríguez Demorizi, Emilio. *Cesión de Santo Domingo a Francia* (Ciudad Trujillo: Impressoro Domina, 1958).

Sánchez, Joseph P. "African Freedmen and the Fuero Militar: A Historical Overview of Pardo and Moreno Militias in the Late Spanish Empire," *Colonial Latin American Historical Review* 3[2] (1994).

Sartorius, David. *Ever Faithful: Race, Loyalty, and the Ends of Empire in Spanish Cuba* (Durham: Duke University Press, 2013).

Saunders, A.C. de C.M. *A Social history of Black Slaves and Freedmen in Portugal, 1441–1555* (NY: Cambridge University Press, 1982).

Schama, Simon. *Rough Crossings: Britain, the Slaves, and the American Revolution* (London: BBC Books, 2005).

Schneider, Elena. "African Slavery and Spanish Empire: Imperial Imaginings and Bourbon Reform in Eighteenth-century Cuba and Beyond," *The Journal of Early American History* 5[1] (2015): 3–29.

Scott, Julius Sherrard. "The Common Wind: Currents of Afro-American Communication in the Era of the Haitian Revolution,' (PhD Thesis, Duke University, 1986).

Scott, Julius Sherrard." Criss-Crossing Empires: Ships, Sailors and Resistance in the Lesser Antilles in the Eighteenth Century," *The Lesser Antilles in the Age of European Empires*, eds. Stanley Engerman and Robert Paquette (Gainesville: University Press of Florida, 1996), 280–301.

Suarez, Santiago Gerardo. *Las milicias: instituciones militares hispanoamericanas* (Caracas: Academia Nacional de la Historia, 1984), 90–5.

Torrão, Maria Manuel Ferraz. "Os portugueses e o trato de escravos de Cabo Verde com a América Espanhola," *Portugal na Monarquia Hispânica. Dinâmicas de integração e conflito*, eds. Pedro Cardim, Leonor Freire Costa, and Mafalda Soares da Cunha (Lisbon: CHAM-Red Columnaria, 2013), 93–106.

Vieira, Alberto. "Sugar Islands: The Sugar Economy of Madeira and the Canary Islands, 1455–1650," *Tropical Babylons: Sugar and the Making of the Atlantic World, 1450–1680*, ed. Stuart B. Schwartz (Chapel Hill: University of North Carolina Press, 2004), 42–84.

Vinson III, Ben. *Bearing Arms for His Majesty: The Free Colored Militia in Colonial* Mexico (Stanford: Stanford University Press, 2001).

Weber, Stephen "Las compañías de milicia y la defensa del istmo centroamericano en el siglo XVII: el alistamiento general de 1673," *Mesoamérica* 14 (December 1987): 511–528.

Wheat, David. *Atlantic Africa and the Spanish Caribbean, 1570–1640* (Chapel Hill: University of North Carolina Press, 2016).

Wright, Irene A. *Historia documentada de San Cristóbal de La Habana en el siglo XVI* (Havana: Impresora El Siglo XX, 1927).

Wright, Irene A, ed. Julian de Castilla, *The English conquest of Jamaica; an account of what happened in the island of Jamaica, from May 20 of the year 1655, when the English laid siege to it, up to July 3 of the year 1656* (London: Offices of the Royal Historical Society, 1923).

INDEX

Acosta, José de 22, 50
African slavery, Iberian road to 51–2
Albaladejo, Pablo Fernández 18
Alexander, James 198
Alexander the Great 214
Ames, Susie M. 238
Andros, Edmund 219
Anglería, Martir de 41
Anglicization, surviving example of 386
Anzoátegui, Víctor Tau 18
Apostolic Bull 22
Archdale, John 39
Articles of Confederation government 386
Artiguaye, Miguel
Astor, John Jacob 342
Atahualpa, capture of 25
Atkins, Jonathan 113
Atlantic, western, and continental early America 321–36, 339–52; alcohol consumption 349; bargaining and the price of furs 344–7; benightedness 327; biological standard of living 350; continental history, detractors of 321; Cree, Assiniboine, Dakota, and Ojibwa traders 347; "Escanxaques" 323; European dynamism, example of 322; European goods purchased by Native traders 347–50; exchange process at Hudson's Bay Company trading posts 343–4; fur trade, structure of 341–2; hierarchical joint-stock company 342; "home guard" Indians 343; Hudson Bay, organization of trade at 342–3; Hudson's Bay Company 322; Indian slavery 322; Jay's Treaty 342; Lewis and Clark Expedition 322; Native–European interactions, place of commerce in 339–40; origins of the North American trade in beaver pelts 340–1; Puebloan communities (New Mexico) 326; Russian-American Company 336; tobacco 348; trade and the living standards of Native Americans 350–2; York Factory 343
Atlantic New England 171–82; Atlantic chasm 177–81; Black and Red Atlantic 174–7; England Atlantic 172–4; Extractive Colonies 177; opportunities for profit 181; settler colonization, process of 177
Atlantic perspectives 5–14; Atlantic chasm 11; boundary making 7; colonial developments and the fate of indigenous polities 10–12; competition, frontiers, and peoples on the borders 12–13; concentration of power 8; imperial experiences, processes common to 6; local experiences, colonial cultures 8–14; morphology and chronology 6–8; revolutions 13–14; slave labor 9–10; Spanish influences 9
Audubon, John James 292
Aztec empire, conquest of 24, 393

Bacon, Francis 50, 281, 287
Bacon, Nathaniel 218
Bacon's Rebellion 194, 218–19, 378
Ballagh, James 236, 238
Barba, Gabriel Dorotea 397
Barbadian code 127
Barbary pirates 11
Barclay, Robert 194
Barr, Juliana 330
Bartram, William 292
Beale, Anthony 349
Becknell, William 323
Benton, Lauren 18
Berkeley, John Lord 194
Berkeley, William 217
Berlin, Ira 51
Biassou, Georges 14, 397
Biassou, Jorge 398

Bienville, Jean Baptist Le Moyne de 358–9, 363
Black Atlantic *see* revolutionary Black Atlantic
Black Legend propaganda 50
Bodin, Jean 18
Bolster, Jeffrey 396
Bolton, Herbert 321
Bourbon Reformers 395
Bowser, Frederick 393
Boyle, Robert 287
Braund, Kathryn 347
Brigidi, Bianca 9, 59
British America, making of 39–52; Anglo-Iberian geopolitics and the making of colonies 44–6; "benevolent" mode of colonization 50; Black Legend propaganda 50; Carolina's Indian slave trade 51; Catholic baptism 43; cosmography and Spanish claims to British America 40–2; dreams of liberation and dreams of emulation 46–9; Elizabethan colonization of America 44; English aspirations in the New World 47; Franciscans 43; from envy to enmity 52; Iberian road to African slavery 51–2; imperial envy 39; Jamestown 44–6; Lascasian moral dimensions of planting 49–51; on the limits of La Florida 42–4; mapping, cartography, and cosmography 40; Munster (Ireland), colonization of 44; *padron real* 40; papal bulls, rejection of 50; Protestant Peru 49; Roanoke 45–6; soldiers of fortune 41; Soto expedition 46; "Treasure House of the Indies" 39; Tudor colonization 44; Virginia 39, 42; Virginia Company 45
Broersz, Jan 307
Brooks, James 9, 59
Brown, Kathleen 11, 235
Bruce, Philip 236
Burbank, Jane 18
Burnard, Trevor 249
Burr, Aaron 201
Byrd, Jodi A. 211

Cabeza de Vaca, Alvar Núñez 59, 323
Cabot, John 47
Calvert, Charles 268
Campanella, Tomasso 29
Cañizares-Esguerra, Jorge 9, 39
Caribbean (early English) 105–16; Barbados 111; "Cormantee Negros" 109; external and internal threats 106–9; Irish landowners with slaves 113; island population, accounting for 112–15; Leeward Islands' census 106; Lords of Trade and Plantations 113; Montserrat 105; Papal Bulls 106; political arithmetic, theories of 109–12; Western Design 107
Carlos, Ann M. 13
Carolina's Indian slave trade 51
Carroll, Charles (family) 249

Carteret, George 194
Casas, Bartolomé de las 20–1
Castillo, Bernal Díaz de 20
Catholicism: baptism (Apalachee population) 43; extreme English view of 266; interimperial wars against Protestants 109; Irish 111; James's conversion to 193, 196; Jesuit 168; Maryland tolerance of 236; monarchy 9; opposition to 263; perception of 268; potential for perfidy posed by 105; protestors of flaws within 267; signer of the Declaration of Independence 249; Spanish instruction to Native Americans 21
Chaplin, Joyce E. 12, 281
Charles V 21
Charlevoix, Pierre-Francois-Xavier de 328
"Charter Generation" 51
Cheeshateaumuck, Caleb 164
Cherokees 215
Chesapeake (putting Maryland on the map) 235–53; emergence of the Chesapeake 242–7; Old Dominion, writing the history of 238; race, slavery, region 238–42; redeeming the south 236–8; return of the repressed 247–51; slaveowning family 236; uncouple of Chesapeake colonies 251–3
Chickasaws 222
Childs, Matt 398
Choctaws 13, 222, 355, 365
Cholulans 25
Chumash (southern California) 339
Clark, William 292
Codrington, Christopher 112
Coercive Acts 386
Cohen, I. Bernard 290
Colden, Cadwallader 201
Columbian Exchange 283
Columbus, Christopher 39
Combes, Thomas 87
Company of the Indies 361
confessional divide 51
continental early America *see* Atlantic, western, and continental early America
Controversy of the Indies 22
Cook, James 292
Cooper, Frederick 18
Copely Medal 12
Corps of Discovery Expedition 292
Cortés, Hernán 19, 41
Covenant Chain 194, 198
Craven, Wesley Frank 238
Cree, as the language of the trade 13
"Creole" slaves 51
Croix, Teodoro de 73–4
Cromwell, Oliver 7, 107, 209, 394
Curse of Ham 126
Cuvier, Georges 293

Dale, Thomas 45
d'Anghiera, Pietro Martire 20
Declaratory Act 382
Delawares 330
Diaz, Francisco 65
d'Iberville, Pierre Le Moyne 356
Diego Martín 394
Disciplined Militias, creation of 395
Dixon, Bradley 9, 39
D'Oyley, Edward 91
Drake, Francis 47, 321
DuBois, W. E. B. 238
"Duke's Laws" 194
Dutch interimperial trade in the Atlantic world 303–14; Barbados 306, 310; Canary Islands 307; connections with French and English America 305–7; Curaçao 308–9; Dutch home ports and the foreign Americas 312; exploring Spanish America 307–8; free trade under fire 313; Middelburgse Commercie Compagnie 312; mule trade 309; St. Eustatius and and St. Martin 309–10; Suriname and Essequibo 310–12; war and trade 303–5
Dutch West India Company 158, 191, 213

East India Company v. Sandys 95
Eden, Richard 48
Edimboro, Felipe 397
Edwards, Jonathan 201
Eliot, John 219, 270
Elizabethan colonization of America 44
Elliott, J. H. 5
Ellis, Elizabeth 13, 355
Ellis, John 49
English imperial experience in the seventeenth century 85–97; colonial merchants 87; intellectual shift 94; Jamestown 86; labor, problem of 86–7; laws aimed at religious nonconformists 91; "Maroons" 89; midcentury turning 88–90; New World diseases 86; political atmosphere 94; privateers 92; Royal African Company, colonial Baor as an interest of the English state 90–5; slavery 87, 95–7; transatlantic empire 85; West India Company 89
Enlightenment 201
Epenow 157
Espejo, Antonio de 328
European dynamism, example of 322

Faragher, John Mack 212
Fergusson, Elizabeth Graeme 201
Fitzgerald, Gerald 44
Five Nations: Central Fire of 194; Middle colony diplomacy and 197
Ford, Lisa 212
Foucault, Michel 19–20

"France's Peru," dismantling the dream of *see* Louisiana (early colonial), Indian and African Influence on the Development of
Franciscans 43
Franklin, Benjamin 198, 202, 382
French and Indian War 380
Frobisher, Martin 45

Gage, Thomas 39
Gallup-Diaz, Ignacio 5, 13, 375, 398
Gálvez, Bernardo de 397
Gates, Thomas 383
Geggus, David 398
Genêt, Edmund 397
Glorious Revolution 8; beginnings of 196; islands under threat during 107; overseas trade in wake of 95; politics of consensus following 375; Protestantism and 377
Gómara, Francisco López de 20
Gorton, Samuel 161
Gould, Eliga 49
Great Migration 10, 157
Greene, Jack 18
Grenville, George 383
Griffin, Eric 47
Guarani language 60, 62

Haitian Revolution 14, 135, 293, 309
Hakluyt, Richard 41, 46–8
Hämäläinen, Pekka 330
Hapsburg supremacy 7
Harriot, Thomas 269
Hartlib, Samuel 287
Haudensaunee leaders 11
Havana, French pirate attack on 393
Hawkins, John 51, 134
Head-Squashed-In 339
Henry, Patrick 236
Hermans, Isaacq 307
Herrera y Tordesillas, Antonio de 21
Herzog, Tamar 18
Hespanha, António Manuel 18
Hoffman, Ronald 249
Hoxie, Fred 210
Hudson's Bay Company 322: tobacco shipped to posts 348; trading posts 343–4
Huguenots 192, 267, 270–1

"Iberian" traders 51
imperial envy *see* British America, making of
imperial experience *see* English imperial experience in the seventeenth century
Inca empire of Peru 393
Indian slavery (New France) 322
indigenous peoples: allies (Brazil) 59; allies (Mexico) 25; beliefs of natural phenomena 68; company-educated children 33; *Conquista*

espiritual 66; daily life for 8; deemed barbarism 333; disease epidemics and 126, 172; French newcomers and 357; imperial experiences 6, 211; interactions between Spaniards and 9; interimperial contestation and 106; Jesuit efforts to settle 28; method through which to explore the history of 6; New Left historiography and 242; opposition to Anglo-American settlement 322; papal designation of responsibility for 266; Paraguay 63; perpetuation of identities at missions 70; of Rio de la Plata 60; segregated 61; Spanish vs. English treatment of 12; treaties with 43; *see also* New England to the 1680s, indigenous peoples and

Indo-Hispano borderlands in the Americas 59–75; colonial Paraguay, entangled worlds in 62–3; conquista espiritual, indigenous ways of being 66–75; Guarani language 60, 62; "haunted frontier" 61; identity management 66; imprisonment 60; indigenous perspectives 67; life-threatening movements 70; medical emergencies and diseases 65; missions 63; "pure ethnicity" 61; Ruiz De Montoya's cartas, anthropology, polygamy, and cacique politics in 64–6; Ruiz De Montoya's writings, indigenous ethnographies in 63–4; Society of Jesus and Friars Minor Capuchin 61

"Invisible College" 287
Irala, Domingo Martínez de 59
Iroquois 210, 213
Isham, James 346

Jacobo, Juan Jorge 398
Jacobs, Margaret D. 211
Jamestown 44–6, 86
Jay's Treaty 342
Jefferson, Thomas 236, 292
Jesuit Catholicism 9, 168
Johnson, Samuel 135
Johnston, Thomas 397

Kennedy, Archibald 198
King Henry VII, oversight of *see* British America, making of
King Philip's War 10, 164, 218, 270
King William's War 112
Klooster, Wim 12, 303, 321
Knox, Henry 52
Kuethe, Alan 395
Kupperman, Karen 45, 268

labor organization 134
Lalemant, Jérôme 210
Landers, Jane 393
Landsman, Ned 11
Las Casas, Bartolomé de 49–50

Law, John 361
Le Clerc, Georges 284
Leisler, Jacob 196
Leni Lenape 195
Leon, Pedro Cieza de 41
Lewis, Frank D. 13
Lewis, Meriwether 292
Lewis and Clark Expedition 322
local colonial cultures 8–14; big picture elements 8; colonial developments and the fate of indigenous polities 10–12; commercial culture 11; competition, frontiers, and peoples on the borders 12–13; monarchy's effective sovereignty 9; revolutions 13–14; Spanish influences 9; trade 13; unfree labor 9–10
Lockhart, James 393
Logan, James 197
Louisiana (early colonial), Indian and African Influence on the Development of 355–66; alliances with Alabamas, Abhikas, and Talapoosas 358; Choctaw nation 355–6, 365; colonial schemes and popular protest 361–6; Company of the Indies 361; enslaved Africans and deposited into the colony 362; enslaved Native men, women, and children 360; Gulf Coast, securing a toehold along 356–61; Natchez Indian nation 363–4; plantation economy 356; War of Spanish Succession 359; Navigation Acts 379
Louverture, Toussaint 14, 397
Lyell, Charles 293

Macaranan, Roque
Mackenzie, Alexander 292
Madera, Gregorio López 21
Madison, James 236
Mancall, Peter 48, 349
Mapp, Paul W. 13, 339
Maracanan, Cacique 73
Marion, Francis 397
"Maroons" 89
Mason, Sally 249
Massachusets 158, 164
Massachusetts Bay Colony Puritans 50
Massasoit 157
Mather, Cotton 171, 180, 266
Mathew, William 105
Mathias, Henrico 307
Maya peoples, effort to subjugate 25
mercantilism, defying *see* Dutch interimperial trade in the Atlantic world
Middelburgse Commercie Compagnie 312
Middle Colonies 11, 189–202; "Bacon's Rebellion" 194; commerce and culture 198–201; Covenant Chain 194, 198; cultural trends 200; diplomacy 195; "Duke's Laws" 194; Enlightenment 201; European arrivals 191–3;

legacies 201–2; origin 190–1; peaceable kingdom 195–6; restoration and consolidation 193–5; revolution, empire, and consolidation 196–7; Six Nations 197; Walking Purchase (1737) 197; wars and violence 197–8
Milne, George 364
Mingo, Alabamon 355
Modyford, Thomas 126
Mohawks 220
Mohicans 156, 330
Montesinos, Antonio de 21
Montezuma 18
Morgan, Henry 112
morphology 6
Murrin, John 377, 384

Nahua groups 25–6
Nairne, Thomas 51
Nanticokes 220, 237
Narragansetts 157, 182
Natchez Indian nation 363–4
Natchez War 366
Navigation Acts 7, 379
New England to the 1680s, indigenous peoples and 153–68; Anglo-Wampanoag trade 157; before New England 153–7; Covenant Chain treaties 167; Dutch West India Company 158; empires, total war, diaspora (1660s–1680s) 164–8; "Great Migration" (1621–43) 157–60; Martha's Vineyard marriage 163; Massachusets 158; Narragansetts 157; networks (1640s–1660s) 160–4; Pawtuckets 158; Pequot alliance 158; smallpox epidemic 158; United Colonies Commissioners 162
Newport, Christopher 46
Nicholson, Francis 196
Ninigret 161
Noell, Martin 87

Oglethorpe, James 396
Ojeda, Jorge Victor 398
O'Neil, Shane 44
Opechancanough 213
Oviedo, Gonzalo Fernandez de 41
Oviedo y Valdés, Gonzalo Fernández de 20
ownership (settler colonialism, native peoples, and imperial balances of power in Eastern North America [1660–1715]) 209–24; aggressive imperial acts 216; Bacon's Rebellion 218–19; balance-of-power policy 222; Dutch West India Company 213; ethnic cleansing, calls for 219; "founders of political orders" 211; Haudenosaunee wars 214; Iroquois 210, 213; Jesuit mission reserves 215; King Philip's War 218–19; naming ceremony 213; Navigation Act 216; political arrangements 210; precolonial flux 211; rival imperial frameworks 210; settler colonialism 209; Seven Years' War 224; "shatter zone" 215; Treaty of Middle Plantation 220–1; Tuscaroras 223; Wamsutta 209; war parties 221; Westos 215; Yamasees 223

papal bulls 50, 106
Papillon, Jean-François 14, 397
Patuxent 237
Pawtuckets 158
Paxton boys 198
Pemaquid Abenaki 157
Penicaut, Andre 360
Penn, William 194–5, 271
Pequots 158, 182, 330
Pequot War 10, 159
Pereira, Juan de Solórzano 20, 22
Pestana, Carla 12, 263
Petty, William 110, 113
Philip II 48
Phillips, Ulrich B. 238
Pierce, James 52
Piscataways 236
Pitt, William 380–1
Pizarro, Francisco 19
Pocahontas 251
Ponsen, Alexander 9, 17
Povey, Thomas 89, 110
Powhatan 46, 49, 213
Powhatans 330
Prieto, Fray Martín 42
Prince, Joseph 350
Protestantism: ascendancy in the Caribbean 107; Dutch 193; English state's relationship to 253; Glorious Revolution and 377; interimperial wars against Catholics 109; Maryland politics and 253; monarch 375; Peru 49; Scots 111
Protestantism as ideology (British Atlantic) 263–74; anti-Catholicism 266; British Atlantic ideologies 266–71; cultural ideology 268; diversity 271; entry into the Atlantic world 263–6; implications of Protestantism as ideology 271–4; "liberation theology" 269; Mexico 49; missionary activity inspired by 273; Native America, Christianization of 270; slaves 269; thralldom to the priestly caste 268; "Three Kingdoms" 270
Purchas, Samuel 41, 48–9
Puritanism: critics within movement 267; dissidents 158, 161; "Great Migration" 157, 195; Maryland tolerance of 236; Massachusetts Bay Colony 50; minister 171; praying towns 215; reliance on slaves in the Caribbean 128; topics of sermons 182

Quakers: antislavery stance of 135; Barbados census and 113; expansionist ambitions of 195; hopes for Jamaica 271; laws aimed at 91;

Maryland tolerance of 236; merchants 196, 199; movement 195; point of concern to 197; refuge, Penn's vision of 194; work ethic 273
Quartering Act of 1765 383

Raleigh, Sir Walter 42, 44, 47–8
Ramusio, Giovanni 41
Rediker, Marcus 396
Restall, Matthew 18, 393
Restoration Settlement 8
revolutionary Black Atlantic 393–9; Admiralty Court 396; "Black Auxiliaries of Charles IV" 398; "black conquistadors" 393; Bourbon Reformers 395; Disciplined Militias, creation of 395; free men of color, acceptance of 394; Havana, French pirate attack on 393; land grants 395; Pardo and Moreno Battalions of Cuba 395; Portuguese settlements 393; prizes of war, Spanish blacks as 396; royalist position 396; second slavery in Cuba 399; slave revolts 399; Treaty of Aix-la-Chapelle 396; Upper Guinea trade 393; War of Jenkins' Ear 396
Richer, Daniel 11, 201
Roanoke 41, 46
Roberts, Justin 10, 123
Rockingham, Marquis of 381–2
Roman law 43
Roullet, Regis du 355–6
Royal African Company (RAC) 10, 90, 134, 216
Royal Philosophical Society 12
Rushforth, Brett 322
Russell, John Henderson 238
Russian-American Company 336

Saint-Pierre, Jacques Legardeur de 323
Salisbury, Neal 10, 153
Saltonstall, Nathaniel 181
Samoset 157
Sandys, Edwin 86
Santa Fe Trail 323
Savage, Perez 180
science (British Atlantic) 281–93; American degeneracy, theory of 284; America the wonderful 283–4; Atlantic epistemologies 291–3; climatic prejudice 284; Columbian Exchange 283; Corps of Discovery Expedition 292; experts and expertise 286–9; "Invisible College" 287; land of opportunity 284–6; marvels of the new world 283; nature and nation 289–91
Scott, Julius 396
Separatist Pilgrims 50
Sephardic Jews 271
Sepulveda, Juan Ginés de 20–1, 50
settler colonialism, imperial colonialism and 211
Seven Years' War 13
Shammas, Carole 349
Shankman, Andrew 13, 375

Shaw, Jenny 10, 105
Shawnees 220, 330
Six Nations 197
slavery, development of (British Americas) 123–39; abolitionist fervor 135; acclimatization and adaptation, Africans undergoing 135; "Atlantic Creoles" 128; Barbadian code 127; Chesapeake plantation frontier 131; Curse of Ham 126; disease epidemics 126; forms of slavery 123; French Empire 136; gang labor 133; Jamaican law 132; labor demands 126; labor organization 134; Lowcountry 130–1; origins of the racially based enslavement 124; Plantation Americas 124; racial divisions 125; resistance, forms of 137; South Carolina, slave codes of 127; "sugar revolution" 128; tobacco plantations 127
slavery: African slavery, Iberian road to 51–2; Chesapeake region 238–42; "Creole" slaves 51; Indian slavery (Carolina) 51; Indian slavery (New France) 322; Louisiana 362; militia rolls, appearance of slaves on 393; Native men, women, and children 360; Protestantism and 269; second slavery (Cuba) 399; slave trade, opening of 95–7
Smith, John 42, 45, 47, 236
Sons of Liberty 382, 385
Soto, Hernando de 46, 215
Spanish imperial sovereignty (1492–1700) 17–29; Aztec empire, mandate to conquer 24; *cabildos* 27; Castilian law 23; celebration 19–21; Chile 28; Columbus' "discovery" of Caribbean islands 19; conquest 25–7; contested boundary line 28; Controversy of the Indies 22; crown rule, partial 19; *encomienda* 21; Hispaniola, Dominican priest in 21; House of Trade 23; imperial authority, renegotiated 18; indigenous sociopolitical organization 26; *indios* 23; integrating a new world 22–5; Isabel and Ferdinand, foundations laid by 19; jurisdictional disputes 24–5; legal theory, key exceptions to 26; limits of imperial sovereignty 27–9; Maya peoples, effort to subjugate 25; messianic discourse 17; Nahua groups 25–6; Native Americans, settler abuse of 22; papal bulls 22; peninsular monarchy to global empire 19; Philippines 28; Pope's secular authority 20; royal treasury 24; social hierarchy 23; terminology 18; vague claims 17; viceroyalties, creation of 24
Spotswood, Alexander 224
Stamp Act 381–5
Stapleton, William 113
Steckel, Richard 350
Stockton, Annis Boudinot 201
Strachey, William 49
Sugar Act 381
Susquehannocks 217, 236
Sutto, Antoinette 253
Sutton, Thomas 109

Swingen, Abigail 9, 85
Sydnor, Charles 236, 238

Tenochtitlan, fall of 25
Thirty Years' War 7–8, 212
Thistlewood, Thomas 132
Thomson, Maurice 87
Tisquantum 157
Tlaxcalans 25–6
Townshend, Charles 384
Townshend Acts Crisis (1767–70) 384–5
"Trail of Tears" 293
transatlantic system, British misperceptions of the sinews of 375–87; Anglicization, surviving example of 386; Articles of Confederation government 386; Coercive Acts 386; colonial political culture(s) 377–8; countercyclical process 376; Court versus Country dynamic 378; crises and Revolution 382–7; Declaratory Act 382; federal empire (imperial regulation, local elites, and voluntarism) 376–81; Glorious Revolution settlement, politics of consensus following 375; keys to success in North America 380–1; king-in-parliament 378; Navigation Acts 379; post-Revolution settlement 378; Quartering Act of 1765 383; social inequality 376; Stamp Act 381–5; Sugar Act 381; Townshend Acts crisis (1767–70) 384–5; White Pines Act 379–80
Treaty of Aix-la-Chapelle 396
Treaty of Munster 8
Treaty of Tordesillas (1494) 106
Treaty of Utrecht 8
Tsenacommacah 49
Tudor, Mary 48
Tuscaroras 215, 223

Upper Creeks 13
Usner, Daniel 349

Valdivia, Pedro de 28
Van Hulten, Philips 307

Veracini, Lorenzo 211
Virginia Company 45
Vitoria, Francisco de 22

Wahunsonacock 42, 46
Walking Purchase (1737) 197
Walpole, Robert 377–8
Wampanoags 164
Wamsutta 209
War of Jenkins' Ear 396
War of Spanish Succession 7, 359
Warren, Wendy 11, 171
Washington, George 236
Weber, Max 273
Welch, Thomas 321
Wertenbaker, Thomas 236
western early America *see* Atlantic, western, and continental early America
West India Company 89
Westos 215
White, John 41
White Pines Act 379–80
William and Mary, accession of 7
William of Orange 193, 196
Williams, Eric 238
Williams, Glyndwr 322
Williams, Roger 50, 158, 161, 269
Willoughby, William 111
Winthrop, John Jr. 194
Witgen, Michael 330
Witherspoon, John 201
Witten, Rafaela 398
Wolfe, Patrick 209
Wraxall, Peter 223
Wright, James M. 238

Yamasees 223
York Factory 343

Zuñiga, Don Pedro de 42–3